Bahamas
Turks & Caicos

Christopher P Baker

D1022872

Bahamas, Turks & Caicos

1st edition

Published by
    Lonely Planet Publications
    Head Office: PO Box 617, Hawthorn, Vic 3122, Australia
    Branches: 155 Filbert St, Suite 251, Oakland, CA 94607, USA
    10A Spring Place, London NW5 3BH, UK
    71 bis rue du Cardinal Lemoine, 75005 Paris, France

Printed by
    Colorcraft Ltd, Hong Kong

Photographs by
    Front cover: Christopher Baker
    All photos by Christopher Baker except those by:
    Bob Krist
    Chris McLaughlin
    Eda Rogers

Published
    May 1998

Although the author and publisher have tried to make the information as accurate as possible, they accept no responsibility for any loss, injury or inconvenience sustained by any person using this book.

National Library of Australia Cataloguing in Publication Data

Baker, Christopher P., 1955-.
    Bahamas, Turks & Caicos.

    Includes index.
    ISBN 0 86442 482 5.

    1. Bahamas – Guidebooks. 2. Turks and Caicos Islands – Guidebooks. I. Title.

917.29604

text & maps © Lonely Planet 1998
photos © photographers as indicated 1998

Christopher P Baker

Christopher grew up in Yorkshire, England. He earned his BA (Honors) in geography at the University of London and gained his first serious suntan in Morocco on a research expedition. He returned to the Sahara in 1976 and also participated in an exchange program at Krakow University in Poland. He later earned master's degrees in Latin American Studies (Liverpool University) and education (Institute of Education, University of London).

In 1978 Chris spent six months bumming around the Caribbean, Mexico, and North America before settling in California, where he received a Scripps-Howard Foundation Scholarship in Journalism to attend the University of California, Berkeley.

Since 1983 Chris has made his living as a professional travel and natural sciences writer for publications such as *Newsweek*, *Islands*, *Elle*, *National Wildlife*, the *Los Angeles Times*, and *Caribbean Travel & Life*. He has authored many travel guidebooks and has contributed chapters to *The Beginner's Guide to Getting Published*, *Traveler's Tales*, Time-Life's *World Travel: A Guide to International Ecojourneys*, and *I Should Have Stayed Home*, an anthology of works by travel writers. His latest project is *Mi Moto Fidel: Motorcycling through Castro's Cuba*, a literary travelogue about a four-month journey by BMW Paris/Dakar motorcycle through his favorite Caribbean isle.

Chris is a member of the Society of American Travel Writers and has been honored with several awards for outstanding writing, including (four times) the prestigious Lowell Thomas Travel Journalism Award and the Benjamin Franklin Award 1995 for 'Best Travel Guidebook.' He appears frequently on television and radio talk shows, regularly lectures aboard cruise ships, and has escorted tours to Hong Kong, Korea, England, and Cuba.

From the Author

Ardent thanks are due to many friends and others who helped in making this book possible. Above all, thanks go to Helen Fillmore and Maura Brassil of the Bahamas Out Islands Promotion Board and to Laura Davidson of Laura Davidson Public Relations, Roberta Garzaroli and Laurie Kaiden of Jensen/Boga, and Mike Sands and Judy Miller of Bahamasair.

I'd also like to thank the following: Karen Adderley of Sandals Royal Bahamian; Pam Armbrister of Fernandez Bay Village; Edwina Arnold of Club Med; David Barlyn of Island Outpost; Cindy Lee Bates of Pittstown Point Landing; Earle Bethel of Radisson Cable Beach; Jeff Birch of Small Hope Bay Lodge; David Brewer of Abaco Beach Resort; Ona Bullard of the Bahamas Tourist Office; Caesar Campbell, director of tourism of the Turks and Caicos; Harold Charles of SkyKing; GianCarlo Corbascio of Club Vacanze; Sarah Dallas of Conch Inn; Jean and Dan Davies of Laughing Bird Apartments; Cheryl-Ann Faessler of the

Turks & Caicos Islands Tourist Board; Wynsome Ferguson of the Abaco Tourist Office; Nicole Fleming of Coco Bay Cottages; Jackie Gibson of the Bahamas Tourist Office; Brent Ingraham of Bahamas Princess; Peter Kline of Hope Town Harbour Lodge; Denis Knight and Marina Darville of Wild Tamarind Pottery & Gallery; Danny and Judy Lowe of Orange Hill Beach Inn; Suzanne McMannus of SuperClubs; Dick and Dawn Meehan of Lochabar Beach Lodge; Heinrich Morio of the Ocean Club; Ann Mullin of The Cove Eleuthera; Eoin O'Sullivan and Tracy Heitzig of Beaches Turks & Caicos; Charlie Pflueger of Club Peace & Plenty; Joanne Robinson of Walker's Cay; Brenda Sawyer of Schooner's Landing; Gladys Saunders of Tangelo Hotel; Norman Saunders of Club Carib Harbour & Beach Resort; Elizabeth Sherman of Bimini Blue Water Resort; Lisa Strachan of the Grand Bahama Island Tourism Board; Nettie Symonette of Casuarinas and Different of Abaco; Cordell Thompson of the Ministry of Tourism; Kim Thompson of Thompson's Rentals; Elizabeth Vance of Stella Maris Resort; Vincent Vanderpool-Wallace of the Bahamas Tourist Office; Peter Whitfield of Emerald Palms by the Sea; the management of Riding Rock Inn Resort; and any others to whom I should apologize for my oversight.

I'd like to offer especially fervent thanks to Maureen Collins, whose memorably passionate contributions proved the adage that it really *is* 'Better in the Bahamas.'

Thanks, too, to all those other Bahamians who displayed great warmth and generosity, and to the many fellow travelers who shared insights and experiences along the way. And lastly I wish to acknowledge Ginny and Jim Craven and all my other personal friends who have lavished their support and forbearance, whether knowingly or not.

From the Publisher

This 1st edition was edited and produced in Lonely Planet's Oakland office. Laura Harger, Susan Charles, and Don Gates edited and indexed the text. Deanna Quinones, Carolyn Keating, and Kate Hoffman proofread it. Sacha Pearson assisted with indexing. Carolyn fact-checked. Amy Dennis drew the maps, with assistance from Cyndy Johnsen, Margaret Livingston, and Deborah Rodgers. David Zingarelli and Arun Rasiah assisted with map proofing and checking layout. Amy designed the book, with assistance from Henia Miedzinski. Hayden Foell and Lisa Summers drew the illustrations. Hugh D'Andrade designed the cover.

Warning & Request

Things change – prices go up, schedules change, good places go bad, and bad places go bankrupt. Nothing stays the same. So if you find things better or worse, recently opened or long since closed, please tell us and help make the next edition of this book even more accurate and useful.

We value all of the feedback we receive from travelers. A small team reads and acknowledges every letter, postcard, and email and ensures that every morsel of information finds its way to the appropriate authors, editors, and publishers. Everyone who writes to us will find his or her name in the next edition of the book and will also receive a free subscription to our quarterly newsletter, *Planet Talk*. The very best contributions will be rewarded with a free Lonely Planet guide.

Excerpts from your correspondence may appear in new editions of this guide, in *Planet Talk*, or in the Postcards section of our website – so please let us know if you don't want your letter published or your name acknowledged.

Contents

Map Legend

BOUNDARIES

—··—··—··— International Boundary

—···—···—··· Provincial Boundary

AREA FEATURES

Park

National Park

National Forest,
Watershed Area

HYDROGRAPHIC FEATURES

Water

Reef

Coastline

Beach

Swamp

River, Waterfall

Mangrove, Spring

ROUTES

Freeway

Primary Road

Secondary Road

Tertiary Road

Dirt Road

Trail

Ferry Route

Railway, Train Station

SYMBOLS

✪	**NATIONAL CAPITAL**	✈	Airfield	⛽	Gas Station	)(	Pass
◉	**State Capital**	✕	Airport	↾	Golf Course	⛤	Picnic Area
●	**City**	∴	Archaeological Site, Ruins	⊕	Hospital, Clinic	★	Police Station
●	City, Small	⑤	Bank, ATM	❶	Information	▭	Pool
●	Town	⌂	Baseball Stadium	⚲	Lighthouse	▽	Post Office
		⚑	Beach	☀	Lookout	≃	Shipwreck
		⚍	Buddhist Temple	⚒	Mine	❖	Shopping Mall
■	Hotel, B&B	⚬	Bus Station, Bus Stop	⚐	Monument	⚡	Skiing, Downhill
⚠	Campground	⊟	Cathedral	▲	Mountain	⚡	Skiing, Cross-country
⚐	Hostel	⌢	Cave	🏛	Museum	🏛	Stately Home
⚏	RV Park	✝	Church	♪	Music, Live	☎	Telephone
⚑	Shelter, Refugio	⊠	Dive Site	⌂	Observatory	▣	Tomb, Mausoleum
▼	Restaurant	◒	Embassy, Consulate	←	One-Way Street	⚑	Trailhead
⚐	Bar (Place to Drink)	⊶	Foot Bridge	⚑	Park	⚲	Winery
⚎	Cafe	❖	Garden	℗	Parking	🐘	Zoo

Note: Not all symbols displayed above appear in this book.

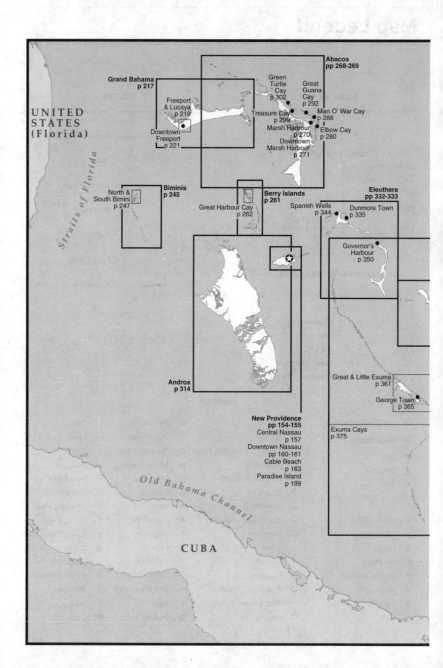

UNITED
STATES
(Florida)

Straits of Florida

Grand Bahama
p 217

Freeport
& Lucaya
p 219

Downtown
Freeport
p 221

Abacos
pp 268-269

Green
Turtle
Cay
p 302

Great
Guana
Cay
p 292

Treasure Cay
p 299

Man O' War Cay
p 288

Marsh Harbour
p 270

Elbow Cay
p 280

Downtown
Marsh Harbour
p 271

Biminis
p 245

North &
South Bimini
p 247

Berry Islands
p 261

Great Harbour Cay
p 262

Eleuthera
pp 332-333

Spanish Wells
p 344

Dunmore Town
p 335

Governor's
Harbour
p 350

Andros
p 314

New Providence
pp 154-155
Central Nassau
p 157
Downtown Nassau
pp 160-161
Cable Beach
p 163
Paradise Island
p 199

Great & Little Exuma
p 361

George Town
p 365

Exuma Cays
p 375

Old Bahama Channel

CUBA

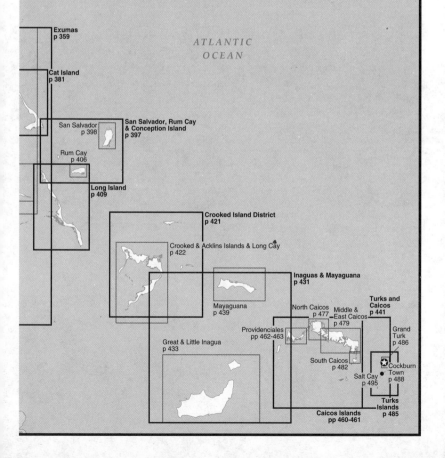

Map Index

Introduction

The Bahamas is part of an archipelago of low-lying islands strewn like pearls in a 750-mile arc from the south tip of Florida to the north shore of Haiti. The archipelago comprises two distinct nations: the independent Commonwealth of The Bahamas (more than 700 islands spread over 100,000 sq miles of ocean – about the same size as the UK) and, immediately to the southeast, the half-dozen or so relatively small islands that make up the Turks and Caicos, a crown colony of the UK. Contrary to popular opinion, the two countries lie outside the Caribbean Sea; they are washed on the north and east by the Atlantic Ocean and on the south and west by the Gulf Stream.

Many visitors think of The Bahamas as a single (and small) island destination and know little of the diversity of individual islands. Some are quite large: Eleuthera, the longest, is 100 miles long. Andros, the largest, covers 2300 sq miles. Though the islands have some things in common, each has its own character and often a distinct culture, usually with a timeless charm and several layers of life to discover.

The Bahamas has long been the major tourist destination in the Caribbean region. In a recent survey of US citizens, the islands ranked as the 'most desirable Caribbean island vacation destination' for the winter months. The Turks and Caicos are far less well known, sparking the nation's tourism board to come up with a marketing slogan: 'Where on earth are the Turks and Caicos?'

The popularity of The Bahamas was tarnished in the 1980s, when it became known as the prime staging point for the South

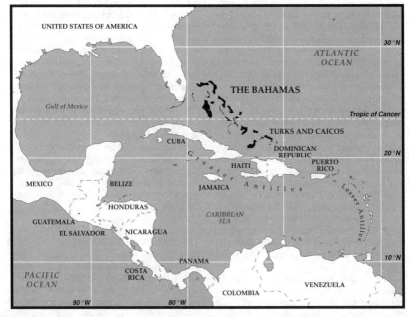

America-to-US drug trade. Political corruption and deteriorating social conditions also fostered a surliness among the people of Nassau (capital of The Bahamas), one felt by tourists. Visitors began to stay away. Fortunately, The Bahamas has bounced back – the mood is now benign and welcoming. And several upscale new properties have energized the marketplace, setting off a scramble among hoteliers to refurbish and renovate.

There are two sides to these islands, but only one is celebrated – the cruise-ship-run-aground world of casinos, rum-swizzle excursions, water sports, and bargain Bulgari shopping . . . and the James Bond world of luxury yachts, golf courses, and grandiose mansions. That's New Providence, especially Nassau; Grand Bahama, seen by 3 million visitors a year; and Providenciales (Turks and Caicos). If you want to be with the pack, these places are for you.

The other side of the coin – one you don't hear much about – is the Out Islands, or Family Islands, the name preferred by the Bahamas Tourist Office, which adopted the new name to impart a sense of community to this necklace of far-flung islands sprinkled like pirate's treasure over thousands of square miles of ocean. The four most-visited members of the family are the Biminis, the Abacos, Eleuthera, and the Exumas. Most of the rest are like beach-fringed pieces of the Third World floating in the shallow emerald sea. There are many pockets where residents lack electricity, many slow-paced towns that live from the sea or by collecting bark for use in aromatic tonics, and many lonesome coral cays (pronounced 'keys') perfect for picnicking under palms. All the islands are rimmed by beaches, talcum-fine between your toes, running from dazzling white, like pulverized sugar, to peachy pink . . . and all are washed by limpid waters like liquid light.

The farther south you go, the hotter things get. Life slows down, too, and the most common vignette is the sight of locals basking like seals under shady trees while dogs – 'potcakes' – snooze in the streets on soft beds of dust. Most Family Islands have populations in the hundreds, not thousands. The more remote islands appeal to vacationers whose idea of a good time is to go with local fishermen far out on the green-blue, where they gather conchs or lobsters on the sandy sea bottom. Attractions are limited to a few Victorian-era lighthouses, roofless plantation houses, and old cannon. And don't expect rousing nightlife. Celebrating the sunset is a prelude to simple evenings spent sampling rum cocktails and listening to native rake 'n' scrape combos.

Some of these gems, once well-kept secrets, are blossoming as resort destinations. Airport expansions for jets began in 1996 on some Family Islands; new roads, water service, and electricity have followed as part of the government's plan to boost the islands. Though the focus is on sun, sand, and 'sin,' opportunities for ecological adventures abound. For example, Great Inagua has a wildlife reserve with one of the largest flamingo flocks in the world. Bird watching is everywhere sublime. And sea kayaking and even biking and hiking programs are taking off, as are whale-watching trips and dolphin swims. The government is wooing ecosensitive hoteliers and tour operators. (Many locals are adamantly opposed to large-scale resort or casino development.) The Turks and Caicos – abounding with wildlife – have made even greater strides in preserving their natural heritage in parks.

Both countries draw thousands of foreign yachters each year, along with anglers and scuba divers – a majority of visitors to the Family Islands come to dive 'the wall,' wrecks, or blue holes, or to cast their lures for feisty game fish.

Enjoy!

THE BAHAMAS IN FOCUS
New Providence

Nassau, the nation's capital, is a historic city with Old World charm. Highlights include casinos, good beaches, quaint colonial-era buildings, an evolved nightlife, shopping and dining, and activities from golf and superb diving to motorboat excursions. The tourist scene is concentrated at Cable Beach, west of Nassau, and Paradise Island, which boasts deluxe resorts, the best casino in the islands, golf, its own airport, and splendid beaches.

Grand Bahama

Freeport, the nation's second-largest city, is unsophisticated and soulless despite promotional hype. But the beaches east of town are excellent, the duty-free shopping is a bargain, golf is top-notch, and there are two casinos and two nature parks. Island highlights include Lucayan National Park, bonefishing at Deep Water Cay, and the funky town of West End, as well as diving, sea kayaking, and day-cruise excursions.

Biminis

The prime attraction is sport fishing – the island group is the site of many annual fishing tournaments. Nightlife is anchored by two famous spots: the Compleat Angler and the End of the World Bar. The bars spill over during spring break, when college kids flock from Florida. The bonefishing is acclaimed and the diving splendid. The beaches are ho-hum.

Berry Islands

These small islands appeal for sport fishing and a few lonesome beaches. Facilities are minimal.

Abacos

This island group is the third-most-visited area in the country. Its Loyalist villages (on a series of cays – Green Turtle, Great Guana, Man O' War, and Elbow) are the prettiest in The Bahamas, with Cape Cod clapboard architecture, museums, art galleries, glorious beaches, and a caught-in-time lifestyle. Waters in the lee of the cays are an acclaimed yachting playground. The east shore is stunning. West of Great Abaco – the main island – are The Marls, with superb bonefishing.

Great Abaco is carpeted in pine forest. To the south lies Abaco National Park, a pristine site for bird watchers and hikers.

Whales pass by offshore. A string of small isles north of Great Abaco ends at Walker's Cay, a prime sport-fishing and dive site.

Andros

Relatively undeveloped for tourism, Andros – comprising three islands – offers superb bonefishing and diving in blue holes and on the wall along the world's third-longest barrier reef. Andros is smothered in pine forests, thick undergrowth, and marshy wetlands. Red Bay is uniquely inhabited by descendants of Seminole Indians and is famous for its beautiful basketry.

Eleuthera

Once popular with wealthy vacationers, mainland Eleuthera has declined in recent years. The happening scene is now the offshore cay of Harbour Island, the choicest place in The Bahamas, boasting Pink Sands, the nation's finest resort; Dunmore Town, a Loyalist village with 200-year-old architecture; and Pink Sands Beach, one of many blush-hued beaches running Eleuthera's length. Eleuthera also offers its visitors scenic headlands and seascapes, plus interesting towns such as Spanish Wells, Governor's Harbour, and quaint Tarpum Bay.

Exumas

A prime cruising ground, the Exumas are a 100-mile-long string of pristine cays. The Exuma Cays Land & Sea Park protects many of these cays and offshore waters. The diving is first class and the bonefishing acclaimed on the flats west of Great Exuma. George Town, the main town, offers an adequate choice of accommodations and restaurants. Site of the annual Family Island Regatta, it briefly becomes the most lively place in The Bahamas.

Cat Island

The heart of traditional Bahamian culture still beats on Cat Island, one of the islands least touched by tourism. Obeah (African-based witchcraft) and bush medicine are still practiced, and many locals make a living from their basketry. Cat has several interesting historic sites, including plantation ruins and the hermitage of Father Jerome. The diving, bonefishing, hiking, kayaking, and bird watching are excellent.

San Salvador

This small island claims (but cannot prove) that it's the site of Columbus' 1492 New World landfall. The island is also known for sport fishing and superb diving. The birding is good, and there's a working lighthouse.

Long Island

This aptly named island is virtually untouched by tourism, despite being the most scenic island. The main base is Stella Maris, the setting for excellent diving, sport fishing, and bonefishing. Its beaches are sublime. Long Island offers intriguing churches, hidden beaches, fine coastal vistas, caves, blue holes, and one of the nation's best offbeat hotels, the Lochabar Beach Lodge. In May the island awakens for the Long Island Regatta.

Crooked Island District

Remote and unspoiled, the island group has few facilities. Attractions are limited to a few splendid beaches, 'bat caves,' and an abandoned lighthouse on an offshore cay. Its birds – especially flamingos – are a good reason to visit. Turtles nest here in season.

Inaguas & Mayaguana

Semiarid, scrub-covered Great Inagua receives few tourists. Beaches are few, but the island boasts the largest flock of flamingos in the Western Hemisphere. Inagua National Park has dozens of other bird species. The island, which has one village and meager tourist facilities, is dominated by the salt industry; a fascinating tour can be arranged. Neighboring Mayaguana is even less prepared for tourism but is slated to become a nature reserve.

TURKS AND CAICOS IN FOCUS

Providenciales

'Provo,' the main island, boasts most of the tourist facilities. The only developed town in the country is here, with modern malls and facilities. There are good bird-watching sites, lonesome beaches, and spectacular Chalk Sound, but otherwise there's only a handful of interesting places. The island offers splendid bonefishing at Sapodilla Bay, plus a rugged drive to Northwest Point Marine National Park, with a lonesome beach where you might stumble upon someone sunning nude, with a dazed, John-the-Baptist look in his or her eyes.

West Caicos

This rugged island south of Provo is known for fantastic diving. It's a popular spot for picnics. Iguanas and flamingos abound, and there are isolated beaches.

North Caicos

This island has minimal tourist facilities but an abundance of plantation ruins and lakes with flamingos and other waders. Seabirds nest in the wetlands of the south shore.

Middle & East Caicos

Middle Caicos, the largest island, features a dramatic coastline, limestone caves, remains of an Indian ballcourt, dense vegetation, secluded beaches, and the country's only developed hiking trail system. The south shore, lined with wetlands, is fabulous for bird watching. East Caicos is a virtually uninhabited, down-at-the-heels island with caves, beaches, and large wetlands.

South Caicos

This island, the center of the fishing industry, is a mecca for bonefishermen and home to the Commonwealth Regatta. There are flamingos close to funky Cockburn Harbour, which has fine historic buildings, a large Haitian community, and an earthy appeal.

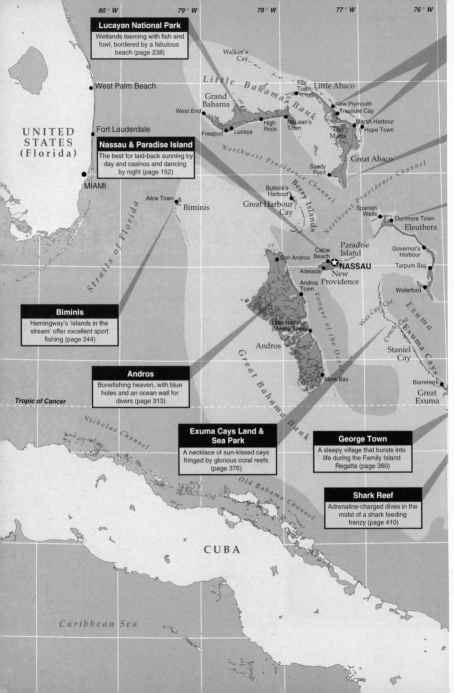

Lucayan National Park
Wetlands teeming with fish and fowl, bordered by a fabulous beach (page 238)

Nassau & Paradise Island
The best for laid-back sunning by day and casinos and dancing by night (page 152)

Biminis
Hemingway's 'islands in the stream' offer excellent sport fishing (page 244)

Andros
Bonefishing heaven, with blue holes and an ocean wall for divers (page 313)

Exuma Cays Land & Sea Park
A necklace of sun-kissed cays fringed by glorious coral reefs (page 376)

George Town
A sleepy village that bursts into life during the Family Island Regatta (page 360)

Shark Reef
Adrenaline-charged dives in the midst of a shark feeding frenzy (page 410)

UNITED STATES (Florida)

West Palm Beach

Fort Lauderdale

MIAMI

Straits of Florida

Tropic of Cancer

Nicholas Channel

Caribbean Sea

CUBA

Old Bahama Channel

Little Bahama Bank

Walker's Cay

Fox Town
Little Abaco

Grand Bahama

West End

Freeport
Lucaya
High Rock
McLean's Town

New Plymouth
Treasure Cay
The Marls
Marsh Harbour
Hope Town

Great Abaco

Sandy Point

Northwest Providence Channel

Berry Islands

Bullock's Harbour

Great Harbour Cay

Alice Town
Biminis

Northeast Providence Channel

Spanish Wells
Dunmore Town
Eleuthera

Governor's Harbour

Tarpum Bay

Waterford

Paradise Island

Cable Beach

San Andros

NASSAU
New Providence
Adelaide
Andros Town

Tongue of the Ocean

Wax Cay Cut
Conch Cut

Exuma Cays

Staniel Cay

Little Harbour (Moxey Town)

Andros

Mars Bay

Barreterre
Great Exuma

Great Bahama Bank

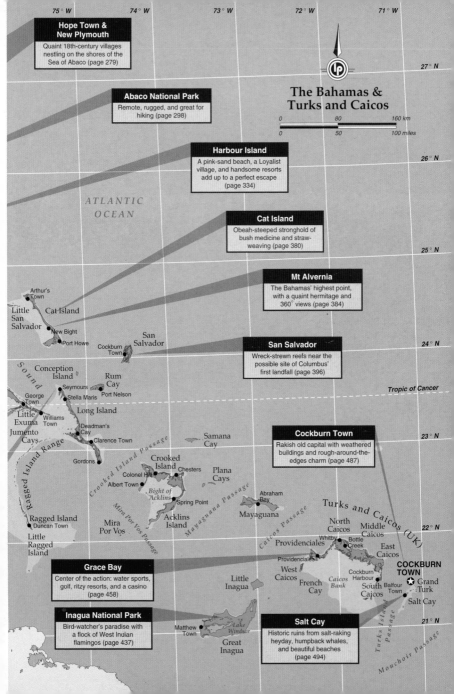

The Bahamas & Turks and Caicos

Hope Town & New Plymouth
Quaint 18th-century villages nestling on the shores of the Sea of Abaco (page 279)

Abaco National Park
Remote, rugged, and great for hiking (page 298)

Harbour Island
A pink-sand beach, a Loyalist village, and handsome resorts add up to a perfect escape (page 334)

Cat Island
Obeah-steeped stronghold of bush medicine and straw-weaving (page 380)

Mt Alvernia
The Bahamas' highest point, with a quaint hermitage and 360° views (page 384)

San Salvador
Wreck-strewn reefs near the possible site of Columbus' first landfall (page 396)

Cockburn Town
Rakish old capital with weathered buildings and rough-around-the-edges charm (page 487)

Grace Bay
Center of the action: water sports, golf, ritzy resorts, and a casino (page 458)

Inagua National Park
Bird-watcher's paradise with a flock of West Indian flamingos (page 437)

Salt Cay
Historic ruins from salt-raking heyday, humpback whales, and beautiful beaches (page 494)

ATLANTIC OCEAN

Tropic of Cancer

Turks and Caicos (UK)

Arthur's Town · Little San Salvador · Cat Island · New Bight · Port Howe · Cockburn Town · San Salvador · Conception Island · Rum Cay · Seymours · Port Nelson · Stella Maris · George Town · Little Exuma · Williams Town · Long Island · Jumento Cays · Deadman's Cay · Clarence Town · Gordons · Ragged Island Range · Crooked Island Passage · Crooked Island · Chesters · Plana Cays · Colonel Hill · Albert Town · Bight of Acklins · Spring Point · Samana Cay · Abraham Bay · Mayaguana · Mayaguana Passage · Mira Por Vos · Acklins Island · Mira Por Vos Passage · Ragged Island · Duncan Town · Little Ragged Island · Little Inagua · Caicos Passage · North Caicos · Whitby · Bottle Creek · Middle Caicos · East Caicos · Providenciales · West Caicos · French Cay · Caicos Bank · Cockburn Harbour · South Caicos · Balfour Town · COCKBURN TOWN · Grand Turk · Salt Cay · Matthew Town · Lake Windsor · Great Inagua · Turks Island Passage · Mouchoir Passage · Sound

0   80   160 km
0   50   100 miles

Top Left: Several unique subspecies of iguanas live in The Bahamas.
Middle Left: The Jesus Christ tree drips blood-red blossoms at Eastertime.

Top Right: A whole lotta yucca
Bottom: Flamingos flock to Great Inagua National Park.

Grand Turk

The islands' capital, Cockburn Town, is surprisingly small and somnolent, with antique, weatherbeaten buildings and the Turks & Caicos National Museum. The island is far from pretty, and shanties abound. If you like sand-blown streets, you may love its rugged, against-all-odds charm. The wall diving is superb. There are also good beaches, bird watching, and windsurfing.

Salt Cay

This tiny cay was once the world's largest salt producer. Steeped in the history of the Turks and Caicos, it boasts fascinating industrial ruins, historic buildings, and great beaches and swimming.

Facts about The Bahamas

HISTORY
The Lucayans
The original inhabitants of the Bahamas were the Lucayans, a tribe of the Arawak Indian group. The Lucayans (a word derived from *lukku-caire*, or 'island people,' the Indians' name for themselves) arrived near the turn of the 9th century, at the end of the great migration of Arawaks from South America. Fleeing the advance of the more militaristic, cannibalistic Caribs, from whom the region gets its name, they leapfrogged from one Caribbean island to another. The Caribs never reached the Bahamas. (Some archaeologists argue that the Lucayans were a separate group altogether and had migrated from the North American continent.)

The peaceful Lucayans lived primarily off the sea. They made bread from manioc and grew corn, yams, and other vegetables. They also evolved skills as potters, carvers, weavers, and boatbuilders, and they spun and wove cotton into clothing (which they traded with neighboring islands) and hammocks. The Indians also wove ropes, carpets, and watertight roofs from the bark of the calabash tree. They got fired up by drinking corn alcohol, smoking dried leaves, and using a powdered drug, blown up the nostrils through a meter-long tube called a *tabaco*. The Lucayans, however, had no conception of the wheel and no written language, and they did not use beasts of burden or metals.

Christopher Columbus, arriving in 1492, considered them 'well-proportioned and good looking.' The Indians, whom he described as the same color as the people of the Canaries ('neither black nor white'), went about painted. Flattened heads were considered beautiful, and babies' heads were thus encased between boards to restrict their development.

They lived in egalitarian communities in caves and thatched shelters. Their villages were comprised of several family clans, each headed by a *cacique*, whose hereditary yet largely nominal title was passed down by primogeniture. Arawak society was communal, and materialism an alien concept. They gladly gave what they had to the greedy Spaniards who arrived in Columbus' wake.

Religion played a central role in Arawak life. They worshipped various gods, who were thought to control the rain, sun, wind, and hurricanes. They believed in a glorious afterlife and would sometimes strangle dying chieftains to speed them to heaven (called *coyaba*). The dead were buried in caves.

Dozens of Lucayan sites have been unearthed, although only very few have been seriously excavated. The little that remains of their culture is limited to pottery shards, petroglyphs, and words such as 'canoe,' 'cannibal,' 'hammock,' 'hurricane,' and 'tobacco.'

The Coming of Columbus
Amerindians had occupied the Bahamas for at least 500 years by the time Christopher Columbus, the visionary Genoese explorer, first sighted the New World on October 12, 1492, during the first of his four voyages to find a westward route to the East Indies. Until Columbus' voyage, the Old World had no idea of the existence of the Americas.

By the time Columbus evolved his grand 'enterprise of the Indies,' rough maps of Asia had been produced. The explorer had also seen Martin Behaim's magnificent globe – the first known globe of the world. Based on Ptolemy's circumference for the earth, which was a quarter too small, the globe excluded the New World.

Though taunted with skepticism and ridicule, Columbus pressed his plan to sail west from Europe to the Orient. King Ferdinand and Queen Isabella of Spain granted him two caravels, and he gained the patronage of the powerful Pinzón family. Finally, on August 3, 1492, Columbus and his crew set out from Palos de la Frontera (Spain) aboard *Santa María*, the flagship, accompanied by two caravels, the *Niña* and *Pinta*, about 20 'friends of the Crown,' and a crew of 90, including a translator versed in Chinese and Arabic.

The expedition sailed west, following the latitude of Japan and China. After 33 days and more than 3000 miles, Columbus recorded that he was now in the vicinity of Japan . . . as indeed he would have been if Behaim's globe and other calculations of the time had been correct.

On October 12 the shout of *'¡Tierra!'* went up, and an island gleamed in the moonlight. Columbus planted the Spanish flag and named the island San Salvador. (The Indians who inhabited it called their island 'Guanahaní.') From here, the fleet sailed south to an island Columbus named Santa María de la Concepción, then west to a large island he named Fernandina. Turning southeast, they touched at a fourth island, christened Isabela, then sailed southwest to today's Ragged Island Range.

The Columbus' First Landing map on the next page shows two courses that have been proposed as the one that Columbus traveled during his exploration. The first, the 'Morison track,' was proposed by Admiral Samuel Eliot Morison, one of the explorer's biographers, and shows Columbus' first landfall as the present-day island of San Salvador. The second, supported by a recent National Geographic Society study, is the 'Judge track.' It proposes Samana Cay as the first landfall. In parentheses below the modern-day names of the landfall islands are the names that Columbus assigned to them.

Everywhere he landed, Columbus found indigenous people who came out to greet the vessels, bearing gifts. He recorded that 'they should be good servants . . . . With fifty men they would all be kept in subjection and forced to do whatever may be wished.'

Columbus and his fellow expeditionaries were underwritten by monarchs and merchants whose interest was economic. Gold, or at least the thought of it, filled the sails. The Spaniards did not linger in these barren coral islands. The Indians told Columbus that gold might be found in Cubanacan (middle Cuba), which he translated as 'Kublai Khan.' Columbus spent 15 days sailing from island to island before cutting south to 'discover' Cuba and Hispaniola, where he wrecked the *Santa María* on a reef. Columbus then took command of the *Niña*, left his crew marooned, and headed back to Europe to report his exciting find. (When he returned to Hispaniola in 1493, the 43 stranded crew members were dead.)

Until his death, Columbus was convinced that these islands were the easternmost outposts of Asia. Since he had traveled west to reach them, he named them the West Indies. Thus their inhabitants became 'Indians.'

Despite three more voyages, he discovered no gold, ivory, or other wealth in any quantity, and his underwriters withdrew their support. On May 20, 1506, he died powerless and relatively poor. It was left for other adventurers to discover the potential of the New World.

Early Years
In 1495 Spanish colonialists established the first settlement in the archipelago. The small stockade, at the southeast corner of today's Cat Island, was named Columba in honor of the explorer. It served as a shipping point for Lucayan Indians, enslaved by the Spaniards and bound for Hispaniola.

There were then perhaps 50,000 Lucayans in the Bahamian islands and only a limited quantity of gold, obtained in trade with other islands. Hispaniola, to the south, held more promise. Here the Spaniards established mines. They so swiftly decimated the native Taino Indians, whom they shackled for labor, that they returned to the Bahamian chain and seized Lucayans for shipment to Hispaniola, Puerto Rico, and Cuba. There the Indians were worked to death. Those who resisted perished by the sword, the rest by European diseases or mass suicide. Within 25 years the entire

Lucayan population was gone. The Spaniards casually sailed away, leaving the island chain devoid of human life (a Spanish slaving expedition in 1511 searched in vain for Lucayans). Columba struggled along for a few years but was eventually abandoned.

In 1513 the Spaniard Juan Ponce de León sailed through the archipelago searching for the fabled Fountain of Youth. Instead Ponce de León, who had been with Columbus on his second expedition, discovered the fast-moving Gulf Stream, which whisked him to Florida and his

discovery of North America. In rapid succession, Spanish explorers came upon the treasure-filled empires of Central and South America. Soon Spanish galleons were passing by the reef-encrusted Bahamas laden with treasure bound for Spain. Many foundered, and the waters of the archipelago were littered with wrecks.

Tales of treasure lured pirates and other adventurers, including Francis Drake and Walter Raleigh, who operated with the sanction of Queen Elizabeth I and used the Bahamian islands as hideaways and bases. San Salvador became the base, too,

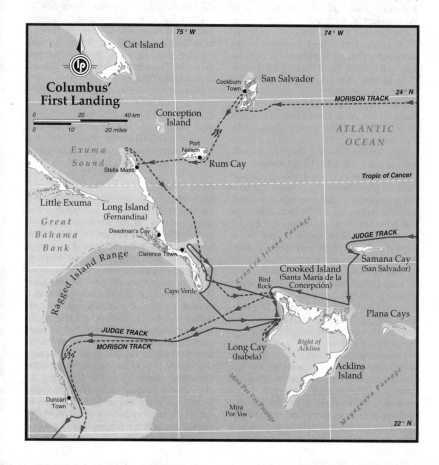

for Raleigh's colony at Roanoke Island, England's first settlement in America. Otherwise the islands remained unsettled and unclaimed for over a century.

In 1629 King Charles I of England granted the islands to his attorney general, Sir Robert Heath, along with the Carolinas, part of Britain's newly founded North American colonies. Four years later, France's King Louis XIII gave the same islands as a gift to one of *his* favorites. But the islands remained neglected, while their neighbors – North America, Hispaniola, Cuba, and Jamaica – grew and prospered.

Beginnings of the Modern Bahamas

The early 17th century witnessed a battle for control of England between Puritans and the Anglican Church. The English Civil War brought religious intolerance and persecution, and many Puritans fled England for the New World. The wave of intolerance arrived in their wake, and the colonies were infected. For the Puritans of Bermuda, it was time to move on.

In 1648 William Sayle, the Puritan founder-governor of Bermuda, outfitted a ship named the *William* and set out with about 60 other islanders, mostly farmers and fishermen, intent on founding a colony of tolerance. The Company of Adventurers for the Plantation of the Islands of Eleuthera arrived at today's Abacos. Political rivalries forced a split, and the majority continued south to the island then known as Cigatoo (the founders renamed it Eleuthera, the Greek word for freedom), where the ship ran aground and sank, taking with it all their provisions. Sayle and a few survivors set out by rowboat to enlist support. They made it to Jamestown in Virginia. Jamestown residents sent provisions to the marooned Adventurers, who founded the first independent republic in the New World, marking the start of the Bahamas' contemporary history.

But the thin Bahamian soil allows root crops little chance to flourish, and the islanders soon began to starve. Some gave up and sailed back to Bermuda (in 1657 Sayle himself left). Others hung on and

Juan Ponce de León

were supplied by the Puritans of Massachusetts, who received in exchange a large quantity of native hardwoods, which funded creation of Harvard College. Other nonconformists arrived, including freed slaves seeking a home.

In 1649, the year the Adventurers founded their republic, Oliver Cromwell's Puritans proved victorious and Charles I lost his head – literally. Cromwell sought to consolidate British holdings in the Caribbean. In 1654 he devised his ill-fated 'Grand Western Design' to destroy the Spanish trade monopoly and secure English holdings in the Caribbean by enticing settlers with land grants and promises of supplies. Puritan settlers were sponsored in the islands. Many of the settlers were free blacks and troublesome slaves evicted from Bermuda and North America. And in 1659 settlers arrived from Providence, in Rhode Island, to found a tiny hamlet named New Providence.

In 1681 Cromwell's reign ended, and Charles II, ignoring the Puritan government of Eleuthera, doled out the islands among six nobles led by Lord Ashley, Lord Proprietor of South Carolina, and sponsored 300 settlers loyal to the crown. New settlements consolidated their hold, notably Charles Town, which was founded in 1666 and favored by its well-sheltered harbor. (In 1695 Charles Town was renamed Nassau in honor of the new king of England, William III, formerly Prince of Orange-Nassau.)

Alas, the six Proprietors were absentee landlords. Soon seafaring rogues were attracted to the new port. When Charles appointed a governor, the populace elected their own governor, Captain Hugh Wentworth. The royal governor died en route to his appointment, foretelling the troubles that ensuing governors would have in establishing a viable government. Wentworth became governor by default over a city that had descended into a 'lewd, licentious' lifestyle. When he decided to take his duties seriously by collecting taxes, he was forcibly removed from office. A replacement was sent from England, but he, too, was sent packing.

Charles Town – an assemblage of sordid elements who gained their livelihood from the salvage trade – grew and prospered. In the age of sail, lacking accurate maps and subject to the vagaries of hurricanes, hundreds of ships foundered in these reef-strewn waters. When times were slow, 'wreckers' would lure hapless ships to their fate by placing shore lights amid the reefs, and then brutishly pick over the bones. Ever-increasing numbers of ruffians came to Charles Town, where the governor served his time at the behest of pirates and outlaws.

Rise of the Buccaneers

During the 17th century, England was constantly at war with France or Spain. Since the Royal Navy couldn't effectively patrol the Caribbean, the crown sponsored sea captains – privateers – to do the job (piracy against a hostile nation was quite legal). Its Letters of Marque authorized privateers to capture enemy vessels and plunder their cities. Scores of ambitious ruffians became privateers. The Bahamas, with hundreds of islets, cays, and complex shoals and channels, lay in the path of treasure fleets bound for Europe and thus was an ideal base for

this fleet of 'common cheats, thieves and lewd persons.'

Many of the 'buccaneers' (from *boucanier*, the French word for a smokehouse worker) were seafaring miscreants, political refugees, or escaped criminals who had gravitated to the tiny isle of Tortuga, northwest of Hispaniola. Spanish authorities resented their presence and made a savage attempt to suppress the buccaneers. Forced out of Hispaniola, they formed the Confederacy of the Brethren of the Coast, committed to a life of piracy against the Spaniards. Gradually they replaced their motley vessels with captured Spanish ships and grew into a powerful force.

The English, who had initially joined the Spaniards in attempts to suppress pirating, rethought this policy with the outbreak of the Second Dutch War against Holland and Spain in March 1664. Pirates were tolerated, and privateers were engaged to act as 'rovers' (pirates by any other name) in the service of the crown. Charles Town took to piracy on an almost industrial scale.

Spain, of course, was outraged, especially since it still claimed title over the Bahamas. It attempted to suppress the buccaneers and on at least four occasions attacked and razed Charles Town, beginning in 1684, when the town was destroyed. Charles Town was rebuilt and returned to its wicked ways.

In 1701 the War of the Spanish Succession broke out, with England pitted against France and Spain. In 1703 a joint French and Spanish fleet destroyed Nassau. Again the pirates and privateers returned. This time, without a governor to control things, they proclaimed a 'Privateer's Republic' without laws or government. This state of affairs lasted until 1714 (Nassau survived Spanish naval assaults in 1704 and 1706), when the combatants signed the Treaty of Utrecht.

No longer under royal patronage, pirates became outlaws. For the next century, even while attempts were made to suppress them, they plundered ships of all nations and raided towns and plantations in the Caribbean and the Carolinas.

The most important pirate in Bahamian history was Henry Jennings, a privateer who had earned the wrath of the English government by attacking Spanish galleons in 1715 (before news of the Treaty of Utrecht reached him) and capturing 5 million pieces of eight. He fled to Nassau and rapidly rose to become its de facto leader. Under his tutelage, the town prospered as a pirate capital, and its wealth attracted merchants, rum traders, vintners, prostitutes, and countless others. Townsfolk even invested in the expeditions in exchange for a share of the booty. No number of taverns and whorehouses seemed enough to slake their thirsts.

Several other pirates rose to infamy. Every English schoolchild has heard of 'Blackbeard' (Edward Teach), who terrorized his victims by wearing flaming fuses in his matted beard and hair. Teach proclaimed himself magistrate of Nassau and used his unique brand of discipline to maintain harmony among the irreverent rabble. 'Calico Jack' Rackham became known for his fondness for calico underwear. He and his Amazonian cohorts, Mary Read and Anne Bonney (who, if drawings of the day are accurate, fought topless), used Bahamian waters as a base. Eventually he was captured and executed.

Pirates Expelled

In 1718 King George II decided to make the Bahamas a royal colony, with direct rule from England. Governor Woodes Rogers (himself a former privateer) was appointed by the king to suppress piracy and install a viable administration. Rogers arrived with three warships and issued the king's ultimatum to pirates: 'death or pardon.' A brief battle ensued, and the royal forces were victorious. Most pirates wisely opted to abandon their lifestyle. Several who refused were promptly hung. The city settled into a period of relative calm. Rogers described his own tenure in words that became the nation's motto: *Expulsis Piratis – Restituta Commercia* (Pirates Expelled – Commerce

Blackbeard

Restored), words that still adorn the official seal of The Bahamas.

England was soon again at war with Spain. Without the presence of pirates to defend Nassau, the crown feared that the Spaniards could attack at will. Hence Rogers fortified the city. When the Spaniards again raided New Providence in 1720, cannon volleys and well-trained former pirates repulsed them.

In 1729 Rogers convened an assembly of prominent Bahamians – the progenitor of one of the oldest parliaments in the New World. It remained virtually unchanged in form until Bahamian independence in 1973. Rogers' Bahamian assembly was notably oligarchic. The elite often acted in their own interests and were frequently and obstinately at loggerheads with the governor and the English crown, setting a tone that lasted two centuries.

Privateering was legalized whenever wars broke out with France and/or Spain (as in 1738, 1748, and 1756), and Nassau benefited from brief bursts of prosperity. But in times of peace and with the heyday of piracy behind them, Nassau and the colonies were depauperate. The islanders scraped by through turtle trapping, salt farming (the collection of salt from evaporation pans), and, most importantly, wrecking. Rogers' attempts to foster agriculture foundered. The Bahamas were so poor that in 1773 the administration declared bankruptcy.

The authorities set up strict rules to govern wrecking, or 'salvage,' as they preferred to think of it. Historian John Old-mixon, in his *History of Providence* (1780), wrote: 'As for Wrecks, all that came ashore was Prize, and if a Sailor had, by better Luck than the rest, got ashore as well as his Wreck, he was not sure of getting off again as well . . . . The Inhabitants looked upon every thing they could get out of a Cast-away Ship as their own, and were not at any Trouble to inquire about the owners.'

By 1850 more than 300 registered salvage ships worked in Bahamian waters, and as much as half of the islands' population made a livelihood from wrecking – as did the government, which took 15% customs duty on the proceeds of sales from salvaged goods. The governor took an additional 10%. The industry became so well organized that many people had a vested interest in causing a ship's demise, including unscrupulous skippers eager to share in the booty.

Those Damned Yanks

The Bahamas lay close to the North American colonies, and the outbreak of the American Revolution in 1775 put the Bahamas in the firing line. The islands' ties to the 13 colonies were intimate, for Charles I's original grant to Sir Robert Heath had lumped the Carolinas and the Bahamas together. Trade and family ties bound the islands to the colonies. Inevitably, although most islanders remained loyal to the crown, sympathies for the rebels ran deep.

When the 13 colonies declared independence, England blockaded North America's eastern seaboard, cutting off trade with the Bahamas, which at the time relied on food imports from North America. The American Navy fell upon Nassau, intent on capturing arms and explosives. This was

the first-ever foreign invasion by US forces. The hapless defenders were overrun, although the governor managed to spirit the explosives away. The Yankees occupied Nassau, carousing their way through Bay St's brothels and bars before sailing away two weeks later.

Nassau again fell victim to the rebels in 1778, and in 1782 a joint Spanish-French-US force took advantage of England's weakened position to capture the city. Spain declared possession of the Bahamas and proceeded to make life intolerable for Nassau's inhabitants.

A year later, the Spaniards evacuated as dupes of a clever ruse. The US colonel Andrew Deveaux, a Loyalist, took it upon himself to recapture the Bahamas for England. With the revolution almost over, he arrived in 1783 with a mere 200 pro-British mercenaries. The Spaniards watched from afar as longboats ferried soldiers ashore. As the landing point was hidden from view, the soldiers lay out of sight for the journey back to the ship, then stood up for the journey back to shore. Thus the Spaniards gained the impression that thousands of troops were landing. The Spaniards packed their belongings and set sail for Cuba.

The Treaty of Versailles formally ceded the Bahamas to England from Spain.

Loyalist 'Invasion'

With the American colonies now independent, English Loyalists began washing up in the Bahamas. Many of them were gentry or successful merchants or farmers. They had remained loyal to the English crown during the bitter years of the revolution and had had their property seized by the victorious Colonials. More than 8000 Loyalists and their slaves resettled in the Bahamian islands between 1783 and 1785, tripling the existing population.

One Loyalist became the new governor. Lord Dunmore, an autocratic and corrupt Scottish earl, had been governor of New York and then Virginia until he was chased out by George Washington's men. In a rage, Dunmore had his ships destroy Norfolk before fleeing to Nassau, where he erected Fort Fincastle and Fort Charlotte to defend against retribution. Dunmore spent lavishly on himself, eventually erecting property on Harbour Island and overseeing construction of a Loyalist settlement that he named Dunmore Town. Dunmore's dissolute ways led to his replacement in 1796.

King George III had guaranteed each of the Loyalist settlers a plot of land. The newcomers – now important landholders – demanded political representation and were supported by Lord Dunmore, who had doled out crown land liberally to gain their support. Soon they were at loggerheads with the existing families, whom the *arrivistes* considered a less noble breed (the Loyalists called them 'conchs,' after the lowly mollusks).

The Loyalists introduced two things that would profoundly shape the islands' future: cotton and slaves. They set up plantations modeled on those in the Carolinas. However, most of the settlers were merchants and craftsmen with little knowledge of farming. And the land was ill suited to cotton. Most of the farms failed within a few years. Many settlers gradually drifted back to the USA or to England. Others stayed, rising to prominence in Nassau and the Abaco Cays.

Plantation Era

Slavery was introduced relatively late to the Bahamas and was comparatively short lived. Slavery here differed from that on neighboring islands or in the US South. The infertile soils of the Bahamas precluded large-scale agriculture. Vast plantations with huge slave populations and their attendant need for barbarous suppression never evolved. Nor did a large slave trade evolve. It was, relatively speaking, a more humane affair, though not wholly free of barbarity. Occasional slave rebellions erupted.

Slavery did have a marked impact: The predominantly white population became predominantly black, weaving African heritage intimately into the weft of English culture. By 1788 the population of the islands was estimated at about 11,200, 75% of whom were black (of these, 25% were freemen, many of whom were themselves slaveowners). That year, almost 1 million lbs of cotton were exported to Britain. In 1789, however, the plantations were struck by an infestation of chenille worms, and most failed within a few decades.

Ambitious public-works programs were initiated to keep slaves employed, resulting in the erection of the fine stone edifices that still grace downtown Nassau.

Demise of Slavery

This period coincided with a time of growing antislavery sentiment, influenced in part by the liberal shock waves of the French Revolution. A humanitarian spirit and a sense that slavery was in conflict with Christian ideals were evolving in England. The British Parliament banned the slave trade throughout the empire in 1807, and Royal Navy vessels intercepted slavers on the high seas. Their captive cargoes were liberated and deposited in the Bahamas. On the eve of emancipation, blacks numbered 12,000 – about three-quarters of the population.

Parliament ended slavery on August 1, 1834. Many of the plantation owners had already departed. After emancipation, many other Loyalists decided to leave, often bequeathing their lands to their former slaves, who turned, like the free blacks around them, to fishing and subsistence farming.

The turmoil of islands such as Jamaica, which had relied on slavery and where the wealthy vigorously opposed emancipation, was avoided. The transition went smoothly. Freemen founded new settlements throughout the islands. And from the very first election, black members were voted into the House of Assembly.

Full equality and political rights, however, proved more elusive, for the post-slavery era was marked by continued colonialism and class and racial discrimination. Voting districts and requirements were gerrymandered to ensure that blacks would be outnumbered in the Assembly.

A minority white elite of merchants and administrators ruled over an ill-represented black majority, a state of affairs that would last for more than a century.

For most of the 19th century, the economy muddled along based on subsistence agriculture, fishing, wrecking, smuggling, and sponging. Thousands of Bahamians – black and white – made a living diving for sponges, which briefly became the islands' most prominent industry under the tutelage of Greeks, who arrived in large numbers. In 1938 a mysterious blight killed the sponges and the industry withered. (See the Andros chapter for more information about sponging.)

As the century progressed, fruit farming evolved into a profitable venture as demand for pineapples and citrus blossomed in England and America . . . until the latter slapped ruinous tariffs on their import. Meanwhile the British erected lighthouses and drew up accurate maps that provided for safer sea passage, bringing on the virtual demise of wrecking.

The US Civil War (1861-65) gave the Bahamas a boost. When US President Abraham Lincoln imposed a naval blockade on the Southern states, Bahamian privateers acted as blockade-runners to supply the Confederacy with armaments and supplies (the British textile industry relied upon cotton from the South; thus Britain favored the Confederacy). The Bahamas became the major trading center for the South. Ships like the *Ballymena* became infamous blockade-runners, running supplies to the South and returning with holds full of cotton. Margaret Mitchell, in *Gone with the Wind*, portrays Rhett Butler as a well-known figure in Nassau, where he loaded his schooner with luxuries for the Confederacy.

Nassau boomed. Fine edifices were erected and the population swelled as out-islanders flocked to reap their share of smuggling fortunes. But the end of hostilities burst Nassau's bubble. Thousands of Bahamians found themselves idle, and the ensuing decades witnessed an exodus of migrant labor to the USA.

A reverse flow also evolved. The rapidly growing wealth in the US created a burgeoning class of people with discretionary money. Many sought vacations in balmy climes. By the turn of the century, Florida was a tourist hot spot and the Bahamas were catching the spinoff, due in large part to Henry Flagler, who created a Miami-to-Nassau steamship service to serve the wealthy.

A Rum Deal

By this time Bahamians of all shades had evolved a fiercely patriotic identity as a British colony. When WWI erupted in 1914, thousands of Bahamians volunteered and gave their lives while serving in the British West Indies regiment.

The war killed the embryonic tourism trade, but in 1920 the islands were again granted divine deliverance – the 18th Amendment to the US Constitution, otherwise known as Prohibition. The Bahamas were ideally situated for running illicit liquor into the USA aboard speedboats, and the Nassau waterfront soon began to resemble a vast rum warehouse. Millions of gallons of alcohol were whisked across the water to Florida or New Jersey's Rum Row. The rumrunners' speedboats led the US Coast Guard a merry chase every night on the mad dash to the USA.

New Yorker William McCoy cleared a profit of over US$130,000 from one such voyage. McCoy handled only fine whiskeys that were guaranteed to be genuine liquor rather than crappy moonshine: one possible explanation of the phrase 'the real McCoy.'

In Nassau and, to a lesser degree, on other islands, construction boomed. New public buildings arose and hotels blossomed like mushrooms on a damp log. And the islands' first casino opened, attracting gamblers and gangsters alongside a potpourri of the rich and famous.

The British Parliament and Bahamian Assembly were hesitant to act against the rum trade. Heck, importing and exporting spirits was no crime. And there were English and Scottish distilleries to support.

In December 1933 the repeal of Prohibition again burst Nassau's bubble. The Depression followed, and the Bahamas hit skid row. Many famous writers, including Ernest Hemingway, Zane Grey, and John Steinbeck, spent time in the Bahamas during this period, and they recorded their impressions in lively prose.

The Bahamas as Duchy

In 1940 the Duke and Duchess of Windsor arrived as governor and governess. Formerly King Edward VIII of England, the duke and Mrs Wallis Simpson (the American divorcée he had married) gave the islands new luster, ensuring that the rich and famous would pour into Nassau in postwar years.

It is argued that the duke, who abdicated the throne in 1936 to marry 'the woman I love,' was given the governor's position – considered lowly – as a punishment. There was, however, evidence that on the eve of WWII, the Nazis were planning to kidnap the duke – who had settled in the south of France – and restore him to the throne as a puppet after Hitler's forces had conquered Great Britain.

Edward had shown sympathies toward Nazism – he even honeymooned in Germany. A photograph later in the possession of US prosecutors at Nuremberg showed him striding down a street lined with Nazis extending their arms in a *Hitlergruss* – and the duke returning a *heil* of his own. (The photo was later touched up to hide the salute.) Winston Churchill, the prime minister, urged King George VI to send his brother to the Bahamas to place him out of harm's way.

Edward, who had suffered great humiliation in Britain, proved just as controversial in the Bahamas. Some claim that he made strides to right the colony's backward and racist politics. Others believe he endorsed the corrupt ways of the 'Bay Street Boys,' an oligarchy of white lawyers and merchants that dominated the islands' assembly for years.

Nonetheless, the duke was beloved by black and white alike and became the topic of endearing songs and poems. One of his favorites was a ditty by Blake Higgs:

It was Love, Love alone
Cause King Edward to leave the throne
It was Love, Love alone
Cause King Edward to leave the throne
We know that Edward was good and great
But it was Love that cause him to abdicate.

Strategic Importance & Civil Unrest

During WWII the islands served as a base for Allied air and sea power. The war also revived the tourism industry. Exhausted Yankee GIs came to the islands to recuperate, joined by wealthy Americans and Canadians seeking a sunny winter retreat.

In 1940 joint US-UK naval bases were established on five islands, not least because German U-boats hid in the interisland canyons. In 1942 the Allied command built a major air base (today's Nassau International Airport) on New Providence.

Local laborers, predominantly black, were hired for military construction at appallingly low (albeit legal) wages. The low pay caused a riot, which erupted into full-scale racial strife. Angry mobs rampaged down Bay St. Eventually the riot was quelled, and wages were raised from four shillings a day to five shillings and free lunch. Nonetheless, as in the USA, black Bahamians were still restricted from entering hotels, restaurants, and theaters . . . a color bar that persisted until 1956.

Thousands of black Bahamians valiantly gave their lives in WWII. The black population, however, remained disenfranchised, and the Assembly remained dominated by the white Bay Street Boys.

Tourism Blossoms

It was clear in the slump that followed the end of WWII that the Bahamas' future lay in the still-embryonic tourism industry. Canadian entrepreneur and philanthropist Sir Harry Oakes, who owned one-third of New Providence and built the Cable Beach Golf Course, the Bahamas Country Club, and much of the tourist infrastructure, had laid the foundation. Oakes' brutal murder in his bed on July 7, 1943, and the subsequent trial of his son-in-law, Duke Alfred de Marigny, reverberated around the world as 'The Crime of the Century,' putting the Bahamas back on the map. The son-in-law was acquitted, and the case remains unsolved.

The decision to promote tourism coincided with the arrival of the jet age and the Cuban Revolution in 1959. During the 1950s, Havana was the mecca for US tourists. In 1961, when Fidel Castro spun Cuba into Soviet orbit, the subsequent US embargo forced revelers to seek their pleasures elsewhere.

Enter Sir Stafford Sands, a wealthy Bahamian who established the Bahamas Development Board, drawing together prominent citizens to formulate a plan for economic development. Sands seized the opportunity presented by Castro and announced that the board would boost tourism from the 32,000 arrivals in 1960 to 1 million a year within a decade. The US air base was expanded and reopened as Nassau International Airport. The harbor was dredged and Prince George Wharf rebuilt to lure cruise ships. A massive advertising campaign was launched.

Sands' board also made a decision to establish the Bahamas as a corporate tax haven, aided by statutes modeled on Switzerland's secrecy laws. The government promoted the nascent banking industry. Tourism and finance bloomed together, with a steadily increasing source of loan capital to support the development boom, further fostered by an influx of capital from British investors escaping onerous taxes imposed by Britain's Labour government. The Bahamas began to prosper, aided by the patronage of many European blue-blood vacationers. Several ultraexclusive resorts were spawned to cater to royals and the social elite.

A major leap forward in tourism was the transformation of Hog Island, facing Nassau Harbour, into chic Paradise Island. A new city – Freeport – sprang up on Grand Bahama under the patronage of prominent businessman Wallace Groves. Sands' goal of 1 million tourists was reached in 1968.

Independence Soon Come

The upturn in fortunes coincided with (and perhaps helped spark) the evolution of party politics and festering ethnic tensions, as the white elite reaped vast profits from the boom.

Only a small number of black representatives (mostly wealthy black businessmen) sat in the assembly, which remained dominated by the Bay Street Boys and by British appointees sent over from London. Blacks were increasingly prosperous, and middle-class blacks' aspirations for representation coalesced with the pent-up frustrations of their brethren who remained impoverished.

In 1953 a local firebrand named Lynden Pindling formed the Progressive Liberal Party (PLP) to seek justice for the nation's majority at the ballot box. In response, the Bay Street Boys and other establishment groups formed the United Bahamian Party (UBP), igniting a long and tenacious feud.

In 1963 the tensions bubbled up into a violent national strike supported by the PLP. A new constitution, proposed by Britain, was drawn up with the aim of creating a more representative legislature and providing for internal self-government. The UBP, led by white Bahamian Roland Symonette, gained power in national elections by a slender majority, and Symonette became premier. White dominance was diluted, but black aspirations had barely been appeased, particularly since voting was restricted to male property owners, a provision overwhelmingly favoring whites. (Women suffragettes, led by Dr Doris Johnson, had won the vote for women in 1961.)

Taking note of the civil rights movement sweeping the USA, Pindling and his party followers brought matters to a head: They refused to recognize the parliamentary speaker's authority. In 1967 the PLP finally boycotted the Parliament altogether, but not before winning an elimination of the property-ownership qualification. A new election was held, and Pindling's PLP came to power, a position it would maintain for the next 25 years.

Naysayers declared that the black government would be an inept one, but Pindling proved them wrong. Britain agreed that the islands were ready for independence, and a new constitution was drawn up, granting islanders autonomy in many internal matters. The independence issue fiercely divided the nation. The PLP was in favor; the UBP, meanwhile, had allied with other minor opposition parties to form the Free National Movement (FNM), which opposed independence. In the Abacos and Eleuthera, ardent descendants of Loyalists plotted to secede and declare their loyalty to Britain if independence were granted. In the September 1972 election, Pindling's party won resoundingly, and the people of the Bahamas prepared themselves for nationhood.

On July 10, 1973, the islands of the Bahamas officially became a new nation, The Commonwealth of The Bahamas, ending 325 years of British rule. That night, thousands of Bahamians gathered at Fort Charlotte to watch the Union Jack lowered a final time and the new flag of The Bahamas raised in its place.

Pindling Era

The postindependence period was a ripe time for the nation. Pindling initially continued the progressive economic policies first adopted by Sands and Symonette, based on tourism and finance. However, foreign-owned development interests enjoyed preferential treatments that fostered land speculation (much of the islands' best land had been bought for development or simply to 'land bank' for speculative investment) and abusive labor practices. Pindling's moves to redress these problems led to a real-estate slump. The economy stalled.

In 1983 the premier became *Sir* Lynden Pindling, knighted by the Queen for his services. His regime, however, had lost its direction and integrity. The administration was mired in corruption, and kickbacks to

government members had become a staple of political life. The international drug trade was also booming, and The Bahamas, with its hundreds of islands, marinas, and airstrips, had become the front-line staging post for narcotics en route to the USA. Bahamians from all walks of life made hay on the trade, and the government seemed disinclined to crack down on it (it was a boon to the nation during a time of shaky financial conditions worldwide).

In 1984 it was revealed that Colombian drug barons had corrupted the government at its highest levels, and the country's drug-heavy reputation tarnished its image abroad. With tourism and financial investment left in the lurch, the government launched a massive crackdown, led by the US Drug Enforcement Administration (US DEA).

Pindling's tenure ended on August 19, 1992, when voters gave the conservative FNM and its leader, Hubert A Ingraham, a resounding victory. The new, intensely probusiness government initiated a privatization plan to sell off many inefficient government-run hotels and is generally credited with putting the bounce back in the economy and restoring a sense of pride. It was returned to power in a landslide victory in March 1997. (See the Government & Politics section in this chapter.)

GEOGRAPHY

The Bahamas archipelago rises from the Bahama Banks, a vast and uniformly flat underwater platform, and consists of some 700 islands and nearly 2500 small islets or cays sprawled across roughly 100,000 sq miles of ocean.

The archipelago stretches 750 miles south from Walker's Cay, about 75 miles east of Palm Beach (Florida), to the Ragged Island Range, which lies 50 miles northeast of Cuba and 55 miles north of Haiti. Yet the islands together add up to no more than 5363 sq miles of land, about the size of Connecticut. The largest island, Andros, takes up 2300 sq miles.

The mostly linear islands are strewn in a general northwest-southeast array.

In or Out?

The Bahamas is geographically *not* part of the Caribbean, as many people think it is. It's part of the North American plate and is bordered on the east by the Atlantic Ocean and on the west by the 'great ocean river,' the Gulf Stream. The *Concise Oxford Dictionary* says that The Bahamas 'is in the West Indies,' the name given to all the islands between North and South America. In general parlance, however, the West Indies is considered to be those islands that encircle and lie within the Caribbean Sea: the Greater Antilles (Cuba, Hispaniola, Jamaica, and Puerto Rico) and Lesser Antilles (the islands between Puerto Rico and Venezuela).

Politically, The Bahamas *is* considered part of the Caribbean (not least by its own government), although one often sees references to 'The Caribbean and The Bahamas.' The British High Commission in Nassau emphatically denies that The Bahamas is in the Caribbean, for the reasons stated above. The US Information Service considers it 'outside the designated Caribbean zone.' It's all a question of perception versus reality! ∎

Several – Great Abaco, Eleuthera, Long Island, Andros – are as much as 100 miles long. Few, however, are more than a few miles wide. All are low lying, the terrain either pancake-flat or gently undulating. Cat Island's Mt Alvernia, the highest point in The Bahamas, is only 210 feet above sea level.

Virtually all the islands are surrounded by coral reefs and sandbanks. Coral reefs, the underpinnings of these painted waters, cement the great banks of shallow seas in place. Most islands have barrier reefs along the length of their windward (east) shores, anywhere from 200 yards to 2 miles out, that offer protection from Atlantic wave action. These shores are lined virtually their entire lengths by white- or pinkish-sand beaches – about 2200 miles in all – shelving into turquoise shallows. In a few places, notably parts of Eleuthera and Cat Island, the Atlantic rollers break through the reefs and crash ashore at the base of limestone cliffs.

The protected sandbanks and shallows extend for miles leeward of most islands. They are usually swampy close to shore, with vast wetlands dissected by serpentine channels. (The Spaniards called the waters *baja mar*, or 'shallow sea'; hence the Bahamas islands are the islands of the shallow sea.) Some islands are separated by great trenches, such as the Tongue of the Ocean, a Grand Canyon-scale crevasse more than 5 miles deep.

GEOLOGY

The Bahamas archipelago sits atop and is formed by one of the greatest masses of limestone in the world: a reef-shelf of solid sea fossils 20,000 feet thick, rising sheer-sided from the seabed. Beneath the sea, division and redivision of the mountainlike landmass formed 20 or so flat-topped summits separated by deep-water gorges. The largest mass is the Great Bahama Bank, encompassing the islands from the Biminis and the Berry Islands south to the Ragged Island Range and Long Island. In the north Grand Bahama and the Abacos rise from the Little Bahama Bank. Crooked Island and those islands to the south and east sit atop their own separate platforms.

The Bahamian islands are composed primarily of oolitic limestone, a sedimentary rock laid down in almost perfect layers and formed by chemical processes in the shallow seas (rather than through the building action of coral normally associated with limestone formation). Over eons, countless tiny marine organisms grew atop the stone and added their skeletal remains to those of their forebears. About 6 miles of limestone rock lie beneath the present-day Bahamas, the result of nearly 150 million years' deposits. The islands as we know them today began to take their present form only about 500,000 years ago.

During the course of millions of years, the region underwent alternating periods of uplift and submergence as the earth's temperature changed. Reddish soils formed during glacial periods, mostly through the accumulation of atmospheric dust (it is caught up in storms over the Sahara and carried west in the upper atmosphere; it still falls today at the rate of about 12 inches every 100,000 years). The islands' surface bears only a thin cover of soil.

Oolitic limestone is relatively soft and crumbly and is easily dissolved by rain and seawater, as evidenced by the honeycombed nature – treacherous to unwary hikers – of the weathered surface rock and, most dramatically, by the numerous caves and 'blue holes' (see below) throughout the islands. Since limestone is unusually porous, rainfall tends to soak into the rock rather than form rivers (the lack of rivers and the silt they deposit into seas helps explain the remarkable clarity of The Bahamas' ocean waters). The limestone filters rainfall, purifying the islands' water supply.

Blue Holes

The islands are pocked by giant sinkholes – water-filled, often fathomless circular pits that open to underground and submarine caves and descend as much as 600 feet.

Sinkholes are formed by rainwater combining with carbon dioxide to form a mild carbonic acid. The acidic freshwater solution dissolves surface rock. Some depressions and pore spaces are enlarged quickly and attract more water, which then further erodes the rock. These holes join into a large depression that grows ever deeper with time. Eventually the fresh water meets saltwater that has seeped into the substrate limestone from the ocean.

Fresh water forms a lens above the separate body of saltwater (the juncture is called a 'halocline'), which mingle at their boundary to form a corrosive mixture capable of dissolving limestone more quickly than either the fresh or saline layers. Since saltwater is denser than fresh water, organic detritus that sinks through the upper layers hits the halocline and stops; here bacteria break it down, generating heat, coloring the water orange, and producing a mild but even more corrosive sulfuric acid – an unnerving environment

> ## What's in a Name?
> *Cay* (pronounced 'key') is an English term meaning 'small island.' The word, however, comes from *cairi*, the Lucayan word for 'island.' Hence the names given to individual islands depended upon who was doing the naming. While Harbour Island is a mere 1 sq mile, Rum Cay has an area of 30 sq miles. ∎

for divers descending into blue holes in search of the narrow sinkholes that lead to chambers below.

Unique creatures have evolved to exist solely within the gloom of the underwater caverns, including blind, pigmentless fish. There are corals and other familiar marine creatures skulking in the enclosed depths, too. And local lore attributes deadly mermaids, mermen, and sea monsters to many of the holes.

For further information, read *Deep into Blue Holes*, by cave explorer Rob Palmer (Palmer and his wife, Stephie Schwabe, founded the Blue Holes Foundation). The book tells the tale of the 'Andros Project,' initiated in 1981 when British cave divers first explored and mapped Andros' cave systems. Alas, Palmer was killed in mid-1997 while deep-diving.

CLIMATE

Upon visiting the Bahamian archipelago in the 1760s, George Washington referred to it as the 'Isles of Perpetual June.' Indeed, the sun shines an average of 320 days a year, with seven hours of sunshine daily in Nassau. Officially, the climate is a tropical maritime wet-and-dry climate. In general, the islands are balmy year-round, with cooling, near-constant trade winds blowing by day from the east. However, the islands are bisected by the tropic of Cancer and span 6 degrees of latitude, a distance north to south of almost 500 miles. Hence significant regional and seasonal variations occur.

Temperature

Temperatures rarely drop below 60°F in winter or rise above 90°F in summer (the coldest recorded temperature is 41.4°F on January 20, 1981). Nationwide, daytime temperatures in the peak-season winter months (December to April) average 70°F, with cooler evenings. However, midwinter temperatures in the northern and western islands *can* be surprisingly cold, especially when northeasters that bring freezing weather to Florida blow in. Then temperatures can plummet into the 50s. In summer the days, averaging 80°F, are breezy and balmy . . . the best time of all, when the water is so warm that you can linger for hours.

The surrounding waters are equally balmy, ranging from about 74°F in midwinter to about 80°F in summer.

Temperatures increase from northwest to southeast, ordinarily reaching 90°F on New Providence and regularly exceeding 100°F in the Inaguas and Turks and Caicos in midsummer.

The breezes generally blow from the east, but tend to become southeasterly May to September and northeasterly October to April, when they can whip in at 25 knots.

Rainfall

Rainfall averages 52 inches yearly. Northern islands receive considerably more rain than do those to the south.

A rainy season begins in May or June and ends in November. About 80% of annual rain falls in these months, normally in short, heavy showers (often accompanied by thunderstorms) and occasionally in protracted rainfall over several days. Towering thunderheads typically develop in midafternoon, fed by updrafts of moist air. They grow to tremendous volume, purpling like a bruise until they let go their torrents of rain.

Summertime sometimes also brings squalls and hurricanes. Still, rain can fall at any time of year. In Nassau rainfall averages 2 inches a month November to April and 6 inches monthly May to October. The islands north of New Providence tend to get more; the southernmost islands receive half that amount and are

virtually rain-barren in summer, often experiencing drought.

Humidity in the northern islands is relatively high year-round, ranging from about 65% to 75% in Nassau – slightly less humid than Florida. Humidity declines from northwest to southeast.

Hurricanes

The Bahamas lies outside the Caribbean belt and statistically has received fewer hurricanes than the Caribbean islands (on average, once every nine years). The past few years have been an exception, and several hurricanes have swept through the country. The 1995 hurricane season was the most active since 1933.

The official hurricane season lasts from June 1 to November 30. August and September are peak months. Usually only one or two islands, or portions of them, are affected by an individual hurricane.

You can get an update on weather information by calling the Weather Channel Connection at ☎ 900-932-8437. It costs US95¢ per minute. The Meteorological Service in Nassau (☎ 915) also has weather forecasts available 24 hours a day, as does the Nassau Marine Operator (channel 27). Radio Bahamas ZNS1 (1540 kHz) offers regular weather broadcasts 24 hours a day.

ECOLOGY & ENVIRONMENT

Coastal mangrove and wetland preserves, pine forests, and other wild places are strewn throughout the archipelago, yet – with the notable exception of the underwater world – few travelers visit the islands to get close to nature. Ecological treasures such as Inagua National Park – protecting the hemisphere's largest colony of West Indian flamingos – go untapped. Ecoconsciousness among the local population is at best embryonic, and existing legislation is largely ineffectual.

The past few years, however, have seen a stirring of ecoawareness. The island governments have adopted a more sensitive approach to development. And entrepreneurs are beginning to open up nature spots to a more sophisticated audience that wants to escape the resort routine.

The archipelago does not display the lushness and physical diversity of neighboring Caribbean islands. But if you're keen to get close to nature, you'll find plenty to keep you enthralled. You'll also be doing the islands a good turn. Nature tourism is one of the most practical ways to save wild places and their wildlife from erosive exploitation: It provides a way of reconciling economic development with species protection while giving local communities a stake in conservation.

Ecological Treasures

The Bahamian archipelago has beaches, but it also has bush. You can forsake sandals for hiking boots to follow coastal trails, explore caverns, and shoot birds through the lens of a camera. Bird watchers are particularly favored. Virtually every island is a birder's haven, for the vegetation is relatively open and the avifauna in plain sight.

The island ecology displays a gradual yet marked change northwest-southeast, becoming more arid and less vegetated as you move south, where hardy droughtresistant scrub and cacti predominate and brackish lakes and ponds are favored by flocks of flamingos. This simple transition masks a more complex matrix of ecosystems, which range from the dense pine forests of Great Abaco and Grand Bahama in the north to the mangrove swamps and wetlands of Andros and North and Middle Caicos to the intricate and absorbing coral reefs.

The Bahamas and the Turks and Caicos governments take their role as guardians of their ecology seriously and work in cooperation with several worldwide conservation bodies. Both nations have designated large areas of land and sea as national parks.

The Bahamas in particular has a long history of conservation activities. For example, as early as 1905, concern was expressed for the West Indian flamingo population in the Caribbean. That year, at the first annual meeting of the National

Big Blows

Hurricanes originate off the coast of Africa, forming as winds rush toward a low-pressure area and swirl around it due to the rotational forces of the earth's spin. The storms move counterclockwise across the Atlantic, fed by warm winds and moisture, building up force in their 2000-mile run toward the Caribbean.

On the islands the first stage of a hurricane's approach is called a 'tropical disturbance.' The next stage is a 'tropical depression.' When winds exceed 40 mph, the system is upgraded to a 'tropical storm' and is usually accompanied by heavy rains. The storm becomes a hurricane if winds exceed 74 mph and intensifies around an eye (a calm center).

Hurricanes can range from 50 miles in diameter to devastating giants more than 1000 miles across. Their energy is prodigious – far more than the mightiest thermonuclear explosions.

Hurricanes are tracked by the National Hurricane Center in Miami. Satellite weather forecasts provide advance warning, but it is difficult to predict a storm's path.

If a hurricane warning is announced, stay sober. A hurricane is no time to be partying. You'll need your wits about you both during and after the storm. For current weather information, you can call WeatherTrak (☎ 900-370-8725). ∎

Audubon Society, a plea was made to The Bahamas' government for the birds' legal protection, and the Wild Birds (Protection) Act was passed. Nonetheless, the late 1940s and '50s saw a sudden decline in the flamingo population. The Audubon Society sent a team to Great Inagua in an attempt to prevent the birds' fast-approaching extinction. After three years' research, the Society for the Protection of Flamingos was formed in 1951 and wardens were hired (paid for by the Audubon Society).

Meanwhile increasing development elsewhere in the island chain was having a damaging effect on other animal and plant

Ten Tips for Environmentally Conscious Travelers

1. *Don't litter.* Remember: Take only photographs, leave only footprints. If you see litter, pick it up. Support recycling programs.
2. *Respect others' property.* Never take 'souvenirs' such as shells, plants, or artifacts from historical sites or natural areas. Treat shells, sea urchins, coral, and other marine life as sacred.
3. *Don't buy products made from endangered species.* Many species of plants and animals are killed to make trinkets for tourists. By buying products made of tortoiseshell, coral, bird feathers, or similar materials, you are contributing to the decimation of wildlife. Shop with a conscience.
4. *Keep to the footpaths.* When you're hiking, always follow designated trails. Natural habitats are often quickly eroded and animals and plants disturbed by walkers who stray off the beaten path.
5. *Don't touch or stand on coral.* Coral is extremely sensitive and is easily killed by snorkelers and divers who fail to honor this law of nature: Human contact is deadly. Boaters should never anchor on coral – use mooring buoys. That's the law!
6. *Sponsor environmental consciousness in others.* Try to patronize hotels, tour companies, and merchants that act in an environmentally sound manner. Consider their impact on waste generation, noise levels and other pollution, energy consumption, and the local culture.
7. *Help local communities gain a share of tourism revenues.* Many local communities are hard pressed to survive and derive little benefit from tourism profits. Educate yourself on community tourism and ways you can participate. Use local guides whenever possible.
8. *Respect others' privacy.* Don't intrude into people's lives or privacy. Ask permission before taking photographs of individuals and before entering private property.
9. *Respect the community.* Learn about the customs of the region and support local efforts to preserve its environment and traditional culture.
10. *Tell others.* Politely intervene when other travelers act in an environmentally or socially detrimental manner. Educate them about the potential negative effects of their behavior.

life. A proposal was made to establish buffer zones, and in 1955 the Crown Lands Office set aside 22 miles of the Exumas for a study (under the auspices of the New York Zoological Society) that spawned the creation in 1958 of the Exuma Cays Land & Sea Park, the first of its kind in the world. One year later, Parliament created a body charged with the park's management and conservation.

Outside the national park system, inappropriate development, pollution, and overexploitation increasingly threaten wildlife and marine resources. Although The Bahamas was the first Caribbean nation to outlaw long-line fishing, a threat to the marine ecology, the islands' stocks of grouper, spiny lobster, and conch all face the consequences of overfishing.

Commercial poaching, mostly by Cuban-Americans from Florida in the west and by Dominicans in the east, has been a significant problem. In the late 1970s the problem stirred several island communities to establish their own reserves, independent of the government.

In 1996 a new government office, Ambassador of the Environment, was created, while the Ministry of Tourism announced a new department to develop ecotourism.

Bahamas National Trust

Today over 238,000 acres of national parks and protected areas are under the jurisdiction of the Bahamas National Trust (BNT). Its headquarters (☎ 242-393-1317) is The Retreat, on Village Rd in Nassau (mailing address PO Box N-4105, Nassau,

Bahamas). It has a second office (☎ 242-352-5438) at the Rand Memorial Nature Centre on E Settlers Way in Freeport.

A nonprofit, nongovernmental organization established in 1959, it has served as a prototype for the development of similar trusts throughout the Caribbean. A collaboration of government, private-sector, and scientific interests dedicated to the conservation and management of the country's natural and historical resources, it is the major force for conservation in The Bahamas and has been at the forefront of saving hundreds of thousands of acres of valuable wetlands, forests, and islands as protected areas.

In addition to an ongoing education campaign, the BNT has achieved such celebrated successes as the preservation of the white-crowned pigeon and repopulation of the endangered hutia, as well as performing important turtle conservation work. The BNT's park management has brought the West Indian flamingo from near extinction to a thriving colony of 50,000 birds in the Inagua National Park. Now it hopes to achieve similar success with the endangered Bahama parrot on Great Abaco.

The BNT advises the government on management programs that reconcile economic development with conservation and has developed a National Strategy for Environment & Development. It is also involved in historic preservation.

FLORA

Compared to neighboring islands, The Bahamas is not species rich; the thin, rocky soil, underlain by limestone, is not conducive to lush vegetation. Nonetheless, the islands together boast more than 1370 species of trees and plants, including 121 endemics, such as Bahamian mahogany and Bahamian pine.

The dominant ecosystem in the northern and western Bahamas is pine forest, characterized by a shrubby understory of palmetto, cabbage palm, and fern, and low-growing thatch palm whose large leaves are used for thatching and weaving. The Caribbean (Cuban) pine and thatch palm have adapted to withstand the wildfires that often decimate competing hardwoods, a natural occurrence that maintains the ecosystem. The red blooms of *Exogonium*, brilliant magenta milk peas, and strange devil's potato flowers entwine the pines.

The forests today bear little resemblance to the original primary cover of subtropical hardwood forests of mahogany, strangler fig, lignum vitae, and gumbo limbo. Most of those forests were felled for boat-building and to clear ground for short-lived cotton plantations. Secondary pine forests grew in their place, many of which (especially those on Grand Bahama, Great Abaco, and Andros) were heavily logged in the decades following WWII. Only in recent years have they recouped their ground.

Mahogany, once common, is now rare, as are ebony (recognizable by its burst of vermilion-bright flowers after rains) and lignum vitae, the beautiful purplish hardwood – and national tree – that you may recognize by its clusters of dark-blue blooms. Its timber is the heaviest of all known woods and much in demand among carvers (its bark, gum, fruit, leaves, and blossoms also serve useful purposes, including medicines for gout and syphilis).

Poisonwood, in the same family as poison ivy, is a very common tree. The waxy branches of the candlewood tree, another endemic species, were once lit as torches by Lucayan Indians. Other natives include the massive silk cotton, the huge buttress flanks of which are unmistakable, and the strangler fig (or ficus), which begins life as an epiphyte on the branches of other trees. It sends down woody roots that attach themselves to the ground and expand – as if in some horror movie – to totally engulf the host tree. Eventually they smother the host, which may die and rot away, leaving a thriving, free-standing fig, the hollow trunk of which may become a habitat for bats, rodents, and other species.

Australian pines (or casuarinas) grow everywhere along the windward shores, providing welcome shade and laying down soft carpets of pine needles. These graceful evergreens were introduced to the islands to anchor the dunes. They outcompeted native vegetation and spread along the coasts, where they exclude understory vegetation.

Many of the leeward shores are fringed by mangroves – the only tree able to survive with its roots in saltwater. All four New World species are found here. The hardy plant puts down a circumference of slender stilt roots, forming a great tangle that helps build up the shoreline and prevents erosion. It also provides rich compost for algae and other microorganisms that draw crustaceans and spawning fish in vast numbers.

Farther south, the drier central islands are dominated by a native coppice of miniature hardwoods, including versions of mahogany, mastic, sapodilla, and lignum vitae. The trees are replaced in the semiarid southern islands by thorny scrub and cactus.

Coconut palms are not as ubiquitous as you may imagine – there are many islands where you are hard pressed to find even a single one.

Blooming Lovely

Flowers abound every month of the year. Many are associated with trees, such as the Pride of India, a large tree that when in flower becomes a cloud of lavender. In spring all the islands are ablaze with the orange blossoms of the croton and the dramatic vermilion of the *Spathodea*, or flame-of-the-forest, also known as the African tulip tree and, locally, the Jesus Christ tree because it blooms blood-red at Easter. It is commonly found outside churches.

Another blooming beauty is the blue mahoe, an endemic form of hibiscus with a ruler-straight trunk reaching 70 feet. Mahoe blossoms blaze from yellow to red.

Ground-loving plants include whisk-broom fern, which is believed to have been the first plant to stand upright in the world. Ernodea and shy little straw-lilies peep up from the pine forest floors.

The long, thin, twirled leaves of the sisal (which rattles in the wind and is therefore also known as mother-in-law's-tongue) are common along roadsides. Sisal is used for making the baskets you see in the straw markets. Agave leaves have been used for generations by islanders as natural needles and threads. And berry- and pod-bearing plants are abundant. Many have uses, such as sea grape, ubiquitous along the shores; its fruits often end up in jams and jellies.

Many plants have long been used for bush medicines, a practice that continues today. Five-finger (also known as chicken-toe) is used to make a tea that relieves body ache. The aromatic leaves of white sage are used as a salve for chicken pox and measles. Wild guava is used to treat diabetes. And several plants are considered to be aphrodisiacs: 'A lot of men lose love life, and they want to make love again. So you boil Gamalamie and strongback and drink a couple of gallons of that, and that straightens you right out – you make love like mad,' says Maggie Nixon of Little Farmer's Cay.

Several species are exotics introduced from abroad, including bougainvillea, whose tissue-paper blossoms blaze purple, pink, and orange, and the frangipani. Pineapple, a bromeliad, is native.

Honeysuckle, jasmine, morning glory, night-blooming cereus, passionflowers, and the rose veil of corallita also mingle their colors and perfumes with the fragrant air. The national flower is the yellow elder, a tubular yellow flower with delicate red stripes on each petal.

Many visitors are surprised to find flowering cacti flourishing in the parched south, notably in the Turks and Caicos, where the national symbol is the Turk's head cactus, named for the similarity of its flower to a Turkish fez.

Opuntia, or prickly pear cactus, is also common and is popular with poorer island residents, who roast and eat it.

FAUNA
Land Mammals

The archipelago has only 13 native land mammal species, all but one being bats. All are endangered. The most common is the leaf-nosed bat. Bats consume large amounts of insects, especially mosquitoes, and act as important seed dispersers and pollinators for flora.

The only native terrestrial mammal is the endangered hutia, a cat-size brown rodent akin to a guinea pig. The Bahamian hutia, a subspecies of a large rodent also found in Cuba and Jamaica, was thought to be extinct until rediscovered in the mid-1960s on East Plana Cay near San Salvador. Once a favorite food of Arawak Indians, the hutia was hunted to near extinction by humans and feral dogs and cats. A population has been re-established on a small cay in the Exumas in an attempt to diversify their range.

Wild boar roam the backcountry on some of the larger islands. And feral cattle, donkeys, and horses, released after the demise of the salt industry, outnumber humans on the southern islands, including the Turks and Caicos.

You might be surprised to find North American raccoons on Grand Bahama. They were introduced to Grand Bahama during Prohibition (they were popular as pets among Yankee bootleggers). Many raccoons escaped or were released, and the population is now well established.

Marine Mammals

The Caribbean monk seal, once common in the southern waters, was hunted to local extinction during the last century. The endangered West Indian manatee has suffered a similar fate. Humpback whales, however, pass through the waters windward of The Bahamas and Turks and Caicos en route to their mating grounds in the warm waters of the Mouchoir Banks, south of Grand Turk. Blue whales are also frequently sighted.

Atlantic bottle-nosed dolphins frequent these waters, as do the less often seen Atlantic spotted dolphins. Several

> **Whales Ahoy!**
> The Bahamas Marine Mammal Survey Team (☎ 242-393-1317), PO Box N-4105, Nassau, Bahamas, part of the Bahamas National Trust, asks mariners to report *any* sightings of dolphins, whales, manatees, and even seals in Bahamian and adjacent waters. You're asked to report the location, date, time, species, size, color, number of animals, and other pertinent information. Take photographs if possible. ∎

individual dolphins, such as 'JoJo' in the Turks and Caicos, have taken a fancy to hanging out with humans in the wild – you may be lucky enough to have one approach you while you're snorkeling. Despite their endearing smile, dolphins can be aggressive (for information on interacting with dolphins, see the Outdoor Activities chapter).

Amphibians & Reptiles

The islands have plenty of slithery and slimy things, including 44 species of reptiles. Lizards (29 species) are seen everywhere in their dusky brown, sky-blue, and rainbow-colored suits. The Bahamas' symbol could well be the curly-tailed lizard, a critter found throughout most of the islands and easily spotted sunning on rocks; its tail is coiled like a spring over its back. Each island has its own subspecies. Some grow to 12 inches in length.

The quick-moving blue-tailed lizard and the well-camouflaged anole are also common. My favorites are the geckos, charming but noisy little creatures that oftentimes can be seen hanging by their suction-cup feet.

None of the islands' 10 species of snakes are poisonous. Corn snakes and brown racers are often seen, as are native Bahamian pigmy boas and blind worm snakes. Snake populations are dwindling, mostly due to the ravages of feral cats.

Many islands have endemic species of reptiles, such as Cat Island, home to the Cat Island terrapin. Great Inagua also has its own terrapin.

There are frogs, too, including the Cuban tree frog, whose mucus is poisonous. The Bahamian crocodile is extinct.

Iguanas Dragonlike iguanas, the archipelago's largest native land animals, can reach 5 feet in length. The islands host several separate iguana subspecies.

Iguanas are shy and harmless vegetarians, feeding mainly on leaves, fruits, and berries. Though they make their homes in shallow burrows, iguanas are sun lovers and spend hours basking. Iguanas reach maturity at the age of six and live for an average of 15 years. The females lay four or five eggs each year. Only the males have spines along their backs.

Humans and feral dogs and cats (the iguanas' only natural predators are larger birds of prey) have completely eradicated iguana populations on virtually every inhabited island. They are now relegated to the outlying isles and cays.

The Central Exuma iguana is known on five small adjacent cays of the Exuma chain; the White Cay iguana is found only on that particular isle, and the Allan's Cay iguana lives on Allan's and one adjacent cay. San Salvador has an endemic subspecies, as do two cays in the Bight of Acklins. Andros has a severely threatened endemic species, and the Bartsch's rock iguana is found only on one cay off Mayaguana.

Crustaceans
Several species of crabs are found in the Family Islands, including giant ochre-hued land crabs. You may see locals chasing them down for the pot. There are also tiny hermit crabs, which make their homes in shells on the beaches. Several species of crayfish (lobsters) inhabit the coral reefs.

Insects
The presence of insects is obvious, notably mosquitoes, which can be ferocious on certain islands in the rainy season. Their presence is limited near the breezy shores, as well as near Nassau and Freeport, where spraying is done to kill larvae.

No-see-'ums (almost microscopic sand flies with a bite quite out of proportion to their diminutive size) are ubiquitous on beaches around dusk.

The air thrums, too, with the buzzing of bees and paper wasps and the steady cadence of cicadas. Grasshoppers are plentiful, as are dragonflies. The Bahamas also has several species of ants and spiders.

About 60 species of butterflies waltz through the islands. Pure yellow sulfurs are common, capering across the roadways in tens of thousands in springtime. You can't miss the zebra longwing, either, with its narrow wings and black and white stripes. The rarely seen giant swallowtail, a mammoth among insects, has a slow-gaited flight and long, sensual tips on its black-and-yellow hind wings.

Moths abound, notably the giant, dark-brown nocturnal fruit moth, called a 'bat' locally and easily mistaken for one because of its size.

Birds
The Bahamas is a bird-watcher's paradise, with about 230 bird species. Only a few are endemic, including the Bahama swallow, Bahama parrot, and the Bahama woodstar hummingbird. The majority of birds in the northern Bahamas are of North American origin. From September through May, the forests swarm with migrants. Vireos, flycatchers, thrushes, and plovers visit, migrating between their summer and winter habitats. Birders can also spot Bahama whistling ducks, guinea fowl, quails, snipes, coots, herons, and gallinules in the wetlands.

The pinelands of the northern Bahamas support a wide variety of resident summer nesters, plus migratory songbirds in winter. With luck, you might see the tiny yet noisy blue-gray gnatcatcher picking insects off trees or the red-legged thrush going about the same business on the ground (another small undergrowth bird is the Bahama yellowthroat; the male has a banditlike black mask). The brown-and-white crested stolid flycatcher prefers its food on the wing, as does the Greater

Antillean peewee, a small, yellowish-brown flycatcher with white eye rings. Stripe-headed tanagers perch in the pines. The white-crowned pigeon is ubiquitous, though the great lizard cuckoo is a secretive bird that you are not likely to see.

The red-tailed hawk is one of several birds of prey commonly seen soaring high overhead, as is the jet-black turkey vulture, which is unmistakable with its undertaker's plumage and bald red head. The beautiful and diminutive osprey and kestrel prefer to spy from atop telegraph poles.

The islands are also home to the burrowing owl and the barn owl. Both are protected species. Alas, a third species – the flightless barn owl – is extinct. According to the Bahamas National Trust, 'screeching, hissing, and clacking its bill in characteristic barn owl fashion, hopping onto its victims or pouncing on them from low tree limbs, [the owl] would have been a memorable sight.' It died out about 300 years ago, and the memory of it probably gave rise to the legend of the 'chickcharnie,' the nasty, leprechaunlike figure of Andros in whose existence many Androsians firmly believe.

You'll see snowy-white cattle egrets everywhere. Roseate spoonbills can be seen in the southern brine lakes, especially on Great Inagua, ornithologically the richest island and boasting a large portion of the world's population of reddish egrets.

At sea, large, graceful pelicans can sometimes be seen diving for fish, while frigate birds – sometimes they're called 'man o' war' birds – soar high above. Offshore cays vibrate with the caterwauling of terns, tropicbirds, and boobies, common in the southern islands.

Flamingos The West Indian (Caribbean) flamingo – the national bird – inhabits Crooked Island, Long Cay, Great Inagua, and, in the Turks and Caicos, Providenciales and North and Middle Caicos. You can also see the birds in botanical gardens and preserves on New Providence and Grand Bahama. Great Inagua has a sanctuary with over 50,000 West Indian flamingos, the largest flock in the hemisphere.

Their orange-pink coloration results from absorption of carolene, a substance found naturally in their diet of tiny algae, crustaceans, and shrimp and insect larvae. Males are generally larger and more brightly colored than females.

Bahama Parrots The only species of parrot in The Bahamas is a close relative of the Amazon parrots of Cuba and the Cayman Islands. The green-and-red parrots were so numerous five centuries ago that Columbus recorded in his log of 1492 that their flocks 'darkened the sun.' Today two distinct populations of this endangered subspecies live on the islands of Great Inagua and Great Abaco. Oddly, there's a genetic split between the two: The Abaco parrots are ground nesters, while the Inagua parrots, which are closer to the Cuban parrot, nest in trees.

In 1997 a forest preserve was under creation on Andros to preserve its small parrot population.

Hummingbirds Restricted to the New World, most hummingbirds are tropical and subtropical, though they thrive in a wide range of climates. There are 163 tropical species, three of which live in The Bahamas.

The only species endemic to The Bahamas is the Bahamian woodstar, known locally as the God bird and found on most Bahamian islands. It weighs less than a nickel yet is pugnacious. The male has a snow-white underbody, red-purple throat, and metallic bronze-green plumage. The female is less ornately adorned, as is typical among hummingbirds. Listen for the birds' '*tit, titit, tit, tit, titit*' or, in song, '*prititidee, prititidee, prititidee.*'

The ruby-throated hummingbird is found only in Cuba, Hispaniola, and The Bahamas. The bright metallic-green Cuban emerald also inhabits Grand Bahama, Green Cay, Great Abaco, and Andros. It darts about like a dragonfly, hovering close to intruders with complete fearlessness and – more peacefully – sipping nectar at flowers.

Caribbean and Bahamian hummers are less territorial than their mainland cousins. They are preyed upon by hawks, orioles, frogs, bass, and even insects like the praying mantis. Their colors serve as both camouflage and attraction. Since most hummers appear green from the back, they blend in with foliage and remain hidden from sharp-eyed predators. But the conspicuous glitter of the male's feathers also dazzles the female.

See the beautifully illustrated *Hummingbirds of the Caribbean* by Esther and Robert Tyrrell for more information on hummers.

Marine Life

The region's marine life is as varied as the islands and coral reefs themselves. The Bahamas has between 900 and 2700 sq miles of coral reef, depending on whom you believe.

The Bahamas' undersea world is enthralling. Frondlike orange gorgonians (named for the trio of snake-haired sisters of Greek mythology) spread their fingers up toward the light. There are contorted sheets of purple staghorn and lacy outcrops of tubipora, resembling delicately woven Spanish mantillas; sinuous, boulderlike brain corals; and soft-flowering corals that sway to the rhythms of the ocean currents. Then there are the sponges, living pumps that take in water through their outer pores, extract the nutrients, and expel the residue.

Countless species of fish zip in and out of the exquisite reefs and swarm through the coral canyons: snapper, bonito, kingfish, jewelfish, deep-blue Creole wrasse, inflatable porcupine fish, moray eel, parrotfish with sharp teeth and a body of iridescent plum-purple and blue-green, and scores of others whose names you may never learn but whose beauty you will forever remember. Their stained-glass brilliance contrasts with the understated colors of the reefs.

The smaller fry are preyed upon by giant groupers, sharks, tarpons, and barracudas, exquisitely patient and facing the current as if they had been frozen by time. Farther

out, the cobalt deeps are run by sailfish, marlins, manta rays, and whales.

The marine world also moves by night, when bioluminescent creatures flit through the dark depths and small transparent fish and shrimp can be seen swimming through the scuba diver's light beam. Lobsters prowl the seabed. Squirrelfish and cardinal fish are also active, scanning the reef with their big, night-perfect eyes.

See the Marine Mammals section in this chapter for details on other underwater life.

Stingrays Some of the islands' creatures have survived quite well, in part because they pose hazards to humans. Stingrays, for example, are feared for their whiplike tails, bearing a spine that can deliver an excruciatingly painful wound. When resting, the rays lie on the seabed and cover themselves with sand. Unwittingly step on one and its tail will whip around and plant a razor-sharp spine in your leg. For your troubles, the 6-inch-long spike is tipped with poison.

Up to 5 feet across, stingrays are in fact quite gentle. As they gather around you, they become gentle birds of the sea. You can even stroke them. These natural bottom-feeders will take food from your hand, though the ray never actually sees its food. Since its eyes are on top of its body and its mouth and nostrils below, it relies on highly developed electroreceptors and a keen sense of smell to find its food.

Sharks Several species of sharks – predominantly nurse, tiger, and Caribbean reef sharks – abound in these waters. *Agh! . . .* those teeth! Sharks' razor-sharp, serrated teeth have kept us rooting for harpoonists and fishermen. But the fact is that more people are killed every year in The Bahamas by falling coconuts than by sharks.

Decades of shark-hunting have led to the near decimation of many species. But a new appreciation has emerged of late as scientists have come to realize the shark's crucial role at the top of the marine food

The Conch

The queen conch *(Strombus gigas)*, a large marine snail with a spectacular pink shell, grazes on seagrasses and looks like a mossy rock crawling slowly along the seabed. The animal doesn't glide like most snails. It uses its large muscular foot to hop along the sea floor. It has a stalked eye to either side of its ungainly proboscis, which it extends like an elephant's trunk to smother a convenient morsel.

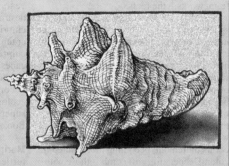

The conch, which can live for 20 years and attain a length of 10 inches and weight of half a pound, begins life as a larvalike creature called a 'veliger,' smaller than a pinhead. It swims at the surface, eating phytoplankton and drifting with the currents. At one month, when it is about 1.2 mm long, it settles to the bottom and undergoes a metamorphosis that includes development of a shell. By night it crawls along the seabed eating algae; by day it burrows. When it is about a year old, it migrates deeper into the ocean to live amid the seagrass meadows, where it continues to feed on algae.

A conch grows its shell in a clockwise direction. The shell expands in order to make way for its growing body. The process lasts for four years, until it is a full-lipped adult with upward-pointing spires. An irregular pink pearl is sometimes found in the shell. The characteristic shell lip forms at about 3½ years, when the animal approaches sexual maturity.

The male and female, now between 20 and 30 cm long apiece, mate sexually and spawn in summer. (Intercourse is a dangerous time for males: The penis, alas, is considered a delicacy by eels, which can often be seen nibbling at copulating couples!) The female lays egg masses up to 10 times a year on the clean coral sands. Each crescent-shaped egg mass may contain up to 300,000 eggs, bonded in a single strand. Only a fraction survive to adulthood – the conch has many predators, including spotted eagle rays, loggerhead turtles, octopi, porcupine fish, spiny lobsters, crabs, and, chiefly, humans.

The conch is the primary source of protein for islanders. It is widely sought after for its sweet white meat, which tastes somewhat like a rubbery scallop. The growing demand for conch has raised the price, leading to overexploitation and the gathering of immature snails. The animal is commercially threatened but not yet biologically threatened. In 1992 the Convention on International Trade in Endangered Species listed the conch one category below threatened status.

For more information, contact the Caribbean Marine Research Center (☎ 703-965-3990), 4905 Indian Draft Rd, Covington, VA 24426. ∎

chain. Now the quest is on to learn how sharks live, reproduce, feed, and survive. Scientists conducting research at Walker's Cay (Abacos) have been surprised, for example, to discover that male sharks migrate seasonally in the winter, leaving female sharks in feeding zones.

Coral Ecology A coral is a tiny animal with a great gaping mouth, surrounded by tentacles for gathering food, at one end. The polyps, which resemble flowers or cushions upholstered with plush fabric, live protected by external skeletons, the production of which is dependent upon algae that live inside the polyps' tissue. The creatures live in vast colonies that reproduce both asexually by budding, and sexually through a synchronous release of spermatozoa that turns the surrounding sea milky.

Together the coral colonies build up huge frameworks – the reefs.

A reef is usually composed of scores of species of coral, each occupying its own niche. However, all corals can only flourish close to the ocean surface, where they are nourished by sunlight in clear, unpolluted waters above 70°F. Each species has its own characteristic shape – bulbous cups bunched like biscuits in a baking tray for the star coral; deep, wending valleys for the well-named brain coral. Deeper down, where light becomes scarcer, massive corals flatten out, becoming more muted in color. Deeper still, soft corals – those without an external skeleton – predominate. These lacy fans and waving cattails look like plants, but a close perusal shows them to be menacing animal predators that seize smaller creatures, such as plankton.

Coral reefs are the most complex and sensitive of all ecosystems. Taking thousands of years to form, they are divided into life zones gauged by depth, temperature, and light. When a coral polyp dies, its skeleton turns to limestone that another polyp may use to cement its own skeleton. The entire reef system is gnawed away by parrotfish and other predators. Fortunately, the reefs of The Bahamas and Turks and Caicos have been spared the discharges of waste and agricultural runoff that have so degraded reefs elsewhere in the world. A few areas have witnessed destruction by

anchors dropped from boats. And in recent years Bahamian fishermen have begun destroying some of the reefs by squirting chlorine bleach into the reefs' nooks and crannies to drive out lobsters. The biggest culprit, however, is Mother Nature: Hurricanes can cause as much devastation as a minor war.

For more information on the fragile reef ecology, pick up Dr William S Alevizon's superb *Caribbean Reef Ecology* (Pisces Books).

Marine Turtles Three species of marine turtles – green, loggerhead, and, more rarely, hawksbill – use the islands' beaches as nest sites. Turtles migrate thousands of miles to nest and lay the eggs for tomorrow's turtles, as they have for at least 150 million years.

Lucayan Indians considered turtles a delicacy. The Lucayans' subsistence needs had as little effect on the vast aquatic herds as the Plains Indians' had on the buffalo. The 'discovery' of the West Indies, however, opened up the waters to rapacious hunting of marine turtles, which are now endangered.

The Dept of Fisheries (☎ 242-393-1777), on E Bay St in Nassau, has established regulations to protect the species, although local fishermen still catch turtles legally for meat. Turtling is prohibited April 1 to July 31. At other times no turtles may be taken on a beach, no eggs may be taken, and no green turtles below 24 inches and no loggerheads below 30 inches may be taken. Hawksbills are protected year-round, but their lustrous shells are much sought after for jewelry. Remember: It is strictly illegal to purchase turtle-shell products, which US or other customs agents are likely to confiscate. You can write the Dept of Fisheries at PO Box N-3028, Nassau, Bahamas.

NATIONAL PARKS

There were 12 national parks and protected areas as of 1997. The newest among them is Abaco National Park, created in 1994 to protect the Bahama parrot. An additional

51 areas in the country are proposed for protection, and large sections of barrier reef off the east shore of Andros are slated to receive national park status.

The 175-sq-mile **Exuma Cays Land & Sea Park**, beginning 30 miles southeast of Nassau, was created in 1958 as the first marine fishery reserve in the world. The park teems with prehistoric life forms, coral reefs, turtles, fish, the endangered rock iguana, and the hutia.

Grand Bahama has **Lucayan National Park**, about 40 miles east of Freeport. This 40-acre ecojewel is leased to the BNT by the Grand Bahama Development Company and boasts 6 miles of underground caverns – one of the most extensive systems in the world – plus large mangrove swamps and native coppice.

The **Peterson Cay National Park** preserves a 1.5-acre cay and surrounding coral gardens off the leeward shore of Grand Bahama.

Also on Grand Bahama is the **Rand Memorial Nature Centre**, a 100-acre reserve of rare palms and native woodland in Freeport, with a captive flamingo flock and populations of native boa constrictors and curly-tailed lizards. The administrative office of the BNT on Grand Bahama is here. Similarly, **The Retreat** is an 11-acre garden of rare palms, native coppice, and exotic plants in residential Nassau. The headquarters of the BNT is here.

The Abacos boast two national parks, including the 2100-acre **Pelican Cays Land & Sea Park**, which contains extensive coral reefs and undersea caves and abundant terrestrial plant and animal life. The 32-sq-mile **Abaco National Park** encompasses the breeding and foraging grounds – some 5000 acres of forest – of the Bahama parrot. The Abacos also have **Black Sound Cay**, off Green Turtle Cay, comprising a thick stand of mangrove vegetation and an important wintering habitat for waterfowl and avifauna, and **Tilloo Cay**, a 20-acre area of pristine wilderness that is a vital nesting site for tropicbirds.

The 287-sq-mile **Inagua National Park**, on Great Inagua, protects the world's largest breeding colony of West Indian flamingos, while the 7-sq-mile **Union Creek Reserve** (at the park's northwest corner, yet separately administered) is an important tidal-creek research site for studying marine turtles.

Green turtles also get star billing at **Conception Island Land & Sea Park**, which is also a sanctuary for seabirds. It lies between Long Island and San Salvador.

See the island chapters for more information on the parks.

GOVERNMENT & POLITICS

Political stability has been a hallmark of the parliamentary democracy that has existed in The Bahamas for almost three centuries. The Commonwealth of The Bahamas has been independent since July 10, 1973, when the current constitution was adopted. The country inherited its political institutions from the UK and is in many regards an England in miniature, attested to by the parliamentary speaker's white wig and the gold scepter at his side.

The Bahamas is part of the Commonwealth of Nations (formerly the British Commonwealth). The British monarch is head of state and is represented by a Bahamian-born governor-general. Duties of this largely ceremonial post include appointing the prime minister, who is always the leader of the party that has won a majority in national elections. At press time the governor-general was Sir Orville Turnquest (deputy prime minister, minister of foreign affairs, and attorney general 1992-95), who was sworn into office on January 3, 1995.

Executive power resides with a ministerial cabinet appointed by and led by the prime minister and responsible to Parliament. Parliament consists of a bicameral legislature – the 49-member elected House of Representatives and the nominated 16-member Senate, nine members of which are appointed by the prime minister, four by the leader of the opposition, and three by mutual consent. The Constituencies Commission is charged with reviewing electoral boundaries every five years. All cabinet ministers must be members of Parliament as well.

The House may override a Senate veto, but any amendment to the constitution must be approved by a two-thirds majority vote in both houses of Parliament and by a national referendum.

A full parliamentary term is five years. The governor-general, however, may call a national election at his or her discretion at any time at the request of the prime minister (that usually means when timing seems propitious for the ruling party) and, in extreme cases, may even dismiss the government.

The Bahamas has a 'first past the post' electoral system; there is no proportional representation. All adults older than 18 may vote.

The political apparatus has traditionally been beset with cronyism and patronage, a fact eagerly anticipated by supporters of the winning party (the ruling party usually dispenses government posts and public-service contracts to favored companies, family members, and friends).

The national flag is a black equilateral triangle on a background of three horizontal bands of equal size: a gold stripe sandwiched between aquamarine stripes. Black supposedly represents the 'vigor and strength of a united people.' The triangle represents the 'enterprise and determination of the Bahamian people,' and the gold and aquamarine represent the land and sea. The nation's motto is 'Forward, Upward, Onward, Together.'

Party Politics & Elections

Island politics was for three decades intimately associated with Sir Lynden Pindling, who led the fight for independence and who served as prime minister from 1967 to 1992. Pindling headed the PLP, which historically has carried the banner of the underprivileged class.

Bahamians have traditionally been fervently partisan about their politics. However, many traditional PLP voters finally came to realize that the Pindling government had become steeped in corruption. In 1992 the PLP's rival, the FNM, took power for the first time, with a 56% majority, under the leadership of the present prime minister, Hubert A Ingraham.

The FNM's prudent policies have made it a beacon of economic stability. Ingraham's first FNM administration spent much of its energy cleaning up the mess created by the 25 years of PLP rule. A majority of Bahamians feel that things improved markedly under Ingraham's tenure (the Family Islands in particular witnessed a wholesale laying of paved roads and an improvement in services). As a result, the FNM was reelected in March 1997 by a landslide, winning an 85% majority with 34 of 40 seats – an unprecedented victory. In the Family Islands the *only* PLP member to win a seat was Sir Pindling, who announced his retirement soon after the election.

Despite Bahamian antipathy for confrontation, outrageous charges – even sexual competence is a favored topic – are made by competing candidates during election time. The islands become charged with election fever. Everyone dons partisan T-shirts emblazoned with emblems of their party, badges are handed out, and posters are plastered on every lamppost and tree. Campaign workers knock on every door, and candidates appear at local cookouts and church fundraisers.

Politics are openly debated between ordinary citizens, who are generally extremely knowledgeable about local issues. The din of disputes on the street astounds many visitors to the islands, who are sure that the arguments must end in fisticuffs. Fortunately, the islands are free of the partisan violence that plagues election time in neighboring countries. On election day voters clog the streets, stand in groups to argue, and display their purple-stained thumbs with pride. Turnout for the 1997 election was over 90%.

Judiciary

The Bahamian judicial system is based on UK common law and practice. A large body of Bahamian statute law also exists.

Magistrates' courts and Family Island commissioners administer summary justice at the local level. There are 10 such courts on New Providence (plus two traffic courts and three drug courts). A superior magistrate reviews appeals, which can then be appealed to the Supreme Court. Further appeal can be made to the Bahamas Court of Appeal and, finally, to Her Majesty's Privy Council in the UK.

The national prison system is one of The Bahamas' more feudalistic institutions and has been decried for its deplorable conditions.

Royal Bahamas Defence Force
Ostensibly The Bahamas has no army, navy, or air force. But in fact, the Royal Bahamas Defence Force, created in 1980 and comprising approximately 1200 members, is a well-armed military unit with its own coast guard and air wing. The Defence Force's primary duty is maritime law enforcement, with a strong focus on drug-traffic interdiction. Its headquarters is in Coral Harbour (New Providence).

ECONOMY
The Bahamas is far more developed than most of its Caribbean neighbors (it is defined by the US Dept of Commerce as a 'stable upper-middle income, developing nation').

The Bahamas' per-capita income is over US$11,000, one of the highest in the region. Its economy has flourished thanks to its stable political climate, liberal laws designed to attract investment, and, undoubtedly, its proximity to North America. The USA is the nation's largest trading partner, accounting for 80% of exports and 65% of imports (excluding oil).

The country's wealth rests on the triumvirate of tourism, banking, and shipping, in addition to – unofficially yet indisputably – drug trafficking. Tourism, however, is the driving engine. About 50,000 people (half of the national workforce) are employed in tourism, which generates about 50% of the gross domestic product (GDP).

One of the country's assets is its large, skilled, well-educated workforce. About 10% of the workforce is employed in banking and insurance industries. Another one-third is employed by the government.

The wealth is concentrated in Nassau, where it is easy to take the relatively high incomes as a matter of course. But there are plenty of pockets of poverty, especially in the Family Islands, where unemployment is high and much of the local economy operates on a barter basis. Still, nowhere will you see the heart-rending poverty of Haiti, Jamaica, or the Dominican Republic.

Because markets are few and far between, many Bahamians rely on traveling tradesfolk, selling their wares like tinkers. Thousands of Bahamians earn their income as itinerant vendors.

Despite the ubiquity of banks, Bahamians are not big borrowers . . . at least not from formal institutions. The 'asue' is a common mode of raising money, involving a specified number of individuals who each contribute an agreed sum of money on a regular, predetermined basis for a specified term. Whenever a contribution is made, the total pool is 'drawn' by a single participant until each of the participants has had his or her draw. For early drawers, the pool operates like a loan that is repaid over regular intervals; for late drawers, it is like a forced savings account.

Large, unexpected debts are often paid for by benefit cookouts, sponsored walkathons, or requests for contributions made through advertisements. Even beauty pageant contestants seek out sponsors, adopting tantalizing names such as 'Miss Flaming Torch' and 'Miss Ooh La La' to attract donations.

Government Policy
The change in government in 1992 brought renewed efforts to expand and diversify the economy. The FNM government, which inherited a US$1.1 billion national debt, introduced new legislation to lure foreign money, including the International Persons Landholding Act of 1993, offering a seductive mix of incentives and privileges to

foreign prospective homebuyers in The Bahamas. The National Investment Policy also includes a provision to spur hotel development. And a highly successful privatization plan has sharply reduced the government's role in the business sector.

The FNM's policies have brought public spending and foreign debt under control. The nation's trade imbalance and US$125 million-a-year budget deficit (1986-92) have been reduced. Inflation is low. And unemployment, previously escalating, had been reduced to 10% by mid-1997. Appropriately, in 1994 the Ministry of Tourism changed its slogan to: 'The Islands of the Bahamas . . . It Just Keeps Getting Better.'

The government derives 90% of its revenue from taxation. Approximately 50% of its income comes from import and export duties. About 75% of government income goes to debt repayment and government salaries.

A Tax Shelter in the Sun

The Bahamas is one of the world's premier tax-free havens. The policy is a linchpin of economic policy and creates a win-win situation for gamblers who get lucky at the gaming tables or for cannier bettors who bone up on tax laws by the hotel pool before hitting the slots. Incentives offered to investors attract millions of dollars every year.

Companies pay no taxes on personal or corporate income, capital gains, dividends, interest, royalties, sales, estates, inheritances, or payrolls. The repatriation of foreign investment funds, foreign assets and dividends, and profits arising from investments is permitted tax-free. Bahamian law strongly protects clients' right to confidentiality and privacy.

The Bahamas Investment Authority (☎ 242-327-5970, fax 242-327-5907), PO Box CB-10980, Nassau, Bahamas, is a 'one-stop shop' for international investors who need information and assistance.

Major Industries

Tourism Tourism is by far The Bahamas' largest industry, accounting for US$1.45 billion in 1996 and producing much of the government's tax revenue. Annual visitor numbers have grown from 1 million in 1970 to 1.5 million in 1980 to 3 million in 1990. Some 3.4 million vacationers (plus cruise-ship day-trippers) arrived in 1996, and there is no sense of coming close to saturation, because many Family Islands still remain virtually undeveloped. The Bahamas aims for 4 million visitors by the year 2000. About 80% of its visitors come from North America.

Passengers from cruise ships comprise a major portion of these visits: Passenger arrivals in 1996 totaled more than 1.6 million, up from 780,000 in 1993. In fact, The Bahamas (predominantly Nassau) receives 50% of *all* passenger visits in the Caribbean region. Most such visitors spend only a day or two ashore.

Tourist facilities (hotels, restaurants, etc) are as good as any in the region, reflecting an investment of US$1.8 billion in tourist infrastructure from 1994 to 1996. In 1992 the Ingraham government began an aggressive development program to maintain competitiveness in the face of rivalry from Florida and the Caribbean islands. Privatization has been central to the government's economic policy; as of 1997 government ownership of hotels had been reduced from 20% to less than 5% of the country's room inventory. And the Hotels Encouragement Act, excepting hoteliers from property taxes, has helped prompt an outburst of construction and renovation. In April 1997 the new tourism minister, Cornelius Smith, announced a whopping increase in the government's tourism promotion budget, to US$65 million.

While most visitors come to the islands to enjoy the casinos, coral reefs, and superlative beaches, Bahamians are beginning to promote the Family Islands (only about 250,000 visitors a year visit them). Vincent Vanderpool-Wallace, director-general of tourism, sees the outlying islands as 'the future.' To support development, the government has invested massive capital in new infrastructure. A provision in the Hotels Encouragement Act that permits hotels with as few as just five rooms to qualify for preferences was designed to spur growth of small properties, to foster tourism at local levels, to stem migration from the Family Islands, and to absorb some of the pressure on the two main islands, where migrants join the ranks of the unemployed.

The Family Islands are working to develop individual identities. Ecotourism is a focal point – for example, the Bahamian government recently announced that Mayaguana, the most remote of the Family Islands, is to be the site of an ecopark. And the government is fostering 'meet-the-people' programs that promote cultural interchange between visitors and residents.

Banking & Finance The Bahamas – specifically Nassau – is one of the world's principal international financial centers. In 1997 over 400 banks from 36 countries were licensed to do business within or from The Bahamas. Almost 200 banks had a physical presence in the islands. Together they manage more than US$200 billion in assets. Financial services annually contribute about US$200 million to the economy (about 10% of GDP). Financial markets are regulated by the independent Central Bank of The Bahamas.

A large body of accountants, legal experts, administrators, and other service providers has evolved. The system primarily serves as a tax-planning haven and place of asset security for wealthy individuals and corporations. Assets are protected from foreign creditors; financial records cannot be subpoenaed or released. However, the FNM government has made sweeping changes in banking laws to help the US DEA and the US Internal Revenue Service combat money laundering, and Bahamian-held assets are no longer secure from US federal agencies.

In 1997 the government began aggressively positioning The Bahamas as a premier offshore insurance center.

Shipping The Bahamas is one of the world's leading shipping registries, with more than 1500 international vessels registered (the world's fifth-largest fleet) – a 25-fold increase since 1983. Today the requirements of Bahamian flag owners are overseen by the Bahamas Maritime Authority, established in 1995 as a semiautonomous government-owned corporation.

In addition to revenue from international shipping registry, the nation earns about US$200 million annually from the import and re-export of crude and refined oil.

A world-class container transshipment terminal was scheduled for completion at Freeport Harbour in 1998.

Agriculture & Fishing The establishment of viable farming on the islands has proved elusive for many centuries. Less than 5% of the workforce is employed in agriculture, which contributes only 2% of GDP, predominantly from fruit crops. Only about 12,000 acres – 1% of the land area – is farmed.

Pineapples were once a staple of the economies of Eleuthera, Cat Island, and Long Island, which were briefly the world's leading suppliers of the fruit (the islands supplied the USA before the plant was introduced to the Hawaiian Islands in the 1890s). They are still grown, though in vastly reduced quantities. Citrus fruits are important on Great Abaco (where 98% by value of agricultural exports are grown), with 5000 acres planted in grapefruit, lemon, and lime trees. Other fruits, tomatoes, and cucumbers are grown commercially on Great Abaco and North Andros, where a crop-diversification scheme introduced in 1983 has fostered production of onions, potatoes, and pigeon peas. There are small papaya orchards on Eleuthera.

The Bahamas has large tracts of unused fertile land and plentiful supplies of fresh water on Grand Bahama and in the Family Islands, where a large percentage of the population raises crops on a level barely above subsistence. The fertile flatlands are mostly in the hands of large-scale commercial operations. Small-scale operators tend to farm rock-strewn patches, often coaxing their products to ripen in the bottom of limestone pits, where soils and water collect.

Logging, once a major industry, has declined markedly in recent years.

A viable cattle industry evolved on Eleuthera in the years following WWII. It is now defunct. However, chickens are commercially reared on Great Abaco.

Countless Family Islanders derive their income from the sea. Conch and scale fish are taken year-round, mostly for local needs. Commercial fishing is of only marginal importance. The major export is lobster. The seasonal trade involves thousands of small-scale fishermen as well as locally owned, capital-intensive, large-scale operations based in Spanish Wells (Eleuthera). It is only in recent years that lobster has become a major export, as Bahamians traditionally considered it an unclean meat and used it as fish bait!

The FNM government continues to invest in schemes to hold farmers and fishermen in the Family Islands and has made promoting agricultural investment a major goal. The government hopes to thus reduce food imports and staunch the flow of capital out of the country.

Manufacturing The major industries are brewing and rum manufacture (valued at US$35 million in annual exports) on New Providence and petrochemicals on Grand Bahama. Annual crude salt exports, predominantly from Great Inagua, are valued at over US$20 million.

Drug Trade No discussion of the economy would be complete without an account of the vast impact of narcotics and drug money. Domestic drug sales are slight. But many Bahamians are involved in illicit narcotics trading, using boats or planes to whisk drugs flown in from Colombia and other drug-producing nations to the USA. An estimated 50% of the cocaine entering the USA passes over or through here.

Eluding drug-enforcement authorities is made easy by dozens of remote airstrips on the countless tiny cays and by the thousands of miles of indented shoreline that are impossible to police.

The traffic evolved during the late 1970s and peaked in the early '80s, when drug-laden planes and cigarette boats zipped in and out 24 hours a day. Thousands of Bahamians were involved in the trade, even otherwise respectable, church-going citizens and high-ranking government officials. Everyone else turned a blind eye, the legacy of a long history of wrecking and smuggling.

Following a scandal in 1984, when it was revealed that drug money had tainted the highest levels of government, the US DEA and Royal Bahamas Defence Force initiated a massive enforcement program. The DEA put three AEROSTAT surveillance balloons over Grand Bahama, Great Exuma, and Great Inagua to track air traffic (the balloons have since been replaced by radar). In 1987 the Biminis were quarantined, as US Coast Guard vessels were given permission to search every vessel entering and leaving the islands.

Bahamian banking laws provided a safe haven for drug cartels to launder their money. As a result, the government recently introduced legislation criminalizing money laundering.

Despite the government's efforts to eradicate the trade, drug trafficking is still very much alive, pumping millions of dollars into the economy each year. The latest crime reports show that trafficking is prevalent on every Bahamian island.

Wrecking still occurs, too. When a ship wrecks – albeit less often than in days of yore – skiffs from local hamlets (called 'settlements') can soon be seen piled high with brass fittings and other treasure plundered from the wreck. 'It's the law of the land,' say the locals.

POPULATION & PEOPLE
The Bahamas has approximately 290,000 people, up from 210,000 in 1980. Life expectancy is 76 years for women and 70 years for men, on a par with the USA.

The birth rate is a low 20 per 1000, and population growth is only 1.5% (until the advent of television, The Bahamas had the second-highest birth rate in the world). More than 64% of the population in The Bahamas is younger than 30.

About 80% of the population is urban. Nearly two-thirds of the population live in Nassau, and approximately 40,000 live in Freeport, the only other major city.

The remainder of the population is scattered among about a dozen Family Islands (predominantly the Abacos, Andros, and Eleuthera, each with about 10,000 people) and a few dozen offshore cays. As you move south, the islands tend to be less populated, and the southern islands are suffering significant declines in population: Cat Island's fell from 2215 in 1980 to 1678 in 1990; Ragged Island's declined from 164 to 89.

About 85% of the population is black (including 'browns,' who have a multiracial ancestry). Whites constitute 14% of the population; most are of British and to a lesser degree US, Irish, and Greek descent. The minuscule remainder are of Chinese, Middle Eastern, or other descent. The vast majority of Bahamians is to some degree of mixed ancestry, and distinctions are sometimes muddied.

The Bahamas prides itself on its harmonious race relations. Indeed, Bahamian islands are refreshingly free of racial tensions, and class divisions are markedly *less* related to color than on many neighboring islands. Middle-class Bahamians will tell you that they measure people not by the color of their skin but by the content of their character. Everyone can socialize together.

Nonetheless, color is still perhaps the ultimate status symbol in a society that exhibits great admiration for status symbols. Many darker Bahamians (who make up a good portion of the poorer classes) attempt to 'lift' their color by marrying a lighter-skinned person. On some of the Abaco Cays, few white descendants of the Loyalist settlers would even dream of

dating or – heaven forbid! – marrying a black person, though the two groups get along fine. Discrimination extends beyond white prejudice against blacks: The most virulent prejudice – among both black and white Bahamians – is against Haitians, a recent immigrant underclass.

The nation's politics and businesses were, until independence, dominated by whites and light-skinned 'brights,' otherwise known as Long Island or Eleuthera 'reds' (Bahamians whose predominantly white ancestry, with a dash of black, is reflected in their mahogany complexions).

There are no descendants of the indigenous Lucayans. But in and around Red Bay (Andros), you may note the distinct features of Seminole Indians, whose forefathers fled Florida and settled here two centuries ago.

Bahamian Blacks
The vast majority of blacks trace their ancestry to slaves brought from the Carolinas. They in turn were drawn predominantly from West African tribes such as the House, Ibo, Mandingo, and Yoruba. To a much greater degree than elsewhere in the Caribbean region, Bahamian blacks have historically favored their African heritages less than that of their former masters.

Various groups of blacks arrived in the Bahamas during the era of slavery. When Loyalists arrived in the islands, they brought with them their most trusted and able slaves. Slavetraders often called into Nassau en route to other destinations and sold Africans to local slaveholders. Scores of free blacks fled the USA for the islands, where many became large landholders (often slaveowners themselves) and prominent citizens. And thousands of runaway slaves – people of immense courage and imagination – and blacks liberated from slave ships by the British and landed in the islands as free people.

The brief-lived slave system was much less rigidly controlled than plantation systems elsewhere in the Americas. When slavery was abolished, the transition to a postemancipation society was relatively peaceful.

Bahamian Whites

Outside Nassau, most whites live in a few settlements where they are a conspicuous majority: Marsh Harbour, Cherokee Sound, and Treasure, Green Turtle, Great Guana, Elbow, and Man O' War cays (Abacos); and Spanish Wells and Harbour Island (Eleuthera). Each settlement has only a few family names – virtually everyone is an Albright on Man O' War. Other Loyalist names are Malone, Pinder, Sawyer, and Saunders.

Most whites in these settlements can claim descent from the earliest English settlers, Loyalists who fled the American Revolution. Others claim descent from Southerners escaping the US Civil War. A few like to claim ancestry from the English ruling elite. A far greater number are descended from pirates and vagabonds.

The white community in Nassau remains somewhat clannish and dominates the upper echelons of economic life. The British tend to excel in the financial industry. Greeks, Jews, and Lebanese (who form less than 1% of the population) have been successful in their own businesses and are insular and protective of their cultural heritage.

Then there are the thousands of part-time and full-time residents – predominantly North Americans – who have chosen The Bahamas as an escape from the prying eyes of the world. Expats' houses are sprinkled throughout the archipelago. Longtime residents can provide insights into local culture that lift away the idyllic veneer.

Conchy Joes Every Loyalist descendant and other Caucasian born in the islands is known as a 'Conchy Jo.' Family Island Conchy Joes are readily identifiable by their distinctive features: usually blue or green eyes, freckled skin, and blondish hair. They follow their own patterns of dress, speech, and behavior, distinct from those of black Bahamians and rather similar to stereotypical middle-American

ways. For a hilarious look at what it means to be a Conchy Jo, see *How to Be a True-True Bahamian* (Guanima Press) by Patricia Glinton-Meicholas.

Haitians

The islands have been 'invaded' in recent years by thousands of job seekers from other islands, predominantly Haiti and, to a lesser degree, the Dominican Republic and Jamaica. Most are illegal immigrants seeking a better life. Haiti is, after all, the poorest of all Caribbean countries, and The Bahamas the wealthiest! The Bahamian government tried repatriating the early refugees, but Haiti refused them.

Haitians (sometimes called 'Hyshuns' locally) fulfill menial tasks – farm labor, domestic work – that few Bahamians are willing to do. Thus they are hired illegally and exploited at below-minimum wages. Nonetheless, there is lingering resentment among Bahamians, who look down on Haitians and even despise them, based on the old bugbear that the immigrants have 'stolen jobs.' The prejudice, however, perhaps derives from a sense of racial superiority: Haitians are in general relatively darker-skinned and shorter than Bahamians.

Many Haitians and 'Bahatians' (Haitians born in The Bahamas) live in squalid conditions, often without sanitation or utilities. A recent Human Rights Watch report revealed that 90% of prisoners in The Bahamas are Haitians. The government seems to have given little thought to the problem.

EDUCATION

During the late 19th century, the British established the foundations of The Bahamas' admirable education system, based on their own model of schooling. More than 95% of the population is literate.

School attendance is compulsory through age 16 (up from 14). Some 80% of schools are government run. Most independent schools – called 'colleges' – are affiliated with a church body. Students work toward earning the Bahamas General Certificate of

Secondary Education in each subject (it is equivalent to the English GCE 'O' level but encompasses a broader range of abilities). Private postsecondary schools provide education in academic subjects and secretarial and technical skills. All students wear uniforms. Each school district has its own colors.

Few schools have computers or advanced teaching aids. However, the FNM administration has boosted spending on education and school construction and scrapped political appointments of school principals.

There are four bodies of higher learning. The University of the West Indies (UWI) has a campus in Nassau, attracting students from English-speaking Caribbean nations. It has a Center for the Hotel & Tourism Industry. The government-run College of the Bahamas, with two campuses in Nassau and one in Freeport, offers advanced-level ('A') certificates, diplomas, and degrees in the arts, sciences, humanities, and banking and finance. The Bahamas Hotel Training College provides training in hospitality fields. The Industrial Training Programme offers training in trade skills.

ARTS

Relative to its neighbors, The Bahamas is an arts backwater. The intellectual tradition is comparatively weak (compared to Jamaica or Cuba, for example). For a capital city, Nassau is surprisingly unsophisticated in the visual and performance arts. A wider search, however, reveals an evolving artistic tapestry. Quintessential Bahamian styles *have* evolved in music, dance, fine arts, and drama.

Music & Dance

From hotel beach parties to the raw 'sound system' dance clubs of Over-the-Hill, Nassau's poorer quarter, The Bahamas reverberates to the soul-riveting sounds of calypso, soca, reggae, and its own distinctive music, which echoes African rhythms and synthesizes Caribbean calypso and soca and English folk songs into its own 'goombay' beat.

Goombay This type of music – the name comes from an African word for 'rhythm' – derives its melody from a guitar, piano, or horn instrument accompanied by any combination of goatskin goombay drums, maracas, rhythm (or 'click') sticks, rattles, conch-shell horns, fifes and flutes, and cowbells to add a uniquely Bahamian *kalik-kalik-kalik* sound. It's typified by a fast-paced, sustained, infectious melody. Goombay is to The Bahamas what reggae is to Jamaica.

Goombay draws on a heritage of folk music introduced by African slaves from North America, Jamaica, and other neighboring islands. Particularly important are the 'talking drums,' once used to pass along information, and folk songs developed in the cane fields to ease the backbreaking labor. Over generations, European elements, such as the French quadrille introduced by planters, were absorbed as well, creating a unique style.

Goombay is most on display during Junkanoo celebrations (see the Junkanoo sidebar in the Facts for the Visitor chapter). The terms 'goombay' and 'Junkanoo' have become virtually interchangeable: 'Junkanoo' is often used to refer to this type of music, but it means, more strictly, the quintessential African-Bahamian celebration held at Christmastime.

Almost every major resort hotel has a goombay band or show, with male musicians and dancers of both sexes dressed in bright flounced costumes.

Rake 'n' Scrape In The Bahamas the down-home, working-class music is rake 'n' scrape, which usually features a guitar, an accordion, shakers made from the pods of poinciana trees, and other makeshift instruments, such as a saw played with a screwdriver.

Rake 'n' scrape music can be heard at local bars throughout the islands.

Calypso, Reggae & 'Chatting' Though calypso and reggae are more closely associated with Trinidad and Jamaica, many hotels feature a steel-drum band or reggae musicians in their weekly repertoire of entertainment.

Dance hall, which is a kind of Caribbean rap and the in-vogue working-class music of formerly British Caribbean islands, has evolved its own style in The Bahamas, where it is known as 'chatting.' It is performed entirely in local dialect. The music has its origins in the USA's urban ghettos of the 1990s, and usually has a monotonous yet fast-paced, compulsive beat, often with vocals added to the rhythms. It is most often performed by local DJs with their own mobile discos. The lyrics are generally sexually explicit and often glorify violence. Check out Tony Mackay's 'Natty Bon Dey' on his *Canaan Lane* album (1994).

Chatting has an ancestor known as 'rigging' – see the Traditional Culture section in this chapter.

Other Sounds The Bahamas has evolved its own church music, too. Spirituals were brought to the islands by Southern Loyalists' slaves, then adapted to incorporate purely Bahamian 'call and answer' techniques, rhyming exchanges of voices. Many secular songs took on a quasicalypso beat and addressed local events, be it a sex scandal or local superstition.

The 1990s have witnessed an upwelling of Bahamian popular music, and the new diversity has been carried to Nassau's radio stations. The music blends reggae and rap with goombay. The lyrics tend to be more upbeat, however, than those of reggae, which was born in the ghettos of Kingston. Bahamian musicians reflect the relative lack of tensions and simmering social protest, and turn to praise of God, fast sex, and the female form. The calypso-soca songs of popular local artist KB, for example, have titles like 'She Fat,' 'Juicy Suzy,' and 'Only Meat,' which bring on a good chuckle among hip Bahamians, reflecting as they do a preference among Bahamian men for full-bodied women.

Sexual relations are a steadfast source of musical inspiration. One of the nation's most popular songs is 'Shame and Scandal in the Family,' an amusing and lively ditty about 'outside' children, those birthed or sired by someone other than the mother's or father's spouse.

Watch for performances by the Baha-Men, the top island group. The 'Obeah Man,' alias Tony Mackay, a flamboyant performer and musical superhero from Cat Island (he now lives in Miami), has become a bit of a cult figure in the USA. His wild costume includes waist-length braided hair – 'Junkanoo locks' – an elaborate hat, and bells and other musical contraptions strapped to his body. His music is pure goombay. His recordings are available on the Mercury Records label and Mackay's own Nassau label. In 1987 he was awarded the British Empire Medal, thus becoming Sir Tony. 'No, no, no,' he laughs, 'Grassroots, man. Gotta stay with de people.'

Literature

While The Bahamas has produced no writer of world renown, the nation does have its literati. Few, however, are known even within the Caribbean region.

The most popular body of homegrown work draws on The Bahamas' unique Loyalist history. The authors themselves tend to be descendants of Loyalists. A good example is Captain Leonard M Thompson, a WWII Royal Canadian Air Force veteran and former prisoner of war who is considered the father of modern tourism in The Bahamas. His autobiographical *I Wanted Wings* is a perennial favorite among Bahamians and a splendid introduction to Bahamian history and ways.

Bahamian Anthology (College of The Bahamas) is a selection of poetry, stories, and plays by Bahamian writers. In a similar poetic vein, try *Bahamas: In a White Coming On* by Dennis Ryan (Dorrance).

Other works view Bahamian society through the eyes of foreigners who have traveled through the islands or settled there in recent decades. Perhaps the most famous example is *Out Island Doctor* by Evans Cottman, a Yankee teacher who fell for Crooked and Acklins islands in the 1940s.

Architecture

The islands have their own architectural styles. The Spaniards left few architectural traces, despite their early presence. Not so the early Bermudian settlers and US Loyalists, who brought their separate influences to bear.

Most plantation and government buildings were built of local sandstone and limestone, as were the homes of the wealthy. The stones were fixed and finished by mortar and plaster containing lime produced by burning conch shells. Being thick – sometimes as much as 3 feet – these massive walls became 'temperature sinks,' keeping the building relatively cool even during the heat of midday. To assist in cooling, breezes were permitted to flow through trellised windows, louvers, grills, and partition walls that didn't quite reach the ceiling.

The Family Islands are peppered with tiny square stone buildings – 'slave homes' – that have survived decay and natural disasters. Many are still inhabited. Each is the size of a pillbox, with a steep-angled, four-sided roof and an open kitchen in back, but no toilet. Communal outhouses (they, too, still stand) were built along the shore, where one would make a deposit straight into the sea.

Two common features on historic buildings are steep-pitched roofs and an absence of roof overhangs. Designed to reduce wind resistance during hurricanes, the steep pitch aids in rigidity and also prevents airfoil uplift (the process that 'lifts' an aircraft off the ground) when strong winds blow across it. The lack of overhang prevents the wind from peeling back the roof. Those shady verandahs you see everywhere are invariably separate 'sacrificial' extensions to the roofs, designed so that the wind may tear them away without taking the roofs as well.

On many islands, wooden houses are more prevalent. On Eleuthera and the Loyalist Cays of the Abacos, a distinctive style evolved that has been likened to that of Cape Cod in Massachusetts. The most splendid examples are in Dunmore Town and Spanish Wells (Eleuthera) and in Hope Town, New Plymouth, and Man O' War Cay (Abacos). The Bahamian clapboard house has been widely copied throughout the Caribbean. In the Turks and Caicos a uniquely Bermudian influence has been at work. Often the houses are made of ship-timber driftwood and planking, the framework filled with cemented rubble rock and finished in plaster. A close look at many of the pitched roofs reveals them to be stone that is stepped in the Bermudian fashion.

Smaller wooden homes in The Bahamas were elevated atop a masonry ground floor, with balconies supported by stilts or masonry pillars. Not only did this allow airflow beneath the living quarters, it also kept them above water level in the event of a hurricane surge.

Paint finishes were applied to the houses of the wealthy. These were produced from linseed oil, wood spirits, or turpentine derived from pine and mixed with ochre, sienna, and other mineral or organic pigments: iron oxides for barn red, copper oxides for green, cobalt for blue, and zinc for white. The latter two were expensive, and a white house with blue shutters became a true status symbol.

Film & Theater

The Bahamas is relatively theater-starved. There is no homegrown movie industry, although the islands are a popular locale for shoots (see the Facts for the Visitor chapter), which is why the Bahamas Tourist Board doubles as the Bahamas Film & Television Commission.

Visual Arts

The islands' plastic arts (ceramics, sculpture, painting, woodcarving, and textiles) have been late in flowering. Perhaps for this reason, The Bahamas as yet has no national gallery, although at press time plans were in the air to convert Dunmore House, the old governor's residence in Nassau. There are many commercial art galleries, mostly in Nassau, Marsh Harbour, and the Abacos. (The exceptional ones are discussed in the island chapters.)

Bahamian art has its origins in the 18th and 19th centuries, when itinerant English and American artists visited the islands and recorded their impressions in pen-and-ink sketches and paintings that reflected colonial society in an idyllic, romanticized light, and always from a Eurocentric point of view that totally ignored or mocked the African heritage.

Well into this century, the few leading artists were establishment figures who looked to Europe for inspiration. The Bahamas was spared the unfulfilled yearnings and turbulence of nationalism and black pride that erupted on several neighboring islands, and the lack of a truly national consciousness precluded the evolution of an expressive indigenous artistic movement.

Until recently there were very few artists painting full time: Brent Malone, Max Taylor, Rolph Harris, and Alton Roland Lowe – The Bahamas' artist laureate for more than three decades – come to mind. But today local talent is blooming. A collective visual style is evident, tending to portray a simple, idyllic notion of The Bahamas: shining-white clapboard houses, lush gardens, evanescent skies and seas, royal poincianas ablaze with orange. Junkanoo dancers and revelers are a common subject, as are sponge collectors, children fishing, and church congregations.

The oils of Alton Lowe, a seventh-generation Loyalist Abaconian, are much sought after by blue bloods and corporations. You may recognize Lowe's work on the nation's postage stamps, rendered in miniature.

Another of the country's leading artists is Eddie Minnis, a cartoonist, songwriter, and recording artist who is inspired by his devotion to the church of Jehovah's Witnesses. His limited-edition prints are popular, and his original oils, works of intricate detail and vibrant color (he paints less than a dozen per year), command thousands of dollars. Several galleries sell his prints; you can contact him directly at ☎ 242-335-1360, General Delivery, Current, North Eleuthera, Bahamas.

Minnis' two daughters, Nicole and Roshanne, have followed in his footsteps. Nicole is acclaimed for her depictions in oils of people and traditional island life. Roshanne's works tend to depict ocean scenes in soft pastels.

The so-called father of Bahamian art is Amos Ferguson, the foremost folk artist. Like Minnis, Ferguson is intensely spiritual. His palette-bright canvases focus upon religion, history, nature, and folklore, or 'ol' story.' Though sometimes crude – oil-based paint on cardboard, bearing his trademark childlike signature: 'Paint by Mr Amos Ferguson' – his works wear price tags of US$1500 or more. Recently Ferguson has begun making bird figurines (about US$20 each), tumblers, and jars for the tourist trade. You can see a permanent collection of his works in the Pompey Museum in Nassau.

Ferguson's abstract expressionism ripples through the world of Bahamian art, influencing important young artists such as Eric Ellis, two generations his junior. Ellis is one of five prominent artists who comprise BCAUSE – Bahamian Creative Artists United for Serious Expression.

The most noteworthy experimental artist is Janine Antoni, from Grand Bahama. Antoni made headlines at the Whitney Biennial in 1993 when she lowered her naked body into a bathtub filled with animal fat. Antoni's unique art includes painting the floor with her hair and gnawing on huge blocks of chocolate and lard. 'A confectioner's day ruined by a beaver,' reported one witty reviewer.

Another artist is Sonia Isaacs, famous for her paintings' bright tropical colors and for her unglazed pottery. Isaacs depicts local culture and personalities in a kind of paint-by-numbers style, with a uniquely intuitive, often hallucinogenic manner.

Ceramics has blossomed in recent years, thanks in large part to the influence of Denis Knight, a septuagenarian British expat acclaimed for his ceramic murals, which adorn several public buildings. Several other expats have brought their own influences.

A splendid coffee-table book on the subject is *Bahamian Art* by Patricia Glinton-Meicholas, Charles Huggins, and Basil Smith (The Counsellors Press, Nassau).

Crafts

Bahamian artisans produce basketry and other straw-work from native thatch palm. But as tourism has increased, cheap straw goods have been imported from Asia to augment local supplies. These imports have virtually killed off native weaving. Pockets of weavers remain, particularly on Cat Island and in Red Bay, where beautiful straw baskets are woven watertight! (See the Things to Buy section in the Facts for the Visitor chapter for more information.)

With the exception of straw-work, the crafts industry is relatively undeveloped. It has been influenced in recent years by the influx of Haitians, who have inspired intuitive hardwood carvings, often brightly painted and highlighted by pointillist dots.

SOCIETY & CONDUCT
Traditional Culture

Very few traces remain of the indigenous Lucayan Indian culture, though many words have been passed down into common parlance. Much of what remains of traditional culture is a legacy of the African slaves who brought their music, folktales, and religious beliefs.

Folktales Bahamian folktales have a tradition dating back to the slavery era. Storytellers have maintained an oral literature of folk stories, many of which bear a similarity to those of black residents of the US South. Particular favorites are tales of animal trickster-heroes such as Bredda (Brother) Rabbie and Bredda Bookie, who survive against the odds by virtue of quick wit, intelligence, cunning, and ingenuity.

Other purely local figures have evolved and found their way into folktales, many of which are firmly believed as fact. Perhaps the best known are the mischief-making chickcharnie of Andros and the sirens and Loch Ness Monster-like creatures of the blue holes of Andros and Cat Island. The 'bunce' is a bogeyman, an evil spirit that inhabits forests.

Ad-libbing or 'rigging' lyrics as part of the chanting and telling of myths has traditionally been used to pass down morals to children. Spiritual and folkloric figures abounded in rigged tales. Adults, as salacious in past years as now, were subtle in disguising much that was implied in the songs. Thus guileless children could hardly guess the truth of things when they heard that 'Mama look up in daddy's face all night long.'

Several books trace the evolution and meaning of Bahamian folktales, including *Bahamian Lore: Folk Tales and Songs* by Robert Curry and *An Evenin' in Guanima: A Treasury of Folktales from The Bahamas* by Patricia Glinton-Meicholas.

Spirit Beliefs Many Bahamians still keep spirit beliefs held over from slave days, when African religions melded with Christianity. Rooted in the animist beliefs of West Africa (animism has nothing to do with animal spirits; the name is derived from the Latin word *anima*, meaning 'soul'), they are based on the tenet that the spiritual and temporal worlds are a unified whole.

A core belief is that spirits live independently of the human or animal body and can inhabit inanimate objects. They can communicate themselves directly to humans and are usually morally neutral; it is the service to which humans call them that determines whether they will be a force of good or evil. Cantankerous, onerous people beget evil 'sperrids'; kind and thoughtful people beget good spirits. Spirits particularly like to live in silk cotton trees, of which many Bahamians are extremely wary.

Spirits reveal themselves on a whim; not being able to see them doesn't mean they aren't there. Many Bahamians believe that if you take the 'bibby' (mucus) from a dog's or horse's eye and put it in your own, you can actually see a spirit.

All kinds of practices have evolved to guard against evil spirits. An example is

'Moonshine Babies,' an almost defunct children's game played by moonlight. One person lies on the ground while others outline his or her body with pieces of broken glass. The person is then lifted up without disturbing the glass fragments, in the belief that this takes away evil spirits or illness. Even physicians are known to tie a black cord around a newborn baby's wrists to guard against evil spirits. A Bible is often placed at the head of a sleeping child, for the same reason. And if this fails, a Bahamian may attempt to dispel a malicious spirit by marking Xs all around and repeating the all-powerful phrase, 'Ten, 10, the Bible 10.'

For more information, see the sidebar on obeah – the practice of African witchcraft – in the Cat Island chapter, and pick up *Ten, Ten, the Bible Ten – Obeah in The Bahamas* by Timothy McCartney.

Bush Medicine Traditional folk healing is still alive, especially in the Family Islands, where locals have a suspicion of doctors and cling to folk remedies. Bush-medicine healers, often respected obeah practitioners, rely on native herbs, which they mix into concoctions, using recipes that have been handed down through many generations.

The sovereign ingredient is cerasee *(Mormodica charantia)*, an orange-fruited vine credited with resolving every imaginable human ailment. Aloe is also used for curing many ills, from sunburn to insect bites. Breadfruit leaves are said to cure high blood pressure.

Not all the cures use berries and leaves. For example, 'goat nanny' (goat droppings) is said to cure whooping cough, while congested air passages are cured by pouring 'chamber lye' on the head. This golden liquid is named for the pot into which a person relieves himself at night when not blessed with an indoor toilet.

A good reference is *Bush Medicine in The Bahamas* by Leslie Higgs.

Modern Culture

Contemporary Bahamian culture revolves around the family, the church, and, away from Nassau, the sea. Many cultural influences seep in from the USA.

National Character The population is perhaps the *least* Caribbean in style and attitude of any in the region. The culture might strike the experienced traveler as rather soft-edged, devoid of nuance and piquancy. The islanders have not developed a uniquely identifiable character, as have the Rastafarians of Jamaica. The nation hasn't evolved the intellectualism of Cuba, a well-defined art school, or a sharp-edged, pithy wit. But Bahamians *have* developed their own eccentricities.

In some ways Bahamians are terribly British. During the colonial era, white society was divided between Bahamian whites, or 'colonials' (those born in the islands), and English émigrés, who considered themselves an elite. Many wealthy Bahamian whites were accepted into the latter class, which established strict barriers to maintain the purity of the social hierarchy. To progress in society required one to become as British as possible in all spheres of life.

Although the nation has been independent since 1973, many British traditions and attitudes remain. Perhaps this is why Bahamians are notably pacific, quiescent, and noncommittal. It is often said that they avoid direct eye contact because they are shy.

The islanders have nonetheless melded their Britishness with certain classically Caribbean behaviors. They move with an air of un-American casualness. Fortunately, their easygoing gait is not without purpose. They simply carry on their affairs with a benign, nonchalant calm, like the measured sway of marine plants in the flow of a current. Traffic jams in downtown Nassau and Freeport are often chaotic, yet you won't hear swearing or deafening honking.

Bahamians are very relaxed toward rules and regulations, and they seem to regard set times for appointments as general guidelines. 'Fashionably late' is the white Bahamians' term for this attitude; black

Bahamians, on the other hand, call it 'BT' (Bahamian Time).

The proximity of North America has had a profound influence on contemporary Bahamian life and society. North American values and consumer tastes have especially influenced the middle classes. Fast-food franchises abound. There's a telephone for every second person. The Bahamas has more satellite systems per capita than any other nation. And the destination of choice is south Florida, where Bahamians flock to malls and car dealerships.

Wit & Humor Though Bahamians – in contrast to the infamously unsheepish Jamaicans – have no great love for drama, they *do* appreciate a somewhat understated yet sardonic wit and keen sense of humor, preferably laced with sexual undertones. They like to make fun of people, usually in the subtlest way, but they accept being the butt of others' humor in good grace. Individual foibles and physical abnormalities are good sources of fun.

Being a reticent people, however, Bahamians will rarely direct their humor at you, the foreign visitor. If they do, take it in good humor. Their deprecating and self-deprecating wit is never meant to sting. You'll be an instant hit if you give as good as you get, but the key is subtlety, not malice.

Work & Social Ethic Bahamians are very contented, with few of the anguishes suffered by other island peoples in the region. The work ethic is pronounced. Few Bahamian workers arrive late or call in sick. One rarely sees the malingerers of other countries, such as work crews snoozing beside the road. And most service staff display eagerness to please. It's true that, in general, The Bahamas offers service with a smile. It just might take a while.

Most Bahamians understand that their lifeblood is tourism. This recognition bolsters their natural sense of courtesy and a desire to please. But they are a proud, self-secure people who request the same respect that they willingly offer to tourists. Most

Bahamians do not tolerate even a hint of condescension. Anyone who treats hotel staff like hired help is likely to be told, 'Don't disrespect me. Make me feel like you know me.'

Bahamians regularly perform acts of great kindness, and not only toward those they know – the calendar is filled with events in aid of charity.

Urban Culture There are really two Bahamian cultures: that of Nassau and Freeport and that of the more lackadaisical Family Islands.

In Nassau and Freeport most working people are employed in banking, tourism, or government work and live a nine-to-five lifestyle. The maturation of the banking and finance industries has fostered the growth of a large professional class, many of whom have grown extremely wealthy. The streets thrum with expensive new cars. Men and women alike dress in elegant clothes, and stores stocked with Armani suits and Donna Karan blouses serve the local nouveau riche as well as the well-heeled tourist. The poorer classes, when 'dressed to the nines,' tend to adopt a 1960s hip look – a polyester suit, white tie over black shirt, alligator shoes, and fedora are typical. Bright colors and tight clothes are de rigueur for younger women, as are Nike and Fila athletic shoes, oversize shirts, baggy jeans, and plenty of gold for young males.

There are few airs or pretenses, although such attitudes are beginning to seep into the behavior of some younger adults. A growing number of younger Bahamian men, influenced by the symbolism of US and Jamaican gangsta rappers, have an 'I' mentality, act arrogantly, and, alas, adopt a threatening swagger. Fortunately, such behavior is the exception, not the rule. For every wisecracking tough wanting to separate you from your money, you'll meet dozens of genuinely charming people with a friendliness that never pales.

It is generally acknowledged that Nassau and Freeport went through a character crisis in the 1980s, when a surly mood was evident. Past visitors and local business-people alike will tell you that until a few years ago, many people in Nassau and Freeport were cursed with an aggressive, devil-may-care attitude that contributed to a bad reputation abroad.

Today people are markedly friendlier and the level of service is very high. To cement the turnaround, the FNM govern-ment has initiated programs to get locals involved in tourism and educate them about its fragility. 'Tourism 2000' gives hospitality employees and students a chance to be hotel guests themselves. And the 'People-to-People' program (see the sidebar on the program in the Facts for the Visitor chapter) matches tourists with locals for meals, religious services, and other aspects of daily life.

Family Islanders The folks of the Out Islands – the Family Islanders – live lan-guid lives in the sun and are altogether more at ease and neighborly than people in Nassau and Freeport. Unspoiled by city life, Family Islanders are friendliness per-sonified, displaying a gentle wisdom and ever-present caring for other people. They take time to chat and to invite strangers to their homes. Traditional courtesies and a sense of integrity and dignity remain firm, untainted by tourism, which has barely touched many islands.

Family Islanders are an honest, hard-working lot. They have little in the way of material goods, but 'their character and dig-nity are gold,' says author Harvey Lloyd. They have manners and pride. They are also far more traditional in outlook than their urban counterparts. Thus the practice of obeah, bush medicine, and folkloric songs and tales still infuse their daily lives, reflecting their bonds with nature.

After emancipation, most former slaves turned to fishing and subsistence farming, which have supported Family Island com-munities for generations. Many families don't need employment, getting by through fishing, catching conch and lobster, and raising corn, bananas, and other crops for the kitchen. Some people earn a little from straw weaving; many still hunt tusked wild boar with dogs in the scrub and pinelands.

There is plenty of poverty in the Family Islands. Most people live a hand-to-mouth existence alleviated by the govern-ment's social security system. At best, the local soils support only subsistence crops, and local economies are underdeveloped. Throughout, you'll see tiny square stone houses with steepled roofs (see the Archi-tecture section in this chapter). Many are nearly derelict and yet still inhabited, often by entire families.

In recent decades a desire for paid jobs has shrunk the settlements. Nassau has absorbed half of all Bahamians. Those who remain still live in the close-knit, tiny vil-lages where they were born. They're curi-ously uncurious about life in distant places.

The islanders are raised from torpor by the unpredictable arrival of the mail boat, upon which most of them rely to ship their fruit, vegetables, and straw-work to market and to deliver basic necessities. The circus often begins even before the boat docks, as everyone gathers, carrying burlap sacks of potatoes or balancing their bundles and boxes.

Children Bahamian children are one of the joys of the islands. Raised with love and firm discipline, schoolchildren with cheery smiles and uniforms stream up and down the streets on the way to or from school. They are orderly and courteous; you'll rarely see bad behavior among children of school age. In groups, they are not wild or out of control. 'When a child sick, teacher say, "Be silent, close hands, close eyes," and we bow heads and pray for child.'

Tittle-Tattle Isolation and the small scale of things have fostered another integral component of Bahamian culture: gossip, called 'sip-sip,' incorporating everything from political events to who's sleeping with whom. Everybody knows everyone else's business. And they're sure to share it. The more salacious, the better.

Patricia Glinton-Meicholas, author of The Island Life Series of books about The Bahamas, says that men tend to talk about 'women, sex, sports, politics, cars, and money,' and, more specifically, 'fast women, clandestine sex, fast sports, clandestine politics, fast cars, and fast and clandestine money.' Women, she says, like to talk about 'their weight, their clothing, their men, their marriage, their children, their hair, their religions, their careers, their education,' and, more specifically, 'other women's men, marriages, children, hair, religion, careers, and education.'

Names Black Bahamians hold great store by Christian names, and the biblical patriarchs and matriarchs offer steadfast favorites. A 'true-true' Bahamian may also be named for a celebrated personality or event or may have a purely homegrown name that combines established favored syllables.

For girls, favored prefixes are 'La,' 'De,' 'Sham,' or 'She,' followed by a favored suffix such as 'kera,' 'meka,' 'nika,' 'tika,' 'tishka,' 'neisha,' 'tisha,' or 'essa.' The prefix 'sha' or 'shan' is often used as a middle syllable, as in Lashandra. Thus you may meet Shanae, Latishka, Shameka, Denae, or Shakera. Any combination is permitted. The same prefixes are favored for boys, often with such suffixes as 'ario,' 'ardo,' 'ron,' and 'vaughn,' forming popular names like Danardo, Devon, Demark, Rashad, and Shevaughn.

White children are usually given plain, old-fashioned English names (Andrew, Charles, William, Edward, Susan, Elizabeth), or other names drawn from the land of their cultural heritage.

You'll see the same surnames over and over again, regardless of color. Many Bahamian blacks inherited their last names from slaveowners. On Great Exuma, where Lord Rolle had his estates, half the population still bears his name.

Pastimes On weekends Bahamians follow social pursuits similar to those of Europeans or Floridians, taking to the basketball court, soccer field, or the beach, where they may gather the family, set up a barbecue grill, and turn up the goombay music. Bahamians tend to avoid touristed beaches in favor of more secluded spots. They spend a lot of time just hanging about in the water (the ocean shallows are also favored for making love). Bahamians, however, are *not* swimmers, although they are great sailors and fisherfolk. Every second household seems to have a boat or Jet Ski.

Bahamian kids play basketball with a passion. The islands' patron saint is Mychal Thompson, a Los Angeles Lakers player from Harbour Island and the first Bahamian to make it to the NBA. Most towns have a small court with makeshift stands. Bahamians follow the US basketball and baseball leagues with intensely loyal fervor.

Of late, body sculpting has become popular, perhaps because hardly a weekend goes by without a beauty pageant or 'sexiest-swimsuit' (interpret that as 'sexiest-body') contest.

Being a gregarious people, islanders have pastimes that revolve around their extended families. No excuse is needed for a family cookout. Weddings, birthdays, christenings, and other family events bring in the most distant of blood relatives. Bahamians are also great joiners of choirs, youth groups, and above all, church groups and charity organizations. Fraternal lodges such as the Rotary Club are particularly popular among both males and females; you'll often see lodge members marching down the street in groups.

Sex & Family Life Despite their Christian beliefs and demure exterior, Bahamians are relatively sexually promiscuous, beginning at an early age. (Couples may marry as young as 15 with parental consent, and even 13-year-olds may marry if given special permission by the courts.) The joy of sex seems to be acknowledged as one of God's blessings. Extramarital affairs are common, as are unwed mothers. About 57% of all births in The Bahamas are to single females, and 24% of these mothers are teenagers.

Though Bahamian men tend to act publicly with due respect toward women, the women live unhappily with the knowledge that a large percentage of island males are philanderers. Many women, it seems, hope for a better man to come their way; hence they, too, are prone to discreet trysts. It is part of the accepted way. 'Outside children,' the offspring of an illicit union between a married man and a woman other than his wife, are accepted into the man's home (his wife often ends up raising the child). A woman who becomes pregnant by another man, however, is usually cast out of the house. Thus the standard joke: 'You can ask who yo mama is, but don't ask who yo daddy is!'

Again, there are differences between blacks and whites and between the urbane of Nassau and the Family Islanders. Conchy Joes, it is claimed, retain more courtly habits between the sexes. Homegrown Family Islanders still like their women 'to stay to home.'

A rule of thumb in the islands is: 'If you've got it, flaunt it!' Scores of Bahamian women sign up for beauty contests to do just that. 'Sexiest Male' competitions are equally popular, when otherwise discreet Bahamian women jostle for seats and whoop and scream at every flex of a muscle. Iron-hard biceps and tight jeans seem to be what counts.

Women Bahamian women are strong and fiercely independent, again a legacy of surviving the hardships of a slave society. Although the first female member of Parliament, Jane Bostwick, was elected only in 1982, women have progressed markedly in recent years in politics and business.

Despite recent progress, however, The Bahamas is still a chauvinistic place. The menfolk, for example, expect their working spouses to cook their meals and clean house. Younger women in particular frequently complain that local males treat them as chattel, talking down to them and ordering them about.

Female visitors to the islands, however, shouldn't encounter any problems. (See Women Travelers in the Facts for the Visitor chapter.)

Dos & Don'ts

Do relax. Time (and service) seems to move at a slower pace in the islands. 'Soon come,' a favorite expression, means 'it'll happen when it happens.' Don't expect that you can improve the situation by being rude or throwing tantrums. Most Bahamians will probably simply shrug their shoulders.

Don't call Bahamians 'natives.' Bahamians may be natives of the islands, but the term is laden with racial connotations that can be taken as slurs. 'Islanders' (or simply 'Bahamians') is more appropriate.

Do ask before snapping a photo. Most Bahamians enjoy being photographed, but occasionally you may find someone who prefers not to pose for tourists.

Don't teach children to beg. Begging is virtually unheard of in The Bahamas. However, in the Family Islands children often ask tourists for money. Giving it sets a bad precedent. If your conscience is tweaked, it is far better to give a useful item, preferably something educational.

RELIGION

The Bahamian people are almost pathological in their religious fervor. The overwhelming majority of islanders are devout believers who profess to live by the word of God. Every coincidence, good piece of luck, stroke of ill fortune, or other noteworthy occurrence is credited to His will or that of Satan.

Virtually every taxi driver has a Bible at hand, as do many office workers. State functions and the school day begin with prayers. Church affairs make headline news, while major international events are relegated to the inside pages. Every political speech is peppered with biblical quotations. And the nation claims the greatest number of churches per capita in the world.

The vast majority of Bahamians are mainstreamers – Baptists (32%), Anglican (20%), Catholic (18%), or Methodist (6%). The official state religion is the Anglican

Church. Many Christian priests hedge their bets and mix a little good-willed obeah into their practice.

Every island is a veritable jumble of chapels and churches – usually Baptist revival centers, referred to as 'jumper churches' by locals – with every conceivable body in the world represented (one of my favorites is the Feed My Sheep Church of God). Even the tiniest settlements boast two or three churches, and it is quite possible to see as many as a dozen churches, many quite small, in settlements with barely 200 people. Fundamentalists have made serious inroads in recent years. Some Family Islands have been won over by a single church (Seventh-day Adventists, for example, predominate on Crooked Island).

The smallest congregations are often served by itinerant priests who make the rounds between islands. Sometimes you might come across a lay preacher giving a sermon beneath a shade tree, complete with amplifier and speakers, the better to attract the masses with his – it's always a man – hip 'chattin' rap in praise of de Lord.'

On any day or night you'll pass services in progress. On Sunday every church in the country seems to overflow with the righteous. The women arrive in high heels, glittering silk dresses, and fancy hats, accompanied by girls in white dresses trimmed with ruffled lace. The boys and men don their best suits and ties. They arrive by car or walk along country roads, holding their Bibles and braving the infernal heat.

The old fire-and-brimstone school of sermonizing is still the preferred mode. Crowded church pews rock with rapturous clapping and lusty hymn after hymn until it seems they'll raise the dead. Bible-waving congregations sway to and fro, roll their heads, and wail, 'Hallelujah!' and 'Amen, sweet Jesus!' while guitars, drums, and tambourines help work the crowds into a frenzy. Often a church will have its own five-piece electric band.

The Bible is taken as divine instruction, not just a good-living guidebook written by the ancients, but some patterns of daily behavior don't square well with professed Christian tenets. Witness, for example, the astonishing degree to which God-fearing islanders are involved in the drug trade. A far more righteous attitude is displayed toward alcohol than toward narcotics. These hypocrisies are especially apparent on Saturday; many believers hold that though Sunday is dedicated to the soul and the Lord, the first day of the weekend may be given to the pursuit of pleasure.

Funerals

Some of the most important events on a Bahamian family calendar are funerals. The national newspapers dedicate a huge percentage of space to announcing deaths and funerals (weddings get little play). Radio programs are frequently interrupted by death and funeral announcements that mournfully recite tedious lists of all the bereaved family members and friends.

Bahamian funerals are grand social events. People buy new clothes to wear. Musicians are hired, politicians fly in to offer eulogies, and the affairs are often dragged out for a full day (that's why they're almost always held on weekends). Some funerals are straight out of a melodramatic Hollywood epic, with alternating frenzies of exaltation and fits of tribulation that seem designed to send weak-hearted members among the mourners into the grave, too.

Bahamians keen like the Irish, although the nature of the wake differs from town to town and from religion to religion. Usually the wake has light-hearted moments, when tongues loosed by an excess of cheap rum tell tales of the deceased's past deeds and misdeeds. Then someone may sing a traditional dirge, says Patricia Glinton-Meicholas, in 'a voyeuristic urge to see the floodgates open in a proper display of grief.' The mourners descend into a miasma of wailing so as not to be accused of lacking respect for the dead.

Six-handkerchief tributes – billed under the title 'As I Knew Him' in funeral programs – are offered, in which the deceased's good character is often embellished to a degree that a spouse or close friend may be tempted to check the coffin to make sure it is occupied by the correct person. Tributes sound like idyllic nursery rhymes laced with lurid metaphor. The only thing missing is the gypsy violin. As soon as the funeral is over, the competing family groups begin gossiping about how such-and-such looked or behaved (see the Tittle-Tattle section in this chapter).

LANGUAGE

English, the official language and that of business and daily life, is spoken by everyone but a handful of Haitian immigrants, who speak their own creole.

'True-true' Bahamians, mostly black, usually speak both Bahamian Standard English (BSE) and their own distinct island patois, a musical Caribbean dialect with its own rhythm and cadence. Bahamian patois is less pronounced than many other Caribbean dialects. Though there are variances among the islands and between blacks and whites, all sectors of Bahamian society understand patois, the language of the street. Even polite, educated Bahamians, who tend to speak in a lilting Queen's or Oxford English, lapse into patois at unguarded moments.

See Books in the Facts for the Visitor chapter for titles on Bahamian English and patois.

Understanding Patois

When Bahamians speak patois, foreigners may find the discussion difficult to follow. However, rarely is it entirely incomprehensible, as it is, say, in Jamaica.

Bahamians have difficulty pronouncing 'th' and often drop the 'h,' as they may also do in words such as ''ouse' (for 'house'). Hence, 't'ree' for 'three,' 't'anks' for 'thanks,' and 'rat' for 'wrath.' 'The' is often pronounced as 'de' and 'them' as 'dem.' They also sometimes use 'v' in lieu of 'w' or drop the 'w,' as in ''ooman.' And the 's' sometimes disappears from the beginnings of words, as when cars ''mash up.' It also frequently disappears from the

ends of plurals, which are thus pronounced as singulars.

Bahamians often use transliteration, such as 'flim' for 'film.' They rearrange syllables and give them their own inflection, such as 'fillymingo' for 'flamingo.' 'Only' becomes 'onliest.' And 'fishing' is 'fishenin'.' The 'ed' is often dropped from the end of verbs – thus a 'slipped disc' becomes a 'slippy dick.' And someone with an 'onion' is really suffering from a hernia. Words are often repeated for emphasis, as in 'true-true.' Verbs are often deleted entirely: 'How de children?' or ''im lazy, yo know.'

Patois is not gender specific. People and things are simply ''im' or 'dem.' Possessive pronouns such as 'my' and 'mine' are often replaced by these words.

Hand-Me-Down Words

Many words in the Bahamian lexicon are carryovers from the early English colonial days – true Shakespearean English. The language is imbued with terms otherwise considered archaic. You may, for example, be served a drink in a 'goblet.'

Other words have been passed down from Africa, such as 'bo-bo' (fool) and 'nyam' (to eat).

A Manner of Speech

Female friends and acquaintances tend to address each other as 'chile' (for 'child'). Males generally prefer to use the term 'man.' Both words liberally spice general conversations. Both men and women commonly refer to members of the other gender (even strangers) as 'baby,' 'darling,' 'my love,' and similar endearing terms without any hint of sexist connotation or flirtation.

When Bahamians 'conversate,' they tend to inquire about the background of people they talk to, usually as a matter of establishing possible kinship. This is especially true of fellow Bahamians, who may be asked, 'Man, where you people from?' Likewise, 'Who yo daddy is?' and 'I bet you know my gran'daddy' are typical attempts to find some blood linkage.

Bahamians have a highly colloquial style of phrase. For example, typical greetings are: 'All is well?' (male) or 'Hey man, what happ'nin'?' and 'Chile, how you do? Me don't know de las' time I see you' (female). Expect to hear rejoinders such as: 'Tryin' to keep up wid' you rich people' or 'Right 'ere 'mong de strong.'

A woman with an ample posterior has a 'peas 'n' rice boungy.' A 'Gussy Mae' is a term of affection meaning a portly woman and reflecting the Bahamian male's penchant for flesh. And a Bahamian who intends to party is about to go 'spillygatin'.' No matter how wild they get, on Sunday Bahamians 'dress down to a fowl feather' for church service.

Bahamians have their own medical lexicon, too. You may hear terms such as 'cascating' for 'vomiting' and 'bound' for 'constipated.'

Another phrase you'll hear often is 'reach,' meaning 'arrive.' Thus, when you hear that 'de plane dun reach,' this means 'the airplane hasn't arrived.'

Talking Conchy Jo

Conchy Joes – Loyalist descendants and other Caucasians born in The Bahamas – have evolved their own unique dialects that, in general, sound vaguely Australian and have been described by several writers as Elizabethan in form and cadence. Personally, I detect a Cornish or Somerset accent (the closest English dialect to Elizabethan English) on Harbour Island and in Spanish Wells. For example, listen for 'horbor' for 'harbor,' 'cor' for 'car,' and 'Cholly' for 'Charlie.' Typically the 'h' is dropped from words, as it is in Yorkshire, and added to others where it doesn't belong. Thus, ''am and heggs.'

Conchy Joes have also evolved their own unique colloquialisms, such as 'A'am got to go.' They don't sound at all like black Bahamians.

Facts for the Visitor

PLANNING
When to Go

The Bahamas is a year-round destination. Its trade breezes ensure cool temperatures, so weather isn't a strong factor in determining when to go unless you're visiting the southern islands, especially the Turks and Caicos, which get infernally hot in summer. Winter months are preferable, with balmy weather and fewer mosquitoes, though 'snow birds' should be prepared for the possibility of cooler, cloudy days.

The so-called rainy season extends from May to November. This time of year is more humid than winter and receives 80% of the total annual precipitation, though usually rain falls only for short stints in late afternoon. Occasionally prolonged rain may fall for several days. Hurricanes are a slim possibility, and when they strike the entire island chain can come to a virtual standstill. Flights and sea traffic cease operation. You may wish to ensure that you have a few days' leeway during these months. Also see Climate in Facts about The Bahamas.

The peak season typically runs from mid-December to mid-April, when hotel prices are highest. This is the busiest period, when snow birds from North America flock.

Some hotels are booked solid around Christmas and Easter. You can save money and will find fewer foreign visitors if you visit in the low or off season (the remainder of the year), when many hotels reduce their rates by as much as 60%.

Some Family Island hotels close for the low season.

Maps

The Bahamas Tourist Office (see Tourist Offices, later in this chapter) distributes a pocket-size map to the islands that is widely available at hotel tour desks and tourist-information booths. It is a handy general reference, though many roads are inaccurately drawn.

You can order a series of Bahamas maps from Omni Resources (☎ 910-227-8300, 800-742-2677, fax 910-227-3748), PO Box 2096, Burlington, NC 27216. The series includes a 1:1,000,000 physical map (for US$14.95), separate 1:500,000 road maps of the northern and southern Bahamas (US$7.95 each), detailed 1:25,000 topographic maps (US$8.95 each), and also a Nassau city atlas (US$12.95).

You'll need a good road map for getting around New Providence. Car-rental companies can give you a basic (not entirely trustworthy) pocket map; ask for one at the rental counter. The most accurate and detailed map of New Providence is the 1:32,000 scale road map, with a 1:7000 scale inset of downtown Nassau, published by Island Maps, PO Box WK485, Warwick WKBX, Bermuda. It's available at a few stores in Nassau or from Holdfast Productions (☎ 242-323-7421), PO Box N-9562, Nassau, Bahamas. Dupuch Publications (☎ 242-323-5665, fax 242-323-5728) publishes *Bahamas Trailblazer Maps*, detailed street maps for Nassau and Freeport. These are readily available at tour desks in major hotels and resorts.

On the main islands, you'll find tourist newspapers with maps of varying accuracy (see island chapters for information). Many hotels provide local maps for their clients, but most are hand-drawn.

Few good maps of the Family Islands are available. The Bahamas Out Islands Promotion Board (see the Tourist Offices section) can supply *The Bahama Out Islands Travel & Map Guide*, a handy newspaper-size foldout with maps and descriptions of hotels, airlines, and other services. You can order it from Star Publishers (☎ 242-322-3724, fax 242-322-4527, boipb@ix.netcom.com), PO Box N-4855, Nassau, Bahamas.

Detailed maps of individual islands (except for the cities of Nassau and Freeport) are mostly limited to navigation maps and charts for pilots and mariners. See the Private Yacht section in the Getting There & Away chapter for information about maritime maps and charts; see the Private Plane section in that chapter for information about aeronautical charts.

The islands are neither mountainous nor challenging enough to require detailed Ordnance Survey maps. Still, if you plan to explore the remoter wilds, there are no better maps to be had. You can order individual Ordnance Survey sheets from the following companies:

France
Espace IGN, 107 rue la Boétie, 75008 Paris (☎ 01.43.98.85.00)
UK
Ordnance Survey International, Romsey Rd, Maybush, Southampton SO9 4DH (☎ 0703-792000, fax 0703-792404)
Stanfords, 12-14 Long Acre, London WC2E 9LP (☎ 0171-836-1321, fax 0171-836-0189)
USA
Map Link, 30 S La Patera Ln, Unit 5, Santa Barbara, CA 93117 (☎ 805-692-6777, fax 805-692-6787, fax 800-627-7768)
Rand McNally, 8255 N Central Park, Skokie, IL 60076 (☎ 847-329-8100)

What to Bring

Travel light! The Bahamas generally basks in subtropical warmth, and you shouldn't need much clothing. My motto is: If you can't take your main bag as carry-on onto an aircraft, you've packed too much for a one-week visit. I manage to survive adequately with a single small piece of luggage for a month or longer. What you'll need depends on where you'll stay. The fancier the resort, the more you will want to pack a selection of fancy clothes.

Keep in mind that Immigration officials have the authority to refuse entry to anyone they deem undesirable. They guard their image carefully, and travelers who look like vagabonds may be required to demonstrate sufficient financial means for their stay.

Clothing Loose-fitting, lightweight cotton clothing is best because it allows air to flow in the hot and sometimes humid climate. Tight clothing tends to make you sweat more and can get uncomfortable, as do synthetics like nylon. T-shirts and tank tops are the perfect wear for outdoors and are best worn without being tucked in.

White is the best color for reflecting the sun's rays but has the disadvantage of getting dirty quickly. You're going to sweat a lot, so unless you plan on doing laundry, consider darker colors that hide the stains! A long-sleeved shirt and long pants are useful in case you get sunburned. You'll also need long pants for more upscale dance clubs, casinos, nightclubs, and restaurants.

Don't forget one or two pairs of shorts, which can be your normal daywear, plus swimwear. Dress modestly in towns.

A light sweater might prove handy at night and in winter months, when it can get surprisingly cool.

Some hotels require casual eveningwear at dinner. Several of the posher hotel restaurants even require jackets (and ties in winter) for men and elegant dresses for women. Elsewhere fancy togs may be taken as a statement of the wearer's insecurities or snootiness. The casinos permit casualwear, but tank tops and skimpy clothes are frowned upon. You should also pack several fancy items if you're traveling on a cruise ship. Each company will provide specific information on dress formalities.

You'll get by with a pair of sneakers, sandals or flip-flops (thongs), and lightweight casual shoes for eveningwear.

If you plan on hiking, bear in mind variable weather conditions. Rain can fall at any time of year. Check the forecast and dress accordingly. Usually lightweight cotton clothing will suffice. Trousers rather than shorts are best for hiking through bush, as they protect against thorns. Often sneakers or tennis shoes are fine for hiking, but lightweight canvas hiking boots are better. You'll want something sturdier than sneakers to handle the sharp limestone found on many islands. And sturdy sandals are perfect for walks around the mud flats and coral shorelines.

Toiletries You will find toiletries widely available in Nassau and Freeport; however, bring them along if you plan on spending most of your time in the Family Islands. If you buy them in the islands, you'll pay a higher price than you would at home.

Generally only the top hotels in The Bahamas provide complimentary toiletries. Don't forget a washcloth: Many hotels don't have them. Unless you're staying at an upscale hotel, bring a beach towel or buy one in The Bahamas.

Supplies Bring a flashlight to use in the event of a blackout and to find your way along unlit streets or paths at night. I also consider a Swiss Army knife essential. Other essentials include zip-lock bags (for toiletries), a small laundry bag (for dirty and/or wet clothes), a small fold-up umbrella (which will also prove a handy parasol), plus a side-brimmed sun hat or baseball cap for shade (alternately, you can buy a straw hat in The Bahamas). Make sure your hat fits snugly; it's often breezy.

Camping & Sports Gear The Bahamas actively discourages campers. If you insist, bring everything you need. Make sure your tent is bugproof and capable of withstanding a good downpour. The few beachside sites that exist have barbecue pits, but you can't count on there being a restaurant nearby. You'll need to bring cooking gear if you plan on camping in the boondocks.

Some resorts with golf or tennis facilities rent equipment, as do scuba diving and snorkeling outlets. However, you may wish to bring your own.

SUGGESTED ITINERARIES

The following itineraries are for travelers *not* pursuing a particular interest (such as sailing, sport fishing, or scuba diving) and who are arriving and traveling by air. Scheduled air service between islands is limited (see the Getting Around chapter)

and has not been factored into the itineraries below.

Weekend in Nassau

Assuming that you don't simply want to laze by the hotel pool sipping cocktails and getting a tan, I recommend the following plan:

Day One – Take a walking tour of downtown Nassau, checking out Bay St for shopping, the Straw Market, and the Pompey Museum; the Junkanoo Expo; and Rawson Square and Fort Fincastle for historical highlights. Climb the water tower for a bird's-eye view. Better yet, hire a surrey (horse-drawn cab) and get a guided tour.

Day Two – Assuming you don't scuba dive, visit the underwater observatory at Crystal Cay, with a conch luncheon on Arawak Cay; or take a water taxi from Prince George Wharf and visit the marine park at Atlantis on Paradise Island. At night, visit a casino and/or take your pick of the Silk Cotton Club (for jazz), The Zoo (for disco), or the 601 Club (for upscale disco).

Week in Nassau

Assume two or three days at the beach, and use the weekend itinerary above as a base:

Day Three – Visit Ardastra Gardens and the nearby Botanical Garden to check out displays of The Bahamas' wildlife.

Day Four – Rent a car and drive around the island, with a stop for lunch and drinks with locals at Honeycomb Beach Club in Adelaide. En route, stop at Compass Point. Maybe you'll lunch here. If not, determine to return for dinner.

Day Five – Play a round of golf or tennis, followed by a three-hour underwater adventure aboard the *Atlantis TS-1* submarine.

Day Six – Enjoy a full-day powerboat ride to the Exumas, where you'll snorkel and meet the iguanas. Alternately, take a boat ride from Paradise Island to Blue Lagoon Island, where you can swim with dolphins.

Day Seven – You're out of here!

Extra nightspots to visit include Joker's Wild, Club Waterloo (for the wild and young-at-heart), and – to be one with the locals – the Same Ol' Place, to listen to rake 'n' scrape music. Also, treat yourself to dinner at Graycliff.

Weekend in Freeport

This one is easy:

Day One – Laze a little on the beach (preferably Taino); then maybe go shopping for duty-free goods at International Bazaar or Port Lucaya Marketplace. Enjoy lunch at Kaptain Kenny's at Taino Beach. If gambling is your thing, take in a casino.

Day Two – Perhaps a round of golf at any of three golf courses? Later, sign up with UNEXSO for a dolphin encounter.

Week in Freeport

Away from Freeport and Lucaya (twin towns), Grand Bahama offers limited attractions but enough to fill a week if you're active. Building on the weekend itinerary, try the following plan:

Day Three – Head to Rand Memorial Nature Centre, the Garden of the Groves, and Lucayan National Park to get close to nature. Pack a picnic and spend the afternoon at Gold Rock Beach, fronting the park.

Day Four – Take a glass-bottomed boat ride from Port Lucaya. Then, how about horseback riding at Pinetree Stables? Or sign up for a ride aboard the *Bahama Mama*.

Day Five – Head to McLean's Town, and then take a water taxi to the Deep Water Cay Club for lunch. Spend the afternoon bonefishing or lazing in a hammock. Or sign up at Port Lucaya to go sport fishing.

Day Six – Go sea kayaking in the mangroves, picnic lunch included.

Would-be scuba divers should pencil in three full days for certification training. Make sure to head out to Taino Beach on Wednesday night for the traditional fish fry.

Week in the Abacos

Two or three islands should do it. Here's my recommendation:

Day One – Fly to Marsh Harbour and take a water taxi to Elbow Cay. Explore the Loyalist village of Hope Town. Eat dinner at Hope Town Harbour Lodge.

Day Two – Laze on the beach. Explore the island by bicycle.

Day Three – Return to Marsh Harbour. Take a guided snorkel or dive trip or go fishing. Alternately, rent a boat and go to Man O'

War Cay to visit Joe Albury's boatbuilding studio or to Great Guana Cay for lunch at Nipper's.

Day Four – Rent a car and drive south to Little Harbour. Visit the studio and museum of Randolph Johnston, and enjoy a cocktail and lunch at funky Pete's Pub. Continue south to Different of Abaco (an alternate spot for lunch). Spend the afternoon bonefishing here or at Cherokee Sound, or continue south and endure the bone-rattling drive through Abaco National Park to the lonesome lighthouse. Take a coastal hike.

Day Five – Drive or take a taxi north of Treasure Cay, and then take a ferry ride to New Plymouth on Green Turtle Cay.

Day Six – Explore the Loyalist village of New Plymouth. Tonight, have a Goombay Smash or two at Miss Emily's Blue Bee Bar.

Day Seven – Return to Marsh Harbour and – *sigh!* – home.

12 Days in the Family Islands

Let's assume you want a rounded and diverse experience taking in three or four islands. I recommend the following plan:

Day One – Fly to Marsh Harbour and take a water taxi to Elbow Cay. Explore the Loyalist village of Hope Town. Have dinner at Hope Town Harbour Lodge.

Day Two – Laze on the beach. Explore Elbow Cay by bicycle. Check out the local night scene.

Day Three – Return to Marsh Harbour. Fly to Cat Island, using Fernandez Bay Village as your base.

Day Four – Rent a car and explore the island, stopping to chat with locals. Don't fail to climb Mt Alvernia to marvel at the hermitage of Father Jerome.

Day Five – Go snorkeling, diving, or fishing. Relax. Down a beer or two and play pool with locals.

Day Six – Fly to Stella Maris (Long Island). Go snorkeling at Cape Santa Maria and eat a picnic lunch; if you're hale and hearty, ride a bicycle to the Columbus Memorial.

Day Seven – Go diving. If you're certified, visit Shark Reef.

Day Eight – Rent a car and explore south to enjoy the seascapes, stopping at the Wild Tamarind Pottery & Gallery, the bat caves, Turtle Cove, and Clarence Town. Alternately, you may wish to overnight on Days Six through Eight at Lochabar Beach Lodge, spending your time relaxing, diving, snorkeling, and exploring.

Day Nine – Fly to North Eleuthera. Transfer to Harbour Island. If your budget allows, stay at Pink Sands. At the very least, dine here tonight.

Day 10 – Laze on Pink Sands Beach and explore Dunmore Town. Tonight, check out the action at the Vic Hum Club.

Day 11 – Take a day excursion to Spanish Wells.

Day 12 – Time for home.

For the Offbeat Traveler

To be a 'true-true' offbeat traveler, you'll move around by mail boat, and you'll need considerable time to do so (at least a day *each way* per island). Hence, here's a medley of recommended things to do:

Abacos – Join Bahamas Naturalist Expeditions and go kayaking, snorkeling, bird watching, hiking, and even swimming with dolphins. You'll want to overnight in rustic accommodations at Hole-in-the-Wall Lighthouse in Abaco National Park. At Walker's Cay, dive with the sharks at the famous Shark Rodeo, and then hitch a ride to Grand Cay and spend a few days fishing and hanging out with the locals.

Cat Island – Go hiking at Turtle Cove and canoeing at Armbrister Creek. Have a local guide take you bonefishing. Take time to get scuba certified. Immerse yourself in obeah culture.

Eleuthera – Hang with surfers at Surfer's Beach. Go sponging and lobstering with locals in Gregory Town.

Exumas – Go blue-hole diving and visit the cays for birding and local wildlife. Deposit yourself for a few days at Bowe Cay, where you can live a simple life on your lonesome, like Robinson Crusoe.

Great Inagua – Donate some time at the turtle reserve at Union Creek. Go bird watching in Inagua National Park, where a hike takes you into the heart of the flamingo preserve. Overnight at the rustic camp.

THE BEST

Dolphin Encounters – Nothing can prepare you for the thrill of an exalted encounter with dolphins on their own terms and on their own turf. Several operators offer swim-with-wild-dolphins trips that are guaranteed to leave you filled with boundless joy (see the Outdoor Activities chapter).

Abaco National Park – Few spots are as dramatic and serene as the lonesome headland at Hole-in-the-Wall, highlight of this forested park – a last refuge for the Bahama parrot. The hiking is splendid. It's a true escapists' dream for those who don't mind rustic accommodations.

Abacos' Loyalist Villages – The fistful of bicentenary Loyalist villages on Elbow, Man O' War, and Green Turtle cays exude irresistible charm. Splendidly preserved, gaily decorated clapboard houses have been pickled in aspic, and the Loyalists' descendants have managed to retain some of their old ways, adding a living-museum quality.

Inagua National Park – If the rewards of standing in the midst of the Western Hemisphere's largest flock of flamingos weren't enough for bird watchers, Great Inagua's saline ponds also attract countless other water birds.

Journeying by Mail Boat – You may choose only to do it once, or it may become the *only* way you travel between the islands, but a journey by mail boat is one to remember forever. Far from cushy, this is down-to-earth travel guaranteed to show you a side of life far from the tourist mainstream, and it's sure to bond you to the Bahamian people.

Family Island Regatta – Put yourself in a party mood and fly down to Great Exuma for the best time in the islands. This traditional sailing regatta pits local skippers against each other, while onshore the crowds whoop it up in a four-day party.

Harbour Island – This is *the* 'in' spot of the moment. Besides the charming historic village of Dunmore Town, 'Briland' boasts a stunning pink-sand beach, great nightspots, and a choice range of accommodations, including Pink Sands, my favorite spot to lay my head in the entire Bahamian chain.

Sport Fishing – Fisherfolk claim that wrestling a big one from the 'great blue river' is a tip-top thrill. If you can stomach it, your options are legion. Or for smaller yet no less challenging fry, try your hand at bonefishing; adherents swear that even great sex can't compare. You decide!

Swimming with Sharks – Phewee! You can go swimming with sharks while they feed at several locales. At Stella Maris and at Walker's Cay, you can witness a feeding frenzy just a few feet away. At Freeport and Nassau the sharks are hand-fed by a diver clad in chain mail. It's not for the timid!

Compass Point – Pay one visit to this brazenly colorful, unpretentious gem west of Nassau –

a sibling to Pink Sands (see Harbour Island, above) – and you'll understand why I try to end every Bahamas vacation here.

Cuba Excursions – If you like The Bahamas, you'll *love* Cuba, a one-hour flight away. Several tour companies offer single- to multiday excursions to this fascinating and friendly island of sensual charms. *One million* tourists visited in 1996! Be prepared to be pleasantly surprised. See the *¡Cuba Sí!* sidebar in the New Providence chapter.

THE WORST

This is where I lose friends and make enemies. Many hotels and attractions are dismal letdowns, despite being lauded. Here are a few of my least favorite things:

Bahamasair – Locals call it 'banana air.' Bahamians don't ask if their flight is on time; they ask, 'How late is the flight today?' Often flights are canceled. Just when you figure you have it worked out and can afford to dally on the way to the airport, the plane will take off 20 minutes early! Guaranteed, the next flight is in two days' time. Do you laugh or cry?

Conch – What *is* the big deal?

Freeport – It's hard to find anything encouraging to say about the town itself. 'Creeping, soulless, and dead as a doornail' about sums it up, though the golf courses are acclaimed, the duty-free shopping is passable, and the Bahamas Princess Resort & Casino is an admirable retreat. It's a poor man's Las Vegas. At least the beaches outside town make amends.

Island Transportation – Getting around on most of the islands is a harpy. In general, there's no such thing as public transportation. And name-brand car-rental companies give most of the islands a wide berth. Thus entrepreneurs have you by the short hairs and charge accordingly for beat-up vehicles that can't be guaranteed to last out the day.

TOURIST OFFICES

The Bahamas Tourist Office (BTO, ☎ 242-322-7500, fax 242-328-0945; in the USA ☎ 800-422-4262; in Canada 800-667-3777), PO Box N-3701, Nassau, Bahamas, publishes maps, directories, guides, and brochures on the islands. It has offices in most major tourist destinations, and its staff are usually very helpful. The office itself does *not* act as a reservation service, but it has a reservation service, Bahamas Reservations (in North America ☎ 800-700-4752). It also has a useful website; see Internet Resources in the back of the book.

In addition, the Family Islands are represented by the Bahamas Out Islands Promotion Board (☎ 954-359-8099, 800-688-4752, fax 954-359-8098, boipb@ix .netcom.com), 1100 Lee Wagener Blvd, No 204, Fort Lauderdale, FL 33315-3564. The board represents the interests of member hotels and other tourism suppliers. It also serves as a one-stop reservation center and should be the first place to call when planning a vacation to the Family Islands. The staff – Maura Brassil and Helen Fillmore – are incredibly helpful. They'll send you hotel brochures, lists of marinas and other special-interest facilities, the *Bahama Out Islands Travel & Map Guide*, and the Family Islands *Getaway* magazine.

See also Information & Reservations in the Accommodations section, later in this chapter.

Local Tourist Offices
BTO
    Airport Arrivals Terminal, Nassau
    (☎ 242-377-6806)
    Rawson Square, Bay St, Nassau, Bahamas
    (☎ 242-326-9781)
    International Bazaar, Freeport, Bahamas
    (☎ 242-352-8044)
    Queen Elizabeth Dr, Marsh Harbour,
    Abacos, Bahamas (☎ 242-367-3067)
    Queen's Hwy, Governor's Harbour,
    Eleuthera, Bahamas (☎ 242-332-2142)
    Bay St, Harbour Island, Eleuthera, Bahamas
    (☎ 242-333-2621)
    Queen's Hwy, George Town, Exumas,
    Bahamas (☎ 242-336-2430)
Grand Bahama Island Tourism Board
    International Bazaar, PO Box F-40252,
    Freeport, Grand Bahama, Bahamas
    (☎ 242-352-8044, fax 242-352-2714)
Nassau/Paradise Island Promotion Board
    Hotel's House, Dean's Ln, Nassau,
    Bahamas
    (☎ 242-322-8383/4, fax 242-326-5346)

Tourist Offices Abroad

The BTO has a central information office in Denver, CO, that sends out literature (in the USA ☎ 800-422-4262). In addition, there are various regional offices in the USA and offices in other countries as well:

Canada
 121 Bloor St E, No 1101, Toronto, ON
 M4W 3M5
 (☎ 416-968-2999, fax 416-968-6711)
France
 60 rue Saint Lazare, 75009 Paris
 (☎ 01.45.26.62.62, fax 01.48.74.06.05)
Germany
 Leipzigerstrasse 67D, 60487 Frankfurt
 Main (☎ 69-970-8340, fax 69-970-8343)
Italy
 via Cusani N7, 20121 Milano
 (☎ 2-72-02-30-03, fax 2-72-02-31-23)
UK
 3 The Billings, Walnut Tree Close,
 Guildford, Surrey GU1 4UL
 (☎ 01483-448900, fax 01483-448990)
USA
 California
 3450 Wilshire Blvd, Suite 1204, Los
 Angeles, CA 90010
 (☎ 213-385-0033, fax 213-383-3966)
 Florida
 1 Turnberry Pl, 19495 Biscayne Blvd,
 Aventura, FL 33180
 (☎ 305-932-0051, fax 305-682-8758)
 Georgia
 2957 Clairmont Rd, No 150, Atlanta,
 GA 30345
 (☎ 770-270-2836, fax 770-633-1575)
 Illinois
 8600 W Bryn Mawr Ave, No 820, Chicago,
 IL 60631
 (☎ 773-693-1500, fax 773-693-1114)
 Massachusetts
 PO Box 1039, Boston, MA 02117
 (☎ 617-485-0572, fax 617-426-3372)
 New York
 150 E 52nd St, 28th Fl, New York, NY
 10022 (☎ 212-758-2777, fax 212-753-6531)
 North Carolina
 11133 Leaden Hall Ln, Charlotte, NC
 28213 (☎ 704-543-0991, fax 704-549-9540)
 Texas
 World Trade Center, No 525, 2050
 Stemmons Fwy, Dallas, TX 75258
 (☎ 214-742-1886, fax 214-741-4118)
 PO Box 2190, Sugarland, TX 77487
 (☎ 713-265-2190)

Other tourist information bureaus in the USA include the Grand Bahama Island Tourism Board (☎ 800-448-3386) and the Nassau/Paradise Island Promotion Board (☎ 305-931-1555, fax 305-931-3005), which shares the BTO's regional office in Aventura, FL (see above).

VISAS & DOCUMENTS

Canadians and citizens of the UK and Commonwealth countries may enter The Bahamas without a passport or visa for up to three weeks. For longer stays, a passport is required. However, UK citizens need to show a passport to re-enter their home country. US citizens do not need a passport for stays of less than eight months but must show proof of citizenship (a passport, voter registration card, etc). Regardless, it is wise to travel with your passport.

Citizens of most European countries, Turkey, and Israel require passports but no visas for stays up to three months. Visitors from most Central and South American countries, including Mexico, require passports but no visas for stays up to 14 days. Visas are required for longer stays.

Citizens of the following countries require passports and visas for stays of any duration: Dominican Republic, Haiti, South Africa, and all Communist countries. Citizens of other countries should check current entry requirements with the nearest Bahamian embassy or with the Immigration Dept (☎ 242-322-7530, fax 242-326-0977), PO Box N-831, Hawkins Hill, Nassau, Bahamas.

If you lose your passport while in The Bahamas, you'll need to visit your embassy, consulate, or high commission. If your country does not have such a facility in The Bahamas, contact the Ministry of Foreign Affairs (☎ 242-322-7624/7590), E Hill St, Nassau. Its postal address is PO Box N-3746, Nassau, Bahamas.

Photocopies

You should make two photocopies of your most valuable documents before leaving home. You should include your passport, your driver's license, airline ticket, hotel vouchers, health insurance, etc. Keep one copy at home. Carry the second copy with you, but keep it separate from the originals.

Travel Permits

No travel permits are required for standard visitors. However, you'll need to fill out an immigration card upon arrival (usually this is handed out onboard the aircraft, but if not, you'll find them in the arrivals lounge). You must show it when you depart and also for bank transactions and currency exchange. Cruise-ship passengers are cleared en masse by the cruise company.

Private skippers need a cruising permit, issued upon arrival (see the Getting There & Away chapter).

Onward Tickets

Immigration formalities require that air passengers have in their possession a return or onward airline ticket when arriving in The Bahamas. You will also be asked to declare where you'll be staying.

Travel Insurance

However you're traveling, it's worth taking out travel insurance. You may not want to insure that grotty old army surplus backpack, but everyone should be covered for the worst possible event: an accident, for example, that requires hospital treatment and a flight home. If you are planning to travel for a long time, travel insurance may seem rather expensive, but think of it this way: If you can't afford insurance, you certainly won't be able to afford a medical emergency overseas.

A travel insurance policy that covers theft, loss of luggage, and medical treatment is a good idea. You might also consider trip-cancellation insurance if you have booked a prepaid package with cancellation penalty clauses. Any travel agent can recommend an appropriate package. The international student travel policies handled by STA Travel and other student travel organizations are usually a good value.

Check the fine print to see if there are exclusions for any 'hazardous activities'

you may be contemplating, such as riding motorcycles, diving, or mountain hiking.

See also Medical Assistance Organizations in the Health section in this chapter.

Driver's License

To drive in The Bahamas, you must have a current license for your home country or state. A visitor can drive on his or her home license for three months. An International Driver's License, required for longer stays, can be obtained in The Bahamas for US$50 from the Road Traffic Dept, Clarence A Bain Bldg, Thompson Blvd and Moss Rd, Nassau. You can also obtain an International Driver's License by applying with your current license at any American Automobile Association (AAA) office. In the USA it costs US$10 and can be issued on the spot at AAA offices (two passport photographs are required).

Other Documents

The Bahamas has no youth hostel system, though there *is* a hostel in Nassau – the International Traveller's Rest – that at press time was planning to become a member of the International Youth Hostel Association (IYHA). Unless you plan on combining your visit to The Bahamas with other destinations that have youth hostels, you can leave your IYHA card at home.

The same is true for student, youth, and seniors' cards. Nobody in The Bahamas honors them.

EMBASSIES & CONSULATES
Bahamian Embassies & Consulates Abroad

Canada
    Bahamas High Commission, 360 Albert St, Suite 1020, Ottawa, ON K1R 7X7 (☎ 613-232-1724, fax 613-232-0097)
UK
    Bahamas High Commission, 10 Chesterfield St, London W1X 8AH (☎ 0171-408-4488, fax 0171-499-9937)
USA
    Embassy of The Commonwealth of The Bahamas, 2220 Massachusetts Ave NW, Washington, DC 20008 (☎ 202-319-2660, fax 202-319-2668)

Florida
Bahamas Consulate General, 25 SE 2nd
Ave, No 818, Miami, FL 33131
(☎ 305-373-6295, fax 305-373-6312)
New York
Bahamas Consulate General, 231 E 46th St,
New York, NY 10017
(☎ 212-421-6420, fax 212-688-5926)

Embassies & Consulates in The Bahamas

Most countries are represented by honorary
consuls, individuals appointed to represent
the respective country. They change frequently. Check the Yellow Pages under
Consulates.

Exceptions are the following:

British High Commission
    Bitco Bldg, East St, Nassau
    (☎ 242-325-7471)
Canadian Consulate
    Shirley St Plaza, Nassau
    (☎ 242-393-2123/4, fax 252-393-1305)
US Embassy & Consulate
    Mosmar Bldg, Queen St, Nassau
    (☎ 242-322-1181, fax 242-328-7838)

The US Embassy & Consulate in Nassau is
also responsible for consular services in the
Turks and Caicos.

CUSTOMS
Entering The Bahamas

All baggage is subject to customs inspection, and Bahamian Customs officials are
serious about their business. Although foreign visitors are usually waved through
after a cursory inspection, you should not
be surprised if your luggage is searched.
All visitors are required to complete a
Baggage Declaration Form.

Individuals are each allowed to import
US$10,000 cash, plus 50 cigars, 200 ciga-
rettes, or 1 lb of tobacco, plus 1 quart of
spirits free of charge. Purchases of US$100
are also allowed for all arriving passengers.
You are allowed to bring in a reasonable
amount of personal belongings free of
charge. However, you may need to show
proof that laptop computers and other
expensive items are for personal use. You
should declare these upon arrival.

Excess items deemed to be imported
goods are subject to 35% duty (25% for
clothing). The tariff varies up to 300% for
certain items.

The following items are restricted:
firearms, drugs (except prescription medicines), flowers and plants, honey, fruits,
coffee, and meats and vegetables (unless
canned).

Also see the Getting There & Away
chapter for information for private skippers
and pilots.

Citizens of The Bahamas are limited to
importing US$300 worth of items duty
free. All excess items are subject to duty,
beginning at 35%. Since most Bahamians
do their big-ticket shopping in Florida,
their luggage is usually searched upon
returning to The Bahamas. Foreign visitors
are rarely searched, but you may be
approached by a Bahamian asking you to
carry his or her possessions through customs as your own. Consider the risks
before accepting.

Leaving The Bahamas

US citizens can purchase up to US$600 of
goods duty free per person, provided they
have not used the allowance within the
last 30 days. In addition, they may each
import 200 cigarettes, 100 (non-Cuban)
cigars, plus 1 liter of liquor or wine. Artworks, handicrafts, antiques, and certain
other items are exempt from duties under
the Generalized System of Preferences.
For more specific information, contact the
US Customs Service (☎ 202-927-6724),
PO Box 7407, Washington, DC 20044.
See the Internet Resources appendix for
its website.

Canadian citizens are once a year permitted a C$300 allowance, plus 200 ciga-
rettes, 50 cigars, 2 lbs of loose tobacco, and
40 ounces of liquor. In addition, they can
mail unsolicited gifts valued up to C$40 per
day. The booklet *I Declare* provides more
information: Contact the Revenue Canada
Customs Dept, Communications Branch,
Mackenzie Ave, Ottawa, ON K1A 0L5.

UK citizens may import goods worth up
to £200 as well as 100 cigarettes, 50 cigars

or 250 grams of loose tobacco, and 2 liters of wine plus 1 liter of spirits (depending on alcohol proof). For further information, contact Her Majesty's Customs & Excise Office, New King's Reach House, 22 Upper Ground, London SE1 9PJ.

Visitors departing Nassau and Freeport international airports for most US destinations clear US Customs and Immigration prior to departure. No further customs formalities are required upon arrival in the USA. European passengers clear customs and immigration upon arrival at their destinations.

MONEY

The Bahamian dollar is the basic currency and is traded at parity with the US dollar. Both are legal tender throughout the islands. Prices in this book are stated in US dollars, although the two are basically interchangeable. European currencies are usually frowned upon. You can bring in as much money as you wish, but any amount over US$10,000 must be declared.

Costs

The Bahamas and the Turks and Caicos are not for the budget-conscious! These are very expensive places. How much you spend, however, depends on your sense of style. Even hardcore budget travelers will need at least US$50 a day. Most foodstuffs and other items are imported from the USA (other than seafood, virtually all foods are imported), with shipping costs and a whopping 35% import duty added. This is reflected in meal prices. You can expect to pay at least 50% more for any item than you would in the USA. A pack of cigarettes will set you back US$5 or so – a very good reason to quit smoking!

Roadside stalls and budget restaurants offer conch and other local meals for as little as US$3. More touristy restaurants, and even most restaurants serving a local clientele, tend to be expensive: Expect to pay at least US$8, for example, for lunch or dinner in modest restaurants, and twice that in more upscale joints. You should budget US$15 to US$30 for the average meal.

Transportation costs vary. Air service between islands costs between US$25 and US$150 one way, according to distance. However, if you plan on island-hopping, remember that unless you charter a small plane (anywhere from US$200 to US$600), you'll usually have to keep returning to Nassau for your next leg, adding to the expense (see the Getting Around chapter).

Accommodations will be your biggest expense (the *average* room rate in 1996 was US$105, up from US$93 the year before). It's possible to find budget accommodations for as little as US$20 a night, though standards are dour. Most budget properties charge US$50 or more, even for mediocre conditions. Medium-range hotels cost US$60 to US$75, though even here, standards are often motley. Deluxe properties begin at about US$150 nightly. Ultra-deluxe accommodations can run as high as US$500 nightly, but some are worth every penny! (Also see the Accommodations section in this chapter.)

Discounts Consider visiting in 'summer,' or low season (mid-April to mid-December), when hotel prices drop significantly and airfares are often reduced. Another good way to spread your dollars is to rent a villa or cottage with several other people. Happy hours and free Ladies' Nights in bars offer further savings for the impecunious. Most of the hip nightspots offer nightly specials and discount coupons. Look in the major tourist rags.

Many larger resorts offer 'Dine-Around' packages for guests to sample local restaurants. These are usually good bargains.

You'll find discount coupons being handed out in Nassau and Freeport, tempting you to eat or shop at specific places. Tourist publications offer discounts, and you can also find discount-coupon booklets at the Ministry of Tourism's information booths.

Carrying Money

Don't rely solely upon cash or upon your credit cards. Carry a combination of cash, credit cards, and traveler's checks, and it's a good idea to carry your cash where it can't be seen: in a money belt or pouch beneath your clothing or in a wallet in your front pocket.

Cash

Carry as little cash as possible when away from your hotel. Keep the rest in a hotel safe. You can rely on credit cards and traveler's checks for most of your purchases in major tourist centers. However, you'll need cash for most transactions in rural areas.

Set a small sum (US$100 or so) aside as a secret stash for emergencies in case you get ripped off.

Traveler's Checks

US-dollar traveler's checks are widely accepted as currency throughout The Bahamas, except on more remote Family Islands. They are convenient and can be replaced if they're lost or stolen; emergency refunds can usually be arranged. Traveler's checks in other currencies are generally only accepted by banks.

You can purchase checks at virtually any bank, lending institution, or currency-exchange service worldwide prior to departing for The Bahamas, as well as at banks in the islands. Three of the most popular and widely accepted traveler's checks are American Express, Barclays Bank, and Thomas Cook.

Some hotels, restaurants, and exchange bureaus charge a hefty fee for cashing traveler's checks. Banks do not generally charge commission but levy a tax (usually no more than US$1 for each check). You will need to show your passport.

To report lost American Express traveler's checks in The Bahamas, contact Playtours (☎ 242-322-2931) at 303 Shirley St in Nassau; in the USA call ☎ 801-964-6665 or 800-221-7282.

ATMs

Automated teller machine (ATM) cards are a good way to obtain incidental cash. Punch in your personal identification number (PIN) and the amount of the withdrawal, and the ATM issues local currency (your home account is automatically debited).

There are ATMs in the leading tourist centers. Most accept Visa, MasterCard, and American Express via international networks such as Cirrus (☎ 800-424-7787) and Visa/PLUS (☎ 800-843-7587).

Check with your local bank before departing for The Bahamas to find out how you can use your ATM card.

Credit Cards

Major credit cards are widely accepted throughout the islands. Visa and MasterCard are the mostly commonly accepted, followed by American Express, Diners Club, and Discover.

Most hotels require a credit-card imprint upon registering to cover incidentals such as telephone charges. Without a credit card, you may need to put down a cash deposit.

Credit cards are *not* widely accepted for general transactions in the more remote Family Islands, which for the most part operate on a cash-only basis. Companies that accept credit cards may add an additional charge of up to 5%. You can challenge these charges, which the credit-card companies generally do not permit. If this doesn't work, you can challenge the charge with the credit-card company, but you will need to show original documentation of all relevant transactions.

You can use your credit card to get cash advances at most commercial banks. You will usually be charged a small transaction fee.

To report lost or stolen credit cards, call the following numbers:

American Express	☎ 800-528-4800
American Express Gold	☎ 800-528-2121
Diners Club	☎ 800-234-6377
MasterCard	☎ 800-826-2181
Visa	☎ 800-336-8472
Visa Gold	☎ 800-847-2911

International Transfers

If you need an emergency injection of cash, you can arrange a telegraphic or mail transfer from your account in your home country or from a friend or family member.

You can also arrange a transfer in advance through your local bank. A fee of 5% to 12% applies.

Western Union has an office on Frederick St in Nassau (☎ 242-325-3273) and one on E Mall Dr in Freeport (☎ 242-352-6676). It also has agents throughout the Family Islands. In North America call Western Union Financial Services (☎ 800-325-6000/4176).

Currency & Exchange

The legal currency of The Bahamas is the Bahamian dollar, which is traded at parity with the US dollar. The US dollar is also accepted as legal tender throughout the islands without restriction. You might have difficulty getting locals to accept US$50 and US$100 bills. There are too many counterfeits in circulation, including the much-vaunted new bills meant to deter such activity.

Bahamian coins are issued in denominations of 1¢, 5¢, 10¢, 15¢, 25¢, and 50¢. Bahamian notes are issued in denominations of 50¢, $1, $3, $5, $10, $20, $50, $100, and $500. Oddities include the scallop-edged Bahamian dime (10¢) and the square 15¢ coin, now rare.

You can operate with US currency everywhere and will only need to change other foreign currencies into either Bahamian or US dollars. You can do this at any bank. Note that you may only exchange up to $70 in Bahamian currency for US dollars or foreign currency equivalent. The only bank permitted to exchange greater amounts is the Central Bank of The Bahamas on Market St in Nassau. Hence it's a good idea to spend all your Bahamian dollars prior to departure.

There is no black market.

Tipping & Bargaining

Tipping is expected, and certain US standards are followed. Tipping, however, has not reached the crazed levels of the USA. Gosh . . . you may even come across folks who *refuse* your tip!

The generally accepted rule in restaurants is a 10% to 15% tip. However, many hotels and restaurants automatically add a service charge (usually 15%) to cover gratuities. This will be displayed on your bill. There is no need to offer additional tips unless you believe you have received exceptional service. But it is questionable whether a tip charged to your credit card will ever reach the service staff. Pay restaurant and hotel tips directly to the staff, and ask to have the service charge removed from your bill.

Tip taxi drivers and bellhops at your discretion. Many perform their duties without expectation of a tip. However, bellhops at more upscale hotels and resorts do expect a tip. Sandals Royal Bahamian and SuperClubs' Breezes, both in Cable Beach (New Providence), do not permit tipping.

Most prices are fixed, and bargaining is less of a common practice than on Caribbean islands. You can feel free to bargain, however, at major straw markets and at roadside crafts stalls.

Taxes

A hotel tax of 10% in Nassau and on Grand Bahama and 8% in the Family Islands is levied (the tax is only 4% for hotels that are not members of a major hotel association or promotion board). An additional 2% to 5% charge for housekeeping service is often added.

POST & COMMUNICATIONS

Every settlement has a post office. The smaller ones issue stamps and receive and send letters but otherwise have few facilities. Larger post offices, found only in major settlements, are full service, with telegram facilities and often fax facilities and a philatelic bureau.

Most post offices are open 8:30 am to 5:30 pm Monday to Friday and until 12:30 pm Saturday. Some have restricted hours.

Bahamian stamps are worth more than a passing lick.

Postal Rates

US stamps are *not* accepted by Bahamian post offices. Postcards to the UK, USA, or

Canada cost 40¢. Airmail letters cost 55¢ per half-ounce to the USA and Canada; 60¢ to the UK and Europe; and 70¢ to Africa, Asia, or Australasia. Domestic mail costs 25¢ per ounce.

High-speed delivery costs $1.20 more than ordinary delivery. 'Speed Mail' service is offered ($5 plus regular postage), with a guarantee of expedited service.

Airmail parcels less than 1 lb in weight cost $4.15 to Canada, $5.25 to the USA, and $9.25 to the UK. Each extra pound costs $2.45 to Canada and the USA, and $4.15 to the UK.

Sending Mail

Public mailboxes are few and far between. You will need to go to a post office to mail your postcards and letters. Alternately, you can leave them with the front desk clerk at most hotels.

Alas, the Bahamian postal service is not noted for efficiency. The service is slow. Use airmail unless you have a valid reason not to; mark your mail 'Air Mail.' Airmail to North America usually takes about 10 days to six weeks, despite the proximity. Allow longer to Europe. Surface mail can take forever (at least two months). Even a letter sent from one Bahamian island to another can take a week or longer.

Ensure that parcels are adequately secured. Postal theft is rare, but don't tempt fate by mailing loosely taped packages. *Never* enclose cash or valuables. If you want to mail valuable documents, use an express-mail service such as UPS or Federal Express.

The weight limit is 22 lbs. Parcels may not exceed a combined dimension of 6 feet 7 inches.

Express-Mail Services These are listed in the Yellow Pages. DHL, Federal Express, and UPS have headquarters in Nassau, plus agents on many Family Islands.

UPS offers a money-back guarantee of 24-hour delivery to North America and parts of Europe, plus free customs clearance, for packages sent from Nassau.

Note that 24-hour service is not usually guaranteed from the Family Islands, as the express-mail services tend to rely on Bahamasair or an air-charter service.

Receiving Mail

You can have mail addressed to you 'Poste Restante' care of 'The General Post Office,' E Hill St, Nassau, Bahamas. Mail should be marked 'To be collected from the General Delivery desk.' All correspondence is retained for three weeks.

Receiving parcels is a pain in the arse. You'll have to go down to Customs to clear your package. Incoming packages are charged US80¢, plus any customs assessment. Packages are delivered at Parcel Post after customs is cleared and payment is made.

Postal codes refer to the post office boxes. Thus on New Providence 'N' refers to downtown Nassau, 'SS' to Shirley St, 'CB' to Cable Beach, 'FH' to Fox Hill, and 'GT' to Grant's Town.

You can also receive mail and telegrams via American Express Travel Services in Nassau and Freeport by prior arrangement with AmEx (☎ 800-221-7282) in North America. There's no charge for holders of American Express cards or traveler's checks.

Telephone & Fax

Telephone service throughout The Bahamas is controlled by the government-owned Bahamas Telecommunications Corporation (BaTelCo, ☎ 242-323-4911), which has its headquarters on John F Kennedy Dr on New Providence. BaTelCo has a local office in most major settlements throughout the islands.

Most telecommunications services are up to date. Instantaneous direct international links are provided through a 100% digitized switching system. However, technology has not caught up with all the Family Islands. Many communities still lack telephone hookups and many hotels have a single phone, often antiquated. Generally telephone communication in Family Island settlements is a case of haves and have-nots. Several remote settlements have only radio links, so be prepared for delays in getting calls through.

Phone booths are ubiquitous throughout the islands, and even the smallest settlement usually has at least one roadside phone. Most accept only prepaid phonecards (see below). Some booths still accept US25¢ coins but often don't permit long-distance calls except through an operator or calling-card company.

In October 1996 the nation changed its area code to 242 (previously it was 809, shared with Bermuda and 18 Caribbean nations).

The following are handy numbers:

Current Time	☎ 917
Directory Assistance	☎ 916
Emergency Assistance	☎ 919
International Operator Assistance	☎ 0
Weather Hotline	☎ 915

Calling Cards The majority of public telephones accept only prepaid phonecards issued by BaTelCo and available at stores and other accredited outlets near phonecard booths. You simply insert the card into a slot in the phone, and the cost of your call is automatically deducted from the value of the card until its value is used up. Some cards can be recharged. Others are non-rechargable debit cards. The cards are sold in denominations of US$5, US$10, and US$20.

Unfortunately, the phone systems themselves are not entirely trustworthy. I've experienced problems with feisty phones, which are often placed at dwarf-height in cramped booths and require Houdini-style contortions.

Domestic Calls Local calls are free of charge. Direct-dialed long-distance calls cost US40¢ per minute. Operator-assisted calls cost US$1.80 per three-minute minimum, then US60¢ per minute.

You will need to dial ☎ 1-242, then the seven-digit local number for all interisland calls. Local calls to another number on the same island do not require you to dial the 1-242 prefix.

International Calls Many phone booths and all BaTelCo offices permit direct dial to overseas numbers. Typical costs from The Bahamas to the USA (the cost is the same whether to California or Florida) are US99¢ for the first minute and US80¢ per minute thereafter. Rates to Canada are US$1.25 and US$1.15 respectively, and to Europe, US$2.75 and US$2 to US$2.75 respectively. Lower rates are charged after 11 pm on weekdays.

Operator-assisted calls to the USA cost US$4.50 to US$8.25 for three minutes, depending on the zone. A similar call to Europe or Australia will cost you a whopping US$15.

Almost all the larger or more upscale hotels have direct-dial calling; elsewhere you may need to go through the hotel operator or even call from the front desk. Hotels generally add a government tax for overseas calls. They also impose their own service charge, often at sticker-shock rates – as much as 500%! Some hotels even block access to 'home-direct' services so that they can jack up your bill. Unfortunately, many hotels also charge for an unanswered call after the receiving phone has rung five times.

You can save money by using any of the home-direct services listed below. You dial an access number from any telephone to reach a US operator, who links your call. You can bill to your home phone, phonecard, or collect to whomever you're calling. AT&T phone booths are located at several key places in The Bahamas, and most upscale hotels have signed up with AT&T to offer direct service from room phones. However, many hotels impose a US$5 surcharge for calls made using your calling card or charge card. *Never* give your calling-card number to anyone other than the operator, as scams are frequent. To place collect or calling-card calls, simply dial the appropriate code below:

AT&T	☎ 800-225-5288
MCI	☎ 800-950-5555
Sprint	☎ 800-877-4646

Note that most North American toll-free numbers cannot be accessed from The Bahamas. Usually you must dial ☎ 1-880, plus the last seven digits of the number. You'll be charged US$1 per minute (sometimes more).

Cellular Phones You can bring your own cellular phone into The Bahamas, but you may be charged a customs fee upon entry (refunded upon exit).

Your phone will not operate on BaTelCo's cellular system unless you rent temporary use of a 'roaming' cellular line through BaTelCo (US$3 per day and US99¢ per minute, plus normal cellular rates). Callers from outside The Bahamas must dial ☎ 242-359-7626 to access your line, followed by your 10-digit roamer number. Within the islands, you can be accessed by dialing ☎ 359-7626, then your 10-digit number. Call your cellular company to determine if it has an agreement with BaTelCo.

Cable & Wireless Caribbean Cellular provides no-fee preregistration for your cellular, giving you a Caribbean number before you depart home. There's a US$5 daily activation fee. To get a local Caribbean number, call ☎ 800-262-8366 in the USA, 800-567-8366 in Canada, or 268-480-2628 from elsewhere. If you are already in the islands, call ☎ 0 and SND.

Boatphone, a subsidiary of London-based Cable & Wireless, also provides a cellular network throughout the Caribbean for yachts and cruise ships. By dialing ☎ 0 SND in The Bahamas, you can register your cellular telephone for instant service. You can arrange billing directly to your credit card. For information, call ☎ 800-262-8366 in the USA, 800-567-8366 in Canada, or 268-480-2628 or 268-462-5051 from elsewhere.

Boatphone offers discount rates for use over a six-week period or longer and rents cellular phones and fax machines.

Fax In Nassau, BaTelCo has a fax bureau at its Centralized Telephone Office (☎ 242-323-6414) on East St and at its offices on Blue Hill Rd and Shirley St and in Golden Gates and Fox Hill.

Many other towns have private offices offering fax services; these are listed in the island chapters. You can also send faxes from hotels and major post offices and via regional BaTelCo centers.

Telegraph
You can send telexes from BaTelCo centers. The cost per minute for a telex is US$2.34 to the USA, US$3.50 to Canada, and US$4 to the UK, Europe, and Australia. For information on sending a telex by BaTelCo, call Data Services (☎ 242-328-0299; on Grand Bahama 242-351-6251). Most hotels and large business also have telex service.

The post office handles all telegram services, which cost US24¢ a word from Nassau and Freeport.

Email
In The Bahamas many of the modern and larger resorts have facilities for plugging in your laptop to gain access to the Internet. At press time there were no 'electronic cafes' or Internet service providers catering to itinerant needs.

VHF Radio
Virtually every Bahamian business (and many homes in the Family Islands) communicates by VHF radio, which is usually faster and more flexible and often easier to use than the telephone. Most folks have a call name for their house, boat, or business. The 'coconut telegraph' accounts for the rapid dissemination of news, information, and gossip (you have to assume that many people are listening in to conversations).

Each island has a particular channel for making contact; other channels are then selected for communication.

If you use VHF, you should remember this steadfast rule: *Be brief.* The channels can get crowded.

BOOKS
Information on Bahamian bookstores can be found in the island chapters.

Macmillan Caribbean (☎ 0256-29242, fax 0256-20109), a division of Macmillan Press, publishes a wide range of general guides and special-interest books about the Caribbean, including *The Bahamas: A Family of Islands* and *The Turks & Caicos Islands: Lands of Discovery*. You can order a catalog by writing Macmillan Caribbean, Houndmills, Basingstoke, Hampshire RG21 2XS, England.

The books listed below provide worthwhile background reading.

Lonely Planet

Eastern Caribbean by Glenda Bendure and Ned Friary, *Cuba* by David Stanley, and *Jamaica* by yours truly are invaluable if you're planning to island-hop through the Caribbean.

Also pick up Nick and Corinna Selby's *Florida* for visits to the nearby Sunshine State or their *Miami* guide if you'll be spending much time there.

Guidebooks

A good general guidebook is the *Insight Guide: Bahamas*, complete with color photography. It is strong on Bahamian history and culture but comparatively short on practicalities. There's also the slender *Insight Pocket Guide: Bahamas* by Deby Nash.

The *Bahamas Guide* by Ron Charles provides good coverage of the main Bahamian islands; however, far-flung Family Islands are omitted, and the book's introduction to the country is cursory.

Bahamas: A Traveller's Guide by Mike East and Adrian Jones (Lascelles Caribbean Guides) is a well-researched and comprehensive guide aimed at British travelers. It's also widely available in Nassau.

The comprehensive *Bahamas Handbook* (Etienne Dupuch, Jr) is an excellent almanac catering to the traveler and business community. It provides a thorough background on the tourism, business, and cultural environment, with solid statistical data and information for planning travel or investments.

The US State Dept publishes *Tips for Travelers to the Caribbean* (Publication No 9906, BCA), available from the Superintendent of Documents (☎ 202-512-1800), US Government Printing Office, Washington, DC 20402.

Activity Guidebooks

Pisces Books publishes an excellent series of full-color diving guides and related titles, covering topics from reef ecology and wreck diving to underwater video photography. For dive and snorkel sites in the region, pick up Steve Blount and Lisa Walker's *The Bahamas: Nassau and New Providence* and Stuart and Susanne Cummings' *The Turks & Caicos Islands*. Another guidebook by the Cummings, *The Best Caribbean Diving,* covers the region from The Bahamas down to the Bay Islands, off Honduras.

Underwater Bahamas by Bob Frield (New Edge) is a pocket guide that offers photos and brief commentary on the dive experience. Another guide is *Bahamas Diver's Guide* by Shlomo Cohen (Seapen Books).

For information about sailing guidebooks, see Guidebooks in the Private Yacht section in the Getting There & Away chapter. For books about flying small planes in The Bahamas, see the Private Plane section, also in the Getting There & Away chapter.

Travel

Very few travel books have been written about The Bahamas.

Exceptions include *The Bahamas Re-Discovered* by Dragan and Nicolas Popov, a coffee-table book with text on The Bahamas' history and contemporary scene. Also check out Harvey Lloyd's *Isles of Eden*, a splendid coffee-table book that describes life in the southern Family Islands.

Out Island Doctor by Evans Cottman is an excellent read, profiling the life of a US teacher who takes on the role of doctor when he settles in the Crooked Island District in the 1930s and '40s.

In the same genre, try *Artist on His Island: A Study of Self-Reliance* by Randolph W Johnston (Little Harbour Press, Marsh Harbour), which tells of his and his family's lives in the Abacos.

History & Politics

For a general overview of Bahamian history, I recommend *The Story of The Bahamas* by Paul Albury, which traces events up to independence, and *A History of the Bahamas* by Michael Craton (San Salvador Press), with a strong slant toward the islands' political development.

Buccaneers of America is an entertaining eyewitness account of the sordid acts of the infamous buccaneers, related by John Esquemeling, who partook of the misdeeds. The book was first published in 1684.

Junkanoo: Festival of the Bahamas by Clement Bethel examines the history of this Bahamian festival. *The Lucayans* by Sandra Riley relates the sad tale of the extermination of the indigenous population by ruthless Spanish conquistadores.

Two recommended books tracing the traumas of the slave era are Gail Saunders' *Bahamian Loyalists and Their Slaves* and *Slavery in the Bahamas*. Colin Hughes' *Race and Politics in The Bahamas* takes a more contemporary viewpoint.

For a look at the Duke of Windsor's highly controversial time in The Bahamas, see *The King Over the Water* by Michael Pye (Hutchinson) and *The Duke of Windsor's War* by Michael Bloch (Coward McCann). Likewise, I recommend Charles Highnam's *The Duchess of Windsor – The Secret Life*, which includes sections on the duke's questionable practices in investigating the murder of Sir Harry Oakes, and James Leasor's *Who Killed Sir Harry Oakes?*, a serious look at the infamous and unsolved murder of one of The Bahamas' leading figures and the basis for the TV series *Murder in Paradise*.

Want to know more about drug trafficking in The Bahamas? Check out *The Cocaine Wars*, written by Paul Eddy, Hugo Sabogal, and Sara Walden.

There are several history books about individual islands. *Grand Bahama* by PJH Barratt is an account of the history, geography, wildlife, development, and potential of Grand Bahama, told by a town planner formerly in charge of the development of Freeport. Likewise, look for *Man O' War: My Island Home* by Haziel Albury. The founding era is traced in Everild Young's *Eleuthera: The Island Called Freedom* (Regency Press).

Flora & Fauna

There's no shortage of books on the natural history of The Bahamas and Caribbean islands.

A good starting point is David G Campbell's *The Ephemeral Islands: A Natural History of The Bahamas*. Likewise, check out *Native Trees of The Bahamas* by Jack Patterson and George Stevenson, *Tropical Flowers of the Bahamas* by Hans Hannau, and *Flora of the Bahama Archipelago* by Donovan and Helen Correll (Lubrecht & Cramer Ltd), which has a section on the Turks and Caicos.

For a general overview, *Caribbean Flora* by C Dennis Adams has detailed descriptions of individual species, accompanied by illustrations. In a similar vein are *Flowers of the Caribbean* and *Trees of the Caribbean: The Bahamas and Bermuda*, both by GW Lennox and SA Seddon.

Serious botanists with a practical bent should check out *Caribbean Wild Plants & Their Uses* by Penelope Honychurch and *200 Conspicuous, Unusual or Economically Important Tropical Plants of the Caribbean* by John Kingsbury (Bullbrier Press).

Birders should pick up *Birds of New Providence and the Bahama Islands* by PGC Brudenell-Bruce. Also try James Bond's *Birds of the West Indies*, a classic reference for serious bird watchers, with discussions on habitats and detailed descriptions of each bird. It was recently republished as *Peterson's Field Guide to Birds of the West Indies* in a lavishly illustrated version.

If you're into snorkeling or diving, a standard reference should be Eugene Kaplan's *Peterson's Field Guide to Coral Reefs*. In the same series is *Fishes of the Caribbean* by Ian Took. Both are comprehensive books with detailed information on ecosystems, habitats, and individual species.

Dee Carstarphen's *The Conch Book: All You Ever Wanted to Know About the Queen Conch from Gestation to Gastronomy* is a veritable feast of information on the ubiquitous marine snail.

Cuisine

There are several books on Bahamian cooking that will help you recreate your favorite island dishes in your own kitchen.

Two of the best are *Bahamian Cuisine* by Jeanette Thompson and *Gourmet Bahamian Cooking* by Marie Mendelson and Marguerite Sawyer (Best-Way Publishing, Iowa).

Also look for *Cooking with Caribbean Rum* by Laurel-Ann Morley.

Architecture

Several books have been written on Caribbean and Bahamian architecture, notably *Caribbean Style* by Suzanne Slesin and Stafford Cliff and its pocket-size companion book, *Essence of Caribbean Style*, which explain the evolution and elements of the Caribbean vernacular in architecture. The lively text is supported by stunning photography.

Nassau's Historic Buildings by Seighbert Russell (Bahamas National Trust) provides readers with a detailed review of individual buildings in the capital city.

Folklore, Folktales & Superstitions

Telcine Turner's *Once Below a Time: Bahamian Stories* is an illustrated collection of short stories for children. Likewise, youngsters might enjoy *Climbing Clouds: Stories & Poems from The Bahamas*, also edited by Telcine Turner, and *An Evenin' in Guanima: A Treasury of Folktales from The Bahamas* by Patricia Glinton-Meicholas (Guanima Press).

Bush Medicine in The Bahamas by Leslie Higgs (Nassau Guardian) provides recipes for curing everything from warts to a broken heart. Obeah and other Bahamian folk religions are the subject of *Ten, Ten, the Bible Ten – Obeah in The Bahamas* by Timothy McCartney.

General

Want to find a place or statistic? You'll find it in the *Atlas of The Commonwealth of The Bahamas* (Ministry of Education, Nassau).

Actor Sidney Poitier, star of *Guess Who's Coming to Dinner* and *In the Heat of the Night*, tells of his upbringing on Cat Island in his autobiography, *This Life*.

Ernest Hemingway's *Islands in the Stream* provides a fictitious but factually based look at Biminis life and his own bohemian ways during WWII. In a similar fictional vein, James Frew's *In the Wake of the Leopard* tells of heroes and Nazi villains playing cat-and-mouse in The Bahamas.

Bahamas Crisis by Desmon Bagley is a murder thriller that provides a behind-the-scenes look at the tourism industry – no dry read, this.

To understand a bit more about what makes Bahamians tick, check out *How to Be a True-True Bahamian* by Patricia Glinton-Meicholas (Guanima Press). To understand something of the local dialect, refer to *Talkin' Bahamian*, also by Patricia Glinton-Meicholas, and *The Dictionary of Bahamian English* by John Holm and Alison Shilling.

A handy booklet for trip planning is *Consumer Reports Travel Buying Guide*. This annual pocket-size guide provides assistance in avoiding pitfalls and finding discounts.

Americans Traveling Abroad: What You Should Know Before You Go by Gladson Nwann (World Travel Institute) is another handy international travel resource guide for US citizens planning a vacation. Virtually no stone is left unturned, with chapters on customs, health, security, seniors, etc.

CD ROM

Virtually There: Caribbean is a CD ROM designed to take you on a 'virtual vacation.' The CD ROM, issued by Sabre Interactive, is intended primarily for travel agents to show their clients. You can also buy it through retail computer stores.

Wondering where to stay? Check out *Resorts of the Caribbean* and *Villas of the Caribbean*, interactive CD ROM travel guides issued by Straight Line Medium, Inc (in the USA ☎ 804-784-2690), in association with Island Hideaways. The guides offer an encyclopedic library of accommodations, with cross-referencing, covering 20 islands. The guides sell for US$29.95; if you order both together, the second is half-price.

ONLINE SERVICES

The explosion of cyberspace communications in recent years has fostered numerous travel sites on CompuServe, America Online, and the Internet. The World Wide Web (WWW) is a rapidly expanding behemoth of information, with countless travel-related home pages (resource files). They are no substitute for a good guidebook, but many provide excellent information for planning your trip. They also give you a chance to exchange information and gossip with other in-the-know travelers via email. Some sites are maintained on a daily basis; others are updated only monthly or yearly.

See Internet Resources, in the back of the book, for specific locations providing travel information.

FILMS

The Bahamas has had star billing in dozens of movies and is a favorite of Hollywood, particularly for underwater scenes.

The islands have had strong links to James Bond movies ever since novelist Ian Fleming concocted the suave, macho spy 007. Fleming was so taken by the islands that he made them the setting for several Bond novels in which 007 seduced glamorous women and, of course, hauled in big cash in the casinos of Nassau. Fleming made Great Inagua the setting for *Dr No*, one of his early 007 novels.

Perhaps the movie most associated with the islands, however, is *Thunderball*, filmed in The Bahamas in 1965. The screenplay took full advantage of the islands' beauty, especially its underwater world. Who can ever forget the love scene between James Bond (Sean Connery) and Domino (Claudine Auger), when they meet in an undersea coral garden and swim to a perfect beach to make love on the sugary sand beneath the shade of tall palms? *Phew!* The film starred many local notables in tuxedos and ball gowns, stepping from their yachts to dine on caviar and champagne at the Café Martinique on Paradise Island. Talk about boosting tourism!

Scenes from *For Your Eyes Only* and *The Spy Who Loved Me* were also filmed in The Bahamas. 007 returned to the islands as late as 1983 for the filming of *Never Say Never Again*, in which he's seen strolling through Nassau's Bay St straw market and eyeing a passing cruise ship from an oceanfront bar. The Never Say Never Again wreck off the south coast of New Providence is named for scenes in the movie; the freighter was a drug boat that had been seized by the Bahamian government, and it was sunk especially for the film crew. Nearby is a plane sent to the bottom for the movie *Thunderball*, parts of which were also filmed at namesake Thunderball Grotto in the Exumas.

Scenes from *Jaws; Splash!; Wet Gold; Cocoon; My Father, the Hero; Flipper; Zeus & Roxanne;* and even *20,000 Leagues Under the Sea* were filmed in The Bahamas. In fact, The Bahamas was the setting for the first undersea motion picture in history, filmed by John Ernest Williamson in 1914!

NEWSPAPERS & MAGAZINES
Foreign Publications

Leading international newspapers such as the *International Herald Tribune*, *Miami Herald*, *New York Times*, *The Times* (of London), *Figaro*, and *USA Today;* leading magazines such as *Newsweek, Time, The Economist, Elle, Cosmopolitan,* and *GQ;* and other general-interest publications are stocked by many hotel gift shops, pharmacies, and stationery stores in Nassau, Freeport, and Marsh Harbour. However, you'll be hard pressed to find even a local newspaper on some of the more remote islands.

Caribbean Travel & Life, PO Box 2054, Marion, OH 43305, is a beautiful full-color bimonthly magazine covering travel throughout the Caribbean. It has feature articles and resort reviews, and it's also packed with money-saving tips and advertisements. *Caribbean World,* Albert Hall Magazines, 84 Albert Hall Mansions, Prince Consort Rd, London SW7 2AQ, comes out quarterly and has an upmarket focus. Both are available at a few news agents.

Caribbean Week, Caribbean Communications, Inc, 1320 Route 9, Champlain, NY 12919, is a high-quality biweekly news magazine that covers travel, politics, fashion, economics, and other trends throughout the region. It is widely available in Nassau. *Caribbean Today* (☎ 305-238-2868), PO Box 6010, Miami, FL 33116, is similar.

Bahamian Publications

The two leading dailies are the morning *Nassau Guardian* and the afternoon *Tribune.* Both are published Monday to Saturday and cost US50¢. They are readily available in Nassau, Freeport, and Marsh Harbour, but have delayed and limited circulation in the Family Islands. Few Bahamians outside Nassau read newspapers.

The daily *Freeport News* and twice-monthly *Freeport Times* serve Grand Bahama.

The Bahama Journal is a weekly national newspaper, as is *The Punch,* a British-style tabloid replete with scantily dressed 'Page 3' equivalents: the 'Beauty of the Week' and 'Hunk of the Week.'

Profile, published by the *Nassau Guardian* in small newspaper format, focuses on tourism, with feature articles and plenty of practical information. You can pick it up free at hotels and other locales.

Der Inseln der Bahamas is a German-language tourist newspaper available free at some hotels.

Island Scene (☎ 242-323-3398, fax 242-326-2020), PO Box N-7937, Nassau, Bahamas, is the official magazine of The Bahamas. The slick, full-color magazine is written for travel professionals. The same company publishes another glossy publication, *Islander Magazine,* aimed at the traveler.

RADIO & TV

The government-owned Bahamas Broadcasting Corporation has a virtual monopoly on radio and television broadcasting.

Radio is the most important news medium for islanders. Expect to hear far less music and far more local news items and call-in banter than you may be used to. There is considerable political debate and airing of parochial grievances.

BBC's Radio Bahamas operates four stations using broadcast designation ZNS, for Zephyr (a balmy breeze) Nassau Sunshine. ZNS-1 (AM 1540 kHz and FM 107.1 MHz), on New Providence, broadcasts throughout the islands 24 hours a day. It is described as 'adult contemporary,' with an eclectic base of music, political analysis, call-in discussions, and tedious lists of funerals and personal announcements. ZNS-2 serves New Providence and has a heavy religious and educational bent. ZNS-FM (104.5) offers mostly contemporary music and has a strong focus on sports news. ZNS-3, Radio Bahamas Northern Service, offers a similar service to ZNS-1, transmitting from Freeport to the northern islands.

There are also two private radio stations inclined more toward entertainment and contemporary music.

BBC operates the only local TV station, on Channel 13, which airs six hours daily on weekdays and 10 hours on weekends. It offers mostly news, political commentary, and sports. Most homes have satellite or cable access to US programs.

Most hotels offer satellite or cable TV, and CNN and ESPN are staples. Some hotels subscribe to HBO and other North American cable stations.

PHOTOGRAPHY & VIDEO

The Bahamas is supremely photogenic. You'll want plenty of film. The seascapes are fabulous, as are the sunsets.

Film & Equipment

You'll find camera stores in Nassau, Freeport, and Marsh Harbour, where duty-free shops sell cameras and lenses at prices that offer marginal savings. You may be able to find better deals at discount mail-order photography suppliers in your home country. Check prices before leaving home. Don't count on being able to buy a specific zoom or wide-angle lens, especially for more obscure makes. Few outlets sell film and camera equipment away from major tourist centers.

Film is expensive – about half again what you'd pay in North America – so ensure that you bring enough to last. If you run out, you probably won't be able to find the specific film type you want. Most photo supply stores and drugstores sell a limited range of film. Print film is widely available, but slide (transparency) film is rarer, usually limited to Kodak's Ektachrome and Agfachrome.

Many out-of-the-way places leave film sitting in the sun; avoid this like the plague, as heat and humidity rapidly deteriorate film. Don't forget to check the expiration date, too. You want film that's as fresh as possible. Once you've finished a roll of film, try to keep it cool; don't leave it sitting in the sun. And have it developed as soon as possible. Waiting one or two weeks is OK, but if you'll be traveling around for several weeks, consider having your film developed on the islands or mailing it home for development (you can purchase prepaid mailers for this purpose).

Likewise, don't leave your camera sitting around in the sun. Keep it out of direct sunlight when not in use.

Most shops sell a range of basic filters, including UV and polarizing filters – which are essentials for getting the most out of subtropical conditions.

Photography

Your greatest potential disappointment when you get your processed photographs is a washed-out look. This is due to overexposure. The bright tropical light can fool even the most sophisticated light-metering systems. Your meter may not be set up to register the dazzling ambient light surrounding the subject from which it's reading. Sand and water are particularly reflective.

A separate hand-held meter can provide more accurate readings. It's also often a good idea to 'stop down' one f-stop to reduce the light and thereby get richer color saturation. Most effective of all is taking photographs in early morning and late afternoon to avoid harsh shadows and the glare of the sun.

Your choice of film will also make a huge difference to the color rendition. Fujichrome Velvia gives the best color saturation of any film. It's not cheap, but it pays big dividends. Kodachrome 25 and 64 also give excellent color rendition; the former is good for bright conditions but is too fast to handle dark conditions or great contrasts of light and shade.

When photographing people, you'll need to compensate for the contrast between dark faces and bright backgrounds; otherwise they may turn out as featureless black shadows. The darker a person's skin, the more light you will need to reflect onto his or her face to compensate. Many modern cameras have a fill-in flash for this purpose. Alternately, invest in a small handheld reflector. If you're taking really close-up shots, you can even ask your subject to hold the reflector (out of the camera frame, of course).

Video

Video cameras and tapes are widely available in photo supply stores in Nassau, Freeport, and main settlements. Prices are significantly higher than you may be used to in North America or Europe. VHS is standard.

Photographing People
The majority of Bahamians delight in having their photographs taken and will be happy to pose for your camera. However, many Bahamians do not like having their pictures taken, especially if they're not dressed in their Sunday best. Others have religious proscriptions. If they don't want to be photographed, they may let you know this and can get quite volatile if you persist. Honor their wishes with good grace.

It is a common courtesy to ask permission. On rare occasions you may be asked to pay a small 'donation' to take photographs. Whether you agree to this is a matter of your own conscience: If you don't want to pay, don't take the shot!

In markets it is considered good manners to purchase a small item from whomever you wish to photograph. Don't forget to send a photograph to anyone to whom you've promised one.

Airport Security
Your baggage will be inspected when you're departing Nassau and Freeport airports on international flights. It's a good idea to have your film inspected by hand, since x-ray machines can fog films. Most modern x-ray machines will not produce any noticeable fogging if your film passes through only once or twice, but why take the risk? If your baggage will be passed through several x-ray machines during the course of your travels, you should definitely have it checked by hand. Or invest in a lead-lined film pouch, which you can buy at most camera stores.

Don't forget to have your camera hand-inspected if it has film inside.

X-ray machines are not used nor are security checks made on domestic flights.

TIME
The Bahamas and the Turks and Caicos operate on Eastern Standard Time (EST), five hours behind Greenwich Mean Time

(GMT). Hence, they are in the same time zone as New York City and Miami, and three hours ahead of California.

Both nations operate daylight-saving time, or EDT (four hours behind GMT), from the first Sunday in April to the last Sunday in October, the same as in the USA.

ELECTRICITY
Most hotels operate on 110 volts (60 cycles), the same as in the USA and Canada.

Sockets throughout the country are usually two- or three-pin to US standard. If you're bringing electrical equipment from North America, you will not need to bring adapters. However, you will need a transformer and adapter for electrical appliances from the UK and certain other countries. Most upscale hotels can supply these to guests, but don't expect more moderate properties to do so.

WEIGHTS & MEASURES
The Bahamas uses the British Imperial System, although tentative moves to shift to the metric system have been made. Distances are still shown in miles and inches on most maps, although some official documents now speak of kilometers and centimeters. Road speed limits are given in miles per hour. Most measurements in this book are given in imperial.

Liquids are generally measured in pints, quarts, and gallons, and weights in grams, ounces, and pounds. Most imported food items are in metric.

LAUNDRY
Most large hotels offer laundry and dry-cleaning services at extra charge. Allow at least a day for items to be returned. A few hotels, and many self-catering units, have coin-operated laundromats on-site. You'll also find local laundries in most settlements; where there is none, there'll be someone willing to wash your clothes for a few dollars. In a pinch you might have to wash your underwear and socks in your sink and hang them to dry.

Dry-cleaning services exist in major towns and settlements.

HEALTH

The Bahamas poses few health risks. The water is potable almost everywhere, and food hygiene standards are generally high. However, most local water supplies comes from ground wells that draw water directly from the limestone substrata. It will usually taste slightly brackish. This usually poses no health risk, but you should beware water that smells or tastes foul. If the ground near the water source is contaminated by leaking sewers, then you're asking for trouble. (I got giardiasis from drinking contaminated water.) I suggest you check with your hotel reception desk before drinking tap water (bottled water is available at most resorts).

Your greatest threats, however, are dehydration and an excess of sun and booze.

Travel Health Guidebooks

The following are two of the best books on travel health:

Staying Healthy in Asia, Africa & Latin America (Moon Publications) is probably the best all-around guide to carry: It's compact but very detailed and well organized.
Travel with Children by Maureen Wheeler (Lonely Planet) includes basic advice on travel health for younger children.

Predeparture Preparations

Health Insurance A travel insurance policy to cover medical problems is a wise idea. There are a wide variety of policies, and your travel agent will have recommendations. For more details about health insurance, see Travel Insurance in the earlier Visas & Documents section and Medical Assistance Organizations in this section.

Medical Kit A small, straightforward medical kit is a good thing to carry. A possible kit list includes the following:

- Aspirin or Panadol for pain or fever.
- Antihistamine (such as Benadryl), useful as a decongestant for colds and allergies, to ease the itch from insect bites or stings, and to help prevent motion sickness. Antihistamines may cause sedation and interact with alcohol.
- Antibiotics are useful if you're traveling well off the beaten track, but they must be prescribed and you should carry the prescription with you. Some individuals are allergic to commonly prescribed antibiotics such as penicillin or sulfa drugs; it's sensible to always carry this information when you are traveling.
- Kaolin preparation (Pepto-Bismol), Imodium, or Lomotil, for stomach upsets.
- Rehydration mixture for treatment of severe diarrhea. This is particularly important if traveling with children but is recommended for everyone.
- Antiseptic, such as Betadine, for cuts and grazes.
- Calamine lotion to ease irritation from bites or stings.
- Bandages for minor injuries.
- Scissors, tweezers, and a thermometer (note that mercury thermometers are prohibited by airlines).
- Insect repellent, sunscreen, suntan lotion, lip balm, and water-purification tablets.

If a medicine is available in The Bahamas, it will generally be available over the counter. However, be careful to ensure that the expiration date has not passed and that correct storage conditions have been met. It may be better to leave extra medicines, syringes, etc, with a local clinic, rather than carry them home.

Immunizations No vaccinations are required to enter The Bahamas unless you have visited an area of yellow-fever infection. Yellow fever is not a threat in The Bahamas. However, a yellow-fever vaccination certificate is required for travelers arriving within seven days of traveling in the following countries: Bolivia, Brazil, Burkina Faso, Colombia, Gambia, Ghana, Nigeria, Peru, Sudan, Zaire, and any other infected areas. Vaccination protection lasts 10 years.

Other Preparations Make sure you're healthy before you travel. If you are embarking on a long trip, make sure your teeth are OK. You don't want to seek dental care in The Bahamas, as the cost is equivalent to that in the USA.

If you wear glasses, bring a spare pair and your prescription. Losing your glasses can be a problem, although you can get new ones made up cheaply and competently in Nassau or Freeport.

If you require a particular medication, take an adequate supply, as it may not be available locally. Take the prescription or, better still, part of the packaging showing the generic rather than the brand name (which may not be locally available), as it will make getting replacements easier. It's a wise idea to have a legible prescription with you to prove that you legally use the medication – it's surprising how often over-the-counter drugs from one place are illegal without a prescription or even banned in another. However, the case is usually the reverse in The Bahamas.

Basic Rules
Food & Water Care in what you eat and drink is the most important health rule; stomach upsets are the most likely travel health problem, but the majority of these upsets will be relatively minor. Don't become paranoid – trying the local food is part of the experience of travel, after all.

The Bahamas has its own natural purification system in its limestone base, through which rainwater percolates. Water is usually safe to drink from faucets throughout the islands, but this is not guaranteed. If you don't know for certain that the water is safe, always assume the worst.

Reputable brands of bottled water or soft drinks are generally fine. Only use water from containers with a serrated seal – not tops or corks. Take care with fruit juice, particularly if water may have been added. Boiled milk is fine if it's kept hygienically, and yogurt is always good.

Salads and fruit should be washed with purified water or peeled when possible. Ice cream is usually OK, but beware of street vendors and of ice cream that has melted and been refrozen. Thoroughly cooked food is safest, but not if it has been left to

cool or if it has been reheated. Conch and other shellfish are usually OK. However, be cautious about eating larger fish species such as barracuda, amberjack, and certain groupers, which have been known to cause potentially deadly ciguatera poisoning.

Bahamian restaurants pose relatively few hygiene problems. If a place looks clean and well run and if the vendor also looks clean and healthy, then the food is probably safe. In general, places that are packed with travelers or locals will be fine, while empty restaurants are questionable. Busy restaurants mean the food is being cooked and eaten quickly with little standing around and is probably not being reheated.

Nutrition If your food is poor or limited in availability, if you're traveling hard and fast and therefore missing meals, or if you simply lose your appetite, you can soon start to lose weight and place your health at risk.

Make sure your diet is well balanced. Eggs, tofu, beans, lentils, and nuts are all safe ways to get protein. Fruit you can peel (bananas, for example) is always safe and a good source of vitamins. Try to eat plenty of grains (like rice) and bread. Remember that although food is generally safer if it is cooked well, overcooked food loses much of its nutritional value. If your diet isn't well balanced or if your food intake is insufficient, it's a good idea to take vitamins and iron pills.

The Bahamas' is a hot climate, so make sure you drink enough – don't rely on feeling thirsty to indicate when you should drink. Not needing to urinate or very dark-yellow urine is a danger sign. Always carry a water bottle with you on long walks.

Everyday Health Avoid overexposure to extremes: Keep out of the sun at its peak. Avoid potential diseases by dressing sensibly. You can get infections through dangerous coral cuts by walking over coral without shoes. You can avoid insect bites by covering bare skin when insects are around, by screening windows or beds, or by using insect repellents. Seek out local advice. In situations where there is no information, discretion is the better part of valor.

Medical Treatment

An embassy or consulate can usually recommend a good place to go for medical advice. So can five-star hotels, although they often recommend doctors with five-star prices. (This is when that medical insurance really comes in handy!) In the Family Islands, medical service is generally offered through clinics, and you should bring sufficient supplies of any prescription medicines.

Also see the Medical Facilities section.

Environmental Hazards

Sunburn In the tropics you can get sunburned surprisingly quickly, even through cloud. Many people ruin their holidays by getting badly burned soon after they arrive in The Bahamas. *Don't underestimate the power of the sun*, no matter how dark your skin color. Use a sunscreen with a protective factor (SPF) of 15 or more. Take extra care to cover areas that don't normally see sun – like your feet. Build up your exposure gradually. A hat provides added protection, and you should also use zinc cream or some other barrier cream for your nose and lips.

Calamine lotion is good for mild sunburn. Aloe vera also helps.

Prickly Heat This is an itchy rash caused by excessive perspiration trapped under the skin. It usually strikes people who have just arrived in a hot climate and whose pores have not yet opened sufficiently to cope with greater sweating. For relief until you acclimatize, keep cool, bathe often, use a mild talcum powder, and resort to air-conditioning.

Dehydration & Heat Exhaustion You'll sweat profusely in The Bahamas. Take time to acclimatize to high temperatures, and make sure you drink sufficient liquids. You'll lose quite a bit of salt through sweating. Salt deficiency is characterized by fatigue, lethargy, headaches, giddiness, and muscle cramps, and in this case, salt tablets may help. Vomiting or diarrhea can also deplete your liquid and salt levels. Anhydrotic heat exhaustion, caused by an inability to sweat, is quite rare. Unlike the other forms of heat exhaustion, it is likely to strike people who have been in The Bahamas' hot climate for some time rather than newcomers.

Maintain an adequate level of liquids. Avoid booze by day, as your body uses water to process alcohol. Drink water, soft drinks, or – best of all – coconut water straight from the husk.

Heat Stroke This serious, sometimes fatal, condition can occur if the body's heat-regulating mechanism breaks down and body temperature rises to dangerous levels. Long, continuous periods of exposure to high temperatures can leave you vulnerable to heat stroke.

The symptoms are feeling unwell, not sweating very much or at all, and a high body temperature. Where sweating has ceased, the skin becomes flushed and red. Severe, throbbing headaches and lack of coordination will also occur, and the sufferer may be confused or aggressive. Eventually the victim will become delirious or convulse. Hospitalization is essential, but meanwhile, get victims out of the sun, remove their clothing, cover them with a wet sheet or wet towel, and fan them continuously.

Fungal Infections Hot-weather fungal infections are most likely to occur on the scalp, between the toes or fingers (athlete's foot), in the groin (jock itch or crotch rot), and on the body (ringworm). You get ringworm (which is a fungal infection, not a worm) from infected animals or by walking on damp surfaces, like shower floors.

To prevent fungal infections, wear loose, comfortable clothes, avoid artificial fibers, wash frequently, and dry carefully. If you do get an infection, wash the infected area daily with a disinfectant or medicated soap and water, and rinse and dry well. Apply an antifungal powder like the widely available Tinaderm. Try to expose the infected area to air or sunlight as much as possible, and wash all towels and underwear in hot water; change them often.

Motion Sickness Eating lightly before and during a trip will reduce the chances of motion sickness. While in transit, find a place that minimizes disturbance – near the wing on aircraft, close to midship on boats, near the center on buses. Fresh air usually helps; reading and cigarettes don't. Commercial anti-motion-sickness preparations, which can cause drowsiness, have to be taken before the trip commences; when you're feeling sick, it's too late.

Ginger is a natural motion-sickness preventative, and it is available in capsule form.

Diseases of Poor Sanitation

Diarrhea Despite all your precautions, you may still have a bout of mild traveler's diarrhea, but a few rushed toilet trips with no other symptoms are not indicative of a serious problem.

Dehydration is the main danger with any diarrhea, particularly for children, for whom dehydration can occur quite quickly. Fluid replacement remains the mainstay of treatment. Weak black tea with a little sugar, soda water, or soft drinks allowed to go flat and diluted 50% with water are all good. With severe diarrhea, a rehydrating solution is necessary to replace minerals and salts. Commercially available rehydration salts are very useful. Stick to a bland diet as you recover.

Lomotil or Imodium can be used to bring relief from the symptoms, although they do not actually cure the problem. Only use these drugs if absolutely necessary – for example, if you *must* travel. For children Imodium is preferable, but under all circumstances fluid replacement is the main message. Do not use these drugs if the person has a high fever or is severely dehydrated.

Giardiasis The parasite causing this intestinal disorder is present in contaminated water. The symptoms are stomach cramps, nausea, a bloated stomach, foul-smelling diarrhea, and frequent gas. Giardiasis can appear several weeks after you have been exposed to the parasite. The symptoms may disappear for a few days and then return; this can go on for several weeks. Tinidazole, known as Fasigyn, or metronidazole (Flagyl) are the recommended drugs for treatment. Either can be used in a single-treatment dose. Antibiotics are of no use for giardiasis.

Diseases Spread by People & Animals

Tetanus This potentially fatal disease is present in The Bahamas, as in other tropical and subtropical areas. It is difficult to treat but preventable by immunization. Tetanus occurs when a wound becomes infected by a germ that lives in the feces of animals or people, so clean all cuts, punctures, or animal bites. Tetanus is also known as lockjaw, and the first symptom may be discomfort in swallowing or stiffening of the jaw and neck; this is followed by painful convulsions of the jaw and whole body.

Sexually Transmitted Diseases There are numerous sexually transmitted diseases, and for most of these effective treatment is available. However, there is currently no cure for herpes or AIDS.

Condoms are widely available in pharmacies and general stores throughout the islands. Nonetheless, they may not be available when you need them. It's a good idea for both men and women to take condoms on their trips. After all, this is The Bahamas, you are on vacation, and who knows what passion might brighten your travel experience?

HIV/AIDS The human immunodeficiency virus (HIV) may develop into acquired immune deficiency syndrome (AIDS). HIV is a relatively small yet not insignificant problem in The Bahamas. Any exposure to blood, blood products, or bodily fluids may put you at risk. In The Bahamas transmission is predominantly through heterosexual sexual activities. Apart from abstinence, the most effective preventative is to always practice safe sex using condoms. It is impossible to detect the HIV-positive status of an otherwise healthy-looking person without a blood test.

Insect-Borne Diseases
Malaria Fortunately, malaria isn't present in The Bahamas. Among the Caribbean islands, it's relegated to Hispaniola (Haiti and Dominican Republic) and, to a lesser degree, Cuba.

Dengue Fever Although extremely rare, dengue fever is present on all Caribbean islands, and 1997 saw a marked outbreak in eastern Cuba and Haiti. There is no prophylactic available for this mosquito-spread disease. A sudden onset of fever, headache, and severe joint and muscle pains (hence its colloquial name, 'broken-bone disease') are the first signs before a rash starts on the trunk of the body and spreads to the limbs and face. After a few more days, the fever will subside and recovery will begin. Serious complications are not common.

The mosquitoes that transmit dengue fever most commonly bite from dusk to dawn, and during this period travelers are advised to wear light-colored long pants and long-sleeved shirts, use mosquito repellents containing the compound DEET on exposed areas, avoid highly scented perfumes or aftershaves, and use a mosquito net – it may be worth taking your own.

Cuts, Bites & Stings
Cuts & Scratches Skin punctures can easily become infected in hot climates and may be difficult to heal. Treat any cut with an antiseptic, such as Betadine. When possible, avoid bandages, as they can keep wounds wet. Coral cuts are notoriously slow to heal, as coral injects a weak venom into wounds. Avoid coral cuts by wearing shoes when walking on reefs, and clean

any cut thoroughly with sodium peroxide if available.

Bites & Stings Bee and wasp stings are usually painful rather than dangerous. Calamine lotion will give relief and ice packs will reduce the pain and swelling. There are some spiders with dangerous bites, but antivenins are usually available.

There are various fish and other sea creatures that can sting or bite or are dangerous to eat. Again, local advice is the best preventative. Fortunately, The Bahamas has no venomous snakes.

No-see-'ums These well-named irritants are almost microscopically small fleas that hang out on beaches and appear around dusk (especially after rains) with a voracious appetite. Their bite is out of all proportion to their size. You'll rarely, if ever, see the darn things, despite the fact that they seem to attack en masse, usually when you're not looking. They prefer the taste of ankles and have a predilection for diners at open restaurants by the shore. Cover your ankles if possible. Most insect repellents don't faze them. A better bet is a liberal application of Avon's Skin So Soft (SSS), a cosmetic that even the US Army swears by.

Jellyfish Local advice is the best way of avoiding contact with these sea creatures and their stinging tentacles. Dousing in vinegar will deactivate any stingers that have not fired. Calamine lotion, antihistamines, and analgesics may reduce the reaction and relieve the pain.

Bedbugs & Lice Bedbugs live in dirty mattresses and bedding. Spots of blood on bedclothes or on the wall around the bed can be read as a suggestion to find another hotel. Bedbugs leave itchy bites in neat rows. Calamine lotion may help.

All lice cause itching and discomfort. They make themselves at home in your hair (head lice), your clothing (body lice), or your pubic hair (crabs). You catch lice through direct contact with infected people or by sharing combs, clothing, and the like.

Powder or shampoo treatment will kill the lice, and infected clothing should then be washed in very hot water.

Scabies Scabies is an infestation of microscopic mites and is acquired through sexual contact, but it may also be transmitted through linen, towels, or clothing. Scabies is common among people living in rustic conditions and is endemic throughout The Bahamas and the Caribbean.

The first sign – severe itching caused by infestation of eggs and feces under the skin – usually appears three to four weeks after infestation (as soon as 24 hours for second infestations) and is worse at night. An infestation appears as tiny welts and pimples, often in a dotted line, most commonly around the groin and the lower abdomen, between the fingers, on the elbows, and under the armpits. Other bacterial skin infections may occur.

Treatment is by pesticide-containing lotions (prescription-only in the USA) sold over the counter at local pharmacies in The Bahamas. The entire body must be covered. Often two treatments within 48 hours are required. Personal hygiene is critical to exterminating the mites. At the same time that you use the treatment, you must also wash *all* your clothing and bedding in hot water. Any bedmates must do the same.

Medical Facilities
The Ministry of Health and Environment administers a nationwide health service with 107 clinics. You'll find government health clinics in settlements throughout the islands, plus private clinics in major towns. In addition, most large hotels have resident nurses, and doctors on call. For anything other than minor problems, you'll need to fly to Nassau or Freeport. For major treatments, the best advice is to get on a plane and fly home.

A visit to the outpatient clinic at Princess Margaret Hospital in Nassau costs US$10, although the wait is usually several hours. A room in Princess Margaret Hospital costs US$75 to US$100. Private doctor office calls average US$30 to US$60.

The following are the leading hospitals:

Nassau
    Doctor's Hospital (☎ 242-322-8411)
    Lyford Cay Hospital (☎ 242-362-4025)
    Princess Margaret Hospital
    (☎ 242-322-2861)
Freeport
    Rand Memorial Hospital (☎ 242-352-6735)

Doctor's and Lyford Cay are both private hospitals.

Medical Assistance Organizations
Many companies offer medical assistance for travelers. Most maintain 24-hour emergency hot-line centers that connect travelers to professional medical staff worldwide. Many also provide emergency evacuation, medical attention, and payment of on-site medical treatment. Some provide services for a set annual membership fee; others offer varying coverage levels.

The Council on International Education Exchange (CIEE) offers low-cost, short-term insurance policies called 'Trip Safe' to holders of the International Student Identification Card (ISIC), International Youth Card (IYC), and International Teachers Identification Card (ITIC).

North American medical assistance organizations include the following:

Access America offers travel insurance and 24-hour emergency, travel, medical, and legal assistance. PO Box 6600, W Broad St, No 11188, Richmond, VA 23230 (☎ 800-284-8300)

Air Ambulance Professionals can provide 24-hour worldwide medical transportation; all flights are staffed by 'aeromedically certified medical attendants.' Fort Lauderdale Executive Airport, 1575 W Commercial Blvd, Annex 2, Fort Lauderdale, FL 33309

ICT Travellers Assistance offers free medical aid, including ambulance, hospitalization, medication, repatriation, and emergency evacuation. PO Box 73008, Station G, Calgary, AL T2W 6E4, Canada (☎ 403-228-4685, fax 403-228-6271)

International Association for Medical Assistance for Travelers (IAMAT) is an information service assisting travelers needing medical attention. In the USA, 417 Center St, Lewiston, NY 14092 (☎ 716-754-4883); in Canada, 40 Regal Rd, Guelph, ON N1K 1B5

MEDEX/TravMed advises you on where to obtain medical assistance. It monitors and pays for health care and can arrange emergency medical evacuation and repatriation. ITAA, 5 Business Center Dr, Suite 100, Reston, VA 20190 (☎ 800-732-5309)

Travel Assistance International (TAI) emergency services include on-the-spot payment for medical expenses, medical evacuation, medication, repatriation of children, and other travel costs. 1133 15th St NW, No 400, Washington, DC 20005 (☎ 202-331-1609, fax 202-331-1588)

Travel Care International specializes in medical evacuations around the world. PO Box 1445, Eagle River, WI 54521 (☎ 715-479-8881)

WOMEN TRAVELERS

Many Bahamian men accept a commonly held stereotype that foreign women are promiscuous. This is believed to be especially true of foreign women seen alone in bars or dance clubs. Fortunately, most Bahamian men are not pushy. They understand the meaning of 'no' and will usually take a rejection in good humor.

Bahamian men and women of all ages indulge in salacious dancing, even with complete strangers. Be aware that if a Bahamian man invites you to dance, he will probably 'wine' you – make sexual contact – from front or behind.

Safety Precautions

Sexual assault is comparatively rare in The Bahamas and is almost unheard of in the Family Islands. It is safe to walk virtually anywhere by daylight, although you should be cautious on E Bay St and Delancy St and in the Over-the-Hill district of Nassau. The Family Islands pose few problems, although even here it is wise to avoid walking alone or hitchhiking at night in remote areas. If you're driving alone, be discreet about those you choose to pick up.

Women traveling alone can reduce unwanted attention by dressing modestly away from the beach. It is wise not to walk around in beachwear – including a bikini top and sarong – away from the beach. Put on a T-shirt. You'll *never* see a Bahamian woman in a bikini top around town.

Organizations & Resources

The Women's Crisis Centre (☎ 242-328-0922), on Shirley St in Nassau, can assist in an emergency or if you need emotional support.

The American Women's Club (☎ 242-327-6812) and Canadian Women's Club (☎ 242-323-3117) may prove handy resources.

Good resources include the International Federation of Women's Travel Organizations (☎ 602-596-6640), 13901 N 73rd St, Suite 210B, Scottsdale, AZ 85260. The *Handbook for Women Travelers* by Maggie and Gemma Ross and *The Traveling Woman* by Dena Kaye are also replete with handy tips and practicalities.

GAY & LESBIAN TRAVELERS

Although Bahamians are generally an extremely tolerant people, the pervasiveness of fundamentalist religious beliefs has fostered bigotry and intolerance of progressive lifestyles, particularly toward gays and lesbians. Most Bahamian gays are still in the closet, and the nation has draconian laws against homosexual activity, which is punishable by prison terms. Laws are strictly enforced; public expressions of affection between gays may well bring trouble.

There are no gay bars or clubs.

Organizations & Resources

The following organizations can provide information and assistance in planning a trip:

Lesbian & Gay Community Services Center
   81 rue Marche au Charbon, 1000 Brussels, Belgium (☎ 32-2-502-2471)
   208 W 13th St, New York, NY 10011 (☎ 212-620-7310)
Travel Alternatives Group
   2300 Market St, No 142, San Francisco, CA 94114 (☎ 415-552-5140, fax 415-552-5104, mark8ing@aol.com)

Ferrari Publications (☎ 602-863-2408, fax 602-439-3952), PO Box 37887, Phoenix, AZ 85069, publishes several travel guides

Facts for the Visitor – Senior Travelers

for gays and lesbians, including the *Spartacus International Gay Guide*. Another valuable resource is *Odysseus: The International Gay Travel Planner* (☎ 516-944-5330, fax 516-944-7540), PO Box 1548, Port Washington, New York, NY 11050.

Scuba divers should call Undersea Expeditions (in the USA ☎ 619-270-2900, 800-669-0310), which plans trips to The Bahamas for gays and lesbians.

DISABLED TRAVELERS

Disabled travelers will need to plan their vacation carefully, as few allowances have been made for them in The Bahamas and Turks and Caicos.

Only a small percentage of hotels have facilities for disabled travelers. Check with the individual hotel before making your reservation. Fortunately, many hotels are one-story buildings or have ramp access or elevators, and the casinos have ramp access.

The tourist board can provide a list of hotels with wheelchair ramps, as can the Bahamas Association for the Physically Disabled (☎ 242-322-2393, fax 242-322-7984), on Dolphin Dr in Nassau. Its mailing address is PO Box N-4252, Nassau, Bahamas. The Bahamas Council for the Handicapped (☎ 242-322-4260) can also provide this information.

The Bahamas Association for the Physically Disabled provides a minibus for disabled tourists and will arrange airport transfers and a guided island tour. Wheelchairs and assistance are available at Nassau International Airport.

New construction codes mandate ramps and parking spots for disabled people at shopping plazas and other select sites. Larger hotels are beginning to introduce features such as Braille instructions and chimes for elevators, bathrooms with grab bars, and ramps. However, only the most recent structures in Nassau and, to a lesser degree, Freeport have adopted these features.

Organizations

The Society for the Advancement of Travel for the Handicapped (SATH, ☎ 212-447-7284, fax 212-725-8253), 347 Fifth Ave, No 610, New York, NY 10016, can provide information for travelers. Annual membership costs US$45. The American Foundation for the Blind (☎ 212-620-2000), 15 W 16th St, New York, NY 10011, also has information on travel.

Flying Wheels Travel (☎ 507-451-5005, 800-535-6790, fax 507-451-1685), PO Box 382, Owatonna, MN 55060, is a tour operator and full-service travel agency for the physically challenged.

SENIOR TRAVELERS

One-third of travelers worldwide are over 50, and travel companies court seniors with discounts, usually passed on through members of seniors' organizations. Most US airlines offer senior discount programs for travelers 62 or older. Some car-rental companies also extend discounts – ask and you may receive!

Unfortunately, The Bahamas seems virtually exempt from seniors' discounts. Only a handful of hotels offer them. There's no harm in asking, but don't be surprised to hear 'no' for an answer.

Organizations & Resources

The American Association of Retired Persons (AARP, ☎ 800-441-7575), at 1909 K St NW, Washington, DC 20049, offers discounts on hotels, car rentals, etc, through its Purchase Privilege Program. It also arranges travel for members through AARP Travel Experience. An annual membership costs US$8. The Golden Age Travelers Club (☎ 800-258-8880), Pier 27, The Embarcadero, San Francisco, CA 94111, offers similar services.

SAGA International Holidays (☎ 800-343-0273), 222 Berkeley St, Boston, MA 02116, specializes in all-inclusive tours for seniors. Also check with Elderhostel (☎ 617-426-7788), 75 Federal St, Boston, MA 02110-1941, which may offer trips to The Bahamas.

Another handy source of tips on seniors' discounts is the monthly newsletter of the National Council of Senior Citizens, 925 15th St NW, Washington, DC 20005.

TRAVEL WITH CHILDREN

The Bahamas pursues the family traveler aggressively, and the larger hotels compete by providing facilities for children. Most hotels will provide a babysitter or nanny if you make an advance request. Several all-inclusive resorts, such as Holiday Inn Pirates Cove Sunspree Resort on Paradise Island (as well as Beaches on Providenciales in the Turks and Caicos), cater specifically to families, offering a full range of activities and amenities for their young guests.

Most hotels also offer free accommodations or greatly reduced rates for children staying in their parents' rooms (a child is usually defined as being 12 years old or younger, but some classify those 16 or younger as children).

It's a good idea to prearrange necessities such as cribs, babysitters, cots, and baby food.

Rental villas and apartments are good options for families. Most come fully staffed, allowing you to leave the children with the housekeeper (you'll need to check that this is in accordance with rental terms).

Rascals in Paradise (in the USA ☎ 415-978-9800, 800-872-7225) specializes in family vacation planning and offers all-inclusive group trips limited to six families. It has trips to several Family Island destinations; trips include a tour-guide-cum-nanny.

If you fancy a cruise vacation, consider Premier Cruises (in the USA ☎ 407-783-5061, 800-327-7113), which specializes in family cruises.

Lonely Planet's *Travel with Children* by Maureen Wheeler gives you the low-down on preparing for family travel. Other handy resources are *The Family Travel Guide Catalog* and *Family Travel Times Newsletter* (☎ 212-665-6124), 80 Eighth Ave, New York, NY 10011.

For encouragement, you might also check out Nancy Jeffrey's *Bahamas – Out Island Odyssey*, her tale of traveling through the islands with two teenage sons and an infant.

USEFUL ORGANIZATIONS

Bahamas Historical Society

This nonprofit cultural and educational organization is dedicated to stimulating interest in Bahamian history. It publishes a regular journal and maintains a museum at its headquarters (☎ 242-322-4231) at Shirley St and Elizabeth Ave in Nassau; its mailing address is PO Box SS-6833, Nassau, Bahamas.

Dept of Archives

This department (☎ 242-393-2175, fax 242-393-2855), on Mackey St in Nassau, serves as a repository for government records and archives. It has a microfilm collection of historical documents dating back to 1700, plus a photographic archive and a large collection of maps and charts. It also serves as the official caretaker of the material archives of the culture and antiquities of the nation. It publishes books and booklets relating to historical and cultural aspects of the islands. The department is open 10 am to 4:45 pm daily except holidays. Its mailing address is PO Box SS-6341, Nassau, Bahamas.

DANGERS & ANNOYANCES

The US State Dept publishes travel advisories that alert US citizens to trouble spots. Advisories are available by recorded telephone message (in the USA ☎ 202-647-5225, fax 202-647-3000), at US embassies and consulates abroad, or by writing the Citizens Emergency Center, Room 4811, State Dept, Washington, DC 20520-4818. They're also posted on the Internet (see the Internet Resources appendix). The warnings are often out of date.

Natural Hazards

Undertows & Currents Those gorgeous coral reefs beg to be explored, and the turquoise waters are seductive sirens. How can you resist the temptation? You don't have to . . . but be aware that many places have dangerous undertows and currents. Seek local advice about conditions before swimming.

Hurricanes Public warnings will be issued if a hurricane is due to come ashore. In the event of a hurricane, seek shelter in the sturdiest structure you can find. (For more on hurricane seasons, see Climate in the Facts about The Bahamas chapter.)

Manchineel The manchineel tree, which grows along the Bahamian shoreline, produces small, applelike green fruits. Don't eat them – they're highly poisonous! Take care not to sit beneath the tree, as even raindrops running off the leaves onto your skin can cause blisters.

Social Hazards

Soon Come! This is the Caribbean . . . well, almost. Service may sometimes be slower than you're used to at home. That's fine! You're *not* at home. You're on vacation. So slow down, relax, and go with the Bahamian flow.

Harassment Most Bahamians are cheery, helpful, law-abiding folks concerned with making the foreign visitor's experience as positive as possible. The Bahamas is relatively free of hustlers, the scourge of neighboring islands like Jamaica. Nonetheless, The Bahamas is not immune, although hustlers are almost entirely restricted to Nassau and, to a lesser degree, Freeport. Here hustlers walk the streets looking for potential customers to whom to sell crafts, jewelry, or drugs; they also offer to wash cars, give aloe massages, act as guides, or perform a thousand varieties of service.

Aggressive persistence is key to their success. Hustlers are experts in consumer psychology. They have an instant answer for any excuse you might offer. Putting a guilt trip on you is a favorite trick. 'Sssst . . . hey! Remember me?' is another clever line used to introduce and link themselves to you.

Play to the islanders' innate sense of humor. A wisecrack can often break the icy confrontation and earn you respect.

If you hire a guide, don't expect him to do more than keep you from getting lost or

keep other hustlers at bay. Establish parameters such as what he'll provide and how much you'll need to pay up front.

Drugs Marijuana *(ganja)* and cocaine are prevalent in The Bahamas, which is used as a transshipment point for drug traffic into North America. At some stage, you may be approached by hustlers selling drugs.

Be warned that possession and use of drugs and the 'facilitation of drug trafficking' in The Bahamas are strictly illegal and penalties are severe. The islands are swarming with US Drug Enforcement agents, and purchasing drugs is a risky business. Foreigners *do not* receive special consideration if caught. Bahamian prisons are notoriously nasty places. Likewise, US Customs agents are on the alert – and well trained – to spot drug smugglers.

Also be aware that a local spliff will pack an almighty punch compared to those skinny little joints you're used to back home. It's not unknown, too, to find that the cocaine you might sniff is actually Ajax, or that your ganja has been sprayed by paraquat, is laced with crack cocaine, or is really dried croton. *Caveat emptor!*

Crime Most Bahamians are extremely law-abiding citizens. Their sense of honor and pride runs deep, and their tolerance of thieves and criminals is extremely low. The Bahamas as a whole is relatively crime-free, and the vast majority of travelers return home without having suffered any mishaps whatsoever.

Nassau is a distinct exception, where shootings and violent robberies among locals are frequent. Many of the murders are related to the drug trade. They occur overwhelmingly in the low-income and shantytown areas south of downtown and to a lesser degree in parts of Freetown. Serious crime in the Family Islands is virtually unknown.

Most crime against travelers is petty opportunistic crime, and is overwhelmingly relegated to Nassau and Freeport, where pickpockets – one could be the foreigner by your side – are particularly busy in the casinos.

Take sensible precautions with your valuables. Hold handbags close to your body. Carry your wallet in your front pocket. Leave jewelry in your hotel safe. Never leave valuables in view in your car, and always keep car doors locked. Steer clear of poorer quarters of Nassau and Freeport, including downtown, at night. And don't wander on unlit streets at night; stick close to main thoroughfares.

Keep hotel doors and windows securely locked at night. Don't open your door at night to anyone who cannot prove his or her identity.

EMERGENCY

You can summon an ambulance or the police anywhere in The Bahamas by dialing ☎ 919. In Nassau the emergency number for public ambulances is ☎ 242-322-2221; for the Red Cross, dial ☎ 242-323-7370. For an ambulance in Freeport, call ☎ 242-352-2689.

In the event of an emergency at sea, contact the following organizations:

Bahamas Air-Sea Rescue Association (BASRA), PO Box SS-6247, Nassau (☎ 242-322-3877, VHF channel 16)
Nassau Marine Operator (VHF channel 27 or 2198 SSB)
US Coast Guard, 7th Coast Guard District, Brickell Plaza, 909 SE 1st Ave, Miami, FL 33131 (☎ 305-536-5611, 2182 SSB)

Each can arrange air transportation to the nearest medical facility. You can also reach the Royal Bahamas Defence Force at channel 22A.

A private ambulance service, National Air Ambulance (☎ 954-359-9900, 800-525-0166), operates from Fort Lauderdale International Airport.

LEGAL MATTERS

Bahamian drug and drunk-driving laws are strictly enforced. Don't expect leniency because you're a foreigner. A jail term can ruin your vacation . . . and your life! Still, if you do run afoul of the law and are arrested, insist on your right to call your embassy or consul to request their assistance. They should be able to help with finding a lawyer, advising relatives, and providing counsel. But that's about as far as they'll go.

Gays and lesbians should note that homosexual relations are illegal, even between consenting adults. People caught engaging in homosexual intercourse are subject to prison terms.

A new law recently made sexual intercourse in public a crime punishable by a jail term up to 20 years, for hetero- and homosexuals. If your bartender asks you if you would like 'sex on the beach,' make sure he or she is referring to the drink!

BUSINESS HOURS & PUBLIC HOLIDAYS

Government and private business offices tend to be open 9 am to 5 pm weekdays.

In Nassau and on Grand Bahama, banks are open 9:30 am to 3 pm Monday to Thursday and until 5 pm Friday. Banks can be very busy on Friday afternoon. In the Family Islands, bank hours vary widely. Usually local banks are open only one or two days a week, for two or three hours. See island chapters for details.

In Nassau and Freeport most stores are open 9 am to 5:30 pm weekdays and 10 am to 5:30 pm Saturday. Often they close for lunch. Few stores are open on Sunday, except boutiques and gift shops in Nassau and Freeport, and then only when cruise ships are in town. In the Family Islands, hours are similar, although more fluid.

Post offices are usually open 8:30 am to 5:30 pm weekdays and until 12:30 pm Saturday.

Most restaurants are open seven days a week. Hours vary.

Holidays that fall on Saturday or Sunday are usually observed on the following Monday. Bahamian national holidays include the following:

January 1	*New Year's Day*
Friday before Easter	*Good Friday*
Monday after Easter	*Easter Monday*

Top: The welcome bench at the government dock in Hope Town, Abacos
Bottom: 'I see you!' says the talking skull of Great Guana Cay.

Top Left: The big ones that didn't get away on Walker's Cay, Abacos
Top Right: Preparing the nightly feast at the Abaco Beach Resort
Bottom: A perfect place to picnic: Eleuthera Point, Eleuthera

Seven weeks after Easter	*Whit Monday*
First Friday in June	*Labour Day*
July 10	*Independence Day*
First Monday in August	*Emancipation Day*
October 12	*Discovery Day*
December 25	*Christmas Day*
December 26	*Boxing Day*

SPECIAL EVENTS

The BTO (see Tourist Offices, earlier in this chapter) publishes a monthly list of events, plus a pin-up calendar of events, available from its offices worldwide. It also provides phone numbers and dates for specific events.

Most events run on a predictable schedule. Many annual events occur at the cusp of months, so the specific month may vary from year to year.

No traditional African festivals were retained in The Bahamas. Nonetheless, several folk festivals evolved from the brief slave era, notably Junkanoo (see below) and Emancipation Day. On these days workers on New Providence put down their tools and walk with their families to Fox Hill, going from church to church and ending the day in merrymaking and traditional dancing.

Junkanoo

The nation's most famous festival has been called 'the centerpiece of Bahamian culture.' The event is hosted at various venues around Christmas and New Year's Day, when streets and settlements resound to the calliope of cowbells, whistles, and goatskin goombay drums, drawing in thousands of foreign visitors. Mostly it is a big blow-out for the local masses, and a tropical Mardi Gras with quintessential Bahamian flavor.

Be prepared to throw inhibitions to the wind. As the festivities wear on, becoming a minicarnival, even otherwise staid island folk put on new personas. Bahamians are not shy about wearing as little as possible, nor about wining (making sexual contact while dancing) with complete strangers.

The main festival is held in Nassau, beginning before sunrise on Boxing Day. As many as 20,000 locals and tourists party

the night away or are up before dawn for the parade. Similarly, on Grand Bahama the parade is held on W Sunrise Hwy in Freeport on New Year's Day at 5 am.

In the Exumas a few local characters (such as Josh, 'King of the Junkanoo') add to the color of the festival. It begins at 3 am on Boxing Day (the day after Christmas). Eleuthera's Junkanoo celebration begins at 5 am on Boxing Day. In the Abacos the parades take place on both Boxing Day, when individual settlements celebrate, and New Year's Day, when they come together in New Plymouth. There are *three* Junkanoo celebrations in Alice Town in the Biminis: on Boxing Day, New Year's Day, and July 10, in recognition of independence.

The festival is a street event, so there is no entrance charge.

Caribbean Muzik Fest

This weeklong festival, first held in Nassau in May 1994, is an annual jam with reggae, soca, Junkanoo music, and dance hall under the same billing, showcasing the best talent from the Caribbean's cornucopia of musical genius. Little-known but top-notch locals also perform, such as Visage, a 'Bahamian super group.' The event is now held in June at the Queen Elizabeth Sports Centre and traditionally lasts from 8 pm until dawn. Tickets cost US$30 – not a bad deal considering the number and quality of artists in one show.

Homecomings & Regattas

Most towns in the Family Islands have 'homecomings,' the very heart of the Bahamian social scene, when family members return from Nassau, other islands, or the USA. Usually these homecomings are associated with national holidays, so that participants can stretch the festivities for three to five days. They're social parties, full of Bahamian bonhomie, and a good excuse for local men to get drunk. Other homecomings are 'dry' (the character of a celebration depends on the town: Harbour Island's homecoming is a bit of a revel, with sexy-swimsuit contests and no small

Junkanoo

You feel the music before you see it . . . a frenzied barrage of whistles and horns overriding the *ka-LICK-ka-LICK* of cowbells, the rumble of drums, and the joyful blasts of conch shells. Then the costumed revelers stream into view, whirling and gyrating like a kaleidoscope in rhythm with the cacophony. This is Junkanoo, the national festival of The Bahamas, its equivalent to Carnival or Mardi Gras.

Junkanoo is a traditional Christmas celebration in which revelers parade through the streets dressed in masquerade. It was once the major celebration on the slave calendar and dates from the 18th century, when slaves were granted three days off for Christmas.

The name, pronounced *junk-un-NOO*, is thought to come from a West African term for 'deadly sorcerer.' Others say the festival is named for John Canoe, a tribal leader who demanded that his enslaved people be allowed to celebrate a holiday. Junkanoo, which had its origins in West African secret societies, evolved on the plantations of the British Caribbean among slaves who were forbidden to observe their sacred rites. The all-male cast of masqueraders hid their identity, following West African mask-wearing tradition. (The costumes resembled those of the Yoruba tribe, notably the Egungun cult, a secret group that worshiped ancestral spirits. An Egungun mask often covers the entire body and usually represents the spirit of a particular person.) Some dressed as demons, others wore horse heads, and many were on stilts. The elaborate carnival was accompanied by musicians with drums, fifes, flutes, and rattles.

At first Junkanoos were suppressed by the Bahamian colonial government, which feared they might get out of hand and lead to slave uprisings. Later planters encouraged them. Creole elements found their way into the ceremony, and Morris dancing, polka, and reels were introduced. On Jamaica and other islands Junkanoo was suppressed to the point of virtual extinction, but in The Bahamas it became an integral part of the culture.

Every major hotel now has a Junkanoo band, and no major event on the tourist calendar is complete without Junkanoo music and dancing. But the greatest spectacle is reserved for year's end, when Junkanoo parades flood down Bay and Shirley Sts in Nassau and erupt on other islands with all the energy of an atomic explosion.

In Nassau the first 'rush,' as the parade is known, takes place on Boxing Day (December 26); the second occurs on New Year's Day. The parades begin at about 3 am and last beyond dawn. By noon on New Year's Day, the parades are over. The costumes are abandoned. Scraps of crepe paper float down Bay St.

Junkanoo is fiercely competitive, and participants practice year-round. Many marchers belong to 'shacks,' organized groups with members from many social classes. The shacks vie to produce the best performance, costume, and music. The most elaborately costumed performers are one-person parade floats and are often sponsored by individual companies or stores. Each costume can weigh over 200 lbs, although they're crafted from crepe paper pasted on cardboard or Styrofoam. Most costumes depict exotic scenes or social themes, with plentiful beads, foils, and rhinestones added for glittery accent. Many people spend the entire year planning their costumes, keeping their designs a carefully guarded secret. ■

amount of salacious fun; that of nearby Current, meanwhile, is more of a church-supper affair).

Many of the homecomings are associated with sailing regattas, when locally made sailing craft compete for prizes and partying is taken to its limit. The more famous regattas – the Family Island Regatta in the Exumas and the Long Island Regatta – are tourist staples and have been summed up in three words: 'boats, bikinis, and booze.'

Other Happenings

See the island chapters for contact information and details on these events.

January

Bahamas Princess Resort & Casino Crystal Pro-Am Golf Tournament – This tourney is held at the Emerald & Ruby Golf Courses, Grand Bahama.

Classic Cars Race – Lovers of flashy vintage cars should head to Nassau for this four-day festival. Rare Ferraris, Jaguars, and other classics dating back to the 1920s gear up for a race along Cable Beach.

February

Ebony Fashion Fair – Traditionally held at the Radisson Cable Beach, the fair draws Nassau's socialites and would-be models to 'ooh' and 'aah' at the latest designs of world-famous designers.

International Food Fair – Local Bahamian fare comes to the streets of Nassau, with cookouts and competitions highlighting the bounty of the sea and land.

People of the Bahamas Annual Archives Exhibition – Held in Nassau, the exhibition features exhibits showcasing the contributions of various ethnic groups to the historical and cultural development of the nation.

March

Freeport Rugby Club Annual Easter Rugby Festival – Grand Bahama hosts 15 of the world's top rugby teams, as players from as far afield as Argentina and Wales gather to tussle for the grand prize.

Grand Bahama 5K Road Race – World-class athletes compete alongside locals, with a grand opening featuring spoofy costumes and bed races.

April

Family Island Regatta – This four-day extravaganza of sailboat races and general merrymaking is a highlight of the Bahamian social calendar. It takes place in George Town (Great Exuma), and thousands fly in for the lively social scene, which includes cooking demonstrations, beauty pageants, and plenty of drinking and dancing.

Snipe Winter Sailing Championships – These races pit homemade sailing craft against one other in Montagu Bay, off Nassau Harbour.

May

Bimini Festival – A popular sport-fishing tournament is the highlight of this festival in mid-May, featuring barbecues, cookouts, and general merriment.

Long Island Regatta – A smaller-scale version of the Family Island Regatta with equal amounts of bonhomie, this midmonth festivity sees up to 50 traditional sailing vessels competing for honors. Rake 'n' scrape bands, native food stalls, and party games round out the carnival-like ambiance.

June

Annual Eleuthera Pineapple Festival – This annual festival in early June in Gregory Town (Eleuthera) combines music, games, and festivities with cooking contests, 'best pineapple' contests, beauty pageants, and the crowning of the young Pineapple Queen.

Bahamas Boating Flings – Each June through mid-August, a lead boat guides a flotilla of yachts and other craft from Fort Lauderdale's Radisson Bahai Mar Resort & Yacht Club to the Biminis.

Goombay Summer Festival – Nassau hosts a midyear Junkanoo, with round-the-clock festivities for summertime visitors.

July

All Eleuthera Regatta – This sailing affair melds three days of racing with a festive atmosphere replete with fashion shows, music, and contests. Islanders flock to Rock Sound for the family fun.

August

Emancipation Day – Held the first Monday in August to commemorate the emancipation of slaves in 1834. A highlight is an early-morning 'Junkanoo Rush' at 4 am in Fox Hill.

Fox Hill Day Celebration – Held a week after Emancipation Day, this celebration recalls the day on which residents of Fox Hill learned of emancipation.

Great Abaco Triathlon – Athletes descend on Marsh Harbour to test their mettle. The event includes a kids' triathlon and Sprintman race.

Miss Bahamas Contest – Finalists vie for the coveted title of Miss Bahamas in a much-anticipated gala evening in Nassau featuring stellar entertainment. The winner represents The Bahamas in the Miss World contest.

September

Bahamas Atlantis Superboat Challenge – Life is never so fast in Nassau as in late September, during this annual professional powerboat race. Forty or more teams compete in boats that are to smaller speedboats what dragsters are to the family sedan.

Ladies' Futures Pro-Am Golf Tournament – This is a challenging 54-hole tourney for top-ranked international golfers at the Paradise Island Golf Club (New Providence).

October

Annual Grand Bahama Triathlon – Athletes compete in a challenging 1.5-mile swim, a 15-mile bike race, and a 3-mile run.

Annual McLean's Town Conch Cracking Contest – Participants in this contest on Grand Bahama compete to extract the highest number of conchs from shells in the shortest possible time. Politically incorrect as well as profligate? Ah, well . . . there's 'greasy pole' climbing and other inane amusements to keep everyone happy.

European Golf Weeks – Grand Bahama hosts a monthlong series of golf tournaments for amateurs at the Lucaya Golf & Country Club.

Great Bahamas Seafood Festival – The Arawak Cay Seafood Market in Nassau is the setting for this annual four-day culinary and cultural extravaganza, featuring concerts, Junkanoo, and plenty of food.

International Cultural Weekend – Bahamians celebrate unity among the many nationals residing in the islands with a weekend of float parades, food fests, arts and crafts displays, and concerts, held in Nassau.

International Mixed Championship Golf Tournament – This is a weeklong 54-hole event for amateurs at the Paradise Island Golf Club.

North Eleuthera Regatta – This three-day racing pageant features scores of locally built sloops vying for the championship. Onshore festivities include entertainment by local bands, regional cuisine, and fashion shows.

November

Annual Grand Bahama Conchman Triathlon – Over 200 athletes gather in Freeport to compete in swimming, bicycling, and running. There's a party, too, at Taino Beach.

Guy Fawkes Night – On November 5 Bahamians celebrate retribution for the Gunpowder Plot of 1605 – when Catholic plotters attempted to blow up the Houses of Parliament in London – by lighting bonfires and burning the lead villain, Guy Fawkes, in effigy, accompanied by requisite fireworks. Nassau has a nighttime parade.

December

Christmas Concert Under the Stars – The Garden Theatre, on Green Turtle Cay (Abacos), plays host to an open-air concert of traditional Christmas music and other performances.

Plymouth Historical Weekend – Residents of Green Turtle Cay celebrate their Loyalist heritage with musical concerts, theater, art exhibits, and barbecues.

Police Band Annual Christmas & Classical Concert – The Royal Bahamas Police Force Band performs holiday classics at the Atlantis resort on Paradise Island, with accomplished local musicians assisting.

WORK

There are strict legal limitations against foreigners seeking work in The Bahamas. Competition for itinerant work is extremely high, so no expatriate may be offered employment in a post for which a suitably qualified Bahamian is available. However, a work permit application may be considered if you have already entered the country as a visitor. A permit relates to a specific job for which an employer must show proof of having made adequate attempts to recruit a Bahamian. Permit requests must be made through the Immigration Dept (☎ 242-322-7530), PO Box N-831, Nassau, Bahamas.

A good start would be to contact the Bahamas Contractor's Association, PO Box N-4632, Nassau, Bahamas; the Bahamas Employers' Confederation, PO Box N-166, Nassau, Bahamas; or the Bahamas Hotel Employer's Association (☎ 242-322-2262), PO Box N-7799, Nassau, Bahamas.

ACCOMMODATIONS

The Bahamas has a range of accommodations, from cozy inns and quaint family-run guesthouses to superdeluxe resorts. Where you stay can make or break your vacation, so it pays to research thoroughly. Don't be fooled by such terms as 'first class' or 'deluxe' in promotional material. Price is only one guide – many hotels of similar price vary dramatically in ambiance and value. There are some splendid bargains at all price levels, from cozy budget guesthouses for US$40 nightly to ritzy all-inclusive resorts where you need never open your wallet once inside the gates.

Also consider how many facilities your ideal hotel should have. If you're a serious golfer, you might think about paying a little more to stay at a dedicated golf resort. There are several dedicated scuba resorts for divers, too.

Basically, you have two choices: windward or leeward. The former usually means miles-long beaches washed by Atlantic rollers; the latter means smaller coves, usually secluded, lapped by mint-green waters. Next, consider whether you want a secluded resort or a local guesthouse.

Many older properties suffer from years of neglect.

Rates & Seasons

Low or off season (summer) is usually mid-April to mid-December; high or peak season (winter) is the remainder of the year, when hotel prices increase by 40% or more.

Prices begin at about US$30 a night for budget, no-frills properties, usually swarming with mosquitoes. You will be hard-pressed to find even a room in a modest middle-of-the-road hotel or guesthouse for less than US$60, which seems to be an island price-standard for even the most mediocre properties. Fortunately, you can also find some gems in this range. Upscale resort hotels are priced from about US$80, deluxe properties from US$150. Ultra-deluxe hotels begin at about US$200 and run upward of US$500 nightly. If you have to ask . . . !

If you stay at an all-inclusive resort, you'll pay one price for as much food, booze, and activities as you wish to indulge in, and these resorts can therefore be great bargains. Check the fine print; some all-inclusives will charge for diving and other services.

Ocean-view rooms are usually more expensive than other rooms. To save money, choose a room with a less desirable view. Also consider buying a package, which most resorts and upscale hotels offer. It's possible to buy a three-day/two-night package from New York or Miami for US$199 to US$399, and a seven-day/six-night package for US$350 to US$800, depending on the resort. Special packages, which usually include airport transfers and some extras, are also offered to honeymooners, golfers, and divers.

Unless otherwise stated, prices refer to room only, or European Plan (EP). Many hotels have a price system tiered into peak, shoulder, and low season rates, while others (usually the most select hotels) have year-round rates. Some properties also discount room rates based on the number of nights you stay. *Ask what discounts may be available and feel free to suggest your own.*

Some hotels will quote rates as Continental Plan (CP; room and breakfast), Modified American Plan (MAP; room plus breakfast and dinner), or American Plan (AP; room plus three meals daily). Don't forget to check if the quoted rate includes tax and service charge. If not, a compulsory 8% government tax (10% in Nassau and on Grand Bahama) and a possible 10% to 15% service charge may be added to your bill. Consider, too, whether breakfast is included. In addition, some hotels add miscellaneous charges such as an energy surcharge, 'resort levy,' or a per-diem fee for housekeeping service (US$3.50 is typical). You may challenge these questionable charges. The housekeeping service charge is legal, but the energy tab is left over from the oil crisis days of the mid-'70s and is definitely illegitimate.

The more popular hotels are often booked solid in peak season; at other times of year not only can you find rooms, but you may be given the run of the house. It is advisable to book several months in advance in peak season, especially if you're relying on the mail, which can take several weeks. It's best to phone, fax, or use a travel agent or hotel representative (see below) in your home country.

Hotel Discounts Several organizations offer discounted room rates at savings up to 50%. Most offer discounts to fee-paying members only, but joining is easy. Contact the following organizations:

Entertainment Publications, 2125 Butterfield Rd, Troy, MI 48084 (☎ 248-637-8400, fax 248-637-3992)

Quest International, 402 E Yakima Ave, Suite 1200, Yakima, WA 98901 (☎ 509-248-7512, 800-742-3543, fax 509-457-8399)

Some hotels that do not anticipate filling their rooms sell blocks of rooms in advance to wholesalers at bulk discounts, which the wholesalers pass along as huge savings. Try The Room Exchange (in the USA ☎ 800-846-7000, fax 212-760-1013).

Information & Reservations
The BTO publishes a guide and rate sheet to leading hotels and guesthouses across the islands. You can obtain it from BTO offices worldwide (see Tourist Offices, earlier in this chapter) or from the BTO information booths at Nassau and Freeport airports. All the establishments listed have been inspected and are 'BTO approved.' (Many accommodations that have not been BTO approved are perfectly OK.)

You can make reservations directly with hotels, but you'll find it just as easy to use travel agencies or hotel representatives, notably the Bahamas Out Islands Promotion Board (see Tourist Offices).

Alternately, try the Bahamas Reservation Service (in the USA ☎ 800-327-0787; in the UK 0181-876-1296), which offers a free reservation service (the hotels foot the bill). The BTO also runs a reservation service, Bahamas Reservations (in North America ☎ 800-700-4752).

The Bahamas Hotel Association (☎ 242-322-8381, fax 242-326-5346), Hotel's House, Dean's Ln, Nassau, Bahamas, represents hoteliers and other accommodations owners and tourism service providers.

Another good resource is 'Where to Stay in the Caribbean,' a website that puts more than 300 properties – not all in The Bahamas, but organized by name, island, and topic – at your fingertips (see the Internet Resources appendix).

Camping
Campers are disdained by tourism officials, and the country is not developed for them. A handful of budget properties will let you pitch a tent on their lawns for a small fee. However, camping on beaches is illegal, and there are no official campsites, even in wilderness areas.

Rental & Self-Catering Units
The Bahamas boasts hundreds of private houses for rent, from modest cottages to lavish beachfront villas. Some are in self-contained villa communities. Others are self-catering apartments in plain condo-style units. These units are a great way to establish your independence and are very cost-effective if you're traveling with your family or a group of friends.

Air-con, a TV, radio, telephone, bed linens, and towels are standard. Most have a fully equipped kitchen; some have only a kitchenette, often tiny, with a small one- or two-ring gas burner. A few have their own swimming pool, tennis court, and/or boat jetty. Check carefully as to the number of bedrooms and beds, and ask whether a third and fourth person will sleep on a sofa bed or Murphy bed. Check for incidentals, including electricity (which is usually included).

Good sources are the classified-ad sections of *Caribbean Travel & Life* and *Islands* magazines. In the UK a good starting point is TC Resorts (☎ 0171-486-3560, fax 0171-486-4108), 21 Blandford St, London W1H 3AD.

In the USA rental companies include the following:

At Home Abroad, 405 E 56th St, No 6H, New York, NY 10022 (☎ 212-421-9165)

Condo World, 4230 Orchard Lake Rd, Suite 3, Orchard Lake, MI 48323 (☎ 248-683-0202, fax 248-683-5076)

Property Rentals International, 1 Park W Circle, Suite 108, Midlothian, VA 23113 (☎ 804-378-6054, 800-220-3332, fax 804-379-2073)

Villa Leisure, PO Box 1096, Fairfield, CT 06430 (☎ 203-222-9611)

Villas International, 950 Northgate Dr, Suite 206, San Rafael, CA 94903 (☎ 415-281-0910, 800-221-2260, fax 415-499-9491)

In The Bahamas you can make arrangements through the following organizations:

Caribbean Management, PO Box N-1132, Nassau, Bahamas (☎ 242-393-8618, fax 242-393-0326)

Grosham Property, PO Box N-8189, Nassau, Bahamas (☎ 242-327-0806, fax 242-322-3549)

Ingraham's Real Estate, PO Box N-1062, Nassau, Bahamas (☎ 242-325-2222, fax 242-325-3433)

Several elegant resort hotels offer villa rentals in private homes on their grounds; renters have access to resort facilities.

Upscale villas usually have a private pool, TV-VCR, stereo, and often a tennis court. They're almost always fully staffed with a housekeeper and cook and sometimes with a gardener and night watchman. Some staffs even include a butler and laundress. Your rental agency should supply you with details on staff, including tipping guidelines. Most agencies recommend that your gratuities should total about 7% to 15% of the villa rental cost. It's customary to give the staff one night off per week.

Weekly rental rates begin at US$100 for budget units with minimal facilities. More upscale villas begin at about US$750 weekly for a two-bedroom cottage and can run US$5000 or more for a four-bedroom estate sleeping eight or more people. Cistern Cay (Exumas) will set 10 adults back a whopping US$38,000 per week. Rates fall as much as 30% in summer. A large deposit (usually 25% or more) is required to confirm your reservation; full payment is normally required one month before your rental begins.

You'll pay a premium for being down by the beach. Expect to pay more, too, if your villa is provisioned with food. It's usual to buy your own food (costs generally run about US$100 per person per week). Your cook may stock the food for your first dinner and breakfast and should be reimbursed. He or she normally accompanies you on your shopping spree – a great way to learn about local food and Bahamian dishes. If the cook does your shopping, give explicit written instructions and ask for a strict accounting.

Homestays & Home Exchanges

The Ministry of Tourism's 'People-to-People Programme,' while not specifically designed to provide accommodations with families, is a good starting point. Participants have been screened by the ministry, which can assist in arranging overnight stays. (See the sidebar on the next page for more information.) An international organization that arranges for homestays is Interculture GB (☎ 0181-534-4201, ext 271), c/o CRS Ltd, 78-102 The Broadway, Stratford, London E15 1NL.

You can also make your own arrangements to stay with individuals or families that do not rent rooms as a normal practice. Use your discretion: If you don't feel secure, don't accept.

Another option is to exchange your home with a family in The Bahamas. Two companies that specialize in handling this are Intervac (in the USA ☎ 800-756-4663) and The Invented City (in the USA ☎ 415-252-1141; see the Internet Resources section for website address). Both represent properties in The Bahamas.

Hostels & Guesthouses

The Bahamas has no youth hostel association. However, there's a youth hostel in Nassau (see the New Providence chapter).

People to People

The Bahamas Ministry of Tourism would like you to meet the locals and discover their warmth and congeniality. It has developed the 'People-to-People Programme' to enable visitors to interact with Bahamians and gain an appreciation for island life. Usually participants attend an afternoon tea, dinner, or cocktail party; join a family at a church service or social or civic club; go sightseeing; or even spend a few hours sharing their hosts' work environments.

Visitors are matched with host families that share the visitors' interests or even professions. Volunteer hosts are all approved by the ministry and their homes inspected to ensure that they meet the program's standards. Most are middle-class citizens.

The program is offered on New Providence, Grand Bahama, the Abacos, the Biminis, the Exumas, and San Salvador. There's no charge, but a small gift (or at least picking up the tab) is considered a common courtesy.

Contact The Manager, People-to-People (☎ 242-326-5371, fax 242-328-0945), PO Box N-3701, Nassau, Bahamas; or The Coordinator, People-to-People (☎ 242-352-8044), PO Box F-40251, Freeport, Grand Bahama, Bahamas. You can also register at the tourism information booths at Nassau International Airport and in Nassau's Rawson Square.

The governor-general's wife hosts a People-to-People tea party on the last Friday of each month (January to August) at Government House in Nassau. ∎

Guesthouses are the accommodations of choice for Bahamians when traveling. Usually they're small, no-frills, family-run properties with a live-in owner who provides breakfast and sometimes dinner on-site.

Standards and prices vary enormously. Some are exquisite. Many are no more than a couple of dingy rooms with shared bathrooms and plenty of mosquitoes. Others are self-contained apartments. Some are indistinguishable from hotels or motels.

They're good places to mix with locals, but choose carefully.

The *Nassau Guardian* and the *Tribune* newspapers list guesthouses under 'Boarding Accommodation' and 'Guesthouse' headings in their classified-ad sections.

Hotels

Bahamian hotels run the gamut, but it is unwise to rely solely on a hotel's brochure or promotional literature. Knowing whether a hotel has air-con, TVs, and a swimming pool tells you nothing about its ambiance, so I've tried to provide in-depth descriptions of hotels to help you make a more informed decision based on ambiance as much as amenities.

All-Inclusive Resorts

These resorts are cash-free, self-contained hotels or village resorts; you pay a set price and (theoretically) pay nothing more once you set foot inside the resort.

All-inclusive resorts offer a pampered vacation but tend to shelter guests from mingling with locals and discovering the colorful, real Bahamas. Most resorts offer a range of excursions and shopping tours.

Caution is needed when choosing a resort. Many properties have jumped onto the 'all-inclusive' bandwagon for marketing purposes. Club Med (☎ 800-258-2633), for example, has three properties in The Bahamas and one in the Turks and Caicos and is considered an all-inclusive chain, but in reality you will have to pay for booze and some extras. Check carefully for any hidden charges for water sports, laundry, and other activities or services *not* included in the price. Rates begin at about US$100 per day at the less expensive resorts.

Two companies dominate the Caribbean scene: Sandals and SuperClubs. Their renowned rivalry, which now extends to The Bahamas and the Turks and Caicos, has fostered the highest standards and supreme service. Sandals' resorts, which are marketed as 'ultra-inclusives,' boast the highest occupancy rates of any hotels in the Caribbean! The Royal Bahamian, its flagship resort on New Providence, is for couples only. Contact Sandals at the following locales:

Canada
    4211 Yonge St, Suite 320, Willowdale, ON M2P 2A9
    (☎ 416-223-0028, fax 416-223-3306)
France
    c/o SME, 28 Rue Caumartin, 75009 Paris
    (☎ 01.42.65.90.90, fax 01.42.65.90.91, sandals@club-internet.fr)
Germany
    Walter Kolb Strasse 9-11, 60594 Frankfurt
    (☎ 69-96-20 28-14, fax 69-610-637, sandals@t-online.de)
UK
    32 Ives St, London SW3 2ND
    (☎ 0171-581-9895, fax 0171-823-8758)
USA
    Unique Vacations, 4950 SW 72nd Ave, 2nd Floor, Miami, FL 33155 (☎ 305-284-1300, 800-726-3257, fax 305-667-8996)

SuperClubs at present has one property in The Bahamas: Breezes, on New Providence. For more information, contact SuperClubs at the following locales:

UK
    39a High St, Hoddesdon, Herts EN11 8TE
    (☎ 0992-447420, fax 0279-506616)
USA
    2021 Hayes St, Hollywood, FL 33020
    (☎ 800-859-7873)

FOOD

The Bahamas' cuisine is a fusion of several ethnic traditions. Indigenous people were fond of seafood and also brought callaloo, cassava, corn, sweet potatoes, and tropical fruits to the islands. English and US settlers adopted native spices, enhanced by spices brought from Africa. Basic roasts and stews followed the flag during British rule, as did meat pies and hot cross buns.

The Bahamians melded all these influences into their dishes, although in recent decades many ingredients have been ousted by North American fare. Bahamian food seems to have lost its edge and nuance. Visitors who ask for spicy food may be handed a bottle of Tabasco.

Traditional cuisine is undergoing a renaissance, however. A new generation of Bahamian chefs is reinterpreting traditional dishes and creating new ones. A distinct Bahamian cuisine is emerging, sponsored by the Ministry of Tourism's annual Great Bahamas Seafood Festival competition (see Special Events). Imagine crab-stuffed sweet potato with pineapple and papaya salsa, blackened conch with pigeon-pea relish and pepper coulis, and whelks seasoned in Kalik beer.

However, such recherché influences have not filtered through the islands. For the most part, Bahamian cuisine is comparatively dull.

Out to Eat

There's a full gamut of restaurant types, from funky seafood shacks and burger joints to ritzy restaurants with candelabras. Restaurants range from wildly expensive (the norm) to humble roadside stands where you can eat simple Bahamian fare for as little as US$3. Small hole-in-the-wall restaurants often serve fabulous local fare; don't be put off by their often basic appearance (unless they appear overtly unhygienic).

Most restaurants serve at least one vegetarian meal. Hotels tend to offer buffet meals; larger resorts have a choice of restaurants, with one always serving buffets. The ultradeluxe hotels have restaurants that are among the best on the islands, but they can't replicate the taste and atmosphere of small, locally run eateries.

Many of the more popular upscale resorts sell evening passes that allow you to eat and drink in their restaurants, bars, and nightclubs for a single fee. And larger hotels often offer bargain-priced 'Dine-Around' programs, sometimes included in the hotel rate.

Many of the restaurants geared to the tourist trade are overpriced. An average dinner will cost US$20 or more. Budget at least US$40 a day for food. Groceries are also expensive. Many canned and packaged goods are imported and cost up to three times what you might pay at home.

Bottled water is also costly. Unfortunately, with the exception of Nassau, you will be hard-pressed to find fresh fruits, vegetables, and spices at markets and roadside stalls. Consider taking favorite food items with you.

If your luck runs thin with rod and reel, you'll find fresh fish sold everywhere in the islands. Most settlements have either a makeshift market – where fishermen filet and sell their fresh catches of dolphin (the fish), grouper, conch, and lobster (in season) – or a cache in someone's home.

Dress is casual at all but the most exclusive restaurants, which will expect you to dress 'elegantly casual' (no jeans). A few upscale resorts may require jackets at dinner. With minor exceptions, only beach bars tolerate the shoeless and shirtless. You'll often see signs advising that you'll be refused service if you're not properly attired.

Main Dishes

Rice (imported) is the dietary staple, usually eaten with 'peas,' such as red beans, pigeon peas, or lima beans. Another favorite is 'grits' (ground corn), also usually mixed with peas. Peas find their way into hearty soups, along with okra, meats, and vegetables. Potato salad often takes the place of rice.

Breakfasts tend toward US style, often with grits. Local breakfast favorites are tuna and grits, corned beef hash and grits (one of my favorites), and eggs and grits.

Seafood

Conch, crab, grouper, jack, lobster, shrimp, snapper, turbot, tuna, and whelk are all daily staples of Bahamian cooking, often cooked with carrot, cassava, cucumber, grits, guinea corn, okra, plantain, and wild spinach.

The sovereign dish is conch (pronounced 'conk' in The Bahamas). This tough mollusk is served pounded, minced, and frittered; marinated and grilled; or even raw as a ceviche or 'conch salad' (diced with onions, celery, pepper, and cucumber, and soaked in lime juice).

'Scorched' conch is not sizzled by flames; it's a conch salad in which the conch is scored, not diced. Almost every eatery in the nation serves 'cracked conch' (battered and deep-fried), conch chowder, and conch fritters fried on a grill. Often it is steamed or 'stewed' in brown gravy.

It is somewhat rubbery and relatively tasteless. So why the fuss? Probably because it is considered an aphrodisiac capable of 'givin' men a strong back.' (Recall the scene in *Thunderball* where James Bond offers his delectable dining companion a bowl of conch chowder? She declines, hinting that 007's libidinous allure needs no artifice.)

Lobsters (crawfish) are other favorites, though being pricey they are not as important a staple as you may imagine. Many local cooks have a habit of overcooking lobster meat. Upscale hotel restaurants, such as Graycliff in Nassau, are renowned for their splendid lobster dishes.

Land crabs are also highly prized (and highly priced). Don't be surprised to see a car come to a screeching halt and its occupant hop out to chase down a land crab on the road. Baked crab is most popular, often with crab eggs and meat mixed together, seasoned with bread crumbs, and baked in the shell.

The favorite fish is grouper, a mild-flavored white fish, often served poached, grilled, or steamed in a mildly spiced sauce. It's often eaten as 'grouper fingers' – battered, deep-fried strips.

A favorite breakfast dish is 'boil fish,' a bouillabaisse of grouper boiled with salt pork, onion, potato, and seasonings. It is usually served with grits or johnnycakes (the Bahamian equivalent of Irish soda bread or American biscuits).

The Exumas are most renowned for their turtle dishes. Turtles are a local delicacy, and each community swears by its own version of preparing the meat, which has a high scent that must be eliminated. The turtle is usually marinated and preseasoned, then chilled in aluminum foil to prevent 'freezer burn.' It is served steamed or broiled.

Meat

Chicken is the staple meat, hotly pursued by pork. Meats tend to be fried, grilled, barbecued, or 'steamed,' meaning braised in a broth of meat drippings, tomato, onion, and herbs. By far the most ubiquitous dish is fried chicken and fries (often packaged).

'Mutton' – frequently seen on menus – can be goat or lamb and is frequently served curried.

Weekends (especially Saturday, when many Bahamians shun the home kitchen) are the time for 'souse,' a clear 'mess of pottage' (meats boiled in saltwater) seasoned with lime juice and pepper. The meat is usually that of a sheep, including tongue, trotters, and all. Local men consider it a good cure for a hangover.

Fruit & Vegetables

The islands are not the tropical Eden of exotic fruits one might expect. At one time rare and exotic fruits were synonymous with The Bahamas, most notably pineapple, which during the 19th century enjoyed a worldwide reputation. Only minuscule quantities are produced today, but look for the Eleutheran sugar loaf or Spanish scarlet varieties, considered especially delicious.

Tiny roadside shacks proffer papayas, mangoes, pineapples, limes, and bananas. But have you ever tried jujubes, star apples, pigeon plums, Surinam cherries, sapodillas, or soursops? I recommend the following fruits:

ackee – A tree-grown fruit (native to Africa), the ackee has a daffodil-yellow flesh that bears an uncanny resemblance to scrambled eggs when cooked. Served with johnnycakes and callaloo and flaked saltfish with onion, it makes a fantastic breakfast. It is poisonous when unripe. It is rarely served in The Bahamas.

guava – A small ovoid or rounded fruit with an intense, musky, sweet aroma, it has a yellow-green skin and pinkish, granular flesh studded with regular rows of tiny seeds. It is most commonly used in nectars and punches, syrups, jams, chutney, and even ice cream.

guinep – This small green fruit grows in clusters, like grapes. Each 'grape' bears pink flesh that you plop into your mouth whole. It's kind of rubbery and juicy, and tastes like a cross between a fig and a strawberry. Watch for the big pit in the middle. It peaks in July and August, when every Bahamian seems to have some in his or her hands.

jujube – Similar to the guinep, this grape-size fruit is green when ripe, with yellow meat and a small pit inside.

mammee – Sometimes called 'mammee apple,' this fruit is round. Peel away the brown skin and you discover a bright yellow pulp that is starchy and chewy, somewhat like coconut. You eat it raw.

mango – The mango is a lush fruit that comes in an assortment of colors. You should massage the glove-leather skin to soften the pulp, which can be sucked or spooned like custard. Select your mango by its perfume. Ripe mangoes smell unmistakably exquisite.

papaya – The papaya's cloak of many colors (from yellow to rose) hides a melon-smooth flesh that runs from citron to vermilion. The central cavity is a trove of edible black seeds. Tenderness and sweet scent are key to buying papayas. They are commonly served with breakfast plates, in fruit salads, and in jams and ice cream. They may also be baked in desserts.

soursop – This is an ungainly, irregularly shaped fruit with cottony pulp that is invitingly fragrant yet bland to acidic in taste, hinting at guava and pineapple. It's most commonly used for puddings, ice cream, canned drinks, and syrups.

star apple – This is a leathery, dark-purple, tennis-ball-size, gelatinous fruit of banded colors (white, pink, lavender, purple). Its glistening seeds form a star in the center. The fruit is mildly sweet and understated. Immature fruits are gummy and unappetizing. You should feel for some give when buying.

sugar apple – 'Sugar apple' is a strange name for a fruit that resembles a giant pine cone, with sections that separate when the fruit is ripe. The gray, juicy flesh is sweet and custardy and shot with watermelonlike seeds.

tamarind – There's no mistaking the pendulous 6-inch-long pod that hangs from tamarind trees. When brown, it is ready for picking. The shell will crack open to reveal a sweet green meat that is often used in sauces.

ugli fruit – This fruit is well named. It is ugly on the vine – like a deformed grapefruit with warty, mottled green or orange skin. But the yellow-golden pulp is delicious: acid-sweet and gushingly juicy.

You may also come across breadfruit in various guises. This starchy fruit is popular throughout the islands and grows wild. It was first introduced in 1793 in Jamaica, following Captain William Bligh's second attempt to procure it from the South Pacific (his first attempt ended in the famous mutiny on the *Bounty*). Breadfruit was then introduced throughout the Caribbean region and raised as a staple food source for slaves. The round fruits weigh up to 4 lbs. Young or immature fruit is either added to soups or served as an accompaniment to main dishes. The mature (but not yet ripe) fruit is roasted or deep-fried.

Among vegetables, the Irish potato has traditionally had pride of place, although more creative chefs are now using pumpkin, plantain, and sweet potato.

Desserts

The trademark Bahamian dessert is duff or guava duff, a fruit-filled, boiled jelly pudding served with sauce made of sugar, egg, butter, and rum. It can be steamed, baked, or even boiled. Another favorite is coconut tart, a thin baked pie filled with sweetened shredded coconut filling.

DRINKS
Nonalcoholic Drinks

Coffee drinkers be forewarned: Coffee in The Bahamas is *awful!* The problem is caused by brackish local water. Imagine a dash of salt in your favorite pick-me-up! Few resorts have cottoned on to making coffee with bottled, purified water. Outside upscale hotels and restaurants, most coffee is instant, such as Sanka or Nescafé, served from a jar and whitened with sweetened condensed milk. Only a few places serve espresso or cappuccino.

Tea is served to US standards: a cup of hot water with a teabag on the side. It's enough to make a Brit's heart sink. Bush teas are still commonly brewed by locals, but you'll rarely see these offered commercially.

Soft drinks are readily available. In addition to North American favorites such as Coca-Cola and 7-Up, an assortment of local equivalents are offered, such as Goombay Punch. Ginger ale is very popular, as is nonalcoholic malt stout. Fruit juices are widely available, as is bottled water.

Alcoholic Drinks

The Bahamas rightfully claims one of the world's premier brews: Kalik. This light, sweet, lager-style beer is perfect for hot days (3.5% alcohol). It sells for US$1 to US$3 a bottle, depending on the standard of bar. The more robust and superb Kalik Gold is twice the strength and guaranteed to give you a buzz. Bahamian men also drink locally brewed Heineken, plus Amstel and US and Canadian beers. Bottled Guinness is popular.

The second drink of choice is rum. The poorer classes tend to shoot shots of cheap, overproof white rum, but there is an excellent range of quality rums, including Bacardi, which has a factory on New Providence. A higher-class option is Ron Matusalem. The third local rum producer is Todd Hunter.

Various locally produced rum liqueurs also find their way into cocktails. Nassau Royale is a rumlike liqueur with a hint of vanilla, good on the rocks or mixed with light rum to make a Rum Royal. Other flavored rums include coconut rum, banana rum, and pineapple rum sold under the Ricardo label.

On islands such as the Abacos, almost every bar has a house libation, often concocted through weeks-long taste tests. Some drinks, though widely copied, have become synonymous with their place of origin, such as the Goombay Smash, invented by Miss Emily's Blue Bee Bar on Green Turtle Cay. Most seek to produce an effect – from a mild glow to complete disorientation – by using copious amounts of rum, often married to tequila, whiskey, or vodka. Usually combining three flavors of rum, the drinks include fruit juice to cut the alcohol flavor and lend sweetness.

Each drink's name is a good guide to its potency. Thus, despite banana rum, coconut rum, gin, scotch, vodka, *and*

151-proof rum, the Tranquil Turtle (the house drink at the Bluff House on Green Turtle Cay) is 'very nice because it's not lethal. You can actually get up and walk around after four or five and not make a fool of yourself,' claims manager Martin Havill. The neighboring Green Turtle Club makes no such claim for its Tipsy Turtle.

My favorite is the Goombay Smash, a killer drink made of coconut rum, Bacardi Gold, and fruit punch, and served in a near-pint-size glass.

Cocktails range from US$3 in local bars to twice that in ritzier hotels.

Wines are widely available but costly. Often they have not been well protected from the heat. Wine connoisseurs should head to Graycliff in Nassau; its owner, Enrico Garzaroli, claims the largest wine collection in the Caribbean, with some rare vintages offered at US$5000.

ENTERTAINMENT
Pubs/Bars
In Nassau there are several English-style pubs and others with an international flavor. These get a mixed crowd, as do hotel bars, which range in decor from rustic to elegant, often in a nautical theme.

Watching basketball and other US sports is the main activity of the Bahamian men who hang out in bars. Pool and dominoes are also popular. Throughout the islands, locals tend to sup in 'satellite lounges' (the name refers to a satellite TV on the premises). Most bars are of this type. Most also have a pool table and serve food. A rake 'n' scrape band is often featured. Visitors are always welcome. Very few bars are to be feared.

A fistful of bars should be inducted into the Hall of Fame. At the Vic Hum Club, on Harbour Island, you can groove to disco music while local youths throw down vicious dunks on the indoor basketball court! The bar at Compass Point, on New Providence, is a likely spot for seeing a famous model or TV actor.

You'll rarely see women drinking alone in local bars, although frequently they'll visit with their boyfriends or spouses (or someone else's). Bars are not good places, in general, for male tourists to make a romantic encounter with a Bahamian lass. For female tourists, the opposite holds true.

Dance Clubs
Nassau and Paradise Island have numerous dance clubs popular with foreign visitors and urbane locals. The past few years has seen several additions. The more upscale clubs boast modern decor and are ridiculously expensive. Here dress codes are enforced. These places are for serious dancing and, if a casual affair is in your stars, offer opportunities to meet a classy partner. Few such clubs get going before 11 pm; most usually stay open until 4 am.

More downscale clubs in Nassau and Freeport tend to attract a lot of fun-loving college types, especially during spring break. Wet T-shirt contests and beer-drinking contests are standard fare. One even has bungee-jumping . . . after half a dozen beers, *I don't think so!*

All dance clubs offer Ladies' Nights with free access for women.

The Family Islands are altogether more down-to-earth affairs. Clubs tend, in general, to cater to the local crowd and often feature a live band.

Larger upscale resorts usually have their own clubs for patrons, but they're invariably open to the public for a small cover charge.

Casinos & Floorshows
Gambling is legal, and thousands of people visit The Bahamas to try their hand with Lady Luck. The games include baccarat, blackjack, craps, roulette, and video poker. Some casinos have a Big Wheel and a sports book section.

You must be at least 18 years old to gamble. Only foreigners may gamble; Bahamians may enter casinos but cannot gamble. Admission is free. Free drinks are provided while you play. Bare feet and swimwear are not permitted, and skimpy clothing is frowned upon. Tastefully elegant minimalism, however, such as a

Gambling 101

Daunted by the sight of suave sophisticates calmly moving their tokens into place on the mysteriously patterned green felt of a gaming table? Then take a class. The Paradise Island Casino, at the Atlantis resort on Paradise Island (see the New Providence chapter), offers a crash 'Gambling 101' course each afternoon at 3 pm.

The hourlong sessions are guaranteed to help you take a step up from the slots. The course includes important aspects of casino etiquette. For example, never *ask* the dealer for a card; instead, tap the table lightly. Don't say 'no' or shake your head if you don't want a card; instead, give a slight sideways hand signal an inch above the table.

Larry Lewin, senior vice-president of gaming operations, offers the following advice to novices:

- Remember, you are playing a game. It is for pleasure.
- Make a budget for each day of play. Establish one budget for winning and one for losing.
- Don't touch tomorrow's money.

miniskirt, décolletage, and high heels, is welcomed. Casinos are open 10 am to 4 am daily; the slot machines are open 24 hours a day.

At press time there were four casinos in The Bahamas:

Bahamas Princess Casino, Freeport, Grand Bahama (☎ 242-352-6721)
Crystal Palace Casino, Cable Beach, New Providence (☎ 242-327-6200)
Lucayan Beach Resort & Casino, Port Lucaya, Grand Bahama (☎ 242-373-7777)
Paradise Island Casino, Paradise Island (☎ 242-363-3000)

The Lucayan Casino was closed at press time for approximately one to two years for remodeling.

The casinos each have Las Vegas-style revues featuring comedians, a magician, crooners, and song-and-dance routines. Topless shows are offered, featuring brief seminudity. Otherwise, the religiously inclined local authorities keep a tight rein on things. Tourists seeking voyeuristic pleasures will be disappointed. There are no 'gentlemen's clubs' and only one strip club: a seedy affair in downtown Nassau.

Cinemas

Urbane Bahamians in Nassau and Freeport are serious cinemagoers. Nassau has several cinemas. First-run Hollywood hits are strongly favored. There are very few cinemas in the Family Islands.

Opera & Classical Music

The most important venue is the Dundas Centre for the Performing Arts (☎ 242-393-3728) on Mackey St in Nassau. Its equivalent in Freeport is the Regency Theatre (☎ 242-352-5533), where the Friends of the Arts lure guest artists from abroad.

Look for performances by the Nassau Amateur Operatic Society, Chamber Singers, Diocesan Chorale, and, on Grand Bahama, the Lucayan Players.

The benefit season gets into swing in winter, when concerts are as thick as baubles on a fir tree. At Christmas you can hear the Royal Bahamas Police Force Band and local musicians perform holiday classics at the Police Band Annual Christmas & Classical Concert.

Occasional soirées may be hosted locally. Keep your eyes on local notice boards and newspapers.

Theater, Ballet & Contemporary Dance

The theatrical arts are quite lively. The Dundas Centre for the Performing Arts and the Regency Theatre (see above) are the two most important venues, although local theater groups also use regional venues.

Watch for performances by the Nassau Players, Bahamas School of Theater, Dundas Repertory Company, and, on Grand Bahama, the Freeport Players Guild and Grand Bahama Players.

Traditional Bahamian dialect is increasingly being honored on stage, headlined by the James Catalyn and Friends company.

The National School of Dance, Nassau Civic Ballet, and New Breed Dancers are among the leading dance companies.

Check local newspapers for current and forthcoming performances.

Jazz

Jazz is growing in popularity. Several venues in Nassau and Freeport cater to jazz lovers, and leading jazz artists occasionally perform. In the Family Islands you may chance upon an impromptu jazz session in a hotel bar, but don't count on it. An international jazz festival is held each summer in Nassau.

Folk/Traditional Music

Traditional rake 'n' scrape music is a highlight of many local bars and festivities such as Family Island regattas. The musical form has been incorporated into a handful of 'native shows,' such as the show at the King & Knights Club in Cable Beach, complete with dance.

Rock

Rock is not the music of the islands. Acclaimed rock performers rarely visit, and DJs are disinclined to play rock music. The more popular dance clubs in Nassau, such as The Zoo, occasionally intersperse favorite rock tunes from the 1960s and '70s. Your best bet is probably to head to the Rock 'n' Roll Café in Cable Beach.

Many bars have jukeboxes, usually with some rock sounds.

SPECTATOR SPORTS

The Bahamas is not a major venue for spectator sports. The BTO can provide a calendar of major events, as can the Bahamas Sports Information Centre (☎ 800-327-7678).

Baseball is the primary team sport, and you may chance upon games on any of the islands. Bahamians are also fond of cricket, though not as much as you'd imagine for a former British colony. Rugby is popular: The Bahamas hosts the annual Freeport Rugby Club Annual Easter Rugby Festival on Grand Bahama.

Regattas are held on most of the major islands and feature locally made sailing craft vying against one other. A powerboat race is held off Nassau each September.

Track and field events are hosted at the Queen Elizabeth Sports Centre (☎ 242-323-5163) on Thompson Blvd in Nassau. Several road races are also held (see Special Events in this chapter).

THINGS TO BUY

Nassau and Freeport are renowned as shoppers' paradises, offering duty-free items, arts and crafts, fashionwear, and food items and drinks. There are waterfront markets and roadside stalls selling a range of goods splashed with Caribbean colors, as well as straw-work, carvings, ceramics, leatherwork, naive art, and T-shirts.

You'll also find some duty-free stores in the Family Islands, especially at upscale resorts. Outside main tourist centers, shopping tends to be limited to local crafts.

In general, the closer you get to the source, the lower the price.

Duty-Free Goods

The two main resort towns and the major settlements have a wide choice of duty-free stores stocked with perfumes, Cuban cigars, Italian leathers, and Colombian emeralds. Want to outfit yourself in Parisian fashion? No problem. Duty-free stores also sell china, crystal, gold, silverware, linens, silks, and jewelry. Most upscale hotels also have stores selling name-brand duty-free items.

Since uncut gemstones can be exported duty free, jewelry constitutes a major trade item. Showcases twinkle with emeralds, diamonds, rubies, and sapphires, along with gold settings. Need a new watch? This could be the place for a first-class Swiss or Japanese model. Many items can be bought at up to 30% below US or European retail prices. Prices vary between stores, however, so it pays to comparison-shop. No domestic sales tax is charged on duty-free purchases.

Destination Bahamas, a coffee-table book found in many hotel rooms, provides comprehensive information on where to shop for duty-free goods.

You can use credit cards or traveler's checks. Paying by credit card is best, as this protects you if the item is defective (some card companies provide buyers' insurance). Most items are not bonded: You simply take your purchase away. In certain cases you may find that you cannot walk out with your purchase; instead, the goods will be delivered to your hotel or cruise ship.

For further information, contact the Nassau Tourism & Development Board (☎ 242-394-3575, fax 242-393-0452), PO Box SS-5252, Nassau, Bahamas, which accredits merchants meeting required levels of quality and authenticity. Look for the pink-flamingo logo.

Warning: Not all duty-free items are bargains. Check the price of items prior to leaving your home country, so that you can determine your actual savings.

Arts & Crafts

The Bahamas is well known for its busy straw markets, as Bahamian weavers were among the first in the Caribbean region to take their skills to commercial heights. You'll find crafts stores virtually everywhere, selling baskets, bags, mats, dolls, and hats woven from the top fronds of coconut palms. Other straw crafts are woven from silver-top or pond-top palm, harvested during a new moon according to tradition.

Nassau's Bay St straw market is by far the largest. Freeport has several centers, notably at the Port Lucaya Marketplace.

The local weaving industry withered in recent decades. Much of the straw-work for sale in Nassau is actually imported from Taiwan and the Orient (yes, even if it has 'Made in Bahamas' stitched across the front in blazing colors)! Fortunately, traditional art has begun to make a comeback, especially on Long Island, which is renowned for its more than two dozen plaiting styles. Long Islanders supply Nassau workers, who stitch the plaiting

into finished products with antique pedal-driven sewing machines. Andros can also lay claim to its own unique style of basketry, often decorated with locally made Androsia batik, a colorful, handmade, authentically Bahamian product from which Androsians fashion clothing and fabrics poignantly representing the simplicity and beauty of the Family Islands.

Look, too, for the 'Lil' Locals,' exquisitely handcrafted by Anastasia Charlow. These small sculptures depict straw vendors, fishermen, domino players, and so on and are made of Androsia batik and other products over wire and window screen. They're priced from US$40.

If you're looking for art, you'll find dozens of galleries in Nassau and Freeport, and also throughout the Family Islands. The Abacos are particularly blessed, for here reside some of the islands' most famous artists; originals by collector-name artists can be had for a relative steal.

Cigars

Fine handmade cigars from Cuba are all the rage in The Bahamas. Many locals smoke 'em, and you won't be long in the islands before discovering that many US citizens like to blow smoke at the four-decade-stale US embargo by drawing on a Communist stogie.

Virtually every gift shop worth its salt sells top-class Havana cigars. Cohibas, Montecristos, Romeo y Julietas . . . they're all sold at bargain prices (you can purchase a box of 25 cigars for as little as US$45). Nassau and Freeport boast well-stocked tobacco shops dedicated to cigar lovers.

US citizens should know that it is illegal to purchase any Cuban-made product without a license to do so, whether you're buying inside or outside Cuba. Your Cuban cigars will be confiscated by US Customs agents if discovered (only rarely is anyone ever arrested or prosecuted, and then only for attempting to smuggle large volumes).

If you want to be perfectly legal, you'll also find high-quality cigars from Dominica for sale.

Outdoor Activities

The Bahamas and the Turks and Caicos have a panoply of sports and special-interest activities for those to whom beach bumming spells boredom. See the island chapters for more information, including details on sites of particular interest for each activity and contact information for activity operators.

The Bahamas

DIVING

The islands offer some of the most spectacular and diverse scuba diving in the world, with 2500 miles of ocean wall drop-offs, underwater caverns, and blue holes (see below). Many blue holes are accessible from underwater caverns. Every island is rimmed by coral reefs.

To the west, the warm waters of the nutrient-rich Gulf Stream move northward, protecting The Bahamas from Florida's rain and river runoff and ensuring that the sea remains crystal clear and the coral reefs pristine. Also ensuring clear waters are the deep trenches that separate many of the islands.

The waters offer exceptional visibility – up to 100 feet or more, although winter fronts can stir up lingering silt. Water temperatures range from 74°F to 85°F year-round. Wet suits are not required, though they can prevent scrapes from coral.

The Bahamas boasts a dazzling display of colorful sealife, ranging from the exotic to the eerie. All the favorite stars are on show: moray eels, grunts, barracudas, stingrays, turtles, queen triggerfish, sand tigers, parrotfish and angelfish flashing their neons, and an impressive array of hard and soft coral formations totaling an estimated 5% of the world's coral reefs. The north, central, and south islands (including the Turks and Caicos) each have their own special attractions. Most islands offer shallow and deep reefs, plus seemingly bottomless drop-offs.

There are plentiful wrecks in the waters, including ships, planes, and – wow! – even a wreck of an 1865 train off Eleuthera. The Bahamas even claims part of the 'lost city' of Atlantis, just off the Biminis, popular with celebrity divers like Don Johnson and Jimmy Buffett.

Above all, The Bahamas is renowned for wall dives – descents of the sheer-faced walls at the edges of the Bahama Banks. A wall dive is said to be like 'flying a small plane into the Grand Canyon – and the descent is like falling down a huge mountain face.' Most commercial wall dives go to about 185 feet. The effects of pressure and the dangerous euphoria known as nitrogen narcosis begin to appear at these depths, and your stay is limited to only a few minutes.

Diving is especially spellbinding March to June, when the marine life is spawning and producing megaschools.

Blue Holes

Many of The Bahamas' caves are underwater, accessed either by large 'blue holes,' circular water-filled pits that look like bomb craters (see Geology in the Facts about The Bahamas chapter) or by their egresses in the limestone walls of the Bahama Banks. Most islands in the chain have blue holes.

Many commercial dive operators offer blue-hole dives for certified scuba divers. The visibility is astonishing, the sensations exhilarating. But diving blue holes is not for novices! Diving is legally restricted to an 80-foot depth for holes and 150-foot penetration in walls, and you must remain within sight of the exit. For deeper dives, you need to be cave-dive certified. It can be a dangerous business. The insurgence and resurgence of current can be colossal: 'high to low, suck to blow.' And the waters deep down can be terribly cold.

Recommended dive operators include Small Hope Bay Lodge on North Andros and Exuma Fantasea on Great Exuma. See the Andros and Exumas chapters, respectively, for contact information and details.

Organizations

The following organizations are good to know:

Divers Alert Network (DAN) offers divers' health insurance, covering evacuation and treatment in emergencies. PO Box 3823, Durham, NC 27710 (☎ 919-684-2948; 24-hour emergency line 919-684-8111)
National Association of Underwater Instructors (NAUI), 9942 Currie Davis Dr, Suite H, Tampa, FL 33619-2667 (☎ 813-628-6284, fax 813-628-8253)
Professional Association of Diving Instructors (PADI), 1251 E Dyer St, No 100, Santa Ana, CA 92705 (☎ 714-540-7234, 800-729-7234, fax 714-540-2609)

Recompression Chambers

There are two recompression chambers in The Bahamas. One is operated by the Underwater Explorers Society (UNEXSO, ☎ 242-373-1244; in the USA 800-922-3483) at Port Lucaya Marina in Freeport (Grand Bahama). The second is at the Club Med Columbus Isle resort (☎ 242-331-2000, fax 242-331-2222; in North America ☎ 800-453-2582, fax 602-443-2086) on San Salvador. This information was current at press time; check before you plan your dive trip.

Operators

There are dozens of licensed dive operators. Many hotels also offer dive facilities, including Club Med, whose Columbus Isle property was rated by *Scuba Diving* magazine as the 1996 'Best Dive Resort in the World.' There are even honeymoon packages for couples who want to learn to dive between moments of nuptial bliss.

Dive operators can also put you up close and personal with hungry sharks. Looking for dolphins? No problem. See the Snorkeling section in this chapter for details.

'Resort courses' (also called 'Discover Scuba' or 'Intro to Scuba') for beginners are offered by most dive operators. They usually last a few hours. You can also take certification courses lasting several days. Licensed dive operators are required to adhere to strict safety standards. *Never* go diving with one of the freelance guides that solicit business on beaches.

Costs average about US$35 to US$60 for a one-tank dive or US$50 to US$80 for a two-tank dive. Introductory half-day resort courses normally cost about US$50, and a full PADI certification course will cost US$300 to US$350. Certified divers should bring their PADI or NAUI certificate.

The Bahamas Diving Association (☎ 954-932-0051, 800-866-3483), PO Box 21707, Fort Lauderdale, FL 33335-1707, publishes a free *Bahamas Dive Guide*, *Dive Guide Video*, and *CD-ROM Dive Guide*.

The Travelin' Diver's Chapbook (Elephant Socks Publishing) is a compendium of opinions on and recommendations of dive resorts and live-aboard boats written by people who've partaken. It has a 12-page section on The Bahamas. It's a handy reference for comparing resorts and making your choice based on unbiased critiques. Contact the publisher at PO Box 1658, Sausalito, CA 94966.

Many dive package tours are available from specialist dive-tour operators in North America. Package tours can offer considerable savings. Reputable companies include the following:

Caribbean Adventures, 10400 Griffin Rd, No 109, Cooper City, FL 33328 (☎ 800-934-3483, fax 954-434-4282)
Tropical Adventures Travel (☎ 206-441-3483, 800-348-9778, fax 206-441-5431, dive@divetropical.com)

See Diving sections in the island chapters for individual dive operators and specifics on the best dive sites.

Live-Aboard Dive Boats

Live-aboards are boats specifically designed for divers, with onboard meals and accommodations, and often with E-6 film processing labs. Most boats are operated by Florida-based companies but are based in The Bahamas, where they roam from site to site on year-round, usually week-long itineraries. Package dive-tour operators (see above) offer charters.

Nekton Diving Cruises (☎ 954-463-9324, 800-899-6753, fax 954-463-8938, nekton1@aol.com), 520 SE 32nd St, Fort Lauderdale, FL 33316, offers weeklong diving vacations aboard the deluxe, twin-hulled *Nekton Pilot*, a state-of-the-art catamaran with an elevated dive platform as wide as its 40-foot-wide stern. Several itineraries are offered that include, variously, the huge coral heads of the Gingerbread Grounds between the Biminis and Grand Bahama, the blue holes of Cay Sal Bank just north of Cuba, and the walls of San Salvador and Conception Island. The company offers free 'Learn to Dive' lessons for novice trip members.

Other live-aboard operators include the following:

Blackbeard's Cruises	☎ 800-327-9600
	fax 305-884-4214
Bottom Time Adventures	☎ 954-921-7798,
	800-234-8464
	fax 954-920-5578
The Dream Team	☎ 800-741-5335
Out Island Voyages	☎ 800-241-4591
Sea Fever Diving Cruises	☎ 800-443-3837
	fax 305-531-3127

Shark Dives
Perhaps the most exhilarating experience you can have is staring eye-to-eye with a shark. Divers rarely see a shark in the wild – the critters are wary of humans and usually give divers a wide berth – unless there's food about. But as several commercial dive operators know, *feed* the sharks and you – yes, *you* – can be there as the toothy horde circles and rips.

UNEXSO, on Grand Bahama, offers you the chance to dive with sharks in 50 feet of water at Shark Junction, where a divemaster wearing chain-mail armor will *hand-feed* Caribbean reef sharks before your very eyes! Similarly, Coral Divers

offers a dive in which you watch sharks being hand-fed at Bull Shark Wall or Shark Buoy, both off New Providence.

A slightly different program is offered weekly by Stella Maris Resort on Long Island, at Shark Reef. A bucket of chum is hurled into the water to feed hungry sharks, while divers safely watch the frenzy from the seabed.

A similar dive is offered at Shark Rodeo at Walker's Cay, in the northern Abacos, where as many as 100 blacktip and Caribbean reef sharks gather to fight over a giant chunk of fish remains.

Shark Research At Walker's Cay in the Abacos, Oceanographic Expeditions (in tandem with the National Marine Fisheries Service, the University of Miami, and the Aquarium of the Americas) conducts research into how sharks mate, migrate, and mature. Volunteer divers are needed to help with the work (see the Abacos chapter for contact information and details).

SNORKELING
If you can swim, you can snorkel, which means donning a swim mask (for better viewing), flippers (for easier movement in water), and a breathing tube that lets you keep your face in the water full time. Snorkel equipment can be rented at most beach hotels, resorts, and dive centers for about US$10 a day.

Out Island Snorkeling Adventures
None other than Jean-Michel Cousteau (son of the late Jacques Cousteau, the world-famous diver and explorer) has designed Out Island Snorkeling Adventures with an emphasis on education and a focus on families. (Cousteau speaks passionately about snorkeling's educational value. He isn't peddling vacations so much as championing family togetherness and nurturing a new generation of conservationists, or as he puts it, 'the constituency of the ocean.')

Over 25 resorts participate in the program, which is designed for a minimum four-day stay and costs US$240 for snorkel instruction, three guided excursions, a snorkel guidebook, and your own mask, fins, snorkel, and gear bag. (The program costs US$97 without the personal gear.) Cousteau has also designed 'get your feet wet' adventures for beginners. Contact the company through the Bahamas Out Island Promotions Board (in the USA ☎ 954-359-8099, 800-688-4752, fax 954-359-8098), 1100 Lee Wagener Blvd, No 204, Fort Lauderdale, FL 33315-3564.

Dolphin Encounters

A specialty of The Bahamas is swimming with dolphins. Who can resist their inimitable smiles and graceful sensuality as they cavort around you, while their gleeful high-pitched songs and staccato clicking ring through the water? You might even feel the dolphins' sonar checking you out. No feeding or touching is allowed.

The animals are far more approachable with snorkels than with noisy scuba gear. But dolphins, despite their cheery smiles, are unpredictable wild creatures. Heed the following advice:

- Remain passive if a dolphin approaches.
- Do not swim or chase after dolphins. They may perceive you as a threat and bite you.
- Never touch a dolphin, for the same reasons.
- Do not lie or swim on your back, as this can make dolphins unpredictable.
- If a dolphin becomes aggressive or unpredictable, exit the water slowly.

Several locales are favored by dolphins on a regular basis, including White Sand Ridge northwest of Grand Bahama. UNEXSO, on Grand Bahama, offers a variety of dolphin experiences, including brief encounters for nondivers, two-tank dives with dolphins, and watching dolphin trainers at work.

Or you can take a half-day 'Dolphin Encounter' with Nassau Cruises from Paradise Island (New Providence) to Blue Lagoon Island, where you can swim with dolphins or wade out to meet them in a protected lagoon. (See the New Providence chapter.) On North Bimini, Bill & Nowdla Keefe's Bimini Undersea offers 'Wild Dolphin Excursions.'

Bottom Time Adventures (see the Live-Aboard Dive Boats section) has a seven-day 'Wild Dolphin Experience,' usually with two or three days of dolphin encounters off the Biminis and Grand Bahama. In 1997 the Florida-based company offered three such trips in June and October aboard the 14-cabin Bottom Time II, an 86-foot catamaran. Rates were US$1295 per person, double occupancy.

The protected inshore waters of the Sea of Abaco immediately southeast of Marsh Harbour are also home to a resident population of about 100 bottle-nosed dolphins. Bahamas Naturalist Expeditions offers a 'Wild Dolphin Tour' here (see trip details in the Abacos chapter).

Natural Habitat Adventures (☎ 303-449-3711, 800-543-8917, nathab@worldnet.att .net), 2945 Center Green Ct, Boulder, CO 80301, offers a summertime 'Dolphin Watch' program that allows you to join a weeklong expedition on the open ocean aboard Jennifer Marie, a 70-foot schooner that accommodates eight guests. The center of action is White Sand Ridge, where Atlantic spotted dolphins are common. Six-night packages begin at US$1895, including all meals. You don't need to be an expert swimmer (flotation equipment is provided for added support).

Oceanic Society Expeditions (☎ 415-441-1106, 800-326-7491, fax 415-474-3395), Fort Mason, Bldg E, San Francisco, CA 94123, invites divers to participate in research trips to learn more about dolphin behavior in Bahamian waters, mostly off Grand Bahama but sometimes farther afield. Weeklong trips are only offered in the summer, with accommodations aboard a 70-foot research vessel; the trips cost US$1499, including meals.

BOATING & SAILING

With more than 3000 islands scattered over 100,000 sq miles of ocean, the chain is a boater's dream.

Favored areas are the protected waters of the Sea of Abaco (between Great Abaco and the Abaco Cays) and Exuma Sound. Both are good for beginning sailors, as the waters are shallow and sheltered, and sailors are always within sight of land. The Sea of Abaco has the advantage of Marsh Harbour, capital of boating in The Bahamas, which is a departure point for sailing to the Loyalist Cays. The Exumas have fewer resorts and marinas but do have the compensation of the Exuma Cays Land & Sea Park.

You *must* have up-to-date charts. The meager shallows, sculpted by chaotic currents and treacherous shoals, are reshaped after each storm. An absolutely indispensable guidebook is the *Yachtsman's Guide to The Bahamas and Turks & Caicos*. See the Sea section in the Getting There & Away chapter for more recommendations, and also check that chapter for details on cruising permits, customs regulations, and official ports of entry.

Boat Charters

Both experienced sailors and novices can charter sailboats, yachts, and cruisers by the day or week. Most marinas offer boats with a skipper and crew, as well as 'bareboat' vessels on which you're your own skipper. Obviously you'll need to be a certified sailor to charter bareboat; usually you'll have to demonstrate proficiency before being allowed to sail away. All boats are normally fully stocked with linens and other supplies. You provide your own food, however. You can hire a cook if you want, for about US$100 a day. A security deposit will be required.

Bareboat charters are usually by the week; prices begin at US$1200, depending on size. Crewed charters normally cost about double that. Skippers can be hired for about US$200 a day.

It's advisable to book well in advance. Two leading companies have home bases in the USA plus bases in the islands:

Florida Yacht Charters
    1290 5th St, Miami Beach, FL 33139
    (☎ 305-532-8600, 800-537-0050,
    boat@floridayacht.com)
    PO Box AB-20511, Marsh Harbour,
    Abaco, Bahamas
    (☎ 242-367-4853, fax 242-367-4854)

The Moorings
    19345 US Hwy 19 N, Clearwater, FL 33764
    (☎ 813-535-1446, 800-535-7289,
    fax 813-530-9747)
    Conch Inn Marina, PO Box AB-20469,
    Marsh Harbour, Abaco, Bahamas
    (☎ 242-367-4000, fax 242-367-4004)

There's also Abaco Bahamas Charters (☎/fax 242-366-0151), Hope Town, Elbow Cay, Abaco, Bahamas. See activities sections in island chapters for details on other charter companies.

Alternately you can use a broker, much like a travel agent, who works with a variety of boat companies for a commission. A broker will prearrange a crewed or bareboat charter based on your budgetary and other requirements, usually without charging a fee. Try the following:

Ed Hamilton & Co, 28 Nilsen Ln,
    Whitefield, ME 04353 (☎ 207-549-7855,
    800-621-7855, fax 207-549-7822)
Lynn Jachney Charters, PO Box 302, Marble-
    head, MA 01945 (☎ 800-223-2050,
    fax 617-639-0216)
Nicholson Yacht Charters, 29 Sherman St,
    Cambridge, MA 02138 (☎ 617-661-0555,
    800-662-6066, fax 617-661-0554,
    nikyacht@tiac.com)

Small Sailboats & Motorboats

Most resorts provide small sailboats called Sunfish, either as part of the hotel package rate or for an hourly rental fee.

You can also rent motorboats, from small fry such as Boston Whalers to giant luxury cruisers with price tags to match, from local marinas. See island chapters for details.

FISHING
Bonefishing

The gin-clear waters of the sand banks that shelve the perimeters of most islands are made for battles with the bonefish: pound for pound, one of the world's fighting champions. The archipelago's sandy flats and channels are rated as perhaps the world's greatest location for stalking the wary *Albula vulpes*, a saltwater specter. The large-eyed, fork-tailed critter, a relative

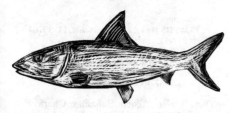

The bonefish, the elusive 'gray ghost'

of the herring, is named for its complex skeletal structure. It makes bony eating.

The fish, which average 5 to 10 lbs apiece, are bottom-feeders and pockmark the sandy bottoms with their snoutlike mouths as they forage for crabs and shrimp, which they root out like vacuums. The fish is also called the 'white fox' or 'gray ghost,' for its flanks are silver mirrors – uncannily efficient camouflage – and when it forages over the green turtle grass, it is nearly invisible. Hushed anglers cast in waters so clear that they can see the fish's shadow before the fish itself appears. It spooks easily, however, and is hard to hook, which adds to the thrill of the chase. The slightest noise will scatter an entire school. All you'll see is a puff of silt where the fish have been.

Finding the fish is half the fun . . . or frustration. The bone is nomadic and fickle about tides, feeding at the flow of one site and the neap of another. It is also highly sensitive to water temperature and will desert waters below 70°F. You can't zip in with an outboard. You need to punt along with a long pole in about 3 feet of water, your osprey-eyed guide standing in the prow. Once the fish is found, you'll have one chance to strike . . . an experience sure to humble even the most experienced caster and a sure bet for piscatorial anecdotes over a consolation cocktail.

Since the fish look down to feed, your bait or fly must be presented below them. You should consult local guides for advice about tackle. Once the fish is hooked, you cannot risk the slightest fault. Despite its small size, it is considered the most sporting of quarries. Once you hook one, it'll

tear away with 150 yards of your line, and you'll think it will never stop. Sometimes it won't. Touch the reel when it flies and the fish may break your line. But once you've won the battle – and to ensure their survival (most bonefish are released) – you must reel them in quickly. Sport-fishermen will tell you that even a blue marlin will hardly cause you such an adrenaline rush.

Light, drab-colored clothing is essential. You'll also need polarized sunglasses and a long-peaked hat, ideally with a dark underside to improve vision. You don't need a permit.

Bonefish can be caught year-round, but April and May – spawning time – are the most productive months: Large numbers shoal, and the flats may become cloudy. Such hot spots are called 'muds,' and here you can expect brisk sport. Look for a tell-tale uniform ripple, or 'nervous water,' on the shallows.

Most of the islands are superb bone-fishing sites. Many lodges are dedicated to bonefishing. The Peace & Plenty Bonefish Lodge on Great Exuma even sponsors an intensive fishing course (see the Exumas chapter).

There are local bonefishing guides on all islands. Rates are about US$150/250 half-/full day for two anglers. If you prefer to go out on your own, bait and tackle are sold near major settlements, where rods are available for rent.

The Bahamas' two prime bonefishing tournaments are the Annual Staniel Cay Bonefish Tournament in the Exumas in August and the Annual Bahamas Bonefish Bonanza at George Town (Great Exuma) in October. The second annual Bahamas National Bonefishing Championships was planned for July 1998.

Sport Fishing

The islands are Main Street for a vast array of game fish that stream along or hang about, just waiting, it seems, for *your* baited hook. As fans of Ernest Hemingway know, the archipelago's ocean waters are a pelagic playpen for schools of blue and white marlin, dolphin fish, wahoo, and tuna. Virtually every island offers world-class fishing. And reef or bottom fishing for snapper, yellowtail, or grouper the size of VW Beetles is sure to bring a succulent taste to your dinner table.

Where & When Any island is good at any time of year. However, individual species have prime seasons and locations:

amberjack – Favors reef areas and wrecks. November to May.
barracuda – Favors reefs but found all over, including shallow water. Year-round.
blackfin tuna – Found all over but especially plentiful near Nassau. May to September.
blue marlin – Gulf Stream waters from the Biminis to Walker's Cay, Chub Cay, the Tongue of the Ocean off Andros, both sides of Exuma Sound, and the Atlantic from Green Turtle Cay (Abacos) to south Eleuthera. Year-round, especially June to August.
bluefin tuna – Gulf Stream waters from the Biminis to Walker's Cay, especially May and June.
dolphin fish – All deep-water regions. Winter and spring.
grouper – All reef areas. Year-round.
kingfish – Throughout the region, especially the Berry Islands and western Abacos. May to July.
sailfish – Berry Islands, Gulf Stream waters from the Biminis to Walker's Cay, and Exuma Sound. Summer and fall.
tarpon – Andros and the Biminis. Year-round.
wahoo – San Salvador, waters south of Cat Island, Exuma Sound, south Eleuthera, and Providence Channel. November to April, especially January and February.
white marlin – Northwest Providence Channel and the Atlantic from Walker's Cay to Exuma Sound. Winter and spring.

Regulations Fishing is strictly regulated. Visiting boaters require a permit to engage in sport fishing (US$20 per trip or US$150 yearly for up to six reels). Vessels with more than six reels are charged US$10,000 annually! No foreign vessels may fish commercially.

You can obtain a permit at your port of entry (see the Getting There & Away chapter for a list of official ports of entry) or in advance (along with a list of current fishing regulations) from the Director of Fisheries, Dept of Fisheries (☎ 242-393-1777), PO Box N-3028, Nassau, Bahamas, who can also supply current fishing rules and regulations.

Scuba equipment and air compressors may not be used to catch fish. The only permitted spearfishing apparatus is a Hawaiian sling, use of which must be approved on your permit. Spearfishing (even with a sling) is prohibited within 1 mile of the coasts of New Providence and Freeport and within 200 yards of the coasts of all Family Islands.

There are bag limits for most fish species. For example, for dolphin fish, kingfish, and wahoo, only six fish (any combination) per person on a vessel are permitted. All other migratory fish *must* be released to the sea without undue injury. Only 20 bonefish per person are permitted. You may catch only 10 conchs, all of which must have a well-formed lip; lobster catch (in season only) is limited to six per person at any one time, and no egg-bearing 'crawfish' may be taken.

The capture, possession, or molestation of coral, marine turtles, and marine mammals is forbidden, as is long-line and net fishing. Other restrictions exist.

Charters Dozens of commercial operators offer sport-fishing charters. Rates for charter boats are US$200 to US$300 for a half-day to US$350 or more for a full day, with bait and tackle provided. You normally provide your own food and drinks. Most charters require a 50% deposit (if you cancel, you should do so at least 24 hours before departure to avoid losing your deposit). Some operators keep half the catch. Discuss terms with the skipper prior to setting out. Never book your trip or negotiate arrangements with bystanders on the dock or beach.

Tours Several companies offer fishing tours to The Bahamas. Try the following organizations:

Angling Travel & Tours, 1445 SW 84th Ave, Portland, OR 97225 (☎ 503-297-2468, 800-288-0886, fax 503-297-3048)

Fishing International, 4775 Sonoma Hwy, Santa Rosa, CA 95409 (☎ 707-539-3366, 800-950-4242, fax 707-539-1320)

Frontiers International, PO Box 959, Wexford, PA 15090 (☎ 412-935-1577, 800-245-1950)

Pan-Angling Travel Service, 180 N Michigan Ave, Suite 303, Chicago, IL 60601 (☎ 312-263-0328, 800-533-4353, fax 312-263-5246)

Tournaments The Bahamas hosts dozens of major fishing tournaments every year (most are April to June), from big-game contests for serious contenders, with stiff entry fees, big prize money, and high-stakes wagers, to the laid-back, family-oriented tournaments.

Key contests include the following:

February
Bahamas Wahoo Tournament – Biminis

March
Bacardi Rum Billfish Tournament – Biminis
Hemingway Billfish Tournament – Biminis

April
Bimini Break (Blue Marlin) Rendezvous – Biminis
Boat Harbour All Fish Tournament – Marsh Harbour (Abacos)
Chub Cay Championship (Bahamas Billfish Championships) – Berry Islands
North Abaco Championship (Bahamas Billfish Championships) – Marsh Harbour

May
Green Turtle Club Fishing Tournament – Green Turtle Cay (Abacos)
Treasure Cay Fishing Tournament (Bahamas Billfish Championships) – Treasure Cay (Abacos)
Walker's Cay Billfish Tournament – Walker's Cay (Abacos)

June
Boat Harbour Championship (Bahamas Billfish Championships) – Marsh Harbour
Cat Cay Billfish Tournament – North Cat Cay

July
Chub Cay Blue Marlin Tournament – Berry Islands
Harbour Island Championship – Eleuthera

August
Big Game Club Family Tournament – Biminis
Bimini Native Fishing Tournament – Biminis

September
Big Game/Small BOAT Tournament – Biminis

November
All Wahoo Fishing Tournament – Biminis

December
Adam Clayton Powell, Jr, Memorial Fishing Tournament – Biminis

KAYAKING

The archipelago has barely been tapped as a venue for canoeing and kayaking, although miles and miles of creeks and flats provide wonderful entrances to the redolent world of the mangroves and wetlands.

Sea kayaks are stable, safe, and perfect for novices. They are light and easily maneuverable . . . and silent, allowing you to glide into areas rich in birdlife.

Many hotels and resorts rent kayaks or provide free use for guests. And kayaking is now being introduced as an organized activity by several tour operators. In the Abacos, Bahamas Naturalist Expeditions offers kayak trips; on Grand Bahama, guided sea kayak tours are offered by Kayak Nature Tours. See the island chapters for contact information.

Ibis Tours (in the USA ☎ 800-525-9411, fax 914-738-1605, ibistours@aol.com) offers weeklong kayak trips from Nassau through the Exuma Cays using stable, 20-foot-long, two-person sea kayaks fitted with sails, paddles, and a foot-operated rudder; trips cost US$1349. *Travel & Leisure* described the experience as 'cruising along on autopilot . . . high-tech drifting riding low in user-friendly waters.' No experience is required. Each day involves about two hours of kayaking in the morning and afternoon. You camp out at night on lonesome beaches, with comfy mattresses and tents (should you choose). Meals are prepared by 'Bardy' Jones, the affable guide, raconteur, and quasigourmet chef.

Ecosummer Expeditions (in Canada ☎ 604-669-7741, fax 604-669-3244; in the USA ☎ 800-465-8884) has similar trips in the Exumas. A one-week trip from Staniel Cay to Norman's Cay costs

US$1345; a two-week trip from Great Exuma to Allan's Cays, which covers 100 miles, costs US$1895. Its mailing address in Canada is 1516 Duranleau St, Vancouver, BC V6H 3S4; in the USA write PO Box 8014-240, Blaine, WA 98230. Ibis and Ecosummer also offer tours in the Exuma Cays Land & Sea Park.

Nature Quest (☎ 714-499-9561, 800-369-3033, fax 714-499-0812) also offers kayak trips in the Exumas. Its mailing address is 934 Acapulco St, Laguna Beach, CA 92651. Most Exumas trips are offered February to May. Bring aquasocks and snorkel fins!

SURFING & WINDSURFING

If you are seeking the ultimate wave, look elsewhere. There are a few spots on The Bahamas' east coasts, however, where surfers can find decent Atlantic waves, notably Surfer's Beach on Eleuthera and, most importantly, the Garbanzo Reef off Elbow Cay (Abacos). Winter months are best.

Virtually the entire east side of the chain is fringed by an offshore barrier reef onto which the waves break, making surfing dangerous far out. The trade winds, however, continue to blow inside the barrier reef, so the placid stretches inside the reef are perfect for windsurfing, in the absence of other coral.

You'll find equipment for rent at leading resorts or from concessionaires on the main beaches of New Providence and Grand Bahama. Many hotels provide free sailboard use for guests. The Clarion Atlantik Beach Resort on Grand Bahama even has a windsurf tuition package. The Romora Bay Club on Harbour Island (Eleuthera) is another good bet for windsurfing.

In January the Bahamas Windsurfing Championship is held in Freeport.

OTHER WATER SPORTS

Most resorts offer water sports, including sailing, windsurfing, and use of Hobie Cats and kayaks. Often these are included in the hotel price, as at the Club Med resorts and Sandals Royal Bahamian on New Providence. At other locales you might have to pay extra, usually by the hour. Motorized water sports, such as water-skiing, jet-skiing, and parasailing, are almost exclusively the domain of private concessionaires (the hotels don't want the liability issues) who rent equipment on the beaches near resorts.

Cable Beach and Paradise Island (New Providence) and Xanadu, Lucaya, and Taino beaches (Grand Bahama) have plenty of operators. The Family Islands have far fewer. Here water-sports facilities are mostly limited to whatever individual resorts and hotels may offer.

See the island chapters' activities and Places to Stay listings for details on local water-sports options.

BIRD WATCHING

The Bahamas is heaven to bird watchers (see Flora & Fauna in the Facts about The Bahamas chapter). More than two dozen reserves protect over 230 bird species. Virtually any island is good, though the southern islands are best, especially Great Inagua.

In the field all you need is a good pair of binoculars and a guide to the birds of the Caribbean (see recommendations in Books in the Facts for the Visitor chapter). The Ministry of Tourism and the Bahamas National Trust (BNT) cosponsor four-day introductory bird courses on a regular basis, based at the BNT's headquarters at The Retreat on New Providence, and the BNT's reserve and museum, the Rand Memorial Nature Centre in Freeport. See the New Providence and Grand Bahama chapters for contact information; the Bahamas Tourist Office can also provide details.

On New Providence, Island Vacations offers a weeklong bird-watching excursion, 'Birding in Paradise.' In the Abacos, Bahamas Naturalist Expeditions has bird-watching trips.

HIKING

Hiking as an organized activity is embryonic in the islands. Mostly you're on your own. Trails are limited, although several wildlife reserves have tracks. You'll also find rough coastal trails on some islands, and several islands have tracks originally cut by lumber companies (others, associated with cotton plantations, were cut two centuries ago).

Many trails are overgrown. You may find hiking even a short way demanding: The oppressive heat and humidity can turn what seems like an easy stroll into a trudge.

Travel light, and always carry plenty of water. Don't attempt to hike farther than your physical health will allow. Take plenty of insect repellent, especially in summer, plus a small first-aid kit when hiking in out-of-the-way places.

Rarely will you be far from a settlement. However, it's easy to become complacent. The limestone terrain is too treacherous to permit you to wander off the track, as thick vegetation hides sinkholes and crevasses. It is easy to injure yourself, and phones and first aid may not be close at hand. Be especially wary of clifftops, which are often undercut and can give way easily. Also, the backcountry of Great Abaco and Andros is popular with hunters seeking wild boar . . . *beware* boars and hunters alike! You may want to consider hiring a hunter as a guide.

Particularly good is Lucayan National Park (Grand Bahama), with short trails leading to caverns and winding through mangroves and woodlands. In the Abacos, Bahamas Naturalist Expeditions offers guided hiking in Abaco National Park on several wildlife-focused trips, as does Sand Dollar Tours.

Cat Island has some of the best hiking. The Fernandez Bay Village resort is a good starting point; the owners can provide maps and even a guide, if required, for hikes along old logging and plantation trails that lead to abandoned ruins, Turtle Cove, and even the site of Spain's first official settlement in the New World.

On Great Inagua, trails lead into Inagua National Park, a semiarid, rugged landscape with fabulous bird watching.

CAVING

The Bahamas has spelunkers salivating. The islands are honeycombed with dozens of limestone caverns, many only partially explored and mapped.

In some, Lucayan Indian petroglyphs add to the allure. Many caverns are also roosts for harmless bats, but you may have to contend with the stench of their manure, which locals collect for fertilizer.

Use extreme caution if you're exploring without a guide. Take a powerful flashlight and spare bulb and batteries.

See Blue Holes, under Diving earlier in this chapter, for information on some of The Bahamas' most fascinating caves.

GOLF

One of The Bahamas' strengths is golf, predominantly on New Providence and Grand Bahama. The nation boasts eight courses, open to visitors for a daily green fee or to guests for free.

For details on The Bahamas' best golfing and for prices at individual courses, see the New Providence and Grand Bahama chapters, as well as the Treasure Cay section in the Abacos chapter and the Cotton Bay section in the Eleuthera chapter.

Listen to your caddy, who undoubtedly knows the course well enough to play in the dark.

The Bahamas hosts several leading international golf tournaments.

TENNIS

There's no shortage of tennis courts. Most upscale resorts have at least one tennis court. Nonguests are usually permitted for a fee.

The largest concentration by far is on New Providence, with over 80 courts. On Paradise Island, Club Med has numerous courts and clinics with professional instruction. You'll also find plenty of tennis courts on Grand Bahama, on Harbour Island, and in Marsh Harbour. Many courts belonging to older properties, however, are run down, especially in the Family Islands.

You should take to the courts in early morning or in the evening, when it's cooler.

HORSEBACK RIDING

Although there are plenty of wild horses and donkeys on the southern islands, horseback riding hasn't taken off as a sport or pastime. The most impressive stable is the New Columbus Horse-Riding Ranch near Cockburn Town (San Salvador), where beach and trail rides are offered and individual and group lessons are available. There are also stables on New Providence and Grand Bahama.

BICYCLING

Relatively few people explore the islands by bicycle, and few locals use bicycles.

Many hotels, resorts, and concessions do rent bicycles (US$8 to US$20 a day). However, they are always heavy single-gear pachyderms called 'beach cruisers,' definitely *not* built for touring. The single gear is fine on the flat, but you can't build up much speed, and the slightest hill or patch of sand will frequently stump you. Often the wheels are bent or the bicycle's seat coil-springs have given way; even if they haven't, you're sure to have a sore behind after a few miles.

A far better option is bringing your own mountain bike. Most international airlines will let you ship it at no extra charge. Bahamasair and charter airlines, however, disdain bicycles. You can ship your bicycle between islands by mail boat. (See the Getting Around chapter for information about mail-boat travel.)

There are virtually no bicycle repair shops. Hence you'll need to carry an adequate repair kit, plus spare parts such as inner tubes.

The three Club Med properties offer guided cycling excursions, as do a handful of other resorts. Only a handful of tour operators offer guided cycling trips. In Nassau, Pedal & Paddle Ecoadventures has an all-day bike ride. And Bottom Time Adventures offers eight-day cycling trips on Eleuthera. (See Bicycling, under Harbour Island, in the Eleuthera chapter for more details.)

Grand Bahama hosts the Tour de Freeport 100-mile road race in spring.

VOLUNTEER RESEARCH

Several scientific organizations offer trips in which participants engage in field research on the natural environment of The Bahamas.

Earthwatch (in the USA ☎ 617-926-8200, 800-776-0188, fax 617-926-8532, info@earthwatch.org; in the UK ☎ 0865-311600; in Australia 03-9600-9100), 680 Mt Auburn St, Watertown, MA 02272, needs participants for its studies of marine environments on San Salvador, the blue holes of Andros, marine mammals, and lemon sharks. Projects, which change year to year, have included caving and archeological digs.

Turks and Caicos

DIVING

Everything that is true of diving in The Bahamas (including prices) holds for the Turks and Caicos, which boast some of the most spectacular wall diving in the world. In fact, you can be among the first to dive these pristine sites. The deep waters of the Turks and Caicos provide endless stretches of walls, breathtaking drop-offs, and a myriad of marine life and wrecks (such as the HMS *Endymion*, a British warship which went down in 1790 and still proudly displays her cannon) that will excite even the most jaded diver. By some estimates, as many as 1000 wrecks may still await discovery amid the 230 miles of unplundered reefs.

The consistently best diving is in midsummer, from June to August. Winter is a time of exquisitely clear water, but it's also a time when storms can sweep in with 15-foot waves. There are no currents, and visibility averages 80 to 150 feet. Water temperatures range from 82°F to 84°F in summer and 76°F to 78°F in winter.

Because most divers who come here are veterans, Turks and Caicos divemasters are willing to take experienced divers on adventurous jaunts. There is plenty of tamer fare for the novice. The pros get the sharks; the novices get the groupers.

Providenciales (or 'Provo,' as it is known) is most developed and quite spectacular, but Grand Turk is perhaps the best island for diving. The west (leeward) side of Grand Turk has a remarkable vertical wall running the island's full length, as little as 400 yards from shore. The wall begins in just 35 feet of water, making it accessible to novice divers, and plunges 7000 feet in the blink of an eye. Salt Cay and South Caicos are also emerging as major dive sites.

North Atlantic humpback whales cruise the Turks Island Passage off Grand Turk in the winter, as do manta rays in summer. Sometimes in winter you can hear the melodic lowing of whales as they cruise to and from their breeding grounds in the Mouchoir Banks southeast of Grand Turk (the *ping . . . ping* that you might hear is said to be the deep-water sonar of Russian submarines. Remember *The Hunt for Red October?*) Schools of dolphins abound, and placid whale sharks, the largest of all fish, are occasionally seen. Even sperm whales are a rare but possible sighting.

See the activities sections in the Turks Islands and Caicos Islands chapters for detailed information on key dive and snorkel sites and local operators. Most of these operators offer PADI and/or NAUI certification courses. Many operators also rent scuba equipment.

There is a recompression chamber at the MBS Medical Clinic (☎ 649-94-64242) on Provo.

Operators

Key dive operators include the following:

Art Pickering's Provo Turtle Divers is the largest operator, with a full range of courses and dives. (☎ 649-94-64232; in the USA 954-467-3460, 800-833-1341, fax 954-467-7544)

Caicos Adventures, on Provo, specializes in West Caicos dives. (☎ 649-94-13346, divucrzy@caribsurf.com; in the USA ☎ 800-513-5822)

Flamingo Divers also has West Caicos and other dives. (☎ /fax 649-94-64193)

J&B Tours runs private dive charters aboard a 24-foot dive boat. (☎ 649-94-65047, fax 649-94-65288)

Oasis Divers specializes in packages on Grand Turk. (☎ /fax 649-94-61122; in the USA ☎ 770-645-8163, 800-892-3995, fax 770-640-7461)

Salt Cay Divers, on Salt Cay, is close to the *Endymion* wreck. (☎ /fax 649-94-66927, scdivers@caribsurf.com)

Sea Eye Diving, on Grand Turk, dives the wall. (☎ /fax 649-94-61407, ci@caribsurf.com; in the USA ☎ 305-670-6149, 800-725-2822)

Silver Deep, on Provo, caters to small groups using a 21-foot dive boat. (☎ 649-94-65612, fax 649-94-64527)

Turtle Inn Divers, on Provo, is a full-service dive center. (☎ 649-94-15389; in the USA 800-359-3483)

Live-Aboard Dive Boats

There are at least three live-aboards:

Island Diver has night- and weeklong trips. (☎ 649-94-15810)

Sea Dancer is a deluxe 110-foot dive boat sleeping 18 divers and offering five dives daily in weeklong packages from Caicos Marina on Provo; contact Ocean Outback (☎ /fax 649-94-65276; in the USA ☎ 305-669-9391, fax 305-669-9475)

Turks & Caicos Aggressor is a 100-foot dive boat with an E-6 photo lab and hot tub. It sleeps 16 divers; contact Aggressor Fleet (in the USA ☎ 504-385-2628, 800-348-2628, fax 504-384-0817)

SNORKELING

Most hotels can provide snorkel gear. All the dive operators also rent gear and offer snorkel trips. Sea Eye Diving offers snorkel trips to Gibb's Cay, an uninhabited island east of Grand Turk. Turtle Inn Divers also offers snorkel excursions.

BOATING & SAILING

The Turks and Caicos, like The Bahamas, offer excellent boating and sailing opportunities. See the Getting There & Away section in the Turks and Caicos introductory chapter for details on boating rules and regulations in the islands.

FISHING
Bonefishing
The Bahamas gets the fanfare for bone-fishing, but the Turks and Caicos give it a run for its money. There are 2000 sq miles of flats between Grand Turk and Provo! No wonder a *Sports Illustrated* writer called the area 'the ultimate bonefishing flat.' You'll find guides on all the islands.

Sport Fishing
The phrase 'summertime blues' takes on a whole new meaning in the Turks and Caicos, which lie on a major route for migrating Atlantic blue marlin, passing by in fantastic numbers from June to August. There are over 35 species of other game fish, too, including black marlin, wahoo, and tuna. Most species can be caught within half a mile of Grand Turk, where the wall drops just a few hundred yards from the beach.

Provo boasts several marinas where you can charter fishing boats (see the Caicos Islands chapter). Prices are similar to those in The Bahamas.

A permit is required. No spearfishing (including Hawaiian slings) or scuba equipment is allowed, nor may visiting vessels take conch or lobster. Information on regulations can be obtained from the Dept of Environment and Coastal Resources, c/o Ministry of Natural Resources (☎ 649-94-62143, fax 649-94-62751).

The island nation hosts several annual competitions, including the Turks & Caicos International Billfish Tournament, held in July on Provo, followed by an Invitational Billfish Tournament. Together they comprise the Turks & Caicos Billfish Challenge.

The annual Grand Turk Game Fishing Tournament is held at the end of July or in early August. The Turks & Caicos International Billfish Tournament comes to Grand Turk in August.

SURFING & WINDSURFING
The islands are virgin territory for surfers but superbly suited to windsurfing. On Provo, Grace Bay is a fabulous location for windsurfing, with the consistent trade winds behind you. Most resorts and several concessionaires along the beach rent sailboards.

On Grand Turk you'll often see wind-surfers whizzing along the waters of North Creek.

BIRD WATCHING
The best sites are the wetlands along the south shores of North and Middle Caicos. The main attraction is Flamingo Pond on North Caicos, one of several lakes on the island where flamingos and other water-fowl gather in large numbers. Another good spot is the Vine Point & Ocean Hole Nature Reserve, an offshore frigate-bird breeding colony near Middle Caicos.

Flamingos also inhabit South Caicos and can be seen at the edge of Cockburn Harbour.

Grand Turk boasts the wetlands of South Creek National Park, good for spotting migrating shorebirds and waders. For rare seabirds, hire a boat and guide to take you to Grand Turk Cays Land & Sea Park, a series of tiny cays east of Grand Turk that are important nesting sites for gulls, sooty terns, frigate birds, and boobies.

On Provo head to Northwest Point Marine National Park, where saline ponds and wetlands attract breeding and migrant waterfowl.

HIKING
The Turks and Caicos are no more attuned to hikers' needs than their northern neighbors. A notable exception is Middle Caicos, where the Middle Caicos Reserve & Trail System has 10 miles of trails along the north coast: an entrance into the shoreline ecosystems, freshwater lakes, and pine forests. The trail system is to be extended along the entire north coast. On Provo you can follow dirt tracks along the east and west shores to Northwest Point Marine National Park.

OTHER ACTIVITIES
The Turks and Caicos have plenty of caves, notably Conch Bar Caves National Park on Middle Caicos, a 15-mile-long system full

of stalactites and stalagmites. A few tour operators offer daylong cave excursions here (see the Caicos Islands chapter), but spelunkers are otherwise on their own.

The Turks and Caicos' sole golf course is at the state-of-the-art Provo Golf Club.

Most resorts feature tennis courts, notably Club Med's facility on Provo.

Horseback riding isn't well developed, and in 1997 there were only two facilities, on Provo and Salt Cay.

See island chapters for details.

Getting There & Away

AIR

The Bahamas is well served by flights from North America and Europe, and abundant direct and connecting airline service puts it within easy reach of anywhere in the world. Its proximity to Florida means regular, relatively inexpensive flights from Miami, Fort Lauderdale, and Orlando, as well as other East Coast gateways. Nassau, the country's capital, is less than three hours' flying time from the northeastern USA and only about 30 minutes by jet from Miami.

For specific details on air service to and from The Bahamas, see the Getting There & Away sections of each island chapter. General information about travel between islands is provided in the Getting Around chapter.

Airports & Airlines

The Bahamas has seven international airports, including the two major hubs: Nassau International Airport (New Providence) and Freeport International Airport (Grand Bahama). Some flights also land at Paradise Island International Airport (New Providence), Marsh Harbour (Abacos), North Eleuthera and Governor's Harbour (Eleuthera), and George Town (Exumas).

'Commuter' charters and private planes will deliver passengers to other airfields throughout the archipelago.

The following major airlines have offices in Nassau and/or Freeport:

Air Jamaica
   Nassau   ☎ 800-523-5585
American Airlines/
  American Eagle
   Nassau   ☎ 242-377-5124
   Freeport   ☎ 242-352-5415
Bahamasair
   Nassau   ☎ 242-377-5505
   Freeport   ☎ 242-352-8343
British Airways
   Nassau   ☎ 242-377-8886

Continental Airlines/
  Continental Connection
   Nassau   ☎ 242-356-7314/9
Delta Air Lines/
  Comair
   Nassau   ☎ 242-377-7774
Gulfstream
  International
   Nassau   ☎ 242-356-7314
   Freeport   ☎ 242-352-6447
LB Ltd
   Freeport   ☎ 242-352-3389
Pan-Am Air Bridge
   Nassau   ☎ 242-363-1687

Buying Tickets

Plane tickets will probably be the most expensive items in your budget, and buying them can be intimidating. There are likely to be many airlines and travel agents hoping to separate you from your money. Spend a few hours researching the market, and start early. Some of the cheapest tickets must be bought months in advance, and some popular flights sell out early.

Flight schedules and fares are subject to change, especially in the transition from winter to summer seasons. Most airlines charge different fares according to the season (highest fares are normally mid-December through mid-April, the peak season). Fares are reduced up to 30% or more in low season (usually mid-April to mid-December) and shoulder seasons (between peak and low seasons). Traveling on a weekday (Monday through Thursday) may also reduce the cost. Booking early is the key to the best deals. Use the fares quoted in this book only as guides. They're approximate and based on the rates advertised by travel agents at press time. A quoted airfare doesn't necessarily constitute a recommendation for the carrier.

Once you have your plane ticket, write its number down, together with the flight number and other details, and keep the information separate from the ticket. If the ticket is lost or stolen, this will help you get a replacement.

It's sensible to buy travel insurance as early as possible (see Visas & Documents in the Facts for the Visitor chapter). If you buy it the week before you fly, you may find, for example, that you're not covered for delays to your flight caused by strikes or other industrial action.

Departure Taxes

Each individual aged six years or older must pay a US$15 departure tax upon leaving The Bahamas by air (US$18 from Freeport).

The USA

You have numerous options. Most major US carriers, including American Airlines/ American Eagle, Continental Airlines/ Continental Connection, and US Airways Express, fly to The Bahamas. This allows you to use frequent-flyer and other discount promotions. The most popular routings are via Miami and New York, but The Bahamas is also served by direct flights from a dozen or so other cities.

Some airlines offer special rates at select hotels in conjunction with the purchase of a ticket. For example, guests at Sandals (a leading resort chain) who are members of American Airlines' AAdvantage frequent-flyer program are awarded 1000 miles for a stay of three or more nights.

The most frequent service to Nassau is offered by American Airlines/American Eagle (☎ 800-433-7300 for information and reservations in the USA, Canada, Mexico, or the Caribbean). All American Airlines' Bahamas-bound flights are routed via Miami; American Eagle flies turbo-props from Miami almost hourly to Nassau. American also flies from Miami to Freeport, Governor's Harbour, Rock Sound (Eleuthera), Treasure Cay (Abacos), and George Town.

Bahamasair (☎ 800-222-4262, fax 305-593-6246), the national airline, flies jets several times daily from Miami to Nassau in winter. It also offers direct flights from Miami and several other Florida cities to destinations throughout the islands. It has a frequent-flyer discount and a 'Great Value Airpass' (see Air Passes in the Getting Around chapter for details). For details on Bahamasair service to the islands, see the Getting There & Away sections of the island chapters.

The lowest fares – albeit for bare-bones in-flight service – are offered by Carnival Air/Pan Am (☎ 800-437-2110, 800-824-7386), which serves Nassau from Newark

---

Travelers with Special Needs

If you have special needs of any sort – you've broken a leg, you're vegetarian, traveling in a wheelchair, taking the baby, terrified of flying – you should let the airline know as soon as possible so that it can make arrangements accordingly. You should remind the airline when you reconfirm your booking (at least 72 hours before departure) and again when you check in at the airport.

Airports and airlines can be surprisingly helpful, but they do need advance warning. Most international airports will provide escorts from check-in desk to plane when needed, and there should be ramps, lifts, and reachable phones. Aircraft toilets, on the other hand, are likely to present a problem; travelers should discuss this with the airline at an early stage.

Deaf travelers can ask that airport and in-flight announcements be written down for them.

Children younger than two travel for 10% of the standard fare (free on some airlines), as long as they don't occupy a seat. They don't get a luggage allowance either. 'Skycots' should be provided by the airline if they're requested in advance; these will hold a child weighing up to about 22 lbs. Children between two and 12 can usually occupy a seat for about one-half to two-thirds of the full fare and do get a luggage allowance. Strollers (pushchairs) can often be taken as hand luggage. ■

Top: Want to meet a dolphin on its own turf? Head to Grand Bahama.
Bottom: Don't worry, they don't bite . . . much: Diver and reef sharks, Grand Bahama

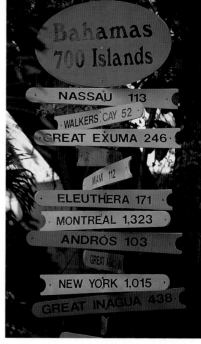

Top: Nassau's Paradise Island Bridge
Bottom Left: Counting the ripples at Gold Rock Beach, Grand Bahama
Bottom Right: No, Montreal and New York are not in The Bahamas.

International Airport and New York's John F Kennedy International Airport year-round. Equally bargain-priced is LB Ltd (formerly Laker Airways, ☎ 800-545-1300), which flies new 727 jets to Nassau and Freeport from several East Coast and Midwest cities.

Continental Airlines' subsidiary Continental Connection (☎ 800-231-0856) has daily flights from Miami and Fort Lauderdale to Nassau.

Delta Air Lines (☎ 800-241-4141, 800-221-1212) has daily jet service to Nassau from Atlanta, GA; Fort Lauderdale; and New York City. Its commuter airline Comair (☎ 800-354-9822) flies turboprops to Nassau and Freeport from Orlando and Fort Lauderdale.

Gulfstream International (☎ 305-871-1200, 800-992-8532) has scheduled service to Nassau, Freeport, and Marsh Harbour and Treasure Cay from 12 Florida cities, plus Atlanta and Mobile, AL. It flies from Fort Lauderdale and Miami to North Eleuthera. Prices are competitive, and service is excellent. It has a code-sharing agreement with United Airlines, whose Mileage Club members can accrue frequent-flyer miles. Gulfstream also offers 'Sun Pac' commuter booklets, offering one free ticket with a pack of five roundtrip tickets (three free tickets with a pack of 10). Tickets are transferable and can be used by anyone you designate. Call ☎ 800-688-7225.

Island Express (☎ 954-359-0380, fax 954-359-7944) offers scheduled daily service to seven Family Islands from Fort Lauderdale, flying in nine-seater Cessna aircraft.

Pan-Am Air Bridge (formerly Chalk's, ☎ 800-424-2557, fax 305-359-5240) offers scheduled daily seaplane flights to the Biminis and Paradise Island from Miami's Watson Island (☎ 305-371-8628) and Fort Lauderdale's Jet Center (☎ 954-359-0329). Pan-Am also serves Walker's Cay (Abacos) from Fort Lauderdale.

Paradise Island Airlines (☎ 954-359-8043, 800-786-7202) serves Paradise Island with daily flights from Fort Lauderdale, Miami, and West Palm Beach.

US Airways Express (☎ 800-622-1015) flies to Nassau from Baltimore; Charlotte, NC; and Philadelphia. It also flies from Fort Lauderdale to two Eleuthera airports, from Orlando and West Palm Beach to Marsh Harbour, and from Fort Lauderdale and Orlando to Treasure Cay.

Air Jamaica (☎ 800-523-5585) offers direct service several times weekly from Chicago to Nassau. A free champagne breakfast is offered in every class. Air Jamaica offers its '7th Heaven Fly Free Program': If you buy six roundtrip tickets in any two-year period, you'll get the seventh free (if three tickets were 1st class, then the free ticket is also 1st class). If you purchase four roundtrip tickets within two years, you'll receive a 50% discount on the fifth.

The *New York Times*, the *Los Angeles Times*, and most other major city newspapers all have weekly travel sections in which you'll find any number of ads quoting airfares. The magazine *Travel Unlimited*, PO Box 1058, Allston, MA 02134, publishes details of the cheapest airfares and courier possibilities for destinations all over the world from the USA.

Council Travel (☎ 800-226-8624) and STA Travel (☎ 800-777-0112) have offices in major cities nationwide.

Charter Flights There are two types of charter flights to The Bahamas. The first, utilizing large-body jets, are chartered by large tour operators. These flights generally offer the lowest fares for confirmed reservations (sometimes one-third or more less than regular airlines' prices), which can be booked through most travel agencies. You can sometimes book one-way tickets with charter airlines for less than half of their roundtrip fares. These flights are usually direct, without the hub stop common on ordinary airline flights. Few charters are listed in airline computer reservations systems, as they're operated by wholesale tour operators with whom you or your travel agent will have to deal directly.

There are drawbacks. Although you can buy the ticket without an advance-purchase requirement, you do have to fix your departure and return dates well in advance; a substantial fee may apply for any changes or cancellations (you should consider cancellation insurance in the event of illness, etc). Seating may be more cramped, planes are usually full, and flight times are often at inconvenient hours. And though US charter operators are bonded with the US government, if the tour operator or airline defaults, you may have problems getting your money back. Also, charter flights are often less organized than those of major scheduled carriers, and processing at airline counters oftentimes is more confused and time-consuming.

Dozens of charter operators serve The Bahamas from the USA. Check the Sunday travel sections of major city newspapers. Your travel agent should also be able to provide a listing. A good resource is *The Worldwide Guide to Cheap Airfares* by Michael McColl. See the island chapters for information on specific charter services and fares.

Key charter operators serving The Bahamas include Apple Vacations (on the East Coast ☎ 800-727-3400; on the West Coast 800-365-2775), the largest operator, flying to Nassau from Baltimore/Washington, DC; Pittsburgh; and Philadelphia. It also flies to Freeport. You must book through a travel agent. Apple will not quote prices directly over the phone.

GoGo Worldwide Vacations (☎ 800-821-3731) flies to Nassau from Newark, using Carnival Air. Sunquest Holidays (☎ 805-578-9860, fax 800-497-3171) has direct flights to Nassau from Los Angeles. TNT Vacations (☎ 617-262-9200) serves Nassau and Freeport from Boston.

Typically, three-, five-, and seven-night packages are offered in conjunction with flights. For example, Island Hoppers (☎ 800-467-7595) offers air-hotel packages to Nassau, Grand Bahama, and the major Family Islands from as little as US$163 in summer, including roundtrip airfare from Miami and two nights of accommodations. You can fly from other cities for add-on fares.

The second charter group, often called 'commuter' airlines, uses small planes (usually carrying up to 10 passengers; larger craft are sometimes used). Individual seats are sold, but small groups may charter the planes. Fares are generally much lower than on larger carriers but are nonrefundable (nor can you get a credit if you miss a flight). Rarely are scheduled departures offered. Flights are also more subject to cancellation in the event that not enough people buy seats.

Island Express (see the USA section) has on-demand charter service from Fort Lauderdale to seven Family Islands.

The following airlines also offer charter service from major Florida airports to The Bahamas:

Abaco Air	☎ 242-367-2266
Air Charter One	☎ 561-750-6200, 800-538-3548
Air Sunshine	☎ 954-434-8900
Cherokee Air	☎ 242-367-2089
Dolphin Atlantic Airlines	☎ 800-353-8010
Island Air Charters	☎ 800-444-9904
Major's Air Services	☎ 242-352-5778
Nassau/Paradise Island Express	☎ 201-467-4670, 800-722-4262
Trans-Caribbean Air	☎ 954-434-5271, 888-239-2929 fax 954-434-2171
Tropical Diversions Air	☎ 954-921-9084, 800-343-7256 fax 954-921-1044
Walker's International	☎ 954-359-1400, 800-432-2092 fax 954-359-1414

Several Family Island hotels offer their own commuter charter services from Florida. (See Hotel Charters in the Getting Around chapter for details.)

Courier Flights Unfortunately, there are very few courier flights to the Caribbean. However, the leading booking agency for courier companies, NOW Voyager (☎ 212-431-1616), 74 Varick St, No 307, New York, NY 10013, does have courier flights to the Caribbean region. You must pay a one-time US$50 registration fee.

Two good resources are *The Courier Air Travel Handbook* by Mark Field and *The Worldwide Guide to Cheap Airfares* by Michael McColl.

Discount Tickets Many discount-ticket agencies sell reduced-rate tickets to The Bahamas and the Caribbean. One of the leading ticket brokers is Pan Express Travel (☎ 212-719-9292), 55 W 39th St, New York, NY 10018. Student travel agencies such as College Travel International (☎ 217-359-9885, wolvie@prairienet.org) offer airfares at up to 50% savings.

Alternately, try Express Discount Travel (☎ 619-521-0549, 800-266-2639), 5945 Mission Gorge Rd, No 10, San Diego, CA 92120.

Standby & Last Minute If you can fly on very short notice (usually within seven days of travel), consider buying a ticket from a 'last-minute' ticket broker. These companies buy surplus seats from charter airlines (and sometimes from scheduled carriers) at hugely discounted prices. The airlines would rather fill the seats than fly empty – you reap the reward. Discounts can be as great as 40% for a confirmed seat.

One of the leading distress-sale brokers is Last Minute Travel Club (☎ 617-267-9800, 800-527-8646), 100 Sylvan Rd, Suite 600, Woburn, MA 01801, which specializes in air/hotel packages to the Caribbean. Other last-minute ticket agencies require you to become a member of their club; annual fees cost about US$40, for which you receive regular updates. Companies you should consider include Moment's Notice (☎ 212-486-0500), 7301 New Utrecht, Brooklyn, NY 11204; and Worldwide Discount Travel Club (☎ 305-534-2082), 1674 Meridian Ave, Miami Beach, FL 33139.

Canada

The Bahamas is a popular destination for snow birds flocking south in wintertime, although summer is peak season for travel from Canada. Most choose charter flights.

However, Air Canada (☎ 800-776-3000) serves Nassau from Toronto and Montreal.

Leading city newspapers such as the *Toronto Globe & Mail* and the *Vancouver Sun* carry travel agents' ads. The magazine *Great Expeditions*, PO Box 8000-411, Abbotsford, BC V2S 6H1, is also useful.

Charter Flights Air Transat (☎ 905-678-1011) offers charter flights to Nassau from Toronto. Regent Holidays (☎ 905-673-3343), 6205 Airport Rd, Bldg A, No 200, Mississauga, ON L4V 1E1, offers charter flights and air/hotel packages using Air Transat. Canada 3000 (☎ 416-674-2661) also flies from Toronto to Nassau.

Conquest Tours (☎ 416-665-9255, 800-268-7063, fax 416-665-6811), 85 Brisbane Rd, Downsview, ON M3J 2K3, flies from Toronto, Winnipeg, and Halifax to Nassau; from Toronto and Ottawa to Freeport; and from Halifax to Freeport.

Canadian Universities Travel Service (Travel CUTS, ☎ 416-979-2406) has offices in all major cities.

Australia & New Zealand

There is no direct service to The Bahamas; travelers from Australasia must fly via the USA.

STA Travel (in Sydney ☎ 02-9212-1255; in Auckland 9-309-9995) and Flight Centres International are major dealers in cheap airfares. Check the travel agents' ads in the Yellow Pages, and then phone around.

The UK

The Bahamas is well served by direct flights from the UK. Several airlines also feed Miami, Orlando, and Fort Lauderdale from the UK, including American Airlines, Delta Air Lines, and Virgin Atlantic. American Airlines and Delta have connecting service to The Bahamas.

British Airways (☎ 0181-897-4000) offers direct service to Nassau and Freeport from Heathrow, plus daily flights to Miami. It also operates a charter service to Nassau from Gatwick. It's advisable to check seasonal variations in schedules.

Bahamasair (☎ 0171-437-8766, fax 0171-734-6460), 79 Dean St, London W1V 6HY, offers a 'Great Value Airpass' for passengers transferring via Florida from Europe (see Air Passes in the Getting Around chapter), although it has no service from the UK to The Bahamas.

Most British travel agents are registered with the Association of British Travel Agents (ABTA). If you have paid an ABTA-registered agent for a flight and the agent then goes out of business, ABTA will guarantee a refund or alternative. Unregistered bucket shops are riskier but also sometimes cheaper.

Caribbean Gold (☎ 0181-741-8491) is a leading air-only travel specialist.

Trailfinders (☎ 0171-937-5400), 194 Kensington High St, London W8 7RG, produces a lavishly illustrated brochure that includes airfare details. STA Travel also has branches in the UK. Look in the listings magazine *Time Out*, plus the Sunday papers and *Exchange & Mart* for ads. Also look out for the free magazines widely available in London – start by checking outside the main railway stations.

The Globetrotters Club, BCM Roving, London WC1N 3XX, publishes a newsletter called *Globe* that covers obscure destinations and can help in finding traveling companions.

Charter Flights The Bahamas is a major charter destination from the UK. Many tour operators have contracted seats with airlines.

Thomson Holidays (☎ 0171-387-9321, 0990-502555, fax 0171-387-8451), Greater London House, Hampstead Rd, London NW1 7SD, flies to Nassau from Gatwick and Manchester using Britannia Airways. Other leading charter operators include the following:

Airtours, Wavell House, Holcombe Rd, Helmshore, Rossendale, Lancashire BB4 4NB (☎ 01706-260000)

British Airways Holidays (☎ 01293-723210)

Caribbean Connection, Concorde House, Forest St, Chester CH1 1QR (☎ 01244-341131)

Caribtours, 161 Fulham Rd, London SW3 6SN (☎ 0171-581-3517, fax 0171-225-2491)

Cosmos (☎ 0161-480-5799)

Harlequin Worldwide, 2 North Rd, South Ockenden, Essex RM15 6QJ (☎ 01708-852780, fax 01708-854952)

Jetlife Holidays (☎ 01322-614801)

Kuoni (☎ 01306-742222)

Simply Caribbean (☎ 01423-526887)

Thomas Cook (☎ 01733-332255)

Unijet Travel (☎ 0990-114114)

Virgin Holidays (☎ 01293-617181)

Continental Europe

There are few direct flights to The Bahamas from Europe. You should plan on flying via Florida.

Although it does not fly from Europe, Bahamasair has offices in Frankfurt (☎ 69-25-32-44), Milan (☎ 2-89-01-03-68), and Paris (☎ 01.43.65.36.04). Its 'Great Value Airpass' can be purchased in Europe.

LTU International Airways (☎ 0211-9-41-8888, fax 0211-9-41-8881) in Germany has flights from Dusseldorf and Munich to Nassau. Contact LTU at the following locales:

Parsevalstrasse 7a, D-40468 Dusseldorf (☎ 0211-9-41-0952)

Eisenhelmerstrasse 61, D-80687 Munich (☎ 89-57-09-29-30)

Modul A, Munich Airport (☎ 89-97-59-19-16)

From Italy, Club Fortuna operates biweekly charter flights to Eleuthera year-round. In The Bahamas contact Club Venta Eleuthera (☎ 242-334-4055).

In Denmark, Cruise & Travel (☎ 33-11-95-00, fax 33-11-95-01), Bredgade 35C, Copenhagen DK1260 K, specializes in travel to the Caribbean.

In France contact Alternative Travel (☎ 01.42.89.42.46, fax 01.42.89.80.73), 8 Ave de Messine, Paris 75008, or Austral, 29 rue Dupuits Mauger, Rennes 35000.

In Italy try the following tour companies:

Hotelplan Italia, Corso Italia 1, Milan 20129 (☎ 2-72-13-61, fax 2-87-75-58)

Viaggiare, via San Nicola da Telentino 18,
     Rome 00187
     (☎ 6-47-46-751, fax 6-48-20-022)
Viaggidea SRL Caribbean, via Biondelli 1,
     Milan 20141
     (☎ 2-89-52-91, fax 2-84-67-71)

Asia

There are no direct flights; travelers fly via London or Florida. Hong Kong is the discount plane-ticket capital of the region. Its bucket shops are at least as reliable as those of other cities. Ask the advice of other travelers before buying a ticket.

STA Travel has branches in Hong Kong, Tokyo, Singapore, Bangkok, and Kuala Lumpur.

In Japan you might try one of the following agencies specializing in Caribbean travel:

Alize Corporation, Aoyama Kyodo Bldg,
     No 803, 3-6-18 Kita Aoyama Minato Ku,
     Tokyo 107
     (☎ 3-3407-4272, fax 3-3407-8400)
All Nippon Airways World Tours,
     Kasumigaseki Bldg, 3-2-5 Kasumigaseki
     Chiyoda-ku, Tokyo 100
     (☎ 3-3581-7231, fax 3-3580-0361)
Island International, 4-11-14-204 Jingumae,
     Shibuya-ku, Tokyo 150
     (☎ 3-3401-4096, fax 3-3401-1629)
L&A Tours, No 608, 3-1-19 Nishi Azabu,
     Minato-ku, Tokyo 106
     (☎ 3-5474-7723, fax 3-3746-2478)

The Caribbean

Air Jamaica flies from Montego Bay to Nassau, with connecting flights via Mo' Bay from several eastern Caribbean islands. Cubana (☎ 53-7-78-4961, 53-7-33-4949) flies from Havana to Nassau.

Gulfstream International flies charters to Havana from Nassau.

Private Plane

About 45,000 private pilots fly to The Bahamas annually. An aircraft is an ideal way to get there and around, giving you the flexibility and freedom to flit between islands in a jiff. Distances between islands are short, and the chain boasts dozens of airstrips, ranging from the major international airport at Nassau to short patches of crushed coral. Several of the strips were once US military facilities, with 4500-foot-plus asphalt runways. Many of the strips, however, are private, so check before putting down. Most have tie-downs. Some do not have fuel. Landing fees and per-day parking fees each average US$6.

Your first destination in The Bahamas must be an official port of entry (there's at least one for each island; see island chapters), where you must clear customs and immigration.

Your first step in planning your trip is to contact the Bahamas Pilot Briefing Center via the Bahamas Tourist Office (☎ 800-327-7678) for the latest information.

Step two should be to purchase Betty and Tom Jones' superb *The Pilot's Guide to The Bahamas and Caribbean* (Pilot Publishing), 500 pages of listings on 60-plus airstrips, with details on which have jet fuel and Avgas. It also tells you everything you need to know about permits, entry and departure procedures, customs and immigration regulations, and essentials on ground transportation, etc. Contact Pilot Publishing (☎ 800-521-2120), PO Box 88, Pauma Valley, CA 92061, which also sells a recently updated sectional, covering the entire chain, called *The Bahamas Air Navigation Chart*, as well as the *Bahamas & Caribbean Pilots Aviation Guide*.

Also try *Flying The Bahamas: The Weekend Pilot's Guide* by Frank K Smith (TAB Books). The Aircraft Owners & Pilots Association (AOPA) publishes the *AOPA Flight Planning Guide: Bahamas* and the *AOPA Bahamas Flying Kit*, available for US$8 from the AOPA flight-operations center (☎ 800-872-2672), 421 Aviation Way, Frederick, MD 21701. The latter contains much of the same information as the Joneses' book, plus such handy sections as information for scuba divers on diving-to-flying times.

The Bahamas Aeronautical Authorities (☎ 242-377-7281), Dept of Civil Aviation, PO Box N-975, Nassau, Bahamas, oversees all flights and airports. It has an aeronautical information service (☎ 242-377-7116). Also, make sure to contact US Customs (☎ 305-526-2878) in advance to ensure compliance with regulations, as improper procedures can result in whopping fines.

For weather and flight information, contact Weather & Flight Info, Miami FSS/IPSS (☎ 305-233-2600).

Should things go wrong, you can contact the Bahamas Air-Sea Rescue Association (BASRA, ☎ 242-322-3877, VHF channel 16) or the US Coast Guard's 24-hour Search & Rescue operations center (☎ 305-536-5611, 2182 SSB). Also see the Emergency section in the Facts for the Visitor chapter.

SEA
Cruise Ship

If all you want is a short taste of The Bahamas, consider visiting by cruise ship. The Bahamas is by far the most popular port of call in the Caribbean region for cruise ships.

Almost two dozen cruise companies include Nassau or Freeport on their itineraries. A few also call at their own private Bahamian cays, where passengers alight for beach- and water-based fun. The rest of the Bahamian islands are usually bypassed.

Cruise ships are floating resorts, with all meals, activities, and entertainment included in one price. Most feature a swimming pool, spa, health club, beauty shop, duty-free stores, theater, card room, library, bars and lounges, dining rooms, and medical facilities. Larger, ritzier ships will usually have a casino, orchestras, and lavish Las Vegas-style revues. Always there's a full complement of prearranged activities to keep you amused.

Most days are spent at a port of call; most travel between ports takes place at night. Ashore the cruise companies offer various tour options. Be aware that shore excursions cost extra and can add considerably to the price of a cruise. Or you can sightsee on your own. You're not going to have enough time to get a real feel for the islands.

Cruise experiences vary vastly according to the cruise company and ship you choose. *Caveat emptor!* One person's sugar may be another one's poison. Fortunately, there's something for everyone. It's not simply a matter of cost or length (cruises usually last from one to 14 days). While some cruise lines are relaxed, others are regimented, with neatly choreographed dining and entertainment. Princess Cruises, for example, requires formalwear for dinner (remember scenes from *The Love Boat?*), but Carnival – which bills its vessels as 'Fun Ships' – is carefree. Carnival's ships are all kitschy, razzle-dazzle, Las Vegas-style glitz and appeal to a younger, budget-conscious crowd, perhaps more concerned with partying than with gourmet cuisine (its meals are mediocre).

The Cruise Line International Association (CLIA, ☎ 212-921-0066, fax 212-921-0549), 500 Fifth Ave, No 1407, New York, NY 10110, is a handy resource.

Costs Prices vary widely according to how deluxe a ship is, length of cruise, and which cabin you choose. (See cost specifics in the listings below.) Most ships have a range of accommodations. The cheapest cabins are usually in the center of the vessel – midships – and often lack windows, but are less prone to rolling and pitching. You'll pay more for an ocean view and more still for an upper-deck cabin. Suites are often lavish.

You'll save money by booking early. Don't forget to budget for tips. Cruise lines promote tipping to its extreme.

To The Bahamas Most cruises that call in The Bahamas depart from Florida, less frequently from New York. A few depart Los Angeles and travel via the Panama Canal.

Holland America Line's *Maasdam* sails from Lisbon to The Bahamas on 10-day Caribbean cruises.

Crystal Cruises' *Crystal Symphony* includes Nassau on its weeklong itineraries from San Juan (Puerto Rico). Costa Cruises' 1360-passenger *Costa Romantica* also sails from San Juan and calls on Nassau.

In Nassau cruise ships anchor at the Prince George Wharf, at the foot of Rawson Square in downtown Nassau. There is no terminal building. A tourist information booth is opposite the wharf, where the surreys (horse-drawn cabs) also park. There's also an ATM.

Freeport's modern cruise terminal is about 6 miles from downtown Freeport. Taxis are available. The terminal features immigration and customs facilities, duty-free stores, snack bars, and other visitor facilities.

Immigration and customs formalities are handled by the cruise companies upon arrival in port.

Major cruise lines include the following:

Cape Canaveral Cruise Line has two-day budget cruises to Grand Bahama from Port Canaveral aboard the 590-passenger, circa-1955 *Dolphin IV*. Cruises are no-frills; US$100 to US$250 per person daily. 751 3rd Ave, New Smyrna, FL 32169 (☎ 800-910-7447)

Carnival Cruise Lines has three-, four-, and seven-day cruises to The Bahamas and Caribbean aboard its Fun Ships. The 2044-passenger *Fantasea* sails from Port Canaveral each Thursday on a three-day cruise to Nassau, and each Sunday on a four-day cruise to Nassau and Freeport. The *Ecstasy* sails from Miami each Friday on a three-day cruise to Nassau. The ships appeal to young adults who like neon and noise. Per-day rates are US$200 to US$400 per person. 3655 NW 87th Ave, Miami, FL 33178 (☎ 305-599-2600)

Celebrity Cruises includes Nassau on weeklong Caribbean cruises from Fort Lauderdale aboard the deluxe 1750-passenger *Century*. Per-day rates are US$280 to US$900. 5201 Blue Lagoon Dr, Miami, FL 33126 (☎ 305-262-6677, 800-437-3111)

Costa Cruises operates two stylish vessels infamous for their 'Roman Toga' parties. The 1928-passenger *Costa Victoria* includes Nassau on cruises from Miami; US$200 to US$1000 per day. World Trade Center Bldg, 80 SW 8th St, Miami, FL 33130-3097 (☎ 305-358-7325)

Crystal Cruises' 'super elegant' *Crystal Symphony* includes Nassau on weeklong cruises from New York. The crowd is well heeled and mature. The cost? If you need to ask . . . . 2121 Ave of the Stars, Suite 200, Los Angeles, CA 90067 (☎ 310-785-9300)

Discovery Cruises' *Discovery 1* sails to Grand Bahama from Fort Lauderdale every Monday, Wednesday, Friday, and Sunday; *Discovery Sun* sails from Miami on Monday, Tuesday, Thursday, Friday, and Saturday. Packages combine the cruise with one to four nights ashore. Rates are bargain priced, with a four-night stay at the Bahamas Princess Resort for as little as US$269. Air-land-cruise packages are also offered. 1850 Eller Dr, Fort Lauderdale, FL 33316 (☎ 800-937-4477)

Disney Cruise Line plans to introduce the family-oriented *Disney Magic* in 1998, with three- and four-day cruises from Port Canaveral. The mainstays are seven-day packages with stays at Disney World, from US$1409 per person, including airfare from most gateways. 210 Celebration Pl, Suite 400, Celebration, FL 34747-4600 (☎ 407-566-3500, 800-939-2784, fax 407-566-7353)

Dolphin Cruise Lines offers budget-priced three- and four-night cruises to The Bahamas and Key West from Miami aboard the graceful, 780-passenger *Ocean Breeze* on Friday and Monday. The 840-passenger *Sea Breeze* includes Nassau on weeklong Caribbean cruises from Miami, departing Saturday; US$100 to US$250 per day. 901 S America Way, Miami, FL 33132 (☎ 305-358-5122)

Holland America Line's upscale 1500-passenger *Westerdam* and 1266-passenger *Statendam* depart Fort Lauderdale and call on Nassau during seven-day Caribbean itineraries. The *Veendam* and *Ryndam* also call. It's renowned for quality and value for money. The *Westerdam* has facilities aimed at families. Expect to pay US$250 to US$475 daily. 300 Elliott Ave W, Seattle, WA 98119 (☎ 206-281-3535; for brochures 800-626-9900; for reservations 800-426-0327)

Majesty Cruise Line's elegant 1056-passenger *Royal Majesty* sails from Miami on three-night itineraries to Nassau and the company's own 'Royal Isle,' off the Berry Islands. The entertainment and cuisine are said to be lackluster; US$150 to US$450 per day. 901 S America Way, Miami, FL 33132 (☎ 800-327-7030)

Norwegian Cruise Line (NCL) has three- to seven-day itineraries from Miami. The 974-passenger *Leeward* visits Nassau and NCL's own 'Pleasure Isle' (Great Stirrup Cay) on three-day sailings each Friday; US$250 to US$550 per day. NCL's luxury flagship, the 1870-passenger *Norway*, visits Pleasure Isle on a year-round weekly Caribbean itinerary; US$250 to US$775 per day. The

1246-passenger *Dreamward* also visits Pleasure Isle, departing Fort Lauderdale. 'Casually elegant' defines the line. 7665 Corporate Center Dr, Miami, FL 33126 (☎ 305-436-4000)

Premier Cruises has cruises from Port Canaveral to Nassau and Port Lucaya aboard the aging, red-hulled, 1800-passenger *Oceanic*, the sole remaining 'Big Red Boat.' It departs each Friday for a three-night cruise, and Monday for a four-night cruise. You can combine a cruise with a visit to Disney World and Universal Studio in Orlando. The line has a full children's program. Prices begin at US$739 for the cruise only, including airfare from US gateways. 400 Challenger Rd, Cape Canaveral, FL 32920 (☎ 407-783-5061, 800-327-7113)

Princess Cruises' 1200-passenger *Sky Princess,* 1500-passenger *Star Princess,* and 1590-passenger *Crown Princess* visit Nassau on weeklong and 10-day Caribbean cruises from Fort Lauderdale. The clientele spans the ages. These are the 'Love Boats' of TV fame, and a good value at US$190 to US$475 a day. 10100 Santa Monica Blvd, Los Angeles, CA 90067 (☎ 310-553-1770)

Royal Caribbean Cruise Lines offers three-day cruises from Port Canaveral each Friday aboard the *Nordic Empress*, with stops at Nassau and at Coco Cay, the company's private Bahamian island. A four-day cruise departs every Monday and includes a visit to Freeport. The showy 2524-passenger *Sovereign of the Seas* visits Nassau and Freeport on three- and four-day cruises from Miami. The elegant and massive 2744-passenger *Majesty of the Seas* visits Coco Cay on weeklong Caribbean cruises from Miami. Expect to pay US$225 to US$675 daily. 1050 Caribbean Way, Miami, FL 33132 (☎ 305-539-6000)

From The Bahamas

Cruising *from* The Bahamas is generally more offbeat, offering a chance to explore some of the Bahamian islands and other Caribbean locales. Options include the following:

American Canadian Caribbean Line's 92-passenger *Mayan Prince* sails on a 12-day trip from Nassau to Providenciales (Turks and Caicos), stopping at five Exuma cays, George Town, Long Island, Acklins Island, the Plana Cays, and Mayaguana. One trip is offered in December, with a reverse itinerary in April aboard *Niagara Prince*, a sibling ship. A 40-foot bow ramp permits you to descend directly onto beaches. The trips are for nature lovers, not those seeking lavish cuisine and pampering, and cost US$1475 to US$2415, depending on cabin. PO Box 368, Warren, RI 02885 (☎ 401-247-0955, 800-556-7450, fax 401-247-2350)

Windjammer Barefoot Cruises offers a down-home experience on a 13-day cruise from Freeport to Trinidad aboard the *Amazing Grace*, a 'workhouse' vessel supplying the company's clipper ships in the Caribbean (none of which sail to The Bahamas). It has elegant cabins and heaps of charm. It stops at Nassau, Little San Salvador, Conception Island, Little Inagua, and the Plana Cays, plus Grand Turk and Providenciales. Trips cost US$1075 to US$2900, depending on season and cabin. PO Box 190-120, Miami Beach, FL 33119-0120 (☎ 305-672-6453, 800-327-2601, fax 305-674-1219, windbe@windjammer.com)

World Explorer Cruises' 739-passenger *Universe Explorer* retraces the route of Spanish galleons around the Caribbean rim, calling at places steeped in the allure of the old Spanish Main. The itinerary slates 25 hours of informal lectures and educational videos, and there's a plush library with 15,000 volumes. Each winter the vessel departs Nassau for eight- and 14-day voyages. Per-person rates are US$825 to US$1770 for the eight-day voyage; US$1445 to US$3095 for the 14-day program. The fiercely loyal clientele includes many passengers bonded by an experience called 'Semester at Sea,' run by the University of Pittsburgh, which annually charters the vessel as a kind of floating university for two 100-day round-the-world voyages. 555 Montgomery St, Suite 1400, San Francisco, CA 94111 (☎ 415-393-1565)

Private Yacht

The sheltered waters of the 750-mile-long archipelago attract thousands of yachters each year. Winds and currents favor the passage south. If you plan to travel in summer, keep fully abreast of weather reports, as mid- to late summer is hurricane season. Ironically, sailing conditions are at their best in summer.

Upon arrival in The Bahamas, you *must* clear customs and immigration. Specified marinas on each island are designated ports of entry (you may not enter at any other place):

Abacos – Green Turtle Cay, Marsh Harbour, Spanish Cay, Walker's Cay
Andros – Congo Town, Fresh Creek, Mangrove Cay, Morgan's Bluff
Berry Islands – Chub Cay, Great Harbour Cay
Biminis – Alice Town, North Cat Cay
Cat Island – Smith Bay
Eleuthera – Governor's Harbour, North Eleuthera, Rock Sound, Spanish Wells
Exumas – George Town
Grand Bahama – Freeport Harbour, Lucaya Marina, Jack Tar Village Marina (West End), Port Lucaya Marina, Xanadu Marina
Great Inagua – Matthew Town
Long Island – Stella Maris
New Providence – Nassau (any yacht basin)
San Salvador – Cockburn Town

See details on each port's marinas in the island chapters.

You'll require the regular documentation for foreign travel (see the Visas & Documents section in the Facts for the Visitor chapter), including a cruising permit (costing US$10), which is issued at your first port of entry in The Bahamas and is good for 12 months. Don't forget to ask for a fishing permit for your boat if you're planning on baiting a hook. Permits can be renewed annually. Your crew and guests will all need either a passport or birth certificate (a driver's license is not proof of citizenship). Depending on your time of arrival, there may be customs and immigration charges.

You'll need to clear customs again upon arrival at *each* island. It's a hassle, but The Bahamas' drug problem is such that you should be sympathetic to this policy. Anticipate the possibility of being boarded and searched by the US or Bahamian coast guard.

A full description of official requirements is given in the *Yachtsman's Guide to The Bahamas and Turks & Caicos* (see below).

Guidebooks No sailor should set out without the excellent *Yachtsman's Guide*

to The Bahamas and Turks & Caicos, edited by Meredith Helleberg Fields. It provides detailed descriptions of just about every possible anchorage in the archipelago, with handy, accurate sketch maps and charts, and lists full information on marinas throughout the islands as well as approaches and other invaluable information. It's available at bookstores and marinas in The Bahamas or by mail for US$31.95 from Tropic Isle Publishers (☎ 305-893-4277), PO Box 610938, N Miami, FL 33261.

In a similar vein, refer to Julius Wilensky's *Cruising Guide to the Abacos and the Northern Bahamas*. It and other regional guides can be ordered from White Sound Press (☎ 217-423-0511, fax 217-423-0522), 1615 W Harrison Ave, Decatur, IL 62526.

The Bahamas Out Islands Promotion Board (see Tourist Offices in the Facts for the Visitor chapter) also publishes a booklet of marina information, including rates and facilities.

Maps & Charts You'll need accurate maps and charts for any voyage through the region's reef-infested waters. US Defense Mapping Agency charts, British Admiralty charts, and Imray yachting charts are all accurate. You can order them in advance from Bluewater Books & Charts (☎ 954-763-6533, 800-942-2583), 1481 SE 17th St, Fort Lauderdale, FL 33316.

The splendid and indispensable *Yachtsman's Guide to The Bahamas and Turks & Caicos* (see above) has small sketch charts, but they are *not* intended for use in navigation. Larger-scale (11-by-17-inch) versions of the charts can be ordered for US$3.50 each; they're highly detailed, accurate, and durable. A complete set of 72 charts covering The Bahamas as well as the Turks and Caicos costs US$195. Some charts are detailed sections of individual islands. Contact Tropic Isle Publishers (see above).

International Sailing Supply (☎ 800-423-9026), 320 Cross St, Punta Gorda, FL 33950, publishes a series of large-scale waterproof sectional charts of The Bahamas. They mostly show physical features and are of limited use as travel maps.

US government charts of the region can be ordered through most marine stores, as can detailed National Oceanic & Atmospheric Administration (NOAA) charts. Contact NOAA (☎ 301-436-6990), Riverdale, MD 20737-1199, or Better Boating Association, PO Box 407, Needham, MA 02192.

Crewing Crewing aboard a yacht destined for The Bahamas from North America or Europe is a popular way of getting to the islands. You'll need impressive offshore sailing experience to be hired for an Atlantic sailing.

You can ask around in ports or yacht marinas for any irregular passenger services by yacht or cargo boat between the Caribbean islands and The Bahamas. Also, look at the notice boards at marinas. Often you'll find notes advertising for crew. You can also leave your own. Yachting magazines are also good resources.

In the UK contact Alan Toone of Compass Yacht Services (☎ 0181-467-2450), Holly Cottage, Heathley End, Chislehurst, Kent BR7 6AB, a charter company that can help you find a crewing position.

Yacht charter companies are listed in the Outdoor Activities chapter.

Bahamas Boating Flings In summer the Bahamas Ministry of Tourism and the South Florida Marine Industries Association cosponsor 'Bahamas Boating Flings.' These are organized flotillas that cross to the Biminis from Fort Lauderdale in groups of no more than 30 vessels; participation costs US$65.

For information, contact the Bahamas Tourist Office (☎ 800-327-7678, 800-224-3681).

Freighter
Gone are the good ol' days when travelers could buy passage aboard the banana freighters that plied between the Caribbean and North America and Europe.

The one guaranteed option is Windjammer Barefoot Cruises' *Amazing Grace* (see Cruise Ship in this chapter).

Ford's Freighter Travel Guide (☎ 818-701-7414), 19448 Longelius St, Northridge, CA 91324, lists freight ships that take passengers. You can also find listings in *TravelTips* (☎ 800-872-8584), PO Box 580188, Flushing, NY 11358.

In the UK contact Strand Cruise & Travel Centre (☎ 0171-836-6363, fax 0171-497-0078), Charing Cross Shopping Concourse, The Strand, London WC2N 4HZ.

ORGANIZED TOURS
There are dozens of organized tours to The Bahamas. The vast majority are sun-and-sand 'package tours,' usually using charter flights (see Charter Flights in this chapter) and including roundtrip airfare, airport transfers, hotel accommodations, and breakfasts and certain other meals, all for a guaranteed price. Sightseeing tours, entertainment, and other extras may also be included, usually representing a great bargain!

Most per-person prices quoted by tour operators are based on double occupancy (two people sharing a room). An additional charge ('single supplement') applies to anyone wishing to room alone.

Package Tours
The USA Several tour companies in the USA specialize in The Bahamas.

Bahamas Travel Network (☎ 954-467-1133, 800-513-5535, fax 954-467-7544, lori@estreet.net), 1043 SE 17th St, Fort Lauderdale, FL 33316, specializes in Family Islands. Prices for its 1997 packages began at US$307, including roundtrip airfare.

Take A Break Student Travel (☎ 617-292-0200, fax 617-292-9237) offers 'College Spring Break' and 'High School Graduation Trip' programs to The Bahamas. Weeklong packages with roundtrip airfare and accommodations begin at US$299, quadruple occupancy.

And don't forget the airlines, many of which have their own package tours.

Gulfstream International, for example, offers two- and six-night vacation packages at Sandals Royal Bahamian on New Providence, including airfare from eight Florida cities. Two-night package prices start at US$499 for Florida residents, US$666 for nonresidents.

The tour operators listed below are also active in the Bahamas market. Contact them for information about other package-tour options:

American Airlines Fly AAway	☎ 800-321-2121
American Express Vacations	☎ 800-241-1700
Apple Vacations	☎ 610-359-6500
East Coast	☎ 800-727-3400
West Coast	☎ 800-365-2775
Bahamas Travel Network	☎ 954-467-1133, 800-513-5535
Caribbean Concepts	☎ 516-496-9800, 800-423-4433
Caribbean Travel Planners	☎ 212-564-9502, 800-323-2020
Changes in L'Attitude	☎ 813-573-3536, 800-282-8272
Delta Dream Vacations	☎ 800-872-7786
Fiesta Holidays	☎ 305-895-1213, 800-288-1435
Friendly Holidays	☎ 516-358-1320
West Coast	☎ 800-221-9748
Funjet Vacations	☎ 414-351-3553, 800-558-3050
Globetrotters	☎ 617-621-9911, 800-999-9696
GoGo Worldwide Vacations	☎ 800-821-3731
Grand Bahama Vacations	☎ 800-545-1300
Gulfstream Air Holidays	☎ 305-870-9444, 800-870-4786
Inter-Island Tours	☎ 212-686-4868, 800-245-3434
Island Flight Vacations	☎ 310-410-0909
West Coast	☎ 800-426-4570
Island Resort Tours	☎ 212-476-9400, 800-251-1755
Places to Go	☎ 954-714-9994, 800-775-2237
Sun Splash Tours	☎ 212-366-4922, 800-426-7710
Travel Impressions	☎ 516-845-8000, 800-284-0044
US Airways Vacations	☎ 800-455-0123
Vacation Express	☎ 404-321-7742, 800-486-9777
Vacation Network	☎ 305-673-8822, 800-423-4095

Canada The following tour operators specialize in The Bahamas and Caribbean:

Air Canada Vacations, 1440 Ste Catherine St W, Montreal, QC H3G 1R8 (☎ 514-876-0704, fax 514-876-3699)

Air Transat Holidays, 300 Leo Pariseau, No 400, Montreal, QC H2W 2P6 (☎ 514-987-1616, fax 514-987-8029)

Albatours (☎ 416-746-2890, 800-665-2522, fax 416-746-0397)

Canadian Holidays (☎ 416-620-8050, 800-661-8881, fax 416-620-0018)

Conquest Tours, 85 Brisbane Rd, Downsview, ON M3J 2K3 (☎ 416-665-9255, 800-268-7063, fax 416-665-6811)

Regent Holidays, 6205 Airport Rd, Bldg A, No 200, Mississauga, ON L4V 1E1 (☎ 905-673-3343)

Signature Vacation, 160 Bloor St E, No 400, Toronto, ON M4W 1B9 (☎ 416-967-1510, fax 416-967-0334)

Sunquest Vacations, 130 Merton St, Toronto, ON M4S 1A4 (☎ 416-485-1700, fax 416-485-9479)

Australia & New Zealand Contours Travel (☎ 03-9329-5211, fax 03-9329-6314), 466 Victoria St, N Melbourne, Victoria 3051, is Australia's largest tour operator/wholesaler to the Caribbean and The Bahamas.

In New Zealand, Innovative Travel (☎ 3-365-3910, fax 3-365-5755), PO Box 21, 247 Edgeware, Christchurch, is about the only tour operator with an emerging Caribbean/Bahamian specialty.

The UK The Caribbean Centre (☎ 0181-940-3399, fax 0181-940-7424), 3 The Green, Richmond, Surrey TW9 1PL, offers package tours to The Bahamas. Uncle Sam Travel Agency (☎ 0121-523-3141, fax 0121-554-7315), 295 Sotto Rd, Birmingham B21 95A, also offers tours to The Bahamas.

Also see Charter Flights in the Air section in this chapter.

Asia Island International (☎ 3-3401-4096, fax 3-3401-1629), 4-11-14-204 Jingumae, Shibuya-ku, Tokyo 150, specializes in package tours and special-interest travel to the Caribbean and The Bahamas.

Specialty Tours
Very few companies offer specialty tours to The Bahamas.

An excellent resource is *Specialty Travel Index* (☎ 415-459-4900, 800-442-4922), 305 San Anselmo Ave, Suite 313, San Anselmo, CA 94960, a biannual publication that lists companies with special-interest tours worldwide. Tours are cross-referenced in both a geographical and subject index. The *Island Vacation Guide* (☎ 203-655-8091, 800-962-2080, fax 203-655-6689), PO Box 2367, Darien, CT 06820, also lists tours to The Bahamas and Turks and Caicos.

A variety of activity-oriented tours are offered by US operators, as well as nature tours and opportunities for volunteers to participate in research on the flora, fauna, and natural environment of The Bahamas. For details on these trips, see the Outdoor Activities chapter and the island chapters.

Clothing-Optional Tours Only one Bahamian resort – Cutlass Bay – welcomes nudists (see the Cat Island chapter). There are at least three US companies catering to travelers seeking an all-over tan at Cutlass or other sites in the Caribbean region:

Bare Necessities, 1502-A W Ave, Austin, TX 78701 (☎ 512-499-0405, 800-743-0405)

Go Classy (☎ 888-825-2779, goclassy@sprynet.com)

Travel Au Naturel, 35246 US 19 N, Suite 112, Paul Harbor, FL 34684 (☎ 800-728-0185)

WARNING
The information in this chapter is particularly vulnerable to change: Prices for international travel are volatile, schedules change, special deals come and go, and rules and visa requirements are amended. Airlines and governments seem to take a perverse pleasure in making price structures and regulations as complicated as possible. Check directly with the airline or a travel agent to make sure you understand how a fare (and any ticket you may buy) works. The travel industry is highly competitive; there are many lurks and perks.

You should get opinions, quotes, and advice from as many airlines and travel agents as possible before you part with your hard-earned cash. The details given in this chapter are pointers and are not a substitute for your own careful, up-to-date research.

Getting Around

Perusing a map, you may be tempted to think that island-hopping down the chain is easy. It ain't, unless you have your own boat or plane. Interisland air is based on a hub-and-spoke system, with Nassau as the center. Getting between islands without constantly backtracking is a bit of a feat. Even the mail boats are, for the most part, Nassau-centric.

Details – including fare and schedule information – can be found in the island chapters.

AIR

Interisland flights are the only fast and convenient way to get around within The Bahamas.

The scene is dominated by Bahamasair (in Nassau ☎ 242-377-5505; in Freeport 242-352-8343; in the USA 800-222-4262, fax 305-593-6246), the government-owned airline that has preciously guarded its quasimonopoly on scheduled interisland flights. Onboard service is good, the standard of piloting is exemplary, there is just one class, and only rarely is seating assigned. But the airline is beset with mismanagement. In mid-1997 the government initiated the first stage of a business plan that may eventually lead to the airline's long-called-for privatization.

Bahamasair serves New Providence, Grand Bahama, and all the main Family Islands with scheduled flights, using 36-passenger prop planes and small jets. Schedules change frequently and at short notice (and no attempt is made to notify passengers with advance reservations). *You should always double-check your flight times on the day prior to departure!*

The airline operates on a hub-and-spoke system, with Nassau as its hub. Thus, if you want to fly between adjacent islands, such as Cat Island and Long Island, you will have to first return to Nassau. If you do a lot of island-hopping, you'll begin to feel

like a yo-yo. Worse, you may need to overnight in Nassau between flights.

At press time Bahamasair offered flights from Nassau to the following destinations:

Destination	Frequency
Abacos (Marsh Harbour)	Daily
Abacos (Treasure Cay)	Daily
Acklins Island (Spring Point)	Tuesday, Saturday
Andros (Andros Town)	Daily
Andros (Congo Town)	Daily
Andros (San Andros)	Daily
Cat Island (Arthur's Town)	Sunday, Tuesday, Thursday
Cat Island (New Bight)	Monday, Friday
Crooked Island (Colonel Hill)	Tuesday, Saturday
Eleuthera (Governor's Harbour)	Daily
Eleuthera (North Eleuthera)	Daily
Eleuthera (Rock Sound)	Daily
Exumas (George Town)	Daily
Grand Bahama (Freeport)	Daily
Great Inagua (Matthew Town)	Monday, Tuesday, Wednesday, Friday
Long Island (Deadman's Cay)	Four flights weekly
Long Island (Stella Maris)	Four flights weekly
Mayaguana (Abraham Bay)	Three flights weekly
San Salvador (Cockburn Town)	Friday, Sunday

If possible, allow several hours' leeway for connecting flights. Flights are consistently late – often by several hours – or canceled. Occasionally they take off early! You'll often be told that flights are sold out, but don't believe it: Bahamians tend to book the next available flight, then get themselves on the standby list for the flight they really want. You should do as the locals do, calling on the day you wish to fly. Usually a seat will have appeared.

In Nassau anticipate a long wait at the Bahamasair check-in counter. Counter staff are unaccountably *slooowww!* And many locals will be laden with a gross excess of luggage and boxes. Here you may see Bahamians at their worst. Line-jumping is common, and your complaints may be met with an aggressive, in-your-face response.

The luggage limit is 70 lbs per person. Ensure that your bags are tagged with the correct destination.

When flights are turbulent, Bahamian passengers take to wailing as if they were in church: *'Oh, Lord! Oh, Lord Jesus!'* On a *really* bumpy flight, it's quite a giggle!

Air Passes

Bahamasair has a 'Great Value Airpass' for travelers arriving from Florida. It's good for travel to up to three islands plus Nassau (eight flights). The Miami-to-Nassau leg (two flights) costs US$110; that leg plus one island costs US$180; plus two islands, US$250; plus three islands, US$320. You can also fly via Orlando.

You can also purchase an air pass for flights to and from Nassau only (one island, US$90 roundtrip; two islands, US$145; three islands, US$215). Reservations and payment must be made in your country of origin. The air pass cannot be purchased in The Bahamas. No route changes are permitted, nor are refunds given after departure on the first leg. The pass is good for a stay of up to 21 days.

Bahamasair also offers a frequent-flyer discount: Book 10 full-fare legs and you'll get the 11th free.

Charter Flights

Each of the Family Islands is served by commuter airlines and charter flights. Most are based in Nassau, but their itineraries often hop from airstrip to airstrip and may include several islands. Some airlines have

carved out their own turf. Congo Air, for example, is the main carrier to Andros.

You can also charter a small aircraft, usually carrying up to six people, from any of more than a dozen companies . . . a simple solution for island-hopping. Typically, expect to pay US$200 to US$600 one way for the plane, depending on distance. However, if several people share the flight, this option becomes cost-effective. This is especially true if you wish to do some island-hopping and want to avoid the cost of repeatedly returning to Nassau with Bahamasair (think of the time you'll save, too).

Interisland service is offered by the following charter and commuter companies:

Cat Island Air	☎ 242-377-3318
Cherokee Air	☎ 242-367-2089
Cleare Air	☎ 242-377-0341
	fax 242-377-3296
Congo Air	☎ 242-377-5382
	fax 242-377-7413
Falcon Air	☎ 242-377-1703
Island Express	☎ 954-359-0380
	fax 954-359-7944
Long Island Wings	☎ 242-357-1013
Major's Air Services	☎ 242-352-5778
Seaplane Safaris	☎ 242-393-2522
Sky Unlimited	☎ 242-377-8993,
	242-377-8777
Taino Air	☎ 242-352-8885
	fax 242-352-5175
Trans-Island Air	☎ 242-327-5979

Hotel Charters Charter service is offered by a number of hotels and resorts, including the following:

Andros
  Small Hope Bay Lodge
    (☎ 242-368-2014, 800-223-6961,
    fax 242-368-2015)
Cat Island
  Fernandez Bay Village
    (☎ 242-342-3043, fax 242-342-3051;
    in the USA ☎ 954-474-4821, 800-940-1905,
    fax 954-474-4864)
  Greenwood Beach Resort (☎ 242-342-3053)
Grand Bahama
  Deep Water Cay Club (☎ 242-353-3073;
    in the USA 954-359-0488,
    fax 954-359-9488)

Long Island
    Stella Maris Resort
    (☎ 242-338-2051, fax 242-338-2052;
    in the USA ☎ 954-359-8236, 800-426-0466,
    fax 954-359-8238)
San Salvador
    Club Med Columbus Isle
    (☎ 242-331-2000, fax 242-331-2222;
    in North America ☎ 800-453-2582,
    fax 602-443-2086)
    Riding Rock Inn Resort
    (☎ 242-331-2631, fax 242-331-2020;
    in the USA ☎ 954-359-8353, 800-272-1492,
    fax 954-359-8254)

Many resorts also offer charter service to
and from Florida. See the island chapters
for fare information.

Helicopter

Paradise Island Helicopters (☎ 242-363-
4016, pager 242-340-2744) offers transportation between Nassau/Paradise Island
and the Family Islands, as well as Grand
Bahama. The company also offers sightseeing tours. See the New Providence
chapter for details.

BUS

Traveling by bus is a bomb, except in
Nassau, where dozens of private jitneys
(minibuses) are licensed to operate around
the city on pre-established routes. (See the
New Providence chapter.)

Alas, there is no public transportation on
any of the Family Islands. Even Freeport
and Grand Bahama have minimal service.
Some enterprising individuals operate in-
frequent minibus service on a few islands
(see island chapters).

There are no public buses at airports, not
even at Nassau International Airport. When
the airport opened in 1959, public bus service *was* established by the government.
However, local taxi drivers blocked the
roads with their cars to force the government to withdraw the service. When the
government refused, trade union leaders
called a general strike, which lasted three
weeks.

A few larger resorts include airport-hotel
transfers in their room rates. See the Taxi

section in this chapter for information on
getting to and from the airports.

CAR

Driving in the islands is a no-brainer. A
paved highway circles New Providence,
which is also crisscrossed by a small number
of main roads. A single highway runs the
length of most other inhabited islands and
cays, and there are usually side roads
leading to nearby settlements. The islands'
main highways – usually called 'Queen's
Hwy' or 'King's Hwy' – virtually always
consist of one lane in each direction.

Conditions vary from excellent to awful.
Main roads are usually in good condition,
although you're likely to find deep potholes everywhere, especially toward the
end of the summer rainy season. Keep
your speed down! Many minor unpaved
roads are in appalling condition, rutted by
rain and lack of repairs; these are best
tackled with a 4WD vehicle.

Bahamians are generally cautious and
civilized drivers. Unlike in, say, Jamaica,
you will rarely be honked at here; nor do
Bahamians yell cuss words at other drivers.
Traffic jams frequently occur in Nassau,
but most drivers accept things in good
grace (there will *always* be some arrogant
SOB trying to squeeze down the center
divide, however).

A small percentage drive too fast for
local conditions; as a whole they drive
faster than do US drivers in similar conditions. Too many drivers can't stand being
behind another car. You should be prepared
for cars overtaking you with harrowing,
daredevil folly, particularly on New Providence. Use extreme caution and drive
defensively, especially at night.

On New Providence and Grand Bahama
streets are well-signed, as they are in most
major settlements. Since there is usually
only one main road running the length of
each island, getting lost is virtually impossible. Distances may seem minor, but what
may appear on a map to be a 30-minute
journey will usually take longer. Believe
any Bahamian who says that a road is bad.

A good road map is essential for getting around New Providence. Hotels may provide local, hand-drawn maps. (See Maps in the Facts for the Visitor chapter for specific map suggestions.)

Road Rules
Always drive on the *left*. Remember: 'Keep left and you'll always be right.' Another saying worth remembering is: 'De left side is de right side; de right side is suicide!' Speed limits are 30 mph in settlements and 50 mph on main highways. Observe them.

At traffic circles (roundabouts), remember to circle in a clockwise direction, entering to the left. You must give way to traffic already in the circle. *Be cautious!* Not all Bahamians agree on who has right of way, leading to frequent collisions.

The Bahamas has no compulsory seatbelt law (few old cars have seat belts anyway), but you must wear a helmet when riding a motorcycle or scooter.

Gasoline
Esso, Shell, and Texaco maintain gas (petrol) stations on most islands. Even in remote spots, there'll always be a gas station, although it may be no more than a pump in front of a grocery store or in someone's front yard. Gas stations are usually open from 8 am to about 7 pm. Some close on Sunday. In Nassau and Freeport you'll find stations open 24 hours a day. Gasoline costs US$2.35 to US$3.25 per US gallon.

Credit cards are accepted in the major settlements. Elsewhere, it's cash only!

Security
You don't need to be paranoid, especially in the Family Islands, where theft is a minor problem. Still, it's always best to park in an established parking lot when you can, particularly in Nassau. Always remove any belongings from the car, or at the very least, keep them locked in the trunk.

Women need have no fear about driving alone in the Family Islands or in most of Nassau. At night, avoid Nassau's Over-the-Hill area, if possible; lock your doors.

Picking Up Passengers
In the Family Islands, where the income levels are low and few people own cars, an empty seat in your car will go a long way toward easing the burden of Bahamians forced to rely on passing vehicles. You'll often see people waving you down with a lackadaisical sweep of an outstretched hand. You can feel secure offering rides to virtually anyone in the Family Islands, but use common sense and caution when giving rides, especially in Nassau.

Mechanical Problems
There's no national roadside service organization to call when you have car trouble. The larger rental agencies in Nassau and Freeport have a 24-hour service number in case of breakdown or other emergencies. In the Family Islands, where most car-rental agencies are mom-and-pop operations, you may or may not be given a telephone number to call.

If you do break down and must use a local mechanic, you should do so only for minor work; otherwise the rental agency may balk at reimbursing you for work they haven't authorized. If you can't find a phone or repair service, flag down any passing car. The occupant will usually be happy to assist you. Since the islands are so small and everyone knows everyone else, you'll usually quickly find someone who can get a message to whomever rented you the vehicle.

Accidents
Hopefully you won't have one, but if you ''mash up,' there are a few rules to obey. Firstly, don't move the vehicles, and don't let anyone else move them, including the other driver. Have someone call the police, and remain at the scene until a police officer arrives (this may take a while). Make sure to get the name and address of anyone involved in the accident, as well as their license number and details of their vehicle. Take photos of the scene if possible, and get the names and addresses of any witnesses (who may, however, disappear or be noncommittal about what they

saw). Don't get drawn into an argument. Call the rental company as soon as possible.

Rental

Several major international car-rental companies have outlets in Nassau and Freeport, along with smaller local firms (see the Getting Around sections in the New Providence and Grand Bahama chapters). In the Family Islands, there are few established agencies. Usually a few locals earn extra income by renting their private cars.

You usually rent for a 24-hour period. Daily rates begin at about US$60, even for a beat-up old jalopy. In Nassau and in Freeport, modern US-model cars are available at rates starting at US$60, but rates go as high as about US$125 for large 4WD vehicles. You can save as much as 25% by booking through the larger US companies *before* your arrival in The Bahamas:

Avis	☎ 800-331-1212
Budget	☎ 800-527-0770
Dollar	☎ 800-800-4000
Hertz	☎ 800-654-3131
National	☎ 800-227-7368

In peak season, especially in the Family Islands, you may find that vehicles are not available. It's wise to reconfirm before arrival. Usually your car will be delivered to your hotel. Allow for some flexibility in the Family Islands.

In the Family Islands, a cash deposit – up to US$500 – is usually requested to cover the owner's deductible (a similar deposit, payable by credit card, is required by the major companies in Nassau and on Grand Bahama).

There is rarely a difference in rates between low and peak seasons. Most companies include unlimited mileage; a few others set a limit and charge a fee for excess miles.

Keep copies of any paperwork. Mom-and-pop operators usually don't give you any paperwork, however; they simply hand you the keys.

Before signing any paperwork or driving away, go over the vehicle with a fine-toothed comb to identify any dents or problems. Make sure they are all marked up or pointed out to the owner before you drive away. Otherwise you are likely to be charged for the slightest scrape. Don't forget to check the cigarette lighter and interior switches, which are often missing. Make sure there's a spare tire, something my experience tells me you may need.

Except when you're renting in Nassau and Freeport, you'll usually have to take whatever vehicle comes your way. It might be a dilapidated pickup, a large gas-guzzling sedan with bad tires, or a tiny Geo Metro. One price fits all! In any vehicle the steering wheel is guaranteed to be on the left side.

Your hotel or the rental company can usually arrange a driver for an extra fee.

Insurance Before you rent a car, check whether your current insurance or credit card covers you for driving while abroad. In Nassau and Freeport, the major rental agencies will recommend damage-waiver insurance, which limits your liability in the event of an accident or damage. It should cost about US$12 a day – a valuable investment. If you have an American Express card, you can waive this requirement: Most rental companies recognize its policy, which covers car insurance. Mom-and-pop operations don't offer insurance coverage; your deposit covers the owner's deductible.

Driver's License Although the minimum age to obtain a driver's license in The Bahamas is 17, renters must be 21 (some companies only rent to those 25 or older). Mom-and-pop operations may not care and will rarely ask to see your license. For additional details, see Driver's License in the Facts for the Visitor chapter.

You can drive on your foreign license for up to three months.

MOTORCYCLE & SCOOTER

There's a special thrill to exploring on two wheels, and it's a good option for compact resort areas, where a car may be overkill.

Scooters are available in major tourist areas. A few companies also rent motorcycles. These companies are far more lax than the major car-rental companies, though you usually still have to show a driver's license. Scooters cost about US$25 to US$40 daily, including insurance; hourly rental is sometimes offered. Expect to pay US$5 to US$10 more for a motorcycle. A deposit of US$100 is typically required for a motorcycle.

Wearing a helmet is mandatory. Usually the rental agencies offer beat-up old helmets. Count yourself lucky to be given one that fits!

Ride cautiously! Road conditions are extremely hazardous, especially away from major resort areas. You'll encounter potholes, loose gravel, fast drivers, narrow roads, free-roaming goats, and kamikaze chickens. Check the Car section in this chapter for more information about road rules and conditions.

BICYCLE

Cycling is a cheap, convenient, healthy, environmentally sound, and above all *fun* way to travel. Major resort hotels rent bicycles. Typical costs are US$7 to US$20 daily. Unfortunately, the bikes are beach cruisers: They're heavy, have only one gear, and the pedal also acts as the brake. They are not designed for long-distance touring and are virtually guaranteed to give you a sore bum. Mountain bikes are not available.

If you take your own bicycle, go over your bike with a fine-toothed comb and augment your repair kit with every imaginable spare. You won't be able to buy that crucial gizmo when your bicycle breaks down in the back of beyond.

Bicycles can travel by air. You can take them to pieces and put them in a bike bag or box, but it's much easier to simply wheel your bike to the check-in desk, where it should be treated as a piece of luggage. You may have to remove the pedals and turn the handlebars sideways so that the bike takes up less space in the aircraft's hold. Check all this with the airline well in advance, preferably before you buy your ticket.

Also see Bicycling in the Outdoor Activities chapter.

HITCHHIKING

Technically, hitchhiking is illegal in The Bahamas. Still, locals (including women and children) without cars rely on hitchhiking. In the Family Islands, everyone hitchhikes or gives rides as a matter of course. Many Bahamians may offer to give you a ride or tour. Often this is done from the goodness of their hearts; at other times it becomes clear that a monetary donation would be appreciated.

While hitchhiking is never entirely safe and Lonely Planet does not recommend it, hitchhiking in The Bahamas (outside Nassau) is as safe as anywhere. Travelers who decide to hitchhike should understand that they are taking a small but potentially serious risk. Let someone know where you are planning to go.

BOAT

Ferry & Water Taxi

Interisland ferries are *not* as ubiquitous as you may imagine. Nonetheless, a few ferry services exist. Government-run ferries link islands that are a short distance apart, such as North Bimini and South Bimini; Mangrove Cay and South Andros; and Crooked and Acklins islands. Passage is usually twice daily and usually free.

Water taxis ply between Nassau's Prince George Wharf and Woodes Rogers Walk and Paradise Island. Several other offshore islands are served by private water taxis. For example, Harbour Island is served from the government dock at North Eleuthera; Green Turtle Cay (Abacos) is served from the dock a few miles north of Treasure Cay; and water taxis run to Great Guana, Man O' War, and Elbow cays (Abacos) from Marsh Harbour. See island chapters for details.

Private Yacht

Marinas are strewn about the islands like confetti at a wedding. If you plan on boating around, be sure to obtain the booklet of marina information published by the Bahamas Out Islands Promotion Board and the *Yachtsman's Guide to The Bahamas and Turks & Caicos* (see Tourist Offices in the Facts for the Visitor chapter and Private Yacht in the Getting There & Away chapter, respectively). For more information about sailing The Bahamas, see the Outdoor Activities and Getting There & Away chapters.

Although rare, drug-related acts of piracy do occur, though not on the level of the 1970s and '80s, when boating magazines warned skippers to carry guns to guard against drug-runners, who seized 'clean' boats on which to sneak into the USA.

Mail Boat

Mail boats were the only reliable inter-island transportation until regularly scheduled air service between Nassau and the Family Islands began. Nowadays about 29 mail boats under government contract serve most of the inhabited islands from Potter's Cay in Nassau. They traditionally sail overnight on journeys lasting five to 24 hours, carrying passengers going 'down home' and others wishing to get a taste of Family Island life.

Mail boats have etched their names – along with those of skippers such as Edgar Moxey of the *Captain Moxey* – in the maritime history of The Bahamas. Introduction of mail-boat service was first proposed in the House of Assembly in 1819. The first service began in 1832. The principal station was then on Crooked Island, where vessels carrying mail between England and the USA via the Crooked Island Passage called. Packages were distributed from Crooked Island to other islands. Soon the boats were carrying other cargo. The government-subsidized, steel-hulled vessels today carry everything from vehicles and groceries to furniture and passengers.

It all sounds so Conradian and romantic, hopping aboard a beaten-up vessel – most are small general-cargo freighters, long on durability and short on luxury – steered by a cheroot-smoking skipper surrounded by bales of bananas and sacks filled with letters. (Actually, most mail travels by air these fast-paced days, leaving the hold and every conceivable inch of deck space free for beer crates, gas cylinders, bags of potatoes and onions, bananas, and more beer.)

A mail-boat trip does provide a unique sense of adventure and puts you close to the Bahamians. But be prepared to have your carefully made plans shredded. The ladies (in truth, few of the mail boats look female, unless you're thinking of a Russian *babushka*) are wayward tramps: They often travel with flagrant disregard for their schedules. All the vessels are slow and notoriously unreliable. You'll need to be flexible.

Mail-boat travel can also be arduous. Many of the passages, such as the Crooked Island Passage and the crosscurrents in the New Providence Passage, are quite treacherous. Occasional (OK, make that frequent) rough seas and the smell of diesel can induce seasickness. To avoid this, it is best to decline your skipper's invitation to go below to admire the reeking engine room.

Note that a 2nd-class ticket only guarantees passage; you will have to pay extra (usually US$5) for 1st class to secure a coveted bunk about the size of a stretcher. Accommodations vary from Spartan to ultra-Spartan. Often the only sleeping spaces are on wooden benches lining the narrow corridors . . . *and* you'll have to scramble for *your* spot before the savvy islanders. The losers get to sleep on the greasy floor. Sleeping on deck is usually better than the suffering the fetid conditions below. This is not the *Love Boat!*

You may be handed some fruit, a soda, and perhaps a tin of Spam upon boarding, but don't count on it. Take eats and drinks – especially a bottle of rum – to share with locals. A pack of cards comes in handy.

Contact the Dockmaster's Office (☎ 242-393-1064) at Potter's Cay, Nassau, for the latest itineraries and fares. The schedule and one-way fares listed on the next two pages applied at press time.

Destination	Boat	Departs Nassau	Duration	Fare
Abacos (Marsh Harbour, Hope Town, Treasure Cay, Green Turtle Cay)	Mia Dean	8 pm Tuesday	12 hours	US$45
Abacos (Sandy Point, Bullock Harbour)	Champion II	8 pm Tuesday	11 hours	US$25
Andros (Cargill Creek, Bowen Sound)	Lady Gloria	10 pm Tuesday	5 hours	US$30
Andros (Drigg's Hill, Congo Town, The Bluff, Kemp's Bay)	Captain Moxey	11 pm Monday	7½ hours	US$30
Andros (Lisbon Creek)	Mangrove Cay Express	6 pm Wednesday	5½ hours	US$30
Andros (Mastic Point, Nicholls Town, Morgan's Bluff)	Lisa J II	3:30 pm Wednesday	5 hours	US$30
Andros (North)	Lady Margo	2 am Wednesday	5 hours	US$30
Andros (North)	Challenger	Call dockmaster for time, duration, and fare		
Andros (South)	Delmar L	10 pm Thursday	7½ hours	US$30
Andros (Stafford Creek, Blanket Sound, Staniard Creek, Fresh Creek, Behring Point)	Lady D	Noon Tuesday	5 hours	US$30
Biminis & North Cat Cay	Bimini Mack	Call dockmaster for time	12 hours	US$45
Cat Island (New Bight, Bennett's Harbour, Arthur's Town)	North Cat Island Special	1 pm Wednesday	14 hours	US$40
Cat Island (New Bight, Old Bight, Smith Bay)	Sea Hauler	3 pm Tuesday	17 hours	US$40

Destination	Boat	Departs Nassau	Duration	Fare
Crooked Island, Acklins Island, & Mayaguana (Landrail Point, Spring Point, Abraham Bay)	*Lady Mathilda*	Call dockmaster for time and duration		US$70
Eleuthera (Current, The Bluff, Hatchet Bay)	*Current Pride*	7 am Thursday	5 hours	US$20
Eleuthera (Governor's Harbour)	*Eleuthera Express*	7 pm Monday	5½ hours	US$20
Eleuthera (Hatchet Bay)	*Captain Fox*	Noon Friday	6 hours	US$20
Eleuthera (Rock Sound, Davis Harbour, South Eleuthera)	*Bahamas Daybreak III*	5 pm Monday	5 hours	US$20
Second departure		7 am Thursday	5 hours	US$25
Eleuthera (Spanish Wells)	*Eleuthera Express*	7 am Thursday	5 hours	US$25
Eleuthera (Spanish Wells)	*Spanish Rose*	7 am Thursday	5 hours	US$20
Exumas (George Town)	*Grand Master*	2 pm Tuesday	12 hours	US$35
Exumas & Ragged Island (Staniel Cay, Black Point, Little Farmer's Cay, Barreterre)	*Ettienne & Cephas*	2 pm Tuesday	21 hours	US$30
Grand Bahama (Freeport)	*Marcella III*	4 pm Wednesday	Call dockmaster for duration	US$45
Long Island (Seymours, Salt Pond, Deadman's Cay)	*Sherice M*	1 pm Tuesday	17 hours	US$45
Long Island & Great Inagua (Clarence Town, Matthew Town)	*Abilin*	Noon Tuesday	17 hours	US$45
San Salvador & Rum Cay (Cockburn Town, United Estates, Port Nelson)	*Lady Francis*	6 pm Tuesday	Call dockmaster for duration	US$40

Unfortunately, mail-boat service between the islands is limited to these routes. You cannot, for example, catch a mail boat from Cat Island to the Inaguas. Thus, if you plan on island-hopping, you may have to return to Nassau repeatedly or charter aircraft.

Excursions

As you'd expect in an archipelago of 700 islands and cays, boat excursions are a mainstay of exploring. More than a dozen major operators are based in Nassau, Paradise Island, and Grand Bahama, and they take visitors on excursions far and wide. See details in the New Providence and Grand Bahama chapters.

In the Family Islands, you can arrange your own excursions with local boat-owners. Prices are negotiable and range from US$50 for a two-hour excursion by small speedboat to US$300 or so for a day-long excursion on a larger vessel with skipper.

TAXI

There's no shortage of licensed taxis in Nassau and Freeport, where they can be hailed on the streets. Taxis are also the main local transportation in the Family Islands, but you'll rarely find one cruising for business. Usually they must be summoned by radio or telephone. Some taxis are modern US-made minivans. But more often they're old US-model jalopies. The seat belts have usually been removed. Still, the religiously superstitious may consider themselves safe: Most taxi drivers keep a Bible at hand.

All taxi operators are licensed. Fares are fixed by the government according to distance: US$2 for the first quarter-mile and US30¢ for each additional quarter-mile. Rates are usually for two people. Each additional person is charged US$2. Fixed rates have been established from airports and cruise terminals to specific hotels and major destinations. These rates should be displayed in the taxi. Tipping is discretionary and not automatically expected.

Few taxi drivers use their meters. Most taxi drivers are entirely reliable, especially in the Family Islands. However, you should beware some crafty scams in Nassau and Freeport, where an unscrupulous driver may attempt to charge additional people the same rate as the first and second person.

You can hire taxis for long-distance touring at government-fixed rates: US$25 per hour and US$10 per additional half-hour. Minivans can charge more. In some cases rates may be negotiable. A half-day tour may cost about US$100. Expect to pay at least US$150 for a full-day tour. Whatever you choose, agree on a fare *before* setting out.

Some hotels include airport-hotel transfers in their room rates. Otherwise the taxi-drivers' union has you – the money-flush visitor – by the short and curlies.

On New Providence and Grand Bahama, and even in the more remote Family Islands, taxis usually show up to meet incoming flights (if not, someone at the airport will radio for a taxi on your behalf). See the Getting Around sections in the New Providence and Grand Bahama chapters for details.

Local islanders may offer to guide you around in their cars. Some do this for free; others expect payment. They may be too proud to ask you directly for money, so you must judge the mood and act accordingly.

ORGANIZED TOURS

There are plenty of organized tours in Nassau and on Grand Bahama. Several reputable companies offer guided excursions to leading attractions – everything from free guided walking tours of historic Nassau led by Ministry of Tourism guides (☎ 242-322-8634) to a nightclub tour offered by Majestic Tours (☎ 242-322-2606, fax 242-326-5785), the leading tour operator. Majestic also has half-day guided tours of Nassau and New Providence.

Similar tours of Freeport/Lucaya and Grand Bahama are offered by the Grand Bahama Taxi Union (☎ 242-352-7858/7101) and Bahamas Travel (☎ 242-352-3141).

Rather than signing up with a tour company, you might try a fun and romantic way to explore historic Nassau: Take one of the shaded horse-drawn surreys that line up for business at Prince George Wharf. Rates are negotiable, according to the time and distance of your tour.

See the New Providence and Grand Bahama chapters for details on tours.

A variety of nature tours and activity-oriented trips on the islands and on the water are offered by tour operators. For details and contact information, see the Outdoor Activities chapter, and also check the Activities and Organized Tours sections in the island chapters.

New Providence

Pop 171,542

New Providence is the most important island in the Bahamian chain. Nearly two-thirds of the nation's population lives here, overwhelmingly in Nassau, the capital, which sprawls over much of eastern New Providence. More than 70% of all visitors to The Bahamas land in Nassau or on neighboring Paradise Island.

The ovoid island is 21 miles east to west and 7 miles north to south at its widest. The resort zones – a mini-Cancún of ritzy casinos, world-class entertainment, and duty-free shopping – are limited to Paradise Island, just north of Nassau; downtown Nassau; and the north shore, notably Cable Beach, 3 miles west of central Nassau. Paradise Island boasts two of The Bahamas' longest and most stunning beaches, plus its own casino and luxury resorts. Cable Beach has long been the Bahamian Riviera, its gently curving sands lined with hotels and the Crystal Palace Casino.

Residential Nassau spreads south and east for several miles. The rest of the island is humdrum and sparsely populated. Most of the interior is marshy, with large lakes and dense scrub forest favored by locals as impromptu garbage dumps. Bird watchers might do well here, and canoeing is offered on Lake Nancy. Otherwise, the only sites of interest are the scenic northwest shore and the funky village of Adelaide near the south shore. The south shore has a few unremarkable beaches and even fewer hotels, though the diving is superb.

Two notable resorts – the South Ocean Golf & Beach Resort and Compass Point – add luster to the northwest and south shores. Compass Point's 1995 opening blew the dust off the somewhat bah-humbug Bahamian hotel scene. It was followed the next year by Sandals Royal Bahamian. These were the high-water marks of a boom in hotel construction and renovation that has swept Nassau and Paradise Island in the past few

HIGHLIGHTS

- Lively Bay St and Rawson Square, brimming with historic buildings and bustle
- The Same Ol' Place, for a down-to-earth night listening to rake 'n' scrape with the locals
- Paradise Island's Cabbage Beach. And you thought Cable Beach was cool!
- Colorful Potter's Cay, where locals buy fresh fruit and fish
- Compass Point. If you can't stay here, at least treat yourself to a meal
- Blue Lagoon Island, a fabulous cay where you can snorkel with dolphins
- The dive sites north of Paradise Island and southwest of New Providence

years as properties attempt to cash in on the islands' rebirth. The sidewalks are cleaner, public services have been enhanced, and even the locals (who developed a reputation in the 1980s for surliness) are friendlier.

Nassau

Pop 170,000

Nassau, on the island's northeast shore, seems small in scale at first sight. It exudes

152

a special charm, lent by a blend of Old World architecture and contemporary vitality. Modern Nassau is a far cry from the rustic yet rowdy village that once harbored pirates, prostitutes, and ragamuffins. The city is steeped in modern US ways, which meld well with a quasi-Caribbean flavor. The historic downtown core – some 10 blocks long and four blocks wide – is replete with colonial edifices. Some are quite grand neocolonial government buildings; others are quaint wooden and limestone homes and office buildings in a pastel-painted vernacular style, usually with large louvered windows, wide balconies supported by wooden knee braces or pillars, and slate or shingle roofs.

But downtown is more than a pretty snapshot. It is also the center of commerce and government, policed by officers in immaculately starched white jackets and black pants or skirts trimmed with a red line (some wear white pith helmets to beat back the sun). The city is world renowned as a lively financial center where Brits in pinstriped shirts manage billions of dollars of wealthy folks' assets. Yet it lacks the high-rises one associates with international finance centers.

The heart of touristic affairs extends along the waterfront and along Bay St, one block inland. It's a beehive of activity when the cruise ships disgorge their hordes. The city's cash registers tinkle to the sound of the tourists' silver dollars, many of which come rolling down the gangplanks. Wherever you are in downtown Nassau, the ships loom over you; when in port, their presence is overwhelming. A half-dozen ships at a time often berth, their white hulls sleekly reflected in the turquoise waters.

The town extends inland for miles, with low-income and middle-class suburbs edging as far as the south coast. The government ministries, modern shopping malls, and colleges also lie south of downtown along Thompson Blvd in areas where few tourists venture. There are few sights of interest in this area.

Beyond town there's no shortage of water-based activities to keep you amused, from jet-skiing and parasailing to diving and snorkeling to exciting excursions on and under the water.

Very few foreign visitors break out of the established tourist routine to engage with the locals or discover what the island is like away from the narrow touristy corridor from Cable Beach to Paradise Island. Nassau is so overwhelmingly geared to the tourist that the 'real' island takes some seeking out. Yet it lies close at hand, in albeit modern (and motley) fishing villages along the south shore; on beaches beyond Nassau, Paradise Island, and Cable Beach; at fishing wharves, where locals gather to chat over conch salads; and, above all, in Over-the-Hill, an African-Bahamian enclave of colorful wooden houses just south of downtown.

The people of Nassau are a particularly Bible-wielding folk as a whole. Everywhere you'll come across folks reading their Bibles and reciting psalms in public. Taxi drivers often have their Bibles on their dashboards. And the number of little churches, many of them built on the most marginal land, is mind-boggling.

HISTORY

Nassau's colorful history is steeped in rumrunning, blockade-running, wrecking, piracy, and all-around roguery. It all began in 1648, when William Sayle and his party of Eleutheran Adventurers briefly landed. The island became known as Sayle's Island, but the party didn't settle. Buccaneers did, establishing a base beyond the reach of any authority. (See History in the Facts about The Bahamas chapter for details on this period.)

The first settlement, established in 1666, was named Charles Town. There was little formal structure. The dirt streets were lined by brothels and taverns for 'common cheats, thieves, and lewd persons.' In 1684 virtually the entire population fled to the American colonies when the Spaniards sacked the town as retribution for relentless attacks by Charles Town's pirates. The town was rebuilt and renamed Nassau in 1695, with Fort Nassau on the site now

NEW PROVIDENCE

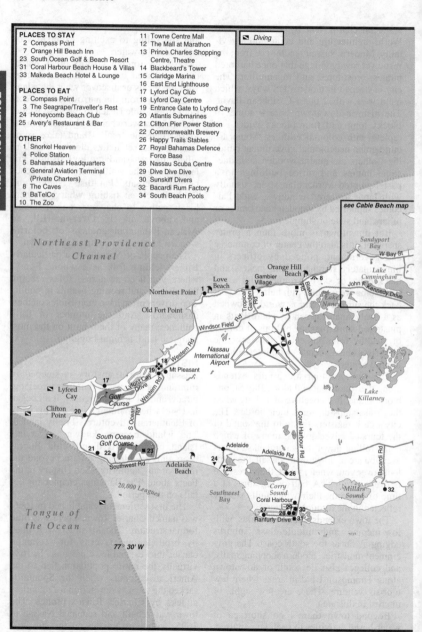

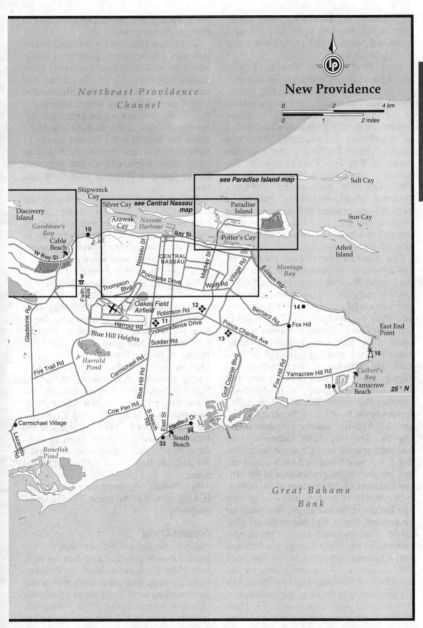

New Providence

Northeast Providence Channel

0   2   4 km
0   1   2 miles

see Paradise Island map

Salt Cay

Shipwreck Cay

Discovery Island

Goodman's Bay

Silver Cay *see Central Nassau map*

Paradise Island

Sun Cay

Arawak Cay *Nassau Harbour*

10

Cable Beach

W Bay St

Bay St

Potter's Cay

Athol Island

9

Faith Ave

Nassau St

CENTRAL NASSAU

Mackey St

Village Rd

Montagu Bay

Thompson Blvd

Poinciana Drive

Wulff Rd

Eastern Rd

Gladstone Rd

Oakes Field Airfield

Robinson Rd

12

Bernard Rd

14

Fox Hill

East End Point

Harrold Rd

11

Independence Drive

Prince Charles Ave

Blue Hill Heights

Soldier Rd

13

Fire Trail Rd

Harrold Pond

Carmichael Rd

Blue Hill Rd

Golf Course Blvd

Fox Hill Rd

Yamacraw Hill Rd

16

Culbert's Bay

15

Yamacraw Beach

25° N

Cow Pen Rd

S Bay Rd

East St

Harbour Dr

34

Carmichael Village

Lazaretto Rd

Bonefish Pond

33

South Beach

Great Bahama Bank

occupied by the British Colonial Hotel. Nassau was attacked again in 1703 by a combined Spanish and French force that destroyed the fort.

In 1718 Governor Woodes Rogers arrived to establish order and an administration answerable to the English crown. Piracy was suppressed. Still, by the middle of the 18th century, the public buildings comprised merely a church, along with a jail, courthouse, and Assembly House in a single, ruinous building at the northeast corner of Bay St – then known as 'The Strand' – and today's Market St. In the 1760s Governor William Shirley, former governor of Massachusetts, brought a Yankee sense of order and ingenuity to the creation of a *real* city. The swamps were drained, the land was surveyed, and tidy new streets were laid.

The American Revolution boosted the city's fortunes, as citizens took to running the English blockade. Meanwhile a flood of Loyalist refugees – many quite wealthy or entrepreneurial – began arriving, lending new vigor to the city. In 1787 the haughty and inept Earl of Dunmore arrived as governor of the Bahamas, despite disgracing himself in the posts of governor of New York and Virginia in events before and during the American Revolution. His critics – there were many – accused him of a reprehensible private life, while bemoaning appointments to office of 'bankrupts, beggars, blackguards, and the husbands of his whores.' The ever-crafty Dunmore, who had been granted use of a home, built himself a *separate* home and then leased the new property to the government as the official residence of the governor of the colony.

His legacy is evident today in several fine buildings, including the two batteries he erected: Fort Charlotte and Fort Fincastle. Alas, Dunmore erected his troops' barracks in the direct line of fire between Fort Charlotte and the town it had been built to defend. An investigation by the Secretary of War was highly critical, but the governor was saved by the outbreak of Britain's war with France in 1793. Dunmore's exorbitant spending was justified.

Meanwhile, many Nassauvians returned to their privateering ways.

By the late 18th century Nassau had settled into a slow-paced, glamorous era in which the well-to-do lived graciously. Gentlemen kept many slaves. Slaves and free blacks (who lived in Over-the-Hill shanties) were banished from the streets after nightfall. Their numbers vastly expanded following abolition of the slave trade in 1807, when the British Navy landed scores of slaves who had been freed on the high seas. Many of the public edifices and sites such as the Queen's Staircase date from this time.

The city's fortunes briefly revived again during the US Civil War, when citizens took to running the Northern blockade on the Southern states. Hotels went up to serve the traders, smugglers, and spies. Many fine homes were erected on the proceeds from blockade-running.

During the 20th century, Nassau witnessed an influx of Greeks, lured by the local sponging industry, which they soon commanded. Wealthy tourists also began to arrive. Their numbers were boosted by Prohibition. While Nassauvians made hay illicitly supplying liquor to the USA, Yankees flocked to make merry in Nassau, where a casino had opened. After the repeal of Prohibition, tourism became seasonal, focused on the 'winter season' from December to March. The major hotels – the Royal Victoria, Fort Montagu, and the British Colonial – were only open for those three months and closed after the annual Washington Ball, when tourists returned home.

For Nassau's contemporary history, see History in the Facts about The Bahamas chapter.

ORIENTATION

Historic downtown Nassau faces north toward Paradise Island and Nassau Harbour. The town rises south to Prospect Ridge, a steep limestone scarp that parallels the entire north shore about a half-mile inland. A second, higher ridge – Blue Hill Heights – rises to 120 feet and runs east to

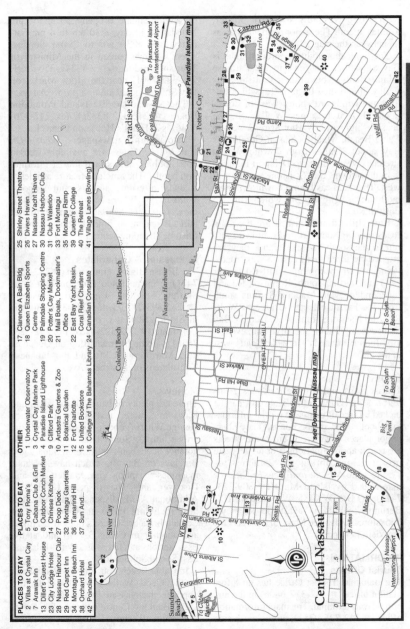

PLACES TO STAY
2 Villas at Crystal Cay
7 Arawak Inn
13 Diller's Guest House
23 City Lodge Hotel
28 Nassau Harbour Club
29 Red Carpet Inn
34 Montagu Beach Inn
38 Orchard Hotel
42 Poinciana Inn

PLACES TO EAT
5 Tony Roma's
6 Cabana Club & Grill
8 Outdoor Conch Market
14 Chinese Kitchen
27 Poop Deck
32 Montagu Gardens
36 Tamarind Hill
37 Sun And...

OTHER
1 Underwater Observatory
3 Crystal Cay Marine Park
4 Paradise Island Lighthouse
9 Clifford Park
10 Ardastra Gardens & Zoo
11 Botanical Garden
12 Fort Charlotte
15 United Bookstore
16 College of The Bahamas Library
17 Clarence A Bain Bldg
18 Queen Elizabeth Sports Centre
19 Palmdale Shopping Centre
20 Potter's Cay Market
21 Mail Boats, Dockmaster's Office
22 East Bay Yacht Basin, Coral Reef Charters
24 Canadian Consulate
25 Shirley Street Theatre
26 Divers Haven
27 Nassau Yacht Haven
30 Nassau Harbour Club
31 Club Waterloo
33 Fort Montagu
35 Montagu Ramp
39 Queen's College
40 The Retreat
41 Village Lanes (Bowling)

Central Nassau

west along Nassau's southern border, 3 miles inland. The major residential areas lie between the ridges.

The main thoroughfare through town is Bay St, which runs east to the Paradise Island Bridge; beyond, it continues as E Bay St and then Eastern Rd, which follows the windward shore. West of downtown, Bay St becomes W Bay St, the coastal 'highway.' W Bay St runs west to Cable Beach, which begins at Goodman's Bay, about 3 miles from downtown, and stretches west 2 miles to Delaport Point.

In downtown, Bay St is one way east to west. The main eastbound downtown thoroughfare is Shirley St, which runs to Eastern Rd.

Blue Hill Rd and East St are the main roads running south from downtown (both run to the south shore). Inland, they are crossed by three main east-to-west roads: Poinciana Dr (becoming Wulff Rd farther east) and, farther south, Robinson Rd and Independence Dr. Mackey St runs south from the Paradise Island Bridge to Wulff Rd. And Nassau St runs south from W Bay St, becoming Thompson Blvd and, eventually, John F Kennedy Dr, which leads west to the airport.

Maps

Tourist maps, notably the *Bahamas Trailblazer Map* (Dupuch Publications), can be picked up free of charge at tourist information booths and major hotels. They show major places of interest, but some streets are rough approximations. For an accurate presentation, obtain the 2-inches-to-1-mile-scale *Nassau and New Providence* map issued by Island Maps (☎ 809-323-7421), PO Box WK485, Warwick WKBX, Bermuda, which is available in major bookstores. (Also see Maps in the Facts for the Visitor chapter.)

INFORMATION
Tourist Offices

The Bahamas Tourist Office has an information office (☎ 242-377-6806) in the airport arrivals terminal. The main information office (☎ 242-326-9781), on the north side

of Rawson Square, is open 8:30 am to 5 pm Monday to Friday, 8:30 am to 4 pm Saturday, and 8:30 am to 2 pm Sunday. There's also a bureau in the Ministry of Tourism headquarters (☎ 242-356-7591, 242-322-7501) near the Straw Market on Bay St; it's open 9 am to 5 pm weekdays.

The Nassau/Paradise Island Promotion Board (☎ 242-322-8383/4, fax 242-326-5346) is at Hotel's House on Deans Ln.

Two monthly newspapers, *What's On* and *Tourist News*, are available free in hotel lobbies, stores, and tourist information booths. They include feature articles, a calendar of events, and discount coupons. *What-to-do: Where to shop, dine, stay, play, invest* is available free at tourist bureaus and most hotel lobbies. It has a fulsome shopping section.

Embassies & Consulates

The British High Commission (☎ 242-325-7471) is in the Bitco Bldg on East St at Shirley St. The Canadian Consulate (☎ 242-393-2123/4, fax 242-393-1305) is in Shirley St Plaza; the US Embassy & Consulate (☎ 242-322-1181, fax 242-328-7838) is in the Mosmar Bldg on Queen St near Marlborough St; and the Japanese Consulate is on Elizabeth Ave.

Money

There are plenty of banks clustered around Rawson Square, just south of Prince George Wharf (good for passengers off the cruise ships). Some banks have ATMs, notably Scotiabank on Rawson Square and Barclays on Bay St, which have 24-hour machines accepting Visa, MasterCard, and Discover cards. They dispense US dollars. Additional ATMs dispense Bahamian dollars, including those at Royal Bank of Canada branches (there's one on E Hill St and another in Cable Beach) and at the Esso stations at Village and Wulff Rds, and East St and Soldier Rd.

In Cable Beach you'll find a Scotiabank in the Cecil Wallace Whitfield Centre opposite the Nassau Beach Hotel, and a CIBC Banking Centre near Sandals Royal Bahamian. Western Union has an office here and another (☎ 242-325-3273) downtown on Frederick St.

American Express is represented by Playtours (☎ 242-322-2931) at 303 Shirley St between Charlotte and Parliament Sts.

Discounts The free *Tourist News* and *What's On* newspapers (see Tourist Offices, above) each have '$500 of coupons inside' for discounts on restaurants, entertainment, sightseeing excursions, and shopping.

Post & Communications
The main post office (☎ 242-322-3025), on E Hill St at Parliament St, is open 8:30 am to 5:30 pm weekdays and 8:30 am to 12:30 pm Saturday. There is also a post office at Cable Beach.

Federal Express (☎ 242-323-7611) has an office downtown on Frederick St.

BaTelCo has an office (☎ 242-323-6414) on East St a half-block south of Bay St, with public phone booths for international calls. It's open 7 am to 10 pm daily. BaTelCo's headquarters (☎ 242-323-4911) is on John F Kennedy Dr.

See Post & Communications in the Facts for the Visitor chapter for details on other services available in Nassau.

Bookstores
Many of the larger resort hotels have gift shops stocking international magazines and a limited range of newspapers and books. Several stores on Bay St stock a wide range of magazines, newspapers, and books. Try the Island Shop (☎ 242-322-4183) at the corner of Frederick St, on the 2nd floor. Anglo-American Book Store (☎ 242-325-0338), in Nassau Arcade on Bay St, has men's and women's magazines and popular literature, plus a secondhand book section in the back. It's also a stationery store. It's open 8 am to 5 pm weekdays and 8 am to 1 pm Sunday.

For a larger selection, try the United Bookstore (☎ 242-325-0316) in the Oakes Field Shopping Centre on Poinciana Dr at' Nassau St. It also has outlets at The Mall at Marathon (☎ 242-393-6166) at Robinson and Marathon Rds, and in the Palmdale

Shopping Centre (☎ 242-322-8597), located on Madeira St.

Libraries
The paltry public library (☎ 242-322-4907) at Shirley and Parliament Sts is dedicated mostly to works of popular fiction, and it has an eclectic miscellany of magazines, most of them rather tattered. Its hours are 10 am to 8 pm Monday to Thursday, 10 am to 5 pm Friday, and from 10 am to 4 pm Saturday.

You will also find public libraries at Fox Hill (☎ 242-324-1458), on Mackey St (☎ 242-322-1096), and on Blue Hill Rd (☎ 242-322-1056).

The largest collection is at the College of The Bahamas Library (☎ 242-323-8552) on Poinciana Dr, open 8 am to 9 pm weekdays year-round, and also 9 am to 5 pm Saturday except July to September.

See also the Historical Library & Museum section in this chapter.

Publications
The Bahamas Historical Society (☎ 242-322-4231), PO Box SS-6833, Nassau, Bahamas, sells booklets and the *Journal of the Bahamian Historical Society*, an annual report with scholarly articles on the islands. The Bahamas Information Services (☎ 242-328-1345), in the Rodney E Bain Bldg at Shirley and Parliament Sts, publishes a monthly newsletter called *Infoserve*; the mailing address is PO Box N-8172, Nassau, Bahamas.

Laundry
Most hotels will arrange laundry and dry cleaning. Self-service laundromats are scattered around residential districts; there are none at Cable Beach. The nearest to downtown is Superwash (☎ 242-323-4018) at Nassau St and Boyd Rd. Main Street Laundromat (☎ 242-394-8196) has a pickup and delivery service 7 am to 9:30 pm daily.

Medical Services
The main facility is the government-run, full-service Princess Margaret Hospital

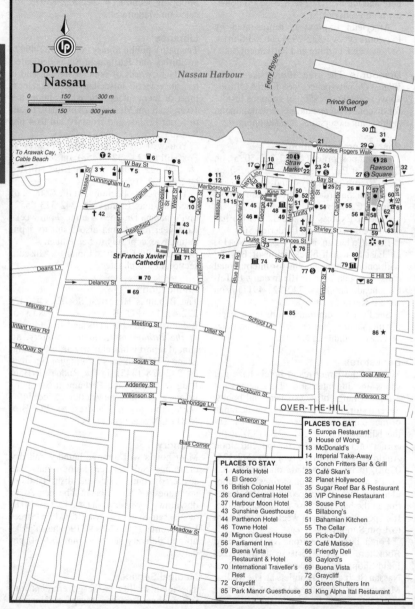

Downtown Nassau

Nassau Harbour

Prince George Wharf

To Arawak Cay, Cable Beach

Straw Market

Rawson Square

St Francis Xavier Cathedral

OVER-THE-HILL

PLACES TO STAY

1 Astoria Hotel
4 El Greco
16 British Colonial Hotel
26 Grand Central Hotel
37 Harbour Moon Hotel
43 Sunshine Guesthouse
44 Parthenon Hotel
46 Towne Hotel
49 Mignon Guest House
56 Parliament Inn
69 Buena Vista
     Restaurant & Hotel
70 International Traveller's
     Rest
72 Graycliff
85 Park Manor Guesthouse

PLACES TO EAT

5 Europa Restaurant
9 House of Wong
13 McDonald's
14 Imperial Take-Away
15 Conch Fritters Bar & Grill
23 Café Skan's
32 Planet Hollywood
35 Sugar Reef Bar & Restaurant
36 VIP Chinese Restaurant
38 Souse Pot
45 Billabong's
51 Bahamian Kitchen
55 The Cellar
56 Pick-a-Dilly
62 Café Matisse
66 Friendly Deli
68 Gaylord's
69 Buena Vista
72 Graycliff
80 Green Shutters Inn
83 King Alpha Ital Restaurant

NEW PROVIDENCE

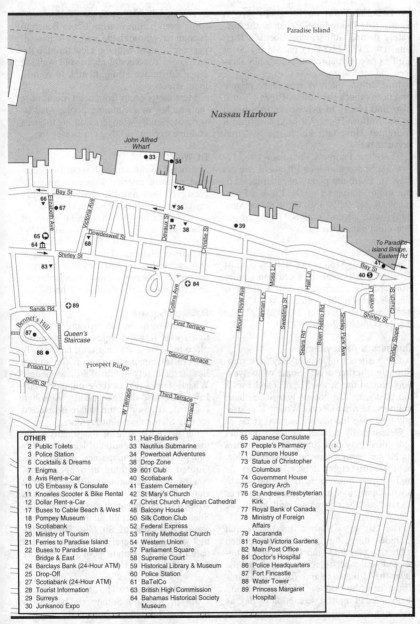

Paradise Island

Nassau Harbour

John Alfred Wharf

● 33

■ 34

▼ 35

▼ 36

Bay St

66 ◄
● 67

Elizabeth Ave

Victoria Ave

Dowdeswell St

■ 37 ▼ 38

Devaux St

Christie St

● 39

65 ⌖
64 🏛

68

Shirley St

To Paradise
Island Bridge,
Eastern Rd

Bay St

41 ▼

83 ▼

Collins Ave

✚ 84

40 🅢

Mount Royal Ave

Moss Ln

Cannan Ln

Hall Ln

Lovers Ln

Church St

Shirley St

Sands Rd

✚ 89

First Terrace

Sweeting St

Sears Rd

Buen Retiro Rd

Shirley Park Ave

Shirley Slope

Bennet's Hill

87 ●

Queen's
Staircase

Second Terrace

Prison Ln

88 ●

North St

Prospect Ridge

Third Terrace

W Terrace

E Terrace

OTHER		
2 Public Toilets	31 Hair-Braiders	65 Japanese Consulate
3 Police Station	33 Nautilus Submarine	67 People's Pharmacy
6 Cocktails & Dreams	34 Powerboat Adventures	71 Dunmore House
7 Enigma	38 Drop Zone	73 Statue of Christopher
8 Avis Rent-a-Car	39 601 Club	Columbus
10 US Embassy & Consulate	40 Scotiabank	74 Government House
11 Knowles Scooter & Bike Rental	41 Eastern Cemetery	75 Gregory Arch
12 Dollar Rent-a-Car	42 St Mary's Church	76 St Andrews Presbyterian
17 Buses to Cable Beach & West	47 Christ Church Anglican Cathedral	Kirk
19 Scotiabank	48 Balcony House	77 Royal Bank of Canada
20 Ministry of Tourism	50 Silk Cotton Club	78 Ministry of Foreign
21 Ferries to Paradise Island	52 Federal Express	Affairs
22 Buses to Paradise Island	53 Trinity Methodist Church	79 Jacaranda
Bridge & East	54 Western Union	81 Royal Victoria Gardens
24 Barclays Bank (24-Hour ATM)	57 Parliament Square	82 Main Post Office
25 Drop-Off	58 Supreme Court	84 Doctor's Hospital
27 Scotiabank (24-Hour ATM)	59 Historical Library & Museum	86 Police Headquarters
28 Tourist Information	60 Police Station	87 Fort Fincastle
29 Surreys	61 BaTelCo	88 Water Tower
30 Junkanoo Expo	63 British High Commission	89 Princess Margaret
	64 Bahamas Historical Society	Hospital
	Museum	

(☎ 242-322-2861) on Elizabeth Ave at Sands Rd. Immediately east is the privately owned, full-service Doctor's Hospital (☎ 242-322-8411) on Shirley St at Collins Ave. Both provide emergency services and acute care.

In addition, many doctors have private practices (check the Yellow Pages). You'll also find plenty of private dentists listed in the Yellow Pages. Or head to Princess Margaret Hospital, which has a dental department.

There's a People's Pharmacy (☎ 242-356-9806) downtown on Elizabeth Ave off Bay St. There are plenty of pharmacies in the major shopping malls. Lowe's Pharmacy (☎ 242-322-7430) is the major company, with several outlets. There are no late-night pharmacies.

Emergency

There are pea-green police stations in most districts; you'll rarely be more than 2 miles from one. For emergencies, call ☎ 919. You can also reach the police at ☎ 242-322-4444, an ambulance at 242-322-2221, or the Red Cross at 242-323-7370.

Dangers & Annoyances

A few hustlers hang around Bay St, surreptitiously offering drugs. Some of the vendors around the Straw Market can be a bit too pushy, as can one or two of the hairbraiders at Prince George Wharf. They usually take your 'no thanks' in good grace.

Occasionally a hotel doorman or other individual may hint subtly that drugs or a nighttime partner can be made available, but these are offered in an offhand way. At night a few hookers hang around downtown, hoping to snare the amorous sailor or tourist, but their presence will hardly be noticed.

The city does have a rough side that includes muggings and murders, armed robberies of banks and stores, and drug-related violence, relegated mostly to the Over-the-Hill area (Bains Town and Grants Town neighborhoods). This area should be avoided at night. Use caution by day, as the area's down-at-the-heels quality is aggravated by the presence of 'Jonesers' (drug users). Jitneys from Cable Beach to Nassau pass through the area; most passengers are content with the view through the windows. You should also avoid walking alone downtown at night; stick to well-lit main streets.

Most thefts occur from hotel rooms or at the beaches or swimming pools. Also be wary of friendly strangers wanting to assist you in carrying your bags or belongings.

DOWNTOWN

The heart of downtown Nassau is a compact historic district whose many well-preserved 18th- and 19th-century buildings evoke the colorful past.

Before setting out on a walking tour of downtown, obtain a copy of *Nassau's Historic Buildings* by C Sieghbert Russell (Bahamas National Trust). If the heat is oppressive, hop aboard a canopied surrey, the picturesque horse-drawn coaches available for hire at Prince George Wharf.

Rawson Square

The heart of town, the zero milestone for tourists, is Rawson Square. It's a natural place to begin a walking tour, particularly for cruise-ship passengers, as the square lies immediately south of Prince George Wharf, within two or three minutes' walk from the cruise-ship gangplanks. Although it is pedestrian-only, the square is bisected by Bay St, the main thoroughfare.

On the north side of the square is the main tourist information office, where you can pick up free maps and information. Guided walking tours also begin here. Nearby, note the patinated life-size bronze statue **Bahamian Woman**, which honors women's role during 'years of adversity.' She holds a small child. In the center of the square is a **bust of Sir Milo Butler**, the first governor-general of the independent nation, and a fountain pool with leaping bronze dolphins.

Parliament Square The area immediately south of Rawson Square on Bay St is known as Parliament Square for its con-

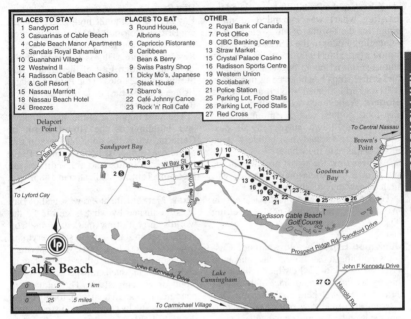

PLACES TO STAY
1 Sandyport
3 Casuarinas of Cable Beach
4 Cable Beach Manor Apartments
5 Sandals Royal Bahamian
10 Guanahani Village
12 Westwind II
14 Radisson Cable Beach Casino & Golf Resort
15 Nassau Marriott
18 Nassau Beach Hotel
24 Breezes

PLACES TO EAT
3 Round House, Albrions
6 Capriccio Ristorante
8 Caribbean Bean & Berry
9 Swiss Pastry Shop
11 Dicky Mo's, Japanese Steak House
17 Sbarro's
22 Café Johnny Canoe
23 Rock 'n' Roll Café

OTHER
2 Royal Bank of Canada
7 Post Office
8 CIBC Banking Centre
13 Straw Market
15 Crystal Palace Casino
16 Radisson Sports Centre
19 Western Union
20 Scotiabank
21 Police Station
25 Parking Lot, Food Stalls
26 Parking Lot, Food Stalls
27 Red Cross

NEW PROVIDENCE

clave of all-important public buildings. On three sides of the square, they are the office of the Lead of the Opposition (on the left), the House of Assembly (right), and the Senate (facing Bay St). It's amazing to think that these three twee buildings are the center of government! The pink-and-white Georgian neoclassical buildings – built between 1805 and 1813 – are modeled on Governor Tyron's Palace in New Bern, the ancient capital of New Carolina. In their midst, facing north over Bay St, is the **Queen Victoria Statue**, unveiled in 1905 yet portraying the monarch as a young woman. She gleams alabaster-white in the sunlight but looks decidedly unamused as she peers down on passersby.

You can peek inside the House of Assembly to watch proceedings when it's in session. Arrangements can be made at the House Office of the Clerk of Courts (☎ 242-322-7500). Note its green carpet, symbolizing the English meadow where

King John was forced to sign the Magna Carta in 1215. The Senate also has a visitors' gallery, with tickets given out free on a first-come, first-served basis.

Supreme Court Immediately south of Parliament Square is the Supreme Court, a newer Georgian edifice between Parliament St and Bank Ln. Here bewigged and be-gowned judges perform their duties.

A few yards farther north is the small **Garden of Remembrance**, with a cenotaph honoring Bahamian soldiers who died in the two world wars (note the plaque to four members of the Royal Bahamas Defence Force killed in 1980 when their patrol vessel, *Flamingo*, was attacked by Cuban MiGs).

Prince George Wharf
The historic cruise-ship wharf, north of Rawson Square and Bay St, is the gateway to Nassau for 1.6 million visitors a year! It

dates back to the Prohibition era, when the existing wharf was expanded to make room for the dozens of ships engaged in smuggling liquor to the USA. After Prohibition's repeal in 1933, it sat virtually idle until the tourist boom began in the 1960s and cruise ships began arriving in earnest.

The wharf is fronted by bustling **Woodes Rogers Walk**, lined with souvenir stalls, fast-food outlets, and a canopied stand where horse-drawn surreys await customers. There's a shady hair-braiders' stand at the entrance to the wharf.

At press time the wharf area was in the midst of a handsome makeover that will include new digs for the Junkanoo Expo.

Ferries to Paradise Island also leave from Woodes Rogers Walk (see the Getting There & Away section).

Junkanoo Expo The old wharfside Customs building today houses the Junkanoo Expo (☎ 242-356-2731), which tells of the history and cultural importance of the annual Junkanoo festival held each Boxing Day (December 26) and New Year's Eve throughout the islands. The museum displays some of the elaborate winning costumes and floats, plus goatskin drums, cowbells, and other paraphernalia that make Junkanoo the colorful highlight of the social calendar. It's open 9 am to 5 pm daily except holidays; US$2/US50¢ adults/children.

Hair Braids

If your hair is more than an inch long, you won't get 5 yards along the beach or Prince George Wharf before someone will approach you and ask if you'd like your hair braided. Braiders even have their own braiding booth just outside the wharf.

Some people choose to get a token braid or two, while others have all their locks braided and laced with colored beads. Braiding costs US$2 per braid or about US$20 for a headful.

Once you're braided, you may need to apply sunscreen to protect newly exposed scalp. ■

Bay St

Bay St runs west to the high-rise, colonial-era **British Colonial Hotel** at the junction with Navy Lion Rd, five blocks west of Rawson Square. This is the heart of the shopping district. East of the square, Bay St runs about 2 miles to the Paradise Island Bridge (see the East of Downtown section in this chapter).

The most imposing of the many impressive buildings is the **Royal Bank of Canada**, which has done business in this grandiose stone structure since 1919. Opposite is another notable edifice: the **Masonic Temple**, dedicated in 1885.

Straw Market Life at the west end of Bay St is dominated by what is said to be the world's largest straw market. Some 160 vendors set up stalls daily to sell everything from straw-work to T-shirts, woodcarvings, shell souvenirs, and other island handicrafts. You can watch craftspeople whittling wood or weaving straw. The undisputed matriarch is Diana Thompson, fondly called 'Aunt Di.' She has been selling straw since the early 1930s (from the age of 10), when the market was in Rawson Square and received most of its trade from cruise ships such as *The Monarch of Bermuda, The Queen of Bermuda*, and *The Normandy* during the winter season.

Pompey Museum The Bahamas' history is told through displays at this small museum (☎ 242-326-2566) in Vendue House, one block west of the Straw Market. The building was once a slave-auction site, and the museum is named in memory of a slave who led a rebellion. The exhibits include artifacts, historical documents, and drawings tracing events from the Lucayan period to the bootlegging era. It also features an exhibit of naive paintings by noted artist Amos Ferguson. It's open 10 am to 4:30 pm Monday to Friday and 10 am to 1 pm Saturday; US$1/US50¢ adults/children.

Balcony House This beautiful two-story cedar structure – a restored 18th-century merchant's house that was named for its

The Supreme Court and cenotaph

prominent balcony supported by wooden knee braces – is on Market St just off Bay St. The original slave kitchen remains, as does the staircase, taken from a sailing ship. It is now a local history museum, open 10 am to 1 pm and 2 to 4 pm Monday, Wednesday, and Friday; donations are accepted. Call the Pompey Museum (see above) for more information.

Shirley St
Shirley St parallels Bay St at the foot of Prospect Ridge. Its attractions include historic buildings, museums, and gardens.

Trinity Methodist Church This delightful church, at the west end of Shirley St on Frederick St at Trinity Pl, was originally planned for a congregation of 800 people. Alas, the four carpenters sent from Scotland all succumbed to yellow fever, and a more modest church was built in 1861. It had only been open a year when it was blown down by a hurricane. The current church dates from 1869 and was significantly repaired following damage in the 1928 hurricane.

Historical Library & Museum The library (☎ 242-322-4907), between Parliament St and Bank Ln one block south of Rawson Square, is housed in an unusual octagonal building erected in the 1790s as a jail (the dungeon still exists below ground). Convicts gave way to books in 1873. Note the model of the *Arethusa*, the rumrunning schooner of Captain Bill McCoy.

A museum on the second floor, dedicated to the peaceful Lucayan Indians, has a motley collection of artifacts, including bones, a few old maps, engravings, photographs, a bell, a coin press, shells, stamps, and old parchments.

Both are open 10 am to 8 pm Monday to Thursday, 10 am to 5 pm Friday, and 10 am to 4 pm Saturday; admission is free.

Royal Victoria Gardens This opulent garden, across from the library on the ridge to the south of Shirley St, is on the site of the sprawling Royal Victoria Hotel (now partly in ruins). Pathways lead past more than 300 species of tropical plants, many sown when the resplendent three-story Royal Vic opened in 1861 – a true relic of the US Civil War. Overnight the hotel established itself as a popular rendezvous for blockade-runners, Confederate officers, Union spies, and other colorful characters attracted by the salubrious climate and boisterous parties. After the war, the hotel went through lean times. Alas, she breathed her last as a hotel in 1971, when she was consumed by flames. Parts of the extant remains house government ministries.

Bahamas Historical Society Museum
This impressive little place (☎ 242-322-4231), on Shirley St at Elizabeth Ave, has a modest miscellany of artifacts and documents tracing the islands' history from Lucayan times to Blackbeard to the contemporary era. It's worth the admission merely to admire the beautiful model of the Spanish galleon *Santa Luceno*. A free history lecture is offered at 6 pm every last Thursday of the month. The mailing address is PO Box SS-6833, Nassau, Bahamas. It's

Slaves built Nassau's Queen's Staircase.

open 10 am to 4 pm weekdays and 10 am to noon Saturday; US$1/US50¢ adults/children.

Collins House Continue east to Collins Ave and you'll come upon this imposing neoclassical building, built in 1929 by the Honorable Ralph Gregory Collins, a respected citizen, to replace the family home destroyed in a hurricane the prior year. The beautiful two-story property was later used as a school and in 1971 took on its present role as the government's Ministry of Education and Culture.

Bennet's Hill
Elizabeth Ave slopes south past Princess Margaret Hospital, uphill to Bennet's Hill (part of Prospect Ridge).

Queen's Staircase At the south end of Elizabeth Ave, a passageway and 90-foot-deep gorge in Prospect Ridge lead to Fort Fincastle and a water tower (see below). The staircase at the end of the passageway, a much-touted curiosity, was cut from solid limestone by slaves, beginning in the 1790s, with the intent of constructing a roadway through Prospect Ridge. Emancipation was proclaimed before it could be finished.

The box canyon is cool and shady, and it has been beautified with towering palms. Rainwater oozes from the walls, feeding prolific epiphytes. The passageway is also lined with souvenir stalls. At its end, the Queen's Staircase (also known as the '66 Steps') leads up to the fort. Freelance guides will hustle you at the top. They'll immediately launch into the staircase's history. If you don't want their services, say so at this stage and they'll accept in good grace. But the guides can provide some intriguing anecdotes to liven up your viewing. They'll expect a tip (what you pay is up to you, depending on the length and quality of the spiel).

Fort Fincastle This tiny fortress was built in 1793 by Lord Dunmore. Why it was whimsically built in the shape of a paddle-wheel steamer isn't clear. The fort faces east and was intended to guard 'all the Town and the Road to the Eastward.' It was never put to the test and later served as a lighthouse and signal station. It lies partly in ruins but retains intriguing old cannon. Many devout locals gather at lunchtime and on weekends to the north of the fort for a little (but voluble) wailing in praise of the Lord. Admission is free.

Water Tower The tall tower (☎ 242-322-2442) behind the fort was erected in 1928 to maintain water pressure on the island. It is 126 feet tall and provides a marvelous panoramic view of Nassau. You can walk up the narrow, winding staircase – there are 216 steps – or take the elevator. Tours are offered 8 am to 5 pm daily except Thursday; US50¢.

W & E Hill Sts

These two streets, which run parallel to Nassau Harbour along the north side of Prospect Ridge, extend from West St to East St. The two streets are joined by Duke St, running east to west for one block between them. They're lined with important historical buildings, including impressive old homes such as **Jacaranda**, at the corner of E Hill and Parliament Sts. Once owned by Sir Harry Oakes, it was also home to the Duke of Windsor during part of his tenure in The Bahamas.

St Francis Xavier Cathedral This Roman Catholic cathedral, at the corner of West and W Hill Sts, dates from 1885. It has a long, slender nave topped by a bell tower, illumined within at night. Many prominent Protestants of the time resented the incursion of the Catholics and ascribed to the hands of God the bolt of lightning that struck the church during construction, killing a workman and doing significant damage. Further confirming their suspicions, Rev Robert Dunlop, the Presbyterian minister who sold the original site to the Catholics, died of a heart attack while preaching at *his* pulpit at St Andrews Presbyterian Kirk.

Dunmore House The huge three-story balconied mansion, across from the cathedral on W Hill St, was erected by Lord Dunmore after his arrival as governor in 1787. Dunmore leased it to the government as his official residence and finally sold it to the local government in 1801. It later became an officers' quarters and a military hospital, and also served as a Roman Catholic mission and the private residence of Chief Justice William Doyle (it is still colloquially called 'Villa Doyle').

The mansion was in great disrepair at press time, but a restoration was soon to begin. The National Art Gallery of The Bahamas was to take over the mansion and open its doors in 1998. Don't hold your breath: An anonymous donor contributed US$1.5 million for the restoration, but most of the additional US$3 million needed hadn't yet been secured.

Graycliff This beautiful building, on W Hill St at the corner of Blue Hill Rd, began life as the home of privateer John Howard Graysmith and was built partly on the ruins of the oldest church in The Bahamas, erected in 1694 but destroyed by the Spaniards in 1703. It became a hostelry in 1844, when it was known as 'Victoria House,' where 'Gentlemen and Ladies can be accommodated with Board and Lodging.' It later passed into the hands of the Earl and Countess of Dudley; in 1974 it again became a hotel.

Over the years it has received many prominent guests, including Sir Winston Churchill, who lodged as the guest of the Dudleys. Today it is owned by a prominent Italian, Enrico Garzaroli, who is setting up a **cigar factory** next door, employing Cuban cigar rollers. It is perhaps the city's finest hotel and restaurant, flush with antiques and redolent with charm . . . but it is not a museum! (See the Places to Stay section for more details.)

Government House The conch-pink Georgian structure commanding the city from atop Mt Fitzwilliam, just south of W Hill St, is the official residence of The

Bahamas' governor-general. The site has been in government hands since 1799, although governors lived there prior to that time; the original home was built in 1737 by Governor Fitzwilliam (1733-38). A new structure was built in 1806. Additional wings were added during the 20th century, including a ballroom, but the entire house was swiftly destroyed by a hurricane in 1929. The current building was completed in 1932. The lavish decorations date from 1940, when the Duke of Windsor arrived to take up his post as governor of the colony.

Visitors can walk the grounds for a close look at the building, but you'll have to request permission from the guards, who must accompany you. *One two! One two!* You can 'have a cuppa' with the governess (see the People to People sidebar in the Facts for the Visitor chapter) or watch the Changing of the Guard twice a month.

Check out the **statue of Christopher Columbus**, depicting him in rather jaunty outfit on the steps overlooking Duke St. It was designed by US writer Washington Irving – who dressed the 15th-century Genoese explorer in the garb of Irving's day – and was presented to Governor Smythe in 1830. At night Columbus is suffused by the glow of colored spotlights.

A stone arch topped with iron railings – **Gregory Arch** – spans Market St (cutting through Prospect Ridge) at the east end of Government House grounds. It was named for Governor John Gregory in 1852.

St Andrews Presbyterian Kirk 'The Kirk,' below Government House on Duke and Market Sts, is a handsome crenellated church that owes its existence to a Loyalist who settled in Nassau at the end of the American Revolution. In 1798 he established the St Andrew's Society of 55 Scots to 'cultivate good understanding and social intercourse.' The Freemasons laid the cornerstone in 1810, and the church has since undergone many architectural changes. Its ministers traditionally were culled from the Presbyterian clergy of Edinburgh and Glasgow.

Follow the curling road uphill past Gregory Arch to continue along E Hill St.

Ministry of Foreign Affairs East of Gregory Arch at the corner of Glinton St, boasting a fine view over the city, is a beautiful pink Georgian edifice fronted by cannon. The government's foreign affairs are handled within. Outside you'll see a modern purple sculpture – *El Vigía* (The Old Man) – by Mexican sculptor Sebastian. It was a gift from the Mexican government for the 1992 quincentennial of Columbus' landing.

Marlborough St & W Bay St
The area west of Bay St is dominated by Marlborough St, a busy three-block-long street that leads to W Bay St and thence to Cable Beach. Much of the north side of Marlborough St, once occupied by Fort Nassau, is taken up by the **British Colonial Hotel**, fronted by a statue dedicated to Governor Woodes Rogers, plus a rusty anchor and cannon. Remnants of the old walls can be seen on the hotel grounds. Out front are the remains of a well said to have been used by the notorious pirate Blackbeard.

Marlborough St runs east into King St, which parallels Bay St for two blocks. This is the heart of financial affairs, concentrated between Cumberland and Market Sts. Several old cut-stone buildings here are now fine restaurants.

Queen St, which ascends south from Marlborough St, is lined with fine balconied colonial homes, notably the **Devonshire House** at No 11. Two blocks east, Cumberland St boasts **Cumberland House** and **The Deanery**, described as 'the quintessential trademark of colonial Bahamian architecture.'

At Marlborough St's west end, it becomes Virginia St. Prim **St Mary's Church** is found on Virginia St; it was built in 1868 and could have fallen out of a postcard depicting the English countryside. The junction of Marlborough and West Sts has several fine old balconied houses.

Greek Orthodox Church Nassau has a large Greek community, which is served by the Kurikon, also called the Greek Orthodox Church of the Annunciation, erected in 1932. One block south of the Marlborough and West Sts junction, it's intimate and beautiful within, with an exquisite gilt chandelier. Most mornings a small congregation can be found here, chanting you back in time and place to Mykonos or Crete. *Marvelous!* About 70 local families religiously attend (pardon the pun).

Christ Church Anglican Cathedral This striking cathedral on King St dates from 1753, with additions built during the last century. Its splendid interior includes a wood-beamed roof, stained glass, and pendulous Spanish-style chandeliers. The cathedral is topped by a square bell tower.

The current structure is the fourth. The original church was destroyed in 1684 by the Spaniards. Its successors were leveled during the French-Spanish invasion in 1703 and by the ravages of weather and termites.

OVER-THE-HILL

This middle- and low-income area – bounded by East St and Blue Hill Rd to the east and west, and Prospect and Blue Hill ridges to the north and south – is the heart and soul of African-Bahamian life in Nassau and the source of its most passionate politics (former Prime Minister Sir Lynden Pindling hails from here).

The area began as a settlement for free blacks and slaves liberated from slave ships after 1807 by the British Navy. After emancipation in 1834, the area – comprising the villages of Grants Town and Bains Town and, farther east, Fox Hill – expanded. Most inhabitants were destitute and lived in squalor.

As incomes rose during the 20th century, the area picked itself up by its bootstraps. Over-the-Hill, however, is still Nassau's seedy side, although the worst shanties are gone, and there are pleasant middle-class pockets amid the potholed roads lined with wood-and-tin huts and renovated cottages gaily painted in prime Caribbean colors.

This is where you'll find lively traditional culture. Games of *warri* – an African board game – are played beneath shade trees. Many locals paint or make handicrafts. The local bars have rake 'n' scrape bands. And the churches here are among the more lively on New Providence. Worth visiting are **Wesley Methodist Church** (dating from 1847) and the **St Agnes Anglican Church** (one year younger), both at Market and Cockburn Sts.

This is not Haiti or Jamaica. Over-the-Hill is a veritable utopia compared to the sordid ghettos and slums of some Caribbean islands. But caution is needed, as Nassau's ruffians and drug users and pushers are concentrated here.

EAST OF DOWNTOWN
Potter's Cay

The liveliest market in town takes place daily beneath the Paradise Island Bridge, on a manmade cay where fishing boats arrive each day from other islands, carrying conch, crab, jack, mackerel, spiny lobster,

A messy day's work at Potter's Cay

fruit, and vegetables. Locals sell the harvest – alive, dead, dried, filleted – from stalls. You can watch them dicing vegetables, chopping up turtles, and preparing conch. Some of the friendly sellers might jest or even play tricks with you. If tamarind is proffered, don't pop it into your mouth. It tastes ghastly!

The mail boats serving the Family Islands also berth here. It's a great place to hang out and watch the pandemonium whenever a boat arrives or prepares to embark.

Eastern Cemetery

Near the juncture of Bay and Dowdeswell Sts, this grassy cemetery holds the remains of pirates and other rascals executed during the past three centuries. The tumbledown tombs are above ground.

Behind is **St Matthew's Church**, a handsome, tall-steepled edifice. Dating from 1802, it was originally built with a low roof to avoid hurricane damage. The cemetery to the west of the churchyard is called the 'Jew's Cemetery.'

The Retreat

This 11-acre garden, 200 yards south of Shirley St on Village Rd, is the headquarters of the Bahamas National Trust (BNT, ☎ 242-393-1317, fax 242-393-4978), housed in a 150-year-old building. It claims one of the largest private collections of palms in the world (176 species, many quite rare, representing more than half of all known genera of palms), begun in 1925 by original property owners Arthur and Margaret Langlois. The star of the show, at least until 1989, was a rare and awesome Ceylonese talipot palm that expended all its energy in 1986 on a once-in-a-lifetime bloom and then died. But other prize species live on, including the Cuban petticoat palm and fan palms from Borneo, growing vigorously beneath a forest canopy.

Other specimens include hardwoods such as mahogany. Native orchids grace the trunks, and splendid ferns nestle in the limestone holes in which the palms are planted.

Half-hour tours are offered, beginning at 11:45 am on Tuesday, Wednesday, and Thursday; US$2. The mailing address is PO Box N-4105, Nassau, Bahamas.

Fort Montagu

There's not much to draw you to this diminutive fort, though the place is intact and the cannon *in situ*. The oldest of Nassau's remaining strongholds, it was built in 1741 to guard the eastern approach to Nassau Harbour. It never fired its cannon in anger. It's closed to the public and is merely a curiosity in passing.

Eastern Rd

The shoreline park south of Fort Montagu – a shady picnic and trysting spot – is lined with palms and casuarina trees. Two hundred yards from the fort, at the junction of Shirley St and Eastern Rd, is **Montagu Ramp**, a wharf where locals bring fish and conch ashore to clean and sell. It's a very colorful place. You'll smell it well before you see it!

Eastern Rd skirts Montagu Bay through the subdivision of Blair. This windward shore is quite scenic as far as the **East End Lighthouse** on McPherson's Bend at the easternmost point of New Providence. Just south is **Yamacraw Beach**, where the road turns west and heads inland through a middle-class residential area, ending at **Her Majesty's Prison**.

Eastern Rd is paralleled by a slope lined with upscale villas that are festooned in bougainvillea and framed by lush lawns. Sitting atop the ridge 2 miles south of Fort Montagu is **Blackbeard's Tower**, a semi-derelict cut-stone tower that, according to local lore, was built by Edward Teach – 'Blackbeard' – as a lookout tower. Historians point out that it was actually built in the late 18th century, long after the infamous pirate had been killed. The view is good, but the place isn't worth the journey in its own right.

To reach it, you nip up an unmarked path next to a green-and-white house called 'Tower Leigh,' 400 yards south of Fox Hill Rd.

Fox Hill

Fox Hill Rd leads half a mile south from Eastern Rd, over the hill to the village of Fox Hill (also known as Sandilands), which has a simple, rural charm, drawn from its many old wood-and-limestone houses set amid copses. It began life in the 18th century as a free-slave settlement named Creek Village. Last century, Robert Sandilands, Chief Justice of the Bahamas, bought much of the area and distributed land grants to blacks for £10 or the equivalent in labor. The recipients named their settlement after their benefactor.

Freedom Park, at the juncture of Fox Hill Rd and Bernard Rd, is the center of town and the setting each year for Emancipation Day celebrations on August 1.

Other highlights include **St Anne's Anglican Church** on Fox Hill Rd, dating from 1867; and fortresslike **St Augustine's Monastery** (☎ 242-364-1331) atop a rocky perch on Bernard Rd. This working monastery was designed by Father Jerome, the itinerant architect-cleric who blessed Cat and Long islands with beautiful churches (see the sidebar on Father Jerome in the Cat Island chapter). The imposing building dates from 1947 and is still used by Benedictine monks, who give guided tours (donations are appreciated) . . . a fascinating glimpse of monastic life. A college – it's run by the monks – is attached.

WEST OF DOWNTOWN

W Bay St leads westward along Nassau Harbour. About a half-mile from the British Colonial Hotel, you'll see remains of a battery of cannon on the harbor side, immediately next to the road. A cricket ground – **Clifford Park** (also called 'Haynes' Oval') – is to the south; it's the site of the annual Independence Day festivities on July 10.

Fort Charlotte

This fort (☎ 242-322-7500), the largest in The Bahamas, was built between 1787 and 1790 to guard the west entrance to Nassau Harbour. Sitting on the ridge above Clifford Park, it is intact and today is painted white. The deep moat and exterior walls were cut from solid rock and the walls buttressed by cedars. Lord Dunmore estimated its cost as a 'trifling' £4000, and to ensure the approval of the crown, proposed to name it Charlotte, after the consort of King George III. Within a year Dunmore had exceeded all resources. Reluctantly the English War Office forwarded the extra £17,846 required to complete the fort. Dunmore's folly was ill-conceived, with the troops' barracks erected directly in the line of fire!

Today its moat, dungeon, underground tunnels, and bombproof chambers make an intriguing excursion, enhanced by a re-creation of a torture chamber, much like Madame Toussaud's house of horrors. Tours, led by guides in period costume, are offered every half-hour from 9 am to 4:30 pm daily.

Botanical Garden

Immediately west of the fort is the botanical garden (☎ 242-323-5975), on Chippingham Rd 200 yards south of W Bay St. It was constructed in 1951 on the site of an old rock quarry (known as 'the pit') that once supplied stones for construction during colonial times. The lush 26-acre Fantasia has more than 600 species of tropical plants – many indigenous to The Bahamas – plus lily ponds, grottoes, and a waterfall fountain donated by the government of China. Poincianas explode in riotous color. There's even a re-creation of a Lucayan village with thatched *bohios*. The gardens slope uphill to the east, offering fine views. The garden is open 9 am to 4:30 pm weekdays and 9 am to 4 pm weekends; US$1/US50¢ adults/children.

Ardastra Gardens & Zoo

The most impressive of Nassau's several gardens-cum-zoos, this privately run 6-acre lot (☎ 242-323-5806, fax 242-323-7232) is on Columbus Ave off Chippingham Rd, 100 yards southwest of the Botanical Garden. Its lush confines boast about 50 species of animals, birds, and reptiles from around the world. Indigenous species of flora and fauna include agoutis, hutias, snakes, and the endangered Bahama parrot, which, uniquely, is bred in captivity here. The zoo also has a large collection of non-native species, including monkeys, caimans, and sleek cats such as jaguars and ocelots. The undisputed highlight, however, is the gang of West Indian flamingos trained to strut their stuff on voice command at 11 am and 2 and 4 pm daily. The birds get Sunday off.

Facilities include a snack bar and toilets. It's open 9 am to 4:30 pm daily (last admission is at 4:30 pm). It is closed Christmas Day. Admission costs US$10/US$5 adults/children.

Arawak Cay

This manmade 'island' lies north of W Bay St in front of Fort Charlotte. It serves as a commercial dock and water-storage area for the barges that bring Nassau's water supply from Andros. The entrance to the cay gets lively at lunchtime and on weekends, when locals gather for conch and fresh fish sold from fancifully decorated wooden stalls. It's *the* local hangout, made more endearing by hot music.

Crystal Cay Marine Park

One of Nassau's renowned landmarks is a white spaceship-shaped structure hovering above the ocean off Silver Cay. The structure – the entrance to an underwater marine observatory – is the showpiece of the enticing Crystal Cay marine park (☎ 242-328-1036, fax 242-323-3202). You can reach it by following the access road that loops west around Arawak Cay.

Meant to familiarize visitors with the life of the seas, the facility, formerly Coral World, claims that it's the 'greatest show of natural marine life' in the Caribbean region. A self-guided tour leads visitors to shark tanks, turtle pools, marine gardens, a stingray pool, and other attractions, including a mangrove display, an educational aquarium, and a 'marine encounter pool' where kids can handle starfish and other seabed critters. The highlight of the

tour is a 20-foot descent below the ocean surface to the observatory to see marine life in its natural environment . . . a fish-eye view, as it were. (Be sure to visit on a calm day; when the sea is turbulent, visibility is greatly reduced.) There's also a circular tank with sharks and other large pelagics that you can watch being hand-fed by a scuba diver. There's even a snorkel trail that you can follow with mask and flippers (US$5 rental). Macaws hang out in the treetops, and there's also a flamingo pool where the national bird struts. A small beach has lounge chairs.

The facility was recently purchased by the Ruffin Group, a prominent investment company at the forefront of the Cable Beach renaissance. In 1997 the company began a grand rejuvenation of the facility that should add several new features, including the Seashells Restaurant, a kiddies' theme park, and putting golf, with the intention of making Crystal Cay a full-day experience.

A ferry service operates between Crystal Cay and the Nassau Marriott (as does a free shuttle); it also runs every 30 minutes to and from Woodes Rogers Walk. Taxis are usually available from the parking lot. A jitney from the lot whisks visitors over the bridge to the park.

It's open 9 am to 6 pm daily; US$16 (US$8 for guests of the Nassau Marriott and Nassau Beach hotels).

CABLE BEACH

Cable Beach is a self-contained resort 3 miles west of downtown Nassau. The beach is named for the telegraphic cable laid from Florida in 1892 that came ashore here. Nassau's major resort hotels are here, hovering over a seemingly endless sliver of pure-white sand shelving into turquoise shallows. Dominating the scene is the garish, purple Nassau Marriott (formerly the Carnival Crystal Palace), even more garish at night, when a rainbow assortment of neon lights rims the exterior of its three towers. There are water sports and restaurants aplenty, plus golf, tennis, and the Crystal Palace Casino, but no *sites* of interest.

Cable Beach lines Goodman's (east) and Sandyport (west) bays, encircled by Delaport Point to the west and Brown's Point to the east. Near Brown's Point, the beach is called Goodman's Beach; it's popular with locals, who flock there on weekends and leave Cable Beach proper to tourists.

One mile east of Cable Beach is tiny **Saunders Beach**, popular with locals at lunchtime (they sit in their cars, munching cracked conch) and on weekends. At the west end of Cable Beach is Delaport Point, where a massive 144-acre, waterfront residential and resort development named Sandyport was only half-completed at press time.

Cable Beach is linked to downtown Nassau by W Bay St, which here becomes a wide boulevard (two lanes in each direction) with a landscaped central median complete with jogging track – the Tropical Walkway. Labels set in the walkway describe the flora. A constant stream of jitneys passes by, going to and from Nassau.

Discovery Island

For a break, you can head out to this small cay – formerly Balmoral Island – about a mile offshore from Cable Beach (see the New Providence map). It is now leased by the Sandals chain but is open to nonguests. It has its own beach, an atmospheric restaurant, and a lively bar with swim-up pool and Jacuzzi. Trails lead to quiet nooks.

Free ferries run regularly from Sandals Royal Bahamian at Cable Beach (for guests only). Ferries also operate from the pier between the Radisson and Marriott hotels on a regular basis, charging US$10 roundtrip.

ACTIVITIES

The Bahamas Sports & Aviation Information Centre (☎ 305-932-0051, 800-327-7678), 19495 Biscayne Blvd, Suite 809, Aventura, FL 33180, can provide information on what's cooking.

Diving & Snorkeling

New Providence offers superb diving close to its shores, including fantastic wall and

---

Dive & Snorkel Sites

New Providence has many excellent sites for diving and snorkeling:

Anchor – A coral head pokes out of a wall 60 feet below the surface, teeming with fish life.

Lost Ocean Blue Hole – This vertical cavern gapes in 30 feet of water on a sand bottom frequented by nurse sharks and stingrays. The cave bells out to 200 feet and deeper. There's a lobster-filled cavern at 80 feet.

Oasis Wall – This deep dive just off Old Fort Beach is known for reef corals all the way down to 200 feet. There's plenty of lobster and pelagics, too.

Razorback – It's named for the arcing ridge of coral-covered limestone that rises from a sand bottom before plummeting into the Tongue of the Ocean. The reef is a menagerie of fish. The wall attracts hammerhead sharks.

School House – This site features endless varieties of coral at depths rarely exceeding 20 feet. Fish life ranges from blennies and gobies to schooling yellowtail.

The Valley – Says *Skin Diving* magazine: 'Into the valley of death swam the 600 groupers. Coral to the left of them, coral to the right, and the Tongue of the Ocean just over the ridge. They spawned like there was no tomorrow.' Imagine . . . just you and the sharks watching the yearly group(er) sex. ∎

---

wreck dives. The most noted sites lie off the southwest coast between Coral Harbour and Lyford Cay, where several dive operators have facilities. There are plenty of operators with offices in Nassau and Cable Beach. Most upscale hotels also offer diving.

All dive operators also offer snorkeling, as do tour companies, which have trips to offshore cays. You can even go snorkeling with dolphins at Blue Lagoon Island; see Dolphin Encounters in the Paradise Island section for details.

Bahama Divers (☎ 242-393-5644/1466, bahdiver@bahamas.net.bs; in the USA ☎ 954-351-9533, 800-398-3483), at Nassau

Yacht Haven on E Bay St, offers a variety of dive trips, including the Lost Blue Hole (famous for its sharks and schools of stingrays) and wrecks. It has a three-hour learn-to-dive course as well as PADI certification courses (US$399). A single dive costs US$40; a two-tank dive costs US$60; a night dive is US$50. It rents equipment.

Coral Divers (☎ 242-362-1263, fax 242-362-2407) offers several dives, including a 'shark dive' for US$100 in which you watch sharks being hand-fed at Bull Shark Wall or Shark Buoy. A two-tank dive costs US$60; a night dive costs US$100. Snorkel trips cost US$25. It rents snorkel and scuba gear. The company will certify you. Write to Coral Divers at PO Box CB-11961, Nassau, Bahamas.

Other companies offering a full range of dive programs include Divers Haven (☎ 242-393-0869) on E Bay St, Diving Safaris (☎ 242-393-2522), and Sun Divers (☎ 242-325-8927).

See the West New Providence and South New Providence sections in this chapter for details on operators elsewhere on the island. For a list of prime sites, see the Dive & Snorkel Sites sidebar.

Boating & Sailing
You can charter boats from any of the following marinas:

Brown's Boat Basin, E Bay St (☎ 242-393-3331)
Claridge Marina, South Nassau near Yamacraw
    Beach (☎ 242-364-2219)
East Bay Yacht Basin, E Bay St
    (☎ /fax 242-394-1816)
Nassau Harbour Club & Marina, E Bay St
    (☎ 242-393-0771)
Nassau Yacht Haven, E Bay St
    (☎ 242-393-8173)

See the Getting There & Away and Outdoor Activities chapter for general information about sailing and chartering boats.

You can rent your own little speedboat from 'Genius' Jeffrey Stubbs at Coral Reef Charters (☎ 242-362-2058) at the East Bay Yacht Basin wharf, immediately south of Potter's Cay. A six-seater Excel costs US$175/350 half-/full day. Genius offers

hotel transfers (US$3.50 to downtown; US$7 to Cable Beach). It sounds like a pretty cool way to take yourself to an offshore cay.

Larger vessels can also be chartered, including the *King Fisher* (☎ 242-393-3739) and the *Chubasco* (☎ 242-322-8148, fax 242-326-4140, chubasco@nsn.com), which charters for US$300/500 half-/full day. Both are based at the wharf beneath the Paradise Island Bridge.

Sport Fishing
Nassau is a good base for sport fishing, with superb sites just 20 minutes away. Charters can be arranged at most major hotels or by calling any of the marinas listed under Boating & Sailing, above. Also try the Charter Boat Association (☎ 242-363-2335) or the following:

Born Free Charter Service ☎ 242-363-2003
Brown's Charter   ☎ 242-324-1215
Chubasco Charters   ☎ 242-322-8148

Several boats operate from Nassau Yacht Haven (see Boating & Sailing, above), from Hurricane Hole Marina on Paradise Island, and from the dock beneath the Paradise Island Bridge.

Boat Excursions
Dozens of day trips are offered, with options for snorkeling, diving, beach time, island visits, partying, sunset and dinner cruises, and other activities. A few vessels depart the Nassau waterfront; most depart the dock immediately west of the Paradise Island Bridge. See the Paradise Island section for details on cruises that depart Paradise Island.

From Nassau, Topsail Yacht Charters (☎ 242-393-0820) offers full-day cruises to Rose Island aboard the *Liberty Call*, *Riding High*, and *Wind Dance* sailboats. Half-day trips cost US$35, with picnic lunch and snorkeling. Full-day trips, a champagne-and-cocktail cruise, and a private dinner cruise are also offered.

The Booze&Cruise Co Ltd (☎ 242-393-3722) has four-hour booze-cruises aboard

Which Beach?

Cable Beach – The most beautiful beach on the main island is about 2 miles long and has plenty of water sports and activity. Hotels, restaurants, and bars line the beach.

Love Beach – This small, little-used beach near Gambier Village is about 12 miles west of downtown. There's good snorkeling, and Compass Point is at hand.

Orange Hill Beach – About 8 miles west of downtown, this small, narrow beach is popular with tourists and local families. There are a few restaurants and bars nearby.

Saunders Beach – Between Cable Beach and downtown, this small beach is favored by local families. It has no facilities.

South Ocean Beach – On the southwest side of the island, this beach is narrow, secluded, several miles long, and trodden by very few people. You'll find great scuba diving offshore. Facilities are limited to the South Ocean Golf & Beach Resort to the west and Adelaide to the east.

Western Esplanade Beach – On W Bay St, downtown Nassau's only beach stretches west from the British Colonial Hotel. Although it has limited attraction and no facilities, it's within minutes of downtown restaurants and hotels. It's popular with local men.

Paradise Island has its own beautiful beaches:

Cabbage Beach – This stunner stretches 2 miles along the north shore, with plenty of activity and water sports. Several resorts have facilities at the west end.

Paradise Beach – This beautiful beach curves gently along the northwest shore of the island; it is very lonesome to the west. The resorts have their own facilities, but nonguests can pay for privileges.

Pirate's Cove – This well-protected beauty nestles in its own cove and is the virtual private domain of the Holiday Inn Pirate's Cove Sunspree Resort. Nonguests can pay for privileges.

Snorkeler's Cove Beach – Another beauty, this beach is east of Cabbage Beach. It is favored by day-trippers on picnicking and snorkeling excursions from Nassau. ■

Lucayan Queen, departing Nassau Yacht Haven on E Bay St at 1:30 pm daily, for US$30. A full-day excursion costs US$50. It also has sunset cruises. Hotel transfers are provided.

Barefoot Sailing Cruises (☎ 242-393-0820, fax 242-393-5817) offers half- and full-day sailing and snorkel cruises to the outlying cays, plus a champagne sunset cruise. Private charters are also offered; prices start at US$370.

Hartley's Undersea Walk (☎ 242-393-8234/7569) offers a four-hour cruise that includes an escorted undersea walk with a difference. You'll don a roomy brass helmet with large glass windows for all-around viewing. You can even wear glasses! The half-day trip begins with a cruise aboard the *Pied Piper*, a 57-foot catamaran with a sun deck and lounge. Trips depart at 9:30 am and 1:30 pm daily from Nassau Yacht Haven. The trip costs US$36.

Powerboat Powerboat Adventures (☎ 242-327-5385, fax 242-328-5212) whisks you out to the Exumas at breakneck speed aboard 900-horsepower boats that depart the dock at Bay and Devaux Sts. The excursion includes shark feeding, snorkeling with stingrays at various cays, a barbecue lunch, and plenty of rum swizzles. Its postal address is PO Box CB-13315, Nassau, Bahamas.

Submarine *Seaworld Explorer* (☎ 242-356-2548), a 45-passenger semisubmarine, operates from Woodes Rogers Walk. Its air-con hull is lined with large windows below water level. The cruise takes in the coral reefs of the Sea Gardens Marine Park off the north shore; US$20.

The *Nautilus* (☎ 242-325-2876), a reconstructed submarine based at John Alfred Wharf at Bay and Devaux Sts, also offers trips.

Other Water Sports

Cable Beach offers every kind of beach and water activity, including parasailing, water-skiing, and windsurfing. Most resort hotels either include water sports in their rates or offer them as optional extras. However, few resorts offer *motorized* water sports, which are the domain of local entrepreneurs such as Sea Sports (☎ 242-327-6200) at the Marriott, which also offers sea kayaks, Hobie Cats, Sunfish, and sailboards.

Golf

New Providence has two championship golf courses, both open to the public. The challenging Radisson Cable Beach Golf Course (☎ 242-327-6000, 800-451-3103) in Cable Beach charges a US$60 green fee (US$45 for nine holes), plus a US$50 cart fee (shared) and US$25 for club rental. The oldest course in The Bahamas, it is managed by Arnold Palmer . . . the very same! Its well-maintained greens and fairways, particularly the back nine, are dotted with water traps. Its vital statistics: 72-par, 7040 yards, 13 lakes and 50 sand traps.

Another excellent course, the South Ocean Golf Course, is at New Providence's western tip; see the West New Providence section for details. Also see the Paradise Island section in this chapter.

Tennis, Racquetball & Squash

Dozens of hotels have tennis courts (in 1997 there were a total of 83), most notably the British Colonial Beach Resort (☎ 242-322-3301), downtown on Marlborough St; and the Radisson Cable Beach Golf Course (☎ 242-327-6000). Nonguests are charged a fee, typically US$5 per person. Night play costs US$10.

The Radisson Sports Centre, opposite the Radisson Cable Beach, has racquetball courts and charges US$6/10 per hour for guests/nonguests. You'll find squash courts at the Nassau Squash & Racquet Club (☎ 242-323-1854) on Independence Dr. It charges US$8 per hour.

Bird Watching

Bird watching on New Providence? Yep . . . it's particularly good on Paradise Island, where the lushly landscaped and woodsy golf course is blessed with migratory birds, waders, and waterfowl. Commonly seen species include the endemic Bahama woodstar hummingbird, the smooth-billed ani, many types of warblers, Caribbean coots, Bahama pintails, moorhens, tricolored herons, snowy egrets, blue herons, yellow- and black-crowned night herons, belted kingfishers, and even predators such as ospreys. You'll need permission to access the golf course (☎ 242-363-3925).

Alternately, sign up with the Bahamas National Trust (☎ 242-393-1317), which offers islandwide guided bird-watching walks every month.

Bicycling

Pedal & Paddle Ecoadventures (☎ 242-362-2772, fax 242-362-2044), PO Box CB-12564, Nassau, Bahamas, has an all-day, 3-mile bicycle ride for US$99. You'll cycle through the pine forests and mangrove creeks of New Providence and paddle in two-person kayaks to a shallow reef for snorkeling. You must be at least 4 feet 6 inches tall to participate.

Spas & Gyms
Gold's Gym (☎ 242-394-6975), on Mackey St at Bay St downtown, charges nonmembers US$5. It claims to be the largest gym in the Caribbean region.

The gym at the Radisson Sports Centre in Cable Beach is free to everyone. The gym and spa at the Nassau Marriott charges even the hotel's guests US$8! Sandals Royal Bahamian has a fitness center and a top-notch full-service spa offering everything from mud baths to Swedish massage and reflexology.

Fitness fanatics can run the shaded jogging trail that snakes along the central median of W Bay St . . . a 1.5-mile-long path from Sandals to the Radisson Cable Beach Golf Course. The Nassau Hash House Harriers have an organized run each Monday (April to October) or Sunday (October to April). Contact Brian Crick (☎ 242-325-2831) or Ewan Tough (☎ 242-323-4966, 242-362-4654).

Other Activities
Village Lanes (☎ 242-393-2427), at Village and Wulff Rds, has a 20-lane bowling alley. It's open 9:30 am to midnight daily; US$2.50 to US$3 per game.

Canoeing trips (☎ 242-356-4283) are offered on Lake Nancy, a shallow lake fringed by marshes near the airport. You can nip through a canal to Lake Killarney, a much larger neighbor. Access is off John F Kennedy Dr near Blake Rd.

ORGANIZED TOURS
City Tours
One-and-a-half-hour guided walking tours are offered by independent BahamaHost guides from the tourist information office (☎ 242-328-7811) or from the Ministry of Tourism's Tour Unit (☎ 242-322-8634) in Rawson Square. Tours run daily between 10 am and 4 pm and cost US$3 per person. They're supposedly offered twice an hour, but times are flexible, as is the itinerary, which usually incorporates all the main downtown sites between Prince George Wharf and Fort Fincastle. The maximum group size is 10.

Bahamas Experience (☎ 242-356-2985, fax 242-356-7118) offers two-hour city tours for US$18, with visits to all the most appealing sites.

Majestic Tours (☎ 242-322-2606, fax 242-326-5785), at Hillside Manor on Cumberland St, has a two-hour city tour for US$20, plus a four-hour tour of Nassau and New Providence for US$25 that takes in the major downtown sites, plus Ardastra Gardens and The Retreat. It even has a nightclub tour four nights a week, including Saturday, for US$25/55 without/with dinner. Its mailing address is PO Box N-1401, Nassau, Bahamas.

Tours are also offered by Happy Tours (☎ 242-323-4555) on Nassau St and Tropical Tours (☎ 242-322-5791) at Palmdale Ave and Mackey St.

Flightseeing
'Seaplane Safaris' down to the Exumas are offered by Paul Harding (☎ 242-393-2522/1179), including three stops, a picnic lunch at Warderick Wells, and snorkeling in Thunderball Grotto.

Nature Tours
Island Vacations (☎ 242-356-1111, fax 242-356-4379; in the USA ☎ 305-748-1833, 800-900-4242, fax 305-748-1965), PO Box CB-13002, Nassau, Bahamas, offers ecoexcursions, including a weeklong 'Birding in Paradise' trip led by Bahamas National Trust guides. The tour explores a different site on New Providence each day, including Malcolm's Creek, a bird-roosting site; The Retreat; and Goulding Cay, a nesting site for dozens of migratory bird species. The tour costs US$1599, including roundtrip airfare from Fort Lauderdale.

Island Getaway (☎ 242-327-2741, 242-300-7433), PO Box CB-13838, Nassau, Bahamas, has three 'getaway' packages from Nassau to Eleuthera.

SPECIAL EVENTS
Nassau hosts the country's largest annual Junkanoo celebrations, beginning before dawn on Boxing Day (December 26) and New Year's Day. There's also the Goombay

Summer Festival, a midyear Junkanoo that is held every June.

Changing of the Guard
This tradition of pomp and ceremony marks the changing of the guard at Nassau's Government House, the residence of the governor-general. The Royal Bahamas Police Force Band performs. It occurs twice a month at 10 am. Call ☎ 242-322-2020 to confirm date and time.

Opening of Parliament
This colorful formal occasion features the Royal Bahamas Police Force Band marching in pith helmets, starched white tunics, and leopard-skin shawls. The governor-general delivers a speech on behalf of Her Majesty, to whom the gathered officials swear allegiance.

Opening of the Supreme Court Sessions
Pageantry also marks the start of Supreme Court sessions in January, April, July, and October. Lawyers and judges in full regalia march to Christ Church Anglican Cathedral for a service followed by an inspection of the Guard-of-Honor.

Classic Cars Race
You don't expect to see vintage race cars tearing down Bay St. But lo! Racing is an island tradition dating back to the 1950s, when Porsches, MGs, Lotuses, and even Formula Ones, driven by the great names of motor sports, challenged the Nassau circuit on an old airstrip that is now the international airport. The annual race was discontinued in 1989 but was resurrected in January 1997 with Cable Beach as its venue.

Bahamas Atlantis Superboat Challenge
The world's fastest powerboats tear it up off the shores of New Providence in this world-class race held each September. Competitors are divided into four categories by size and horsepower. All are veritable rocket ships, most powered by two 1000-horsepower engines. The winner's *average* lap speed over the 12.5 mile course typically exceeds 115 mph! The event is the last in the year's championship calendar, adding to the feverish excitement. You can watch it from the shore as the race passes through Nassau Harbour and under the Paradise Island Bridge; for information, call the Ministry of Tourism (☎ 242-322-7500).

Other Happenings
The BTO (see the Information section) provides complete lists of special events. Dates vary from year to year.

February
Ebony Fashion Fair – Held at the Radisson Cable Beach Casino & Golf Resort, the fair attracts socialites and aspiring models and showcases the latest designs. Call Pilot Club of Nassau (☎ 242-325-6006) for details.

International Food Fair – Features cookouts and contests.

People of the Bahamas Annual Archives Exhibition – Highlights the contributions of various ethnic groups to the nation.

April
Snipe Winter Sailing Championship – Draws homemade boats to race one another in Montagu Bay; contact Royal Nassau Sailing Club (☎ 242-393-0145) for details.

June
Caribbean Muzik Fest – This weeklong festival features a range of music, from reggae to soca to dance hall, at the Queen Elizabeth Sports Centre. It lasts from 8 pm until dawn; US$30. For details, call the Ministry of Tourism (☎ 242-322-7500).

August
Emancipation Day – Celebrated on the first Monday of the month. Fox Hill features an early-morning 'Junkanoo Rush' and holds its own emancipation celebration a week later.

Miss Bahamas Contest – An entertainment-filled evening features contestants vying for the title of Miss Bahamas; the winner represents the country in the Miss World contest. For details, call ☎ 242-393-4041.

October

Great Bahamas Seafood Festival – Held on Arawak Cay, with live entertainment (including Junkanoo) and a cooking competition.

International Cultural Weekend – Bahamians of all shades and cultural backgrounds come together to celebrate their unity; features arts and crafts displays, food fests, float parades, and live music.

November

Guy Fawkes Night – The villain of the Gunpowder Plot is recalled in Nassau's night-time parade.

December

Police Band Annual Christmas & Classical Concert – The Royal Bahamas Police Force Band performs at the Atlantis resort on Paradise Island.

PLACES TO STAY

Nassau isn't cheap or getting cheaper. The average daily room rate in 1996 at the 27 member hotels of the Nassau/Paradise Island Promotion Board was US$108, a 30% increase since 1995. Many hotels are outrageously overpriced, but there are a few bargains. In general, downtown hotels tend to be smaller, quainter, and cheaper than those in Cable Beach, where the more urbane resorts are concentrated.

There's a notice board with information on small hotels in the immigration lounge of Nassau International Airport. Sandals and SuperClubs also have welcome counters here, which you'll spot as you exit Customs.

Caveat emptor! Brochures tell you little and are often more misleading than illuminating. Pay particular attention to my comments on ambiance.

Places to Stay – budget

A less appealing option is the *Delancy Inn* (☎ 242-325-2688) at 4 Delancy St. It has nine simple rooms with ceiling fans and shared bathrooms for US$23 single or double. I received a surly welcome.

If you want to be in Over-the-Hill, check into *Olive's Guest House* (☎ 242-323-5298), a funky little place on Blue Hill Rd. A room should cost about US$25. The

mailing address is PO Box GT-2130, Nassau, Bahamas.

International Traveller's Rest (☎ 242-323-2904), 23 Delancy St, has 14 bare-bones rooms, each meagerly furnished with two single beds, a dresser, and a floor fan. Bathrooms are shared. The rooms abut a cozy colonial house with an aged wooden floor and are adorned with beautiful prints, potted plants, African masks, and a piano. There's a communal kitchen. The place is lovingly tended by Geoffrey Collie. It planned on joining the International Youth Hostel Association in 1998. Shared rooms cost US$26 per person, including breakfast; singles cost US$40. A US$25 key and linen deposit is required. Credit cards can be used for reservations only. Airport transfers are provided for US$12 one way. The postal address is PO Box CB-13558, Nassau, Bahamas.

The *Mignon Guest House* (☎ 242-322-4771), 12 Market St, is favored by budget travelers. It is splendidly situated in the heart of downtown and a veritable bargain at US$34/38 single/double year-round, including tax. There are six small rooms, clean and quaint, with fans and central air-con, but with shared toilet and bathroom. All have a TV. Guests have access to a small kitchen. The Greek resident-owners, Steve and Mary Antonas, run a tight ship: strictly no guests! The mailing address is PO Box N-786, Nassau, Bahamas.

Places to Stay – middle

Downtown The *Parthenon Hotel* (☎ 242-322-2643), on West St, has 18 simply furnished, air-con rooms for US$48 single or double low season, US$64 peak season. They each have a TV, telephone, and '60s utility furniture, and are a bit gloomy but clean and spacious. The building has a quasi-Greek-Revival exterior. A continental breakfast (US$3) is served on the garden patio. The mailing address is PO Box N-4920, Nassau, Bahamas. Next door is the *Sunshine Guesthouse*, 15 West St, which has rooms in a two-story home. The mailing address is PO Box N-535, Nassau, Bahamas.

NEW PROVIDENCE

One of my favorite spots downtown is the simple yet charming *Parliament Inn* (☎ 242-322-2836, fax 242-326-7196) on Parliament St near Shirley St. It's done up in tropical prints and adornments, with wicker furniture. The six air-con rooms have no TVs or phones, but you can't argue at US$50/60/70 single/double/triple, and the inn is superbly situated for downtown exploring. The mailing address is PO Box N-4138, Nassau, Bahamas.

The basic *Harbour Moon Hotel* (☎ 242-323-8120), at the corner of Bay and Devaux Sts, has small, simple rooms for US$50/60, with air-con, color TV, telephone, and a private bathroom with hot water. The beds are oversize. It's nothing inspirational, just a place to rest your head, tho' it's well placed for a stroll into town. Its postal address is PO Box N-646, Nassau, Bahamas.

If you're not fussy, try the *Grand Central Hotel* (☎ 242-322-8368) at Bay and Parliament Sts, with 35 small rooms in a dowdy orange-and-brown decor. Each has a TV, air-con, and phone; there's no pool or restaurant. Singles cost US$53, doubles US$53 to US$71. The mailing address is PO Box N-4084, Nassau, Bahamas.

The modest *Park Manor Guesthouse* (☎ 242-356-5471, fax 242-325-3554), on Market St near Government House, isn't a true guesthouse. It has a range of offerings. 'Efficiencies' for two people cost US$45; studio apartments for up to four people cost US$55. Deluxe apartments for six cost US$78, and a small cottage costs US$50. Most rooms have king-size beds; all have kitchenette, fans, and air-con. There's an amoeba-shaped pool in the forecourt. The postal address is PO Box N-4164, Nassau, Bahamas.

The *Buena Vista Restaurant & Hotel* (☎ 242-322-2811, fax 242-322-5881) is on Delancy St. This grand old mansion, which is acclaimed for its restaurant, has six rooms, all upstairs, each with air-con, TV, radio, and direct-line phones. It is rated highly. I haven't seen inside the rooms, but the rest of the hotel is in need of restoration, and the mood suggests that the accommodations may not be all they're cracked up to be. Rates are US$55/65 in summer and US$80/90 in winter.

When I stay in town, I gravitate toward *El Greco* (☎ 242-325-1121, fax 242-325-1124) at the corner of W Bay and Augusta Sts, at the west end of downtown. The compact family-run hotel, enhanced by Spanish decor, feels like a European B&B; the friendly owners are Greek. The clean, spacious rooms surround a small courtyard with a pool and bougainvillea adds color. The rooms upstairs are larger and offer more light, with balconies over the courtyard. Take a suite in the main building if possible; some of them are huge. It's recommended! Rooms cost about US$65/75 in summer and US$82/92 in winter; the postal address is PO Box N-4187, Nassau, Bahamas.

A more expensive yet soulless option is the *Astoria Hotel* (☎ 242-322-8666, fax 242-322-8660) on W Bay St at Nassau St. Standard rooms cost US$70 single or double; deluxe rooms cost US$100. The 72 recently refurbished rooms are clean and decorated in bright tropical pastels, and each has a balcony, TV, and king-size bed or two doubles. The postal address is PO Box N-3236, Nassau, Bahamas.

The *Towne Hotel* (☎ 242-322-8450, fax 242-328-1512), 40 George St, offers 46 small, dingy air-con rooms, each with fans, king-size bed, and a TV past its prime. Winter rates are US$75 standard, US$85 superior, and US$95 junior suite; a third person costs US$22. The mailing address is PO Box N-4804, Nassau, Bahamas.

21st Century Realtors (☎ 242-327-4486), outside the entrance to Sandals Royal Bahamian at Cable Beach, rents rooms from US$60; the mailing address is PO Box S/S 5363, Nassau, Bahamas.

Farther Afield West of downtown, a basic option is the simple, family-run *Arawak Inn* (☎ 242-322-2638; ask for Lloyd Gray) on W Bay St near Chippingham Rd. It has six small, simple, self-contained, air-con rooms with kitchenette, TV, and ceiling fans. Sizes vary. It's basic but fine. Rates are US$50 for the first night, US$35 per night for stays of two days or more. The postal address is PO Box N-3222, Nassau, Bahamas.

Dillet's Guest House (☎ 242-325-1133, fax 242-325-7183), on Dunmore St at Strachan St, is one of Nassau's true gems, overflowing with homey hospitality. A row of tall palms guides you up the path to the 1920s-era home, with rocking chairs on the veranda. The huge lounge features an Old World fireplace, wicker furniture, and squawking parakeets. The house, bathed in light, is festooned with original art. Each of the seven simple yet graciously decorated rooms has cable TV (all but two have a kitchenette). Six rooms are planned in a new extension, plus a small dipping pool. There are hammocks slung between trees, where birdsong is rife. The place is run by Iris Dillet Knowles. Rates – US$50 single or double in summer, US$68 in winter, and US$15 for a third person – include continental breakfast. Dinners are available on request for US$20. A small gift shop sells quality crafts. The mailing address is PO Box N-204, Nassau, Bahamas.

Hotels east of town include the charmless *Montagu Beach Inn* (☎ 242-393-0475, fax 242-393-6061) on E Shirley St, whose 33 large, pleasantly furnished rooms cost US$55 single or double year-round. The inn has a pool and a nightclub. The postal address is PO Box N-1411, Nassau, Bahamas. Nearby and more appealing is the *Orchard Hotel* (☎ 242-393-1297, fax 242-394-3562) on Village Rd, with 14 cottages set in quiet, lush grounds centered on a small pool. Each is pleasantly furnished and has air-con, TV, and a small kitchen. There's a small bar. Studios cost US$65 to US$85; cottages cost US$100 standard, US$115 superior. The postal address is PO Box N-1514, Nassau, Bahamas.

The *Red Carpet Inn* (☎ 242-393-7981, fax 242-393-9055), on E Bay St, is a contemporary 40-room hotel with adequate but charmless rooms. They're clean, with double beds, air-con and fan, TV, and phone. Some have a kitchenette. The place is well run by a friendly host, Mike Duggan, who oversees personalized service. Rates

range from US$64 standard to US$84 deluxe. The postal address is PO Box SS-6233, Nassau, Bahamas.

The 34-room *City Lodge Hotel* (☎ 242-394-2591, fax 242-394-3636), just off E Bay St, is clean and adequate but dingy. Air-con rooms have TV and phone and cost US$55/67 single/double. There's a pool and small store. Security may be an issue: The front desk is hidden behind thick glass. The hotel's postal address is PO Box SS-6275, Nassau, Bahamas.

A more upscale option, popular with yachters, is the *Nassau Harbour Club* (☎ 242-393-0771, fax 242-393-5393) on E Bay St, which overlooks the marina and has a pool and sun deck suspended over the water. The decor – tropical prints against stark-white walls – is appealing. The 50 air-con rooms and suites are clean, albeit modestly furnished (some are rather dimly lit). Each has a TV and phone. Winter rates run from US$90 single or double for a standard room to US$130 for a deluxe mini-suite. Its postal address is PO Box SS-5755, Nassau, Bahamas.

Family Islanders tend to stay at soulless hotels in nondescript residential areas. Typical is the *Poinciana Inn* (☎ 242-393-1897), southeast of downtown on Bernard Rd, where rooms cost US$35/55. There's a pool and a bar and nightclub popular with locals. The mailing address is PO Box N-7096, Nassau, Bahamas.

Places to Stay – top end
Downtown Dominating the west end of downtown Bay St is the *British Colonial Beach Resort* (☎ 242-322-3301, fax 242-322-2286), a massive, rambling, grande dame of a hotel built in 1922 but now run by Best Western. It has grounds spanning 8 acres and its own beach. The rooms, which vary greatly in size and position, are clean and airy yet modestly furnished. A refurbishment, just beginning at press time, was intended to bring the hotel up to date and attract a more sophisticated clientele. The dowdy grounds are to be landscaped. There are two on-site restaurants, a large swimming pool, tennis courts, and water

sports. Rates range from US$89 (standard) to US$139 (luxury) in summer; rooms cost about 50% more in winter. A great deal is the three-night 'Goombay Fling Package,' from US$139 per person in summer or US$199 in winter. The postal address is PO Box N-7148, Nassau, Bahamas.

Nassau's most venerable hotel is the 250-year-old *Graycliff* (☎ 242-322-2796, fax 242-326-6110), a Georgian home built by a wealthy pirate and loftily situated above town on W Hill St. It is the only *Relais et Chateaux* establishment in the West Indies.

Run by live-in proprietors Enrico and Anna Garzaroli, Graycliff is a veritable museum of period antiques and fine prints. The nine lofty-ceilinged rooms and five romantic cottage suites in the garden have windows on all sides, granting a free flow of air. Bathrooms are exquisite. All rooms come with plump robes and other luxe extras. Feeling opulent? Check out (or into) the Mandarino Suite, done up in Oriental motif with an oversize bathroom and bed. Rooms in the house cost US$150 to US$290; cottage suites range from US$170 to US$365, including continental breakfast. The hotel features a well-stocked humidor, a beautiful garden, and an Olympic-length pool in a stone courtyard. The restaurant is acclaimed. To add to the sense of nobility, guests are met at the airport and whisked to Graycliff in a Mercedes limo. The mailing address is PO Box N-10246, Nassau, Bahamas.

Farther Afield Seeking an upscale villa? Consider *Villas at Crystal Cay* (☎ 242-328-1036, fax 242-323-3202) on Silver Cay off W Bay St. These 22 secluded and handsome one-bedroom villas are lavishly adorned with elegant contemporary decor and offer a breezy setting atop the coral shore. Each has a fully stocked kitchen, satellite TV, and VCR, plus a private courtyard with a deep plunge pool. You can sit with a sundowner cocktail and watch the cruise ships go by at what seems like fingertip distance. There's a private beach two minutes' stroll away. Villa rates begin at about US$185 double in low season, US$235 in peak season.

Cable Beach The 24-room *Sun Fun Resorts* (☎ 242-327-8827, fax 242-327-8802), on W Bay St at the end of Cable Beach, is a dreary hotel that doesn't live up to its billing. Air-con rooms are clean and well lit, with contemporary furniture in a mauve color scheme. But the jerry-built hotel has no atmosphere. Facilities include a restaurant and small cooling pool. The beach is 200 yards away. In summer rates begin at US$65. Winter rates range from US$75 standard to US$115 for a minisuite.

Casuarinas of Cable Beach (☎ 242-327-8153, fax 242-327-8152), near the west end of Cable Beach, spans W Bay St. The rooms are nice enough, with pleasing furnishings, but the public arenas are dowdy. Some are timeworn; others are attractive, especially room No 15 . . . the graciously appointed 'suite.' Cable TV in rooms offers pay-per-view programs, including – a rarity in The Bahamas – adult movies. Telephones are not direct dial. There are two swimming pools, one on each side of the road. It boasts two restaurants: the Round House, serving Chinese; and the basic Albrions, which has an all-you-can-eat special on Friday night for US$12 and also serves bush teas. There's access to a tiny beach. Rates begin at US$95 single or double and run to US$190 for a two-bedroom suite. The mailing address is PO Box CB-13225, Nassau, Bahamas.

I like the *Radisson Cable Beach Casino & Golf Resort* (☎ 242-327-6000, 800-333-3333, fax 242-327-6987; in the USA ☎ 800-432-0221, fax 305-932-0023), next to the Nassau Marriott. It recently emerged from a US$15 million remake that has graced it with a dynamic tropical feel. This vast property (it has 669 ocean-view rooms, all with a balcony) is centered on an exquisitely landscaped, 25,000-sq-foot courtyard with three large pools, cascading falls, whirlpool spas, and shady palms. The spacious, air-con rooms have king-size beds. Rooms cost US$115 to US$125 on average. The resort offers an all-inclusive package costing US$145 to US$150 per day on average, as well as 'Camp Junkanoo,' an extensive supervised program for kids.

Take your pick of several first-class restaurants and activities that include tennis, golf on a championship 18-hole course, racquetball, squash, and water sports. Service in the resort's restaurants is swift and conscientious. One-night hosted off-property dining is included for guests staying four or more nights. It also has a shopping arcade and direct access to the Marriott's Crystal Palace Casino. The postal address is PO Box N-4914, Nassau, Bahamas.

I also like the *Nassau Beach Hotel* (☎ 242-327-7711, fax 242-327-7615; in the USA ☎ 888-627-7282), on Goodman's Bay, an intimate and traditional hotel that was featured in two James Bond movies, then lost its luster. In 1997 it was in the midst of a US$12 million refurbishment, which will add a pool and lavish landscaping. All the rooms are admirable, but those in the East Wing are splendid – they're spacious and have beautiful Edwardian mahogany furniture. Cable TV with optional pay-per-view channels is standard. There's a small shopping arcade and several dining options, including Café Johnny Canoe. Water sports are offered. The hotel has a fiercely loyal clientele. Winter room rates run from US$160 to US$215 and up to US$750 for the penthouse. You can also choose an all-inclusive package. The hotel's postal address is PO Box N-7756, Nassau, Bahamas.

Just west, in garish counterpoint, is the *Nassau Marriott* (☎ 242-327-6200, 800-333-3333, fax 242-327-6801), a purple-and-neon futuristic hotel straight out of a Flash Gordon movie. This megahotel (it has 867 rooms and suites in five towers) underwent a US$30 million renovation in 1997 but retains its Las Vegas gaudiness. The rooms are attractive and tastefully done in contemporary decor. The Galaxy Suite is said to be the most expensive hotel room in the world . . . a mere US$25,000 a night! Mere mortals will pay US$95 to US$225 low season, US$165 to US$275 peak season.

Facilities include the Crystal Palace Casino, a cabaret nightclub, a shopping plaza, and several bars and restaurants. The Sportsbook Sports Bar & Deli offers a splendid buffet. The hotel also has a 'Kids Club,' with supervised activities and theme days, costing US$10 per child per hour. Babysitting costs US$15 per hour. The landscaped beachfront courtyard has a 100-foot waterslide. The hotel's postal address is PO Box N-8306, Nassau, Bahamas.

Immediately west of the Radisson is *Westwind II* (in the USA ☎ 616-942-5555, fax 616-942-0974). This resort boasts upscale self-contained, two-bedroom, air-con villas in lush grounds centered on two swimming pools, and features a clubhouse with bar and grill. Each unit has satellite TV and a fully furnished kitchen. Winter rates range from US$180 to US$220 single and US$220 to US$275 for up to four guests. The local mailing address is PO Box CB-11006, Nassau, Bahamas; in the USA write 3200 Broadmoor St, Grand Rapids, MI 49508.

Near the east end of the beach is *Breezes* (☎ 242-327-5356, fax 242-327-5356; in the USA ☎ 800-330-8272), part of the SuperClubs all-inclusive chain, with a 1000-foot beachfront. The 391 spacious rooms have subdued, tasteful decor and a TV offering German, Spanish, and UK stations. The courtyard boasts five pools, including a huge Jacuzzi and a misting pool. Room rates begin at US$220 double in low season, US$270 in peak season.

Don't come for peace and quiet: The resort is noisy with the sounds of good times. It's perfect for gregarious sorts who don't mind the rattle of Ping-Pong balls and the sounds of live bands. The dining room, which offers lavish buffets, is like a refectory decorated by David Hockney. All the public arenas are gaily painted, suggesting that you are in for a colorful time. The activity is full-bore: pajama parties, Mr & Mrs Bikini Contests, talent shows, Junkanoos, sailing lessons, outdoor games, and even trampoline clinics on the beach (for the less daring, there's a Friday-night outdoor circus show). There's an inline skating and jogging track; the Hurricane dance club, built of Old World stone and timber; and a Queen Anne-style piano bar. A day pass for nonguests costs US$60; an evening pass costs US$50.

Breezes has shuttles to and from the airport. The resort is adding 92 junior suites. The place is often sold out. And guys . . . there are more single women than men! The mailing address is PO Box CB-13049, Nassau, Bahamas.

The most lavish place – for couples only – is *Sandals Royal Bahamian* (☎ 242-327-6400, fax 242-327-6961; in the USA ☎ 800-726-3257). The flagship of the renowned Sandals hotel chain – voted 'World's Best All-Inclusive Resorts' and 'Top Caribbean Hotel Group' three years in a row at the World Travel Awards – gets my vote as the most elegant all-inclusive resort in the region. Stay here and you'll feel it truly is 'better in The Bahamas.' The resort was formerly the glamorous Balmoral Club and later Le Meridian Royal Bahamian. Beyond the marble-sheathed lobby are 196 air-con rooms, from beachfront rooms and villas to suites. All feature regal handcrafted mahogany furniture and king-size beds. Suites have their own concierge. Per-person rates range from US$580 to US$885 for two nights March 30 to December 19 (US$645 to US$925 the rest of the year). A seven-night all-inclusive package costs you US$1695 to US$2575 (US$1885 to US$2710). Once inside the doors, you pay nothing extra.

Sandals has six restaurants (two gourmet), a lively nightclub with superb entertainment, and various bars, including an authentic pub brought over from England. The property extends over 13 landscaped acres, including a private beach with water sports; there are also four whirlpools, a misting pool, and a vast swimming pool, centerpiece of an opulent architectural fantasy with statues and stately columns. A second pool, Jacuzzi, and the atmospheric Café Goombay are on Sandals' private island, Discovery, with its own beach. The resort is also a full-service spa resort with a splendid fitness center and a 'Wellness Centre.' An additional 210 rooms and a second pool were scheduled for early 1998, as were new Italian and Japanese restaurants.

Golf at the Cable Beach Golf Club and scuba diving are included at no extra cost. Sorry, no singles or children allowed. The mailing address is PO Box CB-13005, Cable Beach, Nassau, Bahamas.

Guanahani Village (☎ 242-327-5236, fax 242-327-5059) has oceanfront rental units. You can also try *Cable Beach Manor Apartments* (☎ 242-327-7785), which offers long-term rentals, and *Sandyport* (☎ 242-327-4641, fax 242-327-3663), the snazzy new residential-resort complex and marina at the west end of Cable Beach. Sandyport's postal address is PO Box N-8585, Nassau, Bahamas.

PLACES TO EAT
Nassau's eateries run the gamut from colorful local establishments serving downhome dishes to chic restaurants offering world-class gourmet fare. Also consider Paradise Island, which offers several fine restaurants, and additional eateries to the west and south of Nassau. See the other Places to Eat sections in this chapter for details.

Budget
Downtown Vegetarians should head to the *King Alpha Ital Restaurant*, on Elizabeth Ave at Shirley St, a genuine and duly colorful Rastafarian eatery festooned with inscriptions honoring Jah. It serves such fare as fried snapper for US$6, a 'veggie plate' for US$5, and patties for US$2, washed down with sorrel and other natural drinks.

I recommend the *Bahamian Kitchen* (☎ 242-325-0702) on Trinity Pl, a local favorite specializing in seafood dishes from US$7, but also serving salads and sandwiches from US$3, plus okra soup, curried chicken, boil fish, and hashed beef and grits. It's a great value! It also has a takeout service.

Conch Fritters Bar & Grill (☎ 242-323-8778), on Marlborough St, is a fast-food-style joint specializing in conch dishes that's handy for a quick snack downtown. It's open 11:30 am to midnight.

A good place for breakfast or lunch is *Café Skan's* (☎ 242-322-2486) on Bay St at Frederick St. It's clean and offers a large US-style breakfast menu, including pancakes and omelets from US$5 and steak and eggs for US$9.50. Locals eat here, too. There's often a wait.

The *Yard Style Restaurant*, at Bay St and Elizabeth Ave, has breakfasts for US$2. Its local fare runs to curry mutton and steamed fish. The place is gloomy but clean and favored by locals. The funky roadside *Souse Pot*, a tiny shack at Bay and Christie Sts, offers cheap local dishes on the hoof. How about munching on takeout sheep's tongue for US$6?

You can also stroll to Over-the-Hill and dine with locals at *Royal Castle*, about half a mile south of Government House on Blue Hill Rd. It's full of offbeat ambiance. It advertises breakfasts for US99¢, befitting the income level of the region. Take care hereabouts at night!

If you really must pretend that you're at home, you'll find a *McDonald's* on Marlborough St, where there's a splendid fast-food Chinese takeout – *Imperial Take-Away* – opposite the British Colonial Hotel.

Nassau has a handful of cafes, including *Jitter's Coffee House*, downtown on Bay St above The Girls from Brazil swimwear store. *Friendly Deli*, on Elizabeth Ave off Bay St, is good for fresh salads, soups, etc. And *Planet Hollywood*, at the corner of Bay and East Sts, has a juice bar.

Need a frozen-yogurt antidote to the heat? *TCBY* has outlets at the West Bay Shopping Centre on W Bay St, and on Nassau St near Poinciana Dr.

Farther Afield West of downtown, the undisputed place to be as one with local residents is the *Outdoor Conch Market* between Arawak Cay and W Bay St. Locals flock there on weekends to the two dozen or so stalls with names like 'The House of Love' and 'Andros Hide-Out.' It's a great place to hang out and sample

conch. Typical prices include US$1 for fritters, US$3 for conch salad, and US$5 for cracked conch. You can wash your conch down with fresh fruit drinks or coconut juice ('sky juice') bought at the Daiquiri Bar. The Great Bahamas Seafood Festival is held here each October.

A sign at the entrance to the cay reminds you that conch is an aphrodisiac:

First the conch
Then the love
What? Not without
    the glove!

A glove, of course, is a condom!

East of downtown, an alternative is *Montagu Ramp* at the east end of Shirley St, where conch is landed and cleaned. A couple of small stalls also sell pineapple, coconut, and raisin cake for US$1 a slice. You can get a grouper dinner for US$7. *Bistro Bahama*, in the Nassau Arcade on E Bay St, is also a favorite of locals. It serves a wide range of genuine Bahamian dishes: Try the delicious curry mutton rice for US$5; for breakfast, try ackee and codfish for US$6.50.

The *Cappuccino Café* (☎ 242-394-6332) on Mackey St serves inexpensive and tasty homemade soups, creative salads and sandwiches, and health foods.

I like the simple *Tamarind Hill* (☎ 242-393-1306), in a gaily painted wooden home on Village Rd. Fare includes Bahamian dishes, plus sandwiches averaging US$5, quiche for US$6, and eclectic entrées. It has a happy hour from 5 to 7:30 pm.

If you're exploring south of town, have lunch at the *Corner Hotel* in Carmichael Village. See the South New Providence section for details.

Cable Beach One of the few places to find cheap beef patties (for US$1) is the *Swiss Pastry Shop* on W Bay St near Sandals Royal Bahamian; it also serves fresh-baked pastries and desserts.

Sbarro's (☎ 242-327-3076) has a fastfood outlet outside the Nassau Beach Hotel. You can fill up on pizzas, calzones, salads, or US-Italian fare for less than US$6 with a drink. Sbarro's also offers daily Italian and Bahamian specials.

Cafes in Cable Beach include *Caribbean Bean & Berry* in the shopping strip opposite Sandals. Here, too, is *Carpelago Café*; in the West Bay Shopping Centre, it serves iced coffee for US$1.50.

Middle

Downtown You'd swear you were in an old inn in Surrey upon entering the *Green Shutters Inn* (☎ 242-325-5702) at 48 Parliament St. Its beamed ceiling, leather chairs, and tartan carpet are matched by a menu that includes a ploughman's platter for US$7.25, calf's liver for US$9, and bangers and mash for US$8.50 . . . all washed down with a pint of English ale. It has a three-course dinner for US$23. It's closed Sunday evening.

The Cellar (☎ 242-322-8877), 11 Charlotte St, is another agreeable, oak-beamed, English-style pub. It's elegant and intimate and serves some of the best continental cuisine in Nassau, including superb pastas, and a tasty steak and mushroom pie. Entrées cost US$8 and upward.

Billabong's, on Cumberland St, has a warm ambiance and a snug, 'down-under' feel. This pub is housed in a 200-year-old building with rough-hewn whitewashed walls and a black ceiling scribbled with chalk marks like the aboriginal drawings of Australia. Its eclectic menu includes lasagna for US$9, and pies and fries. Portions are filling.

If you're browsing the Rawson Square area, try *Pick-a-Dilly* (☎ 242-322-2836) at the Parliament Inn. Simple fare includes burgers, salads, and Bahamian fare, but you'll also find creations such as smoked mahi-mahi, beer-battered shrimp in honey mustard, and green rice loaf with cheese. Most dishes cost less than US$10. Pick-a-Dilly specializes in daiquiris. On Bay St try the *Dockside Bar & Grill*, upstairs in Prince George Plaza. It finds inspiration from Greece in such dishes as spicy chicken in pita for US$8. Also here is *Iguana*, serving Bahamian and continental fare.

Another of my favorite places is the *Sugar Reef Bar & Restaurant* (☎ 242-356-3065) on Devaux St off Bay St. It's a cool place . . . colorful, too. A shaded, terra-cotta-tiled terrace faces the harbor. Potted plants abound, and everything is done up in a rainbow of Caribbean colors. The wide-ranging menu includes traditional Bahamian dishes, plus salads for US$6 and up, sandwiches for US$8 and up, burgers for US$7 and up, barbecued ribs, and creative pastas. Happy hour is from 5 to 7 pm.

For Chinese food, I recommend the *House of Wong* (☎ 242-326-0045) on West St in the heart of town. It's clean and airy and serves filling and tasty dishes prepared by a chef from Hong Kong. Lunch specials cost US$6.95. Dinner entrées begin at US$12. The egg rolls, costing US$4, are a meal in themselves. It's open 11:30 am to 3 pm and 6 to 11 pm. The *VIP Chinese Restaurant* (☎ 242-322-1599), at the corner of Bay and Devaux Sts, offers Szechwan and Cantonese cuisine. Entrées cost upward of US$8.

Care for a sonata with your pasta? Then head to the *Caffé dell'Opera* (☎ 242-356-6118), on Marlborough St, serving regional Italian dishes amid suitably Sicilian decor. It's also known as the Restaurant & Bar Italiano.

The Indian cuisine at *Gaylord's* (☎ 242-356-3004), on Dowdeswell St, is excellent. Chicken marsala costs US$9 and tandooris begin at US$12, but the rice is a whopping US$4. Budget a minimum US$25. The restaurant is part of the acclaimed Gaylord's chain, with outlets in New Delhi, Bombay, London, New York, and San Francisco.

German visitors with a longing for home cooking should head to the *Europa Restaurant* on W Bay St. It serves Bavarian knockwurst for US$9.50 and wiener schnitzel for US$12, plus Bahamian fare and Italian pastas starting at US$13.

Farther Afield For barbecued ribs, try *Tony Roma's* (☎ 242-325-2020) at Saunders Beach between downtown and Cable Beach. The burgers and onion rings are good. Tony Roma's also offers late-night specials 9 to 11 pm for US$9.95.

The *Cabana Club & Grill* on W Bay St overlooks Arawak Cay. It specializes in seafood and has a sports bar and small swimming pool.

An option for Chinese west of downtown is the *Chinese Kitchen* near the junction of Nassau St and Boyd Rd. East of downtown, a good option for Chinese food is the *Double Dragon* (☎ 242-393-5718) on Mackey St at the foot of the Paradise Island Bridge. No menu item is more than US$13 (for lobster chop suey).

For a restaurant on a nautical theme, try the *Poop Deck* (☎ 242-393-8175) at Nassau Yacht Haven on E Bay St. It combines Bahamian and continental fare and offers a fine harbor view from the 2nd floor.

Cable Beach I like *Dicky Mo's Seafood Restaurant* (☎ 242-327-7854), just west of the Radisson. The place is atmospheric, done up in a rustic wharflike motif, and the servers wear captains' uniforms. The wide-ranging menu is reasonably priced. It has daily specials such as pan-fried snapper for US$8 and minced lobster for US$13. Try the black bean and onion soup for US$4.50. There's an English-style pub inside.

Another of my favorites is *Café Johnny Canoe* (☎ 242-327-3373), adjoining the Nassau Beach Hotel. You can sit on the rustic yet atmospheric outside deck (lit up at night by Christmas lights), or in the brightly colored, air-con, delightfully funky interior. The wide breakfast menu includes US or Bahamian fare for US$6 or less, plus burgers, sandwiches and local favorites for lunch and dinner. Try the spiced tuna-salad sandwich. The cocktails are bucket-size!

Rock 'n' Roll Café (☎ 242-327-7639), between Breezes and the Nassau Beach Hotel, is much more than a cafe. This sports bar in an old beachfront mansion serves US fare such as nachos and chicken wings, and grilled steaks for US$5 to US$25. It also has vegetarian dishes and is favored by those folks who like a rowdier scene.

The *Japanese Steak House* (☎ 242-327-7781), adjoining Dicky Mo's, boasts genuine Asian decor. The sushi, for US$20, is excellent, though portions are small. The various hibachi dishes are cooked at your table and are pricey, beginning at US$20. You can ring up US$80 for two with no problem.

For Italian, head to the small, cozy, family-run *Capriccio Ristorante* (☎ 242-327-8547) opposite the entrance to Sandals Royal Bahamian. Its romantic ambiance is enhanced by classical music. The dishes are superb – you're sure to find your Italian favorite! – and reasonably priced, from US$5 to US$19. *Mama mia!* . . . there's *real* espresso, too.

Don't forget the hotel restaurants. The Radisson Cable Beach offers the atmospheric *Tequila Pepe's* for Mexican food; *Avocado's* for nouveau California cuisine; *Amici* for Italian; and *The Forge*, where grilled meats are prepared at your table. The all-you-can-eat buffet breakfast in the *Bimini Restaurant* is a bargain at US$11.50.

Also praiseworthy are the expensive *Black Angus Grill* in the Nassau Marriott and the more moderately priced *Beef Cellar* in the Nassau Beach Hotel, serving various types of steaks. The Marriott's *Sole Mare* Italian restaurant is also good.

The *Round House* (☎ 242-327-8153), in a historic structure at the Casuarinas hotel, serves Chinese; it's open noon to 3 pm and 6 to 10 pm. Entrées cost US$10 to US$17.

Top End
Downtown If your budget allows it, head to *Graycliff* (☎ 242-322-2796) on W Hill St, whose restaurant fills a glass-enclosed wraparound balcony of an exquisite colonial mansion. Lace tablecloths, gilt porcelain, and silverware add a regal note to The Bahamas' only five-star restaurant. Its beautifully rendered, French-inspired cuisine will burn a hole in your pocket. The cheapest soup costs US$9! Typical entrées include rack of lamb for US$42 and filet mignon for US$34. The signature dish is lobster. Steep, yes, but it has been rated

among the world's 10 best restaurants by *Lifestyles of the Rich and Famous*. The wine cellar claims the largest collection – supposedly 175,000 bottles – in the Caribbean region, and there is no better selection of fine Cuban cigars with which to end the evening. Understandably, jacket and tie are required.

The *Buena Vista* (☎ 242-322-2811) on Delancy St also has elegant (albeit jaded) silver-and-crystal dining in a period setting. You can also dine on a patio. The creative menu has strong French and Italian influences. It has received rave reviews that are, I suspect, a bit overblown. Entrées begin at US$27; it's open 7 to 11 pm.

Even better is chic *Café Matisse* (☎ 242-356-7012) on Bank Ln, blending contemporary and classical elements such as leopard fabrics, rich hardwoods, bare limestone walls, and Matisse prints. You can dine outside beneath huge shade trees, where a jazz band plays on weekend evenings. The lunch menu boasts an Italian flair at bargain prices: homemade pastas and pizzas for less than US$10 and seafood from US$12. Dinner entrées include such winners as shrimps in red curry sauce for US$22.

Farther Afield For surf 'n' turf, head to *Montagu Gardens* (☎ 242-394-6347) on E Bay St. This casually elegant place serves a wide range of continental fare alongside steaks, seafood, ribs, lamb dishes, and burgers. Prices run US$8 to US$35 for entrées.

An acclaimed option is the oddly named *Sun And . . .* restaurant (☎ 242-393-1205), in a converted home on Lakeview Dr, a cul-de-sac off the east end of Shirley St. Its homey yet elegant ambiance matches its highly acclaimed menu, offering superb French cuisine as well as Bahamian dishes with a French twist. The rack of lamb will set you back a staggering US$72, but the veal sweetbreads will cost you just US$32. The desserts are equally renowned. It's open 6:30 to 9:30 pm only, daily. Reservations are recommended.

Perhaps the finest cuisine on the island is offered at *Compass Point*, west of Nassau.

For details, see Places to Eat in the West New Providence section of this chapter.

ENTERTAINMENT

Downtown Nassau is virtually dead at night, even when cruise ships are in port. The night scene is concentrated in Cable Beach and on Paradise Island (see the Paradise Island section in this chapter).

The earthy nightlife that is a feature of other countries in the region is absent here. Unlike neighboring islands (like Jamaica), where go-go clubs are a staple, The Bahamas' nocturnal scene is held in tight rein by the overriding influence of the Christian community, including the Bahamas Christian Council.

At the other end of the spectrum, afternoon tea parties are held regularly at Government House as part of the People-to-People program, designed to put tourists in closer contact with locals. (See the People to People sidebar in the Facts for the Visitor chapter.)

Dance Clubs

The dance club of choice is *The Zoo* (☎ 242-322-7195), near Saunders Beach on W Bay St. This ultramodern club has the de rigueur laser-light show and piped fog, plus house, techno, R&B, and reggae music. Five bars boast individual decor. It gets packed with a youngish crowd. Eats are available, and there's an open 'VIP Lounge.' Admission costs a whopping US$40 Thursday to Saturday (US$20 Sunday to Wednesday) but is free to guests of Sandals Royal Bahamian, Breezes, and Club Med (you'll need your ID). You can also get in free if you dine at Café Johnny Canoe, which has the same owner. Look for coupons (found, for example, on the back of the *What-to-do* tourist guide), good for US$5 admission. A cocktail can set you back US$6 or more. It has a Ladies' Night.

Recently opened upscale nightclubs include *Enigma*, 300 yards west of the British Colonial Hotel off W Bay St. There are several lounges and dance floors on two levels, each playing its own music, from reggae to house to techno. It has theme nights and stays open Wednesday to Saturday until 5 am, sometimes longer. Dress code is 'casually elegant,' and admission costs US$30.

The snazziest place is the *601 Club* at 601 Bay St. The club's dress code forbids sneakers, and jackets are standard for men. No one under 25 is admitted. The resident band is the six-member BahaMen, the top island group, with a style that blends goombay with modern R&B and rap rhythms. Thursday is Ladies' Night, with free entry for women. Admission otherwise costs US$20 (a VIP entrance costs US$35 and allows you to sit upstairs in a more exclusive environment where you can literally look down on the hoi polloi).

The BahaMen also play at the rather sparse *BahaMen Culture Club* (☎ 242-356-6266) at Nassau and W Bay Sts. Dancing is offered Wednesday to Sunday for US$20. Cocktails here are expensive. Thursday is Ladies' Night.

Several resort hotels have their own dance clubs, too, including *Sandals Royal Bahamian*, which is private. Nonguests can buy an evening pass to *Breezes*. And the *Fanta-Z Disco* at the Radisson Cable Beach is open to all comers.

Casinos & Floorshows

The *Crystal Palace Casino* (☎ 242-327-6200), at the Nassau Marriott in Cable Beach, boasts 800 slot machines, 51 blackjack tables, nine roulette wheels, and other games. It's open to anyone over 21 years of age. (Bahamian residents, however, may not gamble.) It's open 10 am to 4 am daily, but a video slot-machine section operates 24 hours. A second casino is located on Paradise Island (see the Paradise Island section).

The 800-seat *Palace Theatre* (☎ 242-363-3000), at the Crystal Palace Casino, hosts the 'Jubilation' show nightly except Monday. This Las Vegas-style revue blends comedy and a fantastic magician act with sexy routines by leggy showgirls and male dance troupes. You'll see bosoms briefly flaunted; here this is euphemistically termed 'tasteful cultural nudity.' Covered shows

suitable for the entire family are offered at 7:30, 9:30, and 11:30 pm on Tuesday and Saturday. The show costs US$30, including two drinks. You can also take in a dinner show for US$45. No photos are allowed.

The *King & Knights Club* (☎ 242-327-7711), at the Nassau Beach Hotel in Cable Beach, offers a native dance show that includes traditional rake 'n' scrape music, limbo, a fire dance, and Junkanoo music. Shows are at 8:30 and 10:30 pm nightly and cost US$20 per person, including one drink.

Peanut Taylor's *Drumbeat Club* (☎ 242-322-4233), on W Bay St, offers a revue combining traditional Junkanoo and limbo with comedy, including a female impersonator.

Pubs/Bars

Most resort hotels have at least one bar, ranging from the traditionally English motif of the *Nassau Beach Hotel* to more lively options at the *Nassau Marriott*, *Breezes*, and *Sandals Royal Bahamian* (you can purchase evening passes for the latter two resorts, which are all-inclusive; you won't get in without a pass).

Most other bars in Nassau bill themselves as either English-style pubs or US-style sports bars. Many are hybrids.

Quieter bars are represented by the oh-so-English *Palm Patio Bar* in the British Colonial Hotel on Marlborough St. English pubs are represented by *Green Shutters*, *Billabong's*, *The Cellar*, and the *Europa* (see the Places to Eat section). Also check out the bar at *Compass Point* (see the West New Providence section).

The *Drop-Off* (☎ 242-322-3444), on Bay St between Charlotte and Frederick Sts, is a popular basement bar and dance club that attracts a mix of locals and staff from the cruise ships (plus an occasional working girl hoping to snare a randy seaman). It has a suitably international flavor, plus cool, hip music and occasional live bands. Dig the walls, lined with faux aquariums – the water is real, but the fish are fake. Its eclectic fare includes Boddington's draft ale for US$5 a pint, pork pies for US$5, and bacon 'direct from England.' It starts to jam after midnight, especially on weekends when the ships are in port.

The *Pick-a-Dilly* (☎ 242-322-2836) has pool tables, darts, and a sexy 'Girls from Brazil' swimwear show at noon each Wednesday. Want to check out the football game? Then head to the *Dockside Sports Bar*, upstairs in Prince George Plaza; or the basement bar in The Cellar.

The *Sand Dollar Bar*, at W Bay and Augusta Sts, attracts expats and locals for darts and pool. *Cocktails & Dreams* (☎ 242-328-3745), across the street, has three pool tables and a dance club and is popular with locals.

The wild side of things is represented by the Shooters Bar at *Club Waterloo* (☎ 242-393-7324), near Fort Montagu on E Bay St. It's popular with the younger college crowd, which flocks to do shooters and leap from the bungee tower! The club has a separate dance club and a quieter, more sober lounge popular with locals. There's live music Tuesday to Saturday. It's open 9 pm to 4 am nightly; admission costs US$20.

The fun starts at *Cuda Bay*, on the waterfront at the Nassau Harbour Club on E Bay St, which is open 4 pm to 7 pm and has shots for US$1. You are advised to 'get screwed' (with vodka and orange juice)!

You won't experience local color by playing the tourist, however. For that, you need to hang out at satellite lounges (so named for their satellite TVs). Although middle-class locals tend toward the same places as out-of-towners, there are plenty of funky watering holes where the non-monied classes down beers and play dominoes. Most have a TV and pool table.

On Bay St downtown, try the quiet *Pacific Bar*, just west of Victoria St; *Millie's Place*, just west of Devaux St; and the nearby *Drop Zone* (not to be confused with the Drop-Off). One block west of the Drop-Off is a dark, conspiratorial, and uniquely salacious *basement bar* with go-go dancing; US$10. The dancers also hang around the bar soliciting good prospects, but if you turn down their invitations for

extracurricular pleasures, they'll accept your 'No thanks!' graciously.

Farther afield, try the *Silver Dollar* at Farringdon and Eden Rds and *The Outback*, opposite the Esso station on Thompson Blvd. If you're passing by the Paradise Island Bridge, live music wafting across the harbor may lure you to the *Whip Sea Lounge* on Potter's Cay. This small, funky bar is popular with the Bahamian underclass, and it's earthily appealing. It offers live music on Friday, Saturday and Sunday. Beers cost US$3. There's no cover.

Cinemas

Bahamians are big moviegoers. You can choose the *Prince Charles Theatre* in the Prince Charles Shopping Centre on Prince Charles Ave, southeast of downtown, or the *Shirley Street Theatre* (☎ 242-393-2884) on Shirley St. Tickets cost US$5.

Theater

The most important venue is the *Dundas Centre for the Performing Arts* (☎ 242-393-3728) on Mackey St. Plays, dance, and (occasionally) ballets are held here. Watch for 'Summer Madness,' when popular local theatrical troupes such as James Catalyn & Friends use humor to address contemporary issues in Bahamian society. The National Youth Choir holds an annual concert in late April or early May.

Jazz

The *Silk Cotton Club* (☎ 242-356-0955), on Market St, is *the* place to hear jazz, performed by owner Henry Moss and guest stars. 'Late Night Jazz' is offered 8:30 pm to 2 am Thursday, Friday, and Saturday. Wednesday is 'Blues Night.' It's also open for dinner Tuesday to Sunday. There's no cover.

Enigma, on W Bay St, offers jazz 3 to 6 pm Sunday. *Café Matisse* (☎ 242-356-7012), on Bank Ln, also offers live jazz while you dine alfresco.

Folk/Traditional Music

For rake 'n' scrape music, check out the *Same Ol' Place,* in the Oaksfield area on

Thompson Blvd. This earthy Over-the-Hill place is the domain of less-monied locals and guarantees a warm welcome and a richly rewarding experience.

Rock

Rock music ain't big in The Bahamas. A noted exception is the *Rock 'n' Roll Cafe* (☎ 242-327-7639) in Cable Beach. This sports bar is popular with both tourists and locals. It gets rowdy late at night, especially during Saturday-night parties.

SPECTATOR SPORTS

Cricket is played on weekends from March to December at Clifford Park (☎ 242-322-1875/3622), below Fort Charlotte on W Bay St. There's no charge to watch.

Baseball games are hosted at the Queen Elizabeth Sports Centre (☎ 242-323-5163) off Thompson Blvd.

Also see Special Events and Spectator Sports in the Facts for the Visitor chapter.

THINGS TO BUY

Bay St is one of the Caribbean region's great shopping streets. It is lined with arcades (such as Prince George Plaza) and ritzy duty-free stores selling everything from Swiss watches and Colombian emeralds to Milanese fashions and lacy lingerie. You'll find great bargains on island-made products as well as imported goods. And dozens of stores sell T-shirts and kitschy souvenirs. The side streets are favored by stores selling leather goods, artwork, and collectibles. Most of the stores close at night and on Sunday, even when the cruise ships are in.

Upscale resorts also have jewelry and gift stores. The largest are the 'malls' in the Radisson Cable Beach and Marriott.

Before going on a mad spending spree, obtain a copy of *What-to-do: Where to shop, dine, stay, play, invest* (see the Information section).

Most Bahamians do their shopping in Miami, but they are also served by major shopping malls in the residential areas south of downtown. The largest, with 70 stores, is The Mall at Marathon (☎ 242-393-4043) at Marathon and Robinson Rds (you can take the shuttle that leaves from outside KFC on Woodes Rogers Walk for US$1 one way). The Towne Centre Mall (☎ 242-326-6992), at Blue Hill Rd and Independence Dr, is another multilevel mall.

Duty-Free Goods & Collectibles

Dozens of stores on Bay St sell duty-free items. Savings are not guaranteed. It pays to check out prices at home before visiting The Bahamas.

Jewelry is the big-ticket item, including watches. The largest chain is Colombian Emeralds (☎ 800-666-3889), with several outlets, and The Colombian (☎ 242-325-4083). John Bull (☎ 242-322-4252) and Little Switzerland (☎ 242-322-8324) are also represented, with a vast selection of jewelry, perfumes, leather goods, and accessories.

Most duty-free stores stock perfumes. For the best selections, try The Perfume Shop at Bay and Frederick Sts, or Lightbourn's Perfume Centre at Bay and George Sts. Even better, drive out to the Caribe Bahamas Perfume Factory (☎ 242-393-2755) for a self-guided tour; there's a gift shop.

For porcelain and crystal, check out Treasure Traders (☎ 242-322-8521) at Bay and Market Sts. For linens, head to The Linen Shop at Bay and Frederick Sts. The best places for leather goods are Fendi at Bay and Charlotte Sts, The Brass & Leather Shop on Charlotte St off Bay St, and The Leather Shop on Bank Ln off Bay St.

You can buy rare coins and postage stamps at Coin of the Realm (☎ 242-322-4497) on Charlotte St. The main post office has a philatelic bureau (☎ 242-322-3344) at E Hill and Parliament Sts. For antique maps and etchings, try Balmain Antiques (☎ 242-323-7421) at Bay and Charlotte Sts, on the 2nd floor of the Mason's Bldg.

See the Facts for the Visitor chapter for general information on buying duty-free goods.

Straw-Work & Native Items

The Straw Market at the west end of Bay St is a veritable Bahamian souk, bustling with vendors selling T-shirts, wood carvings, and straw baskets, mats, dolls, hats, and other items woven with skill and loving care. Many of the straw items are imported from Asia. The vendors expect you to bargain – it's part of the fun. Don't hesitate to beat the price down. However, most of the vendors are among the islands' poorer folks, so don't be *too* miserly! Prices for straw pieces range from about US$5 for a minipurse to US$25 for a large handbag.

The best place for genuine locally made woven items is The Plait Lady (☎ 242-356-5584) at Bay St and Victoria Ave, with everything from straw-work to conch-shell mats made on-site.

You'll also find a large straw and crafts market across from the Radisson Cable Beach, and another in the gorge leading to the Queen's Staircase on Elizabeth Ave.

Also check out Island Tings (☎ 242-326-1024) at Bay St and East St. The Bahamas Plait Market (☎ 242-326-4192) on Wulff Rd also sells straw bags, hats, and place mats.

A more diverse range of island-made items is offered at the Green Lizard (☎ 242-356-5103) on W Bay St, with everything from straw goods, hand-printed Androsia batiks, and sarongs, to guava jams, pepper sauces, and even Haitian artworks and hammocks.

Artwork

You can admire – or purchase – originals by leading contemporary artists such as Eddie Minnis and Chan Pratt at Unique Gifts (☎ 242-326-0522) on Charlotte St. Nearby, also exhibiting original works, is Charlotte's Gallery (☎ 242-322-6310). On W Bay St, Caripelago Café (☎ 242-326-3568) features an exhibit by a different artist each month. Also check out the Kennedy Gallery (☎ 242-325-7662) on Parliament St, the Nassau Art Gallery (☎ 242-393-1482) in the East Bay Shopping Centre just east of the Paradise Island Bridge, and the Andrew Aitken Art Gallery (☎ 242-328-7065) on Madeira St in the Palmdale district.

Clothing

You'll find T-shirts and resortwear at all the resort boutiques and in dozens of stores downtown. Several stores also sell simple casualwear made from Androsia batiks.

There are few bargains on high-fashion clothing. Try Coles of Nassau (☎ 242-322-8393) on Parliament St, selling designer fashions such as Calvin Klein, Vittadini, and Mondi. The Bay (☎ 242-356-3918) and, for men, Bonneville Bones (☎ 242-328-0804), both on Bay St, also sell elegant designer duds, as does Gucci (☎ 242-325-0561) on Saffrey Square off Bay St. An eclectic range of upscale clothing is available at Barry's Ltd (☎ 242-322-3118).

Se-Kelele Fabrics (☎ 242-394-6337), 100 yards north of the junction of Wulff and Soldier Rds, sells traditional African fashions and prints. It's open 9 am to 6 pm Monday to Saturday.

To pick up some designer leathers, head over to Leather Masters (☎ 242-322-7597) on Parliament St.

Women seeking something *totally* sexy for the beach should head to The Girls from Brazil (☎ 242-323-5966) on Bay St at Parliament St, selling a wide assortment of Brazilian-made bikinis . . . you know, the dental-floss kind your momma wouldn't want you to wear. Tell her you also bought one of their beautiful cover-ups. A good selection of beachwear is also sold at Mademoiselle (☎ 242-322-5130) at Bay and Frederick Sts.

Cigars

Now that *everyone's* smoking stogies, you may want to take home a box of premium Cuban cigars, which you can buy for a song in Nassau. The Pipe of Peace (☎ 242-325-2022), at Bay and Charlotte Sts, has a fine selection, as does Graycliff (☎ 242-322-2796) on W Hill St, which even plans to open a cigar factory – *holy smoke!* – next door, staffed by Cubans.

Remember, Uncle Sam prohibits US citizens from buying Cuban cigars – *that's* 'trading with the enemy' – and US Customs agents will confiscate 'em if they find 'em.

Antiques

Seeking island antiques? Then head to Marlborough Antiques (☎ 242-328-0502) at the west end of Marlborough St near the British Colonial Hotel. It has a wide range, including many items on a nautical theme. Prices are high!

Music

Most upscale hotel gift shops sell island music on CD and tape. If you're serious about music, head to Cody's Music & Video Centre (☎ 242-325-8834) at E Bay and Armstrong Sts. It carries perhaps the largest stock of native and Caribbean music in The Bahamas. The owner, Cody Carter, can guide you.

Want to take a Junkanoo drum home? Head to Pyfroms (☎ 242-322-2603) on Bay St, which sells drums and other musical instruments.

Sex Potents

If you want to put some pep in your love life, buy some Ginseng ('The Sexy Thing') Golden Tonic, a herbal medicine made from ginseng and bee-pollen tonic. Please let me know if it adds a sting to your love life. Its proclaimed attributes include 'restoring the sexual life of men and women in a simple everlasting way.' *Everlasting?* Many stores sell it, or you can call Luden Ltd (☎ 242-322-2117).

Alternately, look for 'strongback,' a local herb used by practitioners of bush medicine to put vim back into wilted willies.

Photographic Equipment

Nassau has few professional photo stores and equally few camera stores. One of the best selections is at John Bull (☎ 242-322-4252) on Bay St, which sells a wide variety of cameras and accessories. Also try Mr Photo on Frederick St off Bay St, which has one-hour developing.

Cameras are often advertised as, say, '20% below manufacturer's suggested retail price.' But that 'retail price' may be much higher than what you'd actually pay for the same item at home. Check prices at home beforehand.

GETTING THERE & AWAY
Air

Nassau is served by direct flights from numerous US cities, Canada, the UK, Jamaica, Cuba, and the Turks and Caicos. See the Getting There & Away chapter for airlines' and charter companies' international and Nassau telephone numbers.

The vast majority of visitors to The Bahamas arrive at Nassau International Airport (☎ 242-377-7035), about 8 miles west of downtown Nassau. Nassau serves as the hub for air service to all the other islands (however, at press time, the Biminis were served solely from Paradise Island International Airport, which also receives international flights; see the Paradise Island section in this chapter).

Immigrations and customs are usually a breeze, although there may be a lengthy wait if there are several flights arriving at once from Miami that are full of Bahamian nationals. Customs officials tend to go through their baggage with a fine comb. Fortunately, there's an express lane for foreign visitors.

You'll find a tourist information desk with maps and pamphlets beyond Immigration. The car-rental agencies are located just beyond Customs. The corridor straight ahead, which leads to the domestic departure terminal, has a post office, open 9:30 am to 1 pm and 2 pm to 4:30 pm weekdays; and a bank, open from 9:30 am to 3 pm Monday to Thursday and 9:30 am to 5 pm Friday. The bank has an outside ATM linked to Cirrus. There's also a telephone exchange. See the Getting Around section for information on local transportation to and from the airport.

Services in the airport's rather spartan domestic departures lounge include a meager cafe, bar, telephones, and TV. All flights to the US depart a new, comfortable terminal 100 yards west of the arrivals terminal. Departures to all other international destinations leave the terminal between the domestic and US departure terminals, east of the arrivals terminal.

Interisland private charter planes arrive at and depart the General Aviation Terminal

---

¡Cuba Sí!

You won't be long in The Bahamas (or the Turks and Caicos) before you notice advertisements for excursions to Cuba, which lies a mere 100 miles from Nassau. Despite its hardships and faults, Cuba offers a profound experience that far exceeds most visitors' expectations.

In 1995 more than 1 million Canadians, Europeans, and Mexicans visited Cuba, as did 20,000 US citizens, mostly through Mexico and Nassau. For US citizens, the temptation to visit an island that Washington, DC, has dubbed off-limits holds a compelling allure (see What Uncle Sam Says, below).

All you need to fly from Nassau is your passport and a tourist visa issued on the spot by any of the Bahamian companies that specialize in excursions to this intriguing island of socialism and sensuality. Flight times vary according to the aircraft used: Havana is about one hour from Nassau and about 90 minutes from the Turks and Caicos.

Contrary to outdated rumors of 'tourist apartheid,' foreign visitors can travel freely and mingle with Cubans without restraint. Getting around is easy via taxi or rental car, though the numerous public buses are crowded and dismal. Now is a particularly fascinating time to visit. The island is awakening from a political time warp and inching toward a market economy.

Three decades of negative reporting have led foreign visitors to expect a dour experience. It's true that the average Cuban's standard of living has plummeted since the collapse of the Soviet Union, Cuba's erstwhile umbilical cord during almost four decades of a far-reaching US trade embargo. And much of Havana is seedy and crumbling and sorely in need of a pot of paint. But the conditions and standards of living are no worse than you can find on almost every Bahamian island, and Cuba's art, dance, and music scenes are truly vibrant.

I recommend a visit to Havana. I *love* this city of tropical charms! Walking Havana's streets is otherworldly. The Spanish colonial buildings hard up against the Atlantic are handsome indeed. Old Havana (proclaimed a World Heritage Site by UNESCO in 1982

---

on Coral Harbour Rd, a half-mile east of the main terminal. There's a snack bar, restrooms, taxis, and telephone, plus an Immigration and Customs office. Porters will charge you US$3.

To/From the USA American Eagle offers turboprop service almost hourly from Miami to Nassau (one hour); its fares range from US$108 roundtrip to US$121 one way, depending on when you book.

Bahamasair, the national airline, flies from Miami to Nassau (40 minutes) up to eight times daily in winter. It flies from Orlando on Thursday, Friday, and Sunday, and from West Palm Beach daily except Tuesday and Thursday. Its headquarters are at the airport.

Low-priced fares are available from Carnival Air, which flies from Newark and New York's John F Kennedy International Airport daily (except Tuesday and Wednesday) year-round.

Continental Connection has regular daily flights from Miami (from US$98 roundtrip) and Fort Lauderdale (from US$104). Delta Air Lines flies jets twice daily from Atlanta, GA; daily from Fort Lauderdale; and daily from New York's La Guardia Airport in winter. Its commuter airline Comair has turboprop flights from Orlando and Fort Lauderdale.

Gulfstream International flies to Nassau from 12 Florida cities, plus Atlanta and Mobile, AL. Inexpensive LB Ltd (formerly Laker Airways) flies jets to Nassau from Baltimore, MD; Chicago; Cincinnati, OH; Cleveland, OH; Fort Lauderdale; Hartford, CT; and Richmond, VA.

US Airways Express flies daily from Baltimore and Charlotte, NC; it flies from Philadelphia on Saturday.

As of July 1997, Air Jamaica flew from Chicago four times weekly; roundtrip prices began at US$426/510 in low/peak season.

NEW PROVIDENCE

and currently being restored to haughty grandeur) is an exhilarating 350-acre repository of castles, churches, and columned mansions dating back centuries. Bohemian cafes spill onto colonial plazas, and at bars such as La Bodeguita and El Floridita you can sit with Ernest Hemingway's ghost and savor the proletarian fusion of dialectics and rum.

And Cuban communism doesn't mean you can't have fun. Cuba blends Caribbean rhythms with Latin sensuality. Music – salsa, rumba, and hip-swiveling *despolete* – is everywhere. Dance clubs throb to the latest sounds: world beat, hip-hop, and soca. And the Cuban people are incredibly gifted, generous, courteous, and intellectual – they will steal your heart!

What Uncle Sam Says The US Government's Trading with the Enemy Act, while not actually barring its citizens from traveling to Cuba, prohibits them from spending money there or otherwise engaging in financial transactions with Cuba. To spend even a cent, US citizens have to obtain a Treasury Dept license, which is granted only to journalists, academic researchers, and Cuban-Americans with family in Cuba. *However, if you purchase an all-inclusive package in The Bahamas or the Turks and Caicos and don't actually spend any money in Cuba, your visit is entirely legal!*

The Cuban government has an open-door policy and welcomes US tourists. Savvy to the complications faced by US tourists, Cuban immigration officials don't stamp passports.

Getting There & Away Several Bahamian tour companies offer weekend and longer excursions using Cubana Airline charters from Nassau. Several airline charter companies in the Turks and Caicos offer their own flights from Providenciales. Most include airfare, transfers, city tours, some meals and entertainment, and accommodations for overnight trips. You can pay for your tour with a US credit card. However, US credit cards cannot be used in Cuba.

See island chapters for details. ■

Charter companies that serve Nassau include Sunquest Holidays, with direct flights from Los Angeles every Sunday (prices begin at US$319 roundtrip); TNT Vacations, flying from Boston on Saturday; and Island Hoppers, which offers air-hotel packages for as little as US$163 in summer, including roundtrip airfare from Miami and two nights of accommodations.

Apple Vacations offers charters from Baltimore/Washington, DC; Pittsburgh; and Philadelphia on Monday and Friday. GoGo Worldwide Vacations offers charters to Nassau from Newark five times weekly.

To/From Canada Air Canada flies to Nassau once weekly from Toronto, with peak fares from C$447 roundtrip; it also flies from Montreal.

Air Transat flies charters from Toronto for as little as C$300 in low season (summer). Regent Holidays offers charters and air/hotel packages using Air Transat. Canada

3000 flies from Toronto; Conquest Tours flies from Toronto on Thursday and Sunday, and also flies from Winnipeg and Halifax.

To/From the UK & Continental Europe British Airways flies directly from Heathrow and offers charters from Gatwick. It also offers flights to Miami. UK charter services include Thomson Holidays, flying from Gatwick and Manchester each alternate week.

LTU International Airways flies from Dusseldorf and Munich.

To/From the Caribbean Air Jamaica flies from Montego Bay twice weekly (fares start at US$207 roundtrip for a seven-day excursion). Cubana has flights from Havana four times weekly, and Gulfstream International offers charter flights *to* Havana.

To/From Elsewhere in The Bahamas Service to neighboring islands is offered by Bahamasair and local charter airlines. Nassau is Bahamasair's hub, and its service to all other Bahamian islands is centered here. See the Getting Around chapter and the island chapters' Getting There & Away sections for details on flights, times, and fares.

Boat

More than a dozen cruise lines offer cruises from Florida to Nassau or include Nassau on their Caribbean itineraries. All berth at Prince George Wharf. See the Getting There & Away chapter for details.

Private Yacht Nassau has several marinas, including the following:

East Bay Yacht Basin (☎ /fax 242-394-1816)

Lightbourne Marina, PO Box N-4849, Nassau (☎ 242-393-5285, fax 242-393-6236)

Nassau Harbour Club & Marina, PO Box SS-5755, Nassau (☎ 242-393-0771, fax 242-393-5393)

Nassau Yacht Haven (☎ 242-393-8173)

The Yacht Haven is a modest affair: There's a pool, restaurant, and bar, plus showers and a private beach, and the club offers sailing programs, including a summer course for kids. But it gets few in-transit yachters (charged US$10 per day) and has no diesel or gasoline.

Moorings are at a premium. Reservations are advised. All vessels must clear themselves with Nassau Harbour Control (VHF channel 16) when entering or departing Nassau.

Paradise Island also has marinas; see the Paradise Island section for details.

Ferry & Water Taxi The Paradise Island Ferry leaves from Prince George Wharf every half-hour, 9:30 am to 6 pm (US$2 per person). Water taxis also operate from Woodes Rogers Walk, departing when full. Other water taxis operate from near the Sugar Reef Bar & Restaurant at John Alfred Wharf. You'll see the signs or be hustled aboard by touts.

Also see the Boating & Sailing section.

Mail Boat Mail boats regularly depart Potter's Cay for Grand Bahama and all the Family Islands. See the Mail Boat section in the Getting Around chapter for a complete schedule of departures, plus island chapters' Getting There & Away sections. You can call the Dockmaster's Office (☎ 242-393-1064) for the latest information.

GETTING AROUND
To/From the Airport

There are no buses to or from the airport. The taxi-drivers' union has things sewn up. Only a handful of leading hotels provide shuttle services. If you're prebooked into one of the major hotels, you'll be steered to minibuses operated by the bigger tour operators. They're parked to the left as you exit the arrivals hall.

Taxis are available immediately outside the arrivals lounge. There's an official dispatcher (☎ 242-323-5111) and no hustlers. Rates are fixed by the government. A taxi to Lyford Cay for two people costs US$10; to Cable Beach, US$12; to downtown and Prince George Wharf, US$18; to Paradise Island, US$18 (plus US$2 bridge toll). Each additional person costs US$3. Some taxi drivers may try to charge the third or fourth person the same rate as for two people. Don't fall for this rip-off!

Taxis generally take you into town along W Bay St, and *to* the airport along John F Kennedy Dr.

There's a telephone desk for limousine services immediately beyond Immigration.

Bus

Nassau is well served by Japanese minibuses called 'jitneys,' operated by private companies (about 40 companies in all). Jitneys run throughout the day, 6 am to 8 pm. There are no fixed schedules.

The main westbound service departs a stop by the British Colonial Hotel at the corner of Navy Lion Rd and Bay St; eastbound service departs the intersection of Frederick and Bay Sts near the straw market downtown. Bus stops are well marked, but you can also wave the jitneys down or request a stop anywhere along their routes.

To request a stop when you're onboard, simply shout, 'Bus stop!'

The standard fare is US75¢ (children US50¢). No change is given for dollar bills, although the drivers will change US$5 bills (you receive US$4 back). You pay the driver upon exiting the bus.

Buses No 10 and 38 serve Cable Beach and downtown, running as far east as Sandy Point. They stop in front of each hotel in Cable Beach, and you'll rarely have to wait more than five minutes for a bus. Westbound, they run along Bay St. Eastbound, they turn inland at Goodman's Bay and take a circuitous route through town, passing through Over-the-Hill and eventually depositing you at Prince George Wharf.

Buses No 24 and 30 run to the Paradise Island Bridge but *not* to the island.

Car & Scooter

Most downtown streets are one way and often congested. Parking downtown is at a premium. It's easiest to head for the public parking lot on Charlotte St (there are several others nearby), where you can park all day for US$7.50 maximum (US$2.50 the first hour). You'll also find parking lots on Elizabeth Ave, which charge US$3 per day.

You really don't need a car to explore Nassau. If you intend to explore farther afield, the following US companies have rental booths at the airport:

Avis	☎ 242-377-7121
Budget	☎ 242-377-7405
Dollar	☎ 242-377-7301
Hertz	☎ 242-377-8684
National	☎ 242-327-8231

Avis' rates begin at US$70 for a subcompact automatic (Geo Metro or Suzuki Swift) and run up to US$109 for a Ford Taurus. It also has offices at Cable Beach (☎ 242-322-2889) and downtown (☎ 242-326-6380) on W Bay St. Budget and Dollar also have offices downtown. Budget has slightly lower rates.

Several local companies also rent cars. Orange Creek Rentals (☎ 242-323-4967, fax 242-356-5005) has cars from US$39 a day for a minimum of three days. You can also try Kemco (☎ 242-323-2178), Wallace's (☎ 242-393-0650), or Teglo Car Rentals (☎ 242-362-4361). Rates begin at about US$60. Insurance policies vary, so check the costs and details carefully before making a commitment. Usually collision damage waiver insurance costs US$12 a day, with a small deductible that you'll be required to pay in the event of an accident.

Scooters are widely available and can be found outside most major hotels. Downtown, try Knowles Scooter & Bike Rental (☎ 242-356-0741), outside the British Colonial Hotel. It rents scooters for US$25 for two hours, US$35 half-day, and US$45 full day.

You'll also find scooters for rent opposite the resort on the south side of W Bay St in Cable Beach.

Taxi

Taxis wait outside all major hotels. Rarely, you may be able to flag down a taxi passing on the road. Usually taxis are radio-dispatched. Summon a taxi by calling Meter Cabs (☎ 242-323-5111) on Davis St or the Bahamas Taxi Cab Union (☎ 242-323-4555/5818) on Nassau St.

Taxis are metered, though few drivers use them. All drivers quote set fares determined by the government. Short rides cost US$2 for the first quarter-mile and US30¢ for each additional mile, for two people (additional passengers are charged US$2 each). If you cross the Paradise Island Bridge, you must pay the US$2 bridge toll.

The fare from Cable Beach to downtown is about US$9 to US$12, depending on where you're dropped off. A trip between Cable Beach and Paradise Island costs about US$13 (plus bridge toll). A ride from downtown to Paradise Island costs about US$9.

You can negotiate with a driver for a guided tour of the island. The legal maximum charge for a tour is US$20 per hour for a five-passenger cab, plus US$10 per extra half-hour; minivans cost US$25 per hour.

Bicycle

Ask if your hotel rents bicycles. Few do, but most places that rent scooters also rent bicycles. Knowles (see Car & Scooter, above) charges US$15 per day. The bicycles are beach cruisers, single-gear bikes on which the pedal functions as the brake, too! They're not very comfortable or agile and are not recommended for pregnant women or men with hernias.

Surrey

Nassau's quaint horse-drawn surreys are a great way to explore downtown Nassau at an easy pace. They begin and end from Woodes Rogers Walk at Prince George Wharf. A 30-minute ride costs US$5 per person. Negotiate a price before climbing aboard if you want to hire a surrey for longer touring. They're available 9 am to 4:30 pm daily, except 1 to 2 pm (November to April) and 1 to 3 pm (May to October), when the horses are rested.

Paradise Island

Part of Nassau or separate from it? Paradise Island lies almost shouting distance across the harbor from Nassau, to which it is linked by a great arcing bridge. Despite its proximity, its level of sophistication and markedly contemporary development make it distinct, with a mood wholly different from the city across the 'bay.'

The island boasts many ritzy hotels, The Bahamas' most sophisticated casino, and, rimming its entire north coast, gorgeous white beaches that outclass all others on New Providence. In general, it attracts a more monied crowd than does Nassau's Cable Beach, which is a sort of Reno to Paradise Island's Las Vegas.

In prior centuries it was used for raising pigs and became known as Hog Island. Boatbuilding also thrived during the 18th and 19th centuries, when the isle was already a tourist mecca, replete with Victorian bathing houses, for Nassauvians making picnicking day trips.

Early in the 20th century, a few wealthy socialites – they formed the Porcupine Club, for *multi*millionaires only – built homes, including Joseph Lynch, founder of the Merrill-Lynch investment company. In 1939 Dr Axel Wenner-Gren, a wealthy Swedish industrialist, bought much of the island, including the Lynch estate. After the war he developed a hideaway, which he called 'Shangri-La,' with a terraced garden modeled on Versailles. Wenner-Gren later sold the property to wealthy scion Huntington Hartford II. The playboy millionaire built a 52-room hotel – the Ocean Club – on the estate, convinced the Bahamian legislature to rename the island 'Paradise Island,' and then added a marina, an 18-hole golf course, and even a 14th-century cloister that he purchased from newspaper magnate William Randolph Hearst.

No bridge existed back then, and the island boasted super-snob appeal: 'There will be no automobiles, no roulette wheels, no honky-tonks on Hog Island,' Hartford proclaimed. The Ocean Club became the home-away-from-home for the Shah of Iran while in residence in the Bahamas. But the club did not fare well, and the island was sold to the Mary Carter Paint Company. As Resorts International, the company built the magnificent bridge in 1967 and set up the Paradise Island Casino before falling into the hands of Donald Trump and Merv Griffin, who built other resorts nearby, as well as the airport. After a brief construction surge, when dozens of expensive homes went up, the island felt the effects of a worldwide economic recession.

In 1994 billionaire Sol Kerzner's Sun International, a South African company that now owns 70% of the island, scooped up three resorts – the Paradise Island Resort & Casino, the Ocean Club, and Paradise Paradise. The recent emergence of Paradise Island as a ritzy destination has much to do with the massive investment by Sun. The remake of the Paradise Island Resort & Casino as the Atlantis – with a massive expansion underway – inspired

NEW PROVIDENCE

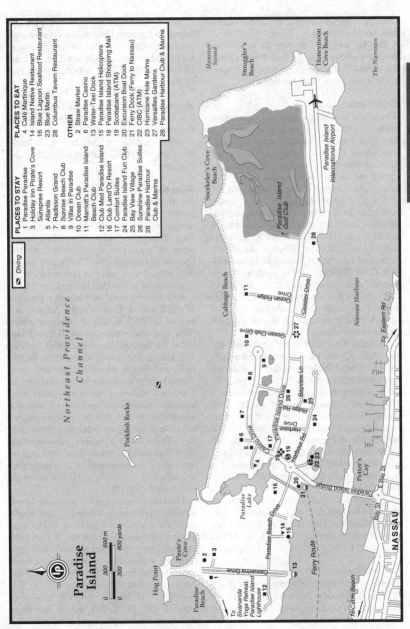

Paradise Island

LP

| 0 | 300 | 600 m |
| 0 | 300 | 600 yards |

Northeast Providence Channel

⊿ Diving

Hog Point

Porkfish Rocks

Paradise Beach

Pirate's Cove

Paradise Lake

Cabbage Beach

Snorkeler's Cove Beach

Paradise Island Golf Club

Hanover Sound

Smuggler's Beach

Honeymoon Cove Beach

The Narrows

Paradise Island International Airport

Ocean Ridge

Ocean Club Drive

Cloister Drive

Casuarina Drive

Paradise Beach Drive

Paradise Island Drive

Casino Drive

Harbour Drive

Ridge Rd

Bayview Ln

Harbour Rd

Ferry Route

Paradise Island Bridge

Nassau Harbour

Potter's Cay

To Eastern Rd

E Bay St

Bay St

NASSAU

To Cable Beach

To Sivananda Yoga Retreat, Paradise Island Lighthouse

PLACES TO STAY
1 Paradise Paradise
3 Holiday Inn Pirate's Cove
5 Sunspree Resort
7 Radisson Grand
8 Sunrise Beach Club
9 Villas in Paradise
10 Ocean Club
11 Marriott's Paradise Island Beach Club
12 Club Med Paradise Island
16 Club Land'Or Resort
17 Comfort Suites
24 Paradise Island Fun Club
25 Bay View Village
26 Sunshine Paradise Suites
28 Paradise Harbour Club & Marina

PLACES TO EAT
4 Café Martinique
14 Island Native Restaurant
16 Blue Lagoon Seafood Restaurant
23 Blue Marlin
28 Columbus Tavern Restaurant

OTHER
2 Straw Market
6 Paradise Casino
13 Water-Taxi Dock
15 Paradise Island Helicopters
18 Paradise Island Shopping Mall
19 Scotiabank (ATM)
20 Excursion Boat Dock
21 Ferry Dock (Ferry to Nassau)
22 CIBC (ATM)
23 Hurricane Hole Marina
27 Versailles Gardens
28 Paradise Harbour Club & Marina

other hoteliers to invest, and the island is now on an upswing.

Despite this, and despite its small size, there are plenty of sequestered coves along the sand-lined shores and plenty of lonesome spots away from the hordes.

Orientation

The island is 4 miles long and a half-mile wide, tapering to the west. It is divided in two by a narrow manmade waterway linking Nassau Harbour to the north shore (the channel opens to a lagoon that is being 'waterscaped' into a vast new marine park – Paradise Lake – as part of the Atlantis project).

The road across the bridge from Nassau descends to a tollbooth and roundabout (traffic circle) just east of the waterway. It continues as Casino Dr to the Atlantis and 2-mile-long Cabbage Beach. Farther east, separated by a small headland, is Snorkeler's Cove Beach, another stunner that is usually deserted except for the few hours each midday when excursion boats disgorge passengers for snorkeling and picnics. Virtually deserted Smuggler's Beach lines the east shore.

Paradise Beach Dr leads west from the roundabout, over the waterway and a half-mile to Club Med, intersecting Casuarina Dr, which runs north to Pirate's Cove. The cove is separated by a small peninsula – Hog Point – from 2-mile-long Paradise Beach, with sand as white and fine as pulverized sugar. It curls west to the red-and-white-striped Paradise Island Lighthouse at the tip of the island. West of Club Med's sprawling property, the peninsula is accessible only by water or by walking the beach.

Harbour Rd leads east from the roundabout past Hurricane Hole Marina to Paradise Island Fun Club. Paradise Island Dr, a block north of the roundabout, leads east to the Ocean Club, golf course, and airport.

Information

There is no tourist information booth on the island. *Paradise Islander* is a slick full-color magazine. Most hotel rooms stock a free copy for guests.

You'll also find sections on Paradise Island in Dupuch Publications' two handy guides to shopping, sightseeing, restaurants, and entertainment, available at hotel lobbies and the tourist information bureaus in Nassau.

Scotiabank has a branch by the roundabout on the north side of the bridge. CIBC has a branch at Hurricane Hole Marina. Both have outdoor ATMs.

For information on nearby tourist facilities, see the Information section under Nassau in this chapter.

Atlantis

No trip would be complete without a visit to the Atlantis' 14-acre waterscape, the source of the hotel's slogan: 'An ocean runs through it.' Here the world's largest open-air aquarium teems with over 100 species of tropical fish. The facility has its own map, which you can pick up from the concierge or at the Hospitality Cavern.

Sun International remade the Paradise Island Resort & Casino as the Atlantis at a cost of US$195 million. It now has waterfalls and the quarter-mile 'Lazy River Ride' for tubing, plus six exhibit lagoons filled with live coral, more than 14,000 fish, and heaps of other sea life, best viewed from a 100-foot-long underwater Plexiglas walkway or from other subaqueous tunnels surrounded by massive aquariums through which 3 million gallons of ocean water are recycled four times each day. There's the Predator Lagoon, with nine fish species, more than 100 sharks, and even a gargantuan jewfish, a behemoth sea bass that can grow to 10 feet in length and weigh 1000 lbs!

The best time to check it out is the 10 am feeding on Tuesday, Thursday, and weekends. At noon or 4 pm, head to the Seagrapes Lagoon to watch the 9-foot-long sawfish being fed. And the kids will love running across the bouncy rope bridge spanning the manmade rock cliffs. Indiana Jones never had it so good!

Atlantis is hugely popular and successful, and justifiably so: It has more diversions than a circus and is a destination in its own right, day or night. Phase II of the project is ongoing (scheduled for completion in 1998) and will add yet more vast expanses of shark-infested waterways and landscaped grounds.

Guided walking tours are offered from the Coral Towers Lobby at 10 am and at 1 and 4 pm. For details, call ☎ 242-363-3000 and ask for Guest Services, ext 28. There's no admission charge.

Versailles Gardens

Dr Axel Wenner-Gren's ostentatious binge resulted in the creation of this sweeping 35-acre garden, stepped in tiers and lined with classical statues depicting the millionaire's heroes. They span the ages: Hercules, Napoleon Bonaparte, and Franklin D Roosevelt are here, to name a few.

Paradise Island Dr runs through the gardens, which fall away on both sides. At the crest is a classical gazebo of columned arches – **The Cloisters** – where weddings are often held. This genuine 600-year-old structure was originally part of an Augustine estate in France, and had languished in crates in Florida, intended for William Randolph Hearst's estate in California.

Huntington Hartford II bought it and shipped it piece by piece to Paradise Island.

Activities

Water sports are available at all the resorts along Paradise and Cabbage beaches. Most of the motorized sports are operated by local entrepreneurs (the resorts post signs disclaiming responsibility). Typical prices include US$30 for 30 minutes' jet-skiing; US$10 per person for a 15-minute banana boat ride, and US$20 for 10 minutes' parasailing. The main outlet is Sea & Ski Ocean Sports (☎ 242-363-3370) on Cabbage Beach, which also offers snorkeling for US$25 and scuba diving for US$35 per single-tank dive.

Paradise Island Golf Club (☎ 242-363-3925, 800-321-3000), at the Ocean Club, is a Dick Wilson-designed championship course known for its rippling fairways, woodsy copses, and strange hazards such as a water pipe, windmill, and the world's largest sand trap. Its 14th hole is legendary for its splendid vistas. Green fees are US$50/80 summer/winter, including a golf cart. Vital statistics: 72-par, 6776-yard, five bunkers per hole.

Wedding Bells

The Bahamas is a popular destination for honeymooners, many of whom tie the knot in the islands. The requirements are easily met. A wedding license is normally granted if either party can prove that he or she is staying in The Bahamas for a minimum of three days.

The license costs US$40 and can be obtained from the Registrar General's Office (☎ 242-326-5371, 242-328-7810) in the Rodney E Bain Bldg on Parliament St in Nassau. You'll need photo identification, proof of citizenship, proof of status if you are divorced or widowed, and an 'Affidavit of Competency to Marry' from the US Embassy & Consulate (it costs US$10). No blood test is required. Anyone under 18 years of age requires notarized parental consent.

The Ministry of Tourism's 'Weddings in Paradise' service will put you in touch with local consultants who can plan a wedding. Most major hotels and tour operators can also make arrangements; they usually ask couples to send notarized copies of required documents at least one month in advance. Major resorts have special honeymoon packages and can arrange a wedding with a minister. ■

Saying 'I do' at The Cloisters

The club hosts the Ladies' Futures ProAm Golf Tournament, featuring top international players, each September; in October the International Mixed Championship Golf Tournament draws amateurs to compete.

Sport fishing is available from charter boats at Hurricane Hole Marina and beneath the Paradise Island Bridge. The bulletin board at Hurricane Hole Marina lists skippers with boats for charter.

All the resorts have tennis courts. The main venue, however, is Club Med Paradise Island (☎ 242-363-2640), with 20 courts, professional instructors, and special tennis clinics with one-on-one teaching by seeded professionals.

The Ocean Club (☎ 242-363-3000) also has a major tennis program, and it hosts tennis championships.

Dolphin Encounters Wow! Kids (regardless of age) can swim with trained Atlantic bottle-nosed dolphins in a protected lagoon at Blue Lagoon Island (☎ 242-363-3578/3577, fax 242-363-1657), PO Box N-7366, Nassau, Bahamas. The movies *Zeus & Roxanne* and *Flipper* were both filmed at this 2-sq-mile private cay and featured the aquatic stars Jake, MacGyver, and Fatman. Scenes from *Splash* were also filmed here.

You can take a half-day 'Dolphin Encounter' trip to the island with Nassau Cruises (☎ 242-363-3577, fax 242-363-1657, cruise@bahamas.net.bs) from Paradise Island that includes a 30-minute swim with these clever mammals; the trip costs US$85. The animals will swim around you and even let you touch them. Nonswimmers and toddlers can opt for a more sedate option, standing in a shallow lagoon, where the dolphins will also let you touch them. A 'Stingray Snorkel' is also offered at Blue Lagoon for US$45.

Boat Excursions Most cruises depart Paradise Island from the dock immediately west of the Paradise Island Bridge. See the Nassau section for cruises that depart marinas on New Providence.

Several uninhabited cays are sprinkled northeast of New Providence, most enticingly Blue Lagoon Island (see above), featured on several day cruises. It's a 30-minute ride from Nassau. Here you can create your own desert-island fantasy. Choose among snorkeling, parasailing, volleyball, or even a dolphin encounter. A live band plays. There's a craft center, the Stingray City Marine Park – where you can swim with the rays – and helicopter tours. There are nature walks, changing rooms, restrooms, showers, and 250 hammocks slung between palms.

A half-day excursion to Blue Lagoon Island with Nassau Cruises (see above)

costs US$20 per person; a six-hour trip costs US$35; a full day costs US$45, including hotel transfers, unlimited water sports, and lunch. The company operates the 100-foot-long, three-deck *Calypso I* and *Calypso II*, taking up to 125 people at a time. Each boat has a bar and dancing. Departures are offered at 10 and 11:30 am daily, returning to Paradise Island at 1:30, 3, and 4 pm. Its mailing address is PO Box N-7366, Nassau, Bahamas.

The same company also offers a 'Historical Harbour Cruise' around Paradise Island, passing the lighthouse, Arawak Cay, pirate homes, and other sites, tracing The Bahamas' colorful past. The trips depart at 9:30 am daily; they take about 90 minutes and cost US$20.

Flying Cloud Catamaran Cruises (☎ 242-393-1957) offers similar cruises aboard the *Flying Cloud*, a 57-foot catamaran that departs Paradise Island 200 yards west of the Paradise Island Bridge. It sails daily except Thursday and Sunday. A half-day cruise costs US$30; a dinner cruise costs US$50. Out Island Voyages (☎ 242-394-0951) offers excursion cruises from the same dock.

For adventures farther afield, Island World Adventures (☎ 242-363-3577, fax 242-363-1657, cruise@bahamas.net.bs) offers daylong excursions to Saddleback Cay (Exumas), whisking you there aboard the 45-foot, high-powered *EcoTime*. You can skinny-dip on any of six beaches, take guided hikes, snorkel, etc. The trips depart daily from Paradise Island Canal Dock at the foot of the bridge and include a stop at Leaf Cay to commune with iguanas. The mailing address is PO Box N-7366, Paradise Island, Bahamas.

Organized Tours

Island Ranger Helitours (☎ 242-363-1040) has breathtaking whirlybird tours over Nassau and Paradise Island and out to Blue Lagoon Island. The 10-minute escapade, which costs US$25, is a good way to get your bearings . . . and some spectacular photos. Longer tours are offered. Trips are

offered 9 am to 6 pm daily from the Paradise Island Heliport on Paradise Beach Dr.

Places to Stay

Paradise Island is not a budget-traveler's haven. Nonetheless, there are a few gems.

Places to Stay – budget & middle

In the heart of luxe is *Sivananda Yoga Retreat* (☎ 242-363-2902, 800-783-9642, fax 242-363-3783, syvcnas@100jamz.com), a reclusive gem amid lush, tranquil grounds on the slender western peninsula of Paradise Island. The place – also known as 'Club Meditation' – is the epitome of calm simplicity. It has dozens of tent sites beneath shady palms (watch out for falling coconuts), where you can camp for US$40. Dormitory rooms in the main building cost US$45. Other accommodations are in rustic yet cozy cabins in the Oriental garden or facing the beach; rates are US$50 for a 'semi-private' share, US$60 for oceanfront, and US$75 single.

The daily schedule is based on Swami Vishnu-devananda's 'Five Points' for a long and healthy life, based on meditation, yoga, proper exercise, etc. Classes are offered daily, including intensive training and residential study. Two buffet-style lacto-vegetarian meals are served daily. Reservations are essential. Bring your own towel. Families with children are welcome. You can reach it by walking along Paradise Beach. A free water taxi – *Godavri* – also operates from Sugar Reef Bar & Restaurant in Nassau. The retreat's postal address is PO Box N-7550, Nassau, Bahamas.

The *Howelton Rose House* (☎ 242-363-3363), a B&B also known as the Pink House, is a showpiece in more ways than one. The Georgian-style inn, which operates like a family-owned manor, dates from 1927, when it was owned by the Sears (as in Sears-Roebuck) family. It starred in the 1994 movie *My Father, the Hero*, in which the father (Gerard Depardieu) and daughter take a Caribbean vacation. It nestles amid 15 acres of tropical gardens toward the west end of the island. Each of the four bedrooms opens onto its own balcony or patio. The lounge and other public arenas are jammed with antiques, wicker furniture, blue-and-white chintz sofas, and other faded mementos of genteel grandeur, lending the home a charming French-chateaux feel. Gracious owner Minni Winn oversees your comfort. Rooms rent for US$80/90 in summer/ winter. A bargain!

Another gem lies 400 yards west of the Yoga Retreat. *Chaplin House* (☎ 242-363-2918) is a delightfully funky old home lived in by Ronnie and Joan Carol, who rent three charming and romantic (albeit simple) cottages of whitewashed rough-hewn hardwoods. The cottages vary in size. Each has a kitchen, air-con, and fan. Verandahs look out over lush grounds where macaws hang out freely in fruit trees. The Carols prefer long-term rentals. It's perfect for island-style living! Studio apartments cost US$95; one-/two-bedroom cottages cost US$100/110. A third person sharing costs US$20. No credit cards are accepted. A water taxi ride from Sugar Reef Bar & Restaurant in Nassau costs US$2. The postal address is PO Box SS-6034, Nassau, Bahamas.

Places to Stay – top end Near Paradise Beach, *Paradise Paradise* (☎ 242-363-3000, 800-321-3000, fax 242-363-2540), owned by Sun International, has 100 unsophisticated, modestly appealing rooms. It has a range of water sports, including sailing and windsurfing. Free transportation is offered to Atlantis, where guests have free use of facilities. Winter rates are US$120/ 140 standard/superior. All-inclusive packages are offered. The postal address is PO Box N-4777, Nassau, Bahamas.

The *Paradise Harbour Club & Marina* (☎ 242-363-2992, fax 242-363-2840), on Paradise Island Dr, is a small, attractive, Swiss-run property in a marina setting. It's popular with German tour groups. Rooms are spacious and clean, with large kitchens and contemporary decor. There's

no beach at hand, but the splendid Columbus Tavern Restaurant is here. Winter rates begin at US$130 double. Junior suites start at US$210 in winter, and apartments begin at US$275. Its postal address is PO Box SS-5804, Nassau, Bahamas.

In a decidedly French vein is *Club Med Paradise Island* (☎ 242-363-2640, 800-258-2633, fax 242-363-3496). The resort, spanning the island from Paradise Beach to Nassau Harbour, was created from three turn-of-the-century estates and underwent a US$15 million renovation in 1997; it now has 41 single-occupancy rooms added to its 320 air-con doubles. All are decorated in soft earth tones and exotic art. Per-person rates are US$130 to US$210 for a standard double room. Deluxe rooms cost 10% more. Single rooms cost 20% to 100% more than the standard rates, depending on season.

The club is popular with honeymooners, who can choose the exquisite 'House in the Woods,' a two-story, Bermudan-style private villa with gingerbread trim, housekeeping service, and wraparound porches on both levels, plus a wrought-iron bed with a plump down duvet as soft as a cloud. It costs US$200 per person or US$375 during holiday periods.

The property encompasses 23 beautifully landscaped acres centered on the main dining room, theater, and nightclub. The buffet meals (continental cuisine) have to be seen to be believed! Dining is family-style. There are also two open-air restaurants: One, in an old Italianate villa, offers Italian fare; the other offers seafood. The club boasts an Olympic-size pool, 19 tennis courts, and an intensive tennis program at no extra cost. Bjorn Borg, Rosie Casals, and Virginia Wade are among the pros who have taught here during the 'Legends of Tennis' session each spring. Excursions, water sports, and recreational activities are offered. Club Med is for gregarious folks – if you're reclusive, it could be a banana peel waiting to happen. Its postal address is PO Box N-7137, Nassau, Bahamas.

The aptly named *Holiday Inn Pirate's Cove Sunspree Resort* (☎ 242-363-2100, fax 242-363-2006), immediately east of Paradise Paradise, overlooks beautiful, flask-shaped Pirate's Cove. Suitably, there's a re-created pirate ship in the pool! The 564-room high-rise has modest furnishings. Children are catered to with the 'Captain Kids' program. In winter standard rooms begin at US$150; junior suites begin at US$200. The mailing address is PO Box SS-6214, Paradise Island, Nassau, Bahamas.

Comfort Suites (☎ 242-363-3680, 800-228-5150, fax 242-363-2588) is a soulless US-motel-style option on Casino Dr. Still, all 150 rooms are nicely furnished. Junior suites (most with king-size beds and all with sofa bed, cable TV, minibar, hairdryer, and safe) and the pool and sun deck areas are attractive. Kids under 18 stay free with parents. Guests have free access to all Atlantis facilities and can make charges directly to their rooms. Its winter rates range from US$159 to US$199. The postal address is PO Box SS-6202, Nassau, Bahamas.

Lushly landscaped and reclusive *Sunrise Beach Club* (☎ 242-363-2234, 800-451-6078, fax 242-363-2308), on Casino Dr, is an Italianate complex of upscale villas, beautifully furnished and highlighted within by two-person marble tubs. Other romantic touches include bathrooms with stained-glass windows and a tiny garden with burbling waterfall in each lounge. Some villas have mezzanine bedrooms. There are two small, exquisitely landscaped swimming pools. Daily rates in winter range from US$150 to US$775, depending on villa size. The mailing address is PO Box SS-6519, Nassau, Bahamas.

The *Paradise Island Fun Club* (☎ 242-363-2561, fax 242-363-3803; in the USA ☎ 800-952-2426, fax 212-221-8198) is an all-inclusive resort – a kind of poor person's Club Med – overlooking Nassau Harbour. It has a panoply of activities, including tennis, dive lessons, and 'Camp Fun Club' for kids. There's a lively restaurant, plus a pool and sun deck facing the harbor. The rooms are nicely furnished and have necessary conveniences; they cost US$160 per person double. However, it lacks the engaging spirit of Club Med and Sandals. The local postal address is PO Box SS-6249, Paradise Island, Nassau, Bahamas; in the USA write 120 W 44th St, New York, NY 10036.

Bay View Village (☎ 242-363-2555, fax 242-363-2370), in a leafy, upscale residential area, has cozy and pleasingly furnished rooms. Its rates in the winter run from US$160 for one-bedroom suites to US$420 for six-person villas. Bay View's postal address is PO Box SS-6308, Nassau, Bahamas. It's also popular with German charter groups, as is *Sunshine Paradise Suites* (☎ 242-363-3955, 800-813-6847, fax 242-363-3840), a similar property farther north on Paradise Island Dr, which has 16 self-catering suites for daily, weekly, and monthly rental. In wintertime, Sunshine's suites cost US$165/195 for one/two bedrooms. There's a small pool in the front courtyard. Sunshine's mailing address is PO Box SS-5206, Paradise Island, Nassau, Bahamas.

A high-rise option is the *Radisson Grand* (☎ 242-363-3500, 800-333-3333, fax 242-363-3900) on Casino Dr. It's very contemporary, with 327 air-con rooms and 33 suites – all in quasitropical decor – that overlook the spectacular beach and a huge triangular pool and sun deck. There's a choice of restaurants, plus a dance club. Room rates vary by month; January rates run from US$175 to US$520. The mailing address is PO Box SS-6307, Paradise Island, Nassau, Bahamas.

I like the cozy *Club Land'Or Resort* (☎ 242-363-2400, fax 242-363-3403; in the USA ☎ 804-346-8200, 800-552-2839), which faces onto Paradise Lake and has a contemporary Mediterranean feel. It's centered on a small pool. The one-bedroom 'villas' (rooms) are romantically furnished, with French lace curtains; they sleep up to six people and have splendid kitchens. It boasts the fine Blue Lagoon Restaurant and has a full roster of entertainment, from poolside fashion shows to bingo and guided excursions. A shuttle runs to Paradise Beach at 10 am and noon daily, returning at 2 and 4 pm. Alas, it's overpriced: Rates begin at US$215 single or double in winter. Each additional person costs US$25. The mailing address is PO Box SS-6429, Paradise Island, Nassau, Bahamas.

Take a little bit of Disneyland, add Las Vegas and a splash of Sea World, and you have *Atlantis* (☎ 242-363-3000; in the USA 800-321-3000, fax 242-363-3524). Huge, bustling, and magnificent, it is unlike any hotel this side of Vegas. Hotel? It's a megaresort. The 1150 rooms boast hints of the tropics in their upscale, contemporary feel. All have a balcony, TV with in-room movies, phones, safe, minibar, and soft yellow decor blending with rattan and light wood furniture. The highlight is the resort's waterscape (see the Atlantis section in this chapter). Atlantis also has 12 specialty restaurants, the Paradise Island Casino, a cabaret, a comedy show, and several bars. Winter rates begin at US$300/350 standard/deluxe, single or double. Summer rates are 50% lower. The resort offers special package rates. A MAP (breakfast and dinner plan) package costs US$43 per person per day, and a 'Gourmet Dining Plan' costs US$72. Its postal address is PO Box N-4777, Nassau, Bahamas.

Villas in Paradise (☎ /fax 242-363-2998) on Casino Dr offers one- to four-bedroom villas with private pool, full kitchen, and options for king-size beds. Winter rates range from US$260 to US$485 for two people. A minimum seven-night stay is required at Christmas, New Year's, and Easter. The mailing address is PO Box SS-6379, Paradise Island, Nassau, Bahamas.

Other two-bedroom villas – good for up to six people – are at *Marriott's Paradise Island Beach Club* (☎ 242-363-2814, fax 242-363-2130) on Ocean Ridge Dr. Villas have fully equipped kitchens. Winter rates average US$375/2500 daily/weekly. It has

no restaurant. The postal address is PO Box N-10600, Nassau, Bahamas.

You'll know you've arrived if you can afford to stay at the *Ocean Club* (☎ 242-363-3000, fax 242-363-2424), where rates begin at a whopping US$545! No wonder sightings of Michael Jackson have been reported here. This exquisite colonial property is centered on a large pool at one end of Versailles Gardens and exudes European elegance, with a refined, casual ambiance and exclusive touches such as complimentary shoe shines. The 58 rooms (including four suites and five two-bedroom villas) are capacious, with large his-and-her bathrooms done up in marble, elegant bygone-era decor, and state-of-the-art amenities like a 27-inch TV. Crystal and silver sparkle on linen-draped tables around the courtyard dining area. You can also dine at the Clubhouse Bar & Grill, overlooking the pool and gardens, and at Hartford's Bar, serving complimentary hors d'oeuvres. The resort abuts a splendid section of beach and has its own Bermudan-style bar. The club boasts the Paradise Island Golf Club and nine tennis courts. Guests also have access to Atlantis' facilities. The club's postal address is PO Box N-4777, Nassau, Bahamas.

Sun Cay, a small private island about 1 mile east of Paradise Island and 1 mile west of Rose Island (see the New Providence map), was opened in 1996 with a clubhouse, pool, wharf, and two bars set around an old lighthouse. The island was formerly named Spruce Cay. You can stay in suites opening to a beach. The place is intended to be used by private parties, such as weddings.

Places to Eat

There are few budget options. One of the best, and the only true native eatery on the island, is the unpretentious, family-run *Island Restaurant* (☎ 242-363-3153), hidden off Paradise Beach Dr. A favorite of locals, it serves US breakfasts for US$3 upward; a breakfast of boil fish and grits or johnnycakes, or a lunch or dinner of seafood or pork chops, costs US$8. There's a small bar and a jukebox.

The *Blue Lagoon Seafood Restaurant* (☎ 242-363-2400), at Club Land'Or Resort, offers a US$5 American breakfast special, and a US$19 dinner special (try the lobster fettuccini). The restaurant has splendid decor: Tiffany lamps, plentiful hardwood, and plate-glass windows with views of the gardens below. Or choose burgers and sandwiches at the poolside bar; the chicken-filet burger for US$5 is excellent.

The *Blue Marlin* (☎ 242-363-2660), at Hurricane Hole Marina, has lunch specials for US$5 and sunset dinner specials for US$12.95.

About 1 mile east is the *Columbus Tavern Restaurant*, overlooking Paradise Harbour Club's marina and exuding a maritime air. It offers French and Swiss specialties, such as stuffed escargots in shells for US$10, roast duck à l'orange for US$22, and sirloin steak for US$26.

Julie's (☎ 242-363-3500), in the Radisson Grand, is an Italian deli with a romantic yet simple atmosphere; meals cost US$10 upward. The Radisson also features a rotisserie (☎ 242-363-2011) serving steaks and seafood – budget US$25 per person or more.

The Atlantis boasts several first-class eateries. Take your pick of international cuisines: For Edwardian London, try the *Bahamian Club*, richly upholstered in mahoganies, leathers, and deep greens. It serves seafood and steaks; entrées start at US$25. *Mama Loo's* whisks you across the Pacific. Its ornately carved, dark Asian decor is fabulous. Chinese dishes here begin at about US$20. For Italian, check out *Villa d'Este* in the Atlantis' Coral Tower.

The Boat House, on the grounds of the Atlantis, is an upscale steak house and grill with classy Manhattan-style decor and hibachis at each table. Entrées begin at US$35. Nearby and in the same price range is the ritzy *Café Martinique* (☎ 242-363-3000), which serves French cuisine and has a clubby feel familiar to anyone who has seen *Thunderball*: Agent 007 dined here.

The Martinique has been a favored institution for almost four decades. Nixon and Reagan are among the US presidents who've dined here, along with notables from Kenny Rogers to Oprah Winfrey.

The Ocean Club's *Courtyard Terrace* (☎ 242-363-3000) is favored by monied locals. The setting is splendid (see the Places to Stay section), with a live band playing easy-listening and jazz tunes. The continental cuisine – heavily leaning to seafood – has been acclaimed, but I was disappointed. Expect to pay US$30 per person and up for dinner. The dress code is casually elegant. Reservations are recommended.

Club Med opens its doors to outsiders on Friday and Saturday nights for the finest buffet spread on the island; it costs US$60, including entertainment.

Entertainment
Casinos & Floorshows The only casino on the island is the 30,000-sq-foot *Paradise Island Casino* (☎ 242-363-3000) at the Atlantis. It's the largest and most upscale in The Bahamas. It's not Monte Carlo, but casually elegant dress is appreciated.

The casino theater has a Las Vegas-style revue – 'Sunsation!' – nightly except Sunday. If you've experienced, say, the revue at Tropicana in Havana, you'll be disappointed by this offering. But if you've never seen beautiful befeathered women in G-strings and high heels dancing alongside besequined, leotard-clad male counterparts, you may love it. Comedy and a magician's act are also featured. A dinner show is offered at 7 pm nightly from Tuesday to Saturday.

A steel band, flaming limbo, and Junkanoo are offered at the *Blue Marlin* (☎ 242-363-2660) at 8:30 pm nightly for US$10 (see Places to Eat, above).

Nightclubs & Bars Most hotels have bars. A crooner called Pat Rolle sings nightly at the *Oasis Lounge* of Club Land'Or. I swear he sounds like Nat King Cole!

The *Sports Bar*, which opens onto the casino in the Atlantis, is hugely popular with locals as well as tourists. It's lively and has a large-screen TV, pool tables, and live music on weekends. It's a happenin' spot. Also check out *Club Pastiche* in the Atlantis' Beach Tower.

Dance Clubs *Le Paon* (☎ 242-363-3500), at the Radisson, has a sophisticated ambiance and draws upscale locals. The US$15 cover includes two drinks. A live band plays on Friday and weekend nights.

Club Med and the *Fun Club* have their own dance clubs.

Comedy For giggles, check out the stand-up comedy in *Joker's Wild* (☎ 242-363-2222) in the Paradise Island Casino. It hosts many internationally known comedians. The cocktail show is at 9:30 pm Tuesday to Sunday and costs US$20.

Things to Buy

Duty-free items and resortwear are sold at boutiques in major hotels and at the small Paradise Island Shopping Mall, just north of the roundabout. Greenfire Emeralds (☎ 242-363-2748) and John Bull (☎ 242-363-3956) have stores in The Bird Cage Walk in the Atlantis, where you'll also find Mademoiselle, selling upscale women's fashions and resortwear. Jewels of the Sea (☎ 242-363-3420) has a store in the Holiday Inn Pirate's Cove.

There's a large straw market at Pirate's Cove between the Holiday Inn and Paradise Paradise, and a smaller one at the ferry wharf at the harbor end of Casuarina Dr.

For designer leathers, check out Leather 'n' Things (☎ 242-363-2192) in Hurricane Hole Plaza.

Too lazy to move from the pool? Then settle your buns poolside at Club Land'Or (see the Places to Stay section), which has an alfresco fashion show at 1:30 pm on Saturday.

Getting There & Away

Air Paradise Island has its own tiny airport at the east end of the island. Facilities include a snack bar, phone booths,

and police station. See the Getting There & Away chapter for airlines' telephone numbers.

Pan-Am Air Bridge (formerly Chalk's) flies from Miami's Watson Island twice daily using clipper planes; fares begin at US$88/195 one way/roundtrip. It also flies daily from Fort Lauderdale's Jet Center. Pan Am has been in operation since 1919. You'll drone along at 180 mph in a Grumman-built Mallard, whisking you back to the days of China clippers. The flying boats take off and land right in Nassau Harbour, like speedboats, with water splashing against their windows. *Way to go!*

Pan-Am Air Bridge also flies from Paradise Island to the Biminis at 9:35 am on Monday, Wednesday, Thursday, and Friday; it flies at 2 pm on other days of the week.

Paradise Island Airlines flies daily from Fort Lauderdale, Miami, and West Palm Beach.

Paradise Island Helicopters (☎ 242-363-4016, pager 242-340-2744) offers transportation between Nassau/Paradise Island and the Family Islands, as well as Grand Bahama. Rates are US$750 per hour and include the return trip, with or without passengers (thus you pay for the return trip even if you're only traveling in one direction). The following are sample fares:

Destination	Fare
Abacos (Marsh Harbour)	US$1800
Andros (North Andros)	US$750
Berry Islands (Great Harbour Cay)	US$900
Cat Island	US$1800
Eleuthera (Governor's Harbour)	US$1125
Eleuthera (Harbour Island)	US$1050
Grand Bahama (Freeport)	US$1875
Long Island (Stella Maris)	US$2550
San Salvador	US$2925

The company also offers sightseeing 'helitours.'

Bus There's no bus service to Paradise Island. However, you can catch a bus from Frederick St in downtown Nassau to the Paradise Island Bridge for US75¢ and then walk over to the island. The bridge toll is

US$2 for motor vehicles and US25¢ for bicycles. Pedestrians walk for free.

Boat The Hurricane Hole Marina (☎ 242-363-3600, fax 242-363-3604), PO Box SS-6317, Paradise Island, Bahamas, is just east of the Paradise Island Bridge.

A two-level ferry departs Woodes Rogers Walk (US$2 per person) for Paradise Island every 30 minutes. It deposits and picks up passengers at the Canal Wharf, just west of the Paradise Island Bridge.

Water taxis also ply the same route and will drop you at Club Med or any of the Paradise Island wharfs by request. Other water taxis depart near the Sugar Reef Bar & Restaurant at John Alfred Wharf, east of downtown Nassau.

Another water taxi operates to and from the south end of Casuarina Dr on Paradise Island, serving Club Med, Pirate's Cove, and Paradise Beach.

Getting Around
There are no jitneys. However, the 'Casino Express' runs a clockwise route throughout the day and early evening, picking up and dropping off passengers at major hotels; the fare is US$1.

The Atlantis offers a complimentary island tour at 10 and 11 am and 2 pm daily except Tuesday. It also has a shuttle to downtown Nassau (tickets are available from the bell captain at Paradise Towers).

To/From the Airport
A taxi from the Paradise Island airport to Atlantis or Club Med will cost about US$6 one way, plus US$2 for each additional person.

A taxi from Nassau's airport costs US$21 one way for two people (US$2 for each additional person), plus US$2 bridge toll; from Cable Beach the ride costs US$14 plus toll.

Taxis are available outside all the major hotels.

Car & Moped
You can arrange car rentals through your hotel's concierge. Budget Rent-a-Car (☎ 242-363-3095) has an office

at the Paradise Island airport. It charges US$47 daily for a Suzuki Swift (US$63 automatic) and US$80 for a Toyota Tercel.

Avis (☎ 242-363-2061) has an office at the Holiday Inn.

Mopeds cost US$30 daily from Club Land'Or and Pirate's Cove.

Bicycle
You can rent bicycles from Club Land'Or (US$6 for four hours, US$10 daily) and at Pirate's Cove (US$20 per day). They're single-gear beach cruisers with back-pedal brakes, but the island is flat and should prove no hardship given the short distances.

Club Land'Or offers a midwinter coupon for 50% discount on rentals.

West New Providence

Running west from Cable Beach on the island's north shore, W Bay St offers a beautiful drive. There's little traffic, and all along the route you'll find little beaches where you can escape the madding crowd. A narrow and forested limestone ridge south of the road parallels the shore. The area is favored by the wealthy, who have their upscale homes atop the ridge (one belongs to Julio Iglesias).

One-and-a-half miles west of Delaport Point you'll pass The Caves, just east of Blake Rd. This large cavern system once sheltered Lucayan Indians. You can peer into the entrance and maybe go farther with a flashlight and guide.

Just west of The Caves is Orange Hill Beach, shaded by sea grapes and palms. It is undeveloped (except for the Orange Hill Beach Inn, hidden on the bluff overlooking the beach) and very popular with locals on weekends. The owners of the hotel caused a storm in 1997 when they cut down the casuarinas (the trees drop pine needles onto the sands), causing the government to seize the beach.

Other pocket-size slivers of white sand lie along the shoreline farther west. There is little development, except for Gambier Village, a small settlement that was founded for liberated slaves shortly after 1807. At the foot of the village, by the shore, is Compass Point, one of the country's most intimate resorts. It's worth a stop for lunch or dinner.

West of Compass Point is Love Beach, with Snorkel Heaven (☎ 242-327-8676), where a friendly Bahamian named Levi operates a snorkeling operation, charging US$20 for daily rental. A reef lies 50 yards offshore. There's beach volleyball but no other facilities.

The road then turns inland and curls past the small settlement of Mt Pleasant and around **Lyford Cay**, a sprawling estate of manicured, tree-lined streets and canals framed by glorious mansions that have attained staggering market heights – one home recently sold for US$22 million!

Only a lucky few who receive a personal invitation from one of the residents will ever see beyond the walls of Lyford Cay, one of the world's most exclusive residential retreats and the 'Beverly Hills of The Bahamas.' Current residents include Sean Connery, Czech billionaire Victor Kozeny, Greek shipping magnate Stavros Niarchos, Princess Annmarie von Bismarck, Eddie Murphy, and Arthur Hailey (author of *Airport* and *Roots)*, who is in charge of Lyford's own fire and security staff. Mere residence alone, however, does not automatically ensure your acceptance as a member of the prestigious Lyford Cay Club, which offers golf, tennis, and boating.

Although nicknamed 'Lifeless Cay' (because as a winter residence or second home for the rich and famous it was relatively dead except around Christmas and Easter), this exclusive hot property is experiencing a second wind. A six-story commercial center – Lyford Cay House – has sprouted just outside the entrance, opposite the neo-Georgian Templeton Bldg. The tenants? Offshore bank and trust companies. New houses are also sprouting like mushrooms on a damp log.

The new residents – increasingly monied and *young* – tend to live here full time.

The main road – now called Western Rd – continues around the perimeter of Lyford Cay. At the extreme west end you can follow an unmarked turnoff to a little wooden wharf and sheltered beach where you can look over the iridescent waters to some of the ritzy homes. Atlantis Submarines operates its sightseeing submarine from the wharf (see Boat Excursions, below).

Beyond, the road curls around the island's westernmost apex, Clifton Point (the site of old plantation ruins), bringing you to the Clifton Pier Power Station, which supplies the island's electricity. The Commonwealth Brewery is here, too. And petroleum is also unloaded here to supply the island's gas stations. Shell and Esso each have separate offloading stations; fire-red miniature oil tankers bob dramatically at anchor in channels cut into the limestone cliff face – very photogenic stuff!

Beyond the brewery you'll pass the South Ocean Golf Course and a 5-mile-long beach lining Southwest Bay.

Information

There's a shopping center – Lyford Cay Centre – outside Lyford Cay's gates, with a bank, police station, gas station, supermarket, art gallery, and liquor store. Lyford Cay also has a hospital (☎ 242-362-4025).

Diving

The island's finest dive sites lie immediately off Clifton Point, where the coral wall drops away into the deeps. There are also several wrecks, including a WWII bomber in the shallows west of Lyford Cay. Thrilling scenes from *Thunderball* were shot here.

Nearby is Stuart's Cove Dive South Ocean (☎ 242-362-4171, 800-879-9832), based in South Ocean. A two-tank dive costs US$65; an introductory dive costs US$99; and a full PADI certification course costs US$350. The company's highlight is a rendezvous with sharks in a feeding frenzy on a 'Shark Awareness Program' that is preceded by a separate free dive with sharks. Other trips include all-day 'wilderness diving safaris' as far afield as the blue holes of Andros and the walls of the Exumas. Stuart's, run by Stuart and Michelle Cove, has a professional photo center. Its US mailing address is 1045 SE 17th St, Fort Lauderdale, FL 33316.

Golf
South Ocean Golf & Beach Resort (see Places to Stay, below) has a 18-hole championship course, the PGA-championship-rated South Ocean Golf Course (☎ 242-363-4391). Amid rolling uplands at the western tip of the island, it offers marvelous seascapes. It's rated more highly than the Cable Beach course and is considered the most challenging on New Providence. It has several water holes. The green fee is US$80, including cart; US$65 for resort guests. Vital statistics: 72-par, 6707 yards. Reservations are advised.

Boating & Sailing
You can charter boats from the Lyford Cay Club (☎ 242-362-4131).

Boat Excursions
The 'Atlantis Submarine Adventure' is a deep experience! A state-of-the-art, 28-passenger submarine, the *Atlantis TS-1* has glass portholes for viewing marine life and shipwrecks 80 feet down. Trips pass within 5 feet of spectacular reefs. The pilot narrates. The sub operates from near Lyford Cay and takes you out to a wreck used in the movie *Thunderball*. The hourlong trip is offered by Atlantis Submarines (☎ 242-362-5676) and costs US$75/40 for adults/children, including hotel transfers.

Places to Stay
There are very few options. In the medium-price range, check into the family-run *Orange Hill Beach Inn* (☎ 242-327-7157, fax 242-327-5186) on the bluff overlooking Orange Hill Beach, just off W Bay St. It's

splendidly located for people in transit between islands, less than 2 miles from the airport; it's also one of few hotels to offer free airport transfers (a taxi costs US$6). The entrance sign reads 'Fawlty Towers,' but I think it's just Danny and Judy Lowe's idea of a joke! They run their no-frills place with an informality and casual familiarity that particularly appeals to Europeans. The cozy lobby is brimful of wickerwork. The 32 rooms, in modern albeit soulless units, are modest, with hardwood floors and contemporary furniture. There are also studios and apartments, both with kitchens. Winter rates are US$80 single, US$95 to US$120 double (US$10 less in summer).

The inn is named for the orange orchard planted here in the 1920s (there are still fruit trees, which attract birds). A path leads to the beach. The bar-cum-games room has about every board game; check out the photo titled 'Nitrogen Narcosis' in the bar. Is that a mermaid, or merely rapture of the deep? The inn's mailing address is PO Box N-8583, Nassau, Bahamas.

The brightest point – literally – in the island's hotel galaxy is *Compass Point* (☎ 242-327-4500, fax 242-327-3299; in the USA ☎ 305-534-2135, fax 305-672-2881) in Gambier Village. It is one of Island Outpost's acclaimed creations and an idyll beloved by the rich and famous. It's impossible to not fall in love with this shining star, with sublime decor in Junkanoo colors: purples, teal blues, canary yellows, blood-reds, sea-greens, and pinks-turning-to-cherry when fired by the setting sun. No stone or tile or furnishing went unpainted in the decorative abandon. The compact resort looks like it was contrived by Lego and dropped into a Fantasia of palms and sea grapes.

It perches breezily over a coral shore, with 13 huts and cottages and five cozy cabañas edging up to the turquoise water. The octagonal clapboard cottages (some on stilts) boast large windows, cute porches, conical beamed ceilings, and rustic yet tasteful furnishings, as well as rocking chairs, fluffy bathrobes, potpourri bowls, mosquito coils, a CD player with hip CDs, and an oversize bedstead mirror to give lovers a thrill. Mid-April through mid-December, rates begin at US$135 for cabañas and US$160 to US$225 for one- and two-bedroom cottages. In peak season cabaña rates start at US$175 and cottages cost US$225 to US$325. It's a bargain!

The dining is exquisite and attracts locals in the know, as does the bar, whose mood, like that of the resort, is conducive to lingering in detached bliss. Compass Point offers snorkeling for US$25, diving for US$70, water-skiing for US$30, kayaking for US$15, and other water sports. The place is fashionable among models, musicians, and Hollywood stars, as well as families (babysitters are available on call). Its mailing address is Island Outpost, 1320 Ocean Dr, Miami Beach, FL 33139.

The *South Ocean Golf & Beach Resort* (☎ 242-362-4391, fax 242-362-4728) anchors the South Ocean area. This upscale, self-contained community has a country-club feel, with a splendid aesthetic in its public arenas and 250 spacious air-con rooms, each with private balcony, telephone, TV, and ceiling fan. The older rooms are in the 'Club House' and face the golf course; more modern (and appealing) rooms are set dramatically over the beach, where they catch the breezes. A makeover was completed in 1997, adding new, upscale plantation-style features.

There are three restaurants, three bars, a nightclub, and live entertainment, plus two swimming pools, tennis courts, and a jogging trail. A panoply of water sports is offered. 'Camp Jama' offers fully supervised activities for kids. Garden-view rooms cost US$145; ocean-view rooms cost US$175. Three-night winter 'family value' packages begin at US$472 single or double, including Camp Jama; a similarly priced golfer's package includes unlimited green fees. It has its own little straw market, plus scooter rental. The resort's mailing address is PO Box N-8191, South Ocean, New Providence, Bahamas.

Places to Eat

Nesbit's, an unpretentious eatery 400 yards west of Sun Fun Resorts on the road to Lyford Cay, serves Bahamian fare and is very popular with locals.

Orange Hill Beach Inn's restaurant serves mediocre home-style fare. The simple dinner menu changes daily; prices range from US$12 to US$23. The lunch menu includes salads and sandwiches for US$4.

The Seagrape/Traveller's Rest (☎ 242-327-7633), 1 mile west of Orange Hill Beach, offers colorful, Hockneyesque ambiance (it's full of Caribbean artwork) and an eclectic menu, including a seafood platter for US$17.

Perhaps the finest cuisine on the island – and surely the best value – is found at *Compass Point*'s exquisite restaurant. Here chef Richard Haja has evolved a fine fusion of Californian, Mediterranean, Pacific Rim, and Caribbean cuisine, such as pizza with jerk chicken and roasted sweet potatoes; Bahamian sushi rolls with conch, mango, and cucumber; and smoked mahi-mahi on a sweet potato pancake. Better yet, the meals are bargain priced, with entrées typically costing US$10 to US$20 – a steal by Bahamian standards. Imagine fried oysters for just US$8.50! Equally creative breakfasts cost about US$10. Full-bodied specialty drinks cost US$6.50. The ambiance is worth the trip. You can dine indoors or on the breezy waterfront terrace. The place is a favorite of locals, including such reclusive residents as Sean Connery and musicians recording at Compass Point Studios across the road, as well as celebs like Naomi Campbell and Cindy Crawford.

At Compass Point's fashionable bar, the clientele includes movers and shakers from Nassau and around the world. If you want to hang with waifish models, local parliamentarians, Hollywood stars and starlets, and others in the know, this is the place.

Getting There & Away

Western Transportation operates regular bus service to the South Ocean Golf &

Beach Resort from Bay St and Frederick St in Nassau between 7:30 am and midnight. Service runs via Cable Beach and Compass Point. The fare from Compass Point is US$1.75. You have to flag down the bus.

A shuttle runs to downtown Nassau from the South Ocean Golf & Beach Resort every two hours and costs US$1.75 one way.

The South Ocean Golf & Beach Resort also rents scooters.

South New Providence

No road runs directly along the southern shore. From the South Ocean area, Adelaide Rd runs east, about 2 miles inland and parallel to the shore, which is accessed by side roads. East of Coral Harbour Rd, which runs north to the airport, Adelaide Rd becomes Carmichael Rd, passing east to west through Carmichael Village (a lower-income residential area founded last century as a settlement for free slaves) to Blue Hill Rd, which runs north to central Nassau and south to South Beach.

There's little along this shore to lure you. Most of it is backed by mangroves, swampy wetlands, and brine pools, parts of which have been used for years as an impromptu rubbish dump. The roads are lined with every conceivable item of rotting detritus, from mattresses to refrigerators. Curiously, dozens of minor Christian bodies have erected their little churches along these roads.

Adelaide

Adelaide, 17 miles southwest of Nassau, is a quaint and quiet little place whose nostalgic lifestyle revolves around fishing. Visually it isn't noteworthy, but it is about as close as you can get to offbeat life on the island. The village dates back to 1832, when it was founded for slaves freed from a Portuguese slavetrader, on a spit of land jutting into a navigable creek rich in conch,

fish, and lobster. The settlement flourished, a harbor was built, and the villagers established a thriving fishing industry and a tender service to bring people ashore in the days before Nassau Harbour's breakwater was built.

A hurricane in 1926 wrecked the harbor and a heavily laden lumber ship was sunk at the mouth of Adelaide Creek, leaving a meager conduit at the east end of the wetlands. Tidal flow diminished, and eventually the free-flowing creek began silting up. A causeway, built across the creek in 1946 to link the village to the beach, cut off the remaining flow. In ensuing years more causeways were built, and houses were erected along the beach and on subdivided plots. Tidal flow was entirely restricted. The mangroves began to die and the wetlands system – an important fish-breeding area – stagnated. The area became a garbage dump.

In 1990 the Bahamas National Trust initiated a plan to restore Adelaide Creek. An army of volunteers and schoolchildren was gathered, and as news of the project spread, people from all over New Providence showed up to lend a hand. Donations flooded in to replace the crossways with bridges. On Earth Day the creek's mouth was reopened and a tidal creek was reborn. Almost immediately marine life returned: crabs, shads, and even bonefish. Today baby tiger sharks, barracudas, snappers, lobsters, and vast armadas of other young fish journey in and out.

The village is fronted by narrow, white-sand **Adelaide Beach**, extending between South Ocean and the village. Fishing boats are drawn up on the beach.

Coral Harbour

Coral Harbour Rd leads south to this residential marina community. Several dive and sport-fishing operators are based here, and there's a small beach.

Coral Harbour Rd turns west along the shore, becoming Ranfurly Dr, and dead-ends at the base of the Royal Bahamas Defence Force.

Bacardi Rum Factory

After Fidel Castro's expropriation of the Bacardi family's rum factories during the Cuban Revolution, the family set up its business in other locales, including a site on the south shore of New Providence. The plant, which is at the end of Bacardi Rd, east of Coral Harbour and southwest of Carmichael Village, produces Bacardi rum (the family successfully sued the Castro regime for the Bacardi title) from sugar imported from Caribbean islands.

Free 30-minute guided tours (☎ 242-362-1412) are offered at 11 am and 2 pm Monday to Thursday and 11 am Friday. Tours are for eight people or more, but you can hang around in the Pavilion, sampling free drinks in the hope that other visitors achieve a quorum.

South Beach Pools

Locals give the southern beaches a wide berth, preferring instead to bathe at South Beach Pools. These pools have been set in pretty landscaped grounds above the mangrove-lined shore. The place is run by the Ministry of Youth and Culture. There are no snack bars or facilities, so bring your own food and drink. Admission is free.

To get to the South Beal Pools from Nassau, follow Blue Hill Rd (or its parallel, East St) south to the shore, then turn left onto Harbour Dr, the coast road, which dead-ends here.

Activities

Dive operators based at Coral Harbour include Dive Dive Dive (☎ 242-362-1401), Sunskiff Divers (☎ 242-362-1979), and Nassau Scuba Centre (☎ 242-362-1964). Sunskiff and Dive Dive Dive offer dive packages that include self-catering accommodations at a villa or house in or near the South Ocean area.

Happy Trails Stables (☎ 242-362-1820), at Coral Harbour, 2 miles south of Nassau International Airport, offers horseback rides along the south shore and scrubland daily except Sunday. Happy Trails' rides, by

reservation only, cost US$50 for 90 minutes, including hotel transfers.

Cantalupa Riding School (☎ 242-361-7101) in Carmichael Village also offers horseback riding. The school has riding lessons and pony rides for children, starting at US$20 per hour.

Places to Stay & Eat

Coral Harbour Beach House & Villas (☎ 242-362-2210, fax 242-361-6514) is a lonesome eight-unit beachfront property in Coral Harbour good for those seeking a reclusive, breezy escape. Rooms are modestly furnished in wicker, with air-con and fan. Take an upstairs room with a balcony and more light, plus a shower (downstairs rooms have a tub only). There's a barbecue pit and hammocks stretched between the trees. The beach is tiny. Rooms cost US$65; large units sleeping four cost US$85; each extra person must pay US$20. Dorothy Johnson, the live-in owner, is a delight. The mailing address is PO Box N-9750, Nassau, Bahamas.

Family Islanders check into the *Corner Hotel* (☎ 242-361-7445), a dreary institutional hotel on Carmichael Rd in Carmichael Village. Rooms cost US$55. The restaurant is appealing, however, with a large, eclectic menu featuring huge portions of local favorites such as tuna and grits for US$4, sheep's-tongue souse for US$7.50, and fried grouper and chips for US$7.

Budget travelers might check out the *Makeda Beach Hotel & Lounge*, a simple and offbeat little place on South Beach about 400 yards east of East St. It was closed, however, when I called by.

There are two options for eats in Adelaide, though no place to rest your head. The first, *Avery's Restaurant & Bar* (☎ 242-362-1547), is an unassuming place serving Bahamian dishes. It has live entertainment on weekends.

Far more appealing – one of the island's offbeat gems – is the *Honeycomb Beach Club* (☎ 242-362-1417), a delightfully funky place to cool your feet. You can sit on the breezy patio overlooking the beach at tables made from upturned telegraph-cable rollers. The little house behind contains a tiny bar and has a polished wood-beamed roof, pool table, captain's chairs, and plenty of ambiance. The place is run by Catherine, a cheery lady who conjures up cracked conch for US$6, pork chops for US$7, and the like for the locals who gather here to sup, flirt, and laugh. Plan on at least a couple of hours of idling.

Getting There & Away
To get to south New Providence from Nassau, catch Bus No 6 downtown. This bus runs along Blue Hill Rd, Carmichael Rd, and Adelaide Rd.

Grand Bahama

Grand Bahama, an ox-jaw-shaped island 110 miles northwest of New Providence and the northernmost major isle in the Bahamian chain, is the second most popular tourist destination in The Bahamas. Like New Providence, it boasts sugar-white beaches, beautiful waters, and a panoply of lodgings, casinos, excellent golf courses, and water sports concentrated in Freeport and its contiguous, distinctly tourist-oriented enclave, Lucaya.

Grand Bahama takes its name from *gran baja mar*, the Spanish name for the 'great shallow sea.' It is 85 miles long, 17 miles across at its widest, and flat as a pancake. Its south shore is lined with startlingly beautiful beaches – 57 miles in all, many of them as private as your innermost thoughts. The island's north shore comprises mangroves and wetlands: There are few beaches but plenty of birdlife. There's plenty of solitude to be had in the forests, along the pristine shores, and on the cays that lie to the east (which boast great bone-fishing spots).

Most of Grand Bahama is smothered by great stands of Cuban pines, with an understory of dwarf palms (mostly thatch, palmetto, and cabbage). Plump curly-tailed lizards are everywhere, scurrying across the sands or through the undergrowth. There are also raccoons and nonpoisonous snakes. And green and loggerhead turtles (and, infrequently, hawksbills) emerge from the sea to nest at Gold Rock Creek, Hawksbill Creek, and at High Rock (near Freetown). Development and tourist visitation, however, have vastly reduced the turtle population.

Scuba diving is splendid, with options for swimming with dolphins or sharks. And several companies cater to ecotourists with kayak trips, hikes, and jeep safaris. One of the island's most attractive features is stunning Lucayan National Park, east of Freeport. And the sleepy fishing village of

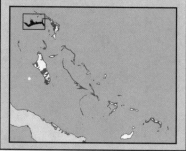

West End, on the island's western tip, is worth a visit.

Still, Grand Bahama is arguably the least attractive Bahamian island – not physically, but because it is surprisingly middle-American. It has rightly been described as 'a culturally antiseptic mecca for fast-lane vacationers.'

In general the island attracts a less sophisticated clientele than do Nassau and the Family Islands. It's a popular venue for Floridians and folks from New Jersey who flock here for a few days of inexpensive fun. Unless you come for the smattering of natural attractions, you'd better be sure that gambling, duty-free shopping, and beach lounging are your things. Freeport and Lucaya are also popular with day-trippers arriving on cruise ships from Florida and

216

GRAND BAHAMA

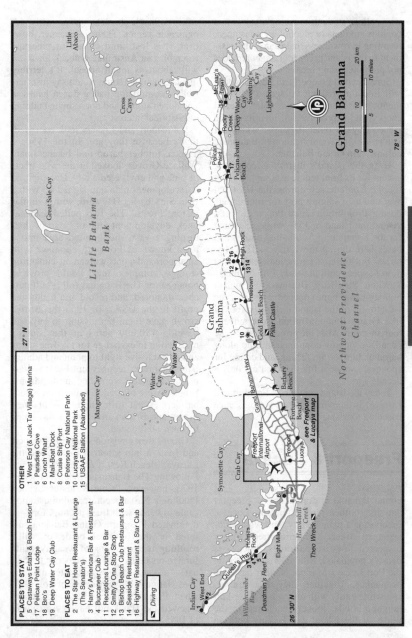

PLACES TO STAY
5 Castaways Estate & Beach Resort
17 Pelican Point Lodge
18 Bro's
19 Deep Water Cay Club

PLACES TO EAT
2 The Star Hotel Restaurant & Lounge
   (The Senator's)
3 Harry's American Bar & Restaurant
4 Buccaneer Club
11 Receptions Lounge & Bar
12 Smitty's One Stop Shop
13 Bishop Beach Club Restaurant & Bar
14 Seaside Restaurant
16 Highway Restaurant & Star Club

OTHER
1 West End (& Jack Tar Village) Marina
5 Paradise Cove
6 Conch Wharf
7 Mail-Boat Dock
8 Cruise Ship Port
9 Peterson Cay National Park
10 Lucayan National Park
15 USAAF Station (Abandoned)

Diving

Grand Bahama

0   10   20 km
0   5   10 miles

78° W

Little Abaco

Little Bahama Bank

Great Sale Cay

Cross Cays

McLean's Town

Sweeting's Cay

Lighthbourne Cay

Deep Water Cay

Rocky Creek

Pelican Point
Pelican Point Beach

High Rock

Freetown

Gold Rock Beach

Pillar Castle

Barbary Beach

Northwest Providence Channel

Grand Bahama

Water Cay

Water Cay

Mangrove Cay

Symonette Cay

Crab Cay

Freeport International Airport

Grand Bahama Hwy

see Freeport & Lucaya map

Fortune Beach

Freeport

Lucaya

Indian Cay

West End

Queen's Hwy

Holmes Rock

Deadman's Reef

Wilischcombe Bay

Eight Mile

Hawksbill Creek

Theo Wreck

27° N

26° 30' N

with college students at spring break (when copious amounts of alcohol are consumed, resulting in rowdiness that is an embarrassment to the island). The tourism board does *not* promote spring break.

Sure, beyond Freeport and Lucaya you'll still find tiny fishing villages, or 'settlements.' But none have the color, soulful energy, and expressive self-identity of the Abaco Cays or other Bahamian islands. If you're seeking sophistication or Bahamian culture, skip Grand Bahama.

Even the island's history is colorless, except for its brief tenure as a supply depot for the Confederacy during the US Civil War and as a staging post for rumrunners during Prohibition. Juan Ponce de León visited the island in 1513 while searching for the Fountain of Youth, and pirates had bases here during the 17th and 18th centuries. But the first permanent settlements didn't appear until the early 19th century.

When Sir Billy Butlins (of English holiday-camp fame) opened a resort at the western tip of the island in 1948, it looked like Grand Bahama might experience a tourism coup. Alas, the project fizzled. The island's economy continued to limp along based on lumbering, fishing, and diving for sponges – ways of life that died out only a decade ago.

Today the island (or at least Freeport and Lucaya) is enjoying a bit of a renaissance based on tourism.

Freeport & Lucaya

Pop 50,000
Grand Bahama is dominated by Freeport and its southeastern extension, Lucaya. Freeport is a planned city with wide, grid-arranged streets and uninspired, widely dispersed low-rise buildings; Lucaya is densely populated, with resorts centered on the Port Lucaya Marina. Neither has edge or nuance. Together, they're a strange, sprawling entity with only a few close-knit neighborhoods, loosely anchored in the midst of the island and lacking both an easily definable character and an easily recognizable center. There *is* a center; however, it is lost amid copses of pine and resembles an Australian outback town . . . with about as much appeal. It's terribly inconsequential (some would say just 'terrible'), comprising half a dozen banks, a few dozen stores, and not a single building of historical interest.

If Freeport and Lucaya look contrived, that's because they are. In the 1950s a Yankee lumber baron and businessman, Wallace Groves, looked at the wild tracts of pine and envisaged a city. He proposed a development plan and signed up with a Brit, Sir Charles Hayward, with a similar vision. Presto! The two pulled a mega-buck development out of a straw hat, turning a vast, uninhabited area into a town known as Freeport, complete with an airport and a port with an oil-bunkering storage complex that would prove a bonanza for The Bahamas (oil is still purchased, stored, and resold at a handsome profit to the USA). In 1955 the British crown gave them permission to buy and develop 150,000 acres of the island's midsection in exchange for tax-free status and an exclusive right to grant and administer business licenses until 2015. Vast marina channels were dug and handsome benefits were offered to waterfront home-builders. What little there was of West Indian and British architecture was sacrilegiously bulldozed.

Groves then envisioned turning Freeport and Lucaya into a tourist mecca, and the Lucayan Beach Resort & Casino went up. Following The Bahamas' independence in 1973, however, Prime Minister Lynden Pindling's Nassau-centered administration came to heads with freewheeling, foreign-dominated Freeport. Grand Bahama suffered in the political battle of wills, resulting in an exodus of wealthy white foreign residents. The island began to stagnate – a state of affairs that lasted until the Free National Movement victory of 1992, when Prime Minister Hubert Ingraham renewed the Hawksbill Creek Agreement of 1955.

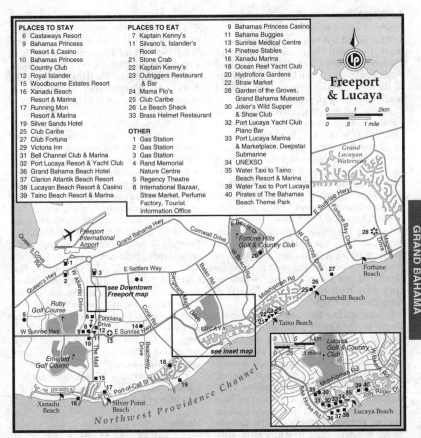

PLACES TO STAY
6 Castaways Resort
9 Bahamas Princess Resort & Casino
10 Bahamas Princess Country Club
12 Royal Islander
15 Woodbourne Estates Resort
16 Xanadu Beach Resort & Marina
17 Running Mon Resort & Marina
19 Silver Sands Hotel
25 Club Caribe
27 Club Fortuna
29 Victoria Inn
31 Bell Channel Club & Marina
32 Port Lucaya Resort & Yacht Club
36 Grand Bahama Beach Hotel
37 Clarion Atlantik Beach Resort
38 Lucayan Beach Resort & Casino
39 Taino Beach Resort & Marina

PLACES TO EAT
7 Kaptain Kenny's
11 Silvano's, Islander's Roost
21 Stone Crab
22 Kaptain Kenny's
23 Outriggers Restaurant & Bar
24 Mama Flo's
25 Club Caribe
26 Le Beach Shack
33 Brass Helmet Restaurant

OTHER
1 Gas Station
2 Gas Station
3 Gas Station
4 Rand Memorial Nature Centre
5 Regency Theatre
8 International Bazaar, Straw Market, Perfume Factory, Tourist Information Office
9 Bahamas Princess Casino
11 Bahama Buggies
13 Sunrise Medical Centre
14 Pinetree Stables
16 Xanadu Marina
18 Ocean Reef Yacht Club
20 Hydroflora Gardens
22 Straw Market
28 Garden of the Groves, Grand Bahama Museum
30 Joker's Wild Supper & Show Club
32 Port Lucaya Yacht Club Piano Bar
33 Port Lucaya Marina & Marketplace, Deepstar Submarine
34 UNEXSO
35 Water Taxi to Taino Beach Resort & Marina
39 Water Taxi to Port Lucaya
40 Pirates of The Bahamas Beach Theme Park

The city of Freeport is now positioning itself as an offshore financial center, the nation's high-technology industrial center, and a prime residential community for second-home dwellers. It is still overseen by the Grand Bahama Port Authority, or 'The Port,' set up by Groves, which maintains strict zoning laws, issues (or denies) all business licenses, and has the same defining role in matters of commercial probity as the Christian Council has in Nassau.

In 1996 a development group, Sun & Sea Estates, started a major redevelopment project in Lucaya. Named the Grand Lucaya Resort & Casino, the five-year project will integrate existing hotels with new hotels, vacation clubs, restaurants, shops, theme parks, a new golf course and golf school, and a marina. And in mid-1997 a Hong Kong-based development group announced plans to take over the government-run Lucayan Beach Resort & Casino and the Grand Bahama Beach Hotel.

Many hope that massive investment will do for Grand Bahama what Sun International's Atlantis resort project did for Paradise Island.

ORIENTATION

Freeport and Lucaya sprawl over west-central Grand Bahama between two waterways: Hawksbill Creek (also known as the Freeport Harbour Channel) to the west and the 7.5-mile-long Grand Lucayan Waterway to the east. Freeport proper – the 'bonded area' – has a slightly smaller compass.

Downtown Freeport, 1 mile south of the airport, takes up eight square blocks west of 'The Mall,' which is E Mall Dr, the main boulevard that leads south from Independence Circle outside the airport on the north shore to Xanadu Beach on the south. The heart of touristy Freeport is 1 mile south of downtown, centered on Ranfurly Circle, the Aladdin-domed Bahamas Princess Resort & Casino, and the International Bazaar.

Queen's Hwy runs southwest from the airport to the Cruise Ship Port via an area of petrochemical industries and some of the island's poorest residential sections, Hawksbill and Pinder's Point. W Sunrise Hwy runs west to the Cruise Ship Port from Ranfurly Circle.

E Sunrise Hwy runs east from Ranfurly Circle to the Grand Lucayan Waterway, beyond which it continues as the Grand Bahama Hwy to the eastern end of the island. Sea Horse Rd leads south from E Sunrise Hwy to the Port Lucaya Marina. East of Sea Horse Rd and south of Midshipman Rd is the area known as Port Lucaya, centered on the Port Lucaya Marina. Between Port Lucaya and Xanadu Beach is Silver Point Beach, a residential marina community with three hotels.

Taino, Churchill, and Fortune beaches extend east from Port Lucaya.

Maps

Etienne Dupuch Publications Ltd publishes a *Bahamas Trailblazer Map* for Grand Bahama. You can pick one up in hotel lobbies and at tourist information booths.

INFORMATION
Tourist Offices

The Grand Bahama Island Tourism Board (☎ 242-352-8044, fax 242-352-2714) has its main office in the International Bazaar. The

postal address is PO Box F-40252, Freeport, Grand Bahama, Bahamas. It also has a US office (☎ 305-935-9461, 800-448-3386, fax 305-935-9464) at 1 Turnberry Pl, 19495 Biscayne Blvd, No 809, Aventura, FL 33180.

The Ministry of Tourism (☎ 242-352-8044) has its main office in the Charles Hayward Library on E Mall Dr near Pioneers Way. The Bahamas Tourist Office (☎ 242-352-8044) is in the International Bazaar. There are also tourist information booths at Freeport International Airport, the Cruise Ship Port, and near the roundabout at the east end of Port Lucaya Marketplace.

What's On, a free monthly tourist newspaper that has discount coupons to a wide variety of restaurants, stores, and excursions, is published by Aberland Publications (☎ 242-351-8051), PO Box F-40517, Freeport, Grand Bahama, Bahamas. Etienne Dupuch Publications Ltd (☎ 242-323-5665, fax 242-323-8722) publishes the biannual *What-to-do in Freeport/Lucaya, Grand Bahama*, a small-format tourist guide full of handy information and discount coupons. The similarly sized *Island Magazine* provides information on shopping, dining, and entertainment. All three are available in hotel lobbies and tourist information booths.

You can pick up a *Discover Port Lucaya* booklet, which has discount coupons and a map of Port Lucaya.

Money

Scotiabank (☎ 242-352-6774), the Royal Bank of Canada (☎ 242-352-6631), CIBC (☎ 242-352-6651), and Barclays Bank (☎ 242-352-8391) maintain downtown branches, as do the British American Bank (☎ 242-352-6676), Western Union (☎ 242-352-6676), and the Bank of the Bahamas (☎ 242-352-7483).

Post & Communications

The main post office (☎ 242-352-9371) is downtown on Explorers Way near E Mall Dr; it's open 9 am to 5:30 pm weekdays.

Federal Express (☎ 242-352-3402) has an office one block south, open 9 am to 5 pm weekdays.

GRAND BAHAMA

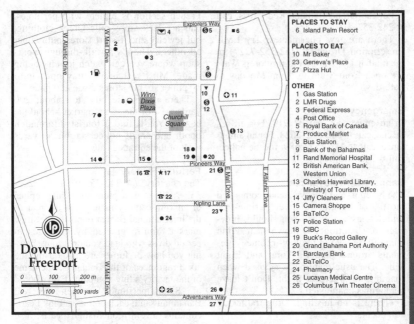

Downtown Freeport

PLACES TO STAY
6 Island Palm Resort

PLACES TO EAT
10 Mr Baker
23 Geneva's Place
27 Pizza Hut

OTHER
1 Gas Station
2 LMR Drugs
3 Federal Express
4 Post Office
5 Royal Bank of Canada
7 Produce Market
8 Bus Station
9 Bank of the Bahamas
11 Rand Memorial Hospital
12 British American Bank,
    Western Union
13 Charles Hayward Library,
    Ministry of Tourism Office
14 Jiffy Cleaners
15 Camera Shoppe
16 BaTelCo
17 Police Station
18 CIBC
19 Buck's Record Gallery
20 Grand Bahama Port Authority
21 Barclays Bank
22 BaTelCo
24 Pharmacy
25 Lucayan Medical Centre
26 Columbus Twin Theater Cinema

GRAND BAHAMA

Travel Agencies

Tour agencies in hotel lobbies may be able to make air and other travel reservations. Or call the Bahamas Travel Agency (☎ 242-352-3141).

Bookstores

Gift shops in major resorts usually sell a small selection of books and magazines. For a larger choice, head to the Freeport Book Centre (☎ 242-352-3759), 14 W Mall Dr, downtown.

Library

The Charles Hayward Library (☎ 242-352-7048), on E Mall Dr near Pioneers Way, is open 10 am to 5 pm Monday, Wednesday, and Friday and 10 am to 2 pm Saturday.

Publications

The *Freeport News* is an afternoon daily, published Monday to Saturday. The *Freeport Times* is published monthly.

Laundry

Upscale hotels will arrange for laundry and dry cleaning. You'll also find a listing of laundries and dry cleaners in the Yellow Pages. One such is Jiffy Cleaners & Laundry (☎ 242-352-7079), downtown at W Mall Dr and Pioneers Way, open 8 am to 6 pm Monday to Saturday.

Medical Services

The main health-care facility is the Rand Memorial Hospital (☎ 242-352-6735) on E Mall Dr near Pioneers Way. Other medical facilities include the Lucayan Medical Centre (☎ 242-352-7288), downtown on Adventurers Way, and Sunrise Medical Centre (☎ 242-373-3333) on E Sunrise Hwy.

If that ol' toothache begins to bite, call Dr Larry Bain (☎ 242-352-8492), in the Sun Alliance Bldg on Pioneers Way, downtown. The dentist's office is open 8:30 am to 4 pm Monday to Wednesday and 8:30 am to noon Thursday and Friday.

For the Grand Bahama Red Cross, call
☎ 242-352-7163.

There are few pharmacies. Try LMR
Prescription Drugs (☎ 242-352-7327) in
the mall at 1 W Mall Dr at Explorers Way;
it's open from 8 am to 9 pm Monday to
Saturday.

Emergency

In an emergency call ☎ 919. For air-sea
rescue, call ☎ 242-352-2628. For an ambulance, call ☎ 242-352-2689; for the police,
call ☎ 242-348-3444.

Dangers & Annoyances

The Freeport and Lucaya area is comprised
mostly of sedate, relatively crime-free
middle-class suburbs. You should, however, use caution downtown near Winn
Dixie Plaza, and in the low-income settlements around Pinder's Point and Eight
Mile. The usual caution is advised when
roaming anywhere at night. Don't leave
belongings unattended.

There is no hustling. Drug trafficking
still occurs.

FREEPORT
Downtown

The official town center lies 1 mile north of
the International Bazaar between W Mall
and E Mall Drs. At its heart is **Winn Dixie
Plaza**. The only noteworthy sightseeing
item is a massive bronze bust of Sir Winston Churchill on a pedestal in the otherwise nondescript Churchill Square.

E Mall Dr is lined with young strangler
fig trees and makes a pleasant walk.

International Bazaar

This compact, hokey, Disney-style emporium, on the northwest side of Ranfurly
Circle, is worth a browse for curiosity's
sake and for shopping. Beyond the Japanese torii gates, a maze of tight-knit
lanes lined with restaurants and shops
imitate international venues, from the
Orient to Scandinavia. Most of the approximately 100 shops are dedicated to duty-
free items from around the world: The

French section is replete with perfumes,
and a Greek store sells Greek clothing,
but jewelry and T-shirt stores outnumber
all others. There's a walk-through workshop where you can watch jewelry being
made. Most restaurants stay open until
10 pm or so, but stores close at 6 pm.

There's a public bus stop about 200
yards west of the straw market behind the
bazaar. You'll find a tourist information
booth and small police station 50 yards
west of the entrance gate.

Perfume Factory

The 'factory' (☎ 242-352-9391, fax 242-
352-9040) is in a plum-and-white replica
of an 18th-century mansion at the rear of
the International Bazaar opposite the straw
market. You're greeted by hostesses in
period dress who lead you on a tour showing you how perfumes are made using the
six 'Fragrances of the Bahamas,' the name
of the factory's tiny company. Every bottle
of 'Sand' perfume for men has real
Bahamian sand; each bottle of 'Pink Pearl'
contains several conch-shell pearls. You
can even mix, bottle, and name your own
fragrance for US$20. Bottles of perfume
purchased here cost about 50% less than
US retail prices. The free five-minute tours
are offered 10 am to 5:30 pm weekdays.

To order Fragrances of the Bahamas
perfumes in the USA, call ☎ 305-294-8681
or 800-628-9033.

Rand Memorial Nature Centre

This natural haven is the headquarters of
the Bahamas National Trust (BNT, ☎ 242-
352-5438) on Grand Bahama. On E Settlers Way about 2 miles east of downtown
Freeport, the center began in 1969 as a
living memorial to Freeport philanthropist
James Rand. It was the first environmental-
education facility in The Bahamas and an
important bird-banding station. In 1991 the
site was transferred to the BNT and opened
as a nature retreat to show off more than
130 types of native plants, including 21
species of orchids. There is even an open,
grassy meadow, highlighted by beautiful

wildflowers in spring and summer, and a native coppice unchanged since before the time of Columbus.

A half-mile-long trail winds through many acres of coppice and pine barrens where a flock of locally bred West Indian flamingos stride about in a freshwater pond adorned with water lilies. (A small native fish, the Bahamian gambusia, keeps the water free of mosquito larvae.) Rand is a gathering spot for wild birds, including Cuban emerald hummingbirds, the tiny yet stunning Parula, and Antillean peewees peering down from their perches in the pines. There are great blue herons and egrets, and even kingfishers and ospreys fish here. Raccoons and red-eared turtles also call it home, as do tree frogs, who often lay their eggs in the birdbaths. Curly-tailed lizards rush down the trails to greet visitors. Butterflies are common. And harmless brown-racer and corn snakes are occasionally seen. A replica of a Lucayan village was under construction in 1997.

Rick and Kathy Oliver, the curators, lead a special bird-watcher's tour and a wildflower tour the first and third Saturday of each month, respectively. A gift shop sells quality nature-related items. Guided walks are offered at 10 am and 2 pm weekdays and 10 am Saturday. They're free with admission: US$5/3 adults/children.

Xanadu Beach
This deep white-sand beach at the south end of The Mall extends westward about a half-mile. It's not as beautiful as Taino Beach but is quite adequate for a day of sunning or splashing around in the shallows. There's a crafts market, snack bar, and plenty of water sports. Lounge chairs rent for US$2. The beach is dominated by the Xanadu Beach Resort & Marina, the former private domain of Howard Hughes, who ensconced himself on the 12th and 13th floors for two years until his death in 1976.

A courtesy bus operates between the Bahamas Princess Resort & Casino and Xanadu Beach.

LUCAYA TO PETERSON CAY NATIONAL PARK
Port Lucaya Marketplace
This 12-acre shopping, dining, and entertainment area fronts the Lucayan Marina Village, a 150-slip marina that is part of a planned waterfront tourism project. It's more couched in Bahamian culture than is Freeport's International Bazaar. Boardwalks lend a Monterey kind of feel; one leads to the beach. At its heart is Count Basie Square, where local musicians perform. There are cultural activities – everything from church choirs to Junkanoo bands – in the evening and on weekends.

Ye Olde Pirate Bottle House (☎ 242-373-2000) is a quasimuseum and antique store with 250 or so bottles dating back to the 17th century. It's open 9 am to 6 pm daily; US$3/2 adults/children.

Balancing Boulders of Lucaya
This man-made fantasy in stone – complete with 20-foot-high waterfall – nestles in a lake surrounding the green of the 18th hole

of the Lucaya Golf & Country Club. It's a curiosity by day; at night it becomes a thing of beauty when colored floodlights are turned on and fire seems to erupt from the rocks.

Hydroflora Gardens
This landscaped garden (☎ 242-352-6052), on E Beach Dr at E Sunrise Hwy, is another lush world of shrubs, tropical fruit trees, and fragrant foliage. Highlights include a rock garden, a 'chapel of blooms,' and a garden of hydroponics where plants grow in soil-free conditions. It is open 9 am to 5 pm Monday to Saturday; US$5/3 guided/unguided.

Garden of the Groves
This 11-acre garden (☎ 242-373-5668), at the intersection of Midshipman Rd and Magellan Dr, is a lush Eden filled with exotic plants and shrubs from around the world – 5000 species in all. There's a 400-foot-long fern gully and a hanging garden, as well as four waterfalls cascading into a placid lake ringed with tropical foliage, and ponds waded by flamingos.

The gardens contain the **Grand Bahama Museum**, dedicated to the history of the island from the time of the Lucayans. There's also a cafe serving snacks and a straw market at the entrance. The mailing address is PO Box 43282, Grand Bahama, Bahamas. It's open 9 am to 4 pm weekdays and 10 am to 4pm weekends; US$5/2.50 adults/children under 10.

Taino Beach
Taino Beach is a miles-long stunner with sand as fine as confectioners' sugar, the setting for water sports and several popular restaurants. To the north is the waterfront settlement of **Smith's Point**, a disheveled cluster of tiny houses; most of its occupants are related to the matriarch, Mama Flo, who at last count had 55 grandchildren.

Churchill, Fortune & Barbary Beaches
Churchill and Fortune, two beautiful beaches, extend several miles east of Taino Beach, from which they are separated by

Sanctuary Bay, a marina complex lined with homes of the well heeled, notably along the beachfront road, Spanish Main Dr (also called 'New Millionaire's Row'). Fortune Beach has several eateries popular with locals on weekends.

Farther east, beyond the Grand Lucayan Waterway, is secluded and seductive Barbary Beach. Each springtime its shoreline bursts into bloom with white spider lilies.

Peterson Cay National Park
This 1.5-acre park, 1 mile offshore and 15 miles east of Freeport, is the only cay on Grand Bahama's south shore. It is one of the Family Islands' most heavily used getaway spots, popular with locals with boats on weekends. Coral reefs provide splendid snorkeling and diving. You can hire a boat from any marina or the Grand Lucayan Waterway. Take snorkel gear and a picnic.

ACTIVITIES
Diving & Snorkeling
Diving is excellent off Grand Bahama. One prime site is the *Theo* wreck, a 240-foot-long sunken freighter with safe swim-throughs in the hold and engine room; the resident moray eels are friendly. Another is East End Paradise, an underwater coral range. Two Spanish galleons filled with gold bullion – the *Santa Gertrude* and *San Ignacio* – ran aground in 1682 off the south shore near present-day Lucaya. The gold and silver coins have been recovered, but the wrecks remain for you to explore.

Experienced divers can check out Ben's Cave, part of the Lucayan National Park, where you can follow permanently installed cable lines through underwater caves for up to 7 miles! The dive is limited to qualified divers, who must obtain a permit from UNEXSO (see below). Only six divers can enter at a time.

The Underwater Explorers Society (UNEXSO, ☎ 242-373-1244; in the USA 800-922-3483), at Port Lucaya Marina, is the best-equipped dive facility. It has a full range of dive programs, from guided reef dives for US$35/65 one-/two-tank to a three-tank all-day dive for US$99. It offers a 20-dive card with no expiration date for US$399. It also offers private instruction for US$50 per hour, an underwater photo certification course for US$349, and cavern diving for US$199. Beginners can take the plunge after three hours of professional instruction in training pools for US$79. It has a fully stocked dive shop, rents underwater photo equipment, and offers film processing. At press time it also had a recompression chamber. I have heard several reports of UNEXSO's dives being oversubscribed and rushed. The local mailing address is PO Box F-42433, Freeport, Grand Bahama, Bahamas; in the USA write PO Box 22878, Fort Lauderdale, FL 33335.

Other dive operators based here include the following:

Caribbean Divers	☎ 800-336-0938
Sun Odyssey Divers	☎ 242-373-4014
Xanadu Undersea	
Adventures	☎ 242-352-3811

Many offer courses that will have novices diving by afternoon; typical three-hour 'learn-to-dive' options cost about US$80. All the dive operators offer snorkel trips that cost US$15 to US$20, including transportation. UNEXSO has a special trip for children for US$10. A good snorkel spot is Paradise Cove, where fish are abundant at Deadman's Reef.

There's a 'SnorkelRama' excursion to Treasure Reef, offered aboard the *Bahama Mama* (☎ 242-373-7863); US$18/14 adults/children.

Dolphin Encounters UNEXSO offers several options for diving with dolphins, including a two-hour 'Dolphin Close Encounter' for US$29 for nondivers, who receive an educational lecture and then stand waist-deep in a sheltered lagoon, where they meet the semiwild dolphins. A full-day 'Dolphin Assistant Trainer' program for US$159 permits you to shadow trainers in the waters at Sanctuary Lagoon. Divers can purchase a two-tank 'Dolphin Dive' add-on to a regular two-dive scuba

package for US$109. Hotel transfers are offered. Reservations are advised.

Shark Dives If too much sun or an excess of rum go to your head, you can swim amid Caribbean reef sharks while a diver wearing a chain-mail suit hand-feeds these notorious predators! Two other divers, armed with sticks, are on hand to ward off wayward sharks. Still, you will have to sign a legal release form saying that it isn't UNEXSO's fault if the sharks decide you look tastier than the fish. A cameraperson will record your swim on video, which costs extra. This event – rated the No 1 photo dive opportunity by *Nikonos Technique* magazine – takes place at Shark Junction. The dive costs an additional US$40 to normal dive rates. Reservations are advised. Contact UNEXSO (see above).

Golf
The island has three championship courses. Emerald & Ruby Golf Courses (☎ 242-352-6721, ext 4600), part of the vast Bahamas Princess Resort complex, are twin, downtown, USGA-rated courses featuring undulating fairways, doglegs, large greens, water, and challenging rough. They're 72-par Dick Wilson creations. Games cost US$50/75 nine/18 holes. Carts rent for US$45; clubs rent for US$20. The fifth is Ruby's signature hole, with a lake wrapped around the fairway and green. In January the Bahamas Princess Resort & Casino Crystal Pro-Am Golf Tournament is held here.

The Fortune Hills Golf & Country Club (☎ 242-373-4500/2222), off E Sunrise Hwy, is a semiprivate, Dick Wilson-designed championship nine-hole course good for beginners. Vital statistics: 36-par, 3458 yards. Games cost US$28, including cart rental. Club rental costs US$9.

Lucaya Golf & Country Club (☎ 242-373-1066, 800-622-6770), at the Clarion Atlantik Beach Resort, is a 6800-yard course featuring well-bunkered greens and generous fairways amid stands of pines and dense tropical undergrowth. It is the oldest club on Grand Bahama and considered a sedate course, yet it's rated one of the top three courses in the Caribbean. There are plenty of water hazards, including a signature 18th hole featuring a lake in front of the two-tiered green that has the Balancing Boulders of Lucaya, a 10-foot-wide, 20-foot-high waterfall (see the Lucaya to Peterson Cay National Park section, earlier in this chapter). Fees are US$70 for 18 holes, including cart rental. It hosts the European Golf Weeks each October.

There is also a run-down nine-hole course with three tee layouts at the old Jack Tar Village Resort at West End. There's miniature golf at Pirates of The Bahamas Beach Theme Park (☎ 242-373-8456) on Jolly Roger Dr in Taino Beach.

Sport Fishing & Bonefishing

The Gulf Stream, off the west coast of Grand Bahama, teems with game fish such as blue marlin. The Northwest Providence Channel drops to 2000 feet just 400 yards off the south shore, where snapper and barracuda are prevalent. And bonefishing is superb on the flats of the Little Bahama Bank to the north and east.

Charter vessels include the well-equipped *Night Hawk*, operated by Viva Cruises (☎ 242-373-7226); half-day fishing trips cost US$35 and depart from Port Lucaya Marina at 9 am and 1:15 pm daily except Friday. Nighttime shark fishing is offered on Tuesday and Thursday for US$40.

Other charter operators based here include the following:

Fisherman's Safari	☎ 242-352-7915
Nautical Adventures	☎ 242-373-7195
Running Mon Marina	☎ 242-352-6834

The Xanadu Marina Offshore Fishing Tournament is held each February with two categories: bottom fishing and deep-sea fishing. There are no cash prizes. Registration costs US$20 to US$50. Call ☎ 242-352-8044 for information.

Boat Excursions

Pat & Diane Snorkeling (☎ 242-373-8681) offers a 'Reef 'n' Wreck' day cruise and snorkel adventure, with a beach party, for US$40/27 adults/children. It also has the 'Sunset Sailing Cruise' aboard *My-Tri*, a 52-foot trimaran, for US$25. Running Mon Marina (☎ 242-352-6834) offers daily deep-sea fishing charters, and it has glass-bottomed boat tours on the *Coral Princess*.

Similar trips are offered aboard the *Bahama Mama* by Paradise Watersports (☎ 242-352-2887). Reef Tours (☎ 242-373-5880/5891) offers party cruises, a nocturnal 'booze cruise,' and snorkel excursions aboard the *Island Princess*, a 72-foot twin-hulled powerboat, and the smaller *Lucayan Princess*. Kids under five go free. Reservations are required.

Several other boats depart Port Lucaya Marina on excursions, including the *Mermaid Kitty*, a massive glass-bottomed boat.

Deepstar Submarine (☎ 242-373-8665, fax 242-373-8667), in Sea Horse Plaza on Sea Horse Rd, dives to 100 feet. The vessel – a COMEX submarine – was constructed specifically to reveal the marvels of the underwater world to nondivers. It claims to be the only submarine in the world with 90% of its hull made of clear acrylic windows. The tour costs US$53/43 adults/children. The postal address is PO Box F-40393, Freeport, Grand Bahama, Bahamas.

Claustrophobics who prefer to be half in and half out of the water can opt for the *Seaworld Explorer* (☎ 242-373-7863), a glass-lined semisubmersible that stays on the surface.

Other Water Sports

Most resort hotels rent snorkel gear, sea kayaks, Sunfish, Windsurfers, and equipment for other water sports. Independent concessions are also located on most beaches. Jet Skis rent for US$30 to US$50 per half-hour. Paradise Watersports (☎ 242-352-2887/6782) offers water sports, including parasailing.

You can learn to windsurf at the Clarion Atlantik Beach Resort (see the Places to Stay section), which has an eight-hour course, from beginners to advanced, for

US$150. It also rents boards for US$25/40 hourly/daily.

The Bahamas Windsurfing Championship is held in Freeport each January.

Other Activities

Pinetree Stables (☎ 242-373-3600) offers horseback rides through the pine forests and along the south shore at 9 and 11 am and 2 pm daily except Monday for US$35. Riding lessons are offered by appointment; the mailing address is PO Box F-42915, N Beachway Dr, Freeport, Grand Bahama, Bahamas.

Tandem Skydive Bahamas (☎ 242-352-5995), at the Taino Air Terminal, offers skydiving in a harness with an instructor and parachute made for two. After a 20-minute flight to 10,000 feet, you'll dive and free-fall for 5000 feet, then float for the rest of the way.

There are at least 50 tennis courts in Freeport and Lucaya. Most resorts have tennis courts, notably the Bahamas Princess Resort with 12 courts. Typical fees are US$5 to US$10 per hour, US$10 to US$20 for night play.

Sea Surf Lanes (☎ 242-352-5784), on Queen's Hwy, has bowling alleys for US$3 per game.

ORGANIZED TOURS
City Tours

Several companies offer half- and full-day sightseeing tours taking in most sites in and around Freeport and Lucaya. Some also offer island tours. Typical prices are US$18/12 adults/children for half-day tours and US$25/15 for a full-day tour as far afield as West End. Companies include the following:

Bahamas Travel	☎ 242-352-3141
Executive Tours	☎ 242-352-8858
Forbes Charters	☎ 242-352-9311
Grand Bahama Taxi Union	☎ 242-352-7858/7101
Inter-Island Adventures	☎ 242-352-9063
Sun Island Tours	☎ 242-352-4811
Sunworld Travel & Tours	☎ 242-352-3717

For a bird's-eye view, try the flightseeing tour with Taino Air (☎ 242-352-8885) or Major's Air Services (☎ 242-352-5778).

Cultural & Nature Tours

East End Adventures (☎ 242-373-6662) offers an all-day ecology-oriented adventure to Sweeting's and Lightbourne cays at the extreme eastern end of the island, including a stop at Lucayan National Park (see the Sweeting's Cay section in this chapter for information).

For an immersion in local culture, try a 'Village Beat' tour offered by Inter-Island Adventures (see City Tours, above). The two-hour guided tour visits settlements such as Eight Mile for US$24. Similarly, the company has a three-hour 'Freeport Heritage Tour' for US$26, as well as two trips to the nearby isle of Great Abaco (see the Lucayan National Park to McLean's Town section, later in this chapter). Its postal address is PO Box F-43216, Freeport, Grand Bahama, Bahamas.

You can also take a guided sea kayak tour into the mangroves. See the Lucayan National Park section for details.

Nautical Adventures (☎ 242-373-7195) has a 'Historic Cave Tour' taking in Lucayan National Park and Gold Rock Beach.

SPECIAL EVENTS

The highlight of the social calendar is the New Year's Day Junkanoo Parade, which kicks off at 5 am downtown, with costumed revelers and a cacophony of sounds.

March traditionally sees the Freeport Rugby Club Annual Easter Rugby Festival, when international teams arrive to compete. Call Bob Davies of the Freeport Rugby Football Club (☎ 242-352-2952) for information. The Grand Bahama 5K Road Race is also held in March. Each spring Grand Bahama also hosts the Tour de Freeport 100-mile bicycle race.

The Annual Grand Bahama Triathlon is usually held in October at the Lucayan Cricket Club; contact Bruce Silvera (☎ 242-352-8137, fax 242-352-6247). In November's Annual Grand Bahama Conchman Triathlon, athletes compete in swimming,

GRAND BAHAMA

bicycling, and running. For details, call John Bradley (☎ 242-373-4521).

PLACES TO STAY

Grand Bahama has about 3000 rooms. If you're looking for budget accommodations or camping options, look elsewhere. Most hotels tack a service charge and government tax onto the room rates that are quoted below.

Places to Stay – middle

Freeport The *Island Palm Resort* (☎ 242-352-6648, fax 242-352-6640), on E Mall Dr at Explorers Way, is a Miami-style property centered on a small pool and landscaped courtyard. It's popular with a local clientele. The 158 modestly furnished rooms cost US$79; some are dingy, as are the bathrooms, but it's advantageously close to the airport. The mailing address is PO Box F-402000, Freeport, Grand Bahama, Bahamas.

Castaways Resort (☎ 242-352-6682, fax 242-352-5087), a stone's throw from the Bahamas Princess Casino and International Bazaar on E Mall Dr, has 130 spacious air-con rooms (bathrooms are small), adequately furnished with one king-size or two double beds, cable TV, and phone. Out back there is a pool and a sun deck with snack bar. Otherwise it's uninspired. Winter rates are US$72 standard to US$98 deluxe, single or double. Its mailing address is PO Box F-2629, Freeport, Grand Bahama, Bahamas.

A better option, across the road from Castaways Resort, is the *Royal Islander* (☎ 242-351-3546, fax 242-351-3546, 800-899-7797), a pleasing two-story property centered on a courtyard with pool and shady palms. Rooms are large and nicely furnished, with heaps of light. Standard rooms cost US$90 single or double in winter; superior rooms cost US$80. Its postal address is PO Box F-2549, Freeport, Grand Bahama, Bahamas.

The *Running Mon Resort & Marina* (☎ 242-352-6834, fax 242-352-6835), 208 Kelly Ct, faces the marina at the south end of The Mall. It has 32 air-con rooms with contemporary furnishings, plus the Mainsail Restaurant and Compass Lounge. Rooms cost US$79 to US$89 single or double in summer, US$99 to US$109 in winter. A deluxe suite for US$219 features a Jacuzzi. It has an on-site dive shop, deep-sea fishing charters, and a swimming pool. Free transport is offered to Xanadu Beach (a 20-minute walk), the Princess Casino, and Port Lucaya. Its postal address is PO Box F-42663, Freeport, Grand Bahama, Bahamas.

Lucaya An option is the *Victoria Inn* (☎ 242-373-3040, fax 242-373-3874), a motel-style hotel at Port Lucaya that serves out-of-towners, spring-breakers, and budget-conscious travelers. The 40 rooms have modest decor, including phone and TV. There's a pool and Jacuzzi. It's overpriced at US$65/75 summer/winter. A meal plan costs US$24 daily. The mailing address is PO Box F-1261, Freeport, Grand Bahama, Bahamas.

Silver Point Beach The condo-style *Silver Sands Hotel* (☎ 242-373-5700, fax 242-373-1039) boasts 144 studio apartments and 20 one-bedroom luxury suites, all done up in contemporary decor with full kitchen; rates begin at US$95. There's a restaurant and a separate snack bar. It has tennis and racquetball courts, two swimming pools, and an on-site basket weaver. Its postal address is PO Box F-42385, Freeport, Grand Bahama, Bahamas.

An alternative hotel is the beachfront, high-rise condo-style *Coral Beach Hotel* (☎ 242-373-2468, fax 242-373-5140), PO Box F-42468, Freeport, Grand Bahama, Bahamas.

Places to Stay – top end

Freeport The grande dame of hotels is the *Bahamas Princess Resort & Casino* (☎ 242-352-6721, fax 242-352-2542; in the USA ☎ 800-223-1818, fax 212-832-1564), a landmark with its plump Arabic domes and minarets crowning Freeport like a mirage. It's popular with package vacationers from New York who flock here for the gambling at the adjacent Princess Casino. The hotel boasts a massive pool with Jacuzzi and a sun deck landscaped with rocks and a waterfall. There are several restaurants and bars and 12 tennis courts, and the Emerald & Ruby Golf Courses are part of the property. Recently upgraded, the 400 rooms in the 10-story Towers are comfortable. Room rates begin at US$95/120 low/peak season. Three-night package rates begin at US$327/336 single/double in winter, US$268/276 in summer. Three-night golf packages start at US$441 per person double occupancy, including roundtrip air transportation, accommodations, golf, and more. Ask about the 'Princess Pizzazz' all-inclusive add-on for US$79, which includes three meals daily, entertainment, unlimited golf, and more. The postal address is PO Box F-40207, Freeport, Grand Bahama, Bahamas.

The *Bahamian Princess Country Club* is part of the same property. The self-contained resort is far more active than the laid-back Towers, though the prices are lower. The 565 rooms in two- and three-story low-rises are tastefully decorated and arranged in a circle around a splendid pool landscaped with waterfalls. It attracts a more upscale crowd. In 1997 it was undergoing renovation. Room rates begin at US$85/110 low/peak season. Three-night package rates begin at US$283/292 single/double in winter, US$224/234 in summer.

Self-catering options include *Woodbourne Estates Resort* (☎ /fax 242-352-4069), at the south end of The Mall, which encompasses three resorts. Coral Court has 20 studios for US$100 and one-, two-, and three-bedroom apartments and efficiencies for US$125 to US$185. Northstar and Woodbourne have 22 and 30 two-bedroom apartments, respectively, sleeping up to six people for US$150. Rates fall for long-term stays. The property serves a mostly Canadian time-share clientele. It rents bicycles for US$10 per day. Its postal address is PO Box F-42453, Freeport, Grand Bahama, Bahamas.

The only beach hotel is the high-rise *Xanadu Beach Resort & Marina* (☎ 242-352-6783, fax 242-352-5799), with its own private beach. It has 137 rooms, all with a private balcony. It has tennis courts, water sports, plus an on-site dive shop. Winter rates begin at US$120 single or double. Suites range from US$195 to US$300. Meal plans are offered.

Lucaya The *Lucayan Beach Resort & Casino* (☎ 242-373-7777) has 243 air-con rooms, including 10 oceanfront suites. The historic property was recently refurbished with distressed oak-style furniture, satellite TV, and direct-dial phones. The resort, managed by Carnival Hotels & Casinos, has a choice of restaurants, entertainment, tennis courts, and water sports, and boasts a 20,000-sq-foot casino. The hotel's signature red-and-white-striped lighthouse rises over the property. Summer rates range from US$130 to US$180; winter rates range from US$155 to US$200. A MAP (breakfast and dinner) plan costs US$35. Special packages begin at US$194 for three nights and US$434 for seven nights in summer; US$217 and US$487, respectively, in winter. The postal address is PO Box F-40336, Lucaya, Grand Bahama, Bahamas.

Next door is the *Clarion Atlantik Beach Resort* (☎ 242-373-1444, fax 242-373-7481; in the USA ☎ 305-592-5757, 800-622-6770, fax 305-592-3715; in Canada ☎ 800-848-3315), a midrange beachfront property that recently underwent a US$10 million renovation. Its Alfredo restaurant (one of three eateries) is among Grand Bahama's better restaurants. The adequate 175 rooms are divided among rooms, suites, and one- to three-bedroom apartments, all with direct-dial telephone, TV, and air-con. It also has an Olympic-size pool, spa, and the hotel's pride and joy – the Lucaya Golf & Country Club. Summer rates are US$100/120 single/double for a standard room, US$155/170 for a junior suite. Apartments begin at US$175/190. Winter rates are US$120/140 for a standard room, US$155/180 for a junior suite. Apartments begin at US$185/200. Golf packages start at US$97 per person per

GRAND BAHAMA

day, double occupancy, including green fees and more. Its postal address is PO Box F-42500, Freeport/Lucaya, Grand Bahama, Bahamas.

The *Grand Bahama Beach Hotel* (☎ 242-373-1333, fax 242-373-8662; in the USA ☎ 305-592-5757, 800-622-6770, fax 305-592-3715) is an older, soulless, 250-room low-rise property centered on a huge sun deck. It has a restaurant and bar, plus swimming pool, tennis courts, and water sports. It was scheduled for a makeover in 1997. Year-round rates run from US$90/105 single/double for an island-view room to US$170/175 for an oceanfront suite. Golf packages begin at US$157/226 in summer and US$175/252 in winter. Contact PO Box F-42496, Freeport, Grand Bahama, Bahamas.

An appealing harborside option is the *Port Lucaya Resort & Yacht Club* (☎ 242-373-6618, 800-582-2921, fax 242-373-6652) on Bell Channel Bay Rd. This new 160-room hotel sits on a peninsula adjacent to the Port Lucaya Marketplace and Marina. Its postal address is PO Box F-42452, Freeport, Grand Bahama, Bahamas. Also at the harborside is the *Bell Channel Club & Marina* (☎ 242-373-2673, fax 242-373-3802) on Jolly Roger Dr. The mailing address is PO Box F-44053, Freeport, Grand Bahama, Bahamas.

The most exclusive resort is *Pelican Bay at Lucaya* (☎ 242-373-9550, fax 242-373-9551), next to the marina. This recently opened 'boutique' hotel boasts exquisite contemporary structures built in classical Bermudan style. It has 48 spacious air-con rooms at the water's edge, each with satellite TV, phone, safe, and minibar, plus private balcony, hot tub, and pool bar! Rates begin at US$150. The mailing address is PO Box F-42654, Freeport, Grand Bahama, Bahamas.

Taino Beach & Fortune Beach
The *Taino Beach Resort & Marina* (☎ 242-373-4677), 5 Jolly Roger Dr at the far west end of Taino Beach near Port Lucaya, is popular with families, though it's appealing to everyone. It has 68 comfortable one-, two-,

and three-bedroom apartments, a nice ambiance, pleasing restaurant, and an array of water sports. Its postal address is PO Box F-43819, Freeport, Grand Bahama, Bahamas.

The Italian-run *Club Fortuna* (☎ 242-373-4000, 800-742-4276, fax 242-373-5555), on Fortune Beach, is an all-inclusive resort that attempts to copy Club Med with modest success. The sprawling 204-room resort is meagerly landscaped but has a large pool and sun deck and backs a beautiful section of beach that is a setting for lively activities, including volleyball, archery, bocce ball, and a full menu of water sports. On the down side, the mediocre cuisine conjures up memories of school-day dining. For a welcome break, walk along the beach to Club Caribe (see Places to Eat, below). Club Fortuna is vastly overpriced at US$220/260 for garden-/ocean-view rooms in low season and US$250/290 in peak season, though the rates include all meals and beverages, water sports (motorized water sports cost extra), and nightly entertainment presented in the impressive open theater. Its mailing address is PO Box F-42398, Freeport, Grand Bahama, Bahamas.

PLACES TO EAT
There's no shortage of places to eat, but finding good value – or even a *tasty* meal – is a challenge. Most serve bland or routine fare, often at New York prices.

Freeport
Downtown, try *Mr Baker* on E Mall Dr. It's a bakery and fast-food deli serving sandwiches and hot dishes such as barbecued ribs, coleslaw, and rice or potato for US$6 and broccoli and garlic potato for US$5. It also has breakfast specials. For lunch, locals head to *Geneva's Place* (☎ 242-352-5085) on E Mall Dr at Kipling Ln, a good place to try Bahamian dishes, including guava duff dessert (dumpling laced with guava purée and drowned in a milky rum sauce). For steaks and Bahamian dishes, check out the *Safari Lounge Disco & Steak House*, a short way up the road. *Pizza Hut*,

on E Mall Dr at Adventurers Way, has an all-you-can-eat luncheon buffet for US$7 each Wednesday.

The *International Bazaar* has more than a dozen places to eat, including an English-style pub. Most serve Bahamian fare. Some have bargain-priced breakfast specials. The restaurants are supposed to serve a free Bahama Mama cocktail with a purchase of lunch or dinner, though none advertise this. *Café Michel's* (☎ 242-352-2191) offers romantic patio dining beneath a suitably French-style awning. A US-style breakfast costs around US$5, as does a sandwich lunch. Its eclectic entrées range from steaks to fish and chips. The food is mediocre. Similarly, *Le Rendezvous* has patio dining and breakfast specials as low as US$1.95. The *Japanese Steak House* (☎ 242-352-9521) looks appealing but is overpriced, and the meals are hit-and-miss; my shrimp teriyaki comprised canned vegetables with shrimp on top for US$12.95. For Greek food, try *The Plaka* (☎ 242-352-5932). It has authentic Hellenic cuisine: souvlaki, kebabs, moussaka, and retsina to wash it all down.

Les Fountains (☎ 242-373-9553), on E Sunrise Hwy, has an all-you-can-eat breakfast buffet for US$8.50, 10 to 11 am. It's open 24 hours daily. The small restaurant in the *Royal Islander* hotel has a bargain-priced US breakfast special for US$3.50.

For Italian fare, try *Silvano's* (☎ 242-352-5110), an elegant restaurant on the northeast side of Ranfurly Circle, suitably Italianate in decor, with a full menu of dishes averaging US$11. It's open evenings only and is closed Monday. It also has an ice-cream parlor, *Gelati Silvano's*, selling homemade ice cream; the factory supplies most of The Bahamas.

In the same price range is *Islander's Roost* (☎ 242-352-5110), adjoining Silvano's. One of the few eateries with a Caribbean flavor, it serves Bahamian and US dishes and offers live entertainment nightly. It's open 5 pm to 1 am Monday to Saturday and is closed Sunday.

Some of the best European cuisine can be found at *Ruby Swiss* (☎ 242-352-8507) on W Sunrise Hwy at W Atlantic Dr. The *Crown Room* (☎ 242-352-7811), at the Princess Casino, claims to serve gourmet continental cuisine; jackets are required.

Lucaya

The Port Lucaya Marketplace has about two dozen choices. You'll find several English-style pubs. Fancy a curry or pizza? Head to *Pisces* (☎ 242-373-5192); plan to spend about US$15. *Zorba's* (☎ 242-373-6137) offers tasty, reasonably priced Greek cuisine, such as chicken souvlaki for US$4.25 and moussaka and Greek salad for US$7.50, to be enjoyed alfresco beneath a canopy of grapevines and pink bougainvillea. The *China Cafe* (☎ 242-373-2398) has lunch specials for US$3.50 and dinner specials for US$8.50, though the cuisine is mediocre. For breakfast specials, try the *Caribbean Cafe* (☎ 242-373-5866), where the menu includes oatmeal and toast for US$3.50, muffins for US$1.75, and pancakes for US$4.50.

Also here is the cozy *La Dolce Vita* (☎ 242-373-8652), decorated in art deco and offering a good selection of continental dishes, including grilled portofino mushrooms, and lobster and linguini in cream sauce. The most sophisticated eatery is *Luciano's* (☎ 242-373-9100), a hip spot lit by halogen spotlights, specializing in Italian and French fare. Try the grilled Dover sole with new potatoes.

The *Brass Helmet Restaurant* (☎ 242-373-2032), above UNEXSO, boasts divers' helmets as decor, plus a great white shark crashing through the wall (oh, go ahead, stick your head in its mouth for the camera). The menu is heavy on seafood. It's reasonably priced, with salads beginning at US$5 and Bahamian dishes such as Andros barbecued chicken for US$10. Start your day with spicy Bahamian hash 'n' grits, locally called 'fire engine.'

Scorpio's (242-352-6969), also at Port Lucaya Marketplace, has been recommended, as has the *Arawak Restaurant* (☎ 242-373-1066), overlooking the golf course at the Lucaya Golf & Country Club and offering specialties such as caesar

GRAND BAHAMA

salad prepared at the table, lobster thermidor, and flambéed desserts. There's live music. It has a Sunday brunch 11:30 am to 3 pm. The *Lucayan Beach Resort* (☎ 242-373-7777) hosts a Sunday champagne brunch in the Buffet Room.

Farther Afield

Some of the best dining lies farther afield, especially at Taino Beach and Deadman's Reef (see the West of Freeport section later in this chapter). In a rambling Cape-Cod-type wooden building near the Cruise Ship Port, *Pier One* (☎ 242-352-6674) serves excellent seafood, such as pan-fried wahoo or shark, at tables that teeter on the brink of the brine. Steady with the rum cocktails . . . sharks circle at the pier in anticipation of a bucket of chum occasionally tossed down from the stilted shack.

At Churchill Beach, *Club Caribe* (☎ 242-373-6866) bills itself as a Boston-style eatery. It's simple yet homey and a marvelous place to hang out on the wooden deck over the beach. A volleyball net may tempt you from indulgent lazing with a cool pint of Fosters. An omelet breakfast or ham and eggs costs US$3. Salads, burgers, and peas 'n' rice are similarly priced. Main dishes begin at US$9. Hotel transfers are provided. A similar, though less atmospheric, option is *Le Beach Shack*, next door.

For a more down-home taste of local color, head to *Mama Flo's* at Taino Beach, alias the White Wave Club Bar & Pool Hall. It's a funky little bar run by a colorful Bahama mama who whips up native fare for a few bucks. The offbeat *Outriggers Restaurant & Bar* (☎ 242-373-4811) is 400 yards west of Mama Flo's and overlooks the beach. It's popular for its fish fry on Wednesday night, when the place gets packed. It's run by Mama Flo's daughter.

For the ultimate in funky Bahamian ambiance, drift to Tony Macaroni's *conch stall* – made of thatch and driftwood – next to the *Surfside Restaurant* (☎ 242-373-1814), which also has a salt-assaulted deck over the beach. Tony is a colorful dude who'll keep you amused while preparing your roast (grilled) conch.

Kaptain Kenny's (☎ 242-373-8689), just west of Outriggers, is an institution . . . and a replay of the popular restaurant in Freeport. This huge, all-timber beachfront bar and restaurant is pervaded by a maritime mood, enhanced by nets and driftwood and waitresses in nautical costume. It offers Bahamian fare, salads, and sandwiches, plus a daily special, including all-you-can-drink Bahama Mamas for US$14. Tour buses unload their cargo here. There are water sports. A weekly afternoon beach party for US$30 and a sunset bonfire for US$25 are offered, with limbo and beer-drinking contests. It's open daily from 9 am until way late.

For upscale dining at Taino Beach, try the *Stone Crab* (☎ 242-373-1442), next to Kaptain Kenny's. It serves steak and seafood averaging US$20 (it also has beach parties for US$40). Nearby is the *Pirates of The Bahamas Beach Theme Park* (☎ 242-373-8456), serving Bahamian dishes. It also offers miniature golf, sea kayaks, paddle boats, and Jet Skis. Also try the *Taino Beach Resort & Marina*.

ENTERTAINMENT
Casinos & Floorshows

The *Bahamas Princess Casino* (☎ 242-352-6721), beside the Bahamas Princess Resort on W Sunrise Hwy, has over 400 slots, 40 blackjack tables, eight dice tables, eight roulette wheels, and other games of chance. Admission is free. No beachwear, bare feet, or bare backs are allowed. The casino also has a sports book section where bets may be placed on sports and other major events.

You can also try your luck at the *Lucayan Beach Resort & Casino* (☎ 242-373-7777), boasting 544 slots, craps, blackjack, roulette, and more. It offers free gaming lessons at 11 am and 7 pm. At press time the casino had closed for one to two years for remodeling.

The Bahamas Princess Casino has a small-scale Las Vegas-style revue, 'Nightlife,' with brief toplessness and dance routines combining classical and contemporary movement. A comedy act is part of the routine.

Shows are at 8:30 and 10:45 pm nightly except Monday; they cost US$25, including two drinks. The *Bahamas Princess Resort* (☎ 242-352-6721) has its own revue, 'The Sultan's Tent,' appealing to lovers of besequined Liberaces.

There are several 'native revues.' One of the best is 'Goombaya' at the *Bahamas Princess Country Club* (☎ 242-352-7811), with singing, dancing, and Junkanoo. Shows are at 6:30 and 7:30 pm Wednesday, Friday, and Saturday. The Bahamas Princess Towers Resort also has a 'Panache Native Show' at 9 pm nightly except Saturday.

A 'Native Floorshow' with calypso is hosted at *The Captain's Charthouse* (☎ 242-373-3900), on E Sunrise Hwy, at 7 and 9 pm nightly except Monday. The *Yellowbird Show Club* at the International Bazaar has a show with fire-eating and limbo dancing at 9 pm nightly except Sunday; it costs US$20, including two drinks. The Lucayan Beach Resort has a similar revue, the 'Flamingo Showcase,' at 8 and 10 pm Wednesday and Saturday; it costs US$25 or US$40 with dinner.

For comedy, check out *Joker's Wild Supper & Show Club* (☎ 242-373-7765) on Midshipman Rd in Lucaya, where a dinner show featuring limbo and 'voodoo' dancers is held at 7 pm nightly except Sunday.

Pubs/Bars

The hot spot is *Kaptain Kenny's* (☎ 242-351-4759) at the International Bazaar. It's the center of action during spring break, and at any time of year attracts a young, beer-guzzling crowd. Happy hour is 5 to 7 pm daily. For a mellower ambiance, try *Sir Winston Churchill Pub* (☎ 242-352-8866), upstairs, next door to Kaptain Kenny's, or the *Prince of Wales Lounge* across the street in the Pub on The Mall.

Bars at Port Lucaya Marketplace include *Bahama Mama's Lounge* (☎ 242-373-8514); *Rum Runners* (☎ 242-373-7233); the *Happy Bar & Lounge* (☎ 242-373-6852), a sports bar with TV; and the *Junkanoo Sports Bar* (☎ 242-373-6170), *the* place to watch the game. Or try the *Red Dog Sports Bar* (☎ 242-352-2700) at the Pub on The Mall opposite the International Bazaar, and boasting a 62-inch TV.

At Taino Beach, *Kaptain Kenny's* and *Le Beach Shack* (☎ 242-373-4525) are happenin' spots.

There are few secret watering holes for locals, who complain that 'there's nothing to do.' The local bar scene is limited to a few vapid 'satellite lounges.'

Live Music

Little Joe Cartwright performs calypso and soca at *Port Lucaya Marketplace* (☎ 242-373-8446) 7:30 to 10 pm nightly. A roller-skating limbo dancer (!) and fire-eaters are featured. Similar sounds can be heard at the lively *John B Bar* (☎ 242-352-7811) at the Princess Country Club, and at *Becky's Restaurant* (☎ 242-352-8717) in the International Bazaar.

For jazz, try the *Port Lucaya Yacht Club* (☎ 242-373-6618), where Mark Carey performs 8 pm to 1 am nightly except Tuesday. *Kaptain Kenny's* (☎ 242-351-4759), at the International Bazaar, occasionally has live jazz.

The *Port Lucaya Yacht Club Piano Bar* is a relaxed spot for sedate listening, as is *Ruby Swiss* (☎ 242-352-8507), next to the Princess Casino. The latter remains open until 6 am.

Big-name performers are often hosted by the Lucayan Beach Resort & Casino.

Dance Clubs

Locals head to *Studio 69* (☎ 242-373-4824), Midshipman Rd, Lucaya, or the *Safari Lounge* (☎ 242-352-2805) at the Freeport Inn. Don't even think of arriving before 11 pm.

The best place is *Club Estee* (☎ 242-373-2777), 5 Port Lucaya, with a large, sweaty dance hall and a smaller, more intimate floor, both with laser lights and a mix of hip-hop, world beat, and island rhythms. No shorts or tank tops; admission costs US$10.

Theater

The Freeport Players Guild puts on four plays each season (September to June) at the

Regency Theatre (☎ 242-352-5533), west of the Bahamas Princess Resort. The Grand Bahama Players (☎ 242-352-7071, 242-373-2299) also perform here. Tickets usually cost US$10. Dinner shows cost US$50, including a bottle of champagne. Also check for performances by the Freeport Friends of the Arts (☎ 242-373-1528).

Cinemas
The only cinema is the *Columbus Twin Theater Cinema* on E Mall Dr at Adventurers Way; admission costs US$5. The *Port Lucaya Yacht Club Piano Bar* (☎ 242-373-9225) shows movies at 7 and 9:30 pm nightly.

THINGS TO BUY
Like Nassau, Freeport and Lucaya are not quite the duty-free shoppers' mecca they're made out to be. There are plenty of stores; the shopping is unsophisticated except for jewelry and perfumes, and real bargains are hard to find. Locals do their shopping downtown at malls such as The Towne Centre and Churchill Square.

What-to-do in Freeport/Lucaya, Grand Bahama (see Information, earlier in this chapter) lists major stores and has maps of the International Bazaar and Port Lucaya Marketplace, plus a handy perfume price-comparison chart.

Take your pick among several dozen jewelry stores, including The Colombian (☎ 242-352-5380), Colombian Emeralds International (☎ 800-666-3889), and Jeweler's Warehouse, all with outlets in the International Bazaar and the Port Lucaya Marketplace.

For embroidered linens, silk pajamas, and the like, try Far East Traders (in the International Bazaar ☎ 242-352-9280; Port Lucaya Marketplace 242-373-8697).

The International Bazaar has approximately 100 stores, including Fendi (☎ 242-352-7908) for Italian leather; Freeport Jewelers (☎ 242-352-2004) and John Bull (☎ 242-352-2626) for jewelry; The Gallery (☎ 242-352-2660) and Island Galleria (☎ 242-352-8194), both specializing in crystal and fine porcelain, including

Waterford and Lladró; and Gucci (☎ 242-352-4580), specializing in Italian clothing, leather, and accessories. The Plaka (☎ 242-352-5932) sells items from Greece. The Taj Emporium (☎ 242-373-5099) sells Indian imports, everything from children's toys to fashionwear.

Several stores in the bazaar sell perfumes. The Perfume Factory (☎ 242-352-9391) is immediately north of the bazaar (see Perfume Factory under Freeport, earlier in this chapter). And the Caribbean Sea Treasures Factory (☎ 242-352-5380) is also here; it offers tours demonstrating how jewelry is made out of shells and coral.

The 6-acre Port Lucaya Marketplace shopping complex has 85 stores. It has Gucci (☎ 242-373-2973), Island Galleria (☎ 242-373-8404), The Jewellery Box (☎ 242-373-8319), Linens of Lucaya (☎ 242-352-8697), and The Nautique Shoppe (☎ 242-373-1522), which specializes in resortwear, silk paintings and other artwork, and custom-made crafts with a nautical theme. Samos of Lucaya (☎ 242-373-5846) sells imports from Greece.

Cigars
Cuban cigars are a great buy. Most quality gift shops sell Cohibas (the Rolls-Royce of cigars), Montecristos, and other notable brands at 50% or more off black-market prices in the USA. The best place is Smoker's World in the Ginza Bldg of the International Bazaar.

US citizens are legally barred from purchasing *any* Cuban products, even if bought in The Bahamas. See the Facts for the Visitor chapter for details on US Customs regulations.

Straw-Work & Native Items
There are several straw markets, notably behind the International Bazaar, where dozens of stalls sell all manner of woven straw crafts, as well as T-shirts, carvings,

and ethnic jewelry. The hustling is light, and it's no gauntlet to browse. You'll find similar markets at the Port Lucaya Marketplace, Xanadu Beach, and Kaptain Kenny's at Taino Beach.

Look for native woodcarvings, especially the simple yet dramatic works by Michael Hoyte, often hewn from ebony driftwood washed ashore from Africa.

For Bahamian sauces and preserves, specialty oils, and other culinary items, head to Solomon's Food Court (☎ 242-352-9681) on Cedar St.

Music
Most gift shops in Freeport and Lucaya sell CDs and tapes. Serious music buffs should head to Buck's Record Gallery, downtown on Pioneers Way near E Mall Dr, or Intercity Music (☎ 242-352-8820) at Port Lucaya Marketplace.

Photographic Equipment
A few stores in the International Bazaar sell cameras and photographic and video equipment, including film. Also try the Camera Shoppe, 20 Pioneers Way, downtown, and the Photo Specialist (☎ 242-373-7858) in Port Lucaya Marketplace.

GETTING THERE & AWAY
Air
Freeport International Airport (☎ 242-352-6020) is 2 miles north of central Freeport. There's a tourist board information booth and exchange office in the arrivals hall. Customs and immigration formalities are straightforward, and usually there are no long lines.

See the Getting There & Away and Getting Around chapters for airlines' and charter companies' international and Freeport telephone numbers.

To/From the USA The following airlines fly to Grand Bahama from the USA: American Eagle, Bahamasair, Delta/Comair, Gulfstream International, and LB Ltd (formerly Laker Airways).

American Eagle, an American Airlines subsidiary, has six roundtrip flights daily from Miami to Freeport, with fares from US$80 roundtrip. Bahamasair has several daily flights from Miami using Dash-8 and Shorts aircraft. Delta's subsidiary Comair flies turboprops from Orlando and Fort Lauderdale. Gulfstream International flies daily from Miami, Fort Lauderdale, Key West, Orlando, Tallahassee, and Naples; on weekends from Tampa and West Palm Beach; and daily (except Saturday) from Gainesville; Jacksonville; Daytona Beach; Atlanta, GA; and Mobile, AL. LB Ltd flies from several East Coast and Midwest cities.

The biggest charter operator is Apple Vacations, with flights from several major cities. American Fly AAway Vacations has two-night packages starting at US$128 at the Bahamas Princess Resort (excluding airfare).

Grand Bahama Vacations, a collective sales arm of six Grand Bahama hotels, has packages using LB Ltd airlines, with direct service from Allentown, PA, on Sunday and Thursday; and Knoxville, TN, on Monday and Thursday. Three-night packages begin at US$269, including airfare. The company also offers packages from Baltimore; Cleveland; Cincinnati, OH; Fort Lauderdale, Richmond, VA; and Raleigh/Durham, NC.

Island Hoppers has air-hotel packages to Grand Bahama that include roundtrip airfare from Miami and two nights of accommodations. Princess Vacations (☎ 800-545-1300) offers all-inclusive packages weekly from Baltimore/Washington, DC; Chicago; Cincinnati; Cleveland; Fort Lauderdale; Hartford, CT; Memphis, TN; Nashville, TN; New York; Raleigh/Durham; and Richmond. Three-night package rates begin at US$365 from New York.

The charter company TNT Vacations has flights from Boston on Monday and Friday.

To/From Canada The charter company Conquest Tours has flights to Freeport from Toronto, Ottawa, and Halifax.

To/From the UK Freeport is served by British Airways, with direct flights from Heathrow.

GRAND BAHAMA

To/From Elsewhere in The Bahamas
Bahamasair flies from Nassau to Freeport daily (US$64 one way). Gulfstream also offers flights several times daily between Nassau and Freeport.

Major's Air Services has flights between Freeport and the Biminis (US$95 round-trip) and Walker's Cay in the Abacos (US$85 roundtrip). Taino Air flies between Freeport and Andros, Eleuthera, and Marsh Harbour (Abacos).

Boat
Cruise Ship Several companies offer cruises to Freeport. For details on cruises, see the Getting There & Away chapter.

The three-pier Cruise Ship Port is about 6 miles west of town. There's a straw market and 'daiquiri bar,' but local attractions are hard to find. Construction of a restaurant and US$10 million 'cruise ship marketplace' was slated to begin in late 1997. Taxis (☎ 242-352-7101) provide service into town and the beaches; rides cost US$12 to US$15 to downtown, US$15 to US$20 to Lucaya.

Private Yacht There are at least half a dozen marinas. The modern Port Lucaya Marina (☎ 242-373-9090, fax 242-373-5884), off Sea Horse Rd, has 150 slips for boats up to 160 feet in length. Dockage costs US$1 per foot in peak season, US75¢ in low season; electricity, water, and cable TV hookup cost extra. Its mailing address is PO Box F-43233, Freeport, Grand Bahama, Bahamas.

Lucaya Marina (☎ 242-373-8888, fax 242-373-7630) also has 150 slips. The Port Lucaya Yacht Club (☎ 242-373-9225), adjacent to the Port Lucaya Marina, is an upscale facility with a top-class lounge and restaurant (and minicinema). It offers a complimentary two-month membership to visiting yachters.

Running Mon Marina (☎ 242-352-6834) is a 60-slip marina with on-site mechanic and repair facilities, including a 40-ton TravelLift.

Bell Channel Club & Marina (☎ 242-373-2673) has 18 slips. Between the two is

Ocean Reef Yacht Club (☎ 242-373-4662), with 52 slips.

You must clear customs and immigration at Lucaya Marina, Port Lucaya Marina, or Xanadu Marina.

Mail Boat The mail boat *Marcella III* sails at 4 pm Wednesday for Freeport from Nassau (US$45 one way). It docks half a mile east of the Cruise Ship Port. There are no services or facilities, but taxis are available.

GETTING AROUND
To/From the Airport
There's no bus service to or from the airport. Taxi rides to the Bahamas Princess Resort cost US$6 to US$8; rides to Lucaya cost US$12 to US$15.

Bus
Freeport lacks a public bus system. However, a handful of private minibuses travel assigned routes from the bus depot downtown at Winn Dixie Plaza, traveling as far afield as West End and McLean's Town. Buses tend to leave when the driver decides he has enough passengers. Fares are US75¢ for travel in town. Several minibuses operate between downtown and Port Lucaya Marketplace (US$1 one way), via E Mall Dr and the International Bazaar, E Sunrise Hwy, Coral Rd, and Royal Palm Way.

The Ministry of Tourism office (☎ 242-352-8044) can provide a list of bus routes.

Free shuttles also run from Bahamas Princess Resort & Country Club and other hotels on The Mall to Xanadu Beach every 30 minutes and to Taino Beach every hour.

Car & Scooter
Freeport's roads are paved, as is the main highway to West End and McLean's Town.

Car-rental agencies include the following:

Avis
　Freeport International Airport
　(☎ 242-352-7666)
　Lucaya (☎ 242-373-1102)
Courtesy Rental
　(☎ 242-352-5212)

Dollar
Clarion Atlantik Beach Resort
(☎ 242-373-9139)

Hertz
Freeport International Airport
(☎ 242-353-9277)

National Car Rental
Freeport International Airport
(☎ 242-352-9308)
Radisson Xanadu (☎ 242-352-6782)

Sears Rent-a-Car
Freeport International Airport
(☎ 242-352-8841)
Clarion Atlantik Beach Resort
(☎ 242-373-4938)

Star Rent-a-Car
Old Airport Rd (☎ 242-352-5953)

A local company named Budget Rent-a-Car should not be confused with the US company of that name.

Cars begin at about US$50 for older, smaller models rented through local companies. The major agencies rent modern cars starting at US$60.

If you like the wind in your hair, consider a street-worthy dune buggy from Bahama Buggies (☎ 242-352-8750), opposite the International Bazaar on E Mall Dr; it costs US$50 for eight hours, US$65 per day, US$50 per day for three to six days, or US$300 weekly.

You can rent a scooter in the forecourt of the Bahamas Princess Towers from Honda Cycle Shop (☎ 242-352-7035) on Queen's Hwy. Expect to pay US$30/40 half-/full day, plus US$100 deposit, including gas and unlimited mileage.

Taxi
Taxis are located at the airport and major hotels. Fares are fixed by the government for short distances (see the Getting Around chapter). Bonded taxis (with white license plates) can't go outside the tax-free zone. Other taxis can take you anywhere on the island for US$25 to US$35 per hour. Expect to pay US$60 to West End.

You can call a radio-dispatched taxi from Freeport Taxi (☎ 242-352-6666) or Grand Bahama Taxi Union (☎ 242-352-7101).

Bicycle
You can rent bicycles in the forecourt of the Bahamas Princess Towers and from the Radisson Lucaya Beach Resort for US$10 daily.

Boat
A water taxi runs between Port Lucaya and the Taino Beach Resort & Marina every hour. It departs Taino Beach on the hour and departs Lucaya at 10 minutes past (US$2 one way).

East of Freeport

East of the Grand Lucayan Waterway, the Grand Bahama Hwy runs inshore to the east end of the island. Side roads lead to the south shore, which boasts white-sand beaches running in endless scallops, as pristine and as dazzling as movie creations. The drive itself is ho-hum. Watch out for the dangerous 90° bends between Rocky Creek and McLean's Town. Other side roads lead to the north shore wetlands.

Water Cay
This tiny, simple settlement is on the cay of that name, 2 miles off the north shore. The community relies on fishing and is as unspoiled as things get on Grand Bahama. You can catch a boat from Hawksbill Creek or the Grand Lucayan Waterway or drive the dirt road from the Grand Bahama Hwy to the north shore dock, where you might be able to hire a boat from a local to Water Cay.

Old Free Town & Owl Hole
The settlement of Old Free Town, 3 miles east of the Grand Lucayan Waterway, was forcibly abandoned in the 1960s when the Port Authority acquired the land and relocated the inhabitants to the new city of Freeport. A few derelict buildings remain. More interesting is the surrounding swamp containing several blue holes (subaqueous caves), notably Mermaid's Lair and Owl Hole, with a flask-shaped opening that

GRAND BAHAMA

drops 35 feet to water level. Stalactites dangle from the roof of the bowl. Owls have nested on the sill as long as residents can remember.

Lucayan National Park

This 40-acre park is Grand Bahama's finest treasure. There are two halves to the park, divided by the Grand Bahama Hwy. On the north side, trails lead from the parking lot onto a limestone plateau riddled with caves, which open to the longest known underwater cave system in the world, with over 6 charted miles of tunnels. (Cave diving is allowed by special permit only under the supervision of UNEXSO in Port Lucaya.)

Two main caves open to the surface, forming blue holes – **Ben's Cave** and **Burial Mound Cave** – where fresh water floats atop saltwater. Steps lead down to viewing platforms above the water level. Colonies of harmless bats use the cave's cool interior as a nursery in summer. Ben's Cave is also the home of a recently discovered and unique class of opaque, blind crustacean – *Speleonectes lucayensis* – that resembles a swimming centipede. Bring some bread to toss into the jade-colored waters and fish will magically appear. In 1986 four skeletons of indigenous Lucayans were found on the floor of one cave, which is thought to have been a cemetery.

The **Creek Trail** (330 yards) and the **Mangrove Swamp Trail** (480 yards), across the road, form a loop, easily walked in 10 minutes, through three distinct shoreline ecosystems (other ecosystems – including rocky coppice and pineland – exist north of the road). Information signs provide edification. The transition zone is formed of bonsai-like ming, cedar, mahogany, and poisonwood, cinnecord, cabbage palms, and agaves, which produce towering yellow flowers favored by insects, hummingbirds, and raccoons. Their low branches are festooned by orchids and bromeliads (with several species found only here, including *Vanilla correllii*).

Between this zone and the shore lies a large mangrove swash dominated by air plants – predominantly the tangled roots of red mangroves and buttonwood. With fortune you might spot a raccoon and land crabs, or even an osprey. Keen-eyed herons wade the shallows on the lookout for tidbits – *pick, pick, pick* – while waterfowl splash about in the sloughs. The marsh is drained by **Gold Rock Creek**. The waters are a habitat for snapper, barracuda, manta ray, and crab (passages lead underground between the creek and the Lucayan Caves so that ocean fish are often seen in the blue holes north of the road).

The third zone is the whiteland coppice, which abuts the sandy shore and is dominated by giant poisonwood trees, pigeon plum, and other trees favored by woodpeckers ('peckerwoods' in local parlance).

Both trails spill out onto the secluded and beautiful **Gold Rock Beach**, fringed by dunes fixed by coco plum, sea grape, spider lily and casuarina (or Australian pine). At low tide the white sand is rippled as far as the eye can see; the wide beach arcs in a seemingly endless scimitar. It's named for the small rock that lies 200 yards offshore.

There were no facilities as of 1997, but a visitors' center is planned. No camping is allowed. Before you set out, take time to study the billboard map at the far end of the parking lot. Bring a picnic lunch and bug spray or, better yet, Avon Skin So Soft (the casuarinas provide a perfect habitat for biting sand fleas). All flora and fauna are protected. The park is open daily year-round. Ben's Cave is closed in June and July to protect the bats' nursery.

For more information, contact the Bahamas National Trust (☎ 242-352-5438), PO Box F-43441, Freeport, Grand Bahama, Bahamas.

Getting There & Away A minivan ('jitney') from Winn Dixie Plaza, downtown Freeport, passes by en route to McLean's Town (about US$3 one way). A taxi from Freeport will cost about US$25.

Erika Moultrie's Kayak Nature Tours (☎ 242-373-2485, kayaknet@mail.batelnet .bs) offers guided sea kayak tours from

Freeport into the wetlands for US$75, including hotel transfers and picnic lunch on Gold Rock Beach, one of the island's most beautiful beaches. Erika acts as guide, pointing out the birdlife, crabs, and other marine life. East End Adventures (☎ 242-373-6662) includes the park in its 'safari trip' to Sweeting's Cay. And a half-day guided excursion (☎ 242-373-7863) is offered with transfers to/from all hotels, with lunch and sunbathing at Gold Rock Beach; US$25/15 adults/children.

Lucayan National Park to McLean's Town

The route to McLean's Town is lined with several tiny settlements, notably sleepy Freetown, now slowly dying since the Gold Rock USAAF Missile Tracking Station – the first tracking station downrange of Cape Canaveral – closed down.

Farther east, you'll pass High Rock, a hamlet with several old wooden homes overlooking the sea from a bluff. The US Drug Enforcement Administration had one of its three drug-surveillance balloons tethered here until recent years.

About 10 miles east, beyond the Burma Oil Depot (with a harbor facility for the world's largest supertankers), is Pelican Point Beach – *fabulous!* – and Rocky Creek, another hamlet known for its blue hole full of marine life.

The fishing village of McLean's Town is a flyblown place surrounded by mangroves at the eastern tip of the island . . . literally the end of the road. It finally got a telephone in 1996. Locals live from conch and lobster fishing, and as fishing guides. The village is the jumping-off place for boat rides to Sweeting's, Lightbourne, and Deep Water cays.

This somnolent hamlet does come alive briefly for the Conch Cracking Contest in October. Contestants compete to be the first person to crack and clean 25 conchs from shells – an ugly business. The foot-long marine snail is torn from its home and butchered, still wriggling! The full-day event includes entertainment such as a greasy-pole climb, bingo, swim races,

amateur boxing, and music performed by live rake 'n' scrape bands.

Places to Stay The *Pelican Point Lodge* (☎ 242-353-6064) is a homey and reclusive place beside the beach at Pelican Point – a perfect escape from tourist traps. It's run by Freddie Long, a friendly chap who lives in the blue-and-white house across the road. He has three family-style units resembling a Midwest trailer park. Each has a kitchenette. Rates are US$60/70 one-/two-bedroom. There's a funky little bar and restaurant – Breezes – attached.

Entering McLean's Town, you can't miss the mint-green, three-story building on the left. This is *Bro's* (☎ 242-353-3440), with a choice of clean yet spartan single rooms and two-bedroom apartments, some with kitchenette. Only one has air-con. Rates are US$25 to US$45 per night, US$350 monthly for an apartment. The owner, 'Doc' Russell, is a friendly guy.

Places to Eat *Smitty's One Stop Shop*, about 5 miles east of Lucayan National Park, offers burgers and basic fare; it also

GRAND BAHAMA

sells gasoline and has a general store. Other basic options include *Receptions Lounge Restaurant & Bar* (☎ 242-353-4063) in Freetown; the *Highway Restaurant & Star Club* at High Rock; and, along the coastal road, the *Bishop Beach Club Restaurant & Bar*. Farther east is the *Seaside Restaurant*. At any of these, you could be the first out-of-towner all week.

In McLean's Town check out the *East Sunrise Bar & Restaurant*, which is inland, serving seafood. There's a basic dance club at night. You can buy groceries at the *Cooper's Convenience Store*, a tiny hut in the middle of the village. *Maxida's*, adjacent to the wharves, offers fish and chips for US$7, pork chops for US$6, and burgers for US$1. It has a pool table and on weekend nights rises from torpor with music and dancing.

Getting There & Away A minibus operates daily from Winn Dixie Plaza in downtown Freeport.

East End Adventures includes McLean's Town on its day trip to Sweeting's Cay (see Sweeting's Cay, below). Inter-Island Adventures (☎ 242-352-9063, fax 242-352-9064) also includes a stop at McLean's Town on its 'Abaco Adventure Tour' for US$99, which includes a trip by hovercraft from McLean's Town. It's offered daily.

Getting Around Freddie Long has a taxi service at Pelican Point Lodge.

Deep Water Cay

Only true isolationists know about this getaway-from-it-all fishing mecca, 1 mile southeast of McLean's Town. Deep Water Cay boasts 250 sq miles of fertile flats and miles-long, crystal-clear creeks darkened by schools of the elusive 'gray ghosts,' or bonefish. The cay is a paradise for anglers hoping to top the record 13.5-lb catch. The Deep Water Cay Club (see Places to Stay, below) has a tackle shop and operates a fleet of custom-designed 16-foot Dolphin Super Skiffs.

There are sharks and barracudas for thrills, too . . . good signs of bonefish being

present. And bountiful birdlife adds to the allure of this small isle.

If fishing isn't your thing, you can sail, dive, snorkel, play croquet, or lounge by the saltwater pool.

Places to Stay The *Deep Water Cay Club* (☎ 242-353-3073; in the USA 954-359-0488, fax 954-359-9488), run by Ed and Carole Dawes, sleeps 18 guests in cottage apartments. It's intimate and a tad exclusive, a feeling enhanced by the decor: an amalgam of a Yukon timber lodge and a Kashmiri houseboat. The air-con cottages have ceiling fan, refrigerator, and coffeemaker, but no telephone or TV. You can relax in hammocks. The clubhouse – you can walk or take the electric golf cart – features a self-service bar and communal dining. Double rooms start at US$950 for three nights, including meals and fishing. Accommodations are available only in three-, four-, and seven-night packages. Reservations are essential. The club is closed mid-July through September. Its mailing address is 1100 Lee Wagener Blvd, Suite 352, Fort Lauderdale, FL 33315.

Getting There & Away The Deep Water Cay Club arranges direct charters from Fort Lauderdale and West Palm Beach to the cay, which has its own tiny airstrip. Alternately, you can take a boat from McLean's Town for about US$40 roundtrip, but you may be able to negotiate a lower price. It's a 10-minute ride.

Abercrombie & Kent (☎ 630-954-4758), 1520 Kensington Rd, Oaksbrook, IL 60523, offers fishing trips to Deep Water Cay.

Sweeting's Cay

This small cay, 3 miles south of Deep Water Cay, is worth a visit for a reclusive escape. Its few dozen residents still make a living from sponging and conching.

Facilities include a small *motel* with cottages for rent. There's *Russell's Restaurant & Bar* on the waterfront and *Seaside Fig Tree*, a cafe owned by Cavil, a fisherman who serves up conch dishes.

You can hire a boat in McLean's Town to get here, but the easiest way is on a full-day 'safari' offered by Tiffany Barrett of East End Adventures (☎ 242-373-6662) in Freeport. The trip to the 'Grand Bahamian Outback' is by jeep and includes time for bird watching and a stop at Lucayan National Park, followed by a speedboat ride to the cays. After roaming and interacting with locals, you're whisked to nearby Lightbourne Cay, where you get a traditional Bahamian lunch. Here you can while away the afternoon sunning, snorkeling, or fishing. The trip costs US$110, including transport from your hotel. East End's postal address is PO Box F-44322, Freeport, Grand Bahama, Bahamas.

West of Freeport

Hawksbill Creek to West End

West of Freeport, a slender, scrub-covered peninsula, separated from the 'mainland' by Freeport Harbour Channel, extends northwest to West End. The main road, Queen's Hwy, runs inland of the coast. A second road parallels the coast but offers little scenic value. There are few beaches until you reach Deadman's Reef.

The channel opens to Hawksbill Creek, named for the once-common marine turtles that now only infrequently come ashore. Fishermen bring conch ashore here; huge shell mounds line the road. Several miles west of the channel is the sprawling, low-income suburb of Eight Mile, fronted by a rocky, shell-strewn, and grossly littered beach. Nearby are several 'boiling holes' (subterranean water-filled holes that bubble under pressure of the tides).

Eight Mile extends to the west to Holmes Rock, another charmless village stretched along the road for several miles. There's good diving offshore, especially at Paradise Cove (see below).

Paradise Cove This private beach operation is perfect for a day of reclusive beach lounging. The setting is splendid, within the cusp of a protected lagoon sheltered by Deadman's Reef. Beach volleyball and water sports are offered. Boats and kayaks cost US$5 per hour, a raft is US$2, and snorkel gear costs US$10. A 'snorkel tour' costs US$18. And you can dine or drink on a large, shaded wooden deck with camp-style tables. It's open 10 am to sunset daily.

Places to Stay & Eat The *Tasty Pot Shop* is a colorful, funky little place on the main road at Holmes Rock, where you'll find several other modest places to eat with locals: *Meka's Place* is one.

Several good options lie west of Holmes Rock, where dirt roads strike out to the shore. The most appealing place, at Paradise Cove, is *Castaways Estate & Beach Resort* (☎ 242-349-2677), a home-away-from-home run by Barry Smith, a friendly and savvy Bahamian. It has one-/two-bedroom apartments sleeping up to six people: US$75 for a one-bedroom apartment, US$105 for a two-bedroom cottage, and US$195 for a two-bedroom suite. Weekly rates are offered. They're large, clean, and well-furnished in contemporary decor, with full kitchen. The snack bar features a menu of sandwiches, burgers, grilled chicken for US$4, and conch dishes. A clubhouse and more apartments are planned. You can write the resort at PO Box F-42629, Freeport, Grand Bahama, Bahamas.

Farther up the road is the supremely atmospheric *Buccaneer Club* (☎ 242-349-3794), centered on a magnificent Old World stone-and-timber structure entered through beaten-copper doors inset with brass portholes. The elegant restaurant is festooned with polished driftwood and nautical regalia. You can also dine outside on a patio shaded by palms. The menu lists native seafood for US$3 to US$7, steaks for US$19, wiener schnitzel for US$19, rack of lamb for US$25, and broiled lobster for US$30, as well as a reasonable wine list. The owners, Heinz and Kitty Fischbacker, host beach parties for US$45, including hotel transfers. It's open 5 to 10:30 pm every day except Monday. Reservations are recommended.

The Buccaneer Club also offers hotel transfers from Freeport and Lucaya.

Harry's American Bar & Restaurant (☎ 242-349-2610), 400 yards farther west, is a basic eatery atop a rocky shore. It was closed when I called in early 1997.

West End

This fishing village, 25 miles west of Freeport, has plenty of funky color. The waterfront could have fallen from the set of Robin Williams' movie *Popeye*, with its tumbledown shacks, half-sunken boats, and piles of sun-bleached conch shells. Pretty the two-street village is not, but there is no denying its somnolent and somewhat sleazy renegade charm.

Amazingly, the down-at-the-heels place was once the center of activity on the island . . . a bustling hive of activity when Prohibition rumrunners ruled the roost and yachters with sterling surnames like Kennedy, DuPont, or Hearst were callers to the Grand Bahama Resort & Country Club, with its own 27-hole golf course, marina, and private airstrip. It became a bit of a Wild West town and blossomed until the development of Freeport knocked the wind out of its sails. West End had a brief renaissance two decades ago when the resort reopened as Jack Tar Village. Alas, it closed again in 1990. There's talk of renovating the hotel and adding a casino, but don't hold your breath.

Lovers of offbeat lifestyles may take pleasure in watching fishermen hang their nets to dry, extract conch from their shells, or live an easy but marginally remunerative life in the shade, where they take their simple pleasures with a beer and dominoes in hand.

This fishing village also boasts one of the island's prettiest churches, the 1893 stone-and-wood Mary Magdalene Church, complete with three small yet beautiful stained-glass windows in contemporary style.

The flats north of West End are good for bonefishing. Bonefish Folley (☎ 242-346-6233) is the area's best-known guide.

Places to Stay & Eat The small, homey *Harbour Hotel* (☎ 242-346-6432), opposite Mary Magdalene Church, has simple rooms and the *Cameo Restaurant*.

The place to groove with the locals is The Senator's, officially *The Star Hotel Restaurant & Lounge* (☎ 242-346-6207), in a weather-worn, two-story clapboard hotel (now defunct). A rusted tug lies capsized opposite the restaurant. The Bahamian fare is simple and cheap. The bar is run by former Bahamian senator Austin Grant, Jr, who revels in telling tales of the days when West End was a sort of Shangri-la for the very rich. Mrs Grant cooks up a mean conch chowder.

Locals will tell you the best conch salad (minced scorched conch) is served at the *Chicken Nest* (☎ 242-346-6440) on the outskirts of town. *Yvonne's Tavern* is recommended for conchburgers.

You can buy fresh-baked goods at *Kerr's Bakery* or the *Seaside Bakery*.

Entertainment When darkness descends, locals gather at the *Double Deuce Nightclub*, overhanging the water at the east end of town.

The *Chicken Nest* has a jukebox, dart board, and pool table. Your alternative is to spend a night slapping down dominoes or playing checkers with the guys (where are the women?) who gather at rickety tables beneath the shady, lopsided eaves of *The Senator's*.

An informal street party called the 'West End Move' is held on the waterfront every Saturday afternoon.

Getting There & Away Franco's Express (☎ 800-448-3386) has a scheduled bus service twice daily from the International Bazaar and Port Lucaya Marketplace for US$10 roundtrip. The bus service runs hourly on Saturday.

A taxi from Freeport or Lucaya will cost up to US$100 for four people.

The Jack Tar Village marina (☎ 242-346-6211) is still open, and lots of yachts from the USA call here. The marina has a fuel dock, slips, electricity and water; it also has telephones. There's a commercial harbor adjacent to the marina that is good for larger vessels.

Several tour operators include West End in their daylong sightseeing excursions from Freeport. See Organized Tours in the Freeport & Lucaya section.

Biminis

Pop 1638

Ernest Hemingway's 'islands in the stream' perch on the edge of the Gulf Stream, just 50 miles east of Miami (the city's glow can be seen at night) and 120 miles northwest of Nassau. The Bimini group – the smallest and westernmost of the Bahamian archipelago – is barely 10 sq miles and flat as a flounder. The name is a Lucayan Indian term meaning 'two islands.'

North Bimini (locally referred to as simply 'Bimini') is shaped like an inverted crab's claw, 7 miles long and no more than 400 yards across at its widest point. Below it and separated by only 150 yards of water lies South Bimini, a chunkier and virtually uninhabited plot of land. A sprinkling of small, slender cays lies farther south. Together the islands have fewer than 1700 full-time residents, known as Biminites, who like to interact with the world on their own laid-back, sometimes lawless, terms. Most everything happens in Alice Town on North Bimini, especially in midsummer, when folks from Florida arrive in flocks to savor a lifestyle that putters along in the slow lane.

North Bimini is also favored by college students whooping it up during spring break, a time for wet T-shirt contests and drunken good times. At other times this is the kind of place to fish, relax, sit around drinking beer, and tell big-fish stories – or listen to even bigger fish stories about Ernest Hemingway, whose ghost still resides, much to local pride. (Back in the '30s, the indomitable author had a standing offer to pay US$100 to any resident of the Biminis who could punch him out. Biminites like to foster the image of their islands as a kind of Wild West, a notion readily supported by macho sport-fishing types who arrive seemingly bent on following Hemingway's example.)

The Gulf Stream brings game fish close to shore in quest of baitfish moving off the

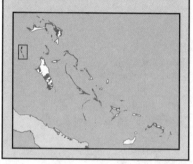

Bahama Banks. The fish really do live up to the stories. You name it – wahoo, tuna, sailfish, mako shark, barracuda, and, above all, blue marlin and other billfish that put up a bruising battle. They're all waiting for you to cast your lure and notch up a record catch that would make 'Papa' Hemingway jealous. Appropriately, the Biminis boast The Bahamas' largest fleet of sport-fishing boats, a mainstay of the local economy. Those who prefer smaller fry look east to the Biminis' flats, where three IGFA world records for bonefish have been set.

Scuba divers are lured to the islands' crystal-clear waters. Water temperatures are about 80°F May through October and hit a seasonal low of 72°F to 75°F in early February. Wet suits are normally worn in winter months. Sunken Spanish galleons and the wreck of a WWI freighter lie in the shallows between South Bimini and North Cat Cay. There's the Bimini Road off North Bimini, alluringly claimed to be part of the 'lost city' of Atlantis. There's the famous Bimini Wall, plummeting over 4000 feet. Wall dives such as Tuna Alley and the Nodules and wrecks such as the *Bimini Barge* host everything from butterfly fish to hammerhead sharks. Shallow reefs such as Kinks and the Strip feature black-bar soldierfish and blue-striped grunts packed in side by side like, well, sardines. See the Dive & Snorkel Sites sidebar in the North Bimini section for the Biminis' other underwater highlights.

The Biminis are also famous for dives with wild dolphins. Pods of rare Atlantic spotted dolphins are regularly seen, and they like nothing better than to cavort and swim nose to nose with humans, whom they attempt to amuse with a constant high-pitched chattering and giggling. Unlike the more well-known bottle-nosed dolphins, spotted dolphins seem to seek out human interaction in the wild (ironically, spotted dolphins do not train well in captivity). Some locals claim that the dolphins are 'ambassadors of Atlantis.'

Biminites are known as creatures of the sea. At least one islander, Ansil Saunders, a famous boatbuilder, is carrying on a family tradition that started last century when, as he says, 'four white men from Scotland moved down from Canada, married four black women from Bimini,' and developed the Bimini Bonefisher boat. His boats – handmade of five-ply, quarter-inch mahogany (the wood is quieter than fiberglass, a crucial advantage in the bonefish game) – can glide through saltwater flats that are barely 6 inches deep.

History

In 1513 the Spanish explorer Juan Ponce de León, then governor of Puerto Rico, drifted through the archipelago seeking the Fountain of Youth. He had heard tales from the Lucayans of a miraculous spring in the Biminis that bestowed youthfulness on whomever bathed in the crystalline waters.

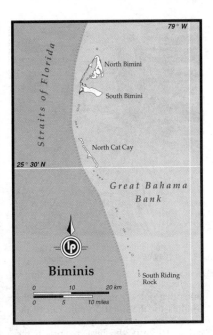

Ponce de León touched ashore at most of the Bahamian islands but missed the Biminis and found Florida instead.

Where the Spaniards went, pirates would later follow. Henry Morgan and other miscreants thought the Biminis a splendid lair in which to lie in wait for treasure fleets making haste homeward via the Gulf Stream. The five founding families who first put down roots here in 1835 did so as licensed wreckers – individuals who 'rescue' ships and their cargoes – and had to haul all manner of pirate wreckage from the shallows to clear a harbor mouth. The advent of steam ships and pilot lights ended the wrecking industry, so Biminites took to sponging – a thriving business that lasted until a blight in the 1930s killed the sponges.

In 1920 the Biminis got a boost from Prohibition. English and Scottish distilleries worked overtime to supply merchant

Pirate Henry Morgan, who found the
Biminis an excellent hiding place

ships that quickly moved whiskey to the
Biminis for the illicit 50-mile run to the
USA. Alice Town became the export capital and briefly the busiest port in the
Bahamas. All sorts of people dabbled in
the dangerous business, not least among
them a daring beauty named Gertrude C
Lythgoe ('The Queen of the Bootleggers'),
who risked the loss of millions and chanced
death from hijackers and drowning before
she reformed and, under guard, spilled the
beans on the rumrunners.

Ernest Hemingway made the Biminis
famous in his best-selling *Islands in the
Stream*, which autobiographically reflects
his hard-drinking, hard-fighting, egotistical
ways. The Biminis' popularity was also
helped along by other notables, including
Kip Farrington, Jr, editor of *Field & Stream*
(who supposedly hooked the first marlin in
1930 and promoted the Biminis as the
'fishing capital of the world'), Howard
Hughes, and Adam Clayton Powell, Jr, the
brash black New York congressman and
Harlem preacher who came to be with his
mistress and, er, lash out at hypocrisies
from his bar by the sea. (More recently, US
presidential contender Gary Hart famously

ruined his career here when he was spotted
cavorting on a sport-fishing boat – appropriately named *Monkey Business* – with a
blonde bombshell who was not his wife.)

In 1936 a chap named Neville Norton
Stuart turned a Prohibition-era bar into the
Bimini Big Game Fishing Club, building
on the tourism boom fostered by the
Bimini Bay Rod and Gun Club, begun in
the early 1920s. Most guests flew in on
'Poppy' Chalk's seaplanes; the company is
still in operation today as Pan-Am Air
Bridge. The opening of an international
airstrip on South Bimini in 1957 boosted
the Biminis' fortunes. Rockwell International even built an executive retreat (now
the Bimini Bay Hotel) here for its top brass
and most important customers.

In ensuing decades the Biminis became a
major stopover for drug transshipments.
Things have definitely quieted since the
local drug lords were put out of business in
the mid-1980s, but plenty of drugs still
come and go through the Biminis. And narcotics agents still blend into the local island
scene.

Hurricane Andrew roared ashore in
1992, and several hotels have never recovered from it. At press time a movie on
Hemingway was to be filmed here, leading
many Biminites to hope for an economic
infusion.

NORTH BIMINI

The main island runs northeast 7 miles,
almost ruler-straight and barely 100 yards
wide, before curling – like a bent straw – to
fan out in a quiltwork of mangrove swamps
and fishing flats. The ocean shore's entire
length is lined by a narrow sliver of white
sand, festooned with sea grape and shaded
by palm and pine trees. The beaches get
better and much prettier to the north, with
the most beautiful beach in Bimini Bay. In
his novel *Islands in the Stream*, Hemingway warned: 'It was a safe and fine
place to bathe in the day, but it was no
place to swim at night. At night the sharks
came in close to the beach . . . and you
could see the phosphorescent wake they
made in the water.'

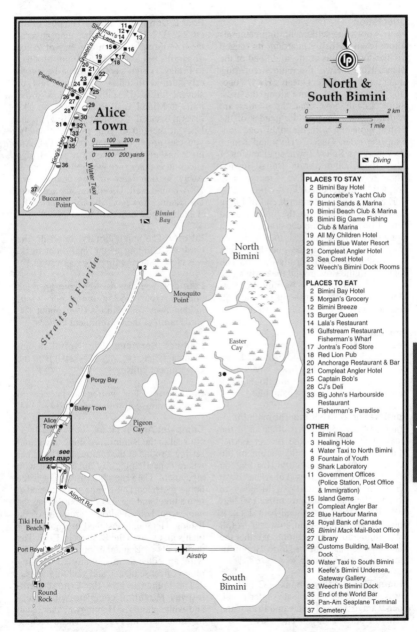

**North &
South Bimini**

⊠ *Diving*

PLACES TO STAY
2 Bimini Bay Hotel
6 Duncombe's Yacht Club
7 Bimini Sands & Marina
10 Bimini Beach Club & Marina
16 Bimini Big Game Fishing
    Club & Marina
19 All My Children Hotel
20 Bimini Blue Water Resort
21 Compleat Angler Hotel
23 Sea Crest Hotel
32 Weech's Bimini Dock Rooms

PLACES TO EAT
2 Bimini Bay Hotel
5 Morgan's Grocery
12 Bimini Breeze
13 Burger Queen
14 Lala's Restaurant
16 Gulfstream Restaurant,
    Fisherman's Wharf
17 Jontra's Food Store
18 Red Lion Pub
20 Anchorage Restaurant & Bar
21 Compleat Angler Hotel
25 Captain Bob's
28 CJ's Deli
33 Big John's Harbourside
    Restaurant
34 Fisherman's Paradise

OTHER
1 Bimini Road
3 Healing Hole
4 Water Taxi to North Bimini
8 Fountain of Youth
9 Shark Laboratory
11 Government Offices
    (Police Station, Post Office
    & Immigration)
15 Island Gems
21 Compleat Angler Bar
22 Blue Harbour Marina
24 Royal Bank of Canada
26 *Bimini Mack* Mail-Boat Office
27 Library
29 Customs Building, Mail-Boat
    Dock
30 Water Taxi to South Bimini
31 Keefe's Bimini Undersea,
    Gateway Gallery
32 Weech's Bimini Dock
35 End of the World Bar
36 Pan-Am Seaplane Terminal
37 Cemetery

BIMINIS

Orientation

There's only one settlement: unpretentious **Alice Town**, raffishly guarding its rugged frontier-town status at the south end of the island. King's Hwy, the main street, runs along the inner shore. Queen's Hwy, a one-lane concrete path, runs along the west shore. Locals joke that the names are switched depending on the gender of the British monarch, with the main road honoring the ruler. Queen's Hwy and King's Hwy merge in Bailey Town, an extension of Alice Town, 2 miles north. Bailey Town – where most Biminites live – merges into Porgy Bay (also spelled 'Poggy Bay').

The road ends at the north end of Porgy Bay at the entrance to the undeveloped Bimini Bay Estate. You can continue north along the dirt road that leads to Bimini Bay. A chain bars your way beyond the Bimini Bay Hotel, but with permission you can continue all the way around the north along a sandy trail cushioned by pine needles. Mangroves line the east shore: The moment you stop, ravenous mosquitoes descend.

Information

Tourist Office Norma Wilkinson runs the local tourist office (☎ 242-347-3529, fax 242-347-3530) in Alice Town. She's quite knowledgeable and has put together a handy tourist information pamphlet.

Immigration & Customs The main Immigration (☎ 242-347-3446) office is in the Government Offices – the former Lerner Marine Laboratory, a field station of the American Museum of Natural History – on King's Hwy at the north end of Alice Town; it's open 9 am to 5:30 pm Monday to Friday. The main Customs office (☎ 242-347-3100) is beside the mail-boat dock. If you're flying to the island, however, you'll clear immigration and customs at either the Pan-Am seaplane port in North Bimini or the South Bimini airstrip.

Money There's a Royal Bank of Canada 50 yards south of the Compleat Angler Hotel, open 9 am to 3 pm Monday and Friday and 9 am to 1 pm Tuesday to Thursday.

Post & Communications The post office (☎ 242-347-3546) is in the main government building at the north end of Alice Town; it's open 9 am to 5:30 pm Monday to Friday. A sign says you must be 'properly attired to enter' (no bare feet or slovenly dress). Despite the Biminis' proximity to Miami, mail to the USA can take several weeks! Consider mailing in the USA at the end of your trip. Alternately, you can drop your mail in the Pan-Am post basket at the Pan-Am Air Bridge check-in counter (see the Getting There & Away section later in this chapter) for USA-bound mail; US stamps are accepted. US stamps, however, are *not* accepted by Bahamian post offices.

Library The small library, opposite the Customs building at the mail-boat dock, was closed at press time for renovation.

Laundry You can use the coin-operated laundry (four US25¢ coins per wash) hidden away from King's Hwy, about 100 yards north of the Government Offices.

Medical Services The North Bimini Medical Clinic (☎ 242-347-3210) is in the Government Offices.

Emergency For police assistance in North Bimini, call ☎ 919 or 242-347-3144.

Compleat Angler Hotel

No visit to the Biminis is complete without raising a round at the famous hotel and bar where Papa Hemingway duked it out with all comers. The venerable structure was the home of Helen Duncombe, who turned it into a hotel and bar in 1935, borrowing the name from Izaak Walton's famous book on fishing. Hemingway stayed in Room No 1 on his first visit to the Biminis in 1935. The dark walls of Bahamian pine are adorned with an eclectic miscellany of angling photos, license plates, and yachting flags.

The lounge is now the **Ernest Hemingway Museum**, complete with black-and-white photos of Hemingway that recall his time here in 1935-37. These include shots of Papa with a submachine gun and Papa with the remains of a 500-lb blue marlin mauled by sharks, the inspiration for his Nobel Prize-winning novel *The Old Man and the Sea*, quotes from which adorn the walls.

Bimini Road

Scuba divers flock to Moselle's Shoal, or 'Bimini Road' – named for the strange underwater formations resembling paving blocks of a giant aqua-highway – off Paradise Point at the north end of Bimini Bay. The enormous limestone blocks are clearly visible in shallow water, resembling the massive hand-hewn building blocks of the Incas. The 'road' stretches for 1000 feet and is the subject of many mystical interpretations. A stylized marble head is said to have been discovered here, too.

No one knows the source of the formations. Adding to the mystery is the disappearance of part of the Bimini Road in 1925 (it may have had something to do with a new jetty being built in Miami; the contractor laid down huge limestone blocks). Tales of strange happenings lured Jacques Cousteau here to film and investigate the formation. Countless other research teams have followed. Explorer Richard Wingate acclaimed the shoal as part of 'The Lost Outpost of Atlantis,' and the concept has become fixed in local lore.

Those who believe in strange sources for the Bimini Road were exhilarated in 1977 by the discovery of a series of 500-foot-long sand mounds in the mangrove swamps in the eastern part of North Bimini. From the air, supposedly, the mounds appear to be shaped like a shark, a square, a cat, and a sea horse, and have been translated by some as guidance beacons for extraterrestrials.

Healing Hole

The Healing Hole is a bubbling freshwater sulfur spring that's said to possess mystical powers.

It's well hidden in a small cove near the Bonefish Hole. The spot is surrounded by mangroves – condominiums for multitudinous mosquitoes – just south of Easter Cay

'Papa' Hemingway

and is accessed by a narrow, 200-yard-long meandering cut barely wide enough for extending your arms. You'll need a guide. The hole is buried deep in the forest. It is about the size of a small motel room, canopied by leafy mangroves through which sunlight dapples down magically, sparkling the water like a disco strobe.

When you're wading, keep to the center, as the slanted edges are slippery. Wear rubber boots for traction and to protect against stubbing your toe on mangrove roots.

Once you're at the hole, ease into the tea-brown water (if only to avoid the mosquitoes). A cool upwelling meets the saline waters, inducing a sudden temperature drop and a nippy surprise for bathers. Fear not crocodiles; the only 'snappers' are juveniles of a nonbiting fish species of that name. The smell is quite nasty, a bit like an unflushed toilet, but it's only natural sulfur. Still, you might want to rinse off at the dock to avoid stares as you head back to your hotel.

It's even possible, especially during each solstice, to come across bands of visitors standing in the chest-deep water, holding hands and chanting incantations to who knows whom . . . perhaps the gods of Atlantis? And what of the hole's healing properties? Well, most visitors seem to experience an enigmatic calming sensation. It all depends on what you are prepared to believe. In 1965 Martin Luther King, Jr, came to the Biminis to meditate and draft his acceptance speech for the Nobel Peace Prize. Knowing King's need for solitude, bonefish guide Ansil Saunders took the civil-rights leader to the Healing Hole. Local lore attributes the inspiration for his 'I Have a Dream' speech to the mystical effect of the waters. (Saunders calls the creek 'Dr King's Creek of Peace.')

Town Landmarks
Sights of interest in Alice Town are limited. There are few edifices of note, though there are plans to restore the old post office opposite the mail-boat dock at the south end of Alice Town and to create a Bimini Museum.

Several restaurants, such as Captain Bob's, have **Fishing Halls of Fame** celebrating those who've made the islands' angling heritage an international draw. Dozens of photos and memorabilia recall celebrities and commoners who have pulled prize-winning fish from the drink.

Ask a local to point out **Memory Ledge**. Locals claim that if you lie down here, you'll be flooded with flashbacks.

The drone of Pratt & Whitney turbo-props, announcing the arrival and departure of the Pan-Am Air Bridge seaplanes, draws visitors to the waterfront to watch them splash down or take off like swans. The activity on the mail-boat dock also adds a note of interest.

Bonefishing & Sport Fishing
The catch of the day is wahoo in winter months; bluefin tuna, blue and white marlin, and sailfish in summer; and grouper, jewfish, kingfish, amberjack, barracuda, snapper, yellowtail, and mackerel year-round. (The biggest fish ever taken in Bahamian waters – a whopping 1060-lb marlin landed in 1979 – is preserved on a wall in the forecourt of the Bimini Big Game Fishing Club.) The hot spots are said to be Moselle's Shoal (or Bimini Road) off the tip of North Bimini, just off Bimini Bay's Three Sisters Rock, and off Great Isaac, 15 miles north.

Bimini Big Game Fishing Club (☎ 242-347-3391, 800-737-1007), Blue Water Marina (☎ 242-347-3166, fax 242-347-3293), and Weech's Bimini Dock (☎ 242-347-3028) all charter boats and skippers and can recommend guides. Typical fees are US$275/400 half-/full day, depending on the size of vessel. Marinas on South Bimini also offer charters; see that section.

Many Biminites also charter boats, including the following:

Frank Hinsey
   Nina, a 28-foot Bertram
   (☎ 242-347-3072)
Captain Bob Smith
   Miss Bonita II, a 51-foot Hatteras
   (☎ 242-347-2367)
Captain Jerome Stuart
   Miss Bonita, a 32-foot Hatteras
   (☎ 242-347-2081)
Captain Tony Stuart
   Sir Tones, a 51-foot Hatteras
   (☎ 242-347-2656)
Captain Alfred Sweeting
   Nutting Honey, a 28-foot Bertram
   (☎ 242-347-3033)

For bottom fishing, you'll need a local guide. The best are talked about reverentially, the way basketball fans talk of Michael Jordan. For snapper, grouper, and grunt, the most highly acclaimed guide is Elvis Saunders (☎ 242-347-3055). For bonefish, try to hire the world-record holder, 'Bonefish' Ansil Saunders (☎ 242-347-2178), who charges US$150/275 half-/full day. Other skilled bonefish guides include Bonefish Cordell (☎ 242-347-2576), Bonefish Ebbie (☎ 242-347-2053), Bonefish Jackson (☎ 242-347-2315), and Bonefish Tommy (☎ 242-347-3234).

You can rent equipment locally. A little store called Bonefish Bill's, opposite the Bimini Big Game Fishing Club, sells bait and tackle.

There are almost a dozen sport-fishing tournaments each year. The Bacardi Rum Billfish Tournament is hosted by the Bimini Big Game Fishing Club in March. The club hosts the Bimini Break (Blue Marlin) Rendezvous each April. Young anglers under 18 are encouraged to participate in the Big Game Club Family Tournament, hosted in early August by the club. The Big Game/Small BOAT Tournament in September pits vessels under 27 feet against one another. In November anglers fly in for the All Wahoo Fishing Tournament. The Annual Bonefish Willies Tournament and the Adam Clayton Powell, Jr, Memorial Fishing Tournament are held in December. See the Outdoor Activities chapter for additional fishing tournaments.

Diving & Snorkeling

Bill & Nowdla Keefe's Bimini Undersea (☎ 242-347-3089, fax 242-347-3079, info@biminiundersea.com; in the USA ☎ 305-653-5572, 800-348-4644, fax 305-652-9148), PO Box 693515, Miami, FL 33269, offers dive trips aboard their dive vessels, the 32-foot *Delphine* and 42-foot *Adventurer*. Trips cost US$39 for the first dive, US$69 for two dives, and US$40 for a night dive. An introductory dive costs US$99, including instruction. They have multiday packages, with three dives daily. They rent cylinders for US$10 per day, regulators for US$15, wet suits for US$10, and other equipment, and offer air fills. Underwater camera rentals cost US$25; US$65 for videos. You need to bring your own lights for night dives. Keefe's also maintains permanent moorings at key dive sites. Call VHF channel 06 to find out which are available.

Snorkel trips at Keefe's cost US$25/15 adults/children; masks, fins, and snorkels go for US$15.

Keefe's takes divers to swim with dolphins. It offers 'Wild Dolphin Excursions'

Dive & Snorkel Sites

Dive Sites

Bimini Barge – The 270-foot *Sapona* wreck lies close to shore in 90 feet of water, just 75 yards from the Gulf Stream drop-off. The result: a one-two punch of prolific reef life and pelagic big boys.

Bimini Road – Some think these stone monoliths were once part of Atlantis!

Hawksbill Reef – This reef is home to large numbers of lobsters and reef fish. The television series *The Last Frontier* was shot here.

Little Caverns – Mountainous coral formations rise on a sandy bottom at 65 feet.

Off the Wall – The Gulf Stream carries you at this popular drift site at 130 feet along the continental shelf. Beyond, the abyss drops to 2000 feet.

Snorkel Sites

Bimini Shoreline – Coral and rock formations here are smothered by sponges.

Eagle Ray Run – The run is a kind of underwater *Star Wars*, with eagle rays in fighter formation.

LaChance Rocks – Lots of small marine critters hang out near these huge rocks.

Stingray Hole – Friendly stingrays glide around waiting to be hand-fed.

Turtle Rocks – Plenty of coral, fish, and turtles can be found here. ∎

---

two or three times each week (US$79/39 adults/children; children under eight free). Interactions usually last about one hour, but the dolphins are in charge. The company has a website (see Internet Resources in the back of the book).

For getting out on your own, Charlie Weech (☎ 242-347-3290) will rent you a boat at Weech's Bimini Dock.

BIMINIS

Kayaking

Sea kayaks are perfect for exploring the shores and mangroves that are inaccessible by boat or foot – and they are easy to use. Take a sun hat and insect repellent to fend off mosquitoes.

Keefe's Bimini Undersea (see Diving & Snorkeling, above) rents one-person sea kayaks for US$7/30 hourly/daily and two-person kayaks and sailboards for US$10/40 hourly/daily.

Boat Excursions

TSL Water Taxi (VHF channel 68), at the mail-boat dock, offers a moonlight cruise on request.

Organized Tours

Ashley Saunders, author of *History of the Bahamas: Bimini*, leads one-hour guided walking tours of North Bimini, beginning at the Government Offices, for US$10. Call the Bimini Tourist Office (see the Information section).

Special Events

The Biminis' party-hearty islanders put on a Junkanoo extraordinaire each Boxing Day and New Year's Day, and on July 10th in celebration of Bahamian independence.

The Bimini Regatta Blast at the end of March features reggae and other live bands. The Bimini Festival in mid-May features a sport-fishing tourney and cookouts.

The Biminis welcome yachters in the annual Bahamas Boating Flings each June through mid-August, when first-time boaters arrive en masse from Fort Lauderdale's Radisson Bahai Mar Resort & Yacht Club. See the Sea section in the Getting There & Away chapter for more details.

Places to Stay

All the hotels in Alice Town are strung along King's Hwy. Hotel rooms are usually sold out during big fishing tournaments: *Book early.*

Weech's Bimini Dock has four bay-view rooms (☎ 242-347-3028, fax 242-347-3508, VHF channel 18) overlooking the marina. They're airy and clean, with plenty of light, and cost US$60 single or double. An efficiency apartment for four people costs US$125. The postal address is PO Box 613, Bimini, Bahamas.

The three-story, all-wood-paneled *Compleat Angler Hotel* (☎ 242-347-3122/3185, fax 242-347-3293) has 12 air-con rooms above the venerable bar. The rooms are dowdy, albeit adequate and quaint, with their original pine walls. Bathrooms vary in size; some are tiny. Want to sleep where Hemingway snoozed and penned parts of *To Have and Have Not*? Then take Room No 1. Expect a *lot* of noise at night from the bar downstairs! Rates range from US$68 to US$83. The mailing address is PO Box 601, Bimini, Bahamas.

Bimini Bay Hotel (☎ /fax 242-347-2171), 3.5 miles north of Alice Town, is an atmospheric 1950s Miami-deco-style entity (originally a Rockwell International retreat) atop a rocky headland at the south end of Bimini Bay. The main house is well kept within and was being slowly upgraded at press time. Light pours in through bay windows, adding a rich glow to tropical pastels. It craves business, however. Some rooms are in rundown apartments; others are in a three-story wooden structure; still others are in the art-deco house, which has a splendidly breezy patio and small pool. Rates range from US$75 to US$125 weekdays, US$95 to US$145 weekends, and US$225 to US$300 for two-bedroom condos. At press time developers were eyeing the hotel and surrounding 700-acre property for expansion, including a golf course and marina. The mailing address is PO Box 607, Bimini, Bahamas.

The modern and modest *Sea Crest Hotel* (☎ 242-347-3071; marina 242-347-3477) has 10 air-con rooms, all with both a single and double bed, TV, and patio with marina view. There's no restaurant or pool. Rooms cost US$85; one-/two-bedroom suites cost US$190/275. Its postal address is PO Box 654, Bimini, Bahamas.

The *Bimini Blue Water Resort* (☎ 242-347-3166, fax 242-347-3293) offers full marina facilities. The rooms in the older building are atmospheric; those in the newer extension have a 1960s cheap-motel feel, with wood-veneer walls and faux-bamboo furniture, plus small TV, mini-fridge, and balcony. Bathrooms have large showers. Rooms cost US$90 year-round. You can also choose a twin-bedroom suite for US$190, the 'Anchorage Cottage' for US$65, or the three-bedroom 'Blue Marlin Cottage' for US$285 (Ernest Hemingway's former home-away-from-home, with a stone fireplace in the wood-paneled lounge). The hotel has a bar and good restaurant – The Anchorage (see Places to Eat, below). The Compleat Angler Hotel is a 40-yard stumble away. A variety of water-based activities is offered, including sport-fishing boats. The pool was derelict in 1997. The mailing address is PO Box 601, Bimini, Bahamas.

All My Children Hotel (☎ 242-347-3334) – the name comes from owner Glen Rolle's 12 children – has modern yet unremarkable air-con rooms with a blue-and-mauve color scheme, large, clean bathrooms, and small color TV. They're overpriced at US$99/110/121 double/queen/king. The hotel also has jaded and soulless rooms for US$68 in an older house (formerly Diandrea's Inn) next door. There's also a cottage with kitchen, plus a huge 'suite' with two double beds for US$231.

The *Bimini Big Game Fishing Club* (☎ 242-347-3391, 800-737-1007, fax 242-347-3392) is a favorite of anglers and yachters. It's the classiest place by far, with grounds festooned with bougainvillea and palms. The self-contained hotel has 49 air-con rooms, cottages, and penthouse suites decorated in rattan, with plate-glass sliding doors opening onto patios or balconies. The cottages each have a kitchenette, but apparently no cooking is allowed! Room rates start at US$149/162 single/double year-round. Cottages cost US$180; suites cost US$298. Facilities include a small, amoeba-shaped pool, two restaurants, three bars, a gift shop, and tennis courts, plus a multitude of water sports and excursion options. It has a large, fully equipped marina, and charter boats are available, as

are bonefishing and deep-sea adventures. The mailing address is PO Box 523238, Miami, FL 33152.

There are several homey properties. At the north end of Alice Town, *Dun's Bay-front Apartments* (☎ 242-347-2093), above Dun's Florist on King's Hwy, has five efficiencies, each with kitchen, living room with TV, and simple furnishings. In Bailey Town the *Admiral Hotel Restaurant Bar & Lodge* (☎ 242-347-2347) has 24 air-con rooms with TV. Choose among doubles, suites, and efficiencies. It's a favorite with Bahamians. To the north in Porgy Bay is *Ellis' Cottage* (☎ 242-347-2483), which has three cottages with full kitchen and living room. There's an indoor whirlpool tub and a private dock. The mailing address is PO Box 611, Bimini, Bahamas. Also in Porgy Bay, Joe and Letitia Jones run the *Sea View Apartments* (☎ 242-347-2444).

Places to Eat

In the morning everybody rubs their eyes and heads to *Captain Bob's* (☎ 242-347-3260), on King's Hwy 50 yards south of the Compleat Angler Hotel. Try the excellent corn-beef hash with eggs for US$6. It serves the usual seafood dishes, too. Also check out *Bimini Breeze* (☎ 242-347-3511), 50 yards north of the Bimini Big Game Fishing Club.

CJ's Deli, opposite the Customs building, is a pleasant hole-in-the-wall run by Cora Dean and her mom, serving breakfast and lunch cooked to order. It also sells ice cream and shakes.

The *Anchorage Restaurant & Bar* (☎ 242-347-3166), at the Bimini Blue Water Resort, serves good breakfasts starting at US$3. Try the Hearty Hemingway with eggs, hash browns or grits, bacon, ham or sausage, and coffee and juice for US$6.25. Lunchtime sandwiches, burgers, and salads are reasonably priced. Dinners – seafood and steaks – begin at US$13. The grouper with spicy sauce is excellent. (The turkey dinner is, alas, canned.) Box lunches cost US$9.25.

The elegant *Gulfstream Restaurant* (☎ 242-347-3391), at the Bimini Big Game

Fishing Club, offers seafood, beef, and chicken dishes beginning at US$13. You'll dine to the toe-tapping sounds of Rattee Sweeting playing his acoustic guitar. Try the spicy Bahamian gumbo, pepperpot stew, or smoked game fish. Reservations are recommended. The place is famous for its punchy rum punch. Also here is the *Fisherman's Wharf*, with a large menu of seafood and steaks starting at US$12 and an extensive wine list; the *Barefoot Bar*, serving snacks; and the resort's *Sports Bar & Grill*, which has three satellite TVs and features Bahamian and US dishes, including conchburgers and pizza.

Edith's Take Out (☎ 242-347-2074) delivers homemade pizza, seafood, and fries. *Lala's Restaurant*, opposite the Bimini Big Game Fishing Club, is a great place to savor fried chicken, fritters, fish fingers, and other fare with the locals. The small and intimate *Red Lion Pub* (☎ 242-347-3259), next to the Bimini Big Game Fishing Club, specializes in steaks and ribs. Try the braised lamb shanks. This pokey little place is famous, too, for its Shrimp Delight, shrimps stuffed with conch, fish, and secret spice, which you should follow with key lime pie or banana cream pie. Entrées begin at about US$10. It's open 6 to 11 pm Tuesday to Sunday.

Snacks are sometimes served at the *Compleat Angler Hotel*, where chef Humphrey Dottin might toss some marlin or other game fish on the grill and offer free sandwiches to all.

At the south end of town is *Fisherman's Paradise* (☎ 242-347-3220), a pleasant place popular with locals. It has indoor and outdoor seating. Try the boil or stew fish breakfast. Pork chops cost US$5; fishpot of the day is US$12. It's open 7 to 11 am, noon to 3 pm, and 6 to 10 pm daily. A similar, smaller option is *Big John's Harborside Restaurant*, a stone's throw north.

You've heard of Burger King, 'Home of the Big Whopper'? Well, head to *Burger Queen*, 'Home of the Little Whopper,' across the street from the All Age School at the north end of Alice Town. (The 'Queen' is Ivy Brown.)

In Bailey Town, I recommend *Sandra's Bar & Restaurant* (☎ 242-347-2336), on King's Hwy, a charming little family-style place serving Bahamian favorites. A conch salad or fish snack costs US$6. You can sit in a captain's chair at the bar and add your autographed dollar bill to dozens of others pinned to the wall. An even smaller dive up the road, *Honey Bun's*, sells burgers and conch dishes for pennies. Turn west here and you'll find another charmer, *ALM Restaurant*, which also serves Bahamian fare. Head to *Jone's Mini-Supermarket* for groceries.

Tiger's Den, in Porgy Bay, sells burgers for US$2 and snacks. It also has a convenience store and serves pig or chicken souse for US$5 on Saturday. North of Porgy Bay, the *Bimini Bay Hotel* (☎ 242-347-2171) has an elegant dining room where you're fussed over by owner Antoinette. It serves three meals daily. Fancy a 'cooling cuppa'? Then head here for afternoon tea, served 3 to 6 pm daily on the patio.

You can buy North Bimini's exquisite, renowned homemade white bread and confections at *roadside shacks* opposite All My Children Hotel and Bimini Big Game Fishing Club. Coconut candy costs US$1, raisin bread is US$2.50, and delicious banana cake is US$5.

Kiddies in tow? A young lady named Tassie sells snow cones outside the Atlantis Spring Water Company toward the north end of Queen's Hwy for US50¢ and US$1.

For groceries, head to *Jontra's Food Store* or *Manny's Supermarket*, opposite Bimini Big Game Fishing Club.

Entertainment

The larger-than-life pub at the *Compleat Angler Hotel* (☎ 242-347-2122), where Ernest Hemingway hung his hat, is still the center of action more than 50 years later. The bar still draws colorful, offbeat characters. It's *the* place to be when the calypso band strikes up and the dance floor begins to cook . . . helped along by a Goombay Smash, a rum-pineapple-coconut concoction for US$4.50, from a bartender known as 'The Devil.' The band plays three to seven nights a week December to April, and Wednesday night and weekends the rest of the year. One of the rooms holds the original bar, fashioned from Prohibition-era rum kegs. The Angler is open 11 am to 1 am daily.

While Hemingway swigged at the Angler, Adam Clayton Powell, Jr, tippled at the *End of the World Bar* (☎ 242-347-2094), a weathered old shack – near the Pan-Am Air Bridge terminal – about the size of a prison cell, where he kept locals amused with his wit and audacity. The floor is still covered in sand, and dogs wander in and out. And you can add your scrawl to the graffiti-covered walls. Bras and panties hang from the rafters and ceiling fans, giving the local health inspector a fit. You don't *have* to whip yours off on-site, but many folks do! If the place seems dead, try again after midnight, when the locals stir. It closes at 3 am.

The *Island House Bar* (☎ 242-347-2439), opposite the Red Lion, has a pool table. It's open 11 am to 3 am. Just up the road is *Bimini Breeze* (☎ 242-347-3511), where The Bahamas' middle-weight boxing champion, Yama Bahama, hangs out. Serious fisherfolk like to gather to tell tall tales at the *Harbour Lounge* in the Bimini Big Game Fishing Club.

In Bailey Town check out the upstairs bar known as the *Specialty Paris* (there's no sign) opposite the Anglican Church, where an octogenarian named Nathaniel Saunders – alias 'Piccolo Pete' – and his rake 'n' scrape band put tunes together on a ukulele, conga drum, and spoon and handsaw. Other similar, no-frills Bailey Town bars include the *Wee Wee Hour's Club*, *Big D's Game Room*, and *Syl's VIP Lounge*.

There's a modest dance club on weekends at *Fisherman's Paradise* and another, *Le Sheriff*, in All My Children Hotel.

Things to Buy

For T-shirts and native crafts, check out the Straw Market opposite All My Children Hotel on King's Hwy, or the Logo Shoppe at Bimini Big Game Fishing Club and Keefe's Bimini Undersea. Gateway Gallery, next to Keefe's Bimini Undersea, is about the only place selling quality arts and crafts with an island theme.

For duty-free perfumes, head to The Perfume Bar, opposite the Customs building. Sue & Joy's Variety Store specializes in jewelry and island-made fragrances; it is open 9 am to 8 pm daily. Island Gems, opposite the Bimini Big Game Fishing Club, sells Cuban cigars and Androsia batik shirts, plus jewelry and perfumes.

The liquor store at Bimini Big Game Fishing Club will deliver to your yacht.

Getting There & Away

Air Pan-Am Air Bridge (formerly Chalk's, in the Biminis ☎ 242-347-3024) flies seaplanes to North Bimini from Fort Lauderdale's Jet Center on N Perimeter Rd. Flights depart daily Sunday to Wednesday and twice daily Thursday to Saturday (US$71 one way). From Miami's Watson Island, seaplanes depart twice daily Monday to Wednesday and Sunday and three times daily Thursday to Saturday (US$71 one way). Pan-Am flies from Paradise Island at 9:35 am on Monday, Wednesday, Thursday, and Friday; it flies at 2 pm on other days of the week (US$78 one way).

Pan-Am's seaplanes 'land' in the water, then waddle ashore at the south end of Alice Town, a short walk from most hotels. An Immigration and Customs office is right there for those arriving from the USA. No hand luggage is allowed.

All other planes land at the airstrip at the east end of South Bimini (see Getting There & Away under South Bimini, later in this chapter).

Boat The official port of entry is in Alice Town. Yachters must clear immigration and customs at the Bimini Big Game Fishing Club. However, there are several marinas to choose among.

The Bimini Big Game Fishing Club (☎ 242-347-3391, 800-737-1007), which is the Biminis' best-equipped marina, has 100 slips for boats up to 100 feet; US$1.25

BIMINIS

per foot per day (with a minimum of US$40), plus US$15 for electricity (mandatory). The Bimini Blue Water Marina (☎ 242-347-3166, fax 242-347-3293) has 32 slips and full facilities, including a 1-ton weigh station to measure the size of your catch. Dockage costs US75¢ per foot; electricity starts at US$10 daily. Smaller marinas include Weech's Bimini Dock (☎ 242-347-3028), which charges US60¢ per foot per day (US$15 minimum), including water. Electricity costs US$7.50 daily (US$15 for 220 volts).

The Biminis and North Cat Cay are served from Nassau by the mail boat *Bimini Mack* (12 hours, US$45 one way). The mail-boat office in Alice Town is on Parliament Ln, 50 yards west of the Customs building.

See the South Bimini section in this chapter for details on water-taxi service between North and South Bimini.

Getting Around
Golf Cart, Moped & Scooter You'll find that most places are within walking distance. However, the fashionable mode of transport is an electric golf cart, which you can rent from the Compleat Angler Hotel (☎ 242-347-3122) or Captain Pat's at the Sea Crest Marina (☎ 242-347-3477). Captain Pat charges US$20 for the first hour, US$10 each additional hour, or US$50/65 half-/full day. He says the prices are negotiable. You can rent golf carts elsewhere; look for posted signs.

You can rent mopeds and scooters from Bimini Rentals (☎ 242-347-3400) or Sawyer's Scooter Rental (☎ 242-347-2555), both near the Bimini Big Game Fishing Club.

Taxi Bimini Bus Service operates a red taxi-van up and down King's Hwy. You can wave it down anywhere. Fares depend on the distance of your trip. A taxi from the Pan-Am seaplane terminal to the Compleat Angler Hotel or Bimini Big Game Fishing Club costs US$3. A tour of the island will cost US$5.

Bicycle Keefe's Bimini Undersea (☎ 242-347-3089, fax 242-347-3079) rents bikes for US$5/12/20 hourly/half-day/full day.

SOUTH BIMINI
Less-developed South Bimini has long been favored by US expats, who as early as the 1930s built plush houses on the island. Today the man-made canals of the Port Royal area, to the southwest, are lined with homes used by Yankees who fly or boat in for weekends. The rest of the 5-mile (east to west) by 2-mile (north to south) island is dominated by mangrove, tropical hardwood forest, and brackish pools. Along the south shore, the mangroves surround Duck Lake, full of waterfowl in season. You can see juvenile fish from the side of the road – they hang around the pipe where tidal waters flow in and out of the lake. (Be careful if you're exploring by kayak, as the tides flow swiftly between North and South Bimini.)

A paved road leads from the water-taxi dock, on the northwest tip, to the airport. A dirt road loops around the west and south shores, connecting with Airport Rd.

There's a public phone at Duncombe's Yacht Club and another at the airstrip. For police assistance in South Bimini, call ☎ 242-347-3424.

Fountain of Youth
Ponce de León's mythical Fountain of Youth is said to be 2 miles southeast of the water-taxi berth on Airport Rd. Look for the sign amid the undergrowth to the side of the road. It's actually a natural, 18-inch-wide hole (often dry) in the limestone, surrounded by a crumbling wall.

Shipwreck
The remains of the *Sapona*, a concrete ship, lie half-submerged offshore, 4 miles south of South Bimini. It was built by Henry Ford during WWI. During Prohibition it was anchored here and turned into a private club – a favored haunt of the rumrunners. Alas, the *Sapona* was wrecked by a hurricane in 1929 and has since been

Top: Sponges soaking up the sun in Gregory Town, Eleuthera

Middle Left: Get your conch from the Frog Man in Marsh Harbor, Abacos.

Bottom Left: Poggy Bay, where even the fish are friendly

Bottom Right: Bringing wood to life at the Straw Market in Nassau

Top Left: At prayer on Long Island
Bottom Left: One, two, three crabs for the pot,
    South Andros

Top Right: One basket, coming up
Bottom Right: A man and his plantains, Eleuthera

used as a bomber's target and smuggler's cache. Today it sits in 15 feet of water and is favored by divers.

Shark Laboratory

Officially named the Bimini Biological Field Station (VHF channel 88), this education and research center east of Port Royal is affiliated with the University of Miami. Most of the research involves the lemon shark, one of the 13 shark species common hereabouts. Visitors are welcome, and staff are glad to give tours of the facility, time permitting (visiting during bad weather is best, when staff are on hand). There are no sharks here, however.

The university offers a 10-day tropical marine biology course open to upper-level undergraduates and graduate students, and a six-day elasmobranch biology course focusing on the life of sharks. Both of these courses are held during intersession and vacation periods. Contact Dr Samuel H Gruber (☎ /fax 305-274-0628, sgruber@ rsmas.miami.edu), 9300 SW 99th St, Miami, FL 33176-2050.

Tiki Hut Beach

This lovely 2-mile strip of white sand lines the west shore. The beach is backed by a beautiful stretch of vegetation, including thatch palm, sisal, beach morning glory, and blooming nightshade.

There's a small shade-hut, 'Tiki Hut,' at the island's south end, where snorkeling is best along the rocky shore running south to Corner Reef. Just offshore, 15 feet down, are rock formations similar to the Bimini Road, off North Bimini. Schools of blue runners and juvenile palometas frequent the shallow areas, and gaily decorated damselfish, parrotfish, and spotted eagle rays can be seen close to shore.

Buccaneer Point, at the north end of the beach, is also good for snorkeling, especially at high tide. Beware of the strong currents. An airplane forced down by the US Drug Enforcement Administration lies just offshore. It's now favored by octopus, eel, and more than 50 fish species.

Corner Reef is a small reef protected by rocks and cays one-half mile south of Tiki Hut Beach, near the Bimini Beach Club. Its flats are popular with spotted eagle rays, and two large schools of grunts sleep here during the day before going out to feed at night in the beds of grasses. The tiny cave and rocks are home to lobsters, octopi, and crabs.

Activities

The Bimini Beach Club & Marina (see Places to Stay & Eat, below) charters boats and skippers for sport fishing, and can recommend guides.

Rodney Rolle (VHF channel 68) rents sea kayaks for US$25/40 half-/full day.

Places to Stay & Eat

Bimini Beach Club & Marina (in the USA ☎ 954-725-0919, 888-824-6464, bimini@ gate.net), at the southwest tip of the island, is popular with scuba divers. It has 40 air-con rooms with rattan furniture, TV, and private bathroom. It also has a pleasant lounge with a stone fireplace and pool table, a large, well-lit restaurant and small bar, and an L-shaped saltwater pool surrounded by a wooden sun deck. It has water sports and dive and sport-fishing excursions. Oceanside rooms cost US$95; bayside rooms cost US$90. Special rates apply for pilots. Its mailing address is 1410 SE 12th St, Deerfield Beach, FL 33441. Scuba Bimini (☎ 954-359-2705, 800-848-4073, fax 954-359-2707), 1043 SE 17th St, Fort Lauderdale, FL 33316, has scuba packages based here.

Bimini Sands & Marina (☎ 242-347-3500; in the USA ☎ 561-739-9008), half a mile south of Buccaneer Point, is a new development due for completion in 2000, when it will have 216 one- and two-bedroom luxury townhouses and 160 boat slips (about 70 of each were ready at press time). The units are splendid – very spacious and flooded by sunlight – and each has a huge kitchen, large patio, and pleasing decor. The exteriors, which look like they're made of cement and stucco, are made of a weatherproof rubber laminate on a steel frame! Weekly rates are US$750/1550 one-/two-bedroom February through September. Low-season rates are US$600/1400. Dockage costs US$1 per foot per night. There is a minimum one-week rental. The postal address is 3469 W Boynton Beach Blvd, No 6, Boynton Beach, FL 33436.

Duncombe's Yacht Club (☎ 242-347-3115) also has 10 rooms, and it serves island meals in its pleasing restaurant.

You can stock up on drinks and snacks at *Morgan's Grocery* or *Morgan's Liquor Store*, the only stores on the island; they're near Duncombe's Yacht Club.

Getting There & Away
Air The airstrip, 3.5 miles east of the ferry dock, has a small snack bar, public phone, and toilets. There is also a cafe, Cox's Snack Bar, next door.

South Bimini is served by Bimini Island Air (in the USA ☎ 954-938-8991). Island Air Charters flies to South Bimini from Fort Lauderdale on Monday, Wednesday, Friday, and Sunday. Major's Air Services has flights between Freeport and the Biminis (US$95 roundtrip).

Sky Unlimited departs Nassau Friday and Sunday (US$68 one way).

Boat TSL Water Taxi operates a water-taxi service between North and South Bimini; the trip costs US$3. PHK Water Taxi also offers a water-taxi service from the North Bimini mail-boat dock to South Bimini. Additionally, tours are offered to the Fountain of Youth and South Bimini for US$5, including bus transfer from your hotel. Both companies can be reached on VHF channel 68.

Getting Around
Shuttle taxis at the airstrip take you to the Bimini Beach Club or Bimini Sands for US$3, or to the water-taxi berth for US$5 per person, which includes a one-way ride to North Bimini. Both TSL Water Taxi and PHK Water Taxi (see above) have minibus taxis waiting at the South Bimini wharf.

Rodney Rolle, who runs TSL, rents bicycles at the South Bimini wharf for US$12/15 half-/full day.

NORTH CAT CAY
North Cat Cay, 10 miles south of South Bimini, is a private island run as an exclusive, members-only club, beloved by magnates and Hollywood stars. The west shore and top half of the east shore are divided into private lots tucked amid bougainvillea and surrounded by sturdy gumbo limbo, hibiscus, and palm. Only club members and their guests may swim in the pool, sunbathe on the diamond-dust beaches, play a round at the nine-hole Windsor Downs Golf Course, or sleep at the club. Nonmembers are restricted to the marina area.

The medical clinic is open daily 10 am to noon. The staff are available at other times for emergencies.

Places to Stay & Eat
Only members and their guests are allowed to rent accommodations on the island. The *Cat Cay Yacht Club* (in the USA ☎ 954-359-8272, fax 954-359-8273) has six hotel rooms with twin beds, TV, and refrigerator for US$150, plus one apartment with king-size bed, TV, and kitchen for US$250. Some of the 70 privately owned villas are also available. The club's postal address is 1100 Lee Wagener Blvd, No 101, Fort Lauderdale, FL 33315.

The *Nauticat* restaurant, overlooking the marina, is open to nonmembers, as is the *Haigh House Bar*. The marina's *Cone Bar & Victoria Restaurant*, the *Kitten Key Club* on the island's southwest point, and the *Pool Patio* are for members and their guests only.

The marina has a *grocery* and a *liquor store*.

Getting There & Away
Air Island Air Charters flies to North Cat Cay from the Fort Lauderdale Jet Center (US$90 one way). Private charters cost US$375 one way for the entire plane.

Pan-Am Air Bridge also offers charters to North Cat Cay from Florida and Paradise Island.

Private pilots with STOL aircraft can use the 1100-foot-long strip for a landing fee of US$25. There's also a seaplane ramp and helipad.

You can clear immigration and customs here 9:30 am to 4 pm Monday to Friday.

Boat North Cat Cay has a new 82-slip marina with commissary (open 10 am to 6 pm Monday to Saturday). All slips have cable TV hookups, metered water, and electricity. Dockage costs US$1.50 per foot per day. 'Transient' boaters are limited to a two-day stay. The *Bimini Mack* mail boat sails here from Nassau weekly (see the North Bimini section).

Getting Around
The island is small enough that you can walk everywhere. Golf carts, however, can be rented at the marina for US$35 daily.

Berry Islands

Pop 634

The 30 mostly uninhabited islands and cays of the Berry Islands are strung out north from Chub Cay, 35 miles northwest of Nassau, to Great Stirrup Cay, a span of about 25 miles. The islands sit atop a plateau rising between the Northwest Providence Channel (to the north) and the Tongue of the Ocean (to the south). The largest and most important island is Great Harbour Cay, a 10-mile-long, 1-mile-wide tendon of limestone composed of scrub-covered rolling terrain.

Birds far outnumber humans in the Berries, and it is quite possible to find your own tiny cay where you can cast cares and clothes to the wind.

The islands' history is inconsequential. In the 1830s King William IV of England decided Great Stirrup Cay would make a good home for freed slaves. A settlement – appropriately named Williamstown – was begun. When the cay's thin soils yielded no produce, the settlement failed.

Little else happened until the 1960s, when Douglas Fairbanks, Jr, and others among the US social elite took the cay to their bosoms. The Great Harbour Cay Club was formed, and nine rippling fairways were sculpted on the rises falling down to the sea. Marinas lined with waterfront homes were constructed. Jet setters briefly flocked, including Brigitte Bardot, Cary Grant, and members of the Rockefeller clan. Even mobster Meyer Lansky had a stake. However, the troubled club was closed and ransacked in the mid-'70s. Nowadays the local property-owners' association subsidizes things to keep the roads in repair and to ensure that the Tamboo Dinner Club – the main social venue – stays open.

Several cays in the Berries are privately owned, such as Bond's Cay, where a private bird sanctuary is maintained, and Cistern Cay, a stone's throw off Great Harbour

- Shelling on scintillating Shell Beach
- Sport fishing in the Tongue of the Ocean
- Down-home eating in Bullock's Harbour
- Escaping to chic Chub Cay, if money's not a problem

Cay's northwest shore. Great Stirrup Cay and Little Stirrup Cay (also known as Coco Cay), two tiny isles, are the private domains of Norwegian Cruise Line and Royal Caribbean Cruise Lines, which deposit their passengers here for a day of R&R. Passengers are tendered ashore by the *Bahama Rama Mama*, based in Bullock's Harbour on Great Harbour Cay.

The Berries were squashed by Hurricane Andrew in 1992 and at press time were still regaining a toehold.

GREAT HARBOUR CAY

Pop 500

The vast majority of Berry Islanders live on Great Harbour Cay in **Bullock's Harbour**, a small settlement on its own island, connected to Great Harbour Cay by a causeway across the Bay of Five Pirates. The somewhat rundown village is raucous with the crowing of cockerels, which pick at the piles of garbage that are strewn everywhere. The first thing you'll notice each day are the roosters, which begin crowing before sunrise. They run around freely, without apparent ownership. Many locals eke a living from sponge diving.

The center of touristy happenings is Great Harbour Marina, built on a narrow channel south of Bullock's Harbour and entered via a slender cut with cliffs to each side. Townhouses line the east and north sides of the marina, adding to the attractive setting.

The cay's main attraction is the 8-mile-long white-sand beach along the windward (east) shore, where the shallows run every shade of jade green. The beach is formed of two great scallops: Sugar Beach to the north and Great Harbour Bay to the south. A few dozen expats have houses along the shore. Great Harbour Bay runs south to Shell Beach and a reef (exposed at low tide) that is good for finding sand dollars.

Shark Creek separates Shell Beach and the northern part of Great Harbour Cay from the wild, uninhabited southern part.

The island's west shore comprises mangroves, flats, and brine pools favored by herons and egrets. Most of the interior is smothered in thatch palm, scrub, and casuarinas; snakes and butterflies abound. There are vast flats for bonefishing. A road – Great Harbour Dr – runs the length of the east coast.

The island held its first Homecoming Regatta in August 1997, with plans for it to be an annual event. There's plenty of home cooking, live music, and fun. Call the local government office (☎ 242-367-8291).

Information
There's no bank. Public telephone kiosks are found at Great Harbour Marina and at the post office in Bullock's Harbour, which is open 9 am to 5:30 pm weekdays. You can buy stamps and drop off mail at Happy People's Gift Shop & Rentals at Great Harbour Marina from 8 am to 5 pm daily.

There's a medical clinic (☎ 242-367-8400) with resident nurse by the post office in Bullock's Harbour, open 9 am to 2 pm weekdays. A doctor makes monthly calls.

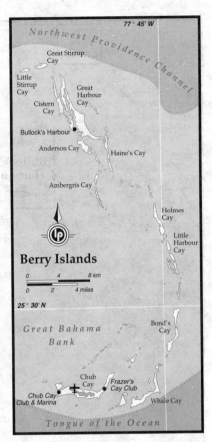

For police assistance, call ☎ 919 or 242-367-8344. The station is in Bullock's Harbour.

Diving & Snorkeling
There are especially good dive and snorkel sites northeast of Great Harbour Cay. You might be able to charter private boats at the Great Harbour Marina (☎ 242-367-8005, fax 242-367-8115), which has daily dive excursions. Percy Darville (☎ 242-367-8119), who has his office at the marina, might also be able to take you diving.

Diving
Fishing
Snorkeling

Bullock's Harbour

0   200   400 m
0   200   400 yards

Bay of Five Pirates

Causeway

Highpoint Drive

Pirates Way Rd

Royal Palm Drive

PLACES TO STAY		OTHER	
1	Tropical Diversions Beach Villas	3	Robert's Lounge & Disco
15	Tropical Diversions	4	Government Dock
		5	School
PLACES TO EAT		8	Police Station
2	Beach Club	12	Post Office, Medical Clinic
6	Watergate	13	Gas Dock
7	Until Then	14	BaTelCo
9	Cooly Mae's Take Away	17	Great Harbour Marina, Happy People's Gift Shop & Rentals
10	A&L Grocery		
11	Pinder's Grocery		
16	Tamboo Dinner Club		
18	The Wharf		

Northwest Providence Channel

Sugar Beach

Bullock's Cay

Cistern Cay

Rat Cay

Great Bahama Bank

Bullock's Harbour

Bay of Five Pirates

see inset map

Bamboo Cay

Pirates Way Rd

Highpoint Drive

Fairway Drive

Great Harbour Cay

Little Petit Cay

Petit Cay

Great Harbour Drive

Royal Palm Drive

Golf Course

Great Harbour Bay

Airport

Shell Beach

Anderson Cay

Shark Creek

Great Harbour Cay

0   1   2 km
0   .5   1 mile

Happy People's Gift Shop & Rentals, at Great Harbour Marina, rents snorkel gear (US$3 for snorkel and fins, US$10 full set). Its postal address is PO Box N-10308, Nassau, Bahamas.

Bonefishing & Sport Fishing

The Berries are superb for fishing, be it for bonefish on the flats, billfish streaming through the Northwest Providence Channel and Tongue of the Ocean, or light-tackle bottom fish such as yellowtail, snapper, and grouper.

The best bonefishing guide is Percy Darville (see Diving & Snorkeling, above). He charges US$215/315 half-/full day, including boat charter. Revis Anderson will take you deep-sea fishing for US$350/500 half-/full day aboard the 28-foot *Five Heart II*.

Happy People's Gift Shop & Rentals (see above) rents a 15-foot bonefishing skiff for US$80/100 half-/full day. It also rents fishing rods for US$15 and sells tackle.

Permits are required for visiting sport-fishing boats (US$20). See the Outdoor Activities chapter for details on how to obtain permits.

Golf

There's a nine-hole golf course a half-mile southeast of the marina. The clubhouse closed a few years ago, but Happy People's (see above) rents clubs for US$15 a day.

Places to Stay

Ruth Adderley (☎ /fax 242-367-8117), alias the Flower Lady, rents four *rooms* in the pink-and-white house on the hill behind Happy People's at the marina. The rooms vary in size, but each is daintily decorated in cool whites, with frilly bedspreads. All have a kitchenette, refrigerator, TV, and air-con. Daily rates range from US$75 to US$95; her postal address is c/o Happy People's, PO Box N-10308, Nassau, Bahamas.

Tropical Diversions (☎ 242-367-8333, fax 242-367-8115; in the USA ☎ 954-921-9084, 800-343-7256, fax 954-921-1044) offers two-bedroom, two-story townhouses with patios and decks overlooking the marina, with private docks below, for US$180 to US$300. All are splendidly decorated and have air-con, TV, washing machine, and full kitchen. The company also has *beach villas* on Great Harbour Bay, with patios facing the ocean. Units vary from single-room efficiencies to an eight-room villa or a luxury suite and rent for US$90 to US$450; prices depend on the number and type of beds. The villas have VCRs and VHF radios. Rates include housekeeping service.

There's also a three-bedroom *beachside house* (in the USA ☎ 937-433-2171) for rent at Sugar Beach.

Places to Eat

Overlooking the marina, *The Wharf* (☎ 242-367-8762) serves hearty US-style and Bahamian breakfasts from US$4 (ask about the daily specials, such as corn-beef hash and grits). It also serves salads, soups, and burgers, plus a wide dinner menu with seafood entrées from US$13 and pizzas from US$8.50. It's open 7 to 11 am and 4 pm to midnight and is closed Tuesday.

In town, *Watergate* (☎ 242-367-8244), opposite the school, is a basic eatery serving huge portions of pork chops, peas 'n' rice, and potato salad (US$8). It's a gas at lunchtime, when the school kids in their vermilion-and-white uniforms pour in like a storm of sweet peas to order takeout meals.

The best cook in town is Liz. At press time she worked at a small restaurant named *Until Then*, southeast of Watergate, but she was planning on opening her own place at the T-junction as you enter the village. Here, too, is *Cooly Mae's Take Away* (☎ 242-367-8730), open for lunch snacks. Cooly will cook and deliver and serve at your home. She offers a vast menu, from lamb stew to pizzas and desserts. You must place your order by 9 am.

Burgers and other snacks are served at the *Beach Club*, a weathered bar overhanging Great Harbour Beach near the airport. It gets few patrons but is a splendid place to chill while marveling at the sugar-white beach.

The elegant *Tamboo Dinner Club* (☎ 242-367-8203), at the marina, is open on Wednesday and Saturday by reservation only (call early). You dine overlooking the water through plate-glass windows that curve along the bayfront. The menu includes boned duck, Bahamian-style spicy chicken, and seafood. Meals cost US$25 to US$30, including soup, salad, entrée, and dessert. When more than 20 people are dining, a buffet is offered, and diners without reservations can sometimes be accommodated.

You can buy groceries and general goods at the *Marina Store* or *Happy People's* at the marina. Every second person in Bullock's Harbour also seems to run a grocery – there's literally one every 100 yards.

Entertainment
The bar with TV at *The Wharf* is favored by young males from Bullock's Harbour; it's a great place to hear local banter, full of wit and wisdom and sexual innuendo. Nearby, *Tamboo Dinner Club* welcomes drop-in guests. It's open Wednesday and Saturday, with an elegant bar, a library, backgammon boards, and a giant TV with VCR. There's a dress code. Local expat homeowners gather here; it's very congenial, and you'll learn a great deal about the cay.

In Bullock's Harbour you can sup with locals at *Watergate*, adorned with signs such as 'No swearing during school hours,' and 'Keep off the grass; take her to a motel.' To boogie down, check out *Robert's Lounge & Disco*, next to the grocery at the north end of town.

Things to Buy
For souvenirs, check out Happy People's or Lilly's Boutique, at the airport. Most of the straw-work is imported from Taiwan, despite the cosmetic adornments reading 'Bahamas.' (Many locals make a killing importing Taiwanese straw hats and selling them on the Stirrup cays to the cruise-ship passengers.)

Getting There & Away
Air See airlines' international and Nassau telephone numbers in the Getting There & Away and Getting Around chapters.

Tropical Diversions Air flies guests in from Fort Lauderdale.

Cat Island Air (on Great Harbour ☎ 242-361-8021) flies from Nassau to Great Harbour daily (US$50 one way). Departure times are tentative; leave plenty of time for connecting flights, especially since the return flight goes via Sandy Point (Abacos). Falcon Air flies twice daily from Nassau, as does Trans-Island Air.

Major's Air Services flies from Freeport to Great Harbour on Monday.

Private pilots must clear entry into The Bahamas on Great Harbour, even if they're heading to Chub Cay.

Boat Boaters and pilots arriving from abroad must clear immigration (☎ 242-367-8112) and customs (☎ 242-367-8207) at Great Harbour Marina.

The marina (☎ 242-367-8005, fax 242-367-8115, VHF channels 16 and 68) has 86 slips for boats up to 80 feet. It has showers, laundry, commissary, fuel, electricity, and water. It charges US80¢ a foot March to September, US60¢ October through February. A US$10 water wash-down charge is mandatory.

Getting Around
Transportation Unlimited (☎ 242-367-8466/8711) provides a taxi service. Reginald Farrington Cay (VHF channel 16) will also taxi you around Great Harbour.

Happy People's rents bicycles (US$2 per hour, US$15 full day, US$90 weekly with eighth day free), Suzuki jeeps (US$40/50 half-/full day or US$300 weekly with the eighth day free), and scooters (US$30/40 half-/full day). Deposits are required.

Happy People's rents boats, including 19-foot Aquasports (US$100/120 half-/full day). Larger boats are available.

CHUB CAY
The southernmost isle in the chain is virtually the private domain of the Chub Cay

Club & Marina. Once the exclusive territory of a small group of wealthy Texans,
today it's a favorite of such moneyed folks
as Quincy Jones and Bill Cosby, though it
is also open to daytime visitors and nonmembers. The cay is also favored for itinerant boats and for sport fishing. It has a
full-service marina and two beaches.
Though trashed by Hurricane Andrew in
1992, the club has arisen like a phoenix
and has a fresh coat of paint.

Chub Cay is shaped like an ox's jaw-
bone. The 4-mile-long island curls north at
its east end; this peninsula is Frazer's Hog
Cay, where hogs were once raised. A small
beach lines the shore.

The cay hosts the Chub Cay Champion-
ship fishing tourney each April and the
Chub Cay Blue Marlin Tournament each
July.

Diving

Chub Cay, which sits at the edge of the
Tongue of the Ocean, offers fabulous wall
diving. One of the best sites is Mama
Rhoda Rock, protected by the Bahamas
National Trust and known for its moray
eels, lobsters, and yellow trumpetfish, as
well as healthy staghorn and elkhorn
coral. There's a shipwreck with cannon
nearby.

The club's Bahama Island Adventures
(☎ 800-329-1337) offers dive packages.

Places to Stay & Eat

The tranquil *Chub Cay Club & Marina*
(☎ 242-325-1490, fax 242-322-5199; in

the USA ☎ 800-662-8555), at the west
end of Chub Cay, faces a splendid horse-
shoe-shaped beach and has eight simply
adorned rooms facing the huge freshwater
swimming pool. Each has cable TV,
refrigerator, and coffeemaker, plus either
a king-size bed or two twin beds. It also
has nine two- and three-bedroom villas
nestled along the beach. Many of the
rooms are reserved for club members. The
club offers tennis and a panoply of water
sports, including scuba diving and sport
fishing. Room rates begin at US$175
year-round; villas begin at US$450. The
mailing address is PO Box 661067,
Miami Springs, FL 33266-1067.

Frazer's Cay Club (VHF channel 16; in
the USA ☎ 305-743-2420), a historic two-
story building on Frazer's Hog Cay, has
rooms, a restaurant, and a bar. Its postal
address is PO Box 500955, Marathon, FL
33050.

The Chub Cay Club's *Harbour House
Restaurant* serves both Bahamian and US
dishes.

Getting There & Away

Island Express flies to Chub Cay from Fort
Lauderdale daily except Wednesday and
Thursday. Private charters also serve the
Chub Cay Club, which provides taxi trans-
fers to and from the airport.

The Chub Cay Club's marina has 76
slips, with full boating services. There's a
commissary. Frazer's Cay Club offers
dockage for boats up to 120 feet, with
water, electricity, fuel, and showers.

Abacos

Pop 10,061

The Abacos – at 649 sq miles, the second-largest land mass in the country – lie at the northernmost end of The Bahamas. The boomerang-shaped chain comprises Abaco (the main island) and the Abaco Cays, a necklace of dozens of smaller cays. Most of the Abaco Cays lie 2 to 4 miles off Abaco's east shore, and they stretch 200 miles from Walker's Cay in the northwest to Cherokee Sound in the southeast. The Sea of Abaco, the protected waters in the cays' lee, is favored by yachters. Indeed, the Abacos and yachting go together like wind and sail, earning the chain the nickname 'The Sailing Capital of the World.' The southernmost island is 106 miles north of Nassau.

The main island, Abaco, technically consists of Great Abaco, the lower part of the island, and Little Abaco, its north-western extension. Inhabitants of the cays often simply refer to Abaco as 'the mainland.' Abaco is 130 miles long yet rarely more than 4 miles wide.

Most folks live in Marsh Harbour (the largest town in the Abacos) or on the Loyalist Cays (the name comes from these cays' early settlers, who arrived here after fleeing persecution during and after the American Revolution). There are four Loyalist Cays: Elbow, Man O' War, and Great Guana cays flank Marsh Harbour; Green Turtle Cay lies farther north. Though edged one to the next, the cays are as different as New York and Paris. The chain's other villages number barely half a dozen.

Spanish explorers, after decimating the Indian population on the island they called 'Habacoa' (a Lucayan word), moved on. The French attempted to establish a settlement – Lucayonique – in 1625, but it quickly failed, and no remains of it have been found.

After the American Revolution, numerous Loyalists who left the newly independent

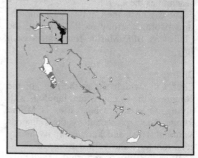

USA settled in the Abacos. Many of the first to arrive were blacks who departed New York in August 1783 aboard the *Nautilus* and *William*, arriving in 'Abbico' near today's Treasure Cay. They founded the village of Carleton (commemorated today by Carleton Point), naming it for Sir Guy Carleton, the commander-in-chief of the British forces in North America. Another group of Loyalists established themselves in an area known as Cherokee Sound.

The Carleton settlers squabbled among themselves and split; some left to found Marsh Harbour and settle the cays, each of which started with only one or two families (the Alburys on Man O' War, the Lowes and Sawyers on Green Turtle, the Malones and Bethels on Elbow). Their names linger on today in quaint communities whose residents cherish their past and independence.

(On the eve of Bahamian independence in 1972, Loyalist Abaconians petitioned the Queen to be separated from The Bahamas as a British crown colony; when they were denied, the most radical elements even contemplated a revolution.) Abaconians talk with an equally quaint Elizabethan lilt, nurtured by the isolation of island life; the accent resembles an Australian talking with mashed potatoes in his or her mouth.

The Loyalist settlers were mostly merchants and craftspeople, and after a brief and unsuccessful tenure as farmers, many moved on. Of the 2000 settlers, only 400 stayed, equally divided between blacks and whites. Those that remained resorted to what they knew best – trading, boatbuilding, and salvaging shipwrecks. By the mid-19th century the Abaconians – especially the citizens of the town of New Providence on Green Turtle Cay – were relatively wealthy, enough so that they loaned money to the government. The cays even evolved a vernacular New England-style architecture, called 'Abaco style,' notable for its high-pitched roofs and wide clapboarding. The form became so popular that in the 1860s many prefabricated houses were made and shipped to Florida.

The Abacos' gaily painted, gingerbread clapboard houses are still framed by white picket fences and set along narrow streets bordered by vivid pink oleander, bougainvillea as red as lipstick, and hibiscus flowers of every hue. And the dour Protestantism of the Loyalists also lives. Each cay has followed its own church (the Gospel Church on Man O' War, the Church of God on Green Turtle) with its own traditions. When the preacher speaks on Green Turtle, the devout shout, *'Hallelujah, brother!'* On Man O' War they mumble, *'Mmmmm-mm.'*

There are no large, showy hotels. Instead the Abacos boast homey cottages and inns on talcum-fine beaches or alongside the many marinas. Walker's Cay, sitting on the edge of the Gulf Stream in the far northwest, is one The Bahamas' prime sportfishing sites. Coral reef gardens fringing the Atlantic beckon divers and snorkelers

(there are also many winding caverns and tunnels full of minnows streaming like silver foil, and even dozens of Spanish galleons resting on the seabed). See the Dive & Snorkel Sites sidebar in the Marsh Harbour section for details on the Abacos' best sites.

Ashore, most of Abaco is smothered with scrub and pine forest, good for bird watching and nature hikes (access is via a web of logging roads) and popular with locals hunting wild boar.

The Abacos boast four national parks, notably Pelican Cays Land & Sea Park, preserving the barrier islands and coral reefs south of Tilloo Cay; and, in the far south, Abaco National Park, protecting the native habitat of the endangered Bahama parrot. The inshore waters of the Sea of Abaco are home to a resident population of about 100 bottle-nosed dolphins.

Off the west shore of central Great Abaco is a vast wetlands area known as The Marls, made up of a mosaic of mangrove creeks and hundreds of tiny isles in the shallow Bight of Abaco. The Marls provide a vital nursery for young fish and invertebrates, plus an important habitat for ducks, egrets, and herons. The bonefishing is superb.

Abaco Life, PO Box 1366, Fort Lauderdale, FL 33302, publishes a detailed foldout map of the Abacos, with separate maps of major settlements. It costs US$3 at retailers (US$5 including postage).

Marsh Harbour

Pop 4000

The boating capital of the northern Bahamas and the third-largest settlement in the country is the nerve center (if not the soul) of the Abacos, with most of the businesses, dive operators, marinas, hotels, and stores. Marsh Harbour is the gateway to exploring the Abaco Cays, a few miles offshore.

The town, which was prosperous in the heyday of sponging and shipbuilding, now has a quiet, small-town Floridian feel – too clean and orderly to be Bahamian. Yet as recently as the mid-1980s, Marsh Harbour had the air of a frontier town. There was no paved road out of town, most roads in town were unpaved, and there were so few restaurants that the Great Abaco Beach Resort (now the Abaco Beach Resort & Boat Harbour) posted information on where guests could get food on particular nights. Then the town boomed, thanks to drug money and, more recently, tourism. Today marinas and jetties jut out from the shoreline like tree branches, festooned with sleek yachts and motorboats as thick as Christmas baubles. Cafes and fine restaurants are springing up, and there is a sense of a resort town on the make.

Many expats have settled here. The wealthiest have their homes along Pelican Shores Rd; at Eastern Shores, lined with beaches and shady casuarinas; and on Sugar Loaf Cay, just offshore. African-Bahamian residents are found northwest of Marsh Harbour in Dundas Town, a down-to-earth, even tumbledown suburb. A large population of Haitians (many of them born in The Bahamas) has settled in the central areas known as The Mud and Pigeon Pea, living in terrible conditions in rough shacks without sanitation or utilities.

The modern suburb of Spring City, south of town, was built to house workers in the lumber industry. Lumbering dominated the local economy for much of the 20th century but was abandoned in the 1970s.

Orientation

The town occupies a peninsula 3 miles northeast of the airport, just off the Great Abaco Hwy, the main road running part of the length of Great Abaco. At the southern edge of town, at the junction with SC Bootle Hwy, Great Abaco Hwy becomes Don McKay Blvd, which leads past the clinic, post office, and leading stores to Queen Elizabeth Dr, in the heart of town. (SC Bootle Hwy leads northwest to Treasure Cay.)

Queen Elizabeth Dr leads west to the mail-boat dock and Dundas Town and east to Bay St, running along the south shore

78° W

Walker's Cay   Seal Cay   Grand Cay

Great Sale Cay

Sponge Cay

Grand Bahama

Abacos

| 0 | 10 | 20 km |

| 0 | 5 | 10 miles |

PLACES TO STAY
1 Tangelo Hotel
4 Sea Shell
5 Different of Abaco Nature
   Park & Bonefish Club
9 Hole-in-the-Wall Lighthouse

PLACES TO EAT
5 Different of Abaco
6 Pete's Pub
8 Leanie's Restaurant & Grocery;
   Trevor's Midway Restaurant,
   Bar & Lounge

OTHER
2 Gas Station
3 Green Turtle Ferry Dock
5 Different of Abaco Nature Park
6 Art Gallery, Bronze Art Foundry
7 Lighthouse
9 Hole-in-the-Wall Lighthouse

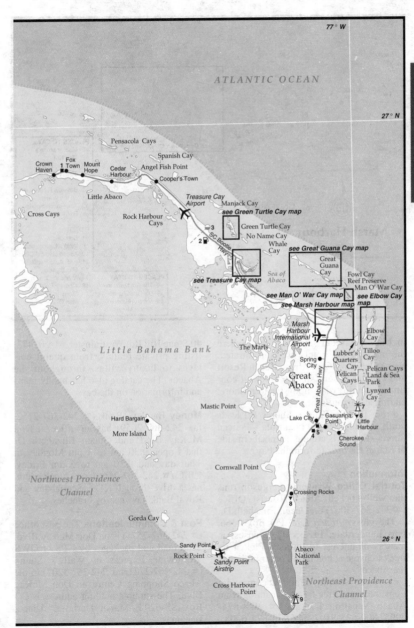

ABACOS

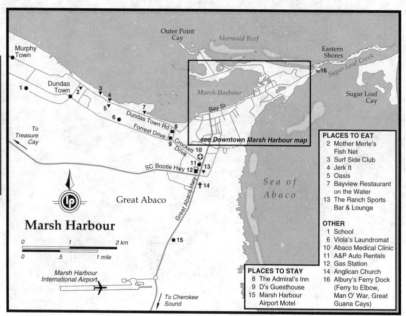

PLACES TO EAT
2 Mother Merle's Fish Net
3 Surf Side Club
4 Jerk It
5 Oasis
7 Bayview Restaurant on the Water
13 The Ranch Sports Bar & Lounge

OTHER
1 School
6 Viola's Laundromat
10 Abaco Medical Clinic
11 A&P Auto Rentals
12 Gas Station
14 Anglican Church
16 Albury's Ferry Dock (Ferry to Elbow, Man O' War, Great Guana Cays)

PLACES TO STAY
8 The Admiral's Inn
9 D's Guesthouse
15 Marsh Harbour Airport Motel

of Marsh Harbour's touristy bay, where the marinas and hotels are concentrated. Bay St leads past the Abaco Beach Resort and ends at Albury's Ferry Dock; it continues as a dirt road along Eastern Shore, ending at Parrot Point.

From Bay St, Pelican Shores Rd leads north around a second peninsula – Pelican Shore – that curls around the northern side of Marsh Harbour to form the bay.

Information
Tourist Office Wynsome Ferguson runs the well-stocked Abaco Tourist Office (☎ 242-367-3067) on Queen Elizabeth Dr.

The glossy *Abaco Life*, PO Box 1366, Fort Lauderdale, FL 33302, focuses on matters of interest to tourists. Pick it up free of charge at hotels and other outlets in the Abacos.

If you're seeking rental accommodations, request a free 64-page catalog from Abaco Vacation Rentals (☎ 978-874-5995, 800-633-9197, fax 978-874-6308),

40 Stone Hill Rd, Westminster, MA 01473, listing private rentals, from quaint cottages to luxury villas, throughout the Abacos. The catalog also has handy maps and information on the cays.

Money Barclays Bank (☎ 242-367-2152, fax 242-367-2659) has an office at Don McKay Blvd and Queen Elizabeth Dr that's open 9:30 am to 3 pm Monday to Thursday and 9:30 am to 5 pm Friday. CIBC (☎ 242-367-2166), one block south, has a drive-through teller. Scotiabank and Royal Bank have nearby branches.

Post & Communications The post office (☎ 242-367-2571) is on Don McKay Blvd. Send mail and packages by UPS or GWS Worldwide Express at Wally's Studio (☎ 242-367-2722, fax 242-367-3207) in the Abaco Shopping Centre on Don McKay Blvd. The studio's mailing address is PO Box SS-6293, Marsh Harbour, Abaco, Bahamas.

ABACOS

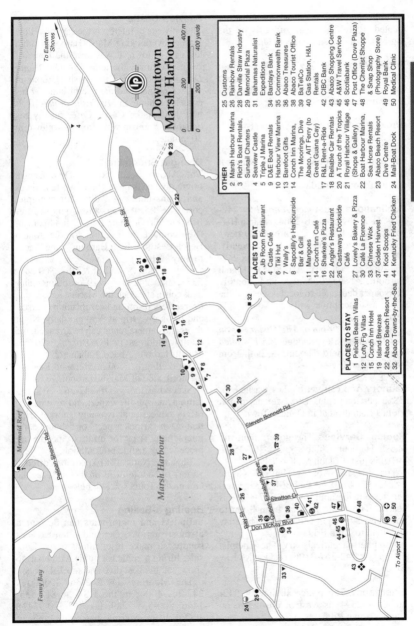

Downtown
Marsh Harbour

To Eastern
Shores

To Airport

Fanny Bay

Mermaid Reef

Marsh Harbour

Pelican Shores Rd

Bay St

Bay St

Queen Elizabeth Drive

Don McKay Blvd

Stratton Dr

Steven Bonnett Rd

0   200   400 m
0   200   400 yards

PLACES TO STAY
1   Pelican Beach Villas
12 Lofty Fig Villas
15 Conch Inn Hotel
19 Island Breezes
22 Abaco Beach Resort
32 Abaco Towns-by-the-Sea

PLACES TO EAT
2   Jib Room Restaurant
4   Castle Café
6   Tiki Hut
7   Wally's
8   Sapodilly's Harbourside
    Bar & Grill
11 Mangoes
14 Conch Inn Café
16 Sharkee's Pizza
26 Angler's Restaurant
    Castaways Dockside
    Café
27 Lovely's Bakery & Pizza
30 Café La Florence
33 Chinese Wok
37 Golden Harvest
41 Kool Scoops
44 Kentucky Fried Chicken

OTHER
2   Marsh Harbour Marina
3   Rich's Boat Rentals,
    Sunsail Charters
4   Seaview Castle
5   Triple J Marina
9   D&E Boat Rentals
10 Harbour View Marina
13 Barefoot Gifts
14 Conch Inn Marina,
    The Moorings, Dive
    Abaco, AIT Ferry (to
    Great Guana Cay)
17 R&L Rent-a-Ride
18 Reliable Car Rentals
20 A Touch of the Tropics
21 Royal Harbour Village
    (Shops & Gallery)
22 Boat Harbour Marina,
    Sea Horse Rentals
23 Abaco Beach Resort
    Dive Centre
24 Mail-Boat Dock
25 Customs
26 Rainbow Rentals
28 Darville Straw Industry
29 Memorial Plaza
31 Bahamas Naturalist
    Expeditions
34 Barclays Bank
35 Commonwealth Bank
36 Abaco Treasures
38 Abaco Tourist Office
39 BaTelCo
40 Gas Station, H&L
    Rentals
42 CIBC Bank
43 Abaco Shopping Centre
45 A&W Travel Service
46 Scotiabank
47 Post Office (Dove Plaza)
48 The Chemist Shoppe
    (Photography Store)
    & Snap Shop
49 Royal Bank
50 Medical Clinic

Public telephone booths are prominently located. BaTelCo's main office is on the south side of Queen Elizabeth Dr.

Travel Agencies Try the Travel Spot (☎ 242-367-2817, fax 242-367-3018) on Queen Elizabeth Dr, or A&W Travel Service near the Abaco Shopping Centre.

Bookstore The Loyalist Shoppe (☎ 242-367-2701), at Don McKay Blvd and Queen Elizabeth Dr, sells paperbacks plus local and foreign newspapers and magazines; it is open 9 am to 5 pm Monday to Friday and until noon Saturday.

Publications The *Abaco Journal* (☎ 242-367-2580), PO Box AB-20642, Marsh Harbour, Abaco, Bahamas, is a monthly news journal; subscriptions cost US$20 yearly. *The Abaconian* (☎ 242-367-2677, fax 242-367-3677), PO Box AB-20551, Marsh Harbour, Abaco, Bahamas, is a monthly newspaper dedicated to local issues and the news; a subscription will cost you US$24 yearly.

Also look for *Abaco: The History of an Out Island* by Steve Dodge and *I Wanted Wings* by Leonard Thompson, both from White Sound Press.

Laundry You can get clothes washed for US$2 per load (plus US$2 for drying) at Viola's Laundromat in Dundas Town.

Medical Services The government-run Marsh Harbour Clinic (☎ 242-367-2510/4010) is just off Don McKay Blvd.

The private Abaco Medical Clinic (☎ 242-367-4240, fax 242-367-3933; emergencies outside hours ☎ 242-367-3159) is nearby. The clinic is open from 9 am to noon and 2 to 4 pm Monday to Thursday and 9 am to 2 pm Friday.

For pharmaceuticals, try The Chemist Shoppe (☎ 242-367-3106) on Don McKay Blvd.

Emergency The police station (☎ 242-367-2560/2594) is west of downtown on Dundas Town Rd.

Seaview Castle
The only site of interest is the canary-yellow 'castle' overlooking Marsh Harbour from a hill east of town. It was once the home of Evans Cottman, the author of *Out Island Doctor*, who settled in Marsh Harbour in 1944. Cottman told the tale of building his crenelated home in *My Castle in the Air*. It now houses the Castle Café, run by his daughter. You can walk from downtown in 20 minutes.

Diving & Snorkeling
The Abaco Beach Resort Dive Centre offers dive packages. Three two-tank dives and a one-tank night dive, for example, cost US$225. It offers dive tours in English, French, German, Italian, and Spanish. (See contact information for the Abaco Beach Resort & Boat Harbour in the Places to Stay section.)

Dive Abaco (☎ 242-367-2787, 800-247-5338, fax 242-367-4779, captain@internetfl.com), at Conch Inn Marina, rents scuba gear, offers resort and certification courses, and has a dive trip at 9:30 am daily. Night dives and camera rental can be arranged; the mailing address is PO Box AB-20555, Marsh Harbour, Abaco, Bahamas.

Snorkeling is good at Mermaid Reef on the north side of Marsh Harbour.

Skeet LaChance (☎ 242-367-2014), a famous marine-life expert and divemaster, offers educational two-day snorkel trips that teach various aspects of fish and coral interaction. Trips for up to six people are preceded by a slide presentation.

Bahamas Naturalist Expeditions offers a variety of snorkel trips on its tours; see the Organized Tours section, below.

Boating & Sailing
Sailboats and motorboats can be rented at most marinas. Demand often exceeds supply, so make reservations early. Consider hiring a guide (or guide with boat) to show you the best dive and snorkel spots.

The Moorings (☎ 242-367-4000, fax 242-367-4004; in the USA ☎ 813-535-1446, 800-535-7289, fax 813-530-9747), at Conch Inn Marina, has seven types of vessel for rent, including sailboats from 35 to 46 feet and catamarans, all fully equipped, with CD/stereo, snorkel gear, and dinghy. Rates vary according to season, beginning at US$260/1820 daily/weekly and rising to US$435/3045. Three-day weekend specials are offered. Skippers, cooks, sailboards, and kayaks are available. In The Bahamas write PO Box AB-20469, Marsh Harbour, Abaco, Bahamas; in the USA write 19345 US Hwy 19 N, Clearwater, FL 33764.

Sea Horse Rentals (☎ 242-367-2513, fax 242-367-2516), at Boat Harbour Marina, has 18- to 24-foot boats for US$80 to US$135 daily, US$495 to US$800 weekly. Its postal address is PO Box AB-20013, Marsh Harbour, Abaco, Bahamas.

The same marina hosts Florida Yacht Charters (☎ 242-367-4853, fax 242-367-4854; in the USA ☎ 305-532-8600, 800-537-0050, fax 305-535-3179, boat@floridayacht.com), which rents boats from US$1200 weekly, offers four-day 'mini-vacations' from US$750, and also has 'day-sails' from US$250. The local mailing address is PO Box AB-20511, Marsh Harbour, Abaco, Bahamas; in the USA write 1290 5th St, Miami Beach, FL 33139.

Also try the following rental agencies:

D&E Boat Rentals, Harbour View Marina
   (☎ 242-367-2182)
Laysue Rentals, Triple J Marina
   (☎ 242-367-4414)
Rainbow Rentals, Union Jack Dock
   (☎ 242-367-4602, fax 242-367-4601)
Rich's Boat Rentals, between Sunsail Charters
   and Fish House
   (☎ 242-367-2742, fax 242-367-2682)

Sport Fishing & Bonefishing

Any marina can arrange sport fishing. Captain Justin Sands (☎ 242-367-3526), PO Box AB-20499, Marsh Harbour, Abaco, Bahamas, will take you bonefishing.

In April the Boat Harbour All Fish Tournament and the North Abaco Championship are held in Marsh Harbour. The Penny Turtle Billfish Tournament is hosted by the Abaco Beach Resort in May. In June the resort hosts the Boat Harbour Championship.

Boat Excursions

The *William H Albury*, a schooner built on Man O' War Cay in 1963, sails weeklong and weekend passages from Marsh Harbour to Little Harbour and Green Turtle Cay for US$150 per day. For details, call Joe Maggio (in the USA ☎ 305-442-9697).

Organized Tours

Bahamas Naturalist Expeditions (BNE, ☎ 242-367-4505, 'BNE Tours' VHF channel 65A), an ecotourism company, offers nature tours exploring the Abacos' wilder side. Its all-day 'Wildlife Tour of Great Abaco' includes a nature walk and bird watching in Abaco National Park and costs US$85; an all-day 'Marls Tour' includes bird watching and blue-hole snorkeling and costs US$95; an all-day 'Wild Dolphin Tour' features dolphin watching and snorkeling in Pelican Cays Land & Sea Park and costs US$95. It also has a half-day (US$50) and full-day (US$95) 'Wildlife Tour of the Sea of Abaco,' combining bird watching, dolphin watching, and snorkeling. Trips include snacks and a deli lunch. Weeklong kayaking, sailing, and camping expeditions are also available.

Special Events

Regatta Week is held in July in Marsh Harbour and other towns, featuring sailing races and festivities. In August the Great Abaco Triathlon is held, including a triathlon for kids and a 'Sprintman' race. Contact the Abaco Tourist Office (see the Information section).

Places to Stay

Bahamians tend to lay their heads at less touristed properties, such as *The Admiral's Inn* (☎ 242-367-2022), a modest property on the edge of Dundas Town, with six simple rooms for US$50 each.

A better option is *D's Guesthouse* (☎ 242-367-3980), at the corner of Crockett and Forrest Drs on the west edge of town. It has six one-bedroom units and also two two-bedroom units in a modern home for US$75. All are clean, with lots of light and simple yet pleasant furnishings. They have air-con, TV, refrigerator, microwave oven, and coffeepot. A small pool and deck were planned. There's a small grocery store next door. The guesthouse's mailing address is PO Box AB-20655, Marsh Harbour, Abaco, Bahamas.

Alternately, try *Pete & Gay Guest House* (☎ 242-366-4139).

I like *Lofty Fig Villas* (☎ /fax 242-367-2681), on Bay St, a calming place tenderly cared for by owner Sid Dawes, comprising six spacious, canary-yellow, air-con efficiency cottages in a serene setting centered on a small pool. Each has a queen-size bed, sofa bed, bright tropical colors, heaps of light, and a screened patio opening onto the lush lawn. Rates are US$80/530 nightly/weekly mid-September through mid-December, US$98/637 the rest of the year. A third person costs US$10/15. Its postal address is PO Box AB-20437, Marsh Harbour, Abaco, Bahamas.

If all you want is a bed by the airport, check into the *Marsh Harbour Airport Motel* (☎ 242-367-4402, fax 242-367-4401), which opened in January 1997 with seven air-con rooms, plus laundry. The spacious, nicely furnished rooms each have a TV and phone and cost US$85 single or double. It plans to add a cafe and swimming pool.

Island Breezes (☎ 242-367-3776), on Bay St, is a small roadside property with

Dive & Snorkel Sites
Dive Sites
Adirondack Wreck – Forty feet below the surface near Man O' War Cay lies this fascinating wreck, with cannon still exposed.

Barge – This WWII landing craft lies 40 feet down and is now home to myriad fish species.

Bonita Wreck – Another WWII wreck, this one is a freighter at 60 feet below the surface, populated by groupers that like to be hand-fed.

Old Wreck – Encrusted by coral and undulating sea whips, this wreck has an octopus that lives in the anchor winch.

Pirate's Cathedral – This swim-through cavern off Walker's Cay offers a religious experience, with rays, parrotfish, and groupers.

Queen's II – Schools of dolphin frequent this spot at the outer edge of the Little Bahama Bank.

Sandy Cay – This cay claims one of the largest stands of elkhorn coral in the world.

San Jacinto Wreck – This Civil War-era steamship sits at 40 feet below the surface, guarded by a friendly moray eel.

Shark Rodeo – One of the Abacos' premier sites: You kneel on the seabed in 35 feet of water off Walker's Cay and watch sharks swirl around you as they feed.

Sue's Reef – WWII relics are scattered 30 feet below the surface; damsels, snappers, and grunts guard the ledges and canyons.

Tarpon Dive – Named for the game fish that swim along this wall, which drops 50 feet off Green Turtle Cay. You can hand-feed a moray eel here. And Big Ben, the oversize grouper, says 'Hi!'

ABACOS

eight modestly furnished, air-con rooms for US$85 per night. There's no pool or restaurant; the mailing address is PO Box AB-20453, Marsh Harbour, Abaco, Bahamas.

The *Conch Inn Hotel & Marina* (☎ 242-367-4000, fax 242-367-4004), on Bay St, has nine spacious air-con rooms, each with a queen-size and a double bed, cable TV, and tiny patio opening to a sand garden with kiddies' playground. Decor is simple yet attractive, with lively tropical fabrics. Rooms cost US$85 double year-round; each extra person costs US$10. There's a 75-berth marina, cafe, and small freshwater pool. The postal address is PO Box AB-20469, Abaco, Bahamas.

Pelican Beach Villas (☎ 242-367-3600, 800-642-7268, pelican@g-net.net; in the USA fax 912-437-6223), nestled amid casuarinas off Pelican Shores Rd at the head of the harbor, has six air-con, two-bedroom cottage villas with ceiling fans, kitchen, phones, and TVs, plus private decks with sliding glass doors. Rattan furnishings are enhanced by a tropical motif and sloped wooden ceilings. Housekeeping is available. Hammocks are slung outside. There's an 87-foot dock. Mermaid Reef lies offshore. Rates begin at US$130/140 single/double nightly, US$910/980 weekly.

Abaco Towns-by-the-Sea (☎ 242-367-2227, for reservations 800-357-7757, fax 242-367-3927) has 64 tastefully appointed

Snorkel Sites

Angelfish Reef – Want to be one with swarms of angelfish? Head here.

Blue Strip Reef – This is a fish-spawning area with lots of tropical fish.

Crawfish Shallows – This is the best place to find lobster . . . and sleeping nurse sharks.

Elkhorn Park – Octopi favor this site, which has acres of elkhorn coral.

Fowl Cay Reef – 'Gillie,' a friendly grouper, guards this reef.

Hope Town Reef – This reef has elkhorn and brain coral, plus schooling fish.

Meghan's Mesa – You'll find corals of every species here.

Mermaid Reef – No, there are no mermaids . . . but there are plenty of big green moray eels and schools of snapper.

Pelican Park – Eagle rays patrol this area, where sea turtles carouse.

The Pillars – Huge coral pillars are found here.

Sandy Cay Reef – This reef is known for spotted eagle rays and huge stingrays.

Sanka Shoal – This is the place to see puffer fish, which inflate like spiked basketballs.

Smuggler's Rest – An upright plane wreck where porcupine fish have taken the controls.

Spanish Cannon – A Spanish galleon hangs on the reef, with cannon scattered about.

White Hole – Grottoes and caverns surround a protected coral basin.

Wrecker's Reef – Once favored by pirates plundering treasures, today it's preferred by sea turtles. ■

two-bedroom self-catering units – billed as 'villas' – nestled in rolling terrain and facing the Sea of Abaco. There's a large pool, tennis courts, and organized activities. Some rooms are a bit dark, but the property is quiet. Rooms cost US$140/160 garden-view/ocean-view. Beachfront rooms cost US$200. The postal address is PO Box AB-20486, Marsh Harbour, Abaco, Bahamas.

The *Abaco Beach Resort & Boat Harbour* (☎ 242-367-2158, 800-468-4799, fax 242-367-2819), formerly the Great Abaco Beach Resort, boasts a Hawaiian feel, with tall palms and lush lawns sloping down to a small beach and the Sea of Abaco. The 80 handsomely appointed rooms have limestone tile floors, gracious contemporary furnishings, elegant bathrooms, kitchenettes, and private patios. It also has six two-bedroom cottage-bungalows with kitchens and private decks. All have air-con, phone, and satellite TV. There's also a suite. Rooms cost US$145 from mid-September to mid-December, US$185 the rest of the year. Cottages cost US$300/350. A four-day/three-night 'Out Island Explorer' package (US$780) includes airport transfers, out-island excursions, and extras. There's an attractive octagonal pool with swim-up bar, a kiddies' pool, tennis courts, scuba diving, and a gift shop and laundry, plus an elegant dining pavilion overlooking the marina. A major upgrading was begun in 1997. Its mailing address is PO Box AB-20511, Marsh Harbour, Abaco, Bahamas.

Abaco Vacation Rentals (see the Information section) offers several rental properties, including *Carambola*, a cottage surrounded by fruit trees on Sugar Loaf Cay, just off Parrot Point; rates here start at US$500 double for three nights. At *Coconut Palm Beach Villa*, custom-furnished island style, a car is included in the US$1010 weekly rate (for up to four people).

Places to Eat

My favorite place to breakfast is the *Conch Inn Café* (☎ 242-367-2319) at Conch Inn Marina. It's also open daily for lunch and dinner (except Tuesday). It serves soups and appetizers such as stuffed jalapeño peppers for US$4 to US$6, as well as burgers, including conch and vegetarian, for US$6 to US$9. Entrées cost US$17 to US$22. Try the tasty grouper calypso. The bar is famous for its Conch Killer. Bring a sweater for evenings.

Also try the US breakfast for US$2.50 at *Castaways Dockside Café* (☎ 242-367-4938), a funky diner-style cafe popular with locals. It also serves grouper fingers, burgers for US$3, and a steak dinner for US$9; it's open 7 am to 7 pm.

For lunch, head to *Castle Café* (☎ 242-367-2315), atop the hill on the east side of Marsh Harbour. Sandwiches cost US$3 to US$7. Gail Cottman's home creations, such as chicken-rice soup for US$3.25, should be washed down by the house drink, the Castle Creeper, for US$3.50. It's open 11 am to 5 pm Monday to Friday.

To be one with local residents, head to *Mother Merle's Fish Net* (☎ 242-367-2770), a down-to-earth spot in Dundas Town. It serves native dishes; it's open for dinner only. Several funky little snack shops line the road in Dundas Town: Try *Jerk It*, selling spicy jerked chicken, pork, and fish, and *Surf Side Club* (☎ 242-367-2762) at Dundas Point.

Craving Chinese or Cuban cuisine? Head to the *Chinese Wok* (☎ 242-367-4129), a hole-in-the-wall on the edge of Marsh Harbour, or the *Golden Grouper* (☎ 242-367-2301) in Dove Plaza. Each night the latter serves a different cuisine: Country-western is served Monday, Cuban on Tuesday, Chinese on Wednesday, Italian on Thursday, Bahamian on Friday, and international on Saturday. It's open 7 am to 3 pm; closed Sunday.

Want to try wild boar? Check out *The Ranch Sports Bar & Lounge* (☎ 242-367-2733), south of downtown on Don McKay Blvd, a satellite lounge that also serves wild boar souse.

Sharkee's Pizza (☎ 242-367-3535), opposite the Conch Inn Hotel, will deliver.

Abaco Beach Resort's elegant *Angler's Restaurant* (☎ 242-367-2871) serves some of the finest and most creative cuisine in town. Appetizers such as lime grouper with wasabi sauce begin at US$4; entrées such as curried shrimp madras begin at US$20. Breakfasts start at US$6. It's open 7 am to 10 pm.

The elegant *Mangoes* (☎ 242-367-2366), on Bay St, serves dinner specials – international dishes with a Bahamian twist – on a shaded deck. It also serves snacks such as popcorn shrimp and steak fajitas. Happy hour is 5 to 7 pm. Wednesday is margarita night.

For romantic, candlelit ambiance, try *Wally's* (☎ 242-367-2074), in a two-story house on Bay St with terrace and indoor dining. Entrées such as coconut shrimp begin at US$18. It also serves soups, salads, and sandwiches. It's open 11:30 am to 3 pm and 6 to 9 pm Tuesday to Saturday. Reservations are suggested.

For colorful, down-to-earth ambiance, try nearby *Sapodilly's Harbourside Bar & Grill* (☎ 242-367-3498), which serves native dishes on a deck with shade trees. Cracked conch costs US$7. It has burgers and sandwiches, plus a catch-of-the-day for US$19. It's open 11:30 am to 3 pm and 6:30 to 9:30 pm Tuesday to Saturday and 1 to 3 pm Sunday.

The *Jib Room Restaurant* (☎ 242-367-2700), at Marsh Harbour Marina, has barbecue specials at 7 pm on Wednesday and Sunday nights, with live island music. Take your pick of chicken or lobster plus ribs (Wednesday) or steak (Sunday).

The *Bayview Restaurant on the Water* (☎ 242-367-3738), on Dundas Town Rd, specializes in Bahamian seafood. It has a Saturday-night prime rib special and a Sunday champagne brunch; it's open 11 am to 11 pm daily. In a similar vein is the waterfront *Tiki Hut*, serving pork chops, peas 'n' rice, and blackened grouper.

Colin, the 'Conch Man,' sells all things conch from his truck. He usually parks about 100 yards east of the Conch Inn Hotel.

Desperately in need of ice cream? *Kool Scoops*, next to the CIBC Bank in town, has a zillion flavors.

For fresh-baked breads and pastries, head to *Flour House Bakery* on Bay St,

open 7 am to 6:30 pm Monday to Saturday; *Island Bakery* in B&V Plaza across from the Abaco Shopping Centre; or *Lovely's Bakery & Pizza* on Queen Elizabeth Dr. *Café La Florence*, a tiny bakery on Queen Elizabeth Dr, also sells homemade pastries and bread; sample their killer lamb curry for US$7.

You can buy meats, canned goods, and produce at *Abaco Market* in the Abaco Shopping Centre and at *Golden Harvest* near the public dock. *Abaco Wholesale* (☎ 242-367-2020) offers galley stocking for yachters, with free delivery.

Entertainment

Mariners gather at the *Sand Bar* (☎ 242-367-2871) at the Abaco Beach Resort. There's live music on Wednesday night at *Wally's*, with dancing helped along by Wally's Special, the lethal house drink guaranteed to wipe out your motor skills. It has live entertainment by Estin on Wednesday and Saturday; several other restaurants also have live music.

Taste-testing? Head to the *Tiki Hut* to sample their Sneaki Tiki. *The Ranch Sports Bar & Lounge*, on Don McKay Blvd, has dart boards, plus pool tables and satellite TV. A dance club gets in the groove on Friday and Saturday night.

Other favorites are *Sapodilly's*, with a pool table and two-for-one cocktails during happy hour (6:30 pm Friday); and, in Dundas Town, the *Oasis* and *Surfside Club*, two satellite lounges doubling as dance clubs.

A 'ladies' luncheon' is hosted once a month at *Mangoes*, where the house drink is named Hurricane Libby after Libby Roberts, the lady of the house.

Things to Buy

Several places offer duty-free watches, jewelry, china, and crystal. Try Little Switzerland, outside Abaco Beach Resort, and the John Bull Shop (☎ 242-367-2473) and Simcoe Jewelers, both next to Mangoes on Bay St.

Royal Harbour Village, opposite the entrance to the Abaco Beach Resort, has handcrafted jewelry at Sand Dollar-Abaco

Gold (☎ 242-367-4405) and a fabulous array of art at the Juliette Art Gallery, with originals and prints by leading Bahamian artists.

Cultural Illusions, downstairs, sells island-made batiks, dolls, and candles.

Don Wood – self-proclaimed 'Carver, Sailor, Rum Barrel Bailer' – at A Touch of the Tropics on Bay St, sculpts wood, gold, and other metals into stunning creations, from earrings to desktop ornaments such as turtles and swordfish.

Be sure to check out Darville Straw Industry (☎ 242-367-2649) on Bay St, where you can watch Mrs 'Parnell' Darville putting finishing touches to straw products at her 1851 foot-treadle sewing machine. She's also a whiz in the kitchen, producing jams, jellies, and coconut cakes. Her hats sell for US$10 and up; a cute little purse with floral motif costs US$4.

The Brass & Leather Shop, in the Abaco Shopping Centre, specializes in fine leather goods. Barefoot Gifts (☎ 242-367-3596), across from the Conch Inn Hotel, sells beautiful resortwear and jewelry, as does Island Gallery (☎ 242-366-0354). Mangoes has a large selection of T-shirts and resortwear.

Getting There & Away

Air Marsh Harbour's airport has restrooms, telephones, and a small snack bar. There's no gift shop or rental-car service. See airlines' international and Nassau numbers in the Getting There & Away and Getting Around chapters.

American Eagle (in Marsh Harbour ☎ 242-367-2231) flies daily from Miami.

Bahamasair flies from West Palm Beach daily except Tuesday and Thursday, and from Miami on Thursday, Friday, and Saturday. It flies daily from Nassau (US$60 one way).

Gulfstream International (in Marsh Harbour ☎ 242-367-3415) flies from 12 Florida cities and from Atlanta, GA, and Mobile, AL. Island Express (in Marsh Harbour ☎ 242-367-3597) flies from Fort Lauderdale, West Palm Beach, and Miami.

US Airways Express (in Marsh Harbour ☎ 242-367-2231) flies daily from Orlando and West Palm Beach.

Taino Air flies between Freeport (Grand Bahama) and Marsh Harbour via Treasure Cay twice daily (US$99). Abaco Air offers charter service from Marsh Harbour.

Boat The Boat Harbour Marina, part of the Abaco Beach Resort (☎ 242-367-2736, 800-468-4799, fax 242-367-2819), has 165 slips for yachts up to 150 feet and a complete range of facilities, including wet storage, cable TV hookup, and commissaries. Dockage costs US80¢ per foot in low season, US$1 in peak season. The mailing address is PO Box AB-20511, Marsh Harbour, Abaco, Bahamas.

The Conch Inn Marina (☎ 242-367-4000, fax 242-367-4004), another full-service facility, charges US40¢ per foot in low season and US60¢ September through March. Facilities include cable TV hookup, provision store, and laundry.

Mangoes Marina (☎ 242-367-4255, fax 242-367-3336) charges US50¢ a foot. Water is free for a stay of three days or longer. Cable TV hookup costs US$2 daily. Its postal address is PO Box AB-20529, Marsh Harbour, Abaco, Bahamas.

Marsh Harbour Marina (☎ 242-367-2700), on the north side of the bay, has 50 slips and a wide range of services.

Albury's Ferry Service (☎ 242-367-3147, fax 242-365-6487) operates water taxis on a scheduled basis to Elbow, Man O' War, and Great Guana cays (see those cays' sections in this chapter for details). The dock is at the east end of Bay St. It has a waiting room and snack bar. There's a coin phone here, plus a little beach if you want to kill time.

Abaco Island Transportation (AIT, ☎ 242-365-6010, fax 242-365-6487, VHF channel 16) operates a water taxi to Great Guana Cay four times daily from Conch Inn Marina (see the Great Guana Cay section).

The mail boat *Mia Dean* departs Nassau for Marsh Harbour at 8 pm Tuesday; the boat returns to Nassau at 7 pm Thursday (12 hours, US$45 one way). The vessel also stops at Hope Town, Treasure Cay, and Green Turtle Cay.

Getting Around

Car, Moped & Motorcycle H&L Rentals (☎ 242-367-2840, 242-367-2854, fax 242-367-4356), at the Shell gas station on Don McKay Blvd, rents economy- to full-size US cars from US$70/350 daily/weekly, with free airport transfers. It also has 100cc mopeds for US$35/175. It's open 7 am to 6 pm Monday to Saturday. Sunday pickup and drop-off can be arranged. Its mailing address is PO Box AB-20438, Marsh Harbour, Abaco, Bahamas.

Reliable Car Rentals (☎ 242-367-4234), near the Conch Inn Hotel, is open 9 am to 5 pm weekdays and until 2 pm weekends; its postal address is PO Box AB-20089, Marsh Harbour, Abaco, Bahamas.

Other companies include A&A Car Rental (☎ 242-367-2148), T&B Car Rental (☎ 242-367-4007), and V&R Car Rental (☎ 242-367-2001).

R&L Rent-a-Ride (☎ 242-367-2744), opposite the Conch Inn Hotel, has 80cc motorcycles for US$40/200 daily/weekly. Credit cards are accepted.

Taxi Taxis run up and down Marsh Harbour. A ride in an unmetered taxi costs about US$1.50 per mile. It's usually best to settle on a fare before getting into the taxi.

A ride from Marsh Harbour's airport to the Abaco Beach Resort will cost you about US$10 for two; a ride from the hotels to Albury's Ferry Dock will cost about US$4. The fare from the airport to the ferry is US$12.

Sue and Joe Knowles (☎ 242-367-3127), who operate Taxi No 81, offer tours.

Bicycle R&L Rent-a-Ride (see the Car, Moped & Motorcycle section, above) rents adults' and kids' bicycles for US$5/8/35 half-day/full day/weekly. Sea Horse Rentals (☎ 242-367-2513, fax 242-367-2516), at Boat Harbour Marina, has bicycles for US$10 the first day, US$5 per extra day, and US$35 weekly.

Loyalist Cays

East and north of Marsh Harbour lie three Loyalist Cays: Elbow, Man O' War, and Great Guana. (The fourth Loyalist Cay, Green Turtle, lies to their northwest; see the Northwest of Marsh Harbour section.)

ELBOW CAY

Elbow Cay, the most-visited Loyalist Cay, is 6 miles east of Marsh Harbour. **Hope Town**, anchored in a well-protected harbor at the north end of the 5-mile-long island, is one of the quaintest of all Caribbean villages, boasting about 100 superbly preserved and gaily painted old homes.

The picturesque hamlet (pop 450) was founded in 1785 by Loyalists from South Carolina (their 300 or so blond, blue-eyed descendants are still here, interacting – but not intermarrying – with a black population). Originally called 'Great Harbour,' the Lilliputian place has a quaintness that you may imagine only Hollywood could create, one contrived for tourists' pleasure. I arrived at the dock uttering, 'Oh, my God. This is fabulous!'

The town, pickled in aspic on the east slope of a splendid harbor, is pinned by a 120-foot red-and-white-hooped lighthouse. Two narrow lanes encircle the village, running past picture-postcard scenes silvered by age; the streets are called 'Up Along' and 'Down Along' (formally, 'Back St' and 'Bay St'), and each is about wide enough for two bicyclists. Most cottages and churches are painted white, with gingerbread trim and shutters of rich pastels, and fronted by gardens full of bougainvillea and hibiscus spilling their blossoms over picket fences and walls.

Today Hope Town is one of the most-visited sites in the Family Islands. A few locals still make a living by boatbuilding or fishing, but most rely on the tourist trade. A town council, however, jealously guards its treasure with strict building and business codes. No cars are allowed in the village.

ABACOS

ABACOS

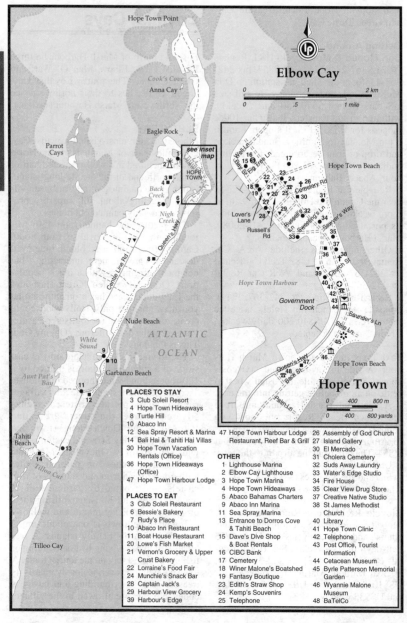

Elbow Cay

Hope Town Point

Cook's Cove

Anna Cay

Eagle Rock

Parrot Cays

see inset map

HOPE TOWN

Back Creek

Nigh Creek

Queen's Hwy

Center Line Rd.

Nude Beach

White Sound

Garbanzo Beach

Aunt Pat's Bay

Tahiti Beach

Tilloo Cut

Tilloo Cay

ATLANTIC OCEAN

Hope Town

Well Ln

Spring Tree Ln

Hope Town Beach

Lover's Lane

Russell's Ln

Sweeting's Ln

Russell's Rd

Cemetery Rd

Sawyer's Way

Church St

Hope Town Harbour

Government Dock

Saunder's Ln

Ship Ln

Queen's Hwy

Back St

Palm Ln

Hope Town Beach

PLACES TO STAY
3 Club Soleil Resort
4 Hope Town Hideaways
8 Turtle Hill
10 Abaco Inn
12 Sea Spray Resort & Marina
14 Bali Hai & Tahiti Hai Villas
30 Hope Town Vacation
   Rentals (Office)
36 Hope Town Hideaways
   (Office)
47 Hope Town Harbour Lodge

PLACES TO EAT
3 Club Soleil Restaurant
6 Bessie's Bakery
7 Rudy's Place
10 Abaco Inn Restaurant
11 Boat House Restaurant
20 Lowe's Fish Market
21 Vernon's Grocery & Upper
   Crust Bakery
22 Lorraine's Food Fair
24 Munchie's Snack Bar
28 Captain Jack's
29 Harbour View Grocery
39 Harbour's Edge

47 Hope Town Harbour Lodge
   Restaurant, Reef Bar & Grill

OTHER
1 Lighthouse Marina
2 Elbow Cay Lighthouse
3 Hope Town Marina
4 Hope Town Hideaways
5 Abaco Bahamas Charters
9 Abaco Inn Marina
11 Sea Spray Marina
13 Entrance to Dorros Cove
   & Tahiti Beach
15 Dave's Dive Shop
   & Boat Rentals
16 CIBC Bank
17 Cemetery
18 Winer Malone's Boatshed
19 Fantasy Boutique
23 Edith's Straw Shop
24 Kemp's Souvenirs
25 Telephone

26 Assembly of God Church
27 Island Gallery
30 El Mercado
31 Cholera Cemetery
32 Suds Away Laundry
33 Water's Edge Studio
34 Fire House
35 Clear View Drug Store
37 Creative Native Studio
38 St James Methodist
   Church
40 Library
41 Hope Town Clinic
42 Telephone
43 Post Office, Tourist
   Information
44 Cetacean Museum
45 Byrle Patterson Memorial
   Garden
46 Wyannie Malone
   Museum
48 BaTelCo

0   1   2 km
0   .5   1 mile

0   400   800 m
0   400   800 yards

The only sounds are the thrum of motor-boats, chimes of church bells, echoes of hammers on wood, coos of doves, and the rustle of the breeze in the palms.

The town has seen several periods of boom, beginning with the US Civil War, when Elbow Cay prospered as a base for blockade-runners carrying English goods and supplies to and from the Southern states. By 1887 Abaconian pineapples were Hope Town's primary export and were shipped to Jacksonville, FL, aboard locally built schooners. By 1897, however, the pineapple trade had been replaced by sponging, plus exports of turtles' shells, oranges, and sisal. In 1938 a blight wiped out the sponge beds and destroyed the industry, too.

In the early 20th century – the zenith of the sponging industry – Hope Town's population peaked at 1200 inhabitants, and Hope Town was home port to over 200 two- and three-masted schooners. Sponging fostered a local shipbuilding industry that reached its peak in the 1920s. During this era, Jenkin Roberts, acclaimed as the premier boatbuilder in the Abacos, oversaw construction of the largest vessel ever built locally, the 484-ton *Abaco*.

Winer Malone, the last of a great generation of Hope Town boatbuilders, still crafts traditional Abaco dinghies entirely from memory, with no power tools whatsoever, from trees he cuts himself on Great Abaco. (In 1997 he placed a notice outside his home and workshop stating that after 40 years of talking to visitors about boat-building, he no longer accepts callers or gives interviews – unless you're interested in having a boat built.)

Most of Elbow Cay is smothered in scrub and sea grape, favored by curly-tailed lizards and feral cats. White-sand beaches rim the Atlantic shore (including a nude beach 1.5 miles south of Hope Town).

North of Hope Town, a dirt road leads past Cook's Cove to Hope Town Point, the northern tip of the island.

Queen's Hwy leads south from Hope Town past White Sound, a large flask-shaped bay that opens to the leeward shore. The road continues to Tahiti Beach at the south end of Elbow Cay. There has been considerable private development in this area in recent years, which has brought a snobbishness that Elbow Cay heretofore lacked.

The intriguing history of the island is related in *A Guide & History of Hope Town* by Steve Dodge and Vernon Malone; it's available at Vernon's Grocery & Upper Crust Bakery in Hope Town.

Hope Town hosts Regatta Week in July, featuring sailing races and festivities.

Information

There's a visitors' information bureau in the peppermint-green building facing the government dock on Bay St. It is not staffed, but you can pick up leaflets here and glean information from the bureau's bulletin boards.

The post office (☎ 242-266-0098) is in the same building, though your mail will travel much quicker if you send it from Marsh Harbour. BaTelCo is at the south end of town.

CIBC (☎ 242-366-0296) has a branch, open 10 am to 2 pm Wednesday only.

Ida Albury at the Suds Away Laundry, on Back St, charges US$2 per pound for washing, drying, and folding. There's no coin machine.

The Hope Town Clinic, also by the government dock, has an emergency room and pharmacy. It's run by Letti and Dick Martz, a couple from New Hampshire.

Should you need pharmaceuticals, try the Clear View Drug Store (☎ 242-365-6217).

Hope Town has a volunteer fire and rescue brigade. If you need emergency assistance, call VHF channel 16, then channel 76; alternately, you can reach the individual volunteers at ☎ 242-366-0087/0363/0023/4044/0143.

Hope Town is the kind of place where children can run free without getting into mischief. There's a kiddies' playground on Bay St. Hilary Albury (☎ 242-366-0290) acts as a babysitter.

Elbow Cay Lighthouse

Hope Town is dominated by the historic, candy-striped Elbow Cay Lighthouse on the harbor's west shore. You can ascend the 100 steps for a picture-perfect view. Construction was begun in 1838 and completed in 1863 after lengthy delays caused by local wreckers fearful of the lighthouse's effects on their profiteering. They vandalized the structure and cut off water supplies to the laborers. But it still shines through a revolving Fresnel lens that magnifies light from a kerosene mantle.

Wyannie Malone Museum

This splendid little museum, on Back St, is a repository for an eclectic miscellany of artifacts and exhibits, including a unique collection of genealogical information pertaining to Loyalist settlers and Lucayan Indians. The kitchen and bedrooms are maintained as they would have looked two centuries ago. Even the outhouse is still in place.

The museum is staffed by volunteers from 10:30 am to 12:30 pm Monday to Saturday (hours are curtailed May to September); US$1. You can call ☎ 242-366-0033 to request a special opening.

Byrle Patterson Memorial Garden

This tiny garden, just northeast of the museum, has two bronze sculptures of dolphins and a seagull shaded by pine trees. It slopes to the ocean, where steps lead onto Hope Town Beach. There's a gazebo for admiring the view.

Cholera Cemetery

These mildewed graves, on a thread-thin lane named Cemetery Rd off Back St, recall the cholera epidemic that swept through Hope Town in 1850, claiming one-third of the population. Note the weathered Betrothal Bench at the crest of the hill.

Cetacean Museum

This tiny museum, in the old peppermint-green building facing the government dock on Bay St, has a few whale bones, charts, a fine mural, and a map showing sightings of whales in Bahamian waters. Eleven species have been sighted in recent years in and around Elbow Cay. Admission is free.

South of Hope Town

South of town, Queen's Hwy swings inland, then turns south as Centre Line Rd, emerging again on the dramatic, wave-pounded Atlantic shore. Nudism is tolerated along a portion of the beautiful beach. The road continues south along a narrow peninsula between the ocean and White Sound, a shallow, mangrove-lined bay with the Sea Spray Resort & Marina at its southern end.

A dirt side road leads west from Sea Spray to a small cove: Aunt Pat's Bay. The handsome yellow house on the hilltop to the right is the vacation home of singer Burl Ives. No trespassing!

Tahiti Beach, at the southwestern tip of the cay, is a stunner. It extends as a sandbar along the peninsula and is backed by an extensive palm grove. Much of the beach is underwater at high tide. Marine turtles still come ashore to nest on the champagne-colored beach.

At Dorros Cove, a half-mile south of Sea Spray, the road passes through a grand entrance to a private residential estate. A sign notes that access is barred to nonresidents. It even says, incorrectly, that there is no throughway to Tahiti Beach. This is a wicked attempt to scare visitors away from one of the most beautiful beaches in the country! The road and the beach are public property and you are quite in your rights to carry on. Don't let anyone tell you otherwise!

Diving & Snorkeling

Reefs off the Atlantic side are excellent for diving and snorkeling. The waters near Hope Town and the northern tip of the cay offer calmer waters and are easily reached by swimming from shore. Staghorn, elkhorn, star, and brain coral are abundant.

Dave's Dive Shop & Boat Rentals (☎ 242-366-0029, fax 242-366-0420) offers daily dive trips (US$50/65 one-/two-tank) and snorkel trips (US$30). It rents equipment. Hope Town Harbour Lodge (see Places to Stay, below) offers snorkel trips and rents snorkel gear.

Sea Spray Marina (☎ 242-366-0065) offers snorkel trips and rents snorkel gear for US$7.50 per day.

Bonefishing & Sport Fishing

Maitland 'Bonefish Dundee' Lowe, the local expert bonefishing guide, operates Wild Pigeon Charters (☎ 242-366-0266). He charges US$190/280 half-/full day for up to four people.

Sea Spray Marina (see Diving & Snorkeling, above) arranges reef fishing and bonefishing for US$100 half-day in your boat; it also arranges deep-sea fishing for up to four people for US$320/500 half-/full day, including boat.

Elbow Cay's weeklong, family-oriented Abaco Anglers Tournament requires little gear and costs just US$70/25 adults/kids. If you enter the bonefishing category, note that Maitland Lowe has won every year since 1972!

Surfing

The offshore waters boast at least six good surfing breaks on the south Atlantic shore, especially in winter months. The Bahamas' top surfing is at Garbanzo Reef, 2 miles south of Hope Town. You can rent surfboards and gear at the Surf Shop (☎ 242-366-0309) at Creative Native Studio in Hope Town. Its hours are 10 am to 2 pm Monday to Friday.

Boat Excursions

Lighthouse Charters (☎ /fax 242-366-0172) has catamaran sailing excursions for US$160/280 half-/full day for up to four people. Don Cash (☎ 242-366-0035) offers guided trips through the cays; US$300 for up to six people, US$50 for a seventh and eighth. Albury's Ferry Service (☎ 242-367-3147) offers sightseeing excursions for US$390 for up to 10 people.

Places to Stay

Hope Town The recently renovated *Hope Town Harbour Lodge* (☎ 242-366-0095, 800-316-7844, fax 242-366-0286), atop a bluff at the south end of Hope Town, is lovingly tended by Peter Kline and his sister Sarah O'Connor. It has 20 simply furnished yet brightly decorated rooms, many overlooking the harbor. Cottages spill down the garden toward the beach. Some have air-con; others have ceiling fans. All have picture-postcard views and lively tropical fabrics. Facilities include a splendid restaurant and bar, a small pool and sun deck, and water sports. Bicycle and boat rentals – including powerboats – are offered, plus snorkel gear. Year-round rates range from US$100/110 single/double harbor-view to US$110/125 ocean-view. An old two-story house, sleeping six, costs US$1000 weekly. The staff, including Junior, the amiable bartender, are super-friendly and efficient. They will prepare a picnic basket on request.

Club Soleil Resort (☎ 242-366-0003, fax 242-366-0254), on the west side of the harbor, offers a taste of the Mediterranean. The hacienda-style resort – accessible only by boat – has six air-con rooms, each with TV/VCR, refrigerator, and coffeemaker, plus a balcony facing the harbor. There's a restaurant, freshwater pool, and bar where you can sip the house special, the Tropical Shock. The resort has diving, snorkeling, and a complimentary boat service. Rooms cost US$110/115 double summer/winter, US$120/125 triple.

Nearby, *Hope Town Hideaways* (☎ 242-366-0224, 800-688-4752, fax 242-366-0434), 1 Purple Porpoise Pl, Hope Town, has villas in an 11-acre complex near the lighthouse. The views are fabulous! All have central air-con, kitchen, housekeeper, 'cathedral' ceiling, gazebos with porch swings, TV/VCR, and exquisite furnishings; many also have a private swimming pool. There's a marina and a sandy harborfront. Rates are US$140 single or double, US$190 triple or quad in low season; US$175 and US$250, respectively, in peak season. A one-week stay costs US$910 single or double, US$980 triple or quad in the low season; US$1099 and US$1260 in peak season. It offers ecoexcursions.

There are dozens of cottages for rent, represented by agents such as Tanny Key's *Hope Town Vacation Rentals* (☎ 242-366-0053, fax 242-366-0051), which offers 17 houses in Hope Town and 13 elsewhere on the island. Tanny has an office at El Mercado on Back St.

Other options include *Hope Town Villas* (☎ 242-366-0030, fax 242-366-0377), comprising two beautifully restored air-con Loyalist cottages; US$150/850 nightly/weekly for four people. Two-story 'Cozy Villa' overlooks a small park 50 yards from the beach; it has three bedrooms and one bathroom. The two-bedroom 'Harbour Villa' faces the harbor and lighthouse and has its own dock. Extra guests at Cozy Villa cost US$50 per week. A 50% prepayment is required. Write to Patte and Michael Myers, General Delivery, Hope Town, Abaco, Bahamas.

Amy and Mac Key's *Turtle Hill Cottages* (☎ /fax 242-366-0557) has beautiful cottage-style villas around a swimming pool, poised over the Atlantic on the outskirts of town. Each handsomely appointed, air-con two-bedroom villa sleeps six people. Rates – US$225/1200 daily/weekly – include use of a golf cart. The Keys also have 'Tres Jolie,' a small cottage for two, with king-size bed and open kitchen, for US$600/2300 weekly/monthly.

South of Hope Town The intimate and unpretentious *Abaco Inn* (☎ 242-366-0133, 800-468-8799, fax 242-366-0113), about 2 miles southwest of Hope Town, crowns a bluff between two beaches at the narrowest point of the island. It has 14 rustic, air-con, wood-shingled cabins surrounded by silver buttonwood, sea grape, and palm. Each has ceiling fans, porches with chaise longues and beach chairs, and hammocks slung between palms. There's a lively bar in the stone-and-wood lodge. Summer rates are US$75/90 single/double harbor-view, US$85/100 ocean-view; in winter, US$105/120 and US$120/135, respectively. A small lap pool sits atop the coral shore, where you can sit under a gazebo sipping a Cranberry Split (the

house drink, blending banana and gold rums with cream of coconut and a splash of cranberry).

The villagelike, pink-and-green *Sea Spray Resort & Marina* (☎ 242-366-0065, fax 242-366-0383) has four one-bedroom and four two-bedroom villas, all 'cottage-style,' with air-con, full kitchen, king-size beds, and sofa beds. One-/two-bedroom harbor-view villas cost US$700/950 weekly; the ocean-view two-bedroom villas cost US$1125. There's a pool, and the clubhouse has a pool table and TV. Free Sunfish sailing is offered, and surfboards, sailboards, bicycles, and snorkel gear are available for rent. There's a free shuttle to Hope Town; water taxis take 20 minutes.

Abaco Vacation Rentals (see Information in the Marsh Harbour section, earlier in this chapter) represents over 30 villas and cottages on the cay, from the deluxe *Bali Hai* on Tahiti Beach (US$350/1080 nightly/weekly) and the 200-year-old *Parliament Hill House* (from US$1235 weekly), to the *Bill-n-Coo*, an exquisite cottage that overlooks Parrot Cay (US$550 weekly). Most properties require a three- or seven-day minimum stay. Bali Hai, *Tahiti-Hai*, and *Tip-o-Tahiti* are also represented by Hope Town Hideaways, based in the exquisite pink-and-white cottage on Bay St.

Places to Eat

Hope Town Hope Town Harbour Lodge's *Reef Bar & Grill* is a good place to savor conch burgers, island nachos with conch salsa, or grouper fritters; meals average US$5. The caesar salad is excellent. Free fritters and veggies are served during happy hour (4 to 5 pm). Similarly down-home and upscale dining, from burgers to seafood platters, is offered at *Club Soleil Restaurant*. The owners will dispatch a water taxi to pick you up and drop you off in Hope Town.

Another favorite for Bahamian seafood is *Captain Jack's* (☎ 242-366-0247) on the harborfront; it's open 8:30 to 10 am and 11 am to 9 pm. Free hotel transfers are offered. In a similar vein, try *Harbour's Edge* (☎ 242-366-0087), a popular eatery on the water; it has a Saturday-night pizza special. Prices at both places start at US$4 for snacks and about US$18 for dinner entrées.

The simple *Main Street Grill* (☎ 242-366-4993) is a good place for burgers and sandwiches, as is *Munchie's Snack Bar*, serving pizzas, burgers, etc, in a little shaded patio with rough-hewn furniture.

The fanciest place is the *Hope Town Harbour Lodge Restaurant* (☎ 242-366-0095), where you can dine in or out. Breakfast is served Monday to Saturday, with daily specials (such as huevos rancheros on Friday) for US$6.50. A Sunday champagne brunch costs US$20 (US$10 for children under 12); reservations are required. Dinner is served 6:30 to 8:30 pm Tuesday to Saturday. Try the grouper and vegetable spring rolls for US$8.50, followed by a pizette, starting at US$12. Nightly specials include tempters such as coconut-battered lobster on Tuesday for US$21. The chocolate brownie and ice cream dessert, for US$4.50, is divine.

Harbour View Grocery sells fresh produce and groceries, as does *Lorraine's Food Fair* and *Vernon's Grocery & Upper Crust Bakery*, transporting you back in time with its country-grocery-store aromas. *Bessie's Bakery*, at Nigh Creek south of town, has been famous for years. Bessie passed away a few years ago, but her husband still bakes.

Robert Lowe (☎ 242-366-0266) has a *fish market* at his house on Russell's Rd.

South of Hope Town The *Abaco Inn Restaurant* has an eclectic menu, including vegetarian meals, but it has a heavy slant toward Bahamian seafood. Reservations are required. The *Boat House Restaurant*, at Sea Spray Marina, serves breakfasts from US$4, plus lunch and dinner, featuring caesar salad for US$7 and entrées (from filet mignon to seafood primavera) starting at US$17. It also has a Sunday brunch for US$16. Reservations are required.

Rudy's Place (☎ 242-366-0062), on Centre Line Rd, serves prix fixe three-course dinners for US$35, including hotel transfers.

Entertainment

Elbow Cay is kinda sleepy. The two happenin' spots are *Harbour's Edge* and *Captain Jack's*. The former, favored by locals, has a pool table and satellite TV, plus live music on weekends. Its Over the Edge drink (Matusalem and banana rums and fruit juices) is the result of a three-week taste-testing. Captain Jack's, which has a live band on Wednesday and Friday, is famed for its Jack Hammer, combining copious rum, vodka, and Tía María, and guaranteed to get you jiving.

Things to Buy

Several stores sell quality crafts, jewelry, and artwork. On Back St try Creative Native Studio (☎ 242-366-0309), Edith's Straw Shop, or Ebb Tide, which has Androsia batiks, locally made spices and preserves, and beautiful artwork. You can buy magazines here. Edith does hair braiding.

Kemp's Souvenirs, on Back St, has pottery, batiks, and spiced coffees. El Mercado sells jewelry and a wide range of resortwear and batiks, as does Island Boutique. For Cuban cigars, try the Fantasy Boutique on Bay St.

For a homegrown souvenir, check out Water's Edge Studio on Bay St, where Russ Ervin crafts superb woodcarvings with a jigsaw and hand tools. You can peer in through the half-doors to watch him at his workbench.

Getting There & Away

Hope Town Harbour has several marinas, including Lighthouse Marina (☎ 242-366-0154, fax 242-366-0171), with the only fuel dock; it charges US75¢ per foot. Hope Town Hideaways (☎ 242-366-0224, 800-688-4752, fax 242-366-0434) has 12 slips with metered water and electricity. It can take vessels up to 70 feet.

Sea Spray Marina (☎ 242-366-0065) has a 24-slip, full-service marina with dockage, exclusively for the use of guests at the Sea Spray Resort. It charges US85¢ per foot; boats under 22 feet may stay free.

Albury's Ferry Service (☎ 242-367-3147, fax 242-365-6487) has water taxis from Marsh Harbour to Elbow Cay at 10:30 am and 12:15 and 4 pm daily, returning at 8 and 11:30 am and 1:30 and 4 pm (20 minutes, US$8 per person one way or US$12 roundtrip same day, children half-price). A charter costs US$50 for up to five people, US$10 for each extra person. The taxi pilot will drop you off and pick you up at specific docks as requested. You can also charter the Albury's ferry to Green Turtle Cay for US$240 for up to 10 people.

A water taxi runs from Man O' War Cay to Hope Town at 7:30 am daily, returning at 4:30 pm.

The mail boat *Mia Dean* sails here from Nassau on Tuesday. See the Marsh Harbour section for information.

Getting Around

You can walk or bicycle everywhere in Hope Town. Vehicular traffic is banned along Bay St and Back St. There's no road on the west side of the harbor. To get there, you can hitch a boat ride from any of the docks along Bay St.

Island Car Rentals (☎ 242-366-0448) and Hope Town Cart Rentals (☎ 242-366-0064) rent golf carts for US$35/210 daily/weekly. They'll deliver free of charge to your hotel.

The Hope Town Harbour Lodge rents bicycles for US$10 daily. Sea Spray Marina rents bicycles for US$10 per day.

Abaco Bahamas Charters (☎ /fax 242-366-0151) rents boats from their base here.

Island Marine (☎ 242-366-0282, fax 242-366-0281) rents 17- to 22-foot boats from US$80/400 daily/weekly. Also try Club Soleil Boat Rentals (☎ 242-366-0003), Sea Horse Rentals (☎ 242-367-2513, fax 242-367-2516), and Dave's Dive Shop & Boat Rentals (☎ 242-366-0029, fax 242-366-0420), which charges US$65 to US$90 daily, US$345 to US$520 weekly.

Sea Spray Marina rents boats from US$90/490 daily/weekly.

LUBBER'S QUARTERS CAY

This 300-acre private island lies between Marsh Harbour and Elbow Cay. A few scattered cottages and villas peek from between the trees. It's a good place for reclusive escapades or prowling the flats for bonefish. There are secluded beaches and short nature trails.

There are no hotels. Abaco Vacation Rentals (see Information in the Marsh Harbour section) offers six properties, including *Refuge* and *Retreat*, two charming cottages on the undeveloped northwest side of the island. Each has solar electricity, propane refrigerator and stoves, VHF radio, and cellular phones. Rates – US$400 to US$620 weekly – depend on the number of people.

There are no stores. You'll want to rent a boat in Marsh Harbour (see that section) for access to the stores in Marsh Harbour and Hope Town.

TILLOO CAY

This 5-mile-long cay, a spitting distance south of Elbow Cay, is renowned for its bonefishing flats and as a nesting site for seabirds, including the rare and beautiful tropicbird.

One of the cay's handful of residents is Brigitte Bowyer, a German-born artist famous for her beautiful watercolor paintings of local scenes. She welcomes visitors to her studio. You can reach her on VHF channel 16 (her call name is 'Honka Loo') or write her c/o Post Mistress, Hope Town, Abaco, Bahamas.

PELICAN CAYS LAND & SEA PARK

This 2100-acre park protects the half-dozen tiny Pelican Cays, south of Tilloo, and their surrounding waters, centered around **Sandy Cay Underwater National Sea Park**, which has great snorkeling. The unique fringing reef provides a habitat for at least 150 species, including turtles and spotted eagle rays. The cays are nesting sites for bridled, sooty, and least terns. The park also boasts shallow coral gardens and underwater caves abounding with marine life.

Bahamas Naturalist Expeditions offers dolphin watching and snorkeling here on its half- and full-day ecoexcursions from Marsh Harbour. For details, see Organized Tours in the Marsh Harbour section.

MAN O' WAR CAY

Pop 250

Fish-hook-shaped Man O' War, 3 miles northwest of Elbow Cay, is as different from Elbow as chalk from cheese. Tourism has barely touched this diminutive, tendril-thin isle and its sole namesake village. As you slide through the narrow inlet into the harbor, the cay is deceptively quiet. A fistful of New England-style homes lines the narrow concrete lanes that creep up the slope. But most houses are modern bungalows, fronted by prim lawns and hedges, with plastic fishing balls hanging from trees.

Behind the misleading tranquillity, Man O' War Cay is an 'industrial boat-building center.' The shore is crowded with marinas and boat sheds that resonate with the thud of hammers and buzz of electrical tools. Virtually the entire population lives off the sea, sailing homemade fiberglass boats or 12-foot wooden crawfish boats. Dozens of Man O' War sailing dinghies dating back half a century are still being used and still in perfect condition, fun to sail and fast as the wind.

Shipbuilding on Man O' War dates back almost 200 years, anchored on Schooner's Landing. Fifty years ago there were about a dozen boatbuilders on Man O' War Cay. Each evolved their own distinct designs – you could tell who built a boat just by looking at it, such as the hourglass-curved transom of Lewis Albury. You can still watch the shipbuilders at work, diligently scraping bottoms, painting hulls, and in one case holding fast to traditional methods of carpentry; the majority, less concerned for their craft, fashion their boats from fiberglass to please the demand for faster, motorized boats. Today fiberglass is the lifeblood of Man O' War's boatbuilding industry.

The boatyards employ black laborers, mostly 'Bahaitians' (Haitians born in The Bahamas) who are also employed as domestic help. They live on the 'mainland' and commute to Man O' War. The island's population – 100% white – is renowned for industriousness, a product of that wholesome Christian lifestyle that still prohibits the sale of liquor. (There are no bars, but you can bring your own booze.) And if you go around wearing skimpy clothing, passing citizens may offer you an indignant reminder of their unwritten rules of decorum. You'll even find religious fliers outside homes for passersby to pick up.

For a history of the cay, read *Man O' War: My Island Home* by Haziel Albury (Holly Press).

Two narrow concrete lanes run parallel to the harbor (the uppermost, Queen's Hwy, continues as a dirt road to the north and south ends of the island). You can walk from one end of the village to the other in 10 minutes, but most locals get around by golf cart or moped (the young men zip around on motorcycles). No one walks.

Calm turquoise waters wash up onto a white beach that stretches lazily along the windward shore. Beyond the village, most of the island is scrub and hardwood forest full of lizards and birdlife. The wreck of the USS *Adirondack*, which went down in 1862, lies offshore in 40 feet of water.

Just northeast of Man O' War Cay, 6 miles north of Marsh Harbour, lies **Fowl Cay Reef Preserve**, a national underwater sea park. It protects a stunning coral reef and, ashore, the nesting sites of sea birds.

Information

The Royal Bank of Canada branch (☎ 242-365-6323) is open 9:30 am to 1 pm Friday only. CIBC (☎ 242-365-6098) is open 10 am to 2 pm Thursday.

Boatbuilding Studio

A handcarved sign on the waterfront points the way to Joe Albury's Studio (☎ 242-365-6082), where you may find Joe Albury standing in his shorts and plaid shirt amid a potpourri of wood chips and shavings in a large shed behind Joe's Emporium.

Joe, Man O' War's finest boatbuilder, crafts traditional Bahamian sailboats with a purist's passion, just as his great-great-great-uncle Billie Bo did 150 years ago when he turned from farming to create Man O' War's first sailboat. Joe began

ABACOS

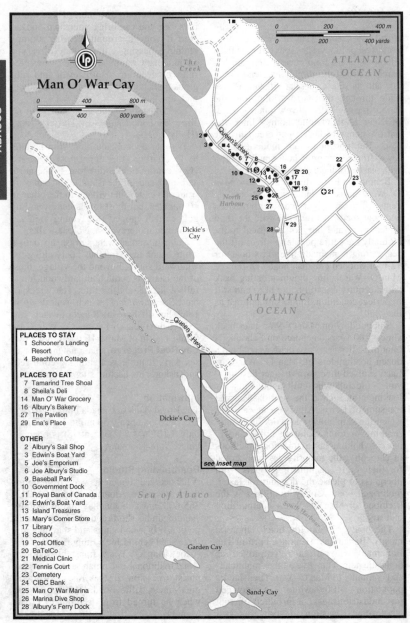

Man O' War Cay

PLACES TO STAY
1 Schooner's Landing Resort
4 Beachfront Cottage

PLACES TO EAT
7 Tamarind Tree Shoal
8 Sheila's Deli
14 Man O' War Grocery
16 Albury's Bakery
27 The Pavilion
29 Ena's Place

OTHER
2 Albury's Sail Shop
3 Edwin's Boat Yard
5 Joe's Emporium
6 Joe Albury's Studio
9 Baseball Park
10 Government Dock
11 Royal Bank of Canada
12 Edwin's Boat Yard
13 Island Treasures
15 Mary's Corner Store
17 Library
18 School
19 Post Office
20 BaTelCo
21 Medical Clinic
22 Tennis Court
23 Cemetery
24 CIBC Bank
25 Man O' War Marina
26 Marina Dive Shop
28 Albury's Ferry Dock

Top Left: Remembering the loved ones in Spanish Wells, Eleuthera
Top Right: Monument, Guanahani Landfall Park, San Salvador
Bottom: The glorious gardens of Eleuthera

Top: Sun, sand, and lunch at Nipper's on Great Guana Cay – what could be better?
Bottom: Sailing on the seas of rum: Funky Pete's Pub, Little Harbour, Great Abaco

carving wood at 15 when he joined his father, Lewis (a sign in the workshop reads: 'Lewis Uriah Albury & Son, Boat Works, Since 1927'). None of the Alburys have ever used blueprints. They've used 'the rule,' an innate knack for dimensions and perfect proportions.

Joe uses cedar, mahogany, and local woods such as madeira (the best timber for boats), which he cuts himself, slogging through the swamps and mangroves of Great Abaco. He then immerses the logs and roots in saltwater to season them against bugs and rot. Then Joe saws the wood, cures and planes it, and starts shaping the boat: mahogany for the transom, white cedar planks for the lower hull, and cypress above to the gunwale; rolled cotton fiber caulks the seams. The planks are dipped in boiling water and bent and twisted to follow the lines of the ribs. Next comes the cedar deck, fastened with brass and bronze affixed to mahogany beams. A handhewn madeira rudder and tiller are added. Then Joe carves the mast and boom from imported spruce, applying his genius with hand plane and adz.

Joe's boats are a thing of joy: all sensuous curves, with surfaces as smooth as a silk-stockinged leg. His hallmark is a lustrous white hull and deck with a yellow stripe, accented with a thin strip of red and a signature coat of lemon-yellow perking up the inside. The end product is nothing short of immaculate: a boat charged with character, purpose, and life.

Joe takes about three months to finish a 12-footer, which he'll sell for US$7500 . . . a bargain! Joe doesn't take orders. His boats go on sale when they're finished. 'I try to sell to people who will take care of it, sail it, and have fun with it,' says Joe, who always sails in the dinghy races popular on Man O' War. Visitors are welcome. Please don't step on any of the 30 cats lying torpid in the shade.

Sail Shop
Albury's Sail Shop (☎ 242-365-6014), on the waterfront at the north end of town, is abuzz with the whir of sewing machines. The hive of activity is overseen by Lois Albury, a 'bag lady' (her term) in the nicest sense of the words. Lois carries on a family enterprise started over 40 years ago by her mother, Selima Albury, who decided to spin off canvas 'ditty bags' from the residual material from her husband's sails and boat canvases. Sails are no longer in production.

Bahamian Sailing Craft
The Bahamas is one of the last strongholds of traditional boatbuilding, thanks to the country's popular work-boat regattas, which have fostered a revival of interest and innovations in design. In days of yore craftspeople built every type of vessel, from dinghies to swift schooners. Today the remaining handful of boatbuilders make only small dinghies with graceful lines. The boats have sea-kindly hulls, fashioned to perfectly suit local waters, and they're piloted by intuitive sailors who can smell bad weather and navigate by reading the seabed. (Every Bahamian sailor worth his or her salt, however, traditionally carries a 'thunderstone,' a smooth, hard stone that is said to bring luck.)

Most dinghies are about 15 feet long and carry only a mainsail (if the boat has a jib, it is a sloop or bare-head smack). They are remarkably strong and flexible, with long, straight keels and flattened, heart-shaped transoms. The boats are built without blueprints, guided only by rules of thumb whose origins are unknown. The stem and stern posts and other timbers are rakes and plumbed by eye alone.

The most beautiful and seaworthy dinghies have traditionally come from the Abaco Cays. The convex 'moon sheer' dinghies of Andros, with minimal transoms and drags, are faster. The flat-bottomed dinghies used in the shoals off Eleuthera copy the style of Chesapeake Bay boats.

To learn more, check out *Bahamian Sailing Craft* by William R Johnson, Jr. ∎

The 30-plus types of bags, duffels, totes, and cosmetic cases made at the Sail Shop – and sold nowhere else – all have their roots in the ditty bag that Lois' mum sewed to hold her little boy's marbles more than 50 years ago. Today Lois is assisted by her daughter, granddaughter, and four other women, who also fashion hats in a rainbow of colors.

Diving & Snorkeling

The Marina Dive Shop (☎ 242-365-6013) rents equipment (except regulators) and provides air fills but does not offer dives. You can rent snorkel gear from the shop for US$8 per day.

Places to Stay

Schooner's Landing Resort (☎ 242-365-6072, fax 242-365-6285) has four modern air-con 'townhouses' with full kitchen. Each two-bedroom, two-story house is roofed with red tile and tastefully decorated with crisp white linens and lace in the bedrooms, plus a TV/VCR, separate dining room, and private patio. There's private dockage, plus a bar and gazebo with barbecue pit and hammocks over the coral shore. Beaches lie a stone's throw in either direction. Rates are US$150 September to mid-May, US$175 the rest of the year (three nights minimum).

An 'idyllic' *beachfront cottage* is offered for rent by CTL (☎ 317-849-5308), 6929 Creekside Ln, Indianapolis, IN 46220. David Albury (☎ 242-365-6059) rents two *houses* in town.

A one-bedroom, gingerbread-trimmed cottage – *Port Deck* – is available on Dickie's Cay, a sliver of land west of Man O' War. It's furnished in nautical decor and done up in light-finished pine. A dinghy is included in the US$850 weekly rental fee. Contact Abaco Vacation Rentals (see Information in the Marsh Harbour section, earlier in this chapter).

Places to Eat

Getting breakfast is difficult. No eatery opens before 10:30 am, although you can

pick up fresh bread and pastries for your morning meal at *Albury's Bakery*.

The Pavilion, on the waterfront, sells burgers and sandwiches for US$3 and upward. It has barbecue specials on Friday and Saturday for US$9 and upward. *Ena's Place* (☎ 242-365-6187) also sells burgers, sandwiches, conch fritters, and homemade pies, along with Bahamian fare enjoyed al fresco on a shady raised porch; it's open 10 am to 6 pm Monday, Tuesday, and Thursday, and 10 am to 9 pm Wednesday, Friday, and Saturday.

Sheila's Deli (☎ 242-365-6118) offers a different dish each night. For US$10, I had steamed pork chops, mashed potatoes, coleslaw, and corn. It opens at 5:30 pm and serves until the food is gone. Don't be late. Locals arrive for takeout, but you can dine in Sheila's home or on the patio.

The only other option is the *Tamarind Tree Shoal* (☎ 242-365-6380), also offering simple fare.

Entertainment

There are no bars or social clubs. The village is still as death after nightfall. Every Thursday a 'social hour' is held at 5 pm at the marina. Bring food to share.

Things to Buy

Albury's Sail Shop (see the Sail Shop section, above) has a wide array of cotton tote bags, purses, hats, and water-resistant jackets that are considered a bit of a highbrow fashion statement among boaters and entertainers from Paul Newman to Perry Como. The jackets cost US$85, and you can pick up a travel bag or purse for as little as US$20 and a T-shirt for US$16.

Joe's Emporium, in front of Joe Albury's Studio, is an Aladdin's Cave of crafts, arts, souvenirs, books, wind chimes, sponges (US$6), and Joe's wooden jewelry boxes, cutting boards, and famous half-ribbed model boats (US$475, or US$680 including crating and shipping). Joe's brother makes custom furniture: An eight-drawer cypress dresser sells for US$2000, a mahogany rocker for US$600.

Island Treasures is a trove of T-shirts, blown-glass figurines, and jewelry. There are several other souvenir stores.

Getting There & Away

Facilities for boaters include the 60-slip Man O' War Marina (☎ 242-365-6008), complete with kiddies' playground, and Edwin's Boat Yard (☎ 242-365-6006), with two locations.

Albury's Ferry Service (☎ 242-367-3147, fax 242-365-6487) operates scheduled water taxis from Marsh Harbour at 10:30 am and 4 pm daily and 12:15 pm Wednesday (US$8 one way, US$12 roundtrip the same day, children half-price). Return service departs Man O' War at 8 am and 1:30 pm daily and at 11:30 am Wednesday. Charters cost US$50 one way for up to six people and US$10 for each extra person. Albury's Ferry Service also has sightseeing trips and charters to outlying cays.

A water taxi also runs to Great Guana Cay at 7:30 am and 3:30 pm Friday; and between Elbow Cay and Man O' War at 7:30 am and 4:30 pm.

GREAT GUANA CAY

Pop 150

Six-mile-long Great Guana Cay, 8 miles north of Marsh Harbour and 5 miles northwest of Man O' War Cay, is the least developed of the Loyalist Cays, with a tiny, unsophisticated fishing village that curls around palm-fringed Kidd's Cove.

The islanders earn most of their income from lobstering. Some of the parochial locals seem to disdain visitors, despite the weathered old sign that reads: 'It's Better in the Bahamas, but . . . It's Gooder in Guana.' When you're browsing the village, you may be taken aback by the skull hanging on a deck opposite Tom's Gift Store on the waterfront. It utters things like: 'I see you!' and 'Where are you going?'

The only noteworthy site is the graveyard on a rise behind the village; the village itself consists of two dozen houses,

an Anglican church, and a one-room schoolhouse. *But what a beach!* The island's claim to fame is a spectacular, seamless, 5-mile-long beach of white sand that runs the length of the Atlantic shore. Several little beaches lie tucked into coves on the leeward shore; a reef runs the length of the cay, 50 feet offshore; and several uninhabited islands lie close at hand. Wild dolphins occasionally call in to frolic in Kidd's Cove.

Cruise ships used to ferry passengers ashore for a few hours on the diamond-dust beach. Most visitors today, however, are day-trippers from Marsh Harbour. A 60-slip marina and 300-foot breakwater are in the works, and new restaurants are planned. The Ritz-Carlton hotel chain reportedly is considering erecting a deluxe 150-room hotel and golf course. And there has been a bit of a boom in home construction to the north during recent years, including a 215-acre tract where million-dollar homes are rising like mushrooms on a damp log.

A rugged sand-and-rock road cuts north through the scrubby undergrowth. At press time you could only travel about 2 miles before the road was blocked by a 20-foot-tall reinforced fence, erected by a politically powerful property owner. It has been

Lobster Fishermen

With luck, you may still see fishermen in 'smacks' up to 40 feet long, catching lobster in time-tested tradition: One man rows while the other looks through a glass-bottomed bucket held in the water. When a lobster's antennae are spotted waving from under a ledge, an L-shaped pole, or 'tickler,' is lowered to entice the creature into the open. It's then snagged in a 'bully' net attached to another pole. A large iron ring, about 4 feet across and spanned by a loose rope netting, is used to catch turtles.

Lobster, fish, and conch are kept alive in a well filled with seawater that circulates through holes in the bottom when the boat's under sail. ■

ABACOS

ABACOS

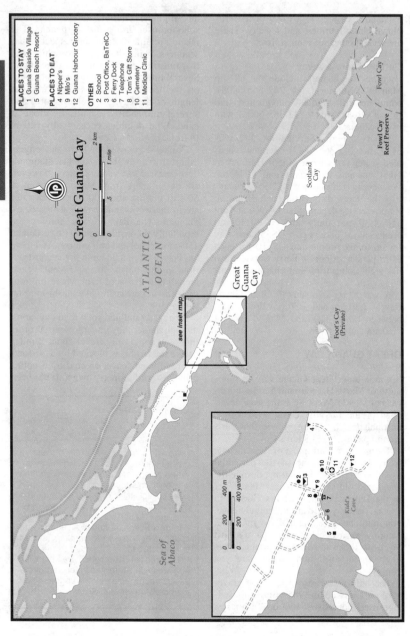

the source of considerable acrimony as well as a court battle to have it torn down.

July's Regatta Week features sailing races and festivities on Great Guana and other towns and cays.

Information

There's a public telephone on the waterfront across from Tom's Gift Store. It takes only phonecards, which you can buy at the BaTelCo office next to the school in the village, open 9 am to 5:30 pm Monday to Friday. The post office is next door.

For laundry, the Guana Beach Resort (see Places to Stay, below) charges US$4 per wash and US$4 per dry.

Activities

Great Guana has superb snorkeling inside the reef along its windward shore; you can rent gear from Tom's Gift Store (see the Things to Buy section) for US$5 per day. You can rent fishing gear at Kidd's Cove Rentals (☎ 242-365-5046).

The Guana Beach Resort offers day trips (with lunch) to Marsh Harbour and dinner cruises from 5:30 pm to midnight.

Places to Stay

A new property, *Guana Seaside Village* (☎ 800-242-0942, fax 242-365-5146, guana seaside@oii.net), opened in November 1996 at Crossing Bay, on a lonesome beachfront north of the village. It has eight nonsmoking rooms, including two ill-lit suites with kitchenette. Cottages were to be added. The two oceanfront rooms have marvelous vistas through plate-glass doors. You can dine on the grassy patio or in the simple restaurant. There's a small bar, plus a poolside bar and grill. The resort has a small dock and a separate bar and grill for 'cruise-by' dining. Sport-fishing boats, motorboats, and tackle will be available for rent, and there's bonefishing right off the dock. Rates range from US$120 to US$145 in January, February, October, and November; US$160 to US$195 in May and August. Its postal address is PO Box 2838, Jupiter, FL 33468.

The *Guana Beach Resort* (☎ 242-365-5133, 800-227-3366; in the USA 954-747-9130) nestles in a coconut grove adjacent to the public dock. It boasts that it was the setting for the Visa Gold Card TV ad showing a couple stranded on an island, but there's nothing spectacular about the beach or the hotel. The eight beachfront rooms (some with king-size beds and kitchenette) and eight two-bedroom suites are spacious. Summertime rates range from US$125 for a beachfront room to US$190 for a two-bedroom suite; they rise to US$140 and US$210 in winter. Rates include water sports, snorkel gear, and water-taxi transfer from Marsh Harbour. Air-inclusive packages are offered from Florida; rates start at US$570 double. There's a pool, sun deck, hammocks, water sports, and volleyball. Boats as long as 150 feet can berth. At press time a renovation of the facilities was planned, including an expansion to 37 rooms and 20 villas. Its mailing address is 10240 NW 47th St, No 43, Sunrise, FL 33351.

A third resort, *Dolphin Beach Resort* (☎ 242-365-5137; in the USA 800-222-2646, fax 800-678-7479), was due to open in 1997, with up to 15 cottages around a four-bedroom central house that will operate like a B&B. The 10-acre site also will include nature trails, a swimming pool, and tennis courts.

There are at least five villas and cottages for rent. One of my favorites is *Penury Hall*, a loftily perched two-story cottage with a wide wraparound deck on two sides. It costs US$720 weekly with a seven-night minimum. It has two double bedrooms upstairs and a separate living area below; they're not rented separately, however. Call Abaco Vacation Rentals (see Information in the Marsh Harbour section).

In the village, *Seafan* is a harborfront home for rent; call Bahama Vacations (in the USA ☎ 603-659-8312).

Places to Eat

Tom Roberts of *Tom's Gift Store* (see Things to Buy, below) serves free coffee

ABACOS

and conversation at his shop every morning from 6:30 to 10 am.

The 'in' spot is *Nipper's*, a timber-frame bar and grill on a bluff overlooking the beach behind the village. It has a large deck with tables and benches painted in tropical pastels and shaded by umbrellas, with views over the beach. The menu includes salads, burgers for US$7, and a seafood dinner for US$14. A pig-roast buffet is offered on Sunday afternoon for US$15. It gets lively at night, when the music is cranked up. Nipper's has an annual Easter-egg hunt in the coral reef (eggs are painted with numbers corresponding to the prize; thus No 100 might equal a US$100 bill). Nipper is a monkey carved from a coconut.

The *Sand Dollar Cafe* has homemade breads and pies, plus casual Bahamian lunches; it's open 10 am to 2 pm Monday to Saturday.

Guana Beach Resort offers mediocre seafood dishes, steaks, and chicken from US$17. The resort hosts a 'Conch Out' on Wednesday night for US$15 and an island-style barbecue with bonfire, limbo, and dancing on Friday for US$15. The house drink – the Guana Grabber – should help get you under the limbo bar.

Guana Seaside Village has an island-style, hickory-smoked barbecue buffet from 12:30 to 9 pm on Saturday for US$14.

For groceries, try *Guana Harbour Grocery*. A crusty local named Milo sells fresh fruit and vegetables from a harborfront stall.

Things to Buy
Tom's Gift Store (☎ 242-365-5021) offers T-shirts, postcards, souvenirs, and bargain-priced Cuban cigars; Cohibas cost US$15 each. The gift shop in the Guana Beach Resort has postcards and resortwear.

Getting There & Away
The Guana Beach Resort has a deep-water marina.

AIT (☎ 242-365-6010, fax 242-365-6487, VHF channel 16) operates a scheduled water taxi from Conch Inn Marina in Marsh Harbour at 9 am, noon, and 4 and 6 pm, plus 11 pm on Wednesday (30 minutes, US$6 one way). Return taxis depart one hour earlier. Albury's Ferry Service (☎ 242-367-3147, fax 242-365-6487) operates a water taxi from Marsh Harbour at 3:30 pm weekdays, returning at 8:15 am. A charter costs US$80 for up to six people, US$12 for each extra person. Both companies will drop off or pick up at the Guana Seaside Village upon request.

You can also charter the *Guana Grabber* motorboat from Guana Beach Resort for US$70 one way.

Getting Around
Donna's Golf Cart & Bike Rentals (☎ 242-365-5195) rents golf carts and bicycles. Guana Beach Resort also has bicycles (free for its guests) and rents golf carts for US$35/200 daily/weekly.

South of Marsh Harbour

The Great Abaco Hwy runs from Marsh Harbour to Sandy Point, at the southwestern end of the island.

Little Harbour
I adore this tiny flask-shaped bay, 20 miles south of Marsh Harbour. The perfectly sheltered crescent bay is held in the cusp of crumbling limestone cliffs topped by wild lilies and plums. The spectacular setting is enhanced by a scimitar-shaped beach along the south shore, where Atlantic rollers crash ashore on the lee side of a narrow peninsula. A kerosene-lantern lighthouse looms over the bay. You can climb to the top for a view of the waves running in toward the reef and the wreck of the *Anne Bonney*.

A few expats have built their houses here, and the bay is popular with yachters and turtles, which swim around the anchorage. The Little Harbour area is protected by the Bahamas National Trust.

Bronze Art Foundry The bay is famous for Randolph Johnston's bronze foundry (☎ 242-367-2720) at the north end of the beach. Johnston, a Canadian, began casting bronze in his teens. In 1952 he settled at Little Harbour with his wife, Margot Broxton (an accomplished ceramist), and three sons. For the first few years, they lived in a cave! Johnston built an electricity-generating plant and a foundry and furnace to cast pieces weighing up to 600 lbs. Today his work adorns many Bahamian public spaces, including Rawson Square in Nassau. He died in 1992 after writing his autobiography, *An Artist on His Island.*

His son Peter still runs the foundry, where he creates marine sculptures and gold jewelry. You can take a guided tour; note *Nine Ages of Man*, a bronze piece showing figures from crawling infancy to the grave. The foundry is open 10 am to noon and 2 to 4 pm Monday to Saturday.

Johnston's works are sold in the adjacent gallery (☎ 242-366-2250), which exudes a Carmel-like artsy ambiance. The place is a repository for works by other leading jewelers, sculptors, and painters. It's open 11 am to 4 pm Monday to Saturday and Sunday by appointment. The mailing address is c/o Cherokee Radio, PO Box AB-20282, Marsh Harbour, Abaco, Bahamas.

Places to Eat 'Funky and fun' describes *Pete's Pub*, the beachside bar and grill knocked together from driftwood, with sand for a floor and T-shirts and ships' pendants for decor. You can sip grog at a bar shaped like a ship's prow and order burgers or barbecue from the open grill. It's a lively place when the sailors are in!

Pete's hosts a four-day 'Dolphin Festival' each May, featuring tennis, cocktails, fishing, more cocktails, the Pirates' Ball (costumes a must), and more cocktails. It costs US$30.

Getting There & Away The turnoff from Great Abaco Hwy is the aptly named Dirt Rd, a hard-packed dirt road 15 miles south of Marsh Harbour. The weathered sign is almost impossible to see; it's 100 yards before a sharp bend with a blue sign announcing, 'Cherokee Sound, Three Miles.' The turnoff from Dirt Rd is 2 miles before Cherokee Sound. Another short but daunting dirt road leads from Great Abaco Hwy

Nine Ages of Man at Randolph Johnston's foundry

over a hill to the bay; 4WD is recommended. Dirt Rd was being paved at press time.

A taxi from Marsh Harbour will cost about US$60 one way.

Cherokee Sound
Pop 150

The small, pin-neat village of Cherokee Sound, 25 miles south of Marsh Harbour, sits at the end of a peninsula jutting out into its namesake sound, surrounded by mangrove shores and miles of turquoise flats. The locals are descendants of Loyalists who arrived in 1783 and passed their genes down in splendid isolation for the next two centuries (note the short triangular noses typical of these parts). Little over a decade ago, the only way to reach this remote fishing village was by boat. Electricity arrived only in 1996, replacing generators hidden in the mangroves.

The clapboard and cement houses are raised off the ground. Most are painted gleaming-white, with pastel shutters and trim, and separated by neatly clipped lawns. The only sites of interest are a marble memorial to sailors of past days, outside the BaTelCo office; the Methodist Church, with its varnished wood ceiling; and the Pentecostal churches, from which hymns waft on almost any night.

Most of the local men make a living diving for lobsters, a dangerous business, and are often gone for weeks at a time. The younger lads – they'll get their turn lobstering in due course – go out at night sharking, looking for jaws to sell to the tourist trade in Marsh Harbour, or hunt foot-long *tiniki* crabs. The men still hunt pigeon and wild boar, too, in the pinelands.

The best time to visit is Cherokee Day, when a large tent goes up outside the schoolhouse, homegrown food is passed around, and everyone participates in quilt auctions and tugs of war.

Places to Stay & Eat There is no inn or restaurant, and there's only one grocery store: the *Food Fair* (☎ 242-366-2022), where Miss Lorraine can arrange cottage

rentals. You can buy homemade bread from Diane – that's 'Dy-yanne' – Sawyer, who will also cook meals in her home on request.

Getting There & Away A taxi from Marsh Harbour will cost about US$60 one way. See Getting There & Away in the Little Harbour section, above, for driving information.

Getting Around Locals such as Tommy and Trevor Sawyer take visitors boating for about US$75 per half-day. Noel Lowe (☎ 242-366-2107) will take you out for US$125 for a full day.

Casuarina Point

This small fishing village lies on the west side of Cherokee Sound, with a beautiful beach shelving into fabulous jade-colored boneflats.

Different of Abaco Nature Park Immediately west of Casuarina Point, Different of Abaco is a kind of natural adventure park where you can go bird watching and hiking in the extensive mangroves and pine forests. It bills itself as an 'eco-resort,' boasting a bird sanctuary and nature trails. You can rent canoes, and guides will take you bonefishing on the extensive flats. There are telescopes for stargazing, and you can commune with wild boar, 'Laro' the donkey, and myriad wildlife, and explore the replica Lucayan Village. The owner, Nettie Symonette, has also created a landscaped garden and intends to create a flamingo park and museum.

Prior to the park's creation, not many folks came this way. Hence the mosquitoes are hungry. *Take repellent!*

Places to Stay & Eat Rustic, eccentric *Different of Abaco Nature Park & Bonefish Club* (☎ 242-366-2150, 800-688-4752, fax 242-327-8152) has eight basic yet nicely furnished rooms with hardwood floors, two double beds, air-con, and screened patios overlooking the swamps. Rooms are a steep US$125 nightly, including all meals; no credit cards. You can also choose among 14 rustic thatched huts with shared bathroom. There's a well-stocked gift shop. The property has a large, surprisingly elegant all-timber restaurant that's gaining atmosphere day by day. The menu includes sautéed grouper and wild boar; meals cost US$16 to US$20. You can also buy bush teas, such as fever grass or Mother's Brew, for US$3. Different's postal address is PO Box AB-20092, Marsh Harbour, Abaco, Bahamas.

At press time Nettie Symonette was also developing a full-service 20-room beachside hotel – the *Sea Shell* – with nearby swimming pool. It was nearing completion in mid-1997, with 10 rooms already open. The rooms cost US$200, with all meals. I expect it to be a hit for bonefishing.

Getting There & Away Most visitors to Casuarina Point drive here. It's 1 mile east of the Great Abaco Hwy (the turnoff is 2 miles south of the turnoff for Cherokee Sound).

Sand Dollar Tours (☎ 242-367-2189), PO Box AB-20538, Marsh Harbour, Abaco, Bahamas, offers guided tours to Different of Abaco on Sunday, including swimming and shelling at Casuarina Point, for US$20 per person.

Crossing Rocks

This forlorn fishing village, 40 miles south of Marsh Harbour, lines the grassy shores of 2-mile-long Long Beach. The white-sand beach has rocks for tidepooling. The residents of the funky, fly-blown hamlet seem to barely eke a living from the sea. Surely the next strong wind will blow down their out-of-kilter shacks.

Crossing Rocks is named for the isthmus where Great Abaco narrows to its slenderest point.

Try *Trevor's Midway Restaurant, Bar & Lounge* (☎ 242-366-2199), on the Great Abaco Hwy at the turnoff for Crossing Rocks, for native dishes.

Sandy Point

South of Crossing Rocks, the Great Abaco Hwy sweeps southwest through vast acres of pineland and ends at Sandy Point, a picturesque fishing community backed by a coconut palm plantation, 60 miles south of Marsh Harbour. Fishing smacks are drawn up on the beach, and nets are lain out to dry. You get the picture.

The Walt Disney Company recently bought Gorda Cay, 8 miles offshore, as a private stopover for its *Disney Magic* and *Disney Wonder* cruise ships, beginning service in 1998.

There's a post office and BaTelCo station in Sandy Point, as well as a government clinic (☎ 242-366-4010), open 9 am to 1 pm weekdays.

Places to Stay & Eat *Oeisha's Motel* (☎ 242-366-4139, fax 242-365-6285), between the airstrip and settlement, has air-con rooms and a restaurant that doubles as a dance club. *Pete & Gay's Guest House*, at the head of the dock, has air-con rooms with TV. It, too, serves meals. The other eatery of choice is *Nancy's Seaside Inn Restaurant & Bar* (☎ 242-366-4120).

Getting There & Away Cat Island Air flies from Nassau to Sandy Point at 8:30 am Wednesday and Friday and 8 am Sunday (US$55 one way). Bahamasair has irregular, seasonal service to Sandy Point.

The *Champion II* mail boat sails from Nassau to Sandy Point at 8 pm Tuesday (11 hours, US$25 one way). It also calls at Bullock Harbour.

On Monday, Sand Dollar Tours (see contact information under Casuarina Point, above) offers a guided tour to Sandy Point and Crossing Rocks, including a visit to Different of Abaco, for US$30.

More Island

More Island, 20 miles northwest of Sandy Point, is the only inhabited island off the west coast of the Abaco mainland. The settlements of **Hard Bargain** and **The Bight** have a long fishing tradition and a wild, rustic spirit. The island has a medical clinic (☎ 242-366-6105).

Tom's Inn, near the airstrip, and *Gator's Inn*, in The Bight, have no-frills rooms.

ABACOS

Sheva Jones' *Cool Spot*, by the dock, and the *Sea View* both serve native dishes. You can buy groceries from *Queenie's* store.

Cat Island Air flies from Nassau to More Island at 8 am Wednesday and Friday and 4 pm Sunday (US$55 one way).

Abaco National Park

The pendulous udder of Great Abaco is smothered in native Caribbean pine and hardwood forest (part of Sandy Point Forest Preserve), much of it within the 32-sq-mile Abaco National Park, established in 1994 to protect the major habitat of the endangered Bahama parrot. About 1100 parrots survive here.

There's also an extensive limestone cave system to explore (the local parrot population is unique – the birds nest in holes in the limestone rocks), plus hiking trails, lonesome beaches, and incredibly wild and spectacular scenery along the Atlantic shore.

Hole-in-the-Wall Lighthouse

The dramatic headland at the southern tip of the island is dominated by this red-and-white-hooped lighthouse, looming over the scrubby shore and reached by a horrendously potholed and tortuous road that adds to the sense of separation from civilization. The whistling wind emphasizes the wild beauty. You can climb to the top of the lighthouse for even more stupendous views.

The lighthouse was recently leased by Bahamas Naturalist Expeditions (BNE), which has renovated the facility as a field research station and ecolodge (see Places to Stay, below). BNE is headed by Diane Claridge, a marine biologist who conducts research on whales and dolphins from the facility. Claridge is funded by a research grant from Earthwatch (☎ 800-776-0188, fax 617-926-8532, info@earthwatch.org), 680 Mt Auburn St, Watertown, MA 02272, a US-based nonprofit organization. Earthwatch groups spend 10 days here learning about the Abacos' marine mammals.

Organized Tours

BNE (☎ 242-367-4505, 'BNE Tours' VHF channel 65A) includes the park in its all-day guided 'Wildlife Tour

of Great Abaco,' departing Marsh Harbour and costing US$85, and in a 'Birdwatching Tour' that departs Marsh Harbour at 5 am and costs US$95.

Sand Dollar Tours (☎ 242-367-2189) also includes Abaco National Park, Hole-in-the-Wall Lighthouse, and the surrounding area on guided nature trips from Marsh Harbour on Thursday, costing US$45.

Places to Stay

At Hole-in-the-Wall Lighthouse, rustic *hostel accommodations* are provided in the lighthousekeeper's former home, an octagonal structure with dormitory beds and a simple kitchen. Nature enthusiasts can stay overnight or use it as a base for expeditions into the forest and along the shore. BNE plans to add tent camping, trail biking, and other activities. Contact BNE (see information above) in Marsh Harbour for details.

Getting There & Away

A turnoff for the park is signed 10 miles south of Crossing Rocks. The road runs south, straight and treacherously potholed, for about 15 miles, then gives way to a dirt-and-rock track that snakes through scrubland for another 5 miles. Just when you and your vehicle are about to pack it in, the lighthouse peeks over the scrub.

Northwest of Marsh Harbour

TREASURE CAY
Pop 1000

Treasure Cay, east of SC Bootle Hwy and 17 miles north of Marsh Harbour, is not a true cay but a narrow peninsula jutting from the mainland like a sea horse's snout. Its north shore flaunts a 4-mile-long, crescent-shaped white-sand beach shelving gently into a vast expanse of turquoise waters extending almost to the horizon. Treasure Cay Beach has been acclaimed as one of the 'ten best in the world' by *National Geographic Traveler*. True, it's stunning, but

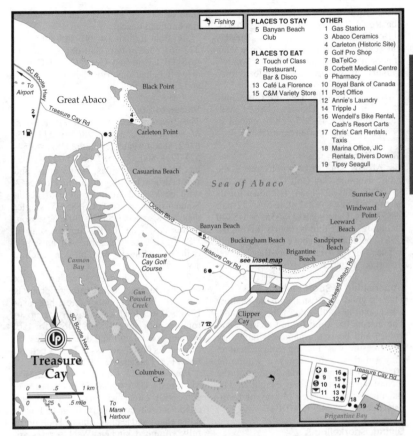

ABACOS

there are better beaches in The Bahamas. The beach is named in sections from west to east: Casuarina, Banyan, Buckingham, Brigantine, Sandpiper, and Leeward.

Treasure Cay boasts Great Abaco's largest residential and resort complex and is popular with North American buyers and with yachters, who call in at the marina.

The Abacos' first Loyalist settlement was founded in 1783 at Carleton Point, at the northwestern end of Treasure Cay; it was later abandoned and only overgrown ruins remain. In the 1950s the first tourist development in the Abacos arose here (thanks to Leonard Thompson, a colorful

character 'born in a hurricane under a coconut tree' who was instrumental in the birth of Bahamian tourism). An 18-hole championship golf course was conjured by legendary designer Dick Jones. The original hotel burned down in 1961, and its replacement has been shuttered since 1990. The cay now features a handsome modern complex of condos, villas, and hotel-style rooms. At press time Sandals, the Jamaica-based hotel chain, had shelved plans to build an all-inclusive resort here.

In May the Annual Bahamian Arts & Crafts Show is held here as part of the Treasure Cay Fishing Tournament.

Information

The Royal Bank of Canada (☎ 242-365-8119) is open 10:30 am to 2 pm Tuesday and Thursday. The post office is open 9 am to noon and 2 to 5 pm weekdays. Annie's Laundry charges US$2.75 per load for a wash and US$2.75 for drying.

There's a doctor at Treasure Cay Clinic (☎ 242-367-3350). The new Corbett Medical Centre (☎ 242-365-8288) opened in 1996; Dr Wilson is often 'gone fishin'.'

Golf & Tennis

The Abacos' sole 18-hole golf course, the public Treasure Cay Golf Course (☎ 242-365-8045, 800-327-1584) is known for its narrow fairways. Vital statistics: 72-par, 6985 yards. Games cost US$35, or US$40 including cart. Tennis courts here cost US$12 per hour. The above rates apply only to guests of the Treasure Cay Beach Hotel Resort & Marina; nonguests will pay more.

Bonefishing & Sport Fishing

There's good bonefishing in the shallow waters on the south side of the peninsula. The marina has sport-fishing charters and guides and hosts tournaments, including the Treasure Cay Fishing Tournament in May (in the 1996 tourney a whopping 1030-lb blue marlin was landed – the second-largest marlin ever caught in The Bahamas). Try Kingsley Murray of Kingfish Charters (☎ 242-365-0104).

Diving, Snorkeling & Other Water Sports

Divers Down (☎ 242-365-8465, fax 242-365-8508, VHF channel 16 or 79), at the marina, rents scuba equipment, offers dives (US$50/70 one-/two-tank; a blue-hole dive costs US$75) and certification. It has snorkel trips for US$35. You can rent a mask, snorkel, and fins for US$10. Its postal address is PO Box AB-22212, Treasure Cay, Abaco, Bahamas.

C&C Boat Rentals (☎ 242-365-8582) offers a snorkel-and-scuba picnic trip with a seafood lunch served on the beach.

Sunfish sailboats (US$10/25 hourly/half-day), kayaks (US$5/15 hourly/full day), and sailboards (US$35 hourly) can be rented on Buckingham Beach.

JIC Boat Rentals (☎ 242-365-8465, fax 242-365-8508) offers half-day excursions to Shell Island and Great Guana Cay. It also offers half-day trips to New Plymouth and Green Turtle Cay.

Places to Stay

The *Treasure Cay Beach Hotel Resort & Marina* (☎ 242-365-8578, fax 242-365-8362, abaco@gate.net; in the USA ☎ 954-525-7711, 800-327-1584, fax 954-525-1699) has hotel rooms, villas, condo units, and two-bedroom homes – 'Treasure Houses' – with decks and stunning interior decor. Standard rooms cost US$85/95 single/double low season, US$120/130 peak season. Suites cost US$115/130 in low season, US$175/190 peak season. All have two twins or a king-size bed, air-con, satellite TV, and patio.

The resort's houses sleep up to six people and are set in exquisite grounds with freshwater pools; rates begin at US$295/365 low/peak season for up to four people and US$395/465 for six people. Special golf and dive packages are offered. Its postal address is 2301 S Federal Hwy, Fort Lauderdale, FL 33316.

Banyan Beach Club (☎ /fax 242-365-8111; in the USA ☎ 888-625-3060, fax 561-625-3060), offers two- and three-bedroom condos, each beautifully furnished with rattan chairs and leather sofas and boasting a fully equipped kitchen. Weekly rates are US$1500 May through October, US$1900 November through April; the mailing address is 2720 Biarritz Dr, Palm Beach Gardens, FL 33410.

Abaco Vacation Rentals (see Information in the Marsh Harbour section, earlier in this chapter) has seven properties on Treasure Cay, including two *condos* and several deluxe *three-bedroom homes*.

Places to Eat

Locals frequent *Touch of Class Restaurant, Bar & Disco*, on the highway 100 yards south of the turnoff for Treasure Cay. It serves native dishes.

Café La Florence sells home-baked cookies, fresh bread, pies, and cakes. It has a patio.

The *C&M Variety Store* stocks a large supply of groceries.

Entertainment

A cocktail party is hosted each Friday evening at the *Tipsy Seagull*, a huge, all-wood bar festooned with nautical paraphernalia and overlooking an amoeba-shaped pool and sun deck.

Things to Buy

Abaco Ceramics (☎ 242-365-8489) has a gift shop, open 9 am to 3 pm weekdays. You can watch Yolanda Smith and LaPage Rolle handmaking and painting kitchenware and adornments in the workshop. A huge serving plate costs US$60. The mailing address is PO Box AB-22117, Treasure Cay, Abaco, Bahamas.

Divers Down has swimwear. Tripple J (☎ 242-367-2163) has a small selection of upscale gifts.

Getting There & Away

Air Treasure Cay airport is located 15 miles north of Treasure Cay. A taxi between the two points costs about US$7 per person.

American Eagle flies daily from Miami. Bahamasair (in Treasure Cay ☎ 242-365-8600) flies directly from West Palm Beach daily except Tuesday and Thursday; from Miami on Thursday, Friday, and Saturday; and from Nassau daily.

Gulfstream International flies daily from Key West, Miami, and Orlando; daily except Saturday from Gainesville, Naples, and Tallahassee; daily except Sunday from Tampa; and on Sunday from Atlanta. It also flies from Mobile, AL.

Island Express flies here from Fort Lauderdale. US Airways Express flies from Fort Lauderdale and Orlando.

Boat The 150-slip full-service marina (☎ 242-365-8250; in the USA 800-327-1584) accommodates yachts up to 140 feet. Dockage costs US80¢ per foot per day (less in low season), including cable TV.

The mail boat *Mia Dean* sails from Nassau to Treasure Cay on Tuesday; see the Marsh Harbour section for details.

Getting Around

Tripple J (☎ 242-367-2163) rents cars for US$75 daily. C&C Boat Rentals (☎ 242-365-8582) rents scooters. Wendell's rents bicycles for US$4/6/35 half-day/full day/weekly.

You can rent golf carts from Chris' Cart Rentals for US$35/175 daily/weekly, and from Cash's Resort Carts (☎ 242-365-8465, VHF channel 16 and 79) for US$20/35/189 half-day/full day/weekly.

C&C Boat Rentals has a wide range of boats, from 17-foot Bone Fishers for US$70/380 daily/weekly to 26-foot Novas for US$135/700.

You can also rent 20- to 26-foot boats from JIC Boat Rentals (☎ 242-365-8465, fax 242-365-8508) from US$90/490 daily/weekly.

GREEN TURTLE CAY

Green Turtle, 8 miles north of Treasure Cay, is the northernmost of the four Loyalist Cays. The town of **New Plymouth** (pop 450) is a time capsule and living museum redolent with Loyalist history.

The town lies on the shore of Settlement Creek, at the westernmost end of a hooked peninsula formed by Black Sound, at the south end of the island. The three-masted schooner that sailed into these sun-dappled waters in 1783 carried 500 New Yorkers (mostly Irish Protestants whose property had been confiscated by the victorious Colonials). In time the town they founded grew to be the second-largest city in the Bahamas in the 19th century, when it was tremendously wealthy. It had the islands' biggest church and bank and its best schools. Sharking, rumrunning, and shipbuilding are no longer important. But the sleepy storybook village has lost none of its venerable charm, thanks to its pastel-painted, clapboarded, gingerbread-trimmed houses and its lively churches (the daffodil-yellow Gospel Chapel, between Crown and Parliament Sts, is renowned for its rousing revival meetings).

ABACOS

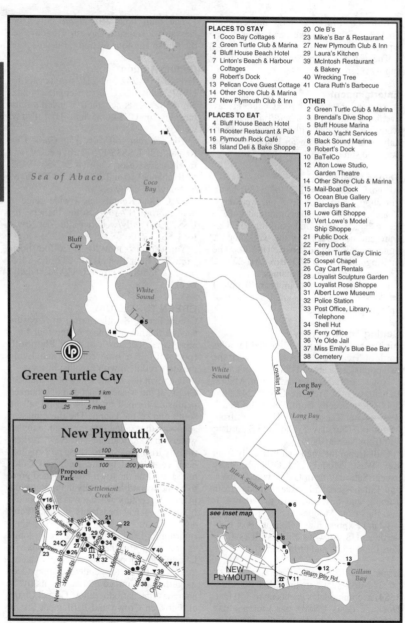

PLACES TO STAY
1 Coco Bay Cottages
2 Green Turtle Club & Marina
4 Bluff House Beach Hotel
7 Linton's Beach & Harbour Cottages
9 Robert's Dock
13 Pelican Cove Guest Cottage
14 Other Shore Club & Marina
27 New Plymouth Club & Inn

PLACES TO EAT
4 Bluff House Beach Hotel
11 Rooster Restaurant & Pub
16 Plymouth Rock Café
18 Island Deli & Bake Shoppe

20 Ole B's
23 Mike's Bar & Restaurant
27 New Plymouth Club & Inn
29 Laura's Kitchen
39 McIntosh Restaurant & Bakery
40 Wrecking Tree
41 Clara Ruth's Barbecue

OTHER
2 Green Turtle Club & Marina
3 Brendal's Dive Shop
5 Bluff House Marina
6 Abaco Yacht Services
8 Black Sound Marina
9 Robert's Dock
10 BaTelCo
12 Alton Lowe Studio, Garden Theatre
14 Other Shore Club & Marina
15 Mail-Boat Dock
16 Ocean Blue Gallery
17 Barclays Bank
18 Lowe Gift Shoppe
19 Vert Lowe's Model Ship Shoppe
21 Public Dock
22 Ferry Dock
24 Green Turtle Cay Clinic
25 Gospel Chapel
26 Cay Cart Rentals
28 Loyalist Sculpture Garden
30 Loyalist Rose Shoppe
31 Albert Lowe Museum
32 Police Station
33 Post Office, Library, Telephone
34 Shell Hut
35 Ferry Office
36 Ye Olde Jail
37 Miss Emily's Blue Bee Bar
38 Cemetery

Sea of Abaco

Coco Bay

Bluff Cay

White Sound

Green Turtle Cay

0   .5   1 km
0   .25   .5 miles

White Sound

Loyalist Rd

Long Bay Cay

Long Bay

Black Sound

see inset map

New Plymouth

0   100   200 m
0   100   200 yards

Proposed Park

Settlement Creek

Charles St

Parliament St

Bay St

Crown St

York St

Hill St

Victoria St

Quarry Rd

Millard St

Gillam Bay Rd

NEW PLYMOUTH

Gillam Bay

The rest of the island is the domain of wealthy expats. No expats own land in town. Loyalist descendants won't sell town property to out-of-towners; they prefer to keep it in the family, undeeded. Many locals make their livings through conching and lobstering.

The Atlantic shore is lined with fabulous white-sand beaches and reefs. Loggerhead turtles still crawl ashore to nest.

A sign over New Plymouth's ferry dock reads 'Remember These Shores.' And indeed you will.

Information
Barclays Bank (☎ 242-365-4144), on Parliament St, is open 10 am to 1 pm Tuesday and Thursday.

The tiny post office is in the historic pink-and-white building on Parliament St at King St.

There are phone booths in several locales: outside the library (you must dial 0 for the operator), by the ferry dock (coin operated), and at the BaTelCo office at the south end of town (it also has fax service).

The library, adjoining the post office, has a good collection of novels and general reference. Books are borrowed on a honor basis.

A government doctor visits the island most Thursdays. The Green Turtle Cay Clinic (☎ 242-365-4028) has a nurse on duty.

Albert Lowe Museum
This exquisite museum (☎ 242-365-4094), at Parliament and King Sts, is housed in a building dating from 1826 that has served as headquarters for the US consul and as home to Neville Chamberlain before he became prime minister of England.

The museum was founded in 1976 by the nation's most prominent artist, Alton Roland Lowe, who has dedicated most of his adult life to preserving the long-neglected history of his native Abacos. The more than 100 Lowe family members on the island contributed the model sailing ships and historical items and documents that tell various chapters of local history. The Lowes are descended from Gideon

Lowe, who was on that first boat in 1783. It's open 10 am to 4 pm daily. Admission costs US$1.

Alton Lowe Studio
Homegrown artist Alton Roland Lowe is the nation's artist laureate and certainly its most successful (his works are sought after by monarchs, prime ministers, and others with heaps of cash to spare). He inherited his artistic skills from his father, Albert, a noted sea captain, inventor, musician, artist, and historian. Alton has built a permanent exhibition hall and cultural center about a half-mile outside town at the head of Black Sound. There's no sign. Look for the tall white gates set back from the road and the pink, white, and peppermint-green house amid trees on the hill above.

Vert Lowe's Model Ship Shoppe
Vert, Alton's brother, makes intricate model sailing ships, a genius he also picked up from his father, a master model-boat builder. When his father died, leaving a presold three-master only partially finished, Vert thought the decent thing to do would be to complete the project. Vert works on commission for a hefty fee but hasn't moved out of his dinky garage, up an alley off Bay St, where you are welcome to watch him conjuring miniature sailing vessels from redwood, spruce, and fir. Many of the beautiful models are displayed in a glass case.

Loyalist Memorial Sculpture Garden
This splendid garden, on Parliament St at New Plymouth St, was conceived by Alton Lowe and brought to fruition through the creative genius of designer-cum-sculptor James Mastin (a Lowe relative by marriage). It features 25 bronze busts of notable Loyalists and slaves from all the Bahamian islands, arranged in the shape of the Union Jack. Two Loyalist women – one black, one white – stand as the centerpiece atop a coral platform, with a bronze plaque written by author Sandra Riley. She movingly describes the abuse of Americans loyal to King George during the American Revolution and their plight, which led to

ABACOS

the settlement of the Abacos. This moving testament to the indomitable spirit of the Loyalists gives equal emphasis to the often forgotten role of slaves and other blacks who fled behind British lines and were guaranteed liberty and protection.

Cemetery
The 200-year-old bones of Loyalist ancestors lie in this twee cemetery at the east end of Parliament St. Many of the graves are so old that they've crumbled and sunk. Even so, descendants of the long-deceased still pretty the graves with flowers and wreaths.

Gillam Bay Beach
This beautiful beach, a half-mile east of town, is as close to Tahiti as you can get in the Caribbean. The 2-mile-wide bay shelves into countless acres of turquoise shallows as limpid and exuberantly blue as anywhere in the world. The large sandbar is good for shelling.

White Sound & Coco Bay
Touristy White Sound, 2 miles north of New Plymouth, is a deep bay protected by a bluff-faced peninsula – the setting for a notably wealthy expat community that other islanders term the 'White Sound Society' for its aloof ways. Pre-Columbian Lucayan artifacts have been found on the bluff.

Dirt roads lead north from White Sound to the wild Atlantic shore and Coco Bay. The latter, a half-mile north of White Sound, is a deep bay with a lovely crescent of powder-soft sand. A more recent, less aloof, crop of expats have homes north of Coco Bay, hidden along the shores amid wild brush. They are very welcoming and can relate marvelous tales of the island . . . like the time a huge section of a US Air Force Titan missile washed ashore from the Atlantic! The Air Force neglected to claim it, until one day a helicopter whirred in, dispatching a military squad and scaring the dickens out of locals (many of whom were involved in drug trafficking). The squad hauled off some of the top-secret components, leaving folks to display parts of the missile in their gardens.

Diving & Snorkeling
Brendal's Dive Shop (☎ 242-365-4411; in the USA 954-467-1133, 800-780-9941), at the Green Turtle Club & Marina (see Places to Stay, below), has dive packages. A two-day, four-tank package costs US$130; 10 one-tank dives cost US$350. Its certification course costs US$450. Beginners can take the plunge for US$85. Snorkel trips cost US$30. You can rent equipment, including snorkel and underwater camera and video gear.

Sport Fishing & Bonefishing
Ken Bower of Barbie Doll Charters (☎ 242-365-5437) can take up to six people deep-sea fishing for US$750 a day.

Guides such as Donnie Sawyer can take you bonefishing.

The Green Turtle Club & Marina hosts an annual billfishing tournament in May.

Boat Excursions
The Green Turtle Club & Marina offers island cruises to guests aboard the 42-foot *Amorosa*.

Brendal Stevens (see dive shop contact information, above) offers daylong sailing cruises with beach cookout and punch on Manjack or No Name cays for US$65. Options include snorkeling, hand-feeding stingrays, diving for lobster, hiking, and shelling. He offers glass-bottomed boat trips for US$40.

Special Events
Green Turtle Cay's traditional Junkanoo parades, held on Boxing Day and New Year's Day, attract scores of visitors. The town's narrow streets are thronged in an extravaganza of clanging cowbells and blasting conch shells. The partying begins before dawn, the formal parade at 2 pm.

Green Turtle's paraders are followed by the Bunce, a bogeyman who lives in the forest, covered in a sheet and propelled down the street in a wheelbarrow, terrifying the kids. (Many islanders firmly believe in the Bunce – or 'Boonce,' as the locals pronounce it – and sleep with a light on at night to keep him away.) The evil spirit is ceremoniously 'captured' and buried during Junkanoo celebrations.

In the weeks leading up to Junkanoo, call in on Corporal Hubert James Smith – Corporal 'Smitty' – the undisputed king of costuming, and watch him make his magical suits. His skill in designing and creating costumes is largely responsible for the huge turnouts at the New Year's Day bash.

The annual highlight is Regatta Week, a weeklong shindig held each July, normally beginning with sailing races and festivities at Green Turtle Cay, followed by more of the same at Great Guana Cay, Marsh Harbour, Man O' War Cay, Elbow Cay, and, again, Marsh Harbour.

During the last week in December, the 'Christmas Concert Under the Stars' is held at the Garden Theatre (see the Entertainment section). An 'Evening of Music and Comedy' is traditionally held here in January. Call Ivy Roberts (☎ 242-365-4094) or Alton Lowe (☎ 242-365-4264).

Also in December, during Plymouth Historical Weekend, Green Turtle residents celebrate their Loyalist heritage with cultural events and barbecues.

Places to Stay

New Plymouth The only hotel in town is the marvelously romantic *New Plymouth Club & Inn* (☎ 242-365-4161, fax 242-365-4138; in the USA fax 908-735-4140), a painstakingly restored colonial inn set amid cloistered gardens replete with cast-iron lampposts and benches. This charmer has nine small air-con rooms with private bathroom and ceiling fan, furnished in period fashion with all the comforts of home, for US$120 single or double year-round. Facilities include a pool and sun deck with hammock in the lush, compact courtyard, and an elegant restaurant serving candlelit dinners, and a bar where jazz music was playing when I dropped by.

The *Other Shore Club & Marina* (☎ 242-365-4195), on the south shore of Black Sound, has rooms and cottages, plus a swimming pool. *Robert's Dock* (☎ 242-365-4105) also has cottages.

Abaco Vacation Rentals (see Information in the Marsh Harbour section) rents the one-bedroom *Pelican Cove Guest Cottage*, on scintillating Gillam Bay Beach, for US$650 weekly.

Linton's Beach & Harbour Cottages (☎ 242-365-4003; in North America 615-269-5682, fax 615-353-1882) comprise two charmers – 'Seagrape' and 'Palmetto' – on Long Bay Beach, 1 mile northeast of New Plymouth, set amid 22 acres. Each has a living room and dining area, plus twin bedrooms, fully equipped kitchen, and patio-garden, but no air-con; ceiling fans and breezes do the trick. Rented together, the cottages accommodate up to 10 people. Each rents for US$150/1000 nightly/weekly single or double mid-September to mid-December. The rest of the year, you'll be charged US$190/1250 single or double; US$220/1450 for three or four people. Bikes are included, and there's a private dock. Credit cards are not accepted.

White Sound & Coco Bay The aptly named *Bluff House Beach Hotel* (☎ 242-365-4247, fax 242-367-4248) is an upscale hideaway centered on a wooden deck, with rooms cascading down toward the Sea of Abaco. Options include air-con rooms, one-to three-bedroom villas, a range of suites, and even 'treehouses' with kitchenette and stove. The rooms all have a refrigerator, hair dryer, and private balcony with marvelous views. Most include a sofa bed. The four 'Upper Suites' have king-size beds, beautiful decor, and a tremendous setting over the water. Rooms cost US$90/100 low/peak season. Suites cost US$105/120. Villas range from US$155 to US$330 in low season, US$170 to US$380 in peak season. The hotel boasts a pool, plus its own private beach, tennis court, boats, fishing tackle, and golf-cart rentals. The resort has lots of steps and is unsuited to the infirm.

Green Turtle Club & Marina (☎ 242-365-4271, fax 242-365-4272; in the USA ☎ 800-688-4752), recently renovated and cradled in the cusp of White Sound harbor, exudes Cape Cod charm. The 26 air-con rooms and cottages and eight villas differ markedly. Deluxe cottage rooms are exquisitely decorated, with hardwood floors, throw rugs, period mahogany furniture, and TV/VCR. Ordinary rooms are simpler. The harbor-front villas are blazing-white, dappled with tropical prints. Deluxe (lowest-tier) rooms begin at US$125 in summer and rise to US$184 during Christmas and New Year's. Suites cost US$160 to US$225. One- and two-bedroom villas begin at US$215 and rise to US$470. Facilities include a pool, English-pub-style lounge, and a restaurant offering candlelit dining. Activities include fishing and diving. Excursions are offered. The mailing address is PO Box AB-270, Green Turtle Cay, Abaco, Bahamas.

Coco Bay Cottages (☎ 242-365-4464, fax 242-365-4301; in North America ☎ 800-752-0166) nestles at the narrowest point of the island, where barely 100 yards of land divide the beaches of Coco Bay from the sandy Atlantic shore. This 5-acre hideaway, with four two-bedroom cottages surrounded by fruit trees, is perfect for an unpretentious, no-frills escape. 'Jamaica' faces the ocean and costs US$200/1200 daily/weekly year-round; 'Tahiti' faces the bay and costs US$150/800; 'Pink' and 'Bali Hai' take in the best of both worlds for US$150/900. Each is adorned with rattan furniture and has a cathedral ceiling, a spacious and fully equipped kitchen, wraparound deck, ceiling fans, and phone. The mailing address is PO Box AB-22759, Green Turtle Cay, Abaco, Bahamas.

The *Treehouse* (☎ 800-942-9304, ext 20510) has octagonal two-bedroom 'treehouses' with living room and full kitchen, each for up to six people, costing US$800 weekly. Contact Janet Curtis, Green Turtle Cay, Abaco, Bahamas.

Patte Myers (☎ 242-366-0030, fax 242-366-0377) also arranges *cottage rentals* from US$850 weekly. Amy Key (☎ /fax 242-366-0557) has four *luxury villas*. Or

you might try *Villa Jamnar* (☎ 242-365-4271, fax 242-365-4272).

Abaco Vacation Rentals (see Information in the Marsh Harbour section) rents two properties by the week. *Cockcroft House*, on 6 acres overlooking Coco Bay, is a charming two-bedroom cottage with cathedral ceiling and its own saltwater pool. It costs US$1160 double, US$1485 for three or four people, US$1742 five or six people. If you want to live like a pasha, try *Villa Pasha*, a traditional Caribbean-style villa on the Atlantic shore. It's luxuriously decorated in period style. There's even a library and master bedroom suite with whirlpool tub, four bathrooms, marble floors, and five TVs. Bicycles and a golf cart are provided, as are a housekeeper and caretaker. Weekly rates range from US$2200 for up to four people to US$2900 for 10 people in low season; peak-season rates range from US$3600 to US$4600.

Places to Eat

New Plymouth US breakfasts and local fare for lunch and dinner are served at *McIntosh Restaurant & Bakery*, where you can also buy carrot cake and homemade desserts.

The *Plymouth Rock Café* (☎ 242-365-4234) has counter dining, including a light breakfast and a luncheon sandwich board. It makes omelets on Wednesday. Another good deli option is *Ole B's*, a US-style diner and ice cream parlor on the Bay St waterfront.

Mike's Bar & Restaurant (☎ 242-365-4219) specializes in conch dishes; it's open 11 am to 2 pm only.

Laura's Kitchen (☎ 242-365-4287), on King St, is lauded by locals. The fare is simple but excellent. The lunch menu includes a tuna sandwich for US$3.50, Bahamian platters for US$8, and a rib-burger special for US$8. The dinner menu changes daily.

The *Island Deli & Bake Shoppe* (☎ 242-365-4082), upstairs from the Lowe Gift Shoppe, specializes in conch dishes.

Two Bahamian-style favorite places include the *Rooster Restaurant & Pub*

(☎ 242-365-4066) and the *Wrecking Tree* (☎ 242-365-4263), with a giant casuarina growing through the deck overlooking the waterfront. The latter serves turtle on request; it's open 10 am to 9 pm daily.

To really be one with the locals, check out Clara Ruth's *backyard barbecue* on Saturday at her home on Hill St.

The *New Plymouth Club & Inn* (☎ 242-365-4161) has one sitting at 7:30 pm, offering a choice among three entrées, preceded by hors d'oeuvres at 6:30 pm. Reservations are due by 5 pm. It also serves breakfast 8 to 9 am and lunch (and Sunday brunch) 11:30 am to 1:30 pm.

White Sound & Coco Bay Reservations are a must for dinner at the elegant, Olde-English-style *Bluff House Restaurant* (☎ 242-365-4247); it's also open for breakfast and lunch.

Green Turtle Club (☎ 242-365-4271), a member of the Chaîne des Rotisseurs, offers breakfast and lunch on the patio and gourmet dinners in its exquisite Queen-Anne-style dining room. You choose among three entrées. Reservations must be made before 5 pm.

Entertainment
Miss Emily's Blue Bee Bar is the legendary watering hole that originated the widely copied Goombay Smash. Miss Emily, a teetotaler who died in March 1997, came up with the bar's trademark drink when she was 'fooling around' with mixes about 20 years ago. The place is now run by her son, Corporal Smith ('Smitty' when out of uniform), and her daughter, Violet, who still brews the secret recipe at home in plastic jugs. The simple wooden hut has only rustic seating, and decor is provided by business cards festooning the walls, T-shirts and underwear hanging from the ceiling, and salutations scribbled by happy customers. The mood is rum-thick when the music gets going. The record number of Goombay Smashes drunk by one man in one night is a whopping 23; he had to be taken home in a wheelbarrow. A woman once drank 19, but her fate is unknown.

You might also nip next door to *Bert's Sea Garden Club* to compare Miss Emily's creation against Bert Reckley's house concoction, made of coconut rum and milk.

The Gully Roosters perform rake 'n' scrape music at the *Roosters Restaurant* on Friday and Saturday nights. The Gully Roosters play at the *Green Turtle Club* on Wednesday night.

On Thursday night there's a beach barbecue with live bands and Junkanoo at *Bluff House*. Live music is offered on other nights.

The open-air *Garden Theatre*, adjacent to the Alton Lowe Studio at Black Sound, hosts comedy, musical, and theatrical concerts throughout the year.

Things to Buy
One visit to Vert Lowe's Model Ship Shoppe will have you reaching for your wallet. A 26-inch one-master costs about US$600. For two- or three-masted ships up to 5 feet long, expect to pay US$1200 to US$2500.

Also look for paintings by Alton Lowe, which are sold at the gallery next to the Albert Lowe Museum. You might see some of his works displayed at the Ocean Blue Gallery in the Plymouth Rock Café, where over 50 artists are represented by their prints, oils, and watercolor paintings. Fabulous originals of local scenes by Jerry Rose and Stan Krieger, his disciple, sell from US$500. Other gems include stained-glasswork by Rome Heyer.

The Sand Dollar-Abaco Gold sells gold jewelry that is handmade using the 'lost-wax' technique. It also has a huge array of resortwear, plus other souvenirs.

The Loyalist Rose Shoppe sells jewelry and T-shirts. And you should be able to find any odds and ends that you need (plus books, postcards, and kitschy souvenirs) at the Shell Hut variety store.

Bluff House has a upscale boutique. The Green Turtle Club Boutique has a wide range of swimwear and casual clothing. The more fashion-conscious might browse the high-class imported ladieswear at Rebecca's, also at the Green Turtle Club.

Getting There & Away

Black Sound Marina (☎ 242-365-4221, fax 242-365-4046) has slips, gas, water, electricity, showers, laundry, and wet storage. The Other Shore Club & Marina (☎ 242-365-4195), also at Black Sound, also has a full-service marina, as does Robert's Dock (☎ 242-365-4105). Abaco Yacht Services, on the north side of Black Sound, has repair facilities. Black Sound is considered a hurricane shelter.

Green Turtle Club has a full-service marina accommodating boats up to 150 feet; US70¢ per foot in summer, US60¢ in winter. Cable TV hookups are available for US$5 daily. The shoreside marina at Bluff House was still open at press time, but an all-new, full-service marina was in the works.

AIT (☎ 242-365-6010, fax 242-365-6487, VHF channel 16) ferries run from the Green Turtle Dock, 2 miles south of Treasure Cay airport, at 2:30 and 4 pm daily, returning at 1:30 and 3 pm (10 minutes, US$8 one way). The skipper will drop you off at the dock nearest to your hotel. If you rented a villa, your skipper will radio ahead so that the caretaker will be waiting for you. Ferries also operate on demand for people with flights; call ahead.

The ferry dock on the mainland has a snack bar. The dock on Green Turtle has no facilities.

A water taxi from Treasure Cay Airport to the dock costs US$6 per person; from Marsh Harbour, it's about US$65 for two people, plus US$5 for each extra person.

The mail boat *Mia Dean* calls in once a week from Nassau; see the Marsh Harbour Getting There & Away section for information.

Getting Around

The preferred mode of transportation is golf cart, available through Cay Cart Rentals (☎ 242-365-4406). Poley Johnson and Don McIntosh of D&P Rentals rent Honda scooters.

There are two taxi services: Omri Taxis and McIntosh Taxis (to reach either call ☎ 242-365-4309, VHF channel 06). A ride

between New Plymouth and Coco Bay or White Sound costs about US$8 for two people.

Brendal Stevens of Brendal's Dive Shop (☎ 242-365-4411) rents bicycles. You can also rent boats from Brendal's for US$15/60 hourly/daily.

Dames Boat Rental (☎ 242-365-4205) has 14- and 17-foot Boston Whalers and 22-foot Markos for US$50 to US$100 daily, US$250 to US$530 weekly. You can also rent boats from Donny's Boat Rental (☎ 242-365-4271) at the Green Turtle Club.

COOPER'S TOWN

This small settlement, the *only* settlement in the 30 miles between Treasure Cay and the northern tip of Great Abaco, is a center for commercial citrus farms, hidden away from the road amid the pine forests that dominate the island. Valencia oranges are grown for export. Most of the residents earn their livings working in Treasure Cay or conching and lobstering. The main street is one block east of SC Bootle Hwy.

The prime minister and FNM leader, Hubert A Ingraham, is the homegrown representative for Cooper's Town.

There's a modern government clinic (☎ 242-365-0019) with dental care and 24-hour emergency room, a gas station open until 11:30 pm, and, next door, Murray's Laundromat and general store.

The delightful *Conch Trawl Inn & Shipwreck Bar*, a weathered-wood restaurant on the waterfront, serves seafood and native dishes amid a motley yet endearing decor of turtle shells and fishing nets. At night it becomes a lively spot. The *Waterfront Privacy Restaurant* also serves seafood.

You can buy fresh bread from Aunt Elvie (hers is the blue house on the waterfront).

SPANISH CAY

This 3-mile-long sliver, once owned by Queen Elizabeth II, is 3 miles off the northern tip of Great Abaco. Most of its 185 acres are covered in palm groves and tropical forest, with a few homes of the international gentry hidden in their midst. Four beautiful beaches line the east shore.

Places to Stay & Eat

The Inn at Spanish Cay (☎ 242-365-0083, fax 242-365-0466; in North America ☎ 800-688-4752) is a small luxury resort with five 'villa-suites' for US$180 year-round, as well as seven one- and two-bedroom apartments starting at US$225. There are two waterfront restaurants and four tennis courts. Golf carts are available, as are boats for fishing or diving. The mailing address is PO Box AB-882, Cooper's Town, Abaco, Bahamas.

Spanish Cay Residence (☎ 242-359-6622) rents rooms.

Point House, at the marina, serves breakfast and lunch. The *Wrecker's Raw Bar*, sitting over the ocean, is open for lunch and dinner; seafood predominates.

Getting There & Away

Spanish Cay has a 5000-foot airstrip for guests arriving by private plane, and a full-service marina with laundry, showers, water, gas, and diesel.

A free water taxi runs from the government dock at Cooper's Town. A taxi from Treasure Cay Airport to the dock will cost US$30 for two people, US$5 per additional person.

LITTLE ABACO

Great Abaco ends 5 miles northwest of Cooper's Town at Angel Fish Point, where SC Bootle Hwy swings west over a bridge onto Little Abaco island.

The population – entirely black – lives in four small and relatively poor settlements: Cedar Harbour, Mount Hope, Fox Town (dominated by the Zion Baptist Church), and Crown Haven. Together the towns bill themselves as 'The Pride of Abaco,' though their few middle-class homes are intermingled with more numerous tumbledown hovels and shacks. This area is an offbeat escape for anyone fleeing the touristy Bahamas. Most of the locals live by conching and lobstering. Crown Haven boasts a lobster business –

Bahasea Products – that exports its product to Japan and Europe.

There are a few modest beaches, and the bonefishing on the south side of Little Abaco is said to be excellent. West of Cedar Harbour, the north shore is lined with mangroves, with scores of little coral heads above water in a long sound. In Crown Haven the road fizzles out at a rickety wharf where in late afternoon you may watch lobster being landed and the day's conch catch being gutted.

The Little Abaco Homecoming is held in early June, with goombay, basketball, barbecues, and general merrymaking.

There's a post office and police station in Fox Town.

Places to Stay & Eat

The *Tangelo Hotel* (☎ 242-365-2222), on the fringe of Fox Town, describes itself as the 'best hotel in Little Abaco.' Indeed, it's practically the only one (notwithstanding, you'll probably be the only guest). Congenially run by Gladys Saunders, this otherwise soulless hotel has 12 modestly furnished air-con rooms, each with TV, ceiling fans, plenty of hot water, and either one double or two twin beds; US$65 single or double year-round. Transfers are offered to and from Treasure Cay Airport. Gladys prepares excellent grouper lunches and dinners for US$8. She hopes to build a marina, which may improve the hotel's fortunes. I wish her luck.

In Fox Town, Merline and Millie McIntosh have a small hotel and restaurant – the *Seaview* (☎ 242-365-2007) – serving seafood.

In Cedar Harbour try *Nettie's Snack Bar*, and in Mount Hope try *EJ's Restaurant & Pool Bar*. Crown Haven boasts *Chile's Bar & Restaurant* and *Black's Restaurant*. All have native food and double as nightspots.

Getting There & Away

A taxi from Treasure Cay Airport will cost about US$60 for two. The Tangelo Hotel will pick you up at the airport for US$10 for two. Most locals hitchhike, including old ladies thumbing a ride to go shopping.

ABACOS

Sand Dollar Tours (☎ 242-367-2189) offers tours to Crown Haven from Marsh Harbour on Wednesday.

At press time Inter-Island Adventures (☎ 242-352-9063, fax 242-352-9064), PO Box F-43216, Freeport, Grand Bahama, was planning a full-day hovercraft excursion to Little Abaco from Grand Bahama for US$99.

Northwest Cays

GRAND CAY

Pop 400

Near the top of the Abacos chain, Grand Cay is as offbeat as things get in The Bahamas. Most of the staff of the Walker's Cay Hotel & Marina live here (see Walker's Cay, below), traveling back and forth by boat, but very few visitors call. You can hop a ride for about US$10 one way.

Grand Cay is divided into the larger, box-shaped, virtually uninhabited isle of that name and, to its east, Little Grand Cay and Mermaid Cay, with small settlements. There are several beaches; the most spectacular is Wells Bay, which runs the length of the 2-mile west shore of Grand Cay. The bonefishing in the area is superb; ask Gerald Rolle or Willard Munnings to guide you.

There's a medical clinic on Grand Cay.

Places to Stay & Eat

Rosie Curry runs the *Island Bay Restaurant & Motel* (☎ 242-353-1200). The 20 modest air-con rooms, for US$50, have a TV; some have a kitchenette. It also has a laundrette.

There are several other eateries, including Eddie Cooper's *Hilltop View Restaurant & Lounge*. You can pick up fresh bread at *Ena's Bakery*.

Entertainment

On weekends the *Island Bay* and *Seaside Bar* get in the groove with dance clubs.

Getting There & Away

Island Bay Restaurant & Motel has a marina with 15 slips, with water, gas, and diesel.

Roosevelt Curry operates a water taxi between Walker's Cay and Grand Cay. There's no charge if you're going to eat at Rosie's (six passengers minimum; otherwise there's a fee). You can call him from the marina. Any local boater will run you between the cays for about US$5.

WALKER'S CAY

Tiny Walker's Cay, the 'Top of The Bahamas,' is a craggy coral outcrop that rises to 50 feet at the uppermost end of the Abacos chain, on the outer edge of the Little Bahama Bank. The isle is dominated by a single marina and hotel, high on the eastern bluff. There's no settlement, and the population is limited to plump curly-tailed lizards and a flock of sooty terns, caterwauling and honking. Frigate birds also wing overhead. The vegetation is mostly cactus and gnarled old trees, with plenty of ficus (strangler figs).

Walker's Cay is acclaimed for diving and sport fishing (it claims 'more IGFA records than any other resort') and hosts the world's largest private billfishing tournament. Barracuda, bonefish, grouper, acrobatic sailfish, and the Atlantic's biggest and heartiest fighter, the mighty blue marlin, are abundant within minutes of the cay.

There's almost nothing to see on the island, although by following the airstrip (stay to the margins, as the strip is very active), you'll reach a slender, scimitar-shaped white-sand beach (there's another teeny beach tucked away at the westernmost end of the airstrip). On the north side of the strip you'll see hundreds of small tanks where tropical fish were once raised for export.

Walker's Cay is surrounded by even tinier cays, to which Walker's Cay Hotel & Marina staff will run you and strand you for an hour or an entire day (after preparing a box lunch for you). Some favorites include Tom Brown's Cay, Seal Cay, and Sit Down Cay.

All visitors from overseas must clear immigration (☎ 242-353-1215) and customs (☎ 242-353-1211) at the airstrip; the office is open 9 am to 5 pm daily.

Diving & Snorkeling

Walker's Cay is fringed by a barrier reef that offers spectacular diving, often in less than 30 feet of water. There's something for everyone: old wrecks, including one WWII relic; Jeanette's Reef, boasting a large population of eels; caverns populated by silver minnows; and the Travel Agent Reef, a beautiful coral garden ideal for snorkelers and novice divers.

The Sea Below Dive Shop (☎ 242-353-1252, 800-925-5377, fax 242-353-1339) has full equipment rental, including 35mm cameras. It offers instruction for PADI certification for US$300. Two dive trips are offered daily (US$40/60 one-/two-tank; US$45 for night dives). Snorkel trips are offered for US$20.

Shark Dives For a real hoot, you can kneel on the sea bottom, 35 feet down, while hungry sharks swirl around you. The island's famous Shark Rodeo (US$65/75 one-/two-tank) often attracts dozens of blacktip and Caribbean reef sharks at a time. They'll swim up close to check you out, but they're more interested in the 'chumsicle' – a plastic trash can filled with stinking fish tails, heads, and entrails – that acts to ravenous sharks as a subaqueous dinner bell. As soon as the bucket hits the water, they rip into the fish. The noise of crunching bones – the water amplifies sound – can be unsettling. All will be fine. Just keep your eyes on the chumsicle and stay clear of sharks fighting for food. And please don't wave your hands, swim erratically, or otherwise act like food.

Shark Research Researchers from the Aquarium of the Americas in New Orleans, along with the National Marine Fisheries Service, the University of Miami, Walker's Cay National Park, and Oceanographic Expeditions, are involved in a long-term effort to study shark behavior around Walker's Cay. Hollywood couldn't have come up with a better name: the 'Apex Predator Project.' The venal-looking critters are tagged underwater by hand with transponders (each with a chip and ID

number that is transmitted and tracked electronically) that are injected into the sharks' skins. Blacktip sharks are an internationally endangered species, and the hard science produced by Walker Cay researchers could prove invaluable in saving them.

Sharks, it seems, are extremely intelligent. One was taught to press a colored button for food; six months later the same shark reappeared with some pals, and all of them pushed the button, demonstrating that sharks have long-term memory and an ability to communicate information to other sharks.

Volunteer divers are needed to study and photograph sharks during monthly trips. To qualify, you must have completed at least 25 logged dives and three night dives in the past five years. The weeklong trips cost US$1395, including roundtrip airfare from Fort Lauderdale. For information, contact Oceanographic Expeditions (☎ /fax 504-488-1573, seascience@aol.com), 4418 St Ann St, New Orleans, LA 70119-3608.

Sport Fishing & Bonefishing

Charter boats are available at the marina from US$200/300 half-/full day, including guide, tackle, and bait. The marina fleet includes flats boats, 50-foot sportfishermen, center consoles, and a drift-fishing boat. Bonefishing costs US$300 (full day only) for a 18-foot skiff. Reservations are recommended for charters.

The North Abaco Sportfishing Championship is held on Walker's Cay each April. In May the cay hosts the Walker's Cay Billfish Tournament and the Bertram-Hatteras Shootout.

Volunteer Research

Oceanographic Expeditions (see Shark Research, above), needs volunteers for its 'Project Reef Spawn' at Walker's Cay. The study seeks to unravel the mystery of coral spawning, when zillions of egg bundles are released simultaneously, like a storm of Alka Seltzer bubbles, on the one night a year that many coral species throughout the hemisphere reproduce. This amazing event occurs predictably in late August. To qualify, you must have completed at least 25 logged dives and three night dives in the past five years. The trips cost US$1395, including roundtrip airfare from Fort Lauderdale.

Places to Stay & Eat

Walker's Cay Hotel & Marina (☎ 242-353-1252, fax 242-353-1339; in the USA ☎ 954-359-1400, 800-925-5377, fax 954-359-1414) is a dedicated scuba-diving and sport-fishing resort nestled over the marina. It has 62 air-con rooms, each with private bathroom and terrace, but no TVs, radios, or telephones. The spacious and functional 'Coral' rooms are short on light and character; they cost US$100 mid-September through March, US$140 in summer – the reverse of normal seasonal rates. Pool-view 'Hibiscus' rooms are slightly better and cost US$110/150. Ocean-view Hibiscus suites cost US$220/275 (one-bedroom) and US$340/435 (two-bedroom). Octagonal 'villas' over the ocean cost US$200/300. A MAP (breakfast and dinner) plan costs US$37.50 per person. A two-night getaway package costs US$339 per person including air, room, taxes, and MAP. Special rates are also offered for divers and private pilots. Small-boaters (with vessels under 35 feet) are offered a special three-day/two-night package for US$355 double, including rooms, dockage, dinner, and extras.

The resort also rents the three-bedroom 'Harbour House,' which boasts a pool table, and Jacuzzi on a deck with views over the marina; US$450/475.

The resort has two swimming pools (one fresh water, the other saltwater) and a Jacuzzi, plus stores, two bars, a volleyball court, tennis, and water sports. The resort's mailing address is 700 SW 34th St, Fort Lauderdale, FL 33315.

The *Conch Pearl* restaurant specializes in seafood and continental favorites of variable quality, with entrées from US$13 upward (my seafood pasta was bland). It's open for breakfast and dinner only. The service is friendly but unsure.

The *Lobster Trap* (☎ 242-352-5252), at the marina, features Bahamian seafood (including a seafood pizza), plus burgers and sandwiches. It has pool tables.

Getting There & Away

Air Pan-Am Air Bridge flies to Walker's from Fort Lauderdale twice daily except Tuesday (US$250 roundtrip). The seaplanes depart from the Jet Center on N Perimeter Rd, on the north side of Fort Lauderdale's international airport. No hand luggage is allowed on board, and luggage is strictly limited to 30 lbs.

Private planes are charged US$10/15 single-/twin-engine, US$25 day visitors. Jet fuel is available.

Boat The marina has 75 slips, plus a bar, commissary, and other services. Dockage costs US$1.25 per foot daily, including electricity (15% discount for a weeklong stay, 25% discount for a monthlong stay). Free winter dockage is provided September to March, where there's a special '50/50' room/dockage program.

Andros

Pop 8155

Andros, 100 miles long and up to 45 miles wide, is the largest island in The Bahamas. It has escaped the commercial development of Nassau, just 25 miles away; in fact, its 2300 sq miles represent one of the largest tracts of unexplored land in the Western Hemisphere.

Andros actually comprises three main islands separated by enormous bights, or sounds, up to 25 miles wide and full of innumerable cays. It is further divided by countless creeks that cut its low surface into a fragmented jigsaw puzzle and either meander tortuously from coast to coast, open to lakes, or meld into endless mangrove swamps. Even at high tide – when the 'Muds' are flooded and the island shrinks considerably – Andros is almost as large as all the other Bahamian islands combined. (Its copious supplies of fresh water led the Spaniards to name it La Isla del Espíritu Santo – 'Island of the Holy Spirit' – after the belief that the Holy Spirit dwells over water.)

Aesthetically, Andros lacks much of the appeal of other Family Islands. It is rough-edged and, at first sight, raw and un-inviting. Most of Andros is covered with acres of palm savannas and eerie primal forests – mahogany, lignum vitae, pine, and palmetto – and by vast mangrove wetlands that form a huge and vital nursery for multitudes of fish and invertebrates.

The forests are home to wild boar, dove, duck, quail, and white-crowned pigeon (each spring a traditional pigeon hunt is held). During late spring and early summer giant land crabs that grow to 5 lbs or more emerge, crossing the road en masse for a paroxysm of mating and egg laying. All are trophies for locals eager to add to their kitchen pots. The skies are patrolled by turkey buzzards (the 'aerial surveillance squadron,' as they are called). And the shrieks of ospreys are commonly heard. Or

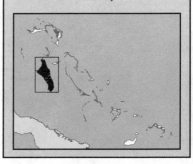

is that the screech of chickcharnies? . . . red-eyed, three-fingered, owl-like elves with beards and feathered scalps who hang by their tails from cottonwood trees. They wreak mayhem on whomever disturbs them. To you or I, the cheeky chickcharnie is a product of local imagination. But to the Androsians, the devil-in-disguise is as real as the nose on your face. The failure of Neville Chamberlain's sisal plantation in the 1890s is blamed on chickcharnies. One thing that *is* real is the fierce horsefly, locally called the 'doctor fly' because its bite hurts like a syringe.

Andros is surrounded by the Great Bahama Bank, a plateau that is about as shallow as the island is high. A 140-mile-long coral reef lies a few hundred yards to 2 miles off the east shore. (Androsians claim that this barrier reef is surpassed in length only by Australia's Great Barrier Reef and the reef off the Caribbean coast of

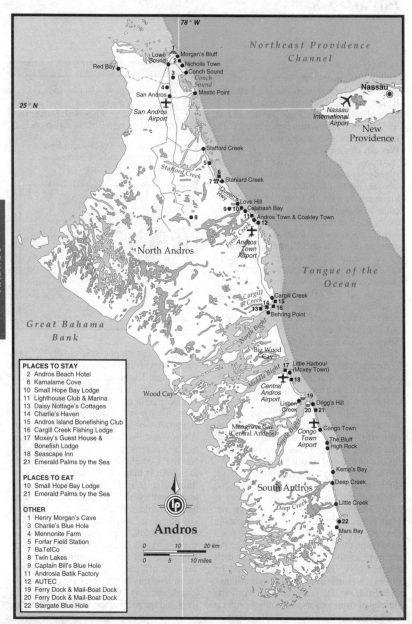

Northeast Providence Channel

78° W

Morgan's Bluff
Lowe Sound
Red Bay
Nicholls Town
Conch Sound
Conch Sound
Mastic Point
San Andros
San Andros Airport

25° N

Nassau
Nassau International Airport
New Providence

Stafford Creek
Stafford Creek
Staniard Creek
Queen's Hwy
Love Hill
Calabash Bay
Andros Town & Coakley Town
Andros Town Airport
Fresh Creek

North Andros

Tongue of the Ocean

Great Bahama Bank

Cargill Creek
Cargill Creek
Behring Point
North Bight

Big Wood Cay

Little Harbour (Moxey Town)
Middle Bight
Central Andros Airport
Wood Cay
Lisbon Creek
Drigg's Hill
Congo Town
Congo Town Airport
The Bluff
High Rock
Mangrove Cay (Central Andros)
South Bight

Kemp's Bay
Deep Creek
Little Creek
South Andros
Deep Creek
Mars Bay

PLACES TO STAY
2 Andros Beach Hotel
6 Kamalame Cove
10 Small Hope Bay Lodge
11 Lighthouse Club & Marina
13 Daisy Nottage's Cottages
14 Charlie's Haven
15 Andros Island Bonefishing Club
16 Cargill Creek Fishing Lodge
17 Moxey's Guest House & Bonefish Lodge
18 Seascape Inn
21 Emerald Palms by the Sea

PLACES TO EAT
10 Small Hope Bay Lodge
21 Emerald Palms by the Sea

OTHER
1 Henry Morgan's Cave
3 Charlie's Blue Hole
4 Mennonite Farm
5 Forfar Field Station
7 BaTelCo
8 Twin Lakes
9 Captain Bill's Blue Hole
11 Androsia Batik Factory
12 AUTEC
19 Ferry Dock & Mail-Boat Dock
20 Ferry Dock & Mail-Boat Dock
22 Stargate Blue Hole

Andros

0   10   20 km
0   5   10 miles

ANDROS

Central America). Beyond it and barely 2 miles from shore, the plateau drops off to a very dark 8700 feet in the Tongue of the Ocean canyon.

The wild island became a refuge for both Seminole Indians and runaway slaves fleeing Florida during colonial days. A community of their descendants still exists in Red Bay on the northwest coast. A string of other small settlements dots the eastern seaboard. Nicely kept modern houses are interspersed with scruffy shacks surrounded by front-lawn furniture such as rusty cars, discarded refrigerators, and other garbage. The settlements sprawl along the one main road and are separated by a flat immensity of scrub, marsh, and pine forest that you might believe really *does* harbor chickcharnies. This is no place for a flat tire!

In the early 1980s Androsians developed a reputation for drug adventures. When you are flying over the island, you'll notice the carcasses of drug planes, some half-submerged, others forlornly bleaching in the bush. From above you can also make out numerous doughnut-shaped blue holes, like patinated copper coins, amid the forests and scrub. The blue holes' levels rise and fall with the tides, alternately pouring water over the surrounding land or draining the brackish streamlets into the underground world to percolate and emerge much, much later from ocean holes inside the fringing reef on the east shore. Androsian blue holes are said to be inhabited by a monstrous octopus called 'Lusca.' Many locals still believe in the creature, although scuba divers have turned up only lobster, shrimp, shark, and smaller fry.

Andros is also renowned for the sponge beds west of the island, which supported much of the population in the late 19th and early 20th centuries until a mysterious blight killed off 99% of the sponges in 1938. The sponges lie in water, or 'muds,' so shallow that they could be pried from the coral with rods. (Some people believe that the island was named by Greek spongers for the Mediterranean island of

Sponging

The sponge is a marine animal composed mainly of microscopic calcareous rods, stars, and hooks held in place by elastic fibers. Nourishment is extracted from water via a vast network of pores and canals. Although they don't have hearts or brains, sponges produce sperm and eggs. There are various species, including the supersoft 'velvet' or wool sponge, and the 'hardhead,' so durable that it has many industrial uses.

Sponging in the Bahamas began in earnest in 1841 after a Frenchman, Gustave Renouard, was shipwrecked here. 'Ooh, la la! Zeez sponges are better zan ze sponges of ze Méditerranée,' said French merchants of the sponges Renouard shipped back to Paris.

Schooners sailed from throughout the Bahamas to gather the prolific wool sponge. Greek deep-sea sponge divers left their homeland to make hay from the Bahamian seabed. Each schooner carried a crew of 20 men, plus six to eight dinghies which were put overboard daily with a crew of two. While one man sculled, the other looked through a glass-bottomed bucket and ripped the sponges from the seabed with a hooked pole. (Today spongers dive with snorkel or scuba gear. They also slice the sponges at the base, leaving the root to regenerate.) Ashore, the sponges were beaten to death and put in shallow-water 'kraals' to allow the flesh to rot and decompose. Then they were rinsed, pounded to a pleasing fluffiness, and strung up to dry before being shipped for sale at the Greek Sponge Exchange in Nassau.

At the close of the 19th century, 500 schooners and sloops and 2800 smaller vessels were working the sponge beds, and in the peak year of 1917, 1.5 million lbs of sponges were exported. 'The Mud,' an extensive 140-mile-long, 40-mile-wide shoal off Andros, was a major source of income for sponge divers. Sponging was the chief source of livelihood on all the Bahamian islands until 1938, when a fungal blight killed the sponges overnight. ■

Dive & Snorkel Sites

Dive Sites

Alex & Cara Caverns – Expert divers can descend to 90 feet to enter these caverns on the edge of the Tongue of the Ocean.

The Barge – This wreck lies 70 feet below the surface and is now a home to large groupers.

The Black Forest – A crop of three dozen black coral trees appears at 70 feet.

The Blue Hole – Large rays and sharks often gather at this tame blue hole with depths down to 100 feet.

Over the Wall – This dive begins at 80 feet and plunges another 100 feet at the edge of the Tongue of the Ocean wall, which itself drops another 6000 feet.

Potomac – This 345-foot British tanker sank in 1929 off Andros' northeast coast.

Snorkel Sites

Central Park – Acres of corals, including elkhorn, are found here.

China Point – Huge fish populations, including blue tangs and sergeant majors, swim here.

The Compressor – Yes . . . a compressor has metamorphosed into a reef!

Davis Creek – This fascinating tidal flat extends into the mangroves.

Goat Cay – These turtle-grass flats are good for hunting sand dollars.

Liben's Point – This is a vast region with tall elkhorn and star coral.

Red Shoal – Schooling grunts frequent this lone patch of elkhorn reef.

Solarium – Lobsters and stingrays favor these shallow flats.

Trumpet Reef – This reef is known for invertebrates such as brittle stars and spiny urchins. ■

Andros.) A few locals still make a living sponging, but most earn a living from fishing (the famous Androsian sloops, however, have been replaced by fiberglass outboards). Agriculture is minimal.

Resort-based tourism has yet to catch on: There are a few homey guesthouses and apartments (dour by Western standards and relying almost exclusively on the Bahamian trade, especially during homecomings) and a fistful of quiet hotels, including a noted scuba resort and several bonefishing camps.

For fisherfolk and divers, there are few more endearing places on earth. Inside the reef's shallows, divers can gambol in an infinite variety of sites. Outside it they can dive the Andros wall, which plunges precipitously to the base of the Tongue of the Ocean.

There are plentiful deep coral canyons, many of which connect to inland blue holes. Gigantic stalactites fill the holes, many of which are entered at depths below 100 feet. The mixing of fresh water and saltwater inside the holes supports some of the most diverse marine life imaginable. There are 178 blue holes inland and another 50 offshore. Blue-hole diving is a specialty of Small Hope Bay Lodge (see the Calabash Bay section).

Andros bills itself as the 'Bonefishing Capital of the World,' and it seems that the experts agree. There are several lodges dedicated to bonefishing. Bonefishing guides can be hired in any community. The Andros Bonefishing Guides Association can provide a recommendation; call Arthur Russell (☎ 242-329-7372) or Andy Smith (☎ 242-368-4261). You should come with all equipment. Pan-Angling Travel Service offers fishing package tours from North America (see the Outdoor Activities chapter for contact information).

Andros also boasts some good hiking spots. However, the island is popular with hunters seeking wild boar, so you should hike with caution. You might want to hire a hunter as a guide.

North Andros

North Andros is the largest of the three Androsian islands. It has some fine beaches and boneflats, the latter concentrated at Lowe Sound in the north and Behring Point in the south. Much of the island is smothered in pine forests that have twice been logged – first to provide pit-props for English coal mines and later for Chicago newspapers. The island's exotic hardwoods, mahogany, and lignum vitae (sometimes called 'sailor's cure' because its sap provided a cure for syphilis in the 19th century), for example, are long gone, but the logging tracks remain, granting access to remote blue holes.

The island hosts the North Andros Thanksgiving Bonefish Tournament each November.

San Andros

This small settlement is lent a semblance of importance by the airport, one of two on North Andros. The town is also served by a commercial harbor at **Mastic Point**, which is 3 miles east of town. Neither place is worth the visit. Much of the land around San Andros is intensively farmed for citrus, potatoes, tomatoes, and other produce. You might wish to visit a community of Mennonite farmers who raise lettuce and other fresh vegetables on a farm north of town.

There's a Canadian Imperial Bank, open 10:30 am to 2:30 pm Wednesday only. There are clinics in San Andros (☎ 242-329-2055) and Mastic Point (☎ 242-329-1849). For the police, call ☎ 919 or 242-329-2353.

Oliver's Guest House (☎ 242-329-3001), in Mastic Point, has simple rooms.

Getting There & Away See the Getting There & Away chapter for airlines' Nassau and international telephone numbers.

Bahamasair (in San Andros ☎ 242-329-2273) offers twice-daily service between Nassau and San Andros (US$45 one way). Island Express flies from Fort Lauderdale.

The harbor here is clogged by sunken boats and is not recommended for private boaters.

The mail boat *Lisa J II* departs Nassau for Mastic Point at 3:30 pm Wednesday (five hours, US$30 one way), with stops at Nicholls Town and Morgan's Bluff.

Getting Around You can rent cars at Mastic Point from either Basil Martin (☎ 242-329-3169) or Cecil Gaitor (☎ 242-329-3043) for US$65 per day.

Lowe Sound

Lowe Sound, just west of the crossroads, 5 miles north of San Andros, is a handsome little fishing village with fishing boats and nets along the beach. Neville 'Uncle JT' Dean might take you out sponging, conching, or lobstering with a long pole. Every morning he leaves at dawn and returns at about 1 pm. You can also watch Arthur Russell (☎ 242-329-7372), a recommended bonefishing guide, carving model ships that he fits with Androsia batik sails.

Kevin's Guest Rooms has air-con rooms and a restaurant. At *Big Josh's Seafood Restaurant* (☎ 242-329-7517), Malvese Bootle conjures up home-style native dishes and seafood; it's open 7 to 11 am and 1 to 11 pm daily (credit cards are OK).

ANDROS

Big Josh's has a satellite lounge, as does the *Twilight Zone* (☎ 242-329-2432), open from 9 pm until late.

Nicholls Town
Pop 600
This coastal settlement, the most important hereabouts, is 3 miles east of Lowe Sound. Palms fringe the beach. The town spreads behind it in a checkered grid, with modern concrete homes and weatherbeaten wooden shacks scattered along the roads, fishing boats out of kilter along the shore, and US-model cars in various stages of rusting on front lawns. It boasts a few small stores, a supermarket, and a gas station.

It is favored for scuba diving. And several North American expats have built homes here and around Conch Sound, a somnolent fishing village 1 mile south of Nicholls Town.

The highlight here is watching septuagenarian William Pratt make wooden boats by hand. You'll usually find him in his workshop, planing and adzing wood and even sewing the sails for boats that he still races himself in the annual regatta.

There's a post office (☎ 242-329-2034); it's open 9 am to 5:30 pm weekdays. For the police, call ☎ 919 or 242-329-2353.

Charlie's Blue Hole This hole near Conch Sound is renowned for its 'boil,' a whirlpool caused by a rapid egress of water during the change of tidal flow, when water is sucked viciously out to sea through the subterranean passages and any boats that happen to be on the surface can be pulled underwater. Several boats have been lost this way, adding to the local legend of the monstrous octopus, Lusca, in residence here ('Mon, dawn't go down der. Nobody go down der!'). Scuba divers who first explored the hole in the 1970s were quite surprised to find sharks swimming in the narrow caverns.

Another hole, **Benjamin's Blue Hole**, has fabulous stalactites and stalagmites gloriously suspended underwater, as if preserved in formaldehyde.

Diving & Snorkeling Andros Undersea Adventures at the Andros Beach Hotel (see Places to Stay, below) offers dives for US$40/60 one-/two-tank and certification courses, plus snorkel trips for US$25.

An Annual Free Diving Championship is hosted at the Andros Beach Hotel each September.

Places to Stay & Eat *Green Windows Inn* (☎ 242-329-2194), in town about five minutes from the beach, has six air-con rooms with shared bathroom and four suites, all with TV. Car and bicycle rentals are offered, and bonefishing trips can be arranged. The postal address is PO Box 23076, Nicholls Town, Andros, Bahamas.

The *Donna Lee Guesthouse* (☎ 242-329-2194), in town, is a simpler affair with 12 air-con rooms.

The coral-colored, motel-style *Conch Sound Resort Inn* (☎ 242-329-2060) has seven large, air-con rooms with pleasant albeit modest furnishings and satellite TV. There are also six concrete cottages with kitchens, an unassuming restaurant and bar, plus a swimming pool. The motel is surrounded by pine forests (good for hiking), with the beach a five-minute walk away. Fishing and other activities can be arranged. The rates are US$80 for rooms, US$180 to US$200 for cottages, including airport transfers. Credit cards are not accepted. Its mailing address is PO Box 23029, Nicholls Town, Andros, Bahamas.

The *Andros Beach Hotel* (☎ 242-329-2582), north of town, was closed at press time, but rumor was that it would reopen. If so, it has 10 comfortable though simply furnished rooms for US$95. There's a restaurant, dive shop, small bar, swimming pool, and dock.

All the hotels have restaurants. Locals gather at *Eva's Picaroon Restaurant* (☎ 242-329-2607) for native dishes; at *Rumours* (☎ 242-329-2398), outside Nicholls Town; and at the *Dayshell Restaurant* (☎ 242-329-2183).

A lively rake 'n' scrape band plays at the Dayshell Restaurant. Rumours also has live bands, plus a dance club on weekends, as does the *Late Night Spot* in the Conch Sound Resort Inn.

Getting There & Away There are six boat slips at the Andros Beach Hotel but no yachting services.

The *Lisa J II* mail boat sails here weekly from Nassau; see the San Andros section for details.

Morgan's Bluff

Two miles northeast of Lowe Sound, the road dead-ends at the tip of the island. There's a nice beach west of the bluff and a wharf where the massive barge that bears 3.2 million gallons of water departs daily for New Providence. The water is drawn from a massive reservoir north of San Andros that is fed by a vast underground aquifer.

If you believe local lore, Henry Morgan, the wily Welsh pirate, hid his treasure in a cave – **Henry Morgan's Cave** – about 30 yards from the road (look for the sign). Like all good pirates, Morgan ravaged throughout the Caribbean, and Andros was not spared. Tree roots wriggle down into the entrance gallery, where the cave slants down just below head height, then opens to a vast Gothic gallery. It would seem from the inscriptions on the walls that the caves are popular trysting spots (not least for bats squirming in the cool shade). Bring a flashlight.

The All Andros & Berry Islands Independence Regatta is held here in mid-July, kicked off by a bonefishing tournament; it features sailboat races, volleyball, boat-building demonstrations, crab cracking, and dominoes. The Police Marching Band and Police Pop Band usually perform.

The bar-cum-restaurant of choice in Morgan's Bluff is Wilmore Lewis' *Willy's Water Lounge*.

The *Lisa J II* mail boat sails here from Nassau each week; see the San Andros section for details.

There's a basic wharf where Patrick Romer sells ice, water, and gasoline. Allen Russell and the Prate brothers rent cars.

Red Bay

Pop 200

This is a colorful albeit down-at-the-heels fishing village, 15 miles northwest of San Andros along a bumpy unpaved road, and it's the only settlement on the west coast of Andros. Uniquely, many of the inhabitants are descendants of Seminole Indians and runaway slaves who fled Florida in the 17th and 18th centuries. Many locals earn an income from weaving, for which they are famed. Using practices passed down from Seminole forebears, they hand-weave watertight straw baskets that sell for US$5 and up. Many are interwoven with locally made batik fabrics. Look for Amelia Marshall, an octogenarian who has been weaving since she was 15.

Other locals are known for their naive wood carvings, notably Henry Wallace, a colorful Rasta character who has exhibited work at the Smithsonian Institution in Washington, DC.

There's no formal restaurant, but you can get snacks at bars such as *Fred Russell's* and the *Marshall Bar*.

Stafford Creek

The road from San Andros cuts inland (due south) through pine forest, then turns east and leaps over the mouth of Stafford Creek. The settlement, north of the creek, is primitive.

On the other side, 1 mile south of the creek, is the **Forfar Field Station** (☎ 242-329-6129), a privately run research station. It's operated by International Field Studies (☎ 614-235-4646, 800-962-3805), 709 College Ave, Columbus, OH 43209, and it is used mostly by North American high school and college students for field studies in geology, marine biology, and ornithology. The main lodge was built as a dive resort by Archie Forfar, who lost his life while attempting to set the world's deep-diving record.

The station has basic accommodations and may be able to take in visitors on an ad hoc basis. *Ellen's Overnight Rest* (☎ 242-329-6111, fax 242-329-6121), in Blanket Sound, has rooms in a basic guesthouse.

ANDROS

The *Lady D* mail boat sails to Stafford Creek and Blanket Sound from Nassau at noon Tuesday (five hours, US$30 one way). It also stops at Staniard Creek, Andros and Coakley towns, and Behring Point.

Staniard Creek

This dispersed, scruffy settlement is on a cay at the south end of Blanket Sound, reached from Queen's Hwy, 25 miles south of San Andros. The place has a backwoods, southern US feel – lots of junked cars rusting outside pastel-colored wooden cabins and mildewed homes. (Beauty is in the eye of the beholder: The *Yachtsman's Guide to The Bahamas and Turks & Caicos* considers the settlement 'attractive . . . [with] each small, neat house in its own garden' and 'a settlement worth visiting.') The 2-mile-long beach rimming its east shore is undisputably lovely.

There's a BaTelCo office just off Queen's Hwy. The Central Andros Clinic (☎ 242-368-2626) is here.

Places to Stay & Eat Staniard Creek has a luxurious rental villa, the four-bedroom *Kamalame Cove* (☎ 242-368-6281, fax 242-368-6279, kamalame@batelnet.bs; in the USA ☎ 305-443-7973), which rents for US$375 per person per night (four people minimum), including meals, a cook, housekeeper, and 16-foot Boston Whaler.

The 'Dickie Brothers' run the modest *Quality Inn Motel* (☎ 242-368-6217) in town. It has a restaurant.

Getting There & Away The *Lady D* mail boat calls here from Nassau on Tuesday; see the Stafford Creek section.

Love Hill

This small settlement astride the main road, about 5 miles south of Staniard Creek, boasts the island's high school. A side road just north of the gas station leads to pleasant Love Hill Beach.

Captain Bill's Blue Hole, hidden amid pine forests, is a popular spot with divers and other guests at Small Hope Bay Lodge in Calabash Bay. There's a ladder and a rope swing for would-be Tarzans. Ducks inhabit the pond. To get there, turn left at the white house with statues of lions on its fence just north of Love Hill; the dirt road – a bumpy old logging road – is good for admiring orchids and butterflies and for bird watching. Turn right at the crossroads; **Desouzas Fruit Farm** is to the left.

Central Andros Inn Motel (☎ 242-368-6209) is a modest, modern motel with 10 rooms for about US$60 per night. It has a small restaurant and characterless bar with a TV and pool table.

There's a gas station in town.

Calabash Bay

This small coastal settlement, at a crook in the road about 2 miles north of Andros Town, is lent a certain charm by its several churches and the flats, which are picked at by herons when the tide is out. (You can also see herons hunting for frogs in the ponds and marshes north of town.)

The bay is also known as Small Hope Bay. Why? 'I'll tell you the same bullshit everybody else does,' says Jeff Birch, owner of Small Hope Bay Lodge, carrying on his father Dick's tall tale (Dick died in 1996.) It seems Henry Morgan and Blackbeard got together here with a cache of treasure. The two rogues rowed ashore with six sailors, buried the loot, then killed the witnesses. As they were rowing back, one said to the other, 'There's small hope that'll ever be found.'

Diving & Snorkeling Small Hope Bay Lodge (see Places to Stay & Eat, below), highly acclaimed by divers, has twice-daily dives for US$45/55 one-/two-tank. It specializes in custom-tailored dives, including blue-hole dives and wall dives to 185 feet. The lodge doesn't have the same restrictions as most resorts do on novice divers; even beginners can dive the wall (free introductory lessons are offered). Only a few people have dived the many sites here. Custom dives cost US$75. PADI certification courses cost US$310. Snorkel trips cost US$15, including a special once-a-week trip with marine biologist Dr Tim

Turnbull. The lodge rents equipment and fills tanks.

Organized Tours Biking and nature tours are offered by Island Vacations (☎ 242-356-1111, fax 242-356-4379), plus a four-day 'Bonefish Heaven' tour. It also offers a 'Water Experience' at Small Hope Bay Lodge, with snorkeling and a learn-to-dive course.

Its mailing address is PO Box 13022, Town Centre Mall, Nassau, Bahamas.

Places to Stay & Eat The family-run *Small Hope Bay Lodge* (☎ 242-368-2014, 800-223-6961, fax 242-368-2015, shbinfo@smallhope.com), just north of Calabash Bay, is a dedicated dive resort and diamond in the rough. Jeff Birch runs the place like one long house party. The large, all-wood lounge with library, games room, large CD collection, and fireplace is a splendid place to relax. There's a bar hewn from half a boat. The 20 large yet spartan pinewood cabins line the beach amid coconut palms. Each has a king-size or double bed. There are four two-bedroom cottages for families (babysitting is offered) and a 'honeymoon' cottage.

Summer rates are US$150/300 single/double with shared bathroom, rising to US$165/325 in winter. The weekly rates are US$1050/2100 with shared bathroom, including airport transfers, three meals daily, all beverages, taxes, service charges, and an introductory scuba or snorkel lesson. Rates for teenagers are US$80 per night; US$40 for children. A private bathroom costs US$45 extra.

The Small Hope Bay Lodge offers self-guided nature walks, plus bird watching and biking tours. A 'Safari to Fresh Creek' offers a chance for you to go snorkeling with a wild dolphin. And what say you to an alfresco hot tub, or a massage for US$30/50 half-/full hour in the thatched solarium intended for all-over tanning? The lodge also has its own charter flights from Fort Lauderdale for US$110 one way. The lodge's local mailing address is PO Box N-1131, Nassau, Bahamas; in the USA you can write to PO Box 21667, Fort Lauderdale, FL 33335.

The restaurant here offers a buffet-style Bahamian lunch with delicious guava duff for dessert. It has a fine US-style breakfast daily, plus a buffet lunch featuring a cold-cuts bar. It also has family-style dining (the cuisine is great) from 7 to 8:30 pm with a choice of entrées. Reservations are essential for nonguests.

Point of View (☎ 242-368-2750), a more upscale, contemporary-style fishing lodge a half-mile south of Calabash Bay, is due to open in late 1997 with 19 rooms.

In town you can try *Sampson's Restaurant* (☎ 242-368-2615) for native dishes.

Getting Around A taxi ride from the Andros Town airport to Small Hope Bay Lodge costs about US$20 for two.

Andros Town & Coakley Town
Pop 500
The main town on North Andros straddles Fresh Creek. The main settlement, Coakley Town, is on the north side of the creek; Andros Town is on the south side. Together they are often referred to as Fresh Creek. The creek extends inland into the depths of Andros. Since 1995 a wild dolphin has returned seasonally (between forays to sea for mating) to live in the creek. You can snorkel with the dolphin, which seems to enjoy human company (see Small Hope Bay Lodge's listing, above).

Swedish industrialist Axel Wenner-Gren launched development here in the 1940s when he bought 35 miles of the east shore and built the Andros Yacht Club (now the Lighthouse Club; see Places to Stay & Eat, below) on the south side of Fresh Creek. The remains of an old lighthouse still stand amid a Fantasia of tropical foliage east of the hotel.

The joint US-UK navies' AUTEC (Atlantic Undersea Test & Evaluation Center) antisubmarine warfare testing facility is 1 mile south of town. The area is strictly off-limits; the same goes for the waters up to 2 miles offshore. Navy personnel often gather to carouse in town.

ANDROS

The Royal Bank of Canada (☎ 242-368-2071) is open 9:30 am to 3:30 pm Wednesday. There's a medical clinic (☎ 242-368-2038) in town. For the police, call ☎ 919 or 242-368-2626.

Androsia Batik Factory No visit to Andros Town is complete without stopping at the factory (☎ 242-352-2255) where the famous Androsia batiks are made. The factory, which employs 45 islanders, is a Birch-family cottage enterprise that exports fashions and fabrics throughout The Bahamas. Melding age-old wax techniques and island motifs, workers create a wide range of fashionwear out of four types of fabrics. It's fascinating to watch the production process; it takes six weeks before the garment is ready for market.

First plain white fabric is stamped with sponge cutouts of shells and other shapes dipped in hot wax and pressed onto the cloth. Then the fabric is steeped in tubs of orange, turquoise, sea-blue, blood-red, pink, or lime-green dye. The waxed surface repels the dye, leaving the desired pattern as plain white. The fabric is then soaked in tubs of extremely hot water that melts and dissolves the wax. The cloth is then hung to dry in the sun before it goes to the cutting and sewing room. You can visit 8 am to 4 pm Monday to Saturday. A guide will show you around.

You can buy at factory prices at the factory outlet. Fabrics cost about US$13 per yard. Kiddies' T-shirts start at US$13, and you'll pay up to US$50 for a dress or shirt.

Twin Lakes At the end of the 19th century, when sisal growers were thriving, young Neville Chamberlain (British prime minister 1937-40) and his father ran a 4000-acre sisal plantation, Twin Lakes Farm, 16 miles inland up Fresh Creek. But the enterprise failed. In 1896 a despondent Neville wrote to his father: 'I no longer see any chance of making the investment pay.' Locals firmly believe that the Chamberlains' effort failed because they disturbed the chickcharnies, who caused Neville no end of grief – not least the scorn of the

Munich Pact. Twin Lakes now lies in ruins, but the two blue holes that lent the plantation its name can still be accessed by a rough, overgrown track.

In recent years Twin Lakes was a haunt for drug-runners. In 1981 two staffers at Forfar Field Station found themselves spread-eagled on the ground with shotguns at their heads. They escaped with their lives but were left with the impression that further forays to the twin lake named Archie's Blue Hole were out of the question.

Somerset Beach This beach is 2 miles south of town. There's not much of a beach at high tide, but when the tide recedes, the miles-long beach is extremely deep and splendid. Wading birds patrol the shore, and you can admire the sand dollars at low tide.

Bonefishing & Sport Fishing Small Hope Bay Lodge and Coakley House (see below) offer bonefishing for US$175/300 half-/full day (add US$40 for fishing North Bight or Stafford Creek). They also have reef fishing for US$220/380 half-/full day and deep-sea fishing for US$275/480 half-/full day. A 36-foot luxury yacht is available for full-day charter for US$800.

The Lighthouse Club & Marina offers bonefishing for US$140/250 half/full day.

Several locals hire out as bonefishing guides. Try Bill Brayden, who has a fleet, for US$150/250 half-/full day for bonefishing and US$300 for full-day deep-sea fishing. Jeff Cartwright is one of the best guides.

Places to Stay & Eat The laid-back, no-frills *Skinny's Landmark Motel* (☎ 242-368-2082), in the heart of Coakley Town, has 15 simply furnished, modestly priced, pine-walled, air-con rooms above a lively restaurant and bar. The rooms have TV, roomy closets, and balconies overlooking the village. Room rates are US$50/65 low/peak season; the motel does not accept credit cards.

Alternately, try Charlie Gay's *Chickcharnie Hotel* (☎ 242-368-2025), with 16 air-con rooms with TV for US$40, shared bathroom; US$60/75 single/double, private bathroom. It's a modest, characterless place, albeit nicely positioned on the waterfront. Bahamian dishes are served in the dining room, which has plate-glass windows overlooking the creek. Charlie, who hangs out in a woolen cap, is a renowned storyteller (who isn't around these parts?).

The most elegant place is government-run *Lighthouse Club & Marina* (☎ 242-368-2305, fax 242-368-2300), on the south side of Fresh Creek. This modern remake of the old Andros Yacht Club has 12 air-con rooms, eight with king-size beds, for US$130 per night single or double, and eight two-bedroom cottages for US$150 for up to four people. All are nicely furnished in Regency reproductions, with TV, air-con, ceiling fan, and tile floors. There is a spacious, elegant restaurant and bar, a games room, bicycle rentals, a swimming pool, two tennis courts, scuba diving, and fishing charters.

The Birch family – which also runs Small Hope Bay Lodge in Calabash Bay – has a luxury three-bedroom villa, *Coakley House*, at the mouth of Fresh Creek in Coakley Town. This beautiful 2100-sq-foot home, amid landscaped grounds, has two large master bedrooms and a third bedroom, all with private bathroom. There's a lounge, dining room, and full kitchen, plus a patio and 120-foot dock. The house sleeps six and is an absolute bargain at US$250/1500 daily/weekly in low season (January and August to mid-December) without housekeeper, US$350/2100 peak season (March, April, and Christmas/New Year's). A housekeeper costs US$35 daily. An all-inclusive plan includes full housekeeping service, with rates for two nights starting at US$770/1000 two/four people in low season, US$970/1200 peak season. A week-long all-inclusive stay costs US$2445/3250 in low season, US$3045/3850 peak season.

Charlie Gay makes a mean conch steak at the Chickcharnie Hotel. Skinny's wife,

Carmetta, brews up a mean hot-pepper sauce to enliven her native dishes at *Skinny's Landmark Restaurant & Satellite Lounge*. Skinny's is also the happenin' place for entertainment. It's lively any night, with live music some weekends when students from the Forfar Field Station come into town.

The elegant Lighthouse Club & Marina restaurant also serves seafood and native dishes, but service is slow. The *Square Deal Restaurant* (☎ 242-368-2593), next to Skinny's, serves simple Bahamian fare.

Getting There & Away Island Express flies from Fort Lauderdale. Bahamasair offers twice-daily service between Nassau and Andros Town (US$45 one way).

The Lighthouse Club & Marina has 18 slips and basic facilities for vessels up to 50 feet. The Chickcharnie Hotel also has slips.

The *Lady D* mail boat calls here from Nassau on Tuesday; see the Stafford Creek section for details.

Getting Around You can rent a car for US$65 to US$85 per day (plus US$200 deposit) from several places. Expect your rental car to be fickle. Try AMKLCO (☎ 242-368-2056) or Bereth Rent-a-Car (☎ 242-368-2102). The road is badly pot-holed; when it's raining, avoid puddles, which often hide potholes deep enough to bend your wheel. Johnny Saunders will run you around in his aging Sedan DeVille.

There's a gas station in Love Hill.

Cargill Creek

Barely anyone resides between Andros Town and the settlement of Cargill Creek, beside its namesake creek, which opens westward into the vast flats of the North and Middle Bights. You are now in bone-fishing territory supreme.

Places to Stay *Cargill Creek Fishing Lodge* (☎ 242-368-5129, fax 242-329-5046; in the USA ☎ 312-263-0328, 800-533-4353) lies on the southern outskirts of the village, beside the creek that offers up prize-winning bonefish. It has 11 simple whitewashed rooms. They're clean, well lit, and tile-floored, with lofty wooden ceilings, air-con, ceiling fan, and hot water. There's also a two-bedroom, two-bathroom cottage. It has a small swimming pool and a lively all-wooden bar and restaurant where fishing types hang out in their gear swapping big-fish stories. Daily rates are US$165/300 single/double (meals are included). Guided fishing costs US$300 daily for two people. Packages are offered. A taxi to/from the airport costs US$30 for one or two people.

Next door is the *Andros Island Bonefishing Club* (☎ 242-368-5167; in the USA 412-935-1577, 800-245-1950, fax 412-935-5388; in the UK ☎ 0171-493-0798, fax 0171-629-5569), of a similar scale and standard. It's run by an amiable host, Rupert Leadon. Most of the 12 spacious cabins are all wood; some are concrete. All have private bathroom, refrigerator, two queen-size beds, and ceiling fans. There's an uninspired restaurant serving native seafood, and a bar with satellite TV. Four-night packages cost US$1465 single, US$980 per person double, including all meals, transfers, and guided fishing; seven-night packages are US$2740/1795, respectively. Extra days cost US$458/295. Rooms cost US$158/146. Its US mailing address is c/o Frontiers, PO Box 959, Wexford, PA 15090-0959; in the UK write c/o Frontiers, 18 Albermarle St, London W1X 3HA.

Places to Eat You can dine at either the Cargill Creek Fishing Lodge or the Andros Island Bonefishing Club. Locals tend to head to *Sea View Restaurant & Bar* (☎ 242-368-4005), 100 yards south of the Cargill Creek Bridge. It's open for breakfast, lunch, and dinner, and serves Bahamian dishes starting at US$5.

Your best bet is *Dig Dig's* (☎ 242-368-5097), a simple roadside restaurant in the home of Liz and Alton Bain (she's Canadian, he's Bahamian). The couple welcomes guests with a splendid house drink (made of gin, condensed milk, and fresh coconut water) before serving their excellent Bahamian cuisine. The entrées average

US$15. You must make reservations beforehand to eat lunch or dinner here.

You can buy groceries at the *Cargill Creek Convenience Store*.

Entertainment The *Cribside Lounge* is the happenin' spot hereabouts; it's open 9 am to 11 pm weekdays and 9 am to 3 am weekends. Leading Bahamian artists perform at least once monthly. A rake 'n' scrape band named Kelly & The Boys often perform. And 'sexiest female' contests are a staple.

Getting There & Away The *Lady Gloria* mail boat sails from Nassau to Cargill Creek and Bowen Sound at 10 pm Tuesday (five hours, US$30 one way).

Behring Point
The Queen's Hwy ends at this pinprick of a hamlet. It sits atop a bluff overlooking the mouth of North Bight, about 20 miles south of Andros Town, at the south end of North Andros. The road continues 1 mile westward in lousy condition along the shore of the bight.

Places to Stay & Eat The small, no-frills *Tranquility Hill* (☎ 242-368-4132) has 10 air-con rooms with lofty wooden ceilings and tile floors. Seven have double beds; three larger, attractive units upstairs have king-size beds and more light. All have TV and fans. Rooms cost an unfathomably steep US$148/155 downstairs/upstairs *per person* in peak season, including three meals daily. A small dining room serves native dishes. There's a small bar with satellite TV. The hotel has five boats; bonefishing costs US$300 full day for two people.

A half-mile farther west is *Charlie's Haven* (☎ 242-368-4087, 888-262-0700), a handsome property of stone and varnished wood, with a lively lounge bar where locals and guests hang out with the proprietor Charlie Smith, alias Bonefish Charlie, an eccentric and colorful character. This outspoken old-timer invented the 'Crazy Charlie' fly. His place has 10 sparsely furnished air-con rooms with ceiling fans and beds covered in tartan blankets for US$130 per person, including three meals daily. Charlie charges US$300 per day for guided fishing. He'll teach beginners the art of casting a lure. Charlie has a loyal following among guests. No credit cards.

At the end of the road, a half-mile west of Charlie's Haven, is *Daisy Nottage's Cottages* (☎ 242-368-4293). Daisy – another animated character who also practices bush medicine – rents 10 modest yet appealing modern rooms, plus five two-bedroom cottages with kitchen and living room. Ya gotta like cats . . . two dozen live on-site! There's a restaurant and bar where Daisy serves conch and other seafood, served with mashed potatoes and fries.

Charlie Smith planned to reopen the *Bang Bang Club*, a famous fishing club on Port Cay, off Big Wood Cay at the west end of North Bight. It was due to open by the end of 1997 with 10 rooms and a four-bedroom cottage, plus dock, pool, kitchen, and dining room. Rates are negotiable, but should be about US$130 daily.

Getting There & Away The mail boat *Lady D* calls here from Nassau on Tuesday; see the Stafford Creek section for more information.

Mangrove Cay

Pop 1500

Mangrove Cay, or Central Andros, is the smallest of the three Andros islands.

Little Harbour is the only concentrated settlement, stretching 2 miles south from the north tip of the cay. It's often referred to as Moxey Town, which is actually the northern division of Little Harbour.

First impressions are of relative wealth, suggested by the predominance of nice concrete housing. Electricity only came to Mangrove Cay in 1989, when everybody gathered under its welcome glow, as if hot showers had arrived. Most locals make an income from lobstering, crabbing, or sponging. Lynward Saunders (☎ 242-369-0414) will show you around his processing shed, where sponges are cleaned and dried and made ready for export, mostly to Belgium.

Farther south, income levels drop and the half-dozen or so tiny settlements are more rundown. If you're into churches, check out the Anglican Church in Dorset, about 4 miles south of Moxey Town.

A narrow beach lines almost the entire east shore, and at least 23 blue holes await exploration.

One road – Queen's Hwy – runs the island's 10-mile length, ending at motley Lisbon Creek, facing South Bight.

Information

The BaTelCo office is a half-mile south of Dorset. The Mangrove Cay Clinic (☎ 242-369-0089) is in Dorset. You can buy pharmaceuticals at Saunder's Drugs, across the road from the White Sand Beach Hotel.

Bonefishing

There is no shortage of potential guides. I recommend Ralph Moxey or 'Bonefish' John, who charges US$250 daily for two people. He's a colorful character with an unlit cigar constantly in his mouth; he'll light up when you strike a 10-lb fish!

Special Events

Little Harbour hosts the three-day August Monday Regatta, when Bahamian skippers congregate to outpace each other. The highlight of the social calendar is the Annual Regatta, also in August, in Lisbon Creek.

Places to Stay

The atmospheric *Moxey's Guest House & Bonefish Lodge* (☎ 242-369-0023), on the shore in Moxey Town, has six rooms and two suites, the latter with four double beds and kitchen. All have air-con and fans and are modestly yet attractively furnished. There's a delightful dining room, plus a splendid and popular bar with a separate pool room.

Fred Sturrup runs *Hellen's Motel Complex* (☎ 242-369-0033), a small, modern complex with 10 rooms across the road from a beach, about 1 mile south of Moxey Town. They're clean, tiled, and have kitchenette and small TV; US$50/65 without/with air-con. There are also air-con cottage minisuites for US$75. Additional rooms are being added on the hill at the back. The hotel has a tiny restaurant and bar with TV. It's popular with Bahamians.

The older *White Sand Beach Hotel* (☎ 242-369-0159), about 400 yards south of Hellen's, has 25 large, carpeted rooms, each capable of sleeping six. They have air-con and fans but are rather dour and dingy. The rooms open to a rundown patio facing the narrow beach, with bonefish flats in front. Newer apartment units are being added.

The snazziest place hereabouts is the *Seascape Inn* (☎ 242-369-0342), 2 miles south of Moxey Town on the beachfront amid palms. Opened in 1997 by Americans Micky and Joan McGowan, it has five small, simple cabins raised off the ground. They're delightfully decorated, with high wooden ceilings, fans, heaps of light, and wooden patios. Three have single beds; two have queen-size beds. There's a lofty all-timber restaurant and bar on tall stilts, with a TV, dart board, and stereo. Dinners include continental fare; on Sunday a fish fry is hosted. The resort has a dive center (you can rent scuba and snorkel gear), and there are bicycles for rent, plus hammocks and lounge chairs for lazing. A guided kayak trip explores the bight and includes a picnic. And there's a small swampland nearby, which is great for bird watching. The US$90 rate includes a daily continental breakfast. The mailing address is PO Box 023824, Mangrove Cay, Andros, Bahamas.

Another attractive option is the modern yet homey *Mangrove Cay Inn* (☎ 242-369-0069, fax 242-369-0014), run by gracious hosts Elliot and Pat Greene (he's from the island, she's from New York). It's set amid lawns and has a path to the beach, about 200 yards away, and to three nearby blue holes. The 12 air-con, dimly lit rooms are carpeted, with wooden ceiling, pink decor, ceiling fan, and a little bathroom; they cost US$65. Bike and snorkel-gear rentals are offered. There's a laundry and a bar with an electric piano.

There are at least three other basic guesthouses: *Cool Breeze Cottage* (☎ 242-369-0465), the spartan *Bannister Guest House* (☎ 242-369-0188), and *Longley's Guest House* (☎ 242-369-0311); the latter two are in Lisbon Creek.

Places to Eat
Hellen's has a restaurant and lounge serving native dishes such as stew conch and fish and grits for US$6.50. Fish and chips cost US$5. Similar dishes are served at *Stacey's Restaurant & Lounge*, about 100 yards south of Hellen's. The restaurant at *Mangrove Cay Inn* has a large menu of salads and sandwiches, plus seafood and meat dishes for US$8 to US$16, best washed down with a superb fruit punch.

Diane Cash will cook you native dishes such as peas 'n' rice; she has a small place about 1 mile south of the Seascape Inn. If you're staying at Mangrove Cay Inn, you might stray down the road to *Auntie B's Restaurant* for simple native dishes.

In Lisbon Creek try the *Aqua-Marine Club*, where Sylvia Bannister cooks up tasty seafood for less than US$10.

You can buy groceries at *McPhee's Food & Variety Store*, opposite Seascape Inn.

Entertainment
The place to sip a drink is at the *Angler's Bar & Grill* at Moxey's Guest House; the hardwood bar provides considerable ambiance. The *Seaman's Club*, on the waterfront in Burnt Rock, 2 miles south of Moxey Town, is another colorful place frequented by locals.

The liveliest place on Mangrove Cay is Henry Rolle's *Happy Tree*, a soca club with live music, dancing, and a pool table. It's in Grants, which is south of Moxey Town. You can also learn some sexy moves at the happenin' *The New Happy Three Soca Club* (☎ 242-369-0030).

Things to Buy
The Hibiscus Gift Shop, opposite the Mangrove Cay Inn, sells painted T-shirts, locally made baskets and straw-work, jewelry, and other island-made items.

Getting There & Away
Bahamasair has seasonal service from Nassau. Congo Air (on Mangrove Cay ☎ 242-369-0021) flies from Nassau to Mangrove Cay at 7:30 am and 4 pm daily, continuing to Congo Town (South Andros). Island Express flies from Fort Lauderdale.

You can catch the small, government-run passenger ferry that runs from Lisbon Creek to Drigg's Hill (South Andros) at 8 am and 4 pm daily. It's free. Mr Moxey, the skipper, will run you across at other times for a fee. There's a telephone but no other facilities at the ferry dock.

The *Mangrove Cay Express* mail boat sails to Lisbon Creek from Nassau at 6 pm Wednesday (5½ hours, US$30 one way).

Hubert King (☎ 242-369-0478) will deliver gas or diesel to boaters in Moxey Town or Lisbon Creek.

Getting Around
There are two taxis run by Sister B ('B' for Bertha) and Rodam Greene. A ride from the airport to Moxey's Guest House costs about US$6; from the airport to the South Andros ferry costs US$17.

South Andros

South Andros is virtually bypassed by tourists, although the bonefishing is superb and there are some beautiful beaches. Sir Lynden Pindling (former Bahamian prime minister) hails from here, and the local citizenry, uniquely among Bahamians these days, remains partisan in his favor. Despite two decades of favoritism under Pindling's tenure, the island is even less developed than North and Central Andros. It is home to a few Androsian iguanas, which can grow to 5 feet in length; they dwell in scattered coppices where wild boars and people rarely venture.

Drigg's Hill to Congo Town
Anyone flying to South Andros will land at the Congo Town airport, 3 miles south of Drigg's Hill, a scrawny hamlet facing onto South Bight at the north tip of the island. The equally diminutive settlement of Congo Town, also known as Long Bay, is 2 miles south of the airport.

There's a BaTelCo office by the ferry terminal at the end of the road in Drigg's Hill.

Stanley 'Jolly Boy' Forbes (☎ 242-369-2767), a good-humored, roly-poly fella, will take you bonefishing for US$300 daily for two people.

A friendly, motivated young chap named Gibson McKenzie leads a walking tour to a blue hole and the swampland. It takes about two hours. Make arrangements at Emerald Palms by the Sea (see below).

Places to Stay The government-owned *Emerald Palms by the Sea* (☎ 242-369-2661, 800-688-4752, fax 242-369-2667), is 3 miles north of the airport, and the only 'resort'-style place to stay on Andros. It conjures up images of Hawaii, with its salmon decor and tall palms lining the beach. The 20 air-con rooms all have ceiling fans, TV/VCR, and refrigerator. They're somewhat small and stuffy, but handsomely appointed with teak reproduction antique furniture, including an option for a king-size four-poster bed with down duvet, crisp linens, and mosquito nets adding a honeymooners' touch. The elegant dining room has plate-glass windows opening to the pool and beach, where buffets are sometimes hosted. There's a tennis court, shuffleboard, Hobie Cats, and Aqua-Views (surfboards that you lie on and marvel at the marine world through a small glass window), plus hammocks slung between palms. Bonefishing, diving, snorkeling, and sightseeing excursions are offered. The staff are super-friendly and eager, and the mood is relaxed. The resort also has a gift shop. Rooms cost

ANDROS

US$80/100/130 single/double/triple; the Lanai suite costs US$135/160/190. A MAP (breakfast and dinner) plan costs US$40 daily. The mailing address is PO Box 800, Drigg's Hill, Andros, Bahamas.

Stuart's Cove Apartments (☎ 242-369-1891) has two modest apartments beside the road 2 miles south of the airport.

The *Congo Town Motel* (☎ 242-329-4777), beside the beach in Congo Town, 2 miles south of Emerald Palms, looked closed in mid-1997.

Places to Eat The *Emerald Palms* serves good meals, including glazed conch, crepe suzettes, stingray, and sea urchin. US or native breakfasts cost US$4 to US$7; dinners are double that. For a more down-to-earth experience, try the *Square Deal*, a native eatery on the roadside 400 yards south of the hotel, or there's the *Bluebird Club* and *Flamingo Club* (☎ 242-369-2671) in Drigg's Hill; the latter serves good cracked conch and native dishes. Both clubs have pool tables and are good spots to get a taste of local nightlife.

Things to Buy Try Gibson's Straw Market in Congo Town. You can buy homemade jewelry crafted from shells at Wendy's Craft Center, opposite the BaTelCo office in Drigg's Hill.

Getting There & Away The Congo Town airport has a snack bar and telephones. If your flight is delayed, you can also buy cooked meals at L&M Restaurant & Take-Away on the roadside 100 yards south of the airport.

Bahamasair (on South Andros ☎ 242-369-2806) flies daily from Nassau (US$45 one way).

Congo Air (in Congo Town ☎ 242-369-2632) flies from Nassau to Congo Town via Mangrove Cay at 7:30 am and 4 pm daily. Return flights depart at 8:15 am and 4:45 pm. Congo Air also flies from Congo Town to Freeport at 11:15 am on Friday and Saturday.

Occasionally (when the driver is on the island) there's a minibus that runs continu-ally between Drigg's Hill and Mars Bay. The fare from Drigg's Hill to Kemp's Bay is US$2; US$5 for destinations farther south.

A small, passengers-only government ferry runs from Lisbon Creek on Mangrove Cay (see the Mangrove Cay section, earlier in this chapter).

The mail boat *Captain Moxey* sails to Drigg's Hill and Congo Town from Nassau at 11 pm Monday (7½ hours, US$30 one way), stopping at The Bluff and Kemp's Bay as well.

Getting Around You can arrange car rentals through Emerald Palms (see Places to Stay, above). You can rent from any local willing to give up his or her car. It's a lackadaisical affair, and your car may not be delivered until midday; if so, bargain a rate other than the standard US$65 per day (a US$100 deposit is normal).

The Bluff & High Rock
Three miles south of Congo Town, The Bluff is the largest and most orderly settle-ment on the island. The government administrative offices for South Andros are here. The village extends south to the suburb of High Rock, a more disorderly affair atop a limestone bluff overlooking fabulously blue flats extending out for more than a mile. Two narrow yet beautiful beaches run north and south.

The Government Administrative Office, at the south end of The Bluff, contains the post office, BaTelCo, and police offices. There's a tiny library at the south end of The Bluff; it's open 10:30 am to 5:30 pm weekdays.

Places to Stay & Eat If you're looking for simple accommodations, try *Lewis' Guest House* atop the bluff, with fine views of the ocean. At press time it had 10 rooms but was adding six more directly over the ocean. Each room has private bathroom, TV, and fan, and costs about US$50. A beautician's shop is to be added soon, and bonefishing and diving will be introduced.

Kemp's Guest House (☎ 242-369-3796) has six tiny and very dark rooms next to the Ocean Restaurant in High Rock. They're scantily furnished but have ceiling fan, TV, and surprisingly large and well-lit bathrooms. Four rooms share a bathroom.

Haylean's Restaurant (☎ 242-369-3505) in High Rock is recommended for chicken 'n' souse and other native dishes. Here, too, is the *Ocean Club*, serving breakfasts for about US$6 and dinners for US$8, and *Big J's*, serving breakfasts such as sheep's-tongue souse and grits, sausage, and eggs for US$5, as well as lunch and dinner.

Getting There & Away The mail boat *Captain Moxey* calls weekly from Nassau; see the Drigg's Hill to Congo Town section for details.

Getting Around Orthniel Lewis is planning to offer car rentals in The Bluff, where there's a gas station.

Kemp's Bay

Kemp's Bay, 5 miles south of High Rock, is a small yet lively center of action, with the island's high school and a concentration of services. The settlement seems to be run by Norman Rahming, the local padrone, who owns the grocery, marina, boatyard (where Rahming Bonefishing skiffs are made), sport-fishing camp, small guesthouse, and car-rental agency.

The local fishermen look toward Tinker's Rock, which is 1 mile offshore. It's favored by schooling groupers on their annual run. In season, hire a boatsman such as Nathaniel Adams and join the other skiffs and sailless yawls running handlines and traps for the big fish, which have been described as 'stacked in countless layers, thick as sand.' You'd have to be a fisherman, I guess, to get off on the sight of these 20-lb-plus fish with their gaping mouths and lustrous reddish bands being clubbed to death by the frenzied locals. The schooling is a major source of local income, and the fishermen's wives wait on shore with bloodstained aprons and machetes, ready to prepare the daily catch,

which will be shipped aboard the weekly mail boat to the Nassau market.

The only bank on the island, Bank of The Bahamas, is here; it's open 10 am to 2:45 pm Wednesday. For the police, call ☎ 919 or 242-369-4733.

Places to Stay & Eat *Rolle's Enterprises* (☎ /fax 242-369-1723) rents apartments in Smith Hill, 1 mile north of Kemp's Bay. A wash house, restaurant, and bar are attached. *Rehring's Food Store* (☎ 242-369-1608, fax 242-369-1934), in Kemp's Bay, also has modest apartments for rent.

Modest *Royal Palm Bonefishing Bay Camp* (in the USA ☎ 813-249-9908, 800-450-9908, fax 813-889-9189) has five carpeted double air-con rooms with TV and minifridge. At press time some were a bit dowdy, with raggedy furniture; others were brighter and better furnished. You can also rent a handsome little two-bedroom cottage made of conch shells! It has a full kitchen and sleeps four people. There's a small restaurant, and a swimming pool was planned. Rooms cost US$100 single or double. Four-night packages cost US$1400 single, US$1100 per person double, including three days' fishing, meals, transfers, and extras. Its mailing address is 5700 Memorial Hwy, No 107, Tampa, FL 33615.

There's a *grocery* and *general goods store* next to Lewis' Guest House, where *Lewis' Restaurant & Bar* offers barbecues on weekends. In Kemp's Bay you can buy groceries at *Rehring's Food Store*.

Entertainment Many locals sup at the *Ocean Club Restaurant & Bar* (☎ 242-369-4796) and at *Big J's on the Bay* (☎ 242-369-1954) in Kemp's Bay. On weekend nights head to Smith Hill, where the beachfront *Cabana Beach Bar* hosts dancing. It has picnic tables and chairs under the palms. *Lewis' Bar* has a dance hall on weekends, when it gets lively.

Getting There & Away A minibus from Drigg's Hill occasionally stops here; see the Drigg's Hill to Congo Town section for information.

ANDROS

The *Captain Moxey* mail boat calls here weekly from Nassau; see the Drigg's Hill to Congo Town section, earlier in this chapter, for details.

Getting Around You can rent cars for US$65 at Rahming's Car Rental (☎ 242-369-1608) at the gas station.

Kemp's Bay to Mars Bay

The road continues south, with bridges skipping over Deep Creek and Little Creek via the settlements of those names, then runs through the tiny settlement of Pleasant Bay before arriving in Mars Bay. Here the road comes to an abrupt halt.

Mars Bay is a colorful seaside settlement with quaint wooden and emancipation-era stone houses painted in bright pastels. You may see old ladies weaving straw, and the fishermen scaling their catch down by the wharf, where a grand old Androsian schooner lies beached.

Stargate Blue Hole This limpidly azure blue hole, looking like a country pond, is actually the local harbor! It descends to about 300 feet, with galleries of stalactites and stalagmites. The experience of diving into its bowels was described by explorer Rob Palmer as like 'swimming down the Grand Canyon at night.' Palmer found Lucayan remains in the subaqueous cave, including an intact canoe!

Places to Stay & Eat *Glato's Apartments* (☎ 242-369-4669), 400 yards north of the bridge over Deep Creek, offers six basic family apartments for US$50. They sit amid lawns within yards of the ocean and are fully furnished but a bit dour. They'd be a good escape from the tourist track for anyone not fussy about aesthetics.

Pure Gold Sports (☎ 242-357-2007), a bonefishing camp at Deep Creek, is run by Stan Clarke. It's more upscale than most fishing camps hereabouts, with a somnolent aura and suites overlooking a vast, blindingly white sandbar.

For a more intimate experience, head to Little Creek and check in at the beachside *Bair Bahamas Guest House* (☎ /fax 242-369-4518), where American man-and-wife team Stanley and Andy Bair play host at their charming, strawberry-pink three-bedroom guesthouse. Imagine, no more than five other anglers at any give time! Local guides take you out on the 17-foot Bonefisher and 18-foot Rahming craft. Meals are also served.

The place to grab a snack in Mars Bay is *Fisherman's Paradise*, which serves Bahamian dishes. Snacks cost from US$4 to US$10.

Getting There & Away A minibus from Drigg's Hill runs to Mars Bay; see the Drigg's Hill to Congo Town section, earlier in this chapter, for more information.

Eleuthera

Pop 10,524

Eleuthera, a slender wisp of an island about 100 miles long yet barely a bowshot wide, arcs on a radius about 50 miles east of Nassau. It has traditionally been the destination of choice for hobnobbing socialites, drawn here by chic club resorts and by sands the delicate hue of Cristal Rosé champagne.

The name 'Eleuthera' comes from the Greek word *eleutheros*, meaning freedom (the Lucayans who originally settled the island called their home 'Cigatoo'). Inarguably, the island is liberating. In 1648 the majority of the 70 Eleutheran Adventurers (see History in the Facts about The Bahamas chapter), who fled religious persecution in Bermuda during the English Civil War era, put ashore on the island's north coast where, apparently, they holed up in Preacher's Cave. Actually, before they found Eleuthera, the island – or rather the Devil's Backbone, an extensive coral reef – found *them*, ripping open the bottom of their boats and forestalling further travel. Thus began English settlement in the Bahamas. They were later joined by Loyalists, who brought their slaves and founded new settlements; the Puritans disdained slavery and *arrivistes*.

Throughout the 18th century, pineapple production blossomed, and a local variety – the Eleutheran sugar loaf – earned recognition as an especially succulent fruit. In 1900 production peaked, and 7 million pineapples were exported. Alas, they were eventually supplanted by fruit from Cuba, Jamaica, and Hawaii (US tariffs were erected on Bahamian pineapples). Eleuthera's pineapple farmers are now a dying breed. Raising pineapples is labor-intensive, requiring backbreaking work that has little appeal for young people, who also have limited patience for the pineapple's 18-month maturation period. Long gone are the days when

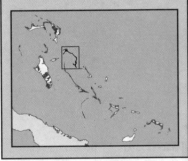

Eleuthera's pineapples were exported to the USA, Europe, and the Caribbean.

Since independence, tourism on the mainland also has withered, and many once-fashionable resort hotels are now closed. A vast number of locals blame the policies of the Pindling government, which chased foreign investment away. Abandoned silos recall the thriving cattle and chicken industries that evolved in the 1950s, concentrated near Hatchet Bay. Alas, following independence the government bought out the farmers, and within a short span the farms were derelict. Numerous fine homes of the American farmers were claimed by squatters and have gone to hell, too!

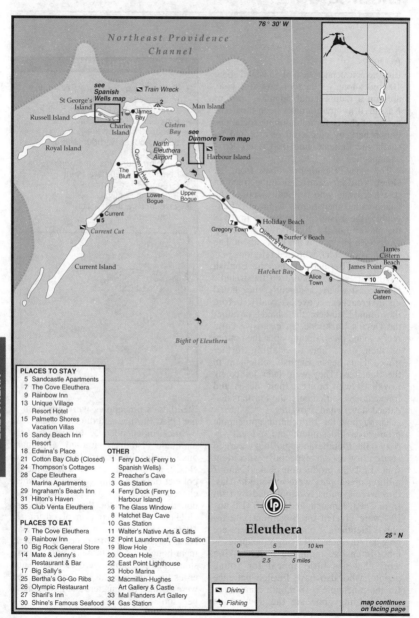

Northeast Providence Channel

76° 30' W

☒ Train Wreck

see Spanish Wells map

St George's Island

Russell Island

Royal Island

Charles Island

James Bay

Man Island

Cistern Bay

see Dunmore Town map

North Eleuthera Airport

☒ Harbour Island

The Bluff

Queen's Hwy

Lower Bogue

Upper Bogue

Current

☒ 5

Current Cut

Current Island

Holiday Beach

Gregory Town

Queen's Hwy

Surfer's Beach

James Cistern Beach

James Point

▼ 10

James Cistern

Hatchet Bay

Alice Town

Bight of Eleuthera

25° N

PLACES TO STAY
5 Sandcastle Apartments
7 The Cove Eleuthera
9 Rainbow Inn
13 Unique Village Resort Hotel
15 Palmetto Shores Vacation Villas
16 Sandy Beach Inn Resort
18 Edwina's Place
21 Cotton Bay Club (Closed)
24 Thompson's Cottages
28 Cape Eleuthera Marina Apartments
29 Ingraham's Beach Inn
31 Hilton's Haven
35 Club Venta Eleuthera

PLACES TO EAT
7 The Cove Eleuthera
9 Rainbow Inn
10 Big Rock General Store
14 Mate & Jenny's Restaurant & Bar
17 Big Sally's
25 Bertha's Go-Go Ribs
26 Olympic Restaurant
27 Sharil's Inn
30 Shine's Famous Seafood

OTHER
1 Ferry Dock (Ferry to Spanish Wells)
2 Preacher's Cave
3 Gas Station
4 Ferry Dock (Ferry to Harbour Island)
6 The Glass Window
8 Hatchet Bay Cave
10 Gas Station
11 Walter's Native Arts & Gifts
12 Point Laundromat, Gas Station
19 Blow Hole
20 Ocean Hole
22 East Point Lighthouse
23 Hobo Marina
32 Macmillan-Hughes Art Gallery & Castle
33 Mal Flanders Art Gallery
34 Gas Station

Eleuthera

0 5 10 km
0 2.5 5 miles

☒ Diving
⚓ Fishing

map continues on facing page

ELEUTHERA

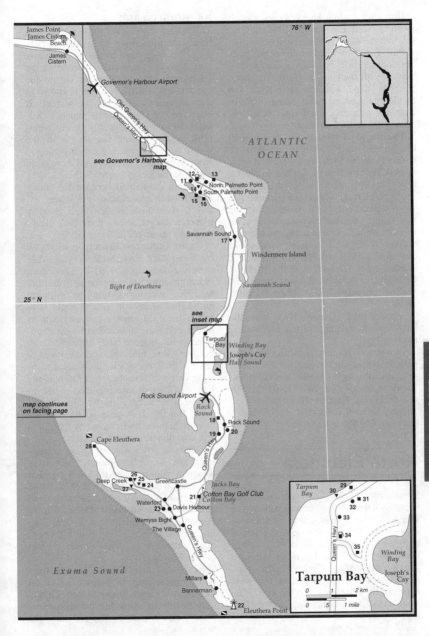

ELEUTHERA

James Point
James Cistern Beach
James Cistern

Governor's Harbour Airport

Old Queen's Hwy
Queen's Hwy

ATLANTIC OCEAN

see Governor's Harbour map

76° W

12 13
11 North Palmetto Point
14 South Palmetto Point
15 16

Savannah Sound
17

Windermere Island

Bight of Eleuthera

Savannah Sound

25° N

see inset map

Tarpum Bay

Winding Bay
Joseph's Cay
Half Sound

Rock Sound Airport

Rock Sound

18 Rock Sound
19 20

Cape Eleuthera

28

map continues on facing page

26 25
Deep Creek 24 Greencastle
27

Jacks Bay

21 Cotton Bay Golf Club
Cotton Bay

Waterford
23 Davis Harbour
Wemyss Bight
The Village

Queen's Hwy

Exuma Sound

Millars
Bannerman

22 Eleuthera Point

Tarpum Bay

30 29
31
32
33
34
35

Winding Bay

Joseph's Cay

Tarpum Bay

0   1   2 km
0   .5   1 mile

Hurricane Andrew knocked the socks off much of North Eleuthera in 1992, rubbing salt into the wounds of a stalled economy.

Still, Eleuthera remains one of the more developed Family Islands, concentrated on two cays off the coast of North Eleuthera: Harbour Island, with Dunmore Town, and St George's Island, with Spanish Wells. Both are booming, the former from lobstering, the latter from tourism.

The island is famous for its stunning blush-pink sands washed by Atlantic rollers (you can even catch a wave at aptly named Surfer's Beach). On the east coast dramatic cliffs, sheltered coves, and offshore coral reefs add to the picture. The Devil's Backbone is still there and in the intervening years has claimed several other ill-fated ships, whose remains await exploration. Divers who 'collect' wrecks will even find a US Civil War-era locomotive submerged at 20 feet. And the Bight of Eleuthera, to the west, is a vast expanse of shallow pavonine waters where bonefish await.

A paved road – Queen's Hwy – runs the length of the island, making exploration simple.

Tarbox Geographix publishes four superb sectional tourist maps of Eleuthera, available through Charlie Moore at the Rainbow Inn (☎ /fax 242-335-0294, 800-688-0047) at Hatchet Bay; its mailing address is PO Box EL-25053, Governor's Harbour, Eleuthera, Bahamas.

North Eleuthera

Eleuthera is neatly divided north and south by a tendril-thin isthmus called 'The Glass Window,' one-quarter of the way down the island. Southward, the island dangles like an umbilical cord. Immediately north, the isle broadens out in a rough triangle shaped like a woodpecker's head, with Current Island to the west forming the long beak. To the east, Harbour Island and neighboring cays enclose a vast harbor.

HARBOUR ISLAND

This island, 2 miles off the mainland and barely 3 miles long by a quarter-mile wide, has been rated by *Travel & Leisure* magazine as 'the prettiest' island in the Caribbean. That's a tall order, but no one can argue that 'Briland,' as it is known to the cognoscenti, *is* picture-perfect. It boasts one of The Bahamas' quaintest villages and an indescribably lovely coral-pink beach running the length of the windward shore, where breakers rolling in from Africa are stopped by offshore coral reefs, guaranteeing superb bathing.

Briland (so-named because the locals have trouble pronouncing the letters 'H' and 'R') blends old and new, highlighted by topnotch resorts, among them Pink Sands, the finest resort in The Bahamas.

Quaint **Dunmore Town** (pop 1500), on the harbor side, harks back 300 years. The town was laid out in 1791 by Lord Dunmore, governor of the Bahamas from 1787 to 1796, who had a summer residence here. This time-warp village could have fallen from an artist's canvas, with its pastel-painted clapboard cottages decorated with filigree and surrounded by bougainvillea, hibiscus, and oleander. In town a gray horse still pulls an Amish-style carriage complete with a swinging lantern. Otherwise the clip-clop of hooves has been replaced with the whir of golf carts. But the daily pace is characteristically Bahamian, underscored by the charm and friendliness of the Brilanders.

Dunmore Town was once a noted shipyard and a sugar-refining center from which a rum-making tradition evolved (fortunes were boosted by Prohibition in 1920). Today many adults are employed at the dozen or so hotels. Others fish, or commute to the mainland to farm land bequeathed to their ancestors in 1783 or to plant and pick in Eleuthera's pineapple and orange groves.

Renowned artist Eddie Minnis lives here, representing his beloved island on canvas. And singer Jimmy Buffett is a regular visitor (piloting his Albatross seaplane), as are many Hollywood stars and

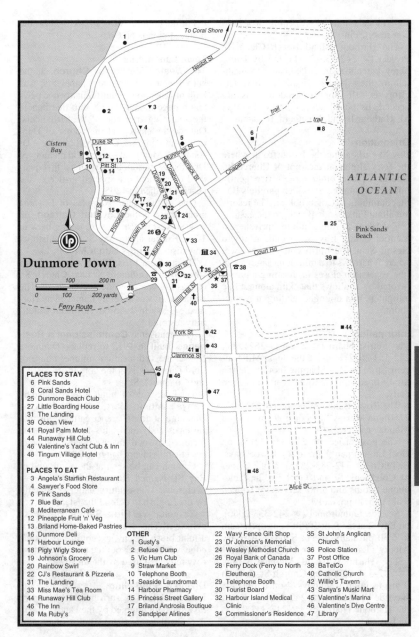

Dunmore Town

ATLANTIC OCEAN

Pink Sands Beach

Ferry Route

To Coral Shore

Cistern Bay

Streets labeled on map: Nesbit St, Duke St, Pitt St, King St, Bay St, Princess St, Crown St, Murray St, Munnings St, Dunmore St, Colebrook St, Barrack St, Chapel St, Church St, Gaol Ln, Hill St, Court Rd, York St, Clarence St, South St, Alice SC

ELEUTHERA

PLACES TO STAY
6 Pink Sands
8 Coral Sands Hotel
25 Dunmore Beach Club
27 Little Boarding House
31 The Landing
39 Ocean View
41 Royal Palm Motel
44 Runaway Hill Club
46 Valentine's Yacht Club & Inn
48 Tingum Village Hotel

PLACES TO EAT
3 Angela's Starfish Restaurant
4 Sawyer's Food Store
6 Pink Sands
7 Blue Bar
8 Mediterranean Café
12 Pineapple Fruit 'n' Veg
13 Briland Home-Baked Pastries
16 Dunmore Deli
17 Harbour Lounge
18 Pigly Wigly Store
19 Johnson's Grocery
20 Rainbow Swirl
22 CJ's Restaurant & Pizzeria
31 The Landing
33 Miss Mae's Tea Room
44 Runaway Hill Club
46 The Inn
48 Ma Ruby's

OTHER
1 Gusty's
2 Refuse Dump
5 Vic Hum Club
9 Straw Market
10 Telephone Booth
11 Seaside Laundromat
14 Harbour Pharmacy
15 Princess Street Gallery
17 Briland Androsia Boutique
21 Sandpiper Airlines

22 Wavy Fence Gift Shop
23 Dr Johnson's Memorial
24 Wesley Methodist Church
26 Royal Bank of Canada
28 Ferry Dock (Ferry to North Eleuthera)
29 Telephone Booth
30 Tourist Board
32 Harbour Island Medical Clinic
34 Commissioner's Residence

35 St John's Anglican Church
36 Police Station
37 Post Office
38 BaTelCo
40 Catholic Church
42 Willie's Tavern
43 Sanya's Music Mart
45 Valentine's Marina
46 Valentine's Dive Centre
47 Library

supermodels since the opening of a popular resort, Pink Sands.

The Harbour Island Beach Clean-Up Project (☎ 242-333-2161), led by Humphrey Percentie, Jr, is dedicated to maintaining the island's pristine quality. The effort is self-supporting; donations are needed. Its postal address is PO EL-Box 61, Harbour Island, Eleuthera, Bahamas.

Orientation

Bay St curls along the harborfront, where the ferry alights at the foot of Church St. Church St and other streets rise gently inland to Dunmore St, which parallels Bay St, continuing to Colebrook St. The resorts are along Pink Sands Beach, to the east.

Colebrook St runs south to a private residential estate. Bay St extends north to Nesbit St at the north end of the town, where it narrows to a mile-long sandy track (the vegetation closes in, forming a tunnel favored by swallows that skim along it like jetfighters in a dogfight) ending at a coral shore.

Information

The tourist board (☎ 242-333-2621, fax 242-333-2622) is above the Sugar Mill souvenir store on Bay St at the foot of Church St; it's open 9:30 am to 1 pm and 3 to 5 pm daily.

The Royal Bank of Canada (☎ 242-333-2250), on Murray St, is open 9 am to 1 pm Monday and Friday.

The post office (☎ 242-333-2215), on Goal Ln, is open 9 am to 5 pm weekdays. BaTelCo (☎ 242-333-2375), at the corner of Colebrook St and Goal Ln, has telephone booths and a fax service; it is open 8 am to 5:30 pm daily.

Seaside Laundromat (☎ 242-333-2066), on Bay St at the foot of Pitt St, is open 6 am to 6:30 pm daily except Sunday. Also try Albury's Laundromat (☎ 242-333-2406).

The Harbour Island Medical Clinic (☎ 242-333-2225), on Church St, is open 9 am to noon weekdays. You'll find the Bayside Drug Store (☎ 242-333-2174) and the Harbour Pharmacy (☎ 242-333-2178) on Bay St.

For the police, call ☎ 242-333-2111; the police station is on Goal Ln.

Town Landmarks

The **Wesley Methodist Church**, at the corner of Dunmore and Chapel Sts, was built in 1843, with beautiful hardwood pews and a huge model sailing ship that honors the seafaring tradition of the Brilanders. Outside the church, at the corner of Dunmore and King Sts, is a small obelisk – Dr Johnson's Memorial – erected in memory of Dr Albert Johnson, the Bahamas' first qualified doctor and a respected justice of the peace who died in 1895.

One of the finest examples of Loyalist architecture is the **Loyalist Cottage**, on Bay St west of Princess St, dating back to 1797. Farther along Bay St is the historic, now disused **Higgs Sugar Mill**.

Dating from 1768, **St John's Anglican Church**, on Dunmore St near Church St, claims to be the oldest church in The Bahamas. It was severely damaged by Hurricane Betsy in 1965 but has been beautifully restored.

The handsome **Commissioner's Residence**, built in 1913 to replace Dunmore House, the 18th-century summer house of Lord Dunmore, is at the corner of Goal Ln and Colebrook St.

The funky side of things is represented by **Sanya's Music Mart**, a small shack on Dunmore St near Clarence St that sells music tapes and videos. It's more interesting for the driftwood, license plates, and other eclectic miscellany hanging outside.

Cannon can be seen at the south end of Bay St. Named **Roundheads**, this now overgrown 17th-century battery was built by the English to defend the island.

Ya gotta see **Pink Sands Beach** to believe it! This deep, miles-long stunner is a faint blush by day, except at the water's edge, which brings out the rouge, turning a rosy red when fired by the dawn.

Diving & Snorkeling

Harbour Island is surrounded by superb dive sites, highlighted by the Devil's Backbone, with more than 3 miles of pristine reefs littered with ancient wrecks. Among them are *Cienfuegos*, a cruise ship; the *Potato & Onion*, a massive 19th-century wreck just 15 feet down; and the Train Wreck, a locomotive that the Confederacy captured from the Union during the US Civil War and sold to a Cuban sugar plantation, but which fell off a barge while on its way to Havana in 1865. A few axles and rusty wheels are about all that remain. See the Dive & Snorkel Sites sidebar for details on other Eleuthera highlights.

Romora Bay Dive Shop, at the Romora Bay Club (see the Places to Stay section), offers resort courses for US$65 and certification courses for US$375, plus underwater photography instruction. It has two 30-foot dive boats. One- and two-tank dive trips cost US$28/50. Night and drift dives are also offered for US$36/48 one-/two-tank, for a minimum of four people. It also rents equipment. Its postal address is PO Box EL-146, Harbour Island, Bahamas.

Valentine's Dive Centre (☎ 242-333-2309), at Valentine's Yacht Club & Inn (see Places to Stay), has complete dive services, including camera and video rental and a range of dives daily: The two-tank dive at 9:30 am costs US$55; the one-tank dive at 1:30 pm is US$30. The center has full dive instruction for all levels, from beginner through divemaster. Night dives cost US$45. A dive at Current Cut costs US$75. It has all-inclusive dive packages.

Romora Bay Dive Shop offers snorkel trips at 2 pm for US$15. Valentine's also has trips daily for US$20. Both companies rent snorkel gear for US$10.

Bonefishing & Sport Fishing

Bonefishing flats extend west and south of the island. Recommended bonefishing guides include Vincent Cleare (☎ 242-333-2072), Vincent Sweeting (☎ 242-333-2145), Maxwell Higgs (☎ 242-333-2530), and 'Bonefish Joe.' Trips cost US$150 a day.

The Romora Bay Dive Shop (see Diving & Snorkeling, above) offers sport fishing for US$395/595 half/full day, including captain, crew, and bait. Two days' notice is required.

Aptly named Pink Sands Beach, Harbour Island

July brings a fishing tournie, the Harbour Island Championship, to Harbour Island.

Boat Excursions

Valentine's Dive Centre (see Diving & Snorkeling, above) offers a sunset cruise on Friday for US$25. 'Uncle Sam' (☎ 242-333-2394) offers boating trips for US$250 a day.

Other Water Sports

Romora Bay Dive Shop (see Diving & Snorkeling, above) rents Sunfish and sailboards for US$15 per hour and US$45/60 half-/full day.

Bicycling

Bottom Time Adventures (in the USA ☎ 954-921-7798, 800-234-8464, fax 954-920-5578) offers eight-day cycling trips along the paved roads of Harbour Island, Eleuthera, and Spanish Wells. You'll live aboard their luxurious 90-foot catamaran, *Bottom Time II*. Trips begin at US$1195 per person, including all meals and use of 12-speed cross-trainer bikes. Bottom Time Adventures can be contacted at PO Box 11919, Fort Lauderdale, FL 33339-1919.

Places to Stay

Pink Sands (☎ 242-333-2030, fax 242-333-2060; in the USA ☎ 800-688-7678) is acclaimed as one of the most unpretentiously chic, contemporary, and calming resort-hotels in the world . . . categorically The Bahamas' finest, and a favorite of shutterbug-shy celebs like Christie

Brinkley and Ed Bradley. There are 29 rooms in 21 exquisite one-bedroom and four two-bedroom cottages, each secluded amid 16 magnificently landscaped acres spilling down to the beach. Each cottage comes with a golf cart. Decor is sublime: throw rugs on rough-cut Italian marble floors, lofty mansard ceilings, and over-size Adirondack chairs with batik fabrics set against a mellow wash of faint blue and the same blush pink as the namesake beach. Each has central air-con, ceiling fans, satellite TV, CD stereo system with choice CDs on hand, two-line telephone, wet bar, private patio with teak furniture, exotic bathrooms with imported tiles, and fine nuances such as fluffy bathrobes fringed with batik.

Facilities include three tennis courts, a gym, freshwater pool, and library with state-of-the-art audio-visual setup, plus diving and water sports. (See Places to Eat for a description of the restaurant.) Service is impeccable and relaxed. Room rates range from US$305 to US$400 from mid-April to mid-December and US$460 to US$595 mid-December to mid-April, including breakfast and dinner. Pink Sands even has a private plane to take guests island-hopping for US$150 per hour. It's worth every cent. Find a lover . . . and *go!* The postal address is PO Box EL-87, Harbour Island, Bahamas.

Neighboring *Coral Sands Hotel* (☎ 242-333-2350, 800-468-2799, fax 242-333-2368), also a legend among sybarites and socialites, is still attractive but comparatively jaded. The place is owned and run by erstwhile Hollywood star Brett King and his wife, Sharon. The 33-room resort extends over 14 acres. There's also a self-contained cottage and a two-bedroom house for rent, and you can dine on the patio at the Mediterranean Café or at the beach bar. There's live entertainment twice

---

Dive & Snorkel Sites

Dive Sites

Fish have long been protected off Harbour Island, where groupers are so tame that they will nuzzle – or gently assault – divers, hoping to be fed. Other hot spots include the following sites:

The Arch – Sharks, rays, and schools of jacks swim through this coral archway that begins at 75 feet below the surface.

Blow Hole – This dramatic cavern, shaped like an amphitheater, is a network of grottoes in the underwater base of Eleuthera. It's only diveable at slack tide. Sponges abound.

Current Cut – On this drift dive for adrenaline junkies, you're whipped along at speeds up to 10 knots, in depths down to 65 feet. You're surrounded by coral walls just 75 feet apart. There's voluminous sea life.

Train Wreck – Imagine! Just 20 feet down lies a Confederate locomotive.

Snorkel Sites

Bird Cay – This cay draws large populations of conch and fish.

Blue Hole – This cavern also features a low-lying reef.

Gaulding's Cay – Soft coral, sea anemone, and bonefish abound across a large area.

Muttonfish Point – This point is a gathering place for mutton snapper.

Oleander Reef – Close to shore, this reef boasts a tremendous variety of tropical fish.

Paradise Beach – This barrier-reef system has heaps of coral and fish species.

Pineapple Rock – Here lies a shipwreck, now claimed by myriad tropical fish.

Seafan Gardens – Gorgonians await, as does 'Baron,' the friendly barracuda. ■

weekly, plus a library, game room with pool table and satellite TV, tennis, and an array of water sports, all included in the rates. You can rent bicycles, scooters, or even a golf cart for sightseeing. Rooms cost US$110/120/155 single/double/suite in summer, US$140/165/210 in winter. The cottage and house cost US$155/210 in summer/winter. A MAP (breakfast and dinner) plan costs US$38.

The equally elegant *Dunmore Beach Club* (☎ 242-333-2200, fax 242-333-2429), due south, has 12 cozy, nicely furnished cottages amid landscaped lawns. There's a clubhouse with bar and lounge complete with fireplace, and a highly rated restaurant requiring jackets and ties at dinner. It's overpriced, however, at US$250/350 summer/winter (closed September and October). The postal address is PO Box EL-27122, Harbour Island, Bahamas.

Next south along the beach is *Ocean View* (☎ 242-333-2276, fax 242-333-2459), whose notably irksome owner, 'Pip' Simmons, runs her beautifully yet eclectically decorated nine-bedroom mansion as an upscale home-cum-house-party to which guests are invited. She has a staunch, predominantly European clientele . . . but the word is that if she doesn't like you, *you're out!* Rooms cost US$300 year-round, including breakfast and dinner. The mailing address is PO Box EL-134, Harbour Island, Bahamas.

The *Runaway Hill Club* (☎ 242-333-2150, fax 242-333-2420), next door, is a contemporary, New England-style hotel amid 7 acres of palm-studded gardens. It attracts a more elderly crowd but seems to be repositioning itself as an upscale place. The 10 voluminous air-con rooms face the sea and have a private patio or balcony, ceiling fans, and decor combining tile floors, rattan furniture, and floral prints. Some are in the main building, others in a villa on the hill. There's a freshwater pool. Choose to dine alfresco on a verandah or in the cozy dining room, with exquisite meals made by Briland-born chef Rica Thompson. Rates run from US$150/170 single/double in summer to US$175/195 in winter. The mailing address is PO Box EL-31, Harbour Island, Bahamas.

The *Romora Bay Club* (☎ 242-333-2325, fax 242-333-2500) faces west, with self-catering cottages spilling down through riotously colorful gardens to wooden sun decks and a Jacuzzi. There are also 33 air-con rooms. All have a splendid aesthetic, plus fans and private patios or balcony views. Sloppy Joe's and the Parrot Bar offer views over the harbor. There's a fine restaurant, plus a clubhouse with lounge and library. It has its own dive facility, plus water sports and tennis, and bicycles can be rented. Summer rates are US$180/200 to US$280/320, including airport transfers, breakfast, lunch, and water sports, plus one scuba dive. Winter rates range from US$230/340 to US$360/450. A MAP plan costs US$38. Seven-night specials are offered, including dive packages.

For a little 'X-rated' fun *(their* description), Romora will whisk you and the one you love to a secluded cay and maroon you for a while with a picnic hamper and drinks. The mailing address is PO Box 7026, Boca Raton, FL 33431.

Ma Ruby has 12 well-lit, air-con rooms in delightful cottages at the casual *Tingum Village Hotel* (☎ 242-333-2161) at the south end of town on Colebrook St. The rooms have stone walls, ceiling fan, and tile floors; they cost US$50/65/75 single/double/triple May through mid-November, US$55/75/85 November through April. A three-bedroom cottage with kitchen costs US$150 and US$175, respectively.

Aqua enthusiasts should head to *Valentine's Yacht Club & Inn* (☎ 242-333-2142, 800-383-6480, fax 242-333-2135), a watersports center on Bay St with 26 air-con rooms, each with pleasing decor and sliding glass doors opening to shady patios. It has a full-service dive shop, lively waterfront bar, attractive freshwater pool and Jacuzzi on a wooden deck, tennis court, and atmospheric restaurant. A shuttle runs to the beach. Rates start at US$80/95 in summer and US$90/120 in winter. Its postal address is PO Box EL-1, Harbour Island, Bahamas.

ELEUTHERA

The hoi polloi might try the modern *Royal Palm Motel* (☎ 242-333-2738, fax 242-333-2528, wgrant@batelnet.bs) at Dunmore and Clarence Sts, with eight air-con rooms, plus six rooms with kitchenette. All are clean, carpeted, and modestly furnished, including king-size bed, ceiling fan, and TV; US$65. Two efficiencies, costing US$80, were to be added. The mailing address is PO Box EL-27059, Harbour Island, Bahamas.

For a B&B-style option, try *The Landing* (☎ 242-333-2707, fax 242-333-2650, landinghl@aol), a colonial-era mansion overlooking the harbor near the ferry dock. This 200-year-old charmer has six gracious air-con rooms (three rooms were to be added), each with ceiling fan and endearing decor of cool whites, old tile floors, rattan furniture, and tropical prints. There's a delightful cottage, too, decorated in lilac blue. The hotel has a splendid restaurant. Tracy and Toby are congenial hosts. Rates are US$100/125 in the winter, US$80/100 in the summer. Suites cost US$125/150 and US$100/125, respectively. The cottage rents for US$150/175 and US$125/150. The postal address is PO Box EL-190, Harbour Island, Bahamas.

Seeking a three-bedroom luxury *lighthouse-turned-home* on the beach? Call David Steigelman (in the USA ☎ 561-395-0483), who rents this unique oceanfront property for US$1260/1575 weekly in summer/winter. *Harbour View* (☎ 242-334-2278) has two nicely decorated two-bedroom cottages with decks.

The *Little Boarding House*, on Bay St at Murray St, is an old gingerbread house for rent.

Edmund Sweating (☎ 242-333-2145) has a small red-and-white *cottage* with kitchen on Princess St for rent for US$40 a day. Check for cleanliness before committing.

Island Real Estate (☎ 242-333-2278) represents about three dozen rental properties, from quaint one-bedroom cottages to deluxe four-bedroom villas. Rates range from about US$500 to US$2500 weekly; its mailing address is PO Box EL-27045, Harbour Island, Bahamas.

Baretta's Town House (☎ 242-333-2361) also rents rooms and townhouses.

Places to Eat

When the cocks crow, head to *Dunmore Deli* (☎ 242-333-2644), on Princess St at King St, for a breakfast of eggs and muffins. The deli also sells gourmet foods, served on a shady deck. *CJ's Restaurant & Pizzeria*, on Dunmore St, is open only for breakfast from 7 am to noon.

For Bahamian home cooking, head to *Angela's Starfish Restaurant* (☎ 242-333-2253) on Nesbit St, serving breakfast at 7:30 am and closing at 8:30 pm (reservations needed for breakfast). Not fussy? Try *Bahama Bayside Café* (☎ 242-333-2174) on the waterfront a few blocks north of the straw market; it's open 7:30 am to 9 pm.

Harbour Island even has its own English pub: *The Inn* (☎ 242-333-2142) at Valentine's Yacht Club & Inn. The food, however, is Bahamian. *Ma Ruby's* (☎ 242-333-2161), at the Tingum Village Hotel, also serves native dishes such as grouper fritter and has daily specials in a bright and airy eatery with upbeat decor. This is the proud home of 'Cheeseburgers in Paradise,' featured in Jimmy Buffett's *Parrot Head Handbook*. It's open from 8 am to midnight.

The *Coral Sands* sun-deck bar and lounge earns rave reviews for its grilled lobster-salad sandwich. The hotel's *Mediterranean Café* offers alfresco dining. The wine list is huge. Dinner reservations are required.

The cozy, pink-and-peppermint-green *Harbour Lounge* (☎ 242-333-2031), on King St, serves such treats as curried pumpkin soup for US$5 and grilled marinated dolphin fish for US$26. It has an outside terrace and is closed Monday.

Hankering for a good burger and buffalo wings? Then check out *George's Sports Lounge* (☎ 242-333-2666), which has pool tables, video games, and satellite TV.

Club sandwiches, gazpacho, and conch salad, costing US$7 and up, typify the lunch menu at the waterfront *Sloppy Joe's*.

The Landing serves wake-me-up espressos and cappuccinos; it's open for breakfast, lunch, and dinner, and serves specialty pastas for US$18 and up, as well as continental dishes. It's closed Wednesday.

Tired of native dishes? Then head to *Pink Sands*, where Chef Stuart Betteridge conjures up such recherché miracles as Bahamian sushi roll with mango, cucumber, and conch, and cornmeal-dusted game hen on spinach with tamarind honey vinaigrette. The fare is superb and the setting sublime. The price fixe four-course dinners cost US$65 and are preset with a different menu nightly, with your choice of meat, fish, or pasta. It's open 7 to 10 pm. Pink Sands' *Blue Bar* serves à la carte lunches, with equally mouth-watering fare and a splendid locale over the beach; it's open noon to 3 pm daily.

Similarly upscale is the *Runaway Hill Club* restaurant, where reservations are required. It's open to the public for dinner only and also has a set menu for US$40.

Ludocic Jarland, the acclaimed chef at the *Romora Bay Club* (☎ 242-333-2325), serves fixed-menu dinners at one seating at 7:30 pm. There's a dress code.

For ice cream, head to *Rainbow Swirl* on Dunmore St; the health-conscious should head to *Island Yogurt*.

Miss Mae's Tea Room (☎ 242-333-2002), on Dunmore St, charges US$3 for a cup of quality tea. It serves afternoon tea on the patio in winter only. Tea parties are occasionally hosted at 3:30 pm at the Commissioner's Residence (see Town Landmarks, earlier in this chapter).

Head to *Patricia's*, on Pitt St just north of the village center, for homemade jams, spices, and hot sauce as well as native fruits; it's open 7 am to 10 pm Monday to Saturday. Plenty of other places sell fresh fruits and vegetables, including *Pineapple Fruit 'n' Veg* (☎ 242-333-2223) on Bay St.

Bakeries include *Home Style Bakery* and *Sybil's*, where you can eat your pastry at a rough-hewn bench beneath a shade tree. You can buy fresh herb bread, scrumptious pastries, croissants, and pies at *Arthur's Bakery & Café* (☎ 242-333-2285), which serves breakfast and lunch specials, and *Briland Home-Baked Pastries* on Pitt St.

You can buy groceries at *Sawyer's Food Store* (☎ 242-333-2356) on Dunmore St and *Pigly Wigly Store* (☎ 242-333-2120) on King St.

Entertainment

Humphrey Percentie, Jr, runs a 'museum,' basketball court, and rough-around-the-edges dance hall named *Vic Hum Club* (☎ 242-333-2161) at Barrack and Munnings Sts. This funky locale is as popular for international model shoots as with locals, who dribble on the checkerboard court that doubles as a dance floor. There's also a pool table. Museum? The banana-yellow walls are decorated with 1960s album covers, Junkanoo costume pieces, vintage posters, and fading photos of US athletes. Inevitably, there'll be a basketball game on the TV and a raw, over-the-rim reggae beat guaranteeing action beneath the full moon. The place also hosts performers from Maxi Priest to the bar's own Paddy 'Big Bird' Lewis. The world's largest coconut sits behind the bar. At press time locals who don't like the noise were attempting to close it down.

Then there's *Gusty's*, in the north end of town, which claims to be Jimmy Buffett's original 'Margaritaville' and where the musician has been known to jam. Reports of Buffett sightings continue to lure crowds nightly.

The Funk Band plays music Wednesday (Ladies' Night) to Saturday nights at *Seagrapes* (☎ 242-333-2389). And the *Harbour View* has live music and a dance club on weekends.

Willie's Tavern (☎ 242-333-2121), on Dunmore St, is another popular, down-to-earth bar with a lofty ceiling festooned with fishing nets. It has a pool table and sports on TV, as does *Baretta's Town House* (☎ 242-333-2361).

Things to Buy

About 20 top artists, most of them Bahamian, are represented at the Princess Street Gallery (☎ 242-333-2788), where a 24-inch original painting by Eddie Minnis sells for US$7500. Prices begin at US$100.

ELEUTHERA

Ceramics are also sold at the gallery, plus pebbles painted as cats in lifelike detail. The Landing also sells beautiful original art, as does Frank's Art Gallery & Souvenirs (☎ 242-333-2121).

Wavy Fence Gift Shop (☎ 242-333-2630) sells antiques and ceramics. For chic casualwear, check out the store at Pink Sands. Colorful batiks made by Androsia Batik are on sale at Briland Androsia Boutique (☎ 242-333-2342). Miss Mae's, on Dunmore St, sells quality prints, batiks, throw rugs, and other souvenirs. And De Island Things specializes in island-made straw hats and bags.

Serendipity will lead you to several other stores. The waterfront boasts a straw market on the north end of Bay St.

Jeanne Davies does hair braiding for US$30 full head, manicures for US$15, and pedicures for US$20 at Tee Jay's (☎ 242-333-2315) on South St.

Getting There & Away
Air Flights arrive at North Eleuthera Airport (ELH), 2 miles inland of the harbor. See the Getting There & Away chapter for the major airlines' phone numbers.

Bahamasair flies Monday and Saturday from Miami, and daily from Nassau (US$40 one way). Gulfstream International flies daily from Fort Lauderdale and Miami. US Airways Express flies from Fort Lauderdale year-round.

Sandpiper Airlines (☎ 242-333-2640), with an office in town on Dunmore St, flies daily from Nassau. Several charter operators also fly to North Eleuthera.

Pink Sands (see Places to Stay, earlier in this chapter) has its own five-seater plane for guests. Flights depart Nassau at 9 am and 5 pm Monday, Wednesday, and Friday, returning at 9:30 am and 5:45 pm. The plane can be chartered for sightseeing.

Boat The Harbour Island Club & Marina (☎ 242-333-2427, 'Jolly Roger' VHF channel 16) has 31 deep-water slips with water, electricity, and gasoline. It has a laundry and bar. There's also a deck and pool, plus a pleasant restaurant and bar (closed

Monday). Valentine's Yacht Club & Inn has a 39-slip, full-service marina for yachts up to 165 feet.

The Harbour Island ferry dock is at the foot of Church St. The dock for ferries *to* Harbour Island is 2 miles east of North Eleuthera Airport. A taxi to the North Eleuthera dock from the airport costs US$4 per person. The 10-minute boat ride to Harbour Island costs US$8 solo, US$4 if shared.

You can also charter a water taxi between Spanish Wells and Harbour Island (US$50 one way).

Getting Around
You'll need to take the ferry or a water taxi to North Eleuthera to get to the airport; see Getting There & Away, above.

On Harbour Island everyone walks or uses a bicycle or golf cart, which you can rent from Big Red (☎ 242-333-2045, cellular 242-359-7399), Michael's Cycles on Bay St (☎ 242-333-2384), or Sublime Rentals (☎ 242-333-2509). Bikes cost US$10; golf carts cost US$35 to US$45.

Taxis cost US$4 to US$6 between any two points in town. Taxi tours are available from Big M Taxi (☎ 242-333-2043), or with Reggie or Jean, who operate the No Problem (☎ 242-333-2116) boat-rental and taxi service. Ross' Garage (☎ 242-333-2122) also rents golf carts and boats (which are good for checking out the beaches on Man Island, north of Harbour Island).

Captain Duke (☎ 242-333-2337) will whisk you around on his water taxi, the *Briland Queen*, as will Keva (☎ 242-333-2287) or Andrew, who has a water taxi called *Lucky Too* at the Government Dock.

SPANISH WELLS
Pop 800
Two miles west of North Eleuthera Airport, the road meets Queen's Hwy (there's a gas station at the T-junction), which runs north about 7 miles to James Bay at the north tip of Eleuthera. The road ends at a ferry dock. St George's Island – dominated by the town of Spanish Wells – lies 1 mile offshore.

Spanish Wells is named for the Spanish galleons that once drew water here before attempting to return home across the Atlantic Ocean. The village dates back to the days of the Eleutheran Adventurers. The deeply religious, somewhat reticent, lily-white population follows a Mid-western US lifestyle, with a surprising level of sophistication, side by side with Swiss-clean orderliness and undaunted quaintness. Intriguingly, generations of isolation have concentrated the gene pool, reflected in prevalent inbred traits. Half the island is named Pinder: 'We wor Pinders b'fore we married, an' we're Pinders now.'

The place has been called the 'Island of the Worker Bees.' Tourism is minimal. Lobstering is its major trade and the source of phenomenal incomes (the locals are among the wealthiest of all Bahamians). Fishermen operate from large state-of-the-art trawlers, and go out as far as 250 miles for a month at a time. Since the best time for lobstering is young adulthood, adolescents tend to leave school (to the frustration of local teachers) by the age of 16 to make the most of their years. When the 'boys' are away, the town is deathly still, with nary a soul on the starkly lit streets. Weird!

A beautiful beach rims the north shore.

Orientation
Spanish Wells is at the eastern end of St George's Island. The main street runs along the oceanside, while a second street runs parallel to it along the harborfront to the south. Charles Island lies off to the southeast, forming the 100-yard-wide harbor channel. Russell Island lies to the southwest and is linked by a bridge (a small community of Haitians lives here in starkly poorer conditions).

Information
The Royal Bank of Canada (☎ 242-333-4131) is open 9 am to 3 pm Monday, 9 am to 1 pm Tuesday to Thursday, and 9 am to 5 pm Friday.

The post office and telephone booths are in the Commissioner's Office on the main street. The BaTelCo station is four blocks to the west of the Commissioner's Office.

A new medical clinic was due to open in 1997 on the main street at Adventurer's Ave. The Spanish Wells Pharmacy (☎ 242-333-4677) is open from 8 am to 5 pm Friday to Monday and 8 am to noon Tuesday and Wednesday.

You can reach the police at ☎ 242-333-4030.

Spanish Wells Museum
The island's history is told in this small museum (☎ 242-333-4710) on the main street; it's ostensibly open 10 am to noon and 1 to 3 pm Monday to Saturday, but at press time it was closed 'until further notice.'

Diving
Manuel's Dive Station, on the main street, is a full-service dive shop. Al Broadstead (☎ 242-333-4427) will take you fishing for US$350 a day.

Places to Stay
The old Spanish Wells Harbour Club, which was destroyed by Hurricane Andrew, has

A typical street scene, Spanish Wells

ELEUTHERA

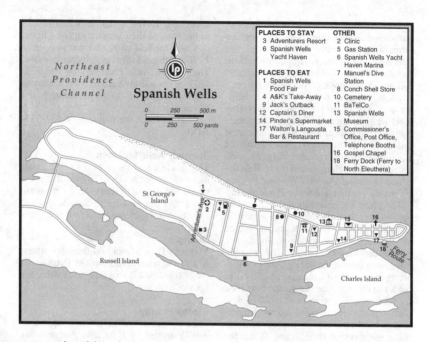

PLACES TO STAY

3 Adventurers Resort
6 Spanish Wells
   Yacht Haven

PLACES TO EAT

1 Spanish Wells
   Food Fair
4 A&K's Take-Away
9 Jack's Outback
12 Captain's Diner
14 Pinder's Supermarket
17 Walton's Langousta
   Bar & Restaurant

OTHER

2 Clinic
5 Gas Station
6 Spanish Wells Yacht
   Haven Marina
7 Manuel's Dive
   Station
8 Conch Shell Store
10 Cemetery
11 BaTelCo
13 Spanish Wells
   Museum
15 Commissioner's
   Office, Post Office,
   Telephone Booths
16 Gospel Chapel
18 Ferry Dock (Ferry to
   North Eleuthera)

metamorphosed into the new *Adventurers Resort* (☎ /fax 242-333-4883, mapeleaf@batelnet.bs), set back off the harbor channel on Adventurer's Ave. It has nine modestly yet nicely furnished air-con rooms for US$75 nightly or US$175 per three-night weekend. It also has seven apartments for US$100/150 single/twin room, US$250/325 weekend. There's a three-room apartment with spacious lounges for US$400 weekend. All have ceiling fans. The resort has a tiny beach with thatched cabañas and a barbecue pit. The mailing address is PO Box EL-27498, Spanish Wells, Eleuthera, Bahamas.

Spanish Wells Yacht Haven (☎ 242-333-4255, fax 242-333-4649), on the harborside, charges US$75/85 summer/winter for its three air-con rooms, US$95/105 for its two apartments. There's a modest restaurant and bar, plus a small swimming pool. Rooms have satellite TV. Bicycles are available for rent for US$6/10 half-/full day. The mailing address is PO Box EL-27427, Spanish Wells, Eleuthera, Bahamas.

Jan and Rick Kurtz (in the USA ☎ 609-652-1551, fax 609-748-0988) rent a two-bedroom *cottage* for US$550 to US$600 weekly.

Places to Eat

A&K's Take-Away, on the main street, offers turtle steak in season, alongside fish or turkey burgers. It has grilled tuna and prime-rib specials on Friday night and cream layer cake on Saturday night.

Other options in Spanish Wells include *Captain's Diner*, on the main street, for lunch and dinner, and *Walton's Langousta Bar & Restaurant* on the dockside.

My favorite place is *Jack's Outback* (☎ 242-333-4219), a dockside eatery done up in mid-American '50s diner style. It serves native fare, including a lobster dinner for US$20 and burgers, as well as a house specialty, 'Island Girls' with fries, for US$7. Be sure to check out the hot fudge sundae! A T-bone special is offered on Friday night for US$12.

You can order homemade pizza from Sheila and Stan (☎ 242-333-4465). For baked goods, try *Dawson's Bakery*; for groceries, try *Pinder's Supermarket* and *Spanish Wells Food Fair*.

Things to Buy
Three Sisters sells clothing and beachwear.

A house one block west of the cemetery on the main street sells conch shells and giant starfish, displayed on the verandah. Prices range from are US$5 to US$10. If no one is home, simply pop the money under the door.

There's a quilt store opposite the museum. And look for the famous Spanish Wells hats, made locally.

Getting There & Away
For information on air travel to North Eleuthera, see Getting There & Away under the Harbour Island section, earlier in this chapter.

Spanish Wells Yacht Haven Marina has 40 slips, a laundry, ice, and showers. It charges US85¢ a foot, plus US$5 daily for cable TV hookup. Boaters between Spanish Wells and Harbour Island are strongly advised to hire a local pilot.

Ferries run all day between Spanish Wells and the ferry dock at James Bay. Caleb Sawyer (☎ 242-333-4254) operates the *Moldie Crab*; Lloyd Higgs has the *Crambone II* (☎ 242-333-4101). Both charge US$5 (US$10 solo) for the five-minute journey. Higgs also charters for sightseeing trips. In Spanish Wells the staff in the blue building in front of Johnson Outboards on the dock will call for a water taxi on your behalf.

A taxi (☎ 242-333-4068) ride from the North Eleuthera Airport to James Bay costs US$10, or US$4 per person if shared. In James Bay there's parking, the Calypso Café, a gift shop, a duty-free liquor store, and a phone booth.

You can also charter a water taxi between Harbour Island and Spanish Wells for US$50 one way.

Two mail boats call here: The *Spanish Rose* departs Nassau at 7 am Thursday (five

hours, US$20 one way); the *Eleuthera Express* also departs Nassau at 7 am Thursday (five hours, US$25).

Getting Around
Most of the locals, from grannies to youngsters, zip around on mopeds (with hardhats for helmets); the rest use golf carts. There's a gas station on the main street.

Anthony and Joanie operate a taxi service. 'Budda' rents himself out as a taxi guide. You can reach them all at ☎ 242-333-4222.

PREACHER'S CAVE
This large cave, at Eleuthera's far northern end, is said to be where the Eleutheran Adventurers found shelter after foundering in 1648. They made an altar here and surely prayed to be rescued. The cavern, which is laced with Swiss-cheese holes, is more a historical curiosity than an engaging site. Light pours down from a large hole in the roof. The cave is fronted by a glorious beach, one of several beaches along the north coast.

Preacher's Cave, which is located about 2 miles east of James Bay, can be reached by traveling down a rough dirt road that leads a half-mile through scrub from Queen's Hwy.

LOWER & UPPER BOGUE
These two small settlements lie 2 miles apart on Queen's Hwy, facing south toward the Bight of Eleuthera amid scrub and marsh (or 'bogue,' a derivative of 'bog'); hence the houses are raised above the ground. Emancipated slaves founded the hamlets 150 or so years ago.

Lower Bogue, the westernmost hamlet, is 2 miles southwest of North Eleuthera Airport. It has a few grocery stores and native eateries, notably *Gullie's Restaurant & Aggie's Bakery* (☎ 242-335-1437) at the corner of Bay St and Cemetery Rd, and *Lady B's Lifesaver Restaurant*, good for cracked conch.

Queen's Hwy turns east to Upper Bogue and The Glass Window. A separate road runs 7 miles west along a slender peninsula to Current.

CURRENT

Whereas the Bogues are populated by blacks, Current is a white community. It is pretty despite its two narrow, parallel concrete lanes crisscrossed by three others and lined with clapboard houses and concrete bungalows. It claims to be the 'Oldest Settlement on the Island.' The townsfolk – some of whom claim to be descendants of Native Americans exiled here after a massacre at Cape Cod – are known for their basketware. The town took Hurricane Andrew on the chin, but except for the disappearance of the Current Club (washed to sea), you'd never know it.

There's a beautiful beach on the west side of town.

Current Cut

This is a half-mile-long channel that separates North Eleuthera from Current Island, a 10-mile-long continuation of the peninsula. The 'cut' narrows down to a mere 100 yards, and during tidal changes the deep waters run at a swift 6 knots, rippling and swirling, creating eddies that stream in the opposite direction close to shore. It is a popular dive and snorkel spot for strong swimmers who want to 'ride' the current.

Everett Griffin (☎ 242-333-4222) can take you fishing; trips cost US$80/150 half-/full day.

Places to Stay & Eat

Monica's Curio Shop, which sells postcards, T-shirts, and souvenirs, also has one-and two-bedroom apartments for US$45/50 daily without/with air-con. Monica also rents a a two-bedroom Loyalist cottage for US$45 and a two-bedroom air-con beach house for US$100.

Sandcastle Apartments (☎ 242-335-1264) rents two beachfront cottages a quarter-mile east of town for US$75. Each has a kitchen and sleeps three people.

The only places to eat are *Griffin's Snack Bar* and *Lim's Take-Away & Bakery*.

Getting There & Away

A taxi from North Eleuthera Airport will cost US$21 one way. The mail boat *Current*

Pride sails here from Nassau at 7 am Thursday (five hours, US$20 one way), also stopping at Hatchet Bay and The Bluff.

THE GLASS WINDOW

Here, about 7 miles east of Lower Bogue, Eleuthera narrows down to a pencil-thin isthmus that separates the deep blue of the thunderous ocean from the placid, teal-green shoals of the Bight of Eleuthera. Atlantic rollers smash against the rocky headlands, throwing spray hundreds of feet in the air, while a mere 20 yards away the bight waters are still as a pond. The arch that formed the 'window' collapsed a few years ago. Queen's Hwy spans the gap by a solid concrete bridge that was heaved 7 feet out of alignment by a massive rogue wave on Halloween in 1991.

Stop and admire the weathered yet barren moonscape of craggy limestone. Be cautious when you're strolling around here. The cliffs are unstable and the pocked terrain is treacherous underfoot.

South Eleuthera

GREGORY TOWN

This large settlement, 5 miles south of The Glass Window, nestles dramatically – like a Cornish village – within a steep-sided cove. Onions, peppers, cabbage, watermelons, and other vegetables are grown locally. Gregory Town is most famous as the center of pineapple farming, though the industry is so atrophied that local farmers could not muster a respectable supply of their usually large and succulent fruits to display at the 1997 Pineapple Festival (the festival championed an ecotourism theme, 'Save the Pine,' an effort to address the lack of interest in pineapple farming among the local youth). As bromeliads, pineapples don't need much rain; they draw dew from the air. Nonetheless, raising pineapples is labor-intensive and today's youth don't have the patience. Increasingly, Gregory Town's young men are turning to lobstering, where the big bucks reside.

Gauldings Cay, 4 miles north of Gregory Town, is a splendid stretch of pure-white sand. The Cove Eleuthera (see Places to Stay, below) offers a daily complimentary shuttle to Gauldings Cay for its guests.

The post office and BaTelCo office are down by the harbor, as is a medical clinic. On the main street, Jay's Laundromat charges US$1.75 per wash.

Activities

Captain Gregory Thompson (☎ 242-335-5357) will take you deep-sea fishing in his 32-foot boat, *Gone Fishin'*, for US$400/600 half-/full day. Warren Cartwright (☎ 242-335-5392) charges US$200/350, respectively.

Charter Cats (☎ 242-335-0186, 800-446-9441) at Hatchet Bay offers full-day sailing trips for US$55 per person, powerboat cruises for US$65 per person, and fishing for US$700, based on a minimum of six people.

Special Events

In early June the town hosts the Annual Eleuthera Pineapple Festival, a good excuse to down a few Kaliks or Gregory Town Specials – made of locally produced pineapple rum or gin-spiked coconut water – as well as conch salad, crab 'n' rice, fried chicken, and Bertha's ribs (see the Cotton Bay to Cape Eleuthera section).

Festival highlights include the 'Miss Teen Pineapple Princess Pageant' and the 'Pineathelon,' which is a swim-bike-run competition. There's also the 'Pineapple-on-a-Rope Eating Contest' in which participants with hands tied behind their backs attempt to nibble a dangling pineapple; a basketball shootout; a kayak race; and the Saturday-night 'Junkanoo Rush,' a street party sure to get you in the groove. Ironically, pineapples are in short supply. You can find nonalcoholic pineapple smoothies at the Corner Bar and pineapple tarts at Monica's Bakery, but that's about it. You should contact the Eleuthera Tourism Office (☎ 242-332-2142, fax 242-332-2480) for more detailed information on the Annual Eleuthera Pineapple Festival.

Places to Stay

The Cove Eleuthera (☎ 242-335-5142, fax 242-335-5338, covelutra@aol.com; in the USA ☎ 800-552-5960), about a mile north of town, is perfect for independent-minded travelers who don't want organized activities. It's aptly named, with views over two coves and its own tiny beach where the snorkeling is splendid (snorkel gear is provided). It has 24 air-con rooms in six cottages fringed by 28 acres of vegetation. Each is furnished in white rattan, with ceramic tiles, a small shower, and private porch. Summer rates are US$79/89/99 single/double/triple garden-view (US$10 more ocean-view). In winter rates are US$99/109/119 (US$20 ocean-view). A MAP plan costs US$33.

There's also a lounge, game room, small library, and VCR, plus tennis, volleyball, badminton, a freshwater pool, and hammocks for alfresco snoozing, which your amiable hosts Ann and George Mullin encourage. Diving can be arranged, and there are bicycles and kayaks you can use. The library has a *huge* map of Eleuthera pinned with photos of points of sightseeing interest . . . perfect for trip planning. The local mailing address is PO Box EL-1548, Gregory Town, Eleuthera, Bahamas.

Cambridge Villas (☎ 242-335-5080, fax 242-335-5308; in the USA ☎ 800-688-4752), beside the road on the edge of town, has modest, fully equipped air-con apartments, plus a choice of rooms and units sleeping two to eight people. Room rates range from US$60/70 summer/winter to US$80/115. A MAP plan costs US$30 per person. There's a pool table and live calypso bands sometimes entertain. Diving, snorkeling, and fishing trips can be arranged. The hotel has a private airplane for island-hopping charters for US$500 daily for up to five people. Its mailing address is PO Box EL-1548, Gregory Town, Eleuthera, Bahamas.

Places to Eat

The Cove Eleuthera's restaurant serves three meals daily; dinner entrées begin at

ELEUTHERA

US$12. The portions are huge. There's a steamed grouper and roast beef buffet on Saturday night. A guitar soloist sometimes plays, and slide shows of underwater life are projected onto a white wall during dinner.

For colorful ambiance in town, check out *Elvira's Restaurant*, with an outside barbecue in the yard; or *Millie's Souce Bowl*, specializing in conch souse for US$2. Millie's is a cool place to play dominoes with locals.

For fresh bread, try *Thompson's Bakery* on Queen's Hwy.

Things to Buy
Cartwright's Straw Market makes and sells baskets, hats, and other straw-work. Terrence Wood sells sponges for US$3 to US$8 at a store opposite Island Made Gift Shop, a splendid little trove run by Pamela Thompson, who handpaints island scenes on shells and driftwood. She also sells jewelry, resortwear, books, and artwork; guests at The Cove Eleuthera get a 10% discount.

Getting There & Away
Gregory Town is midway between the North Eleuthera and Governor's Harbour airports. A taxi from North Eleuthera will cost about US$25 for two people; US$40 from Governor's Harbour.

The mail boat *Current Pride* sails to Hatchet Bay weekly from Nassau, also stopping at The Bluff and Current; see the Current section for details. The *Captain Fox* mail boat departs from Nassau at noon on Friday for Hatchet Bay (six hours, US$20 one way).

Getting Around
There are no major car-rental companies on Eleuthera. However, several people offer cars for rent. Most are beat-up US models. The going rate is US$60 daily. Most rental cars have only 'third party' coverage, meaning that damage to other vehicles or property is insured, but not damage to your car! I had good luck with Hilltop Garage (☎ 242-335-5028), which will deliver to The Cove Eleuthera.

Albury's Taxi (☎ 242-335-1370) and Wendell's Taxi Service (☎ 242-333-0165) both offer guided island tours.

GREGORY TOWN TO GOVERNOR'S HARBOUR
In the 25 miles between Gregory Town and Governor's Harbour – Eleuthera's main settlement – there are only two towns of any size: **Alice Town**, 7 miles south of Gregory Town and just south of Hatchet Bay, the former center of an Angus cattle enterprise; and **James Cistern**, a picturesque albeit wind-battered waterfront hamlet 8 miles farther south, where you might stop off to peek inside Admiral's Arts & Crafts.

The Hatchet Bay Fest in Alice Town each August features dinghy races and partying.

There's a post office and BaTelCo station in James Cistern.

Surfer's Beach
This 2-mile-long, lonesome, sugary beach lives up to its name, especially with southwest winds at low tide, when the surf rolls in nicely. The beach is backed by scrub-covered hills and is reached by a horrendously potholed and rocky track from Queen's Hwy, about 2 miles south of Gregory Town.

A Yankee from New Hampshire named Surfer Pete came to this area, stayed, and married a local woman. He rents surfboards for US$2 and does surfboard repairs. His wife operates Rebecca's Beach Shop.

Hatchet Bay Cave
Spelunkers might enjoy this half-mile-long cave meandering down into the hillside, 5 miles south of Gregory Town (turn south onto the dirt road near the three old silos). From the narrow entrance, a trail connects several chambers, which bear charcoal signatures dating back to the mid-19th century. Some harmless yet fearsome-looking leaf-nosed bats reside within, and deep in the cave stalactites and stalagmites add a touch of romance. No touching! Bring a flashlight and rubber-soled shoes, as the going is slippery. There's a ladder to climb at one stage. You can hire a guide locally.

James Cistern Beach

A bone-jarring dirt road leads north from James Cistern to a 4-mile-long beach good for surfing, where waves sometimes reach 10 feet with a brisk south wind. There's a shipwreck offshore, which is a good spot for snorkeling when the water is calm. The overgrown and arduous Old Queen's Hwy runs the length of the shore, leading north to **James Point**, a lonesome and beautiful setting; 4WD is a must!

Places to Stay

A Bahamian couple, Gilbert and Katherine Kemp, run a quaint guesthouse named *Surfer's Haven* (☎ 242-332-2181, evenings 242-335-0349) on the hillside a half-mile from Surfer's Beach. It has three quaint rooms, each whitewashed, tiled, and simply yet nicely furnished. Katherine cooks native meals, or you can use the kitchen. It's a bargain at US$30 single or double. They have a surfboard for rent.

Surfer Pete may be able to put you up at the *Drifter's Inn* (no telephone).

In Alice Town, Rose Wood operates the *Three Sisters Guesthouse* (☎ 242-335-0482), which has five rooms for US$40 per night. In James Cistern, Hilton and Elsie Johnson run *Island House* (☎ 242-335-6241, fax 242-335-6356), with four modestly yet nicely furnished air-con apartment units with kitchen and lounge for US$90.

The *Rainbow Inn* (☎ /fax 242-335-0294, 800-688-0047; in the UK ☎ 0171-491-1800, 0181-876-1296), on a bluff 2 miles south of Alice Town, offers octagonal villas with one, two, or three air-con rooms surrounded by casuarinas and hibiscus. All have kitchenettes, ceiling fans, and private decks facing onto a beach. The hotel has tennis courts, plus a small saltwater lap pool, snorkeling, fishing, and bicycles for hire. Room rates are US$90 to US$150 year-round. A MAP plan costs US$30. There's also a villa. The postal address is PO Box EL-25053, Governor's Harbour, Eleuthera, Bahamas.

Places to Eat

The *Rainbow Inn*, furnished with varnished, rough-hewn tables and captain's chairs, serves Bahamian and continental dishes, from lobster to seafood crepes to homemade key lime pie; it's open 6:30 to 9 pm Wednesday to Saturday. 'Dr Seabreeze' plays on Wednesday and Friday nights.

In Alice Town try the local hangout, *Forget Me Not Club*, a funky little bar and restaurant. There's a grocery store next door, plus the *Red Dirt Game Room & Snack Shack*. And *Red Rolle's Harbour View Restaurant* gets lively on weekends.

Craving pizza? Try *Juneek's Savoury Snacks* in James Cistern, where outdoor clay ovens are still used. It also sells meat patties and ice cream, as does *Miss Adderley's* in Alice Town.

For groceries, stop at *Big Rock General Store*, 2 miles west of James Cistern.

Getting There & Away

The Governor's Harbour Airport is 3 miles south of James Cistern.

The Hatchet Bay Yacht Club (☎ 242-332-0186) and Marine Service of Eleuthera have slips in Alice Town.

Getting Around

Daniel Ferguson (☎ 242-335-0156) has a taxi for hire. Big Rock General Store (see Places to Eat, above) has gasoline for sale.

GOVERNOR'S HARBOUR

The island 'capital,' midway down Eleuthera, overlooks a broad harbor that runs west along a peninsula to Cupid's Cay, claiming to be the original settlement of the Eleutheran Adventurers; ruins of an old pineapple plantation dating back centuries mark the site, and there are several old homes in semiderelict state. There's a cruise-ship dock, but few ships ever call. Governor's Harbour is also known as Colebrook Town.

During the 19th century, the harbor was filled with schooners shipping pineapples and citrus to New York and New England, or unloading fineries for the wealthy merchants and their wives. The merchants' well-preserved old white clapboard houses, many with ornate gingerbread gable trims, nestle on the hillside east of Queen's Hwy,

ELEUTHERA

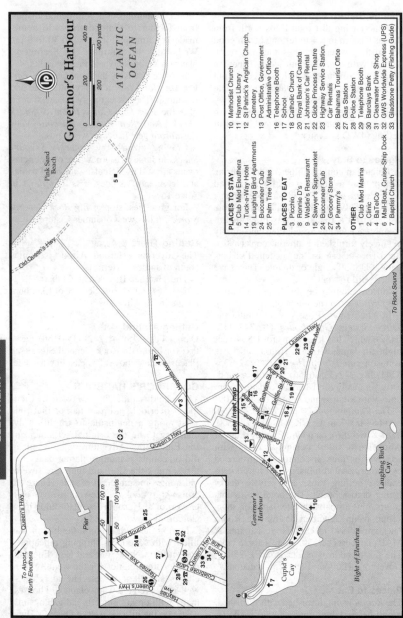

Governor's Harbour

ATLANTIC OCEAN

PLACES TO STAY
5   Club Med Eleuthera
14 Tucka-Way Hotel
19 Laughing Bird Apartments
24 Buccaneer Club
25 Palm Tree Villas

PLACES TO EAT
3   Picchio
8   Ronnie D's
9   Waldie's Restaurant
15 Sawyer's Supermarket
24 Buccaneer Club
27 Grocery Store
34 Pammy's

OTHER
1   Club Med Marina
2   Clinic
4   BaTelCo
6   Mail-Boat, Cruise-Ship Dock
7   Baptist Church
10 Methodist Church
11 Haynes Library
12 St Patrick's Anglican Church,
    Cemetery
13 Post Office, Government
    Administrative Office
16 Telephone Booth
17 School
18 Catholic Church
20 Royal Bank of Canada
21 Johnson's Car Rental
22 Globe Princess Theatre
23 Highway Service Station,
    Car Rentals
26 Bahamas Tourist Office
27 Gas Station
28 Police Station
29 Telephone Booth
30 Barclays Bank
31 Clearwater Dive Shop
32 GWS Worldwide Express (UPS)
33 Gladstone Petty (Fishing Guide)

where royal poincianas blaze vermilion in spring. Many of the fine, well-kept houses are vacation homes for wealthy foreigners.

A stroll along the bayfront passes St Patrick's Anglican Church and cemetery; the historic, pink Commissioner's Office; and the 1897 Haynes Library.

The beach on the south side of the peninsula is a good spot for shelling. The nicest beaches are over the hill on the Atlantic shore.

Information

Jackie Gibson runs the Bahamas Tourist Office (☎ 242-332-2142, fax 242-332-2480) at Queen's Hwy and Haynes Ave.

Barclays Bank has a branch in the town's center. Royal Bank of Canada is on Queen's Hwy at the south end of town. Both are open 9:30 am to 3 pm Monday to Thursday and 9:30 am to 5 pm Friday.

The post office (☎ 242-332-2060) is on the harborfront; it's open 9 am to 4:30 pm weekdays. GWS Worldwide Express, in the town center, acts as a UPS agent; it also has fax service (US$3 local per page, US$5 long distance). There's a telephone booth on Queen's Hwy at Rolle Ln. BaTelCo is atop the hill on Haynes Ave.

There is a laundromat in North Palmetto Point, south of town; see the North & South Palmetto Point section.

The medical clinic (☎ 242-332-2774) is on Queen's Hwy, about 400 yards north of Haynes Ave. Jackie Gleason (☎ 242-332-2496) gives massages.

The police station (☎ 242-332-2111) is on Queen's Hwy in the town center.

Activities

Clearwater Dive Shop in the town center offers dive trips. Gladstone Petty (☎ 242-332-2280) will take you reef- and bonefishing. He has an office on Queen's Hwy, downtown.

Places to Stay

Richard and Carmen's *Tuck-a-Way Hotel* (☎ 242-322-2005, fax 242-322-2775), at Graham St and Rolle Ln, has eight small, dark, air-con units, all with TV. There are two kitchens in the center of the complex, plus an ice machine and free laundry. Rooms without kitchen cost US$52/57 summer/winter; add US$10 for kitchen. Overpriced! The mailing address is PO Box EL-45, Governor's Harbour, Eleuthera.

Laughing Bird Apartments (☎ 242-332-2012, fax 242-332-2358; in the USA ☎ 800-688-4752), on Birdie Ln near Haynes Ave, has cozy, no-frills, one-bedroom studio apartments amid grounds full of hibiscus and palms. Each has a lounge-cum-bedroom and separate kitchen. Some have king-size beds. You can combine rental units to sleep up to six people. The place is run by a delightful English couple, Jean and Dan Davies. A gift shop sells sarongs. Studio apartments cost US$70/80 single/double year-round. Larger apartments closer to town cost US$85/95/105/115 single/double/triple/quad. Ask about weekly rates. The mailing address is PO Box EL-25076, Governor's Harbour, Eleuthera, Bahamas.

Buccaneer Club (☎ 242-332-2000, fax 242-332-2888), on the north side of town, is a handsome remake of a historic three-story farmhouse. It has five small yet tastefully appointed air-con rooms with sliding glass doors opening onto a wide balcony. Each has two double beds and a satellite TV. There's a small pool and a well-tended lawn. Rooms cost US$78/88 low season, US$88/99 peak season. The mailing address is PO Box EL-86, Governor's Harbour, Eleuthera, Bahamas.

Eight modest apartments are available in *Palm Tree Villas* (☎ 242-322-2002, fax 242-322-2479), across the street.

You can also inquire about *apartments* for rent behind the Shell Gas Station in town, and also at Johnson's Car Rental (☎ 242-332-2226). Want a private *beachside villa?* Call ☎ 242-332-2050.

Waldie's Aries (☎ 242-332-2132; ask for Marcus) is a two-bedroom house with loft, two bathrooms, dining room, and kitchen near Club Med for US$500 weekly.

It may surprise you, being greeted most likely by a blond beach bum in nothing more than a loincloth and mirrored sunglasses, to learn that *Club Med Eleuthera*

ELEUTHERA

(☎ 242-332-2270, 800-258-2633, fax 242-332-2271) is a family resort. Couples and singles are also welcome. It is designed for gregarious folks, not clams, and has a large French following. The staff are mostly European (including the chefs), and dining is communal. Accommodations are in two- and three-story beach-front or garden-front lodgings. It has 284 air-con double rooms with one king-size or two full beds and marble-lined bathrooms. Per-person rates range from US$140 to US$235 nightly (US$910 to US$1540 weekly), depending on season, including meals and most activities. Children are charged US$90 to US$155 nightly (US$590 to US$1000 weekly). Single occupancy will cost 20% to 100% more, according to season. It boasts eight tennis courts, a huge swimming pool and sun deck, plus every recreational activity short of hammer-throwing . . . all overseen by GOs (for *gentils organisateurs*, or 'nice organizers'). The club offers special kids' programs, plus excursions. There's also a marina and water-sports center. The postal address is French Leave, PO Box EL-80, Governor's Harbour, Eleuthera, Bahamas.

Places to Eat

For budget meals, try *Pammy's*, a hole-in-the-wall take-away on Pinders Ln that's popular with locals.

The *Buccaneer Club* serves up native dishes, with dinner entrées from US$12. It has live music some nights; it's closed Wednesday. *Picchio* (☎ 242-332-2455), in a delightful gingerbread home just north of town, is recommended for Italian fare.

On Cupid's Cay, *Ronnie D's* serves native dinners, plus a special of macaroni, peas 'n' rice, and potato salad for US$6. A little place called *Waldie's Restaurant* (☎ 242-332-2309), next door, also serves native fare; its open 7 to 11 pm.

Club Med Eleuthera (☎ 242-332-2270) welcomes outside guests, if space is available, including lunch and/or dinner with a dinner show for US$30. Reservations are not accepted, but you must call ahead.

Entertainment

Ronnie D's has a virtual monopoly on nightlife. For dancing, don't even think of arriving before 10 pm. It also has a lively sports bar with pool table and wide-screen TV, plus free shuttles back to your hotel or yacht (on Friday and Saturday shuttles to Club Med leave every 30 minutes from 12:30 until 3 am).

The *Globe Princess Theatre*, on Queen's Hwy, shows movies at 8 pm nightly for US$5.

Also see Places to Eat, above, for Club Med Eleuthera's dinner show.

Things to Buy

Several stores sell resortwear and jewelry. Try Beachcombers, downtown on Queen's Hwy, which has a large T-shirt gallery, or Nicole's Casual Wear, across the road.

Getting There & Away

American Eagle flies from Miami to Governor's Harbour twice daily, with added service on weekends; fares begin at US$119 roundtrip. Bahamasair flies from Miami on Monday and Saturday, and from Nassau daily. US Airways Express has service from Fort Lauderdale.

Club Med has charter flights, with a bus transfer to the club.

The *Eleuthera Express* mail boat sails here from Nassau at 7 pm Monday (5½ hours, US$20 one way).

Getting Around

There are no buses to or from the airport; a taxi will cost about US$20 for two.

To hire a taxi or rent a car, call Tommy Pinder Taxi & Car Rental (☎ 242-332-2568) or Winsett Cooper Taxi & Car Rental (☎ 242-332-1592). Aged US cars can also be rented from the Highway Service Station (☎ 242-332-2077) on Queen's Hwy just south of town, and Johnson's Car Rental (☎ 242-332-2226), nearby on the highway.

NORTH & SOUTH PALMETTO POINT

This budding modern settlement, 4 miles south of Governor's Harbour, is popular with North American retirees. It is divided between North and South Palmetto. The former overlooks a stunning 5-mile-long pinkish beach, with a wreck at the south end. The latter backs a smaller beach and rocky shore, with good bonefishing.

There's a post office, clinic, pharmacy, grocery store, and gas station. Point Laundromat (☎ 242-332-1888) is at the gas station in North Palmetto.

Places to Stay

The modern *Unique Village Resort Hotel* (☎ 242-332-1830, fax 242-332-1838), in North Palmetto Point, enjoys an exquisite setting on a bluff. It has 10 attractively furnished rooms, two two-bedroom villas, and a one-bedroom apartment, all with ocean view, full kitchen, satellite TV, and radio. There's a pleasant restaurant and bar with panoramic windows and outside deck, plus grassy lawns with hammocks slung between palm trees. Rates run US$90 to US$110 in summer, US$110 to US$130 winter. Apartments cost US$130 and US$150, respectively; villas cost US$160 and US$180 (US$25 per extra person). Children under 12 stay free in winter; kids under 18 stay free in summer. A MAP plan costs US$35. Its mailing address is PO Box EL-187, Governor's Harbour, Eleuthera, Bahamas.

Palmetto Shores Vacation Villas (☎ /fax 242-332-1305), in South Palmetto Point, has modest one-, two-, and three-bedroom air-con villas for US$90/100/110 single/double/triple in winter (US$10 cheaper in summer). Money to blow? Take a 'super deluxe' villa for US$180. Children under 12 are half-price. There's tennis and fishing, and other activities can be arranged. Rental cars are available. Its mailing address is PO Box EL-25131, South Palmetto Point, Eleuthera, Bahamas.

A luxury beachfront three-bedroom *'round house'* (in the USA ☎ 914-358-1939, fax 914-358-1974) is also for rent for US$1575 weekly.

Sandy Beach Inn Resort (☎ 242-332-2008), in South Palmetto Point, has apartments and enjoys a nice beachside setting, but the owner was too busy fussing with his car to give me information or permit me to review the hotel.

Places to Eat

I like the warm ambiance of *Mate & Jenny's Restaurant & Bar* (☎ 242-332-1504), in South Palmetto Point, serving tasty pizzas from US$7, as well as broiled grouper for US$16 and other native dishes.

Unique Village Restaurant & Lounge (☎ 242-332-1830) also serves native dishes, plus steaks and fresh seafood. It has a happy hour 5 to 7 pm, live music on Thursday, and a Sunday lunchtime barbecue buffet for US$20.

Things to Buy

Walter Bethel's gift shop, Walter's Native Arts & Gifts, opposite the gas station on Queen's Hwy, sells his scenes of life on the island years ago, rendered in striking oils and acrylics on canvas and driftwood.

Getting Around

Asa Bethel, owner of Palmetto Shores Vacation Villas (see Places to Stay, above), rents cars, scooters, and boats. Arthur's Taxi (☎ 242-332-2006) also rents cars.

SAVANNAH SOUND

This near-destitute hamlet dates back to the 18th century. Goats and chickens roam among tumbledown shacks and collapsed colonial-era buildings. Hurricane Andrew ravaged the already down-at-the-heels settlement, which slopes down to a half-mile-wide channel – Savannah Sound – that separates Windermere Island from the mainland. The channel is good for bonefishing.

Big Sally's, just south of town, serves native dishes and doubles as a bar and dance club.

WINDERMERE ISLAND

Secluded, broom-thin Windermere Island boasts a pristine blush-hued beach running the 4-mile Atlantic shore. It is speckled with snazzy homes (most hidden amid foliage) reflecting its long-standing status as one of the most exclusive hideaways for

ELEUTHERA

the rich and famous. The chic Windermere Island Club, once The Bahamas' most fashionable resort, was a favorite of Lord Mountbatten and, later, his nephew Prince Charles and Princess Diana. Alas, it is closed . . . but may reopen.

The island is reached by a small bridge straddling Savannah Sound (the turnoff from Queen's Hwy is 2 miles south of the village). You'll have to sweet-talk your way past a security checkpoint.

You can rent *villas* and *cottages* by calling VHR Worldwide (in the USA ☎ 201-767-9393, 800-633-3284, fax 201-767-5510).

TARPUM BAY

The road south from Savannah Sound runs along the Bight of Eleuthera, an uninspired drive until you arrive at this delightful seaside fishing village 5 miles north of Rock Sound Airport. It's named for the feisty tarpons that frequent the offshore shallows. The former pineapple-trading port is now a somnolent place comprising quaint old stone buildings and clapboard houses, whitewashed and painted in pretty pastels. This is a perfect spot to cool your heels for a few days, sipping rum cocktails and watching locals cleaning conch on the wharf.

Bonefishing is good in Half Sound, a flask-shaped cove south of beach-lined, crescent-shaped Winding Bay, 1 mile southeast of the town's center.

Macmillan-Hughes Art Gallery & Castle

What, you may wonder, is a long-haired Irishman with a bushy white beard, an Oxford-English accent, and fine whistle doing building a 'castle' of limestone just northeast of the town center? This eccentric, self-promotional fella (he bills himself unabashedly as 'Lord of the Scales Demesne Artist Extraordinaire') offers guided tours of his castle-cum-gallery complete with turret and a 3-D relief of King Neptune – allegorically Macmillan – embracing a mermaid. Here he paints and sculpts in bronze; he has works in the

Royal Collection. Macmillan also holds an annual flag-raising ceremony. Admission costs US$1.

Mal Flanders Art Gallery

Another, less brash, artist has a studio atop the hill south of the town's center. Flanders, a portly American with thick glasses and jet-black hair in Ronald Reagan style, works at a happy, slothful pace in his bright and airy studio. Flanders, once a columnist for the *Miami Herald*, has lived here since 1972 without a car, TV, radio, or even a mailing address. You're made welcome to his studio, where his cartoon-style paintings are done in bright tropical pastels. 'I hope the worms eat my bones here,' he says of the country he loves.

Flanders' canvases and his paintings on driftwood boards sell for US$30 to US$600 on commission. He can paint from photos. You can write to him c/o Tarpum Bay, Eleuthera, Bahamas.

Places to Stay

Ingraham's Beach Inn (☎ 242-334-4285/4066), trashed by Hurricane Andrew in 1992, was scheduled to reopen in 1997 after a well-conceived remake, with eight rooms and four apartments.

Hilton's Haven (☎ 242-334-4231/4125; in the USA 800-688-4752), in town, is an aging property whose 10 rooms each have a private bathroom. Downstairs rooms have air-con; upstairs rooms have ceiling fans. The owner, Mary Hilton, is a delight, but her three-decade-old hotel is jaded (the drop in tourism locally has left few family-scale hoteliers with the funds to upgrade), though fine for anyone not fussy about decor. The restaurant serves native fare. It has bicycles for rent, and diving and other activities can be arranged. Year-round rates are US$50/55 single/double, plus US$10 for an extra person. Apartments cost US$65. The postal address is PO Box N-4616, Tarpum Bay, Eleuthera, Bahamas.

Ethel's Cottages (☎ 242-334-4233) has simple, modestly furnished, air-con, beachfront units. Also try *Cartwright's Ocean View Cottages* (☎ 242-334-4215).

Club Venta Eleuthera (☎ 242-334-4055), on Winding Bay, is an all-inclusive, self-contained village – a remake of a former government property – run by and for Italians (it is not talked of highly by locals because of its aloof, elitist ways). Club Venta operates its own charter flights from Milan to Rock Sound Airport.

Places to Eat

Shine's Famous Seafood is a tiny bayside gem with whitewashed walls and sky-blue shutters, a stone floor, and heaps of time-worn charm. Try the tuna salad and scrambled egg and johnnycake breakfast. Marsha, the robust chef, cooks up seafood and grits. It also serves sandwiches and conch- and fishburgers for US$3.

The menu at *Hilton's Haven* features continental and full breakfasts and native dinners such as pork chops for US$12 and roast beef for US$12, plus homemade cake and pie.

Getting Around

A taxi from Rock Sound (see below) to Tarpum Bay will cost about US$20 for two. There's a gas station on Queen's Hwy south of town.

ROCK SOUND

This small, charming village lies on Rock Sound, a deep U-shaped bay, where early townsfolk set out on their prime occupation – wrecking. Hence the settlement's early name, Wreck Sound. There are several historic buildings of note, plus the Ocean Hole (see below) and, on the bay shore south of town, the Blow Hole, which erupts like a geyser during strong swells.

Rock Sound famously comes alive each summer during the All-Eleuthera Regatta (see below), one of The Bahamas' liveliest let-your-hair-down affairs, and the setting for all-out dinghy races.

There are few beaches hereabouts.

Information

Barclays Bank has a branch on Queen's Hwy, open 9 am to 1 pm Monday to Thursday and 9 am to 1 pm and 3 to 5 pm Friday.

The medical clinic (☎ 242-334-2226) has a nurse and doctor; it's open 9 am to 1 pm weekdays.

You can have clothes washed at CC's Laundromat (☎ 242-334-2236).

For the police, call ☎ 242-334-2244.

Ocean Hole

This crater-like curiosity, along Fish Rd on the south edge of town, is a landlocked, 100-yard-wide, tidal blue hole populated by saltwater fish that move to and fro through subterranean sea tunnels. Take some bread to attract the fish, or descend the steps and hop in for a cool swim.

Be sure to lock your car, as I've heard reports that some of the local kids have taken to stealing.

Special Events

Each July or August, islanders flock to Rock Sound for the All-Eleuthera Regatta, a three-day festive occasion highlighted by regatta sailing. It also features live entertainment and family fun.

Another three-day event – the North Eleuthera Regatta – is held in October. This is one of the granddaddies of Bahamian sailing events and *the* highlight of the Eleutheran year, when islanders with their locally built sloops descend for three days of racing. Ashore the action is just as lively, with native cooks and bands whipping up a storm, while Bahamian lovelies strip down for beauty contests. Special air and boat charters depart from Nassau. Contact the Ministry of Youth and Culture (☎ 242-322-3140).

Junkanoo traditionally begins at 5 am on Boxing Day (December 26), when groups from the various settlements come together at Rock Sound.

Places to Stay

If you seek reclusiveness, try *Edwina's Place* (☎ 242-334-2094), 1 mile north of town. It has nine modestly furnished rooms kept spotlessly clean by live-in owner Edwina Burrows, who cooks for guests; rooms cost US$60/70 single/double. Like most places hereabouts, it is slightly jaded

ELEUTHERA

and hurting for business. The mailing address is PO Box EL-30, Rock Sound, Eleuthera, Bahamas.

Sammy's Place (☎ 242-334-2121), on Albury's Ave on the northeast side of town, has four bare-bones 'comfort suites' with TV; rooms cost US$60 single or double. The mailing address is PO Box EL-7, Rock Sound, Eleuthera, Bahamas.

Serenity (☎ 504-868-4165) is a private villa for rent; for information, write PO Box 9021, Houma, LA 70361.

The *Rock Sound Inn Resort* has closed.

Places to Eat

Take your pick among several down-home eateries serving native fare. Try the *Palm Garden Restaurant & Bar* or *Down Home Pizza*. You need reservations at *The Haven Bakery* (☎ 242-334-2155), which doubles as a pastry shop; it's open 8 am to 6 pm Monday to Friday and 8 am to 7 pm Saturday. Try the delicious coconut tarts.

The hot spot favored by locals is *Sammy's Place*, where Kathleen Cummer serves up everything from conch fritters and burgers to cheese omelets and grouper creole for US$2 to US$11.

Rock Sound Super Market has groceries.

Things to Buy

Almond Tree Arts & Crafts (☎ 242-334-2385) sells handmade gifts and souvenirs, as does Goombay Gifts (☎ 242-334-2191) and Arlicia's Souvenirs (☎ 242-334-2389), which also has jewelry and sportswear.

Getting There & Away

American Eagle flies daily from Miami to Rock Sound Airport, 2.5 miles north of town. Bahamasair has daily flights from Nassau.

A charter flight operates every second week from Milan, serving Club Venta Eleuthera (see the Tarpum Bay section).

The *Bahamas Daybreak III* mail boat calls here twice a week from Nassau, leaving at 5 pm Monday (five hours, US$20 one way) and 7 am Thursday (five hours, US$25). The boat also calls at Davis Harbour.

Getting Around

Dingle Motor Service (☎ 242-334-2031) rents cars.

COTTON BAY

This mile-long bay, off a spur of Queen's Hwy 6 miles south of Rock Sound, is favored by wealthy expats who own fancy villas above the shore. The homes are part of the Cotton Bay Club. Once beloved by hobnobbing socialites, the club has had a troubled history of late and closed in 1995. Wealthy Colombians have bought it with the intent to restore and expand it.

The 18-hole Cotton Bay Golf Club (☎ 800-334-3523), designed by Robert Trent Jones, Jr, was operating at press time, albeit with reduced facilities. The course was scheduled for an upgrade in 1998. It boasts 129 bunkers. Vital statistics: 72-par, 7000 yards. Green fees are US$70 (US$50 for nine holes). Caddies cost US$20 plus tips. You can rent clubs for US$15 per bag.

COTTON BAY TO CAPE ELEUTHERA

South of Cotton Bay, the island flares out in a lopsided, inverted 'T.' At Weymss Bight (pronounced 'wyms'es'), a nondescript settlement 2.5 miles southeast of Cotton Bay, Queen's Hwy splits. One branch leads north 10 miles to Cape Eleuthera via Davis Harbour and the settlement of Deep Creek; the shore is lined by mangrove swamps.

Cape Eleuthera is a good spot to dive for conch. The once-snazzy marina-resort that attracted Wall St and Washington bigwigs, including Richard Nixon, is now a shadow of its former self, and the 18-hole golf course is closed. The government hopes to resurrect it, with a casino and large hotel, but don't hold your breath.

Places to Stay & Eat

Thompson's Cottages has rooms for rent in Deep Creek. The *Cape Eleuthera Marina* (☎ 242-334-8311, fax 242-334-8312) rents swank apartments.

The restaurant and clubhouse at the Cape Eleuthera Marina were closed at press time and had been for some time. But you'll find grub in Deep Creek at the *Olympic Restaurant* and *Sharil's Inn*, which serve native dishes such as peas 'n' rice and cracked conch, and *Bertha's Go-Go Ribs*, serving tasty jerk ribs and pork.

Getting There & Away
When open, Cape Eleuthera Marina (see above) has slips, fuel, water, and electricity, as does the Hobo Marina (☎ 242-334-6101) near Davis Harbour, which has showers, laundry, and a bar and lounge.

The mail boat *Bahamas Daybreak III* calls at Davis Harbour twice weekly from Nassau, also stopping at Rock Sound; see the Rock Sound section for details.

ELEUTHERA POINT
South of Weymss Bight, the paved road runs to the funky settlements of Millars and Bannerman, forlornly set amid scrub and mangroves. One wonders how on earth the folks make a living, miles from factories or fields. Some live in ramshackle huts. Others live in fine houses with flashy cars parked outside. Hmmm . . .

Amazingly, a government-run cruise-ship berth was built on the spit called Princess Cay, just west of Bannerman. Princess Cruises has called here in the past, dispensing its human cargo for beach barbecues.

Beyond Bannerman, the vastly deteriorated road loops back to Millars. Midway, a challenging dirt track (for 4WD only) leads south to exquisite **Lighthouse Bay**. Offshore reefs and two small islands immediately south of the point are good for snorkeling and scuba diving. During tide changes, currents can be strong, so be careful.

At the east end of the bay, a short trail leads up to the historic **East Point Lighthouse**, atop the dramatic headland of Eleuthera Point, the southernmost point of Eleuthera. The lighthouse was restored in 1986. Alas, Hurricane Andrew hit in 1992 and seems to have relegated the lighthouse to its former state.

On the windward side of Eleuthera Point, a stunner of a beach runs north, unbroken, for 6 miles (it can also be reached by side roads from Queen's Hwy). *It doesn't get any more beautiful than this!*

ELEUTHERA

Exumas

Pop 3539

This paternoster of stepping-stone isles is strewn along the eastern edge of the Great Bahama Bank. The Exuma Cays – a necklace of 365 cays, one for each day of the year – begin 40 miles southeast of Nassau and continue in the same direction for over 100 miles, ending at the distant pendants of Great Exuma and Little Exuma, the two largest islands. They are fabulous to view from the air: true pearls in a setting of jade and aquamarine.

Most of the cays are small, uninhabited slips of land. Many are microcays, no bigger than helicopter pads poking out of the ocean. Some are low and barren. Others, like Highborne Cay, are rolling and smothered with dense pine forest and thatch palms and scrub. All are unified by glittering beaches and snug harbors – a boater's dream! Many are inhabited by iguanas, with several subspecies unique to a particular isle. A significant number of the cays are protected within the Exuma Cays Land & Sea Park.

Great Exuma, which is 40 miles long, and Little Exuma are the two main links in the chain. George Town, on Great Exuma, is the administrative center and only town of significance. Other settlements are few and far between and primitive, albeit picturesque. Another necklace of off-the-beaten-track isles, the Ragged Island Range, runs south of Little Exuma toward Cuba. This chain includes the Jumento Cays and Ragged Island.

The Lucayans called the two main Exuma islands 'Yumey' and 'Suma.' During the 17th century, many residents of New Providence settled Great Exuma to escape ruthless buccaneers. They lived as wreckers and salt rakers. By the 18th century the island's salt pans were figuratively producing gold dust. Following the American Revolution, Loyalists under Lord Denys Rolle arrived with 140 slaves aboard a ship

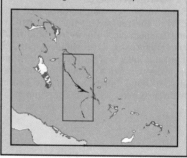

named *Peace & Plenty*. Rolle was granted 7000 acres and planted cotton. His plantations blossomed until the chenille bug arrived, destroying the cotton crop. The salt industry also evaporated, done in by more profitable operations on neighboring islands. In 1834, the year of emancipation, most whites uprooted and left. The newly freed slaves lacked such means and stayed.

Rolle's son, John, who had inherited his father's five plantations and about 400 slaves in 1796, is said to have deeded his land in common to his former slaves, for which he was compensated £4500 by the crown. (Actually, the slaves were in revolt 1828-34 and simply took over Rolle's land after emancipation.) It was common back then for slaves to adopt the names of their masters. Today every second person is a Rolle (locals, however, have a good grip on who their blood relatives are). And since the 1890s every Rolle has been permitted to build and farm on common land. Rolleville and Rolle Town, the two most important historic settlements on Great Exuma, are worth perusal. And forts and ruined plantations lie scattered like pirate treasure, though reclaimed by bush.

Most locals still earn a living from farming and fishing. Sponging, once an important source of income, seems to be enjoying a bit of a revival (today most sponges go to Nassau, and thence to sponge markets in Tampa, Chicago, and Greece).

Many Exumas residents are born to the sea in their shallow-draft sloops: As Yankee skippers read their charts, skilled Bahamian skippers read the reefs and shallows. Regattas earn high points on the social calendar. The tradition began over 40 years ago, when Bahamian sailors gathered in every conceivable craft, all built at home. Hundreds of islanders still make the annual pilgrimage to George Town's Elizabeth Harbour for the Family Island Regatta. The dinghies are shipped from other islands aboard mail boats.

Regattas have helped to revive the spirit of the local population as well as its interest in traditional boatbuilding. Most of the action revolves around the capital city of George Town, a yachter's haven and one of The Bahamas' leading hubs for chartering boats for island-hopping. Jackie Onassis was a regular visitor, and the New England yachting crowd still has a penchant for the Exumas.

As yet there are no flashy resorts or big-chain hotels on the islands (most hotels have fewer than 15 rooms). But that could change. Ritz-Carlton is slated to break ground on a new superdeluxe resort on Great Exuma – the Bahamas Club Resort – with a golf course and casino. The proposed resort, however, is controversial. Many local residents are opposed, fearing the inevitable changes to their bucolic way of life. That said, the locals, especially the

younger generation, are more taciturn than most other Family Islanders.

The Exumas are as good as anywhere in The Bahamas for diving and snorkeling. There are dozens of superb reef sites and wrecks. Dolphins, hammerhead and nurse sharks, and the occasional whale cruise the deep waters. See the Dive & Snorkel Sites sidebar for details on the Exumas' underwater world.

The chain also offers great fishing. The vast flats west and south of the Exumas are bonefish habitat supreme, and you will find good fishing lodges and operators in

EXUMAS

both George Town and Rolle Town. The Exumas Guides Association (☎ 242-336-2222) can provide recommendations for private guides.

Kayaking is also superb in the Exumas. See the Outdoor Activities chapter for details on operators offering trips through the islands.

Great Exuma

GEORGE TOWN
Pop 1000

The main settlement on Great Exuma stands on the west shore of Elizabeth Harbour, a 15-mile-long protected sound sheltered from the Atlantic by Stocking Island, a tantalizing sliver of land lined by fine beaches almost its entire length. George Town is really a village, with one street that encircles a body of water named Lake Victoria. The lake is connected to Elizabeth Harbour by a 50-yard-long channel. It's a quaint, hilly settlement shaded by palms and draped with poinciana.

The tropic of Cancer runs through town. You may feel the bump as you drive over it. If not, drive around the one-way system and try again!

In days of yore the British Navy utilized Elizabeth Harbour and Lake Victoria for refitting warships. The US Navy also had a small base here during WWII. Memories of both are long gone. Today the only noteworthy buildings are the serene St Andrew's Anglican Church, a white confection in stone atop the bluff above Lake Victoria (it's well worth the stroll uphill, at least to peek at the gravestones out back), and the waterside Government Administration Bldg, fronted by a neoclassical pink facade with white columns (it houses the Ministry of Education, post office, police station, magistrates' court, and jail). The rather nondescript Regatta Park, 100 yards south, boasts the weatherbeaten *Patsy*, a diminutive wooden dinghy that first raced in 1953; it now rests on a pedestal beneath thatch.

The hub of village life centers on Government Wharf, where townsfolk gather when fisherfolk return with their catch. It's at its colorful best when the mail boat is in.

Flamingo Bay, 2 miles south of town, boasts a beautiful beach and good bonefishing.

Information

Tourist Office Ona Bullard, a delightful and knowledgeable lady, runs the Bahamas Tourist Office (☎ 242-336-2430, fax 242-336-2431), opposite St Andrew's Anglican Church; it's open 9 am to 5:30 pm Monday to Friday.

Money Scotiabank (☎ 242-336-2651) has a branch in the town center; it's open 9:30 am to 3 pm Monday to Thursday and 9:30 am to 5 pm Friday.

Post & Communications The post office is in the administration building. You can send packages via UPS at Wally's Photographic Studio (☎ 242-336-2148), opposite Regatta Park; it's open 8:30 am to 5:30 pm weekdays and 10 am to 3 pm Saturday. The BaTelCo office is at the south end of town. Exuma Markets (☎ 242-336-2033, fax 242-336-2645) has a fax and phone message service. You can have mail delivered here.

Travel Agency Above Scotiabank, HL Young (☎ 242-336-2703) is a full-service travel agent open 9 am to 5 pm weekdays.

Library A tiny library, opposite the straw market, is open 10 am to noon weekdays May to December. December to May, it's open 10 am to noon Monday to Saturday.

Laundry There's a public laundromat (US$1 per wash) in the Harbour View Apartments on the west side of Lake Victoria; it's open 8 am to noon. You can have clothes dry-cleaned at Exuma Cleaners (☎ 242-336-2038) on the main street.

Medical Services The George Town clinic (☎ 242-336-2088) has three nurses and a

EXUMAS

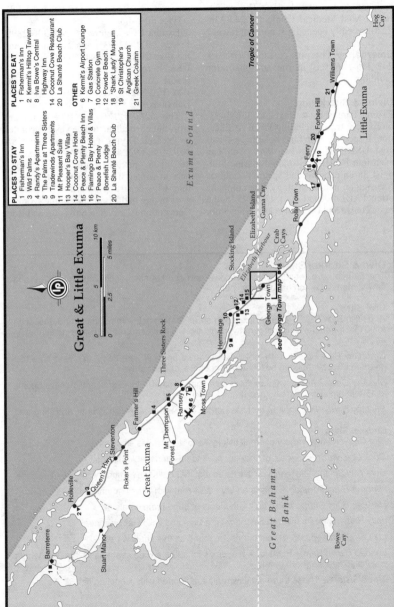

Great & Little Exuma

PLACES TO STAY
1 Fisherman's Inn
3 Wild Palms
4 Randy's Apartments
5 The Palms at Three Sisters
9 Tradewinds Apartments
11 Mt Pleasant Suite
13 Hooper's Bay Villas
14 Coconut Cove Hotel
15 Peace & Plenty Beach Inn
16 Flamingo Bay Hotel & Villas
17 Peace & Plenty
Bonefish Lodge
20 La Shanté Beach Club

PLACES TO EAT
1 Fisherman's Inn
2 Kermit's Hilltop Tavern
8 Iva Bowe's Central
Highway Inn
14 Coconut Cove Restaurant
20 La Shanté Beach Club

OTHER
6 Kermit's Airport Lounge
7 Gas Station
10 Concrete Gym
12 Powder Beach
18 'Shark Lady' Museum
19 St Christopher's
Anglican Church
21 Greek Column

Tropic of Cancer

Exuma Sound

Hog Cay

Little Exuma

Williams Town

Forbes Hill

Ferry

Rolle Town

Guana Cay

Crab Cays

Elizabeth Island

Stocking Island

Elizabeth Harbour

George Town

see George Town map

Hermitage

Three Sisters Rock

Farmer's Hill

Steventon

Rolleville

Barreterre

Queen's Hwy

Roker's Point

Stuart Manor

Mt Thompson

Forest

Moss Town

Ramsey

Great Exuma

Great Bahama Bank

Bowe Cay

10 km

5 miles

EXUMAS

resident doctor and dentist. The private Island Med Medical Clinic (☎ 242-336-2220) recently opened just north of town.

Emergency The police station (☎ 919, 242-336-2666) is in the administration building.

Diving & Snorkeling
Exuma Fantasea (☎ /fax 242-336-3483) offers dive trips, including PADI certification. It specializes in blue-hole dives. Dives cost US$55/85 one-/two-tank. You can even join Ed Haxby, a noted marine biologist, in an ecodive and specialty courses focusing on marine ecology. The company offers PADI instruction for US$495 for the basic course and US$90 for an introductory

resort course. The company also has a full-service dive shop.

Exuma Dive Centre (☎ 242-336-2390, fax 242-336-2391) rents equipment and has dive trips starting at US$50. It charges US$395 for certification and US$75 for a resort course. Its postal address is PO Box EX-29238, George Town, Exuma, Bahamas.

The *Nekton Pilot*, a state-of-the-art, twin-hulled, dedicated dive vessel operated by Nekton Diving Cruises (in the USA ☎ 954-463-9324, 800-899-6753, fax 954-463-8938, nekton1@aol.com) is based here in winter. The company offers week-long trips departing Saturday, with itineraries taking in the best sites of the Exumas, Conception Island, San Salvador, and Rum

Dive & Snorkel Sites
The Exumas are replete with good dive and snorkel sites, including blue holes and caves, many of which have safety lines.

Dive Sites
Angelfish Blue Hole – This vertical shaft starts 30 feet below the surface and descends to 90 feet before leveling into a network of caves. It has heaps of sponges and schooling angelfish.

Crab Cay Blue Hole – A 40-foot-wide crevasse up to 90 feet deep, this blue hole has great archways inhabited by lobsters, snappers, and stingrays.

Mystery Cave – At this vast complex extending south of Stocking Island, access begins at 15 feet below the surface and drops to 100 feet.

Stingray Reef – This shallow reef has hordes of snapper, angelfish, grunts, and stingrays.

Snorkel Sites
Bird Cay – A large variety of small fish jostle for turf on this small cay.

Duck Cay North – Schools of snapper flock to this unusual formation.

Duck Cay South – Life teems on this tiered reef that looks like an underwater wedding cake.

Harbour Buoy Portside – This is a very active reef with lots of marine life.

Harbour Buoy Starboard – You'll find plenty of large brain corals here.

Jolly Hall – This is a favored hatchery for grunts and yellowtail snapper.

Liz Lee Shoals – Lots of brain corals are found on this shallow reef.

Loaded Barrel Reef – Plentiful fish species inhabit the wide seabeds of this reef, where you'll also see staghorn coral.

Three Sisters – These three shallow reefs are flooded with schooling fish. ■

Cay; these cost US$1395 to US$1495, depending on the date.

Exuma Fantasea offers snorkeling, as does Exuma Dive Centre, for US$25. Both rent gear for US$15. Cooper's Charter Services (☎ 242-336-2711) also offers snorkel excursions for US$20. Native Son Tours (☎ 242-336-2950) has two-hour snorkel trips aboard the *African Queen* at 10 am and 1 pm daily for US$25, including gear and instruction.

Sport Fishing & Bonefishing

Rolle's Charters (☎ 242-336-2324) offers sport-fishing charters. Cooper's Charter Services (☎ 242-336-2711) will take you deep-sea fishing. It charges US$300/500 half-/full day. Islan' Time (☎ 242-345-0074) charges US$30 per hour for rod and hand-line fishing.

The Annual Bahamas Bonefish Bonanza, one of The Bahamas' prime fishing tournies, is held in George Town in October.

Boat Excursions

Wendall Cooper of Cooper's Charter Services (see Sport Fishing & Bonefishing, above) offers half-day sightseeing trips by boat to Crab Cay for US$35, as well as snorkeling and fishing trips.

Native Son Tours (☎ 242-336-2950) has 90-minute sunset cruises on Wednesday and Sunday at 4:30 pm for US$25, plus full-day trips as far as Norman's Cay for US$85 for up to four people.

Gym

To counteract your sloth on the beach, check in at the well-stocked Concrete Gym (☎ 242-336-2176) on Queen's Hwy, 2 miles north of town; it's open Monday to Friday and Saturday and costs US$5 per visit.

Organized Tours

Christine Rolle of Island Tours (☎ 242-336-4016) offers two tours to Barreterre and Little Exuma, focusing on bush medicine; one departs in the morning, another in the afternoon. Trips depart the Club Peace & Plenty (see the Places to Stay section) and cost US$15.

Seaside Tours (☎ 242-336-2091, fax 242-336-2092) also has guided tours daily, south and north of George Town. It offers a visit to Crab Cay, plus snorkeling and fishing trips. Its postal address is PO Box EX-29034, George Town, Exuma, Bahamas.

Special Events

The main event is the annual Family Island Regatta, held the last week of April, the premier regatta in the Bahamian islands. See the sidebar on the next page.

In mid-March visiting yachts congregate for the Annual Cruising Regatta in Elizabeth Harbour. It's a general excuse for the social elite to hobnob with the hoi polloi, downing copious amounts of rum and beer and cheering on the sailboats whizzing along in the harbor. Call Kermit Rolle (☎ 242-345-0002) or Mary Dames (☎ 242-336-2176) for information.

Another great time to visit is Christmas, when Junkanoo traditionally starts at 3 am on December 26. The colorful and noisy festival builds beneath the stars as islanders take to the streets for an outpouring of joy and bonhomie. Look for one of the more noteworthy local characters: Josh, 'King of the Junkanoo.'

Places to Stay

George Town For visits during the Family Island Regatta, reserve *way* in advance. Chances for last-minute accommodations are nil.

The tourist office (see the Information section) provides a list of individuals with guesthouses and rental villas starting at US$30 per night.

Marshall's Guesthouse (☎ 242-336-2328), opposite Regatta Park, is a modestly priced, no-frills option with 10 rooms and one apartment for US$40.

Exuma Apartments (☎ 242-336-2506), the green building behind the straw market, has four modestly furnished air-con units, each with fan, TV, carpet, and small bedrooms, for US$68/78 summer/winter. They're stuffy. Some were to be divided and will no longer have a kitchen. The

EXUMAS

Family Island Regatta

The wildly festive, four-day Family Island Regatta is held each April, as it has been since 1953. About 50 Bahamian sailing vessels, all locally made and crewed, race in Elizabeth Harbour, and everyone – landlubbers, yachties, and far-flung Bahamians – within miles who isn't bedridden descends to cheer the sloops. The boats race along with their tall sails billowing, often spilling their drunken crews as they go. The regatta also brings together boatbuilders from throughout the islands to pit their vessels against one another in the ultimate test of their ability to build a winner.

There are races in five classes, including a junior class for youngsters. A hallmark of the races is the 'pry,' a long wooden plank jutting from the side of each dinghy and sloop. The crew – often as many as six or seven people – put their weight on it to keep the boat balanced as it zips along, typically in a stiff 30-knot breeze. The races are highly technical. Knowledge of the winds, currents, and boat-handling is essential to winning.

The celebrated regatta is also an excuse for a bloody good bash! The festivities are massaged until the full week is taken up in support of the Kalik brewery and the rum industry. Speakers are tweaked until the reggae and African-Bahamian riffs create their own ripples on the bay, assisted by a colorful and raucous Junkanoo band. And the locals make hay of all this, too, selling cracked conch and other favorites. The party gets in the groove the week before the regatta, when liquor companies sponsor events.

For information, contact the Bahamas Tourist Office (☎ 242-336-2430, fax 242-336-2431) or call Stephen Hall (☎ 242-336-2685) or Christopher Kettel (☎ 242-358-4034) in George Town. ■

---

postal address is PO Box EX-29050, George Town, Exuma, Bahamas.

In the heart of town is the family-run *Two Turtles Inn* (☎ 242-336-2545, 800-688-4752, fax 242-336-2528), a stone-and-timber lodge with 14 dowdy, uninspired, carpeted, air-con units – three with a small stove and sink. All are modestly furnished and have hardwood walls, ceiling fan, louvered windows, and TV. Rates are US$68 single or double, US$72 triple, US$76 quad in summer; US$88/92/96 in winter, including taxes and continental breakfast. The mailing address is PO Box EX-29051, George Town, Exuma, Bahamas.

If you'd prefer self-catering units with 360° views and a private pocket-size beach, I recommend *Regatta Point* (☎ 242-336-2206, 800-310-8125, fax 242-336-2046), overlooking Kidd Cove at the end of the dock. It has a plantation-style building with four spacious waterfront units, each with high ceiling, kitchen, and patio. Ceiling fans and breezes easing through the jalousied windows keep things cool. There are also two very large and exquisite apartments, one with wooden floors and pinewood paneling, plus lofty ceilings and mosquito netting over the master bed. There's no TV here, but you'll find a book exchange, plus free bicycles, boat rentals, Sunfish, and fishing charters. In the summer room rates range from US$104 for one-bedroom apartments to US$158 for two-bedroom apartments (four people). In winter apartments cost US$122/178 one-/two-bedroom. The inn's postal address is PO Box EX-29006, George Town, Exuma, Bahamas.

Club Peace & Plenty (☎ 242-336-2551, fax 242-336-2093; in the USA ☎ 800-525-2210), at the harbor's edge, is the hub of social activity. Outwardly this two-story, pink-faced hotel resembles a Cape Cod B&B. It was built around a kitchen and the remains of a sponge warehouse; the former cookhouse has metamorphosed into a cozy bar decorated with nautical miscellany. The 35 modern, boxy, air-con rooms face either the small oval-shaped pool or Stocking Island. Each has a small TV and balcony. Facilities include sailboats, scuba diving, snorkeling, and fishing by arrangement. Bicycle, motorcycle, and

EXUMAS

car rentals are also available. Poolside rooms cost US$110 single or double, US$136 triple, and US$166 quad in low season, US$140/168/196 in the winter. Waterfront and garden suite rooms cost US$104 single or double and US$128 triple in the summer and US$128/152 in the winter. They also have more expensive bay-view rooms. A MAP (breakfast and dinner) plan costs US$36 per day. Children under six are not allowed (winter only). Club Peace & Plenty's postal address is PO Box EX-29055, George Town, Exuma, Bahamas.

Harbour View Apartments has modest units set atop the breezy hill on the north side of Lake Victoria.

A hostel-style budget cottage hotel, *The Retreat* (☎ 242-323-2904), was scheduled to open in late 1997; its postal address is PO Box CB-13558, Nassau, New Providence, Bahamas.

Farther Afield *Flamingo Bay Hotel & Villas* (☎ /fax 242-336-2660) sits on a peninsula jutting into Flamingo Bay. The main building has a graciously appointed lounge with New Mexico-style throw rugs,

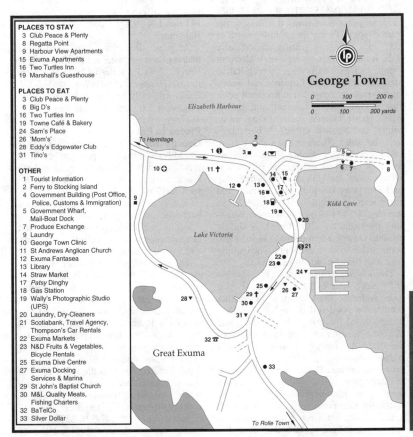

PLACES TO STAY
3 Club Peace & Plenty
8 Regatta Point
9 Harbour View Apartments
15 Exuma Apartments
16 Two Turtles Inn
19 Marshall's Guesthouse

PLACES TO EAT
3 Club Peace & Plenty
6 Big D's
16 Two Turtles Inn
19 Towne Café & Bakery
24 Sam's Place
26 'Mom's'
28 Eddy's Edgewater Club
31 Tino's

OTHER
1 Tourist Information
2 Ferry to Stocking Island
4 Government Building (Post Office, Police, Customs & Immigration)
5 Government Wharf, Mail-Boat Dock
7 Produce Exchange
9 Laundry
10 George Town Clinic
11 St Andrews Anglican Church
12 Exuma Fantasea
13 Library
14 Straw Market
17 *Patsy* Dinghy
18 Gas Station
19 Wally's Photographic Studio (UPS)
20 Laundry, Dry-Cleaners
21 Scotiabank, Travel Agency, Thompson's Car Rentals
22 Exuma Markets
23 N&D Fruits & Vegetables, Bicycle Rentals
25 Exuma Dive Centre
27 Exuma Docking Services & Marina
29 St John's Baptist Church
30 M&L Quality Meats, Fishing Charters
32 BaTelCo
33 Silver Dollar

George Town

Elizabeth Harbour

To Hermitage

Kidd Cove

Lake Victoria

Great Exuma

To Rolle Town

EXUMAS

deep-cushion sofas, and Spanish-style antique glass cabinets. The terrace lounge has lofty views over the bay. Four air-con rooms in the house are similarly appointed. Two are spacious suites with wraparound windows, tropical colors, and fine decor for about US$225 in winter. Rooms can get stuffy. The villas are currently leased to the US Drug Enforcement Administration! The mailing address is PO Box EX-29090, Exuma, Bahamas.

Nellie's Villas (☎ 242-336-2715) is also here, at the foot of Crab Cay. It offers tennis, basketball, and volleyball.

The *Peace & Plenty Beach Inn* (☎ 242-336-2250, 800-525-2210, fax 242-336-2253, ssbpeace@aol.com), a sibling to the Club Peace & Plenty, is 1.5 miles north of town in a suburban section named Jolly Hall. It has 16 deluxe, air-con, waterfront rooms, each exotically done up with Italian tile floors and wicker furniture and boasting a private balcony. There's a small pool, plus a two-story restaurant and lobby. Water sports include scuba diving, snorkeling, and Sunfish sailing. A bar hangs over the water. Summer rates range from US$130 single or double for a sea-view room to US$140 deluxe or efficiency. Winter rates are US$150/176. Three-day package rates (including all meals and other extras) begin at US$720/922 in summer, US$840/1044 in winter. Week-long packages are also offered. A shuttle bus into George Town operates at 9:30 am, noon, and 1:30, 4, 6, and 9 pm. The bathing here isn't the best, due to sea grasses.

The *Coconut Cove Hotel* (☎ 242-336-2659, fax 242-336-2658), next door, is a more romantic nook amid a garden that even has a pond full of reef fish, with a waterfall and footbridge. It was the home of Tom Chimento and Pam Predmore until the Peace & Plenty was built and guests started appearing in their dining room, expecting breakfast! The structure is made of mahogany, with sliding glass doors opening to Elizabeth Harbour. The 11 tastefully decorated air-con rooms each have a ceiling fan, fresh flowers, mosquito nets suspended above the bed, a small TV,

minibar, and thoughtful extras such as his-and-her bathrobes. Feeling frisky? Take the 'Paradise Suite,' complete with king-size bed, marble bathtub, and a hot tub on its own private deck.

Peak-season room rates range from US$120/140 single/double to US$145/165; the Paradise Suite costs US$230/250. Summer rates average US$30 less. Add US$30 for a third person and US$38 for a MAP plan. More rooms were to be added. Barman 'Fuzzy' Beneby can mix any of over 300 cocktails. An elegant dining room overlooks the pool and the ocean. It has bonefishing and dive packages. Free shuttles are offered. The postal address is PO Box EX-29299, George Town, Exuma, Bahamas.

At press time one-, two-, and three-bedroom cottages were to be built at Powder Beach, about 1.5 miles farther north. Here, too, is *Hooper's Bay Villas* (☎ 242-336-2982) with fully furnished air-con efficiencies about 200 yards from the shore.

Places to Eat
George Town The *Club Peace & Plenty* (☎ 242-336-2551) is open for breakfast, lunch, and dinner. Its dinner menu includes blackened mahi-mahi and baked chicken for US$17 to US$28.

The *Two Turtles Inn* hosts its popular barbecue on the patio from 6 to 9 pm Tuesday and Friday evenings. The nondescript restaurant is open daily for lunch and from 6 to 9 pm.

The nonsmoking *Towne Café & Bakery* (☎ 242-336-2194), behind Wally's Photographic Studio, is the place for a morning meal. You can opt for a delicious fresh-baked muffin and fresh-squeezed OJ or sample a Bahamian breakfast: boil fish with onions and hot peppers or chicken souse with grits or mildly spiced johnny cake. Owner Veronica Marshall still 'riddles' (or sifts) her grits the way her 'gran-mama' showed her, using an old corn mill while sensually grinding her hips in the manner proper riddlin' requires.

Sam's Place (☎ 242-336-2579), with a breezy upstairs deck at the Exuma dock, serves cracked conch, grouper fingers, and blackened dolphin (the fish, not Flipper). It serves breakfasts for US$6 and sandwiches and salads at lunch for US$5.

No-frills *Tino's* (☎ 242-336-2838) offers burgers, sandwiches, and native dinners such as turtle steak for US$8 to US$12. It has a boil-fish breakfast.

Gladstone Davis will crack and deftly cut out fresh conch before your eyes. He runs a stall called *Big D's* on the mail-boat dock; ceviche or 'conch salad' costs US$3.

My favorite spot is *Eddy's Edgewater Club* (☎ 242-336-2050) on the south side of Lake Victoria. By day it's a plain-Jane of a place, but it's run by one of the Family Islands' best young chefs, Kevin Brown, who serves splendid Bahamian fare, notably turtle steak, but also broiled grouper, steamed chicken, sautéed liver and onions, and a worthy pea soup with dumplings. The restaurant is hidden away at the back behind the bar. Most dishes cost less than US$10. Native breakfasts cost US$4 and lunch specials cost US$6.

'Mom' sells fresh-baked bread and confections from her van parked outside Sam Gray's.

You can buy groceries and household goods at *Exuma Markets*. Fresh produce can be found at *N&D Fruits & Vegetables* (☎ 242-336-2236), next door, which sells ice cream, doughnuts, and sandwiches; it's open until 10 pm. *M&L Quality Meats* (☎ 242-336-2670, fax 242-336-2671) delivers.

Farther Afield *Nellie's*, at Flamingo Bay, serves native seafood, plus American and continental cuisine. It has a Sunday brunch and a barbecue on Thursday evening. It provides a free shuttle to and from George Town. Other hotels provide free shuttles to restaurants as part of their dine-around program.

The *Peace & Plenty Beach Inn* (☎ 242-336-2250) is open 7:30 am to 9:30 pm and has Bahamian and continental dishes with a French twist.

Locally made dinghies racing in a regatta

The *Coconut Cove Restaurant* (☎ 242-336-2659), with options for indoor or alfresco dining, offers white-glove service. It specializes in Italian cuisine and nouvelle Bahamian dishes such as crab fritters, chicken breast with green pepper sauce, and Bahamian lobster tail, followed by crème brulée or banana flambé. The menu varies daily and can be prepared to order. Pizzas are disappointing. Breakfasts average US$6; dinner entrées are US$13 to US$27.

Entertainment

On Saturday the *Club Peace & Plenty* is *the* place to be. Locals and vacationers alike pour onto the waterfront pool deck to shake their booties with the assistance of copious amounts of rum. During the popular and festive Family Island Regatta, the place packs 'em in like sardines, and there is *no* peace to be had. Any night is good, however, at the hotel's tiny yet cozy English-pub-style bar. Most cocktails are on the expensive side (US$6 for a Goombay Smash), as they are at most hotel bars locally.

Eddy's Edgewater Club is the place to be on Saturday night, when a rake 'n' scrape band pulls 'em in and everyone works up a sweat on the dance floor. It sometimes has live music on Monday, too. The bar is open nightly.

EXUMAS

The *Silver Dollar* (☎ 242-336-2615) bar has dancing every Wednesday evening to a live band called Dry Bread. On Thursday night check out the entertaining limbo show at the *Flamingo Bay* restaurant (☎ 242-336-2660). Otherwise there's usually some action to be found at the patio bar of the *Two Turtles Inn*.

Things to Buy
First stop is the straw market, where women gather beneath the cool dappled shade of a large fig tree.

The boutique at Peace & Plenty sells resortwear and Androsia batik clothing. A similar array of clothing can be had next door at the Sandpiper, which also sells jewelry, fine art, quality locally made souvenirs, and a good collection of trash novels, plus books on The Bahamas. Similarly, Art & Nature has very attractive batik fabrics, native hardwoods, and embroidered T-shirts; it's in front of the Two Turtles Inn.

Scentuous Perfumes, at the marina in George Town, has duty-free perfumes. You can buy huge sponges for US$7 from Exuma Dive Centre. And Rod and Mary Page keep an early 19th-century shell craft alive; they make intricate shell mosaics and 'sailor's valentines,' wooden boxes affixed with shells bearing personalized messages of love.

Getting There & Away
Air The airport is at Moss Town, 6 miles north of George Town. There's a snack bar at the airport, plus Kermit's Harbour Lounge restaurant across the road. Taxis meet all flights. See the Getting There & Away chapter for airlines' international and Nassau phone numbers.

American Eagle flies daily from Miami. Bahamasair (in Moss Town ☎ 242-345-0035) flies between Miami and George Town twice weekly (Thursday and Sunday), and between Nassau and George Town daily (US$60 one way). Island Express flies from Fort Lauderdale.

Private pilots must clear customs and immigration (☎ 242-345-0071) at the airport.

Boat George Town is the official port of entry to the Exumas. Exuma Docking Service (☎ 242-336-2578, fax 242-336-2023) has 52 slips with water, electricity, and gas, plus laundromat and store. Exuma Fantasea Marina also has slips and facilities, including a marine railway for hauling.

The *Grand Master* mail boat departs Nassau for George Town at 2 pm Tuesday (12 hours, US$35 one way).

Package Tours Island Vacations (☎ 242-356-1111, fax 242-356-4379), PO Box CB-13002, Nassau, Bahamas, offers an 'Exuma Historic Excursion' for US$1839, including roundtrip airfare from Fort Lauderdale, that includes a visit to the Kelsall Salt Plantation and to the Shark Lady Museum on Little Exuma, plus a day of bonefishing.

Getting Around
To/From the Airport There's no bus from the airport. A taxi ride from the airport to George Town will cost about US$22 for two (see the Taxi section, below).

Bus A minibus departs George Town and runs east as far as Williams Town at 8 am, noon, and 5:30 pm. Westbound, the bus runs as far as Moss Town and departs at 2:45 and 6:35 pm. The fare is US$3. Inquire at the tourist office for more information.

Car, Moped & Scooter George Town's sole road runs one way, clockwise.

Thompson's Car Rentals (☎ 242-336-2442, fax 242-336-2445), above Scotiabank, rents cars for US$10 per hour, US$45 for four hours, and US$60 daily. It also has minivans for rent for US$15/60/75. There's a deposit of US$200/300 required. Its hours of operation are 9 am to 5 pm Monday to Saturday.

Sam Gray's Exuma Transport (☎ 242-336-2101) has cars at a similar rate. The Two Turtles Inn rents cars for US$55, plus mopeds for US$35. You can also rent scooters from Exuma Dive Centre for US$40/240 daily/weekly.

Taxi Several folks run taxis. Try Sam Gray's Exuma Transport (see Car, Moped & Scooter, above), Leslie Dames Taxi Service (☎ 242-357-0015), or Luther Rolle Taxi Service (☎ 242-345-5003).

Bicycle N&D Bicycle Rental (☎ 242-336-2236) and the Two Turtles Inn rent bicycles for US$10.

Boat Exuma Fantasea (☎ /fax 242-336-3483) rents Boston Whalers for US$75 to US$105 daily, US$375 to US$525 weekly. If all you want to do is beach-hop to Stocking Island, then Exuma Dive Centre (☎ 242-336-2390, fax 242-336-2391) will rent you a 17-foot Polar with Bimini top for US$75/375 daily/weekly, plus security deposit; its postal address is PO Box EX-29261, George Town, Exuma, Bahamas.

Several locals also rent boats.

STOCKING ISLAND

This 600-acre, pencil-thin island parallels Great Exuma about a mile offshore. It's rimmed by talcum-fine beaches and makes a fabulous day trip from George Town. All in all, it's a perfect place to skinny-dip, snorkel, or spend the day gleaning seashells.

Many expats have homes on the island, which is owned by John H Perry, a publisher and communications entrepreneur dedicated to the environment. The Perry Foundation plans a project to power the entire island with clean energy using ocean-current generators, solar cells, wind generators, and hydrogen fuel cells. His Conservation Lodge Foundation was also planning an ecosensitive lodge at the south end of the island. Guests will be permitted to participate in underwater research projects and land-based environmental activities.

There are no roads on the island, and access is by boat. The main hub is Peace & Plenty Beach Club, which offers sailing and snorkeling. The club also hosts Out Island Snorkeling Adventures (see the Outdoor Activities chapter). The best snorkel spots are at the cuts between Stocking Island and Elizabeth Island and between Elizabeth Island and Guana Cay.

Stromatolite Reef

This 400-foot-deep blue hole (also called 'Mystery Cave'), on the Atlantic side, is said to be one of only two living intertidal stromatolite reefs in the world (the other is near Perth, Australia). Stromatolite? Yes, a growing reef of layered limestone – a living fossil – dating back 3.5 million years.

Exuma Fantasea (☎ /fax 242-336-3483) runs dive trips to the reef from George Town.

Places to Stay & Eat

Higgins Landing (☎ /fax 242-357-0008), an upscale guesthouse with four rooms, bills itself as an 'eco-resort.' It also has five handsomely appointed cottages full of antiques, each with a wide balcony and fantastic views. There's a beach bar and restaurant; a single-sitting dinner is offered at 6:30 pm Tuesday to Sunday for US$45, including free shuttle from George Town. Reservations must be made by noon. Free transfers are provided from the Exuma Fantasea dock in George Town. The postal address is PO Box EX-29146, Exuma, Bahamas.

The *Peace & Plenty Beach Club* serves snacks and drinks until 4 pm.

Getting There & Away

A ferry runs twice daily to the Beach Club from Club Peace & Plenty in George Town, departing at 10 am and 1 pm and returning at 12:45 and 3:45 pm (US$8 roundtrip; free for the hotel's guests). A separate ferry departs the Peace & Plenty Beach Inn at 10 am and 12:30 pm, returning at 1 and 4 pm.

BOWE CAY

And what say you to being stranded on a deserted isle? The Robinson Crusoe in you can rent this 220-acre 'Gilligan's Island' about 10 miles east of Great Exuma. There are no headhunters with fake French accents here. It's just you and the sun-baked iguanas. The cay, which is 5 miles around, has a lagoon ringed by mangroves and trails that lead over the blackened coral. You sleep on wooden platforms in tents, with a screened cabaña for shelter, an

EXUMAS

outhouse latrine, and an outdoor shower for bathing beneath the stars. Electricity comes from a battery. The camp, which is rented out to one party at a time (be it one person or a group of 20), comes equipped with stoves, picnic tables, kerosene lamps, fishing gear, and other essential accouterments, including a radio for contact with the mainland.

A company named Ultimate Adventures (☎ 617-397-1481, 800-992-0128), PO Box 1241, Melrose, MA 01176, operates the show on behalf of the cay's owner and will happily maroon you there. A weeklong stay will cost you US$1399 single. For two or three people, it costs US$749 per person; US$599 per person for four to six; US$449 per person for larger groups.

ROLLE TOWN
Pop 300
This small settlement sits magnificently atop a hill with a stunning view over the coastal plains where villagers grow crops of onions, mangoes, and bananas. Vast turquoise boneflats extend beyond. The village was once part of the estate of Lord Rolle. Many of the sun-bleached pastel buildings and clapboard shacks, some of which are in shambles, date back over a century. Goats graze between the homes.

You can follow a wooden path to three 18th-century tombstones, one of which is shaped like a double bed with headboard and footboard; here, according to the marble plaque dating to 1792, the 26-year-old wife of an overseer, Captain Alexander McKay, slumbers with her infant child.

Bonefishing
The Peace & Plenty Bonefish Lodge (see below) is one of the best fishing lodges in The Bahamas. It charges US$290 per day with boat, guide, and tackle for two. The hotel has an intensive seven-day 'bonefish school' package each April and November, with 16 hours of instruction over four days for US$1854. It's billed as 'the ultimate fly fishing school challenge.' Fishing guru Bob Hyde runs the Peace & Plenty Boutique, where you can buy fishing gear.

Places to Stay & Eat
A chap called Charlie (☎ 242-345-5042) rents a fully furnished *two-bedroom home* with lounge and dining room. The bedroom has satellite TV and air-con; US$100/500 daily/weekly double (US$20 each extra person). It comes with a Boston Whaler for an additional US$50 daily.

Serious anglers should head to *Peace & Plenty Bonefish Lodge* (☎ 242-345-5555, fax 242-345-5556), about 3 miles south of Rolle Town at the far south end of Great Exuma. The centerpiece is a marvelous stone-and-timber lodge overlooking landscaped grounds and a stone sun deck. A handsome lounge-cum-bar sports a video library, a pool- and cardroom, plus a restaurant and pro shop. Upstairs, the lodge has a second restaurant and lounge reserved for fisherfolk, with a satellite TV and fax. The eight nicely appointed air-con rooms have two queen-size beds. Each has a balcony and views over the flats. Three-night packages cost US$1504 single (one person per room and boat) and US$854 per person double. A similar weeklong package costs US$3986/2186. Room-only rates are a whopping US$308 single, US$188 per person double. The restaurant is not open for lunch (box lunches are provided). The lodge's mailing address is PO Box EX-29100, George Town, Exuma, Bahamas.

NORTH OF GEORGE TOWN
Queen's Hwy runs north of George Town in good condition through a string of small roadside settlements – Hermitage, Moss Town, Ramsey, Mt Thompson, Farmer's Hill, Roker's Point, and Steventon – with prim little homes painted in Caribbean pastels and shaded by palms. Most are associated with plantation estates that now lie in ruins. The area is important for vegetable and fruit farming; the produce is shipped from the Mt Thompson Packing House.

About a mile offshore from Mt Thompson is the Three Sisters Rock, a trio of craggy boulders rising from the sea. They're supposedly named for three sisters who each drowned themselves here for the shame of bearing a child out of wedlock (the story is apocryphal: The *majority* of children are born so in The Bahamas).

Beautiful beaches line the north shore, including Ocean Bight, between Farmer's Hill and Steventon, the projected site for the Bahamas Club Resort, complete with casino (see the chapter introduction).

There's a BaTelCo station beside the road in Farmer's Hill. Coastline Laundromat is beside the road in Roker's Point. There's a medical clinic (☎ 242-358-0053) in Steventon. Practitioners of 'bush medicine' include Joe Romer (☎ 242-345-7044) in Ramsey, Christine Rolle (☎ 242-358-4016) in Farmer's Hill, and Ira Curry (☎ 242-358-5003) in Roker's Point.

Places to Stay & Eat
Mt Pleasant Suites (☎ 242-336-2960) is a small hotel with modern, modestly furnished, air-con suite units with satellite TV and kitchen. Single rooms cost US$68/85 summer/winter; doubles cost US$80/100. About a half-mile northwest is *Tradewinds Apartments* (☎ 242-336-2697), also with 16 fully furnished, air-con apartments with TV.

The motel-style *The Palms at Three Sisters* (☎ 242-358-4040, 800-688-4752, fax 242-358-4043) looks over a deserted, palm-lined beach in Mt Thompson. It has 12 large, air-con beachfront rooms and two cottages, all modestly albeit nicely furnished, with patios or balconies and satellite TV. Facilities include a weather-worn tennis court, indoor bar, and ocean-view restaurant. The rooms were renovated in 1994, but the hotel still looked a bit raggedy in mid-1997. Summer rates are US$75 single or double, US$90 triple for a beachfront room, US$100 single or double for a cottage. Rates in the winter are US$105 single or double, US$125 triple, and US$125, respectively. It had very few guests when I visited. The mailing address is PO Box EX-29215, George Town, Exuma, Bahamas.

Randy's Apartments (☎ 242-358-0021), about a mile farther north, has four modern, air-con one- and two-bedroom units beside the road, about 100 yards from the beach.

Budget travelers might try *Wild Palms* (☎ 242-345-6036), near Roker's Point, a charming albeit rundown historic two-story wooden home with four rooms.

The *Whale's Tail* (☎ 242-336-2979) restaurant, next to Tradewinds Apartments, is recommended for native dishes. It's popular with locals, who gather for live music on Saturday night. Another acclaimed seafood option is *Iva Bowe's Central Highway Inn* (☎ 242-345-7014), about 7 miles north of George Town. This small, no-frills eatery is popular with locals. Iva is acclaimed for her conch dishes. She also serves tasty shrimp and a crawfish salad with peas 'n' rice.

In Roker's Point you can enjoy a meal at the *Rhodriquez Neighbourhood Club & Restaurant*.

Things to Buy
The Reef, next to Mt Pleasant Suites, sells sporting goods, stationery items, and gifts.

Getting There & Away
Norman Forbes (☎ 242-336-2484/2444) operates a beige Mitsubishi van westbound to Mt Thompson, departing George Town at 8:45 am and 2:30 pm and returning from The Palms at Three Sisters at 9:15 am and 2:55 pm (US$4 one way). He'll operate at other times for a minimum of six people.

Another minibus reportedly runs between Williams Town and Moss Town via George Town. It departs Williams Town at 6:45 am and 12:45 and 5:50 pm. It departs Moss Town at 6 and 8:50 am and 3:15 and 7:10 pm.

Getting Around
Smitty's Taxi (☎ 242-358-4045) is in Farmer's Hill. There's a gas station opposite Iva Bowe's.

Kermit Rolle of Rolleville (see below) offers taxi tours for US$60 to US$140 for four people.

ROLLEVILLE
This historic settlement, 28 miles north of George Town, sits atop a hill at the northern end of Great Exuma. It's a poor village, with many meager shacks and former slave

homes, most in tumbledown condition. In late spring and early summer the village is brightened by dozens of flame-of-the-forest trees. The hamlet is the site of the Rolleville Regatta, held the first Monday in August. Several locals still make boats.

Kermit Rolle (☎ 242-345-0002), one of the island's more successful entrepreneurs, may be free to guide you on a lore-filled tour of the island (try him at Kermit's Hilltop Tavern or Kermit's Airport Lounge).

Do take time for a refreshing drink at *Kermit's Hilltop Tavern* (☎ 242-345-6006), which serves steamed conch, curried mutton, and pan-fried grouper with fresh vegetables from the owner's farm. Reservations are required for dinner. A seat at one of the rooftop tables with a marvelous view makes it well worth the drive. The tavern is the liveliest night spot for miles, especially during the Emancipation Day celebrations. It has open-air dancing and live music on weekends.

There are several other clubs. Try the *Down Home Club*, as you enter town, or the *Club Little Savoy*.

BARRETERRE

About 2 miles south of Rolleville, a potholed side road off the Queen's Hwy leads west to Stuart Manor, where it curls north to the twin Barreterre Cays, which are separated from Great Exuma by waterways (each spanned by a bridge). The road ends at Barreterre, a sleepy, nondescript hamlet that stirs only with the monthly arrival of the mail boat. A few locals still make sailboats. Ask Hughrie Lloyd to show you his regatta-winning dinghies. Everyone seems to be called McKenzie, after a plantation owner.

Keep your ears attuned for the voice of Sonny Lloyd, a blind square-box player and bass singer with a laugh like Ray Charles'. He sings gospel, accompanied by his sister-in-law Evalena. Says author-photographer Harvey Lloyd: 'Their voices are full of the black earth that they farm, of the shallow sea that they fish, of the winds of the sea, of the sweat and the toil and the dignity, the kindness and the pride of the people.'

Sonny's 'rich bass baritone voice fills the dark room with chords struck from the ark of the church.' Evalena sings the melody in 'a sweet high soprano voice – her face lit up like sunshine on the mountain top, her eyes looking straight in the face of God.'

You can rent a 17-foot Boston Whaler from Reverend AA McKenzie (☎ 242-355-5024). Don Smith (☎ 242-345-2323) and Hedley Smith (☎ 242-345-2330), in Stuart Manor, advertise scuba and deep-sea fishing trips.

Places to Stay & Eat

The *Fisherman's Inn* (☎ 242-355-5017), on the waterfront to the left as you enter town, has two simple rooms with ceiling fans and bathroom. The inn is better known as a seafood restaurant and bar; dinner reservations are recommended (US$5 breakfasts, US$8 to US$15 dinners). No-frills eateries include the *Same Old Place* and *Divinche's Take-Away*. You can buy goods at *McKenzie's* grocery store.

Getting There & Away

Bounce's Bus operates roundtrip service to Barreterre at 10 am on Wednesday and Thursday from the Two Turtles Inn in George Town for US$14, including lunch. Check with the tourism office.

The *Ettienne & Cephas* mail boat calls here weekly from Nassau; see the Staniel Cay section in this chapter for details.

Little Exuma

Ferry

This small hillside settlement lies immediately across the 200-yard-wide bight that separates Little Exuma from Great Exuma. It's linked to Great Exuma by a 564-foot-long bridge (before the bridge was built, passengers had to help the ferryman haul their vehicles across the water on a raft drawn by a pulley). The old ferry can be seen, albeit submerged.

A highlight is St Christopher's Anglican Church, a whitewashed chapel festooned with a bougainvillea bower. Supposedly it's the smallest church in The Bahamas.

Just offshore lies Pigeon Cay, a popular spot among day-trippers with well-stocked picnic baskets. You can hire a boat to take you; ask around.

LilyMae Bullard (☎ 242-345-4132) offers Swedish massage at Red Hill Plantation near Ferry; it costs US$40 per hour.

'Shark Lady' Museum The hamlet is most famous for 'Tara,' the home-boutique-museum of Gloria Patience (alias The Shark Lady of the Exumas), a sun-baked old dame whose home abounds with her collectibles and other artistic creations, such as jewelry made from sharks' teeth and spines. For seven years, she captained a yacht with an all-female topless crew! Amazingly, too, this youthful septuagenarian used to snare sharks from her Boston Whaler using a 10-inch hook on a 150-foot hand line! The jaws she sold to tourists; the carcasses she conjured into fertilizer. She likes to dispel the in-vogue notion that sharks are goody-goody creatures with bad press. She has single-handedly hooked and clubbed about 1800 over the years. Her conclusion: 'They're vicious!'

Her simple clapboard house is fronted by a garden full of bougainvillea . . . a far cry from Tara of *Gone with the Wind*. It's roadside, 400 yards south of the bridge.

Ferry to Williams Town

Forbes Hill, 12 miles southeast of George Town, has a 100-yard-wide scimitar of pure white sand with turquoise shallows cusped by tiny headlands. *Idyllic!* Two miles south of Forbes Hill a side road leads east to Tropic of Cancer Beach, another true stunner that runs south, unblemished, for several miles.

The southernmost settlement is Williams Town (pop 300), populated predominantly by Kelsalls, descended from or named for the foremost Loyalist family that founded the settlement. The Kelsalls established a cotton plantation and sold salt drawn from nearby salt ponds. The brush-entangled ruins of the plantation home – Hermitage Estate – are still standing amid the area's pinkish brine ponds.

You can watch locals dressing their fresh catch of fish and conch at the rickety wharf behind and just south of St Mary Magdalene's Church. North of town, on the bluff to the side of the road, you'll pass a tall Doric pillar transporting you metaphorically to ancient Greece. This column and a rusty cannon stand high above the rocky shore. The hulk of a ship lies dramatically on a white-sand beach fronting the village, within calling distance of the column meant to guide mariners.

Marvin and Trevor Bethel act as fishing guides, based at La Shanté Beach Club (see below).

Places to Stay & Eat *La Shanté Beach Club* (☎ 242-345-4136, fax 242-345-4134), at Forbes Hill, is a no-frills place with three modestly furnished air-con rooms with kitchenette and separate dining room. Each has a satellite TV. But what an enviable and lonesome position, right on the scimitar beach! Rates are US$65/85 summer/winter. It serves sandwiches, burgers, and Bahamian dishes in its rather plain restaurant. Breakfast (about US$5) and dinner are provided for guests on request. A seafood platter costs US$25, a T-bone steak costs US$12. There's a free shuttle to George Town. The postal address is PO Box EX-29082, Exuma, Bahamas.

Doris Rahming ('Mom') runs *Mom's Bakery* in Williams Town. She bakes tempting rum cake, banana bread, coconut tarts, and bread. Here, too, is *Nelson's Point* (☎ 242-345-4043) restaurant and lounge and the small *Hilltop Bar*, beside the church. *Bullard's Supplies* sells groceries.

Gordy's Palace, in Williams Town, is a hip-hopping spot on weekend nights.

Exuma Cays

The cays begin at the barren Sail Rocks, 40 miles southeast of New Providence. Though the cays may look alike, each has its own quirky character. Many are privately owned. These waters are acclaimed as the 'finest cruising grounds in the Western Hemisphere.'

Ship Channel Cay & Allan's Cays

Long, narrow Ship Channel Cay is the northernmost cay after Sail Rocks. Allan's Cays, immediately south, comprise about a dozen cays popular with boaters and fisherfolk; one of the prettiest is Leaf Cay, with a splendid beach. An endemic subspecies of iguana, the yellowish 'Bahamian dragon,' lives here. Boaters must keep dogs on board (dogs don't realize that iguanas are a protected species!).

Getting There & Away American Canadian Caribbean Line's *Mayan Prince* and *Niagara Prince* call at Allan's Cays on twice-yearly 12-day cruises between Nassau and the Turks and Caicos. The itinerary also includes stops at Norman's Cay, Warderick Wells Cay, Sampson Cay, Staniel Cay, and George Town. See the Getting There & Away chapter for more information.

Native, dragonlike iguanas can grow up to 5 feet long.

Yachters will find an exceptionally good anchorage at Leaf Cay.

Powerboat Adventures (☎ 242-327-5385, fax 242-328-5212) offers a thrilling powerboat adventure from Nassau at 9 am daily; it costs US$150/99 adults/children. Hang on to your toupee as you zip along first to Allan's Cays for snorkeling. Then it's on to Ship Channel Cay for a barbecue lunch on the beach. The postal address is PO Box CB-13315, Nassau, Bahamas.

Highborne Cay

This private cay, 2 miles south of Leaf Cay, is favored by yachters, who are permitted ashore. A pathway leads from the marina to a small provisions store and pay phone where weathered sailors lounge around swapping shaggy-dog stories while basking in the chairs set outside. You can climb the hill topped by waving palm trees for a view of the most beautiful beach you have ever seen.

There are four *oceanside cottages* for rent. Only yachters and people staying in the cottages are allowed access to the cay. Nightly rates begin at US$200. Contact Highborne Plantations (☎ /fax 242-355-1003), PO Box SS-6342, Nassau, New Providence, Bahamas. The Highborne Cay Marina, which has a *grocery store*, caters to yachts up to 130 feet. Contact Peter and Alison Albury (☎ 242-355-1008, fax 242-355-1003, VHF channel 16), PO Box N-6342, Nassau, New Providence, Bahamas.

Norman's Cay

One look at the stunning beaches and you'll understand why 4-mile-long Norman's Cay was once an idyllic hideaway for the wintering wealthy. In the 1970s most of the island was purchased by Carlos Lehder, a key German-Colombian drug lord who brought in armed thugs, drove out most of the residents, and turned the cay into a landing strip for illegal cargoes. The corrupt Pindling government turned a blind eye (see History in the Facts about The Bahamas chapter) until an NBC documentary blew the lid

EXUMAS

Exuma Cays

Sail Rocks

Ship Channel Cay

Allan's Cays

1 Highborne Cay

Norman's Cay

2

Wax Cay Cut

Shroud Cay

Hawksbill Cay

Exuma Cays Land & Sea Park

3 Warderick Wells Cay

Hall's Pond Cay

Conch Cut

Compass Cay

Fowl Cay

Sampson Cay

Leaf Cay   4

Staniel Cay   *see inset map*

Great Bahama Bank

Black Point

Great Guana Cay

Little Farmer's Cay   5 Big Farmer's Cay

Tongue of the Ocean

6 Lee Stocking Island

ATLANTIC OCEAN

Eleuthera

Little San Salvador

Cat Island

Exuma Cays

Exuma Sound

Staniel Cay

7

8

9

10

Great Exuma

Stocking Island

George Town

Little Exuma

Bowe Cay

Williams Town

see Great & Little Exuma map

Hog Cay

EXUMAS

PLACES TO STAY
4 Sampson Cay Club & Marina
5 Farmer's Cay Yacht Club & Marina
9 Staniel Cay Yacht Club & Resort
10 Happy People Marina

PLACES TO EAT
7 Club Thunderball

OTHER
1 Highborne Cay Marina
2 DC-3 Plane Wreck
3 Ranger Station/Park Headquarters
6 Caribbean Marine Research Centre
8 Thunderball Grotto

0   20   40 km
0   10   20 miles

in 1983. Lehder now idles in jail and many of the residents have returned, but there are still armed police here (mostly to guard against vandalism). Itinerant visitors need permission from the Homeowners Association to explore north of the airstrip.

A DC-3 drug-running plane rusts here in shallow water, having missed the runway. And the boat that is keeled and rotting dockside capsized a few years ago – overloaded with Haitian refugees – taking its cargo with it.

The bonefishing is said to be superb.

Dale or Sally Harshbarger rent beachfront cottages at *MacDuff's* (☎ 242-357-8846), each with island decor, ceiling fans, air-con bedroom, and a fully equipped kitchen. Water sports are offered. The couple will stock the cottages with food by arrangement.

American Canadian Caribbean Line's *Mayan Prince* and *Niagara Prince* stop here. See the Getting There & Away chapter for details.

Exuma Cays Land & Sea Park

This 175-sq-mile protected area of islands and surrounding seas was created in 1958 as the first marine 'replenishment nursery' in the world. It runs 22 miles south from Wax Cay Cut (immediately south of Norman's Cay) to Conch Cut and Fowl Cay. It is 8 miles wide, extending 3.5 miles east and west on each side of the islands. It has outstanding anchorages and even more outstanding dive sites.

All commercial fishing and collecting is banned. (No marine or plant life, whether dead or alive, may be taken, including shells.) The waters teem with marine life, and snorkeling (with an average depth of about 10 feet) doesn't get any better than this – there are miles of sun-dappled coral reefs where groupers and turtles huddle. The waters lap against beaches as private as your innermost thoughts. On land, you may spot the Bahamian mockingbird, Bahamian banana quit, or the rare red-legged thrush. Seabirds abound, including terns, waders, and the elegant, long-tailed tropicbird, which nests in high bluffs. Land animals

include curly-tailed lizards, blue-tailed lizards, plump iguanas and, on several isles, hutias so endangered that messing with them is good for a hefty fine and up to six months in the pokey.

Uninhabited Hawksbill Cay, ringed by stunning beaches, has marked nature trails that lead to the ruins of an old Loyalist plantation. Hall's Pond Cay has a recyclable library (take a book, leave a book) at the abandoned Exuma Cays Club. Warderick Wells Cay, which has 4 miles of nature trails, is said to be haunted by the tormented spirits from a slave ship. Shroud Cay has 'Driftwood Village,' an ever-expanding piece of flotsam folk art. And the Rocky Dundas, two rocks in Conch Cut, have a cave full of stalactites and stalagmites.

The ranger station is on the northwest side of Warderick Wells Cay; it is open 9 am to noon and 1 to 5 pm Monday to Saturday and 9 am to 1 pm Sunday. Trail maps are available, and there's a library. The Bahamas National Trust has posted information leaflets on several cays.

Park access is free.

Places to Stay You can rent a house and two cottages sleeping up to 10 people on *Cistern Cay* (☎ 242-326-7875). But you'd better check with your bank manager before you send your deposit . . . the weekly rent is a withering US$38,000! At least this pays for a gourmet chef, all meals, and as

The endangered hutia

much booze as you can down, plus water sports, a fishing guide, and other extras.

Getting There & Away Several cays have airstrips, many of which are private.

American Canadian Caribbean Line's *Mayan Prince* and *Niagara Prince* spend a week in the park during its twice-annual 12-day Bahamian cruises. See the Getting There & Away chapter for details.

The best access to the park is from Staniel Cay, where you might be able to hitch a ride with the park warden, Ray Darville, on his daily patrol. The journey takes one hour by speedboat. Darville monitors VHF channel 16 from his headquarters at the Warderick Wells Cay anchorage.

Boaters must anchor at Hog Cay at the south end of Warderick Wells Cay. Moorings cost US$15 for two nights. You should call early on the day you plan to visit to check availability.

Out Island Voyages (☎ 242-394-0951, 800-241-4591, fax 242-394-0948), on Paradise Island, offers four- and seven-day 'Exuma Exploration' cruises aboard its 124-foot luxury yacht, the sleek *Ballymena*; these cost US$995 to US$2195. It also offers day trips from Paradise Island to the Exuma Cays for snorkeling and hiking, including gourmet meals.

Island World Adventures (☎ 242-363-3577, fax 242-363-1657, cruise@bahamas.net.bs) offers daylong excursions from Paradise Island to Saddleback Cay aboard the 45-foot, high-powered speedboat *EcoTime*. Trips also stop at Leaf Cay. Its postal address is PO Box N-7366, Paradise Island, Bahamas.

Ecosummer Expeditions and Ibis Tours offer kayak adventures and camping trips in the park; see the Outdoor Activities chapter for details.

Sampson Cay

This popular yachter's haven boasts a small harbor with a beach and nearby beach-lined coves.

Sampson Cay Club & Marina (☎ 242-355-2034, VHF channel 16) has air-con beachside cottages and a restaurant and bar.

Reservations are required for all meals; it's closed Sunday, except to cottage guests. It also has moorings and fuel, oil, ice, water, and groceries for boaters. There's also a 500-foot dock in the outer harbor.

Staniel Cay
Pop 80
This mite of a cay is the main settlement in the Exuma Cays and the main base for visiting the Exuma Cays Land & Sea Park. The small village has a post office, church, library, telephones, and grocery stores. There are peaceful beaches, and bone-fishing is said to be tops.

There's a BaTelCo station and a few phonecard booths. Several local women take in laundry.

The time to visit is during the New Year's Day Regatta, when locally built dinghies compete for prizes. There's also the Annual Staniel Cay Bonefish Tournament in August.

Thunderball Grotto A highlight of any visit to Staniel Cay is a snorkel or dive trip into this grotto, just northwest of the cay, below Crown of Thorns Rock. The exquisite cavern, which is lit by shafts of light pouring in from holes in the ceiling, is named for the James Bond movie *Thunderball*, scenes from which were filmed here. So, too, were scenes from *Splash* and another 007 movie, *Never Say Never Again*. A panoply of colorful fish crowds the crystalline waters. The current is very strong – inexperienced swimmers beware!

Places to Stay The cay's two waterfront hotels play to the boating crowd. *Happy People Marina* (☎ 242-355-2008) has eight rooms with ceiling fans and a decor of rainbow pastels. Upstairs rooms boast marvelous views and have private bathrooms; those downstairs share bathrooms. Rooms cost US$75 to US$90.

The recently renovated *Staniel Cay Yacht Club & Resort* (☎ 242-355-2024, fax 242-355-2044; in the USA ☎ 954-467-8920, fax 954-522-3248) has an exceptional oceanfront setting. Aficionados of

EXUMAS

Sports Illustrated swimsuit issues might recognize it as a setting for a recent shoot. There are six cozy air-con cottages, each sleeping up to four people, plus a guesthouse for six people. All have refrigerators, coffeepots, and fresh water made on-site. The resort offers free use of Boston Whalers, plus Sunfish sailboats and scuba gear rentals. Rates are US$155 single or double, US$230 triple or quad in summer, US$170/265 in winter, including airport transfers.

Rose and Marchus Mitchell rent three simply furnished, modestly priced beachside rooms with kitchenette at *Staniel Cay Colony* (☎ /fax 242-355-2034). A fourth cottage is up the hill. There's a restaurant and bar.

Places to Eat Singer Jimmy Buffett drops in on occasion to play Happy People's *Royal Entertainer's Restaurant*, where locals hang out. It specializes in cracked conch, lobster, pork chops, and other native fare. For lunch, try Theaziel Rolle's 'Theazielburger.'

The *Staniel Cay Yacht Club* restaurant serves three meals daily; it's closed Sunday, except for dinner for cottage guests. Reservations are required for yachters. You can order a boxed lunch for excursions.

Club Thunderball, at the north end of the cay, sits atop the bluff overlooking the Thunderball Grotto. The restaurant serves native fare and often has beach parties. The club also features music, a pool table, and satellite TV.

Several stores sell groceries, ice cream, and snacks. You can buy fresh-baked bread at Berkie Rolle's *Isles General Store*. Other local women sell bread.

Things to Buy There's a straw market, plus a few craft stores selling straw-work and T-shirts. Happy People Marina and the Staniel Cay Yacht Club & Resort have boutiques.

Getting There & Away Island Express offers flights between Fort Lauderdale and Staniel Cay.

Charter flights from George Town cost about US$360 roundtrip for up to five people; flights from Nassau cost US$500. You can charter a plane on Staniel Cay from Solomon Robinson (☎ 242-355-2012) or John Chamberlain (☎ 242-355-2011).

American Canadian Caribbean Line's *Mayan Prince* and *Niagara Prince* cruise ships call at Staniel Cay. See the Getting There & Away chapter for information.

Most people arrive at Staniel Cay by boat. Staniel Cay Yacht Club and Happy People Marina have slips, water, electricity, and fuel (see Places to Stay, above).

The *Ettienne & Cephas* mail boat sails here from Nassau at 2 pm Tuesday (21 hours, US$30 one way), also stopping at Black Point, Little Farmer's Cay, Barreterre, and Ragged Island.

Great Guana & Little Farmer's Cays

The largest of the Exuma Cays, 12-mile-long Great Guana Cay also has the cays' largest settlement – **Black Point** (pop 300). Facilities include an airstrip, post office, BaTelCo station, clinic, and laundry. There is a deep cave worth exploring (Martin Rolle acts as a guide). An Emancipation Day Regatta is held here each 'August Monday.'

Little Farmer's Cay, a stone's throw off the southwest tip of Great Guana, hosts the Annual Farmer's Cay (5F) Festival each first weekend of February and the Full Moon Beer Festival – *oooww-uuwww!* – in July. It also has a post office, BaTelCo station, and clinic.

Places to Stay & Eat The *Farmer's Cay Yacht Club & Marina*, on Little Farmer's Cay, has rooms, and a restaurant and bar (reservations needed for dinner). The *Ocean Cabin Restaurant*, in the hamlet up the hill, serves native fare and bakes bread to order. It has pre-dinner crab races on Wednesday and chicken races on Saturday.

On Great Guana Cay, *Lorene's Café* is recommended for inexpensive native fare and fresh-baked bread and cookies. The *Scorpio Inn* has also been praised; local residents gather at the inn at night to play pool and dominoes and to dance.

Getting There & Away The *Ettienne & Cephas* mail boat sails to Black Point and Little Farmer's Cay from Nassau weekly; see the Staniel Cay section for details.

Lee Stocking Island

Lee Stocking, about 5 miles north of Great Exuma, has an airstrip and the **Caribbean Marine Research Centre** (CMRC). This 100-acre scientific research facility (☎ 242-345-6039; in the USA 561-471-7552) is one of six marine research centers funded by grants from the US National Oceanic & Atmospheric Administration. Its mission is to study underwater ecosystems, such as conch and lobster populations, and broaden understanding to ensure the vitality of the reefs and aquatic life. Visitors are welcome; short tours are given, including the laboratories.

Ragged Island Range

This remote range of tiny islands forms a miniarchipelago poking up along the southeastern edge of the Great Bahama Bank. The crescent of a dozen or so isles and a score of smaller cays begins with the Jumento Cays, about 25 miles south of Little Exuma, and arcs west and south for about 100 miles, ending with Ragged Island, the largest of the half-moon chain.

Like other Bahamian isles, the Ragged Island Range has seen its day in the sun. During the 19th century its flats were utilized for salt-crystal farming. Today they are virtually uninhabited.

Most of the cays here are windswept and barren, increasingly so to the south. The birdlife is varied and prolific. And the cruising is spectacular, though few boaters make it this far. You can stop to admire the lighthouse that is still standing on Flamingo Cay.

The largest and southernmost island, Ragged Island (pop 89), also has the only settlement of any consequence: **Duncan Town**. It's a bit of a flyblown place, and most of the houses are abandoned and boarded up. Most folks who remain eke out a living from fishing.

Sheila's Fisherman's Lounge and *Louise's Sweet Place* serve simple native fare in Duncan Town, as does *Percy's Eagle Nest*, a crashed DC-3 that has creatively been turned into a bar, with a pool table in the shade beneath the plane.

Duncan Town has a 3000-foot paved airstrip. There is no scheduled air service, and the only visitors are the few sailors who call in, often bound for a circuit of Cuba.

The *Ettienne & Cephas* mail boat calls here weekly from Nassau; see the Staniel Cay section.

Cat Island

Pop 1678

Cat Island (not to be confused with North Cat Cay in the Biminis) is another narrow sliver of land, just 48 miles north to south. This slinky, sleepy, little-visited island, south of Eleuthera and 130 miles southeast of Nassau, is one of the most interesting islands in The Bahamas, a true gem for people hoping to discover traditional African-Bahamian culture.

The island is shaped like a long, slender boot, with New Bight, the capital, as the boot's buckle. Cat averages 1 to 4 miles wide before broadening along its 12-mile-wide sole.

How the island got its name is a source of controversy (it was officially known as San Salvador until 1926, when that name was transferred to Watling Island, today's San Salvador). Locals have always called their home 'Cat Island,' for Arthur Catt, a notorious pirate who supposedly had his base here. Local historian Eric Moncur says it was named by the English for the cats that the Spaniards introduced to the island.

A single, well-paved road – Queen's Hwy – runs north to south down the west shore, lined by plantation ruins and ramshackle settlements (few are more than dots on a map) where goats wander amid fallen stone walls. So provincial is the island that many of its inhabitants have never ventured to either its northern or southern end.

Dirt tracks lead from Queen's Hwy to the Atlantic shore (called the 'north' shore by locals), boasting miles-long pinkish beaches. The scenery here is often dramatic, with cliffs that plunge to the breakers. The south offers tranquil sugar-white beaches. The west shore is memorable for bonefish swarming the creeks opening to Exuma Sound. Cat Island is also blessed with rolling hills, crowned by Mt Alvernia (210 feet), itself topped by a

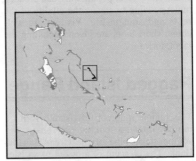

hermitage looking like it was dropped in from King Arthur's Cornwall.

The island is swampy in places and, elsewhere, densely forested with mangrove, scrub, and broadleaf woodland boasting mahogany and cascadilla, a heavily scented tree whose bark is shipped to Italy to be used in wine and perfume manufacture. Many caves, blue holes, and freshwater lakes dot the island, which is known for a species of freshwater turtle. The creatures – called 'Peter' by locals – are endangered but are still taken as a local delicacy or for domestic garden pools. Good places to see them are the shallow freshwater ponds between Tea Bay and Knowles. Small, non-poisonous snakes abound. You're sure to see giant land crabs with pincers the size of plumber's grips; at night, you might see flickering lights amid the undergrowth, those of locals hunting crabs for tomorrow's supper. And Cat Island is famed for ubiquitous monarch moths, dark brown and as large as small bats. Locals call them 'money bats' in the belief that if one lands on you, you'll come into some dough.

Above all, Cat Island has its own raw, time-steeped feel, typifying, as much as anywhere in The Bahamas, how 'the dramatic beauty of the Caribbean is the powerful beauty of decay,' in the words of Anthony Weller. The islanders' simple limestone homes are old and foursquare, with steep shingled roofs. Many are dilapidated, mildewed, leaky, and seemingly ready to tumble in the next heavy wind. Others are gaily painted in faded pastels. Many homes retain traditional African ovens in their yards, still used for baking bread and teacakes. Another oddity is the old public outhouses built over the shore.

Following the American Revolution, many Loyalists brought their slaves and established cotton and cattle estates. In its heyday Cat Island had over 40 plantations.

CAT ISLAND

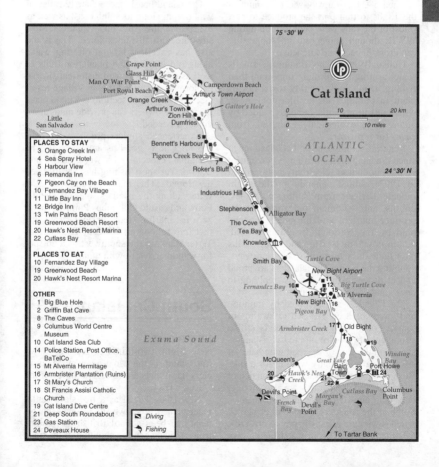

PLACES TO STAY
3 Orange Creek Inn
4 Sea Spray Hotel
5 Harbour View
6 Remanda Inn
7 Pigeon Cay on the Beach
10 Fernandez Bay Village
11 Little Bay Inn
12 Bridge Inn
13 Twin Palms Beach Resort
19 Greenwood Beach Resort
20 Hawk's Nest Resort Marina
22 Cutlass Bay

PLACES TO EAT
10 Fernandez Bay Village
19 Greenwood Beach
20 Hawk's Nest Resort Marina

OTHER
1 Big Blue Hole
2 Griffin Bat Cave
8 The Caves
9 Columbus World Centre
   Museum
10 Cat Island Sea Club
14 Police Station, Post Office,
   BaTelCo
15 Mt Alvernia Hermitage
16 Armbrister Plantation (Ruins)
17 St Mary's Church
18 St Francis Assisi Catholic
   Church
19 Cat Island Dive Centre
21 Deep South Roundabout
23 Gas Station
24 Deveaux House

There were several slave revolts, notably that of 1831 at Golden Grove plantation. In 1834 the abolition of slavery rang a death knell for the estates. Most of the estate-owners left (several were attacked by newly freed slaves as they boarded ships); others stayed and loaned their names to new emancipation settlements.

Pineapple and sisal farming evolved in the mid-19th century. The island was second only to Eleuthera for pineapples (in 1801, 84 million pineapples were shipped). The ports were full of ships bound for Europe and North America, and the population reached 5000. A railway was even built in the 1880s to transport the produce to port (most of the rails were later torn up during WWII, though some remain, supporting cauldrons in backyard kitchens).

Unusually for The Bahamas, small-scale farming is still more important than fishing. Don't look for tidy rows. Locals plant in potholes in the limestone base, where nutritious soils gather . . . aided by guano (bat excrement) gathered from caves for fertilizer.

Materially, things haven't changed much since emancipation for a large percentage of the population (electricity only arrived in 1993), which depends on the slight income derived from selling tomatoes, onions, and succulent pineapples at the produce market, and on small stipends paid by the National Insurance Board. Unemployment is rife, and many folks pass their days lying in shady doorways, counting the hours. The islanders are proud and at peace in their poverty, replying to decay and defeat with humor.

Cat Islanders are anchored by tradition and have not been exposed to swarms of tourists or to TV. Straw-work is still a strong custom; you're sure to pass islanders sitting on the side of the road with bales of silvertip palm, casually waiting for a ride. Bush medicine and obeah – the practice of African-based witchcraft – are also stronger here than anywhere else in The Bahamas. Some of the islanders are said to be skilled witches who are always happy to prescribe a homemade cure from Cat Island's own larder. You won't see dolls pricked by pins, however. Obeah uses bottles as its chief prop. Those trees with bottles dangling from them are not bearing strange tropical fruit . . . the bottles are spells to protect against thieves. So don't go picking fruit! Also stay clear of graveyards, which are littered with bottles meant to indulge the spirits of the dead, who like a tipple and otherwise would come bothering the living for rum. Many houses, especially those north of New Bight, are topped by spindles (like lightning rods) meant to ward off evil spirits.

Cat Island boasts more than 12 miles of wall diving along its south coast as well as exceptional dive sites on all quarters. Most sites are virtually unexplored. The island also has excellent hiking, offering walks along old logging and plantation trails as well as ruins, coves, and historical sites to explore. The Fernandez Bay Village resort (see the New Bight section) is a good place to start; the owners can provide maps and a guide, if needed.

Experienced anglers proclaim the fishing off Cat as good as anywhere in The Bahamas, especially for white marlin and wahoo. Yet sport fishing has hardly been developed. The main grounds are the waters along the island's sole, off Devil's Point and east to Columbus Point – ground zero for marlin. Here currents create rips that trap schools of baitfish. The edge of Tartar Bank, to the southwest, is a hotspot for wahoo and yellowfin tuna.

South Cat Island

NEW BIGHT

New Bight, two-thirds of the way down Cat Island, is the usual gateway for travelers. It sprawls along several miles of the Queen's Hwy.

New Bight began as a free-slave settlement named Freetown. Its original inhabitants had been aboard British slave ships from Africa when the abolition of the trade

Obeah

Obeah is the practice of interacting with the spirit world. Its equivalents are Haitian voodoo and Cuban *santería*, although it differs from both. Obeah is part folklore, part superstition, and part witchcraft, and it is deeply imbedded in the national psyche.

Obeah (the word is Ashanti, from West Africa) was once prevalent throughout the English-speaking Caribbean islands, and the 'obeah man' inspired respect and fear among fellow villagers. He was hired to work magic, much as a modern doctor (or lawyer!) is sought out today. Obeah was prohibited and severely suppressed by colonial authorities.

Father Jerome, Cat Island's saintly hero (see the sidebar on him in this chapter), fought a constant battle to eradicate obeah. Once, for example, hearing that a woman lay dying because she had eaten vegetables from a garden into which an enemy had tossed a cursed rotten banana, Jerome came down from his monastery and ate a sample of every vegetable growing there. Then, to the gasps of the crowd, he ate the rotten banana, too!

The practice of obeah has withered somewhat, and few Bahamians speak openly of it. But obeah still coexists alongside Christianity. There are no formal gatherings or group worship, and the practice has no formal priests. On Cat Island in particular, Bahamians (regardless of their Christian faith) still consult practitioners. Some practitioners operate as 'balmists,' using magic for medicinal purposes, to enact revenge, to influence impending court cases, or to ensure a successful romance on behalf of a supplicant. Firm believers sometimes heal, fall sick, or even die due to their faith in the power of obeah.

'Fixing' is the deploying of a spell to protect property; it also means casting a spell or preventing a casting on or by other people. Fixers advertise in the Yellow Pages under the heading 'Spiritual Healers' or 'Psychic Readers.' Many fixers ascribe their powers to God and place their 'fix' through directions derived from the Bible. For example, an alcoholic can be cured by giving a fixer money; the fixer then reads psalms, places the money in the Bible between the pages of the psalms, and shuts the Bible, thus taking away the spirit of drunkenness.

On Cat Island the center of obeah is New Bight. (Mrs Armbrister – 'Missus A' – at Fernandez Bay Village delights in telling tales of the island's witchcraft). On New Providence it's the working-class area of Fox Hill, once home to Zaccharias Adderley, 'king' of obeah in Nassau.

Obeah is still legally banned, mostly due to pressure from the Baptist church. In recent years obeah has been given a new lease on life by a flood of Haitian immigrants. ∎

was announced. They were put ashore on Cat Island. Much of the land hereabouts has belonged to the Armbrister family since 1780. In the 1950s Frances Armbrister and her son, Tony, returned to the ancestral property and built a serene retreat from stone recycled from the plantation. Today their home, Fernandez Bay Village, is a hotel and the acknowledged center of affairs.

The waters of Pigeon Bay, south of New Bight, were once used by whales weaning their young in summer. Alas, they no longer visit. But there *is* great diving and snorkeling nearby. There are several beautiful casuarina-lined beaches, including Fernandez Bay.

New Bight extends 4 miles north to the tiny settlement of Smith Bay, where there's a hut made entirely of conch shells just north of town, and a bat cave amid the bush behind Hazel's Seaside Bar. A goat track leads east from Smith Bay to Fine Bay, a good surfing beach.

Those with an adventurous spirit can hike east to Turtle Cove, a splendid cove on the Atlantic shore where marine turtles graze in the shallow waters. It's a harpy to get there along a tenuous dirt road.

Information

There are no banks on Cat Island. The post office and BaTelCo office are in the

Government Administrative Complex on Queen's Hwy. The island's main medical clinic (☎ 242-342-3026), in Smith Bay, is staffed by Dr Pablito Tan. The police station (☎ 242-354-5039) is also in the Government Administrative Complex.

Holy Ebenezer Catholic Church
The main attraction in town gleams white beside the main road and looks like it belongs on Mediterranean shores. The church was built by Father Jerome (see the Father Jerome sidebar on the next page), who also blessed Cat Island with its most famous landmark, the pint-size Mt Alvernia Hermitage.

Mt Alvernia Hermitage
Scrub-covered Como Hill, also known as Mt Alvernia – the name bestowed on this incomparably peaceful spot by Father Jerome – rises southeast of New Bight. Here the hermit built himself a simple blanched-stone structure – what Anthony Weller called 'a handmade apartment of faith overlooking the world' – in exquisite Celtic-cum-Mediterranean style.

It is reached by a rock staircase hewn into the side of the hill. Not forgetting his purpose, Father Jerome added simple stone Stations of the Cross that you pass as you climb, while the forest opens up below. From the top, you can marvel at the spiritually reviving 360° view. Try to make it at sunrise or sunset.

The hermitage, which has a bell tower with a pointed fool's-cap roof, looks like something Merlin might have conjured up in the days of King Arthur. You can enter the small chapel, tiny cloister, and a guest cell the size of a large kennel. The only furniture is a writing desk, a stool, and a single cot for guests (Jerome slept on a straw mat on the cloister floor), perfectly befitting its ascetic function. The brass sundial in the grounds to the rear still gleams, and hummingbirds flit about amid the engulfing foliage (the Armbrister family sends men up to clear it several times a year).

The rough track leading to the hermitage begins immediately south of the Government Administrative Complex on Queen's Hwy, north of the ruins of the old **Armbrister Plantation**. You can also take a parallel track, 50 yards south, that squeezes through the plantation estate house's archway.

Diving & Snorkeling
There are several superb sites locally. Dry Head, in shallow water close to shore, has prolific marine life, including a resident barracuda – Barry – who doesn't bite but is curious.

Fernandez Bay Village's Cat Island Sea Club (☎ 242-474-4821) offers beginner to advanced courses, plus group and custom dives. It has full scuba facilities and virtually guaranteed one-on-one diving. ('We're not a dive factory. It's a personal thing,' says divemaster Bill Chapman.) A 'Discover Scuba' course costs US$100; an open-water dive course costs US$370. A night dive costs US$85. Blue-hole and cave dives cost US$25. Scuba gear can be rented. Snorkel trips cost US$25. You can also rent a mask, snorkel, and fins for US$6 daily. Fernandez Bay Village participates in Jean-Michel Cousteau's Out Island Snorkeling Adventures (see the Outdoor Activities chapter for details).

Sport Fishing
Favored bonefishing spots include the flats of Joe's Sound Creek, a 20-minute boat ride south of Fernandez Bay, and Pigeon Creek, a 20-minute ride to the north. Fernandez Bay Village charges US$150/200 half-/full day for bonefishing. Sport fishing costs US$200/300.

Organized Tours
Island Vacations (in Nassau ☎ 242-356-1111, fax 242-356-4379) offers an escorted 'Mystery Island Tour' that explores the history, ecology, and culture of Cat Island.

Andy at Fernandez Bay Village guides trips to the bat caves and blue holes.

Special Events
The biggest event of the year is the Cat Island Regatta, which is on Emancipation

CAT ISLAND

Father Jerome

John Hawes – hermit and humanitarian – was born in England in 1876 to an upper-middle-class family. He practiced as a visionary, prize-winning architect before entering Theological College in 1901, preparing to become an Anglican minister.

Once ordained, he vowed to emulate the life of St Francis of Assisi and lived briefly as a tramp. In 1908 he came to the Bahamas and traveled around the islands rebuilding churches destroyed by a hurricane, utilizing thick stone and Roman arches. Hawes offended local sensibilities, however, while preaching on Harbour Island. He

Mt Alvernia Hermitage, home of Cat Island's builder-priest

asked the congregation why the whites were sitting at the front and the blacks at the back, when all men are created equal. 'The congregation nearly fainted with shock and I was rushed out of the church as quickly as possible,' Hawes recorded.

Between bouts of preaching, the eccentric Englishman did duty as a mule-driver in Canada, a fox-terrier breeder, a cow-puncher, and a sailor. In 1911 he converted to Catholicism and studied in Rome for the priesthood before moving to Australia to serve as a gold-rush bush priest. He stayed there for 24 years and built a renowned reputation until suffering a heart attack.

In 1939 Hawes returned to the Bahamas, washing ashore on Cat Island to live as a hermit. The following year, he began work on his hermitage atop Como Hill, which he renamed Mt Alvernia after the site in Tuscany where St Francis received the wounds of the cross. Meanwhile, like a good hermit, he lived in a cave amid snakes, tarantulas, and crabs, and took unto himself the name Father Jerome.

On weekdays Jerome meditated alone (he also read newspapers, painted, drew cartoons, and wrote essays with a George Bernard Shaw flavor); on weekends he worked in the village. He built four churches on Cat Island, as well as a medical clinic, convent, monastery, technical school, and other projects throughout the Bahamas, all featuring his trademark medievalist architectural motif. His buildings were made of rock quarried on-site, with nothing that could rot or rust away.

Undoubtedly, locals considered him a saintly figure. He strolled around barefoot and lavished charity on the islanders, many of whom climbed the steps to his monastery to ask for money (during this period most Cat Islanders were incredibly poor, described by Father Jerome as 'in a state verging on destitution'). None were denied, and at other times, as during drought, the charity flowed uphill. Jerome became the conscience of the island, acting as a salve to settle disputes. Locals of all denominations attended his sermons, although apparently he converted only five people to Catholicism, as the locals resisted his strictures against 'extracurricular sex.'

He died in 1956 and was buried, per his request, barefoot and without a casket in the cave that had once been his home. ∎

Day (the first Monday in August), when scores of Cat Islanders return from afar. The highlight of this homecoming is the sailboat races. Excursion boats from Nassau call in crammed with spectators. There are domino tournaments, fashion shows, and sometimes a beauty contest, and

rake 'n' scrape bands scratch out narcotic tunes.

Places to Stay

The bland *Little Bay Inn* (☎ 242-342-2004), at the north end of New Bight, has six rooms, each with a ceiling fan and private bathroom. The inn has a single shared kitchen. At US$60 nightly per room, it's overpriced.

The Russells run the simple, motel-style *Bridge Inn* (☎ 242-342-3013, 800-688-4752, fax 242-342-3041), just north of the Government Administrative Complex. It has four single rooms, four double rooms, and four triple rooms. All are handsome, albeit modestly furnished, with bare native-stone walls and lofty wooden ceilings. Each has a private bathroom, porch, TV, potted plants, and ceiling fan. There's a swimming pool, hot tub, and an airy restaurant and bar that doubles as a nightclub. The hotel is on bare grounds about 200 yards from the beach. Rooms cost US$60/70/85 single/double/triple in summer, US$10 more in winter. All-inclusive three-night package stays cost US$430 without air-con (air-con is available at a higher price). It offers diving, snorkeling, sailing, volleyball, and tennis, plus bicycles and island excursions. Free airport transfers are offered.

Worth a trip in its own right is *Fernandez Bay Village* (☎ 242-342-3043, fax 242-342-3051; in North America ☎ 954-474-4821, 800-940-1905, fax 954-474-4864), on a scimitar of perfect white sand near New Bight airport (around one arm of the bay lies an even more private beach, Skinny Dip; two knotty islets rise offshore – perfect for snorkeling over the reefs). Now weather-worn, the resort used to be a bit of a society place (Jackie O's yacht once bobbed at anchor). Tony Armbrister and his wife, Pam, pamper you as if you were family down for the week.

The one- and two-bedroom cottages are hidden amid casuarinas. Six have a fully equipped kitchen. All are of simple stone and timber, with red-brick floors and plate-glass doors opening onto patios. Some have four-poster beds. None have air-con, but you don't need it. Open-air 'garden baths' are surrounded by stone walls, so you can shower or linger on the pot while admiring the stars. Three new rooms were to be added, along with a long-awaited clubhouse. Guests and hosts mingle together at the thatched beach bar

and in the cozy lounge-cum-library. Rates are US$165 to US$195 in summer and US$190 to US$225 in winter, including two meals daily, plus 15% service charge. The hotel offers air charters (see Getting There & Away, below).

Bicycles can be rented for US$7 daily. It offers free use of sailboats and canoes, plus diving and snorkeling. The local mailing address is New Bight, Cat Island, Bahamas; in North America write 1507 S University Dr, Suite A, Plantation, FL 33324.

Nearby is the *Twin Palms Beach Resort*, a modest guesthouse beside the beach just west of the Bridge Inn. Mary Saymore (☎ 242-342-6008) rents a one-bedroom cottage, *Old Dad*, in Knowles, at the north end of Smith Bay.

Places to Eat

The restaurant at the *Bridge Inn* (☎ 242-342-3013) specializes in island-style seafood and Yankee fare such as burgers for US$4 and chicken and fries. It serves breakfast, lunch, and dinner, and has a Friday-night fish fry for US$5.

The misleadingly named *Sailing Club* offers good chicken lunches and dinners (it's not a sailing club; it's just a small building beside the beach). Reservations are required.

The *Blue Bird Restaurant & Bar* (☎ 242-342-3095), on Queen's Hwy near the government complex, serves local fare, with entrées from US$7. For conch, check out *Bachelor's Restaurant* (☎ 242-342-6014) in Knowles. Ruth serves her conch every which way; she keeps it fresh in the sea.

Fernandez Bay Village offers a nightly torch-lit buffet dinner on the beach beneath whispering casuarinas. The Armbristers take pride in their cuisine, amply prepared by Carnetta and two other chefs. On rainy nights dinner is served buffet-style in the handsome stone-and-timber main house, with the soft glow of lanterns adding a romantic touch. There's conch chowder . . . and then there's Fernandez Bay chowder! Dinner, for US$30 (including appetizer and dessert), is by reservation. Breakfasts and lunches cost US$10. Fernandez Bay is open 8 am to 9:30 pm.

You can buy groceries and other supplies at *New Bight Food Store* or several other convenience stores. *McKinney's Bakery* has fresh bread daily.

Entertainment

At night the *Blue Bird Restaurant & Bar* is a good place to play pool with locals and catch up on 'sip-sip' (gossip). So, too, is Iva and Zeffy Thompson's *First & Last Chance Bar*, nearby on Queen's Hwy, known for lively games of dominoes. On Saturday night join the 'all-comers-welcome' dance on the sands at the *Sailing Club* cafe-bar.

The *Bridge Inn* has dancing on Saturday night, plus a pool table and a jukebox with an A-list of favorite tunes, from Nat King Cole and the Isley Brothers to Conway Twitty and Kenny Rogers. On holidays and weekends a local rake 'n' scrape band – Fealy & the Bone Shakers – sometimes plays.

In Smith Bay, *Hazel's Seaside Bar*, hosted by Hazel Brown, is a favorite for domino games. It has the coldest beers around, thanks to a kerosene freezer.

Things to Buy

You can see Iva Thompson making baskets and mats at her small store next to the First & Last Chance Bar (see above).

You can also watch Louise Saunders weaving at Fernandez Bay Village. She'll gladly weave your name into a hat or basket (she'll also put a bead or two in your hair). A beautiful straw rug costs US$80 to US$100, depending on size.

Getting There & Away

Air New Bight airport is 2 miles north of town. There are toilets and a public phone but no other facilities. A chap called Basil sells snacks from his van in the parking lot, offering macaroni and cheese for US$1 and ice cream for US$2. See the Getting There & Away chapter for airlines' international and Nassau phone numbers.

Air Sunshine has flights from Fort Lauderdale (US$225/325 one way/roundtrip) and Sarasota (US$275/425) on Monday, Tuesday, Wednesday, and Thursday. Prices are for a charter for up to six people. Island Express flies from Fort Lauderdale.

Bahamasair (in New Bight call ☎ 242-342-2017 on the day of your flight) flies Monday and Friday from Nassau (US$60 one way).

Sunshine Tours (☎ 242-342-5011; in Nassau 242-377-1703, 242-323-4170) flies between Nassau and New Bight daily except Sunday. Night-Flyer (call Larry or Carol Meredith, ☎ 242-342-3018) offers charters from Nassau for US$70 one way. Other private charters, including Sandpiper Air, serve the island.

Fernandez Bay Village offers air charters from Florida and Nassau (US$95 one way per person, US$70 for children), as does Greenwood Beach Resort near Port Howe.

New Bight is the only port of entry for private pilots. The Customs and Immigration office (☎ 242-342-2106) is here; private pilots can clear customs here before flying on to Arthur's Town airport or the Hawk's Nest airstrip.

Boat There are no marina facilities. Most yachties anchor in Fernandez Bay.

The *North Cat Island Special* mail boat departs Nassau at 1 pm Wednesday for New Bight, Bennett's Harbour, and Arthur's Town (14 hours, US$40 one way). The *Sea Hauler* leaves Nassau at 3 pm on Tuesday (17 hours, US$40 one way), also calling at Old Bight and Smith Bay. This converted tug has 10 bunks in a small cabin that resembles a sauna (I'm speaking *heat*, not pinewood decor).

Getting Around

There's no bus or taxi service from the airport. Your hotel will arrange a free airport pickup with advance notice.

Jason Russell, owner of the New Bight Shell station, rents cars for US$85 (plus gas at US$3 per gallon) for 24 hours, including a rusty '80s-model car that drinks a gallon every 12 or so miles. He'll come down to US$65 if you push him. Weekly rates are negotiable. He plans to begin accepting Visa and MasterCard in 1998. You're asked to sign accepting responsibility for *all* damage that may be done to the car. His hours are 7:30 am to 6:30 pm Monday to Saturday.

Fernandez Bay Village rents small boats for US$25 per hour; larger boats with captain cost US$50 per hour.

OLD BIGHT

This slightly down-at-the-heels settlement, beginning 4 miles south of New Bight, is also called 'The Village.' It straggles along the road for several miles. Impressive plantation ruins abound to its east, shaded by trees festooned with Spanish moss.

Things to See & Do
St Francis Assisi Catholic Church is a twee, mossy stone legacy of Father Jerome. It sits atop a little ridge beside the road. It has a Gothic facade topped by a cross and an engraving of St Francis with a flock of birds. Its interior has frescoes and sculptures. Mrs Burrows, across the road, has the key.

Worth a visit is **St Mary's Church**, fronted by an African flame tree. The church is claimed to be the only monument in The Bahamas to emancipation. It was a gift of the family of Blaney Balfour, the British governor who read the emancipation proclamation.

A track that begins at the rear of the Old Bight primary school leads you along the edge of **Great Lake**. If you keep on along the northeast shore (avoiding side paths), you'll reach an old stone wall that descends into the lake. By following the wall uphill, you'll ascend **Mt View** (150 feet), topped by the ruins of an old home. Continue east along a dirt path (which crosses a semi-paved road) to reach the sea. Refreshments can be had at the Greenwood Beach Resort, 2 miles south along the sandy shore. The hike is about 5 miles one way.

Armbrister Creek
This creek-laced mangrove estuary, near Old Bight, is fabulous for exploring by canoe. It leads inland to a crystal-clear lake called 'Boiling Hole' that bubbles and churns under certain tide conditions, fueling local fears that it is haunted by a monster. Baby sharks and rays can be seen cruising the sandy bottom. Birdlife also abounds.

You can rent canoes at Fernandez Bay Village (see Places to Stay in the New Bight section) for exploring in the mangroves. They're free to its guests. A guided canoe trip from Fernandez Bay costs US$25.

Getting There & Away
The *Sea Hauler* mail boat sails here from Nassau once a week. See Getting There & Away in the New Bight section for details.

BAIN TOWN
About 13 miles south of New Bight on the Queen's Hwy, you emerge by the south shore at a traffic circle, the Deep South Roundabout, ringed by 570 rosy conch shells. Bain Town, 2 miles east of Deep South Roundabout, lies along the shore south of the main road. It has several sites of interest, including St John the Baptist Catholic Church, another inspired Father Jerome creation. At the turnoff for town is the colorful Galleon Club, constructed to resemble a Spanish galleon but now a bit tumbledown. Immediately behind it on the

St Francis Assisi Catholic Church

slope is House Rebecca, built of local lime-stone and conch shells; owners Mr and Mrs Bain may invite you in to peek at the sitting room ceiling, made of 966 shells.

Lotto-Man Hole

This cave, one of the largest on the island, is hidden behind St John the Baptist Catholic Church. It got its strange name, apparently, after an East Indian sailor was marooned here and chose the cave as his home. If you intend to explore beyond the entrance, take a guide.

Mermaid Hole

Quite a few locals firmly believe that this 20-meter-wide blue hole is inhabited by a mermaid. The lake is 10 feet deep, but four holes in its bed lead down into vast under-water chambers and passageways. Your guide may tell you to be quiet as you approach through the brush, as he will want to get a glimpse of the mermaid; she is sure to flee at the sound of humans.

Places to Stay & Eat

Cutlass Bay (☎ 242-342-3085, cutlass-bay@ the-solution.com; in the USA ☎ 800-723-5688) is a secluded, 300-acre, all-inclusive, clothing-optional resort – the only nude resort in The Bahamas – for adult *couples* only. It has 18 rooms and villas overlook-ing palm-shaded lawns sloping down to a beach beckoning you for a perfect all-over tan. Rooms have no TVs or phones. The stone-and-timber clubhouse evokes a plan-tation feel. Bougainvillea bowers add color. There's a swimming pool, tennis court, snorkeling, bicycles, nature trails, games room, and library, plus a private 2500-foot airstrip. Breakfast and lunch are served on the verandah or poolside; dinner is served in the handsome clubhouse, boasting a bar, sofas, and lofty timber ceiling.

Per-couple rates range from US$1340 to US$1590 for three nights for standard rooms and US$1675 to US$1895 for deluxe one-bedroom villas, depending on season. Two-bedroom villas cost US$2680 for three nights. Four- to seven-night packages are also offered. A US$500 deposit is required.

There's no sign . . . look for the rusty gates about a half-mile west of Bain Town, follow the dirt road (the airstrip will be on your right), and then turn left at the T-junction. Casual visitors are *not* welcome. The postal address is PO Box 273767, Tampa, FL 33688-3767.

Mr and Mrs Bain occasionally welcome guests to *House Rebecca*.

The *Galleon Club* has a driftwood bar serving snacks and drinks.

PORT HOWE & VICINITY

Port Howe, a hamlet 5 miles east of Deep South Roundabout, is the most historically important area on Cat Island. Historians believe that Columba, the first Spanish settlement in the New World, was estab-lished here in 1495 as a terminus for Lucayan Indians shipped as slaves to His-paniola. A huge tract that spread from today's Port Howe to Old Bight was

---

Beasts in the Blue Holes

Many of Cat Island's saltwater blue holes are thought to be the home of awesome beasts, including an island equivalent to the Loch Ness Monster. Islanders prefer to find sinister expla-nations for the fact that a piece of wood dropped in an inland lake may re-appear some time later out at sea. In fact, objects are sucked out of blue holes by strong tidal flows through sub-terranean passages that link the holes to the sea.

The monster of Bad Blue Hole, just off Dickie's Rd near Orange Creek, is said to have an appetite for horses. Hence some horses that die on Cat Island are tipped into the lake! And though freshwater lakes are less feared, at least one – Mermaid Hole – is said to be the home of a mermaid, a noted and bewitching siren. Another has a no less seductive merman.

Says local historian Eric Moncur: 'Cat Island fishermen will readily launch a skiff and travel many miles offshore, but these same men cannot be coaxed with any amount of inducement to travel even 50 feet on the lakes.' ∎

cleared for cattle ranches. Columba was later abandoned.

Around 1670 a small group of English settlers arrived from Bermuda and established themselves here, earning a living predominantly as wreckers. Their settlements were attacked by the Spaniards in 1717 and on a regular basis in later years by the Spaniards and pirates. Then, in 1783, 60 English Loyalists arrived from Florida. Their leader, Lt John Wilson, laid out a town named Carlyle. Several important plantations evolved nearby. The harbor later became known as Port Howe, named for Admiral James Howe, a British naval commander during the American Revolution.

The ruins of several fortresses still stand, much overgrown in the years since they were erected to protect against pirates. Take time to browse the old overgrown cemetery on the west side of town.

Deveaux House

This mansion looms foursquare – albeit in advanced dereliction – over the settlement. The two-story edifice was the center of a once-thriving 1000-acre cotton plantation owned by Colonel Andrew Deveaux, the American Loyalist who was granted land here as a reward for saving Nassau from Spanish occupation in 1783 (see History in the Facts about The Bahamas chapter). Note the old slave quarters just alongside.

Columbus Point

Columbus Point, the southeasternmost point of Cat Island, lies 2 miles southeast of Port Howe at the south end of Churney Bay. Cat Islanders cling to the belief – which was effectively debunked by recent evidence – that Columbus anchored here on October 12, 1492.

The shoreline has old coral heads embedded with brain coral. There's a cave said to be worth exploring (it was once inhabited by Lucayan Indians, who left artifacts for posterity) and a tidal geyser in Churney Bay.

There's no road access. You can hike from Port Howe along a dirt track (you

may be able to make it at least part of the way in a 4WD vehicle) that leads east via the ruins of another old Loyalist settlement, Bailey Town. Here, follow the track that begins to the right of the House of Zion Church (keep right at the Y-fork, and after 2 miles, follow the old plantation farm walls to Churney Bay). You can also keep east through Bailey Town to Winding Bay and then walk south to Columbus Point.

Activities

The diving off the south shore is superb along a 12-mile front. The wall begins at 50 feet and drops to 6000 feet, and there are caves and coral canyons to explore. Cat Island's prime dive site is Tartar Bank. A 5-mile boat ride southwest of Port Howe, it's a columnlike plateau covered by coral, sponges, and sea fans. The plateau slopes to a drop-off beginning at 80 feet, where the deep blue goes screaming down. Tartar Bank is good for shark swims and wall dives. Winding Bay offers fabulous gorgonians and black coral.

The Cat Island Dive Centre, at Greenwood Beach Resort (see below), is the island's most complete full-service dive shop. It offers tank fills and maintains two boats in Port Howe. Dives cost US$40/65 one-/two-tank; an open-water certificate costs US$370. It offers PADI certification and resort courses and has day and night dives. Snorkeling costs US$20, including equipment.

There's good bonefishing in the bay off Port Howe. Charles Zonicle (☎ 242-342-5005) offers fishing from Port Howe. The Greenwood Beach Resort charges US$140 to US$200 for bonefishing; sport fishing aboard a 25-foot Bimini top costs US$460.

Places to Stay

The lonesome *Greenwood Beach Resort* (☎ 242-342-3053; in the USA ☎ 800-688-4752), 5 miles north of Port Howe, is a delightful and casual 20-room resort run by a friendly German family. It edges up to an 8-mile-long pink-sand beach running south to Winding Bay. It's favored by divers. The simply furnished rooms are in whitewashed cottages with pastel trim. They feature king-size beds, small patios, ceiling fans, and clean, spacious bathrooms. Facilities include a massive lounge-cum-dining-room, a bar, swimming pool, and full-service dive shop. Bicycles can be rented. Rates are US$65/85 single/double in summer, US$79/99 in winter, including airport transfers from Arthur's Town or New Bight. A 15% service charge is added. A MAP (breakfast and dinner) plan costs US$40.

The resort also has air charters to New Bight airport (see the New Bight section). The postal address is Port Howe, Cat Island, Bahamas.

Places to Eat
The *Greenwood Beach Resort* offers European dishes and local fare, plus specialty buffet dinners on the outside terrace or in the modest dining room.

Otherwise pickings are slim. Try the *Rockum Palace Bar* in Port Howe.

Getting Around
There's a gas station west of Port Howe.

Daisy Mae Hunter of Sunshine Tours (☎ 242-342-5011/5025) will take you sightseeing in her 12-seater bus.

MORGAN'S BAY TO HAWK'S NEST
A badly potholed road leads west (to the right) from the Deep South Roundabout, heading along the shore of Morgan's Bay to Devil's Point. Five miles southwest of Deep South Roundabout, needle-sharp Devil's Point is the southernmost tip of Cat Island. There's a hard-pressed fishing village – also named Devil's Point – nearby, at the end of the road. The scant remains of an octagonal fortress atop the bluff are now foundations for a navigation light.

Just before Devil's Point, an unmarked side road leads north to McQueen's. The lonesome settlement, 4 miles north of Devil's Point, faces Exuma Sound. It was founded in the 18th century by a Scottish Loyalist, Alexander McQueen, and has several paltry yet intriguing old buildings adorned with ornate chimneys.

From the settlement of McQueen's, a dirt road runs southwest along the shore of Exuma Sound to Hawk's Nest Resort Marina (see the Places to Stay & Eat section, below), at the toe of the island. Hawk's Nest is a 15-mile drive from Deep South Roundabout.

Activities
The flats and tidal creeks that meander inland for several miles from the Hawk's Nest channel are said to be 'bonefish city'! Other good sites include the bight east of Hawk's Nest and the lagoon at the entrance to Hawk's Nest channel.

A 26-foot Dusky can be rented from Hawk's Nest Resort Marina (see below) for US$75 hourly or US$350 daily, with captain. Rudy Rolle, the bartender, will guide you. At Devil's Point, Nathaniel Gilbert (☎ 242-342-7003) rents a 14-foot Whaler.

The reefs offshore from Hawk's Nest are splendid for diving and snorkeling. And Devil's Point is noteworthy for large formations of elkhorn and staghorn, tube sponges, and brain coral. Snorkeling is said to be especially good in Morgan's Bay. Hawk's Nest Resort Marina offers diving (US$65/75 one-/two-tank) and snorkeling.

Places to Stay & Eat
Recently renovated *Hawk's Nest Resort Marina* (☎ /fax 242-357-7257, ☎ 800-688-4752, Unicom VHF 122.8 channel 16), at the western toe of Cat Island, has 10 clean air-con rooms, all ocean-view with a king-size bed or two queen-size beds, plus a ceiling fan and a patio facing palm-filled grounds. It also has two-bedroom houses with full kitchen and housekeeping service. There's a bar and restaurant, plus a beach-volleyball court. Fishing, diving, and snorkeling are offered; bikes, mopeds, and golf carts can be rented. Rooms cost US$135 per person double, including breakfast and dinner. Houses cost US$370/2200 daily/weekly. Lunches cost US$10 to US$15.

Getting There & Away
Hawk's Nest has a 4600-foot hard-surface airstrip with tie-downs, plus its own plane

CAT ISLAND

for charters. It also has a protected, deep-water, eight-slip marina with a grocery store. There's gas, diesel, water, electricity, showers, and laundry.

If you're coming from abroad, you must clear customs and immigration in New Bight (see Getting There & Away in the New Bight section).

North Cat Island

Knowles to Industrious Hill

North of New Bight, Queen's Hwy hugs the west shore. Little boats lie upturned beneath spread-fingered palms; tumbledown slave-era homes dot the shore.

Knowles, 8 miles north of New Bight, is the first of a half-dozen small settlements. It boasts the tiny **Columbus World Centre Museum**, which tells the history of the island. The founder and curator, locally born historian Eric Moncur, will gladly show you around.

Farther north, the scenery is splendid as you pass through **Tea Bay** and **The Cove**, where reminders of several nautical mishaps are writ into the landscape, such as the pathway cut into the reef by the ill-fated SS *Modegard*, which ran aground in 1910. Endemic freshwater turtles inhabit the inland lakes and ponds.

Near Stephenson, a dirt road leads east to a splendid beach at **Alligator Bay**, on the Atlantic.

The Caves, a multichambered system just south of the settlement of Industrious Hill and 12 miles north of New Bight, have traditionally been used as a hurricane shelter. They're framed by dramatic fig trees beside the road. Goats prefer the shady entrance and will flee into the dark recesses at your approach. At least one person has disappeared while exploring. You'll need a guide and a strong flashlight.

Roker's Bluff

This small settlement (also called 'Zanicle'), 20 miles north of New Bight, was one of the largest settlements in the mid-19th century. It was founded by Scottish settlers, and many of the locals still have Scottish surnames: McKenzie, McDonald, Hepburn.

A dirt road leads northwest 2 miles to beautiful **Pigeon Creek Beach**.

Pigeon Cay on the Beach (☎ 242-354-5084), northwest of town, has five simple rooms with kitchen, plus eight cottages, a restaurant, and a bar. You can rent boats for fishing, snorkeling, and kayaking, and bikes are available.

You can choose between the *Triple X Bar & Restaurant* and *Mack's Restaurant* for cracked conch and native fare.

Bennett's Harbour

North of Roker's Bluff, the highway climbs Thurston Hill, on whose north slope the settlement of Bennett's Harbour sprawls beneath blazing-bright flame trees that flow down to a picturesque harborfront. The sheltered cove was once favored by pirates waiting to pounce on passing treasure-laden ships. The settlement was founded in the 1830s for slaves freed from captured slavetraders, and it later became a port for the salt trade (you can still see the old salt ponds in the lake to the east).

Little San Salvador, a small, uninhabited island 15 miles west of Bennett's Harbour, is an occasional stopping point for boaters. A lagoon offers superb bonefishing. There are virtually tame iguanas on the island, and plenty of seabirds.

The *Amazing Grace*, the supply ship for Windjammer Barefoot Cruises' sailing fleet, calls on Little San Salvador during its island-hopping voyages. These cruises are offered twice monthly between Grand Bahama and Trinidad, and also include a number of other Bahamian islands on their 13-day itineraries. See the Getting There & Away chapter for details and contact information.

Places to Stay & Eat Patrick Cooper's *Remanda Inn* (☎ 242-354-6973) sits atop the bluff about 200 yards from the shore. It has seven small, simple rooms with fans. One room has air-conditioning. Rooms cost US$35/50 with a shared/private bathroom. There's a small restaurant and a tinier bar.

Alternately, try *Harbour View* (☎ 242-354-2146/6074; ask for Hansel Strachan), down by the shore. Its 10 simple rooms have fans and hot and cold water (two have air-con). At press time it was under renovation and slated to reopen in 1998; rooms will cost US$80.

Peas 'n' rice and conch are served at the *Beverage Restaurant & Disco*, which comes alive on weekends. You can buy foodstuffs at *Len's Grocery*.

Getting There & Away The *North Cat Island Special* mail boat sails here from Nassau; see Getting There & Away in the New Bight section for details.

Dumfries

Named for the hometown of Loyalist settlers who emigrated from Scotland to Virginia to Cat Island, Dumfries lies on the inner shore of a saline lake separated from the sea by the Gossip Bar. A mile-long track that begins just north of the bar leads to Great Crown Caves, a vast cave system hidden amid the mangroves. Finding them ain't easy: an old-timer named Ishmael Gaitor will guide you.

At Zion Hill, 1 mile north of Dumfries, ruins of a Loyalist mansion can be seen, surrounded by stately silk cotton trees.

You can buy straw hats from Minerva Thompson (☎ 242-354-5077), who makes them.

Gaitor's Hole This blue hole is reached by a rough mile-long track running east from Dumfries. It is often a deep purple color, due to a dense bacterial population that thrives on a thick hydrogen-sulfide layer.

Ishmael Gaitor loves to regale visitors with the tale – he sounds sincere – of a young island girl who disappeared years ago while visiting the hole to do laundry. Several months later she reappeared . . . very pregnant! It seems she had encountered a merman (the male equivalent of a mermaid). He had seduced her and she had

lived blissfully with her aquatic lover in his home beneath the waters until homesickness drew her away. Her family was less broadminded than she, and her father and brother stormed off to the lake, armed with shotguns. They trapped the distraught merman and shot him dead. Some weeks later the girl gave birth to a baby merman, with a tail just like a fish's. Mr Gaitor, alas, has no idea what happened to the creature.

Places to Eat You might catch Mr Gaitor telling his merman stories in the *Turning Point Club*, where a sign advises 'Eat Before Drinking!' Try the mutton souse. Another option is the *Gossip Bar & Restaurant*.

Arthur's Town

The island's second-largest town, 30 miles north of New Bight, is also its most handsome settlement.

Arthur's Town is centered on grassy Symonette Square, lorded over by prim St Andrews Anglican Church, dating from the early 1870s. There are several other historic buildings.

The town's main claim to fame is that it was the boyhood home of Sidney Poitier, the Academy Award-winning actor. You can read about his childhood in his autobiography, *This Life*, but there is no museum, and Poitier's childhood home is now derelict.

The road to the airport, just north of town, continues east to Camperdown Beach on the Atlantic shore.

There's a medical clinic (☎ 242-354-4050). For the police, call ☎ 242-354-2046.

The town hosts a heritage festival during the first weekend in May.

Places to Stay & Eat Nellie Rolle (☎ 242-354-2031) rents three *apartments*. Mrs Bertram Dean runs *Dean's Inn* (☎ 242-354-2121), with 10 apartments.

You can buy fresh-baked breads and confections at Pat and Dell Rolle's *Cookie House* (☎ 242-354-2027), 50 yards north of Symonette Square. The Rolles also serve burgers, fish and chips, and other snack lunches costing about US$5, as well as lobster, conch, and grouper dinners from US$12.

Native dishes are also served at *Hard Rock Café*, named for the rocky outcrop on which it rests.

Gina's, a tiny US-style roadside diner near the square, serves hot dogs and burgers.

You can buy fresh bread from Avid Armbrister and produce from *Jabon Convenience Store* or *Campbell's Big Bull* food store.

Entertainment The *Boggy Pond Bar* has a pool table, as does *Lover's Boulevard Satellite Lounge*, with TV and disco on weekends.

Getting There & Away Arthur's Town has a small airport. Bahamasair (in Arthur's Town call ☎ 242-354-2049 on the day of your flight) flies here from Nassau Sunday, Tuesday, and Thursday.

The *North Cat Island Special* mail boat calls from Nassau; see details in the New Bight section.

Getting Around Pat Rolle at Cookie House (see Places to Stay & Eat, above) rents scooters for US$20 per day.

Orange Creek

Orange Creek, near the north end of the island, 3 miles northwest of Arthur's Town, stretches along Queen's Hwy for 2 miles. There's an old and a new section.

The town is named for the creek at its north end, which glows a fiery luminescent orange when certain conditions of wind and wave and the angle of the sun are just right.

Activities There's good bonefishing in the mouth of Orange Creek, where it spills onto a beach. Farther inland, the creek is scum-covered and smells like something the cat fetched up.

Willard Cleare will take you bonefishing, as will Lincoln Cleare; to contact either, call ☎ 242-354-4052.

The turquoise waters offshore are said to be superb for snorkeling, with beautiful fan-coral formations.

There are several good hiking and 4WD trails, especially near the head of Orange Creek. From here, a trail leads west half a mile to Port Royal Beach. Another leads north past Oyster Lake (good for spotting ducks and cormorants) to Sea Cave and Man O' War Point. Take the left-hand trail at the Y-fork just south of the lake.

The right-hand trail leads to a beach (good for snorkeling) east of Man O' War Point. Drip Cave lies hidden behind an old vine-covered tamarind tree farther east along the beach.

A third track leads east from the head of Orange Creek to Glass Hill (162 feet), where you'll have beautiful views south over Blue Hole Lake, north to the beach, and east to Flamingo Pond. Trails descend to all three.

From Queen's Hwy between the Sea Spray Hotel and the Orange Creek Inn, Dickie's Rd runs east to Griffin Bat Cave. Once a home to slaves who built walls and windows into the entrance, the cave is now occupied by leaf-nosed bats. Take a flashlight!

The track also leads to a series of blue holes (a sign in town invites you to 'explore the blue holes'). You can loop north to Big Blue Hole and Glass Hill or continue east to the Atlantic shore and then head south 2 miles to Camperdown Beach.

Willard Cleare (see number above) acts as a guide.

Places to Stay & Eat Charlie Campbell's *Sea Spray Hotel* (☎ 242-354-4116, fax 242-354-4161) has 15 rooms and one suite, all with air-con, cable TV, fans, and sliding glass doors opening onto a waterfront patio. There's a small restaurant and bar but no beach. It's rather nondescript, but a renovation promises to add some luster, along with a swimming pool. Rooms cost US$65 single or double; a small suite costs US$75. The hotel accepts Visa but not MasterCard.

The modern *Orange Creek Inn* (☎ 242-354-4110) sits above the creek. It has 16 rooms with fans (one has air-con). There's a TV lounge and a laundry, but there's no restaurant or bar. It was temporarily closed when I called by.

There's a rental cottage called *Old Stuart Home* at Camperdown Beach.

The *Orange Creek Inn* has a well-stocked food store, open 7 am to 7 pm Monday to Thursday, 7 am to 5 pm Friday, and 8 am to 1 pm Sunday and holidays.

Getting Around The Sea Spray Hotel rents cars for US$65 per day and bicycles for US$7 per day. The Orange Creek Inn also rents cars. There's a gas station in town.

Lincoln Cleare (☎ 242-354-4052) will take you sightseeing.

San Salvador, Rum Cay & Conception Island

Tiny San Salvador, 200 miles southeast of Nassau, is the nation's outermost island. The name, meaning 'holy savior,' was bestowed by Christopher Columbus on the first land he sighted after his daredevil Atlantic crossing in 1492: an island known as Guanahaní to the Lucayan Indians. There is little evidence to support the persistent claim that the explorer landed here, but the belief has become so entrenched that it's accepted as religiously as was the belief Columbus set out to disprove: that the earth was flat. The island was named Watling Island until 1926, when the name was changed to honor the Columbus claim.

Recent discoveries of Spanish artifacts are said to support the landfall claim. It was nonetheless effectively debunked by a study published in *National Geographic* in 1986 that convincingly concluded that Columbus' first landfall was at Samana Cay, 65 miles to the southeast. (However, in 1989 English around-the-world yachtsman Robin Knox-Johnson retraced Columbus' route using 15th-century instruments and ended up at . . . San Salvador!)

San Salvadoreans are partisan on the issue and couldn't give a damn for the Samana Cay theory. Some islanders, equally partisan, may whisper in your ear that in 1926 money changed hands. Until that year, the island had been officially considered the first landfall site. The name change was, in fact, mostly a product of lobbying by Chrysostrom Schreiner, a missionary who dedicated his life to resolving the landfall puzzle. See details of the controversy in The First Landfall sidebar in the Crooked Island District chapter.

Rum Cay, a small isle with beautiful beaches, lies 25 miles to San Salvador's southwest. Uninhabited Conception Island is a protected park northwest of Rum Cay.

HIGHLIGHTS

- Dixon Lighthouse, offering a panoramic view
- Diving the wall...or casting a line for prize-size wahoo at The Hump
- Skinny-dipping at Snow Bay
- Horseback riding on the beach at New Columbus Horse-Riding Ranch
- Letting it rip at the Friday night 'rip' at the Harlem Square Club

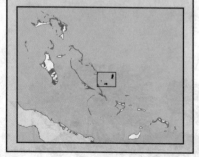

San Salvador

Pop 1200

In the 17th century a British pirate, George Watling, claimed the island for himself and loaned his name to it. In the 18th and 19th centuries Watling Island's history was similar to that of neighboring islands. A fistful of settlers established ill-fated cotton plantations (one of the slave-owners, Henry Storr, was himself black) that faded into obscurity. The remote island wallowed in neglected torpor until the 1930s, when Nassau entrepreneur Sir Harry Oakes built a short-lived hotel. In WWII the hotel was leased to the Royal Navy as a submarine reconnaissance base (it was later turned into a teacher training facility; Club Med Columbus Isle now occupies the site). Later the US government set up a missile-tracking station. It was disbanded in the

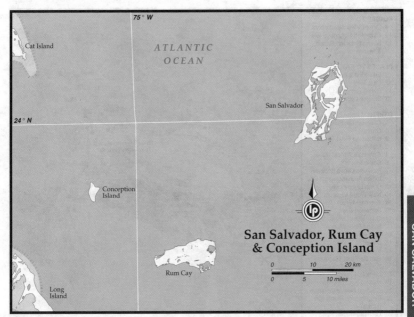

San Salvador, Rum Cay & Conception Island

0   10   20 km
0   5   10 miles

mid-1970s and turned into a biological research station.

The island economy limped along until 1975, when a retired treasure salvager, Bill McGehee, discovered the most beautiful drop-offs he'd seen in his 20 years of Caribbean diving. He began a dive operation. In addition to superb wall diving, there are about a dozen shipwrecks, including the *Frascate*, less than a mile off Riding Rock Point. The canyons and reefs to the southwest are especially awesome. For details on the area's best diving and snorkeling, see the Dive & Snorkel Sites sidebar.

During the 1970s and '80s, a spotted dolphin named Sandy cruised up and down the leeward side of the island. He loved to play with divers, and locals believed he was the 'spirit of Columbus,' returned to bring good luck. Maybe so . . . in 1992 Club Med opened its exclusive resort, which has finally put 'San Sal,' as the island is known, on the map.

San Sal is the tip of a mountain peak that rises 13,000 feet from the ocean floor, and it's bordered by vertical cliffs that plunge into the abyssal deep. Small – 12 miles long by 6 miles wide – and undistinguished, it is nonetheless ringed by superb reefs. The island, with its 41-mile circumference, is also ringed by 30 miles of beaches. Inland it's waterlogged, with acres of mangroves and dozens of briny lakes. The longest is Great Lake, which connects the two major settlements – Cockburn Town and United Estates. It was, prior to the construction of Queen's Hwy, the main highway for locals. Paved along its entire length, Queen's Hwy now girds the island. It's a 90-minute drive or a four- or five-hour bicycle ride. In recent decades part of the population has drifted to Nassau, and settlements along the windward shore have been abandoned.

San Sal offers excellent bird watching. Ospreys (locally called 'chicken hawks') are everywhere. The cays off the north

SAN SALVADOR

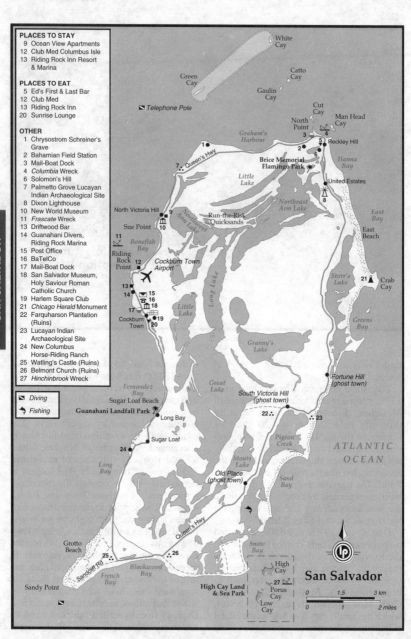

San Salvador

PLACES TO STAY
- 9 Ocean View Apartments
- 12 Club Med Columbus Isle
- 13 Riding Rock Inn Resort & Marina

PLACES TO EAT
- 5 Ed's First & Last Bar
- 12 Club Med
- 13 Riding Rock Inn
- 20 Sunrise Lounge

OTHER
- 1 Chrysostrom Schreiner's Grave
- 2 Bahamian Field Station
- 3 Mail-Boat Dock
- 4 *Columbia* Wreck
- 6 Solomon's Hill
- 7 Palmetto Grove Lucayan Indian Archaeological Site
- 8 Dixon Lighthouse
- 10 New World Museum
- 11 *Frascate* Wreck
- 13 Driftwood Bar
- 14 Guanahani Divers, Riding Rock Marina
- 15 Post Office
- 16 BaTelCo
- 17 Mail-Boat Dock
- 18 San Salvador Museum, Holy Saviour Roman Catholic Church
- 19 Harlem Square Club
- 21 *Chicago Herald* Monument
- 22 Farquharson Plantation (Ruins)
- 23 Lucayan Indian Archaeological Site
- 24 New Columbus Horse-Riding Ranch
- 25 Watling's Castle (Ruins)
- 26 Belmont Church (Ruins)
- 27 *Hinchinbrook* Wreck

🄽 Diving
🄵 Fishing

Dive & Snorkel Sites
Dive Sites
San Sal is one of the best wall-dive destinations in the world. There are more than 40 dive sites within 30 minutes of shore, and more near Rum Cay and Conception Island. The island's waters are known for visibility to 200 feet; on special days it can exceed a miraculous 250 feet! There are more than 20 miles of vertical walls, which begin as little as 40 feet below the surface.

The best sites include the following:

Basket Case – This site is named for the massive basket sponges along a vertical wall beginning at about 30 feet. There's also a deep grotto.

Frascate – This 261-foot-long ship (which sank in 1902) lies just 20 feet down. It's great for novice divers, and there's superb visibility.

Rum Cay Wall – The wall drops from 40 feet to eternity. Nearby are the partial remains of the *Ocean Conqueror*, a 19th-century British steam-powered battleship.

Southampton Reef – This massive reef begins 9 miles north of Conception Island, with fabulous elkhorn and staghorn.

Telephone Pole – This party-line dive begins at 45 feet and angles downward at 45°. You emerge at 100 feet on a wall crowded with large purple sponges and plate coral. Large pelagics abound.

Snorkel Sites
Flower Gardens – These scattered coral heads feature caves for exploring.

The Hump – This formation is a vast undersea condo for small marine life, including countless shrimp.

Natural Bridges – This unusual reef formation features natural arches.

The Rookery – Queen and king helmet conch abound.

Sandy Point – This site, south of Cockburn Town, is one of the best.

Split Reef – Two reefs in one: The first has huge brain corals, the second a long ridge.

Staghorn Reef – You'll find star and staghorn corals aplenty, as well as heaps of other marine life. ■

SAN SALVADOR

shore are favored as nest sites by boobies and other seabirds. And egrets and herons pick in the brine pools. Flamingos were relocated from Great Inagua to San Sal in 1992, when the Brice Memorial Flamingo Park was created in an effort to reintroduce the national bird to the island. Alas, the birds were later removed.

Besides diving and birding, there's not much to do, other than spend your time lying in a hammock.

A warning: Many areas (including Club Med and the Riding Rock Inn Resort) are infested with no-see-'ums, the sand flies so tiny that you never see them. Take Avon Skin So Soft. And be careful if you explore amid the brush. There are quicksands! Poisonwood and manchineel – poisonous to the touch – are ubiquitous.

COCKBURN TOWN
Pop 300
San Sal's major settlement and administrative center, midway down the west coast, is named for Sir Frances Cockburn, governor of the Bahamas from 1837 to 1844. Cockburn (pronounced 'Coburn') Town is a motley affair comprising two parallel roads (1st Ave and 2nd Ave) criss-crossed by five narrow lanes. Tumbledown stone cottages and clapboard shacks in faded pastels mingle with new, often stylish houses

squatting in unkempt yards picked at by goats and cockerels.

A 12-foot plastic iguana guards the entrance to town, where locals gather under the 'Lazy Tree,' a gnarled almond tree whose shade is preferred by locals for loafing.

To get your bearings, you can look out over the town and surrounding mangroves from a derelict observation platform atop a rise 1 mile north of town, to the east of the airport.

Information
There's a BaTelCo office and a post office in town. The medical clinic (☎ 242-331-2105), on the north side of town, is open 9 am to 1 pm weekdays. You can get prescriptions filled and buy over-the-counter drugs at J's Discount Drugs.

To reach the police, call ☎ 242-331-2010.

San Salvador Museum
This small museum is housed in the old jail, in the two-story pink-and-bottle-green building near the north entrance to town. One room displays Lucayan Indian

VERBO AMERICA

Mural, San Salvador Museum

remains, dug up locally. The second room is dedicated to Columbus' discovery of the New World. Note the ceramic mural on the outside wall, bearing a childlike depiction of Columbus (or is it two Lucayan Indians?) paddling ashore.

The doors are usually locked; to visit, ask at the BaTelCo office 50 yards north or call Clifford 'Snake Eyes' Fernandez (☎ 242-331-2676).

Holy Saviour Roman Catholic Church
This pretty pink structure, behind the museum, was established by the Catholic Archdiocese of Nassau in 1992. The church looks much older and fits right in with the museum.

Diving & Snorkeling
Guanahani Divers (☎ 242-331-2631), next to the Riding Rock Inn Resort, has complete scuba facilities, including the Underwater Photo Center, offering camera and video rentals and daily E-6 processing. A one-day underwater photo course costs US$99. It uses custom boats with walk-through transoms and dive platforms. Its one-/two-tank dives cost US$40/60; its night dives cost US$45. A beginner's resort course costs US$105; certification costs US$400. It rents scuba gear. You can have your dives filmed and prepared with music on VHF tape.

Guanahani Divers also offers snorkel trips for US$20, rents snorkel gear for US$10/50 daily/weekly, and participates in Jean-Michel Cousteau's Out Island Snorkeling Adventures (see the Outdoor Activities chapter for details).

Club Med Columbus Isle (see Places to Stay, below) has a full-service dive center offering equipment rental, three 45-foot dive catamarans, and an on-site recompression chamber. Certified divers can dive up to three times daily. Certification costs US$225. It offers a 'special diving and snorkeling' excursion daily, for US$95 including picnic lunch.

Several past guests have complained about the club's dive programs, however, in *The Travelin' Diver's Chapbook* (see the

Outdoor Activities chapter). An excess of divers (dozens at a time) and supercilious staff are among the common gripes.

Sport Fishing

In winter flying fish gather over a group of underwater pinnacles named The Hump, north of San Sal, drawing yellowfin tuna as well as wahoo, which feed on the tuna. At times the waters boil as tunas crash the flying fish, driving them to the surface, where frigate birds scoop them up in flight and boobies and terns wheel thickly over the water. Then the wahoo come in for lunch. (Three world records for wahoo were set here in 1996.)

September through April is the prime wahoo season. In summer blue-marlin fishing is excellent.

You can rent a 30-foot boat and guide from Guanahani Divers (see above) for US$300/500 half-/full day, including tackle. A 42-foot sport-fishing boat costs US$100 extra.

Club Med Columbus Isle has half-day deep-sea fishing excursions for US$95 per person.

Organized Tours

Club Med Columbus Isle offers a half-day island excursion each Tuesday and Thursday for US$25 and a one-hour 'Sunset Cruise' on Thursday for US$22. It also offers a full-day flight excursion to Nassau on Monday, Tuesday, Wednesday, and Friday for US$300.

Mr Forbes gives an island tour from the Riding Rock Inn Resort (see Places to Stay, below) on Tuesday afternoon. You can also book an excursion to the Exumas at Riding Rock Inn Resort; it includes a boat ride to Stocking Island, a meeting with a bush-medicine specialist, and diving at Thunderball Grotto. These trips cost US$150 per person, and there's a minimum of four participants.

Al and Colin, in Cockburn Town, will take you sightseeing to remote spots, including Low Cay, where you'll see iguanas, and High Cay, where you'll be chased by playful ospreys.

Places to Stay

The *Riding Rock Inn Resort & Marina* (☎ 242-331-2631, fax 242-331-2020; in the USA ☎ 954-359-8353, 800-272-1492, fax 954-359-8254, ridingrock@aol.com) is southwest of the airport. Popular with divers, it has 42 nicely furnished air-con rooms, all with cool tile floors, cable TV, couch, and small private patio. Eighteen rooms are classified as 'deluxe' and have a refrigerator and phone. Year-round nightly rates are US$95 single or double for a standard room, US$120 for a deluxe room. Triple rooms cost US$109/135 standard/ deluxe. There are also five handsome stone cottages with a telephone and efficiency kitchen.

A restaurant serves basic meals, and there's a bar, swimming pool, and tennis court. The resort has eight-day dive packages, with three dives daily. A September special includes free dives for a second person; the first person is charged US$950/ 1959 standard/deluxe and the second US$680/780. Rental cars and bicycles are available. In 1996 Hurricane Lili stripped the hotel of its luster, but restoration was ongoing at press time. A nice beach lies a stone's throw away. The postal address is c/o Out Island Service Co, 1170 Lee Wagener Blvd, No 103, Fort Lauderdale, FL 33316-3561.

Club Med Columbus Isle (☎ 242-331- 2000, fax 242-331-2222; in North America ☎ 800-453-2582, fax 602-443-2086), just 200 yards west of the airport, is one of the French hotel chain's flagship properties, spanning 80 acres along 3 miles of shoreline. In 1996 *Scuba Diving* magazine rated it the 'Best Dive Resort in the World.' The low-slung resort, painted in bright Caribbean pastels, boasts a stunning setting and exotic antique art valued at more than US$2.5 million: carved Nepalese doorways, patinated Pakistani urns, Indonesian temple gods, Brazilian headdresses, Turkish rugs, African statues, and masks. The resort is centered on a spacious sun deck and pool; stone pathways lead from the pool through expansive, half-wild grounds.

It has 286 spacious double-occupancy rooms in two-story beachfront units, all with custom-fashioned furniture, ocean views from gingerbread-trimmed private balconies, TV, phone, refrigerator, and safe. There are three gourmet restaurants, 12 tennis courts, a fitness center, and just about every water sport and recreational activity imaginable. Water-skiing is offered May to October. Nighttime is lively, with a show and merry-making led by the party-hearty 'GOs' (quasi-camp-counselors for adults). Nightly rates for standard rooms range from US$170 to US$270 per person, depending on season; weekly rates are US$1100 to US$1750. Ocean-view rooms cost more. No children under 12 are permitted.

Places to Eat

In town Faith Jones runs the clean and tidy *Three Ships* (☎ 242-331-2787), serving boil fish and grits for breakfast on request, plus burgers, turtle soup, and native dinner specials from US$8; dinner reservations are required, and it's closed Sunday. The *Sunrise Lounge*, on Queen's Hwy south of town, also serves native dishes.

The *Riding Rock Inn* restaurant serves set meals. Breakfast costs US$9.25; lunch is US$12.25; dinner, including wine, is US$25.25. A 15% service charge is added. The moderate-quality fare is filling but overly expensive. Two entrée options are offered. Get there by 8 pm or you may be out of luck. Pizzas are served Wednesday night until midnight, as they are on Saturday at *The Shack* in Cockburn Town.

Club Med charges nonguests US$40 for an evening pass, including a splendid buffet dinner, entertainment, and access to its nightclub. *A bargain!*

You can buy groceries at *Jake Jones Food Store*, next to the Sunrise Lounge.

Entertainment

The atmospheric *Driftwood Bar*, at the Riding Rock Inn Resort, is adorned with driftwood carved with names and salacious comments. Popcorn is served. There's a TV. It hosts a party on Wednesday and Friday nights, when it can get lively and noisy.

On Friday night, a bash called 'The Rip' is hosted at the *Harlem Square Club* (☎ 242-331-2777), a lively place with live music and revelry. There's dancing, too, on Saturday, and you can join the locals for a lively game of dominoes. An alternative is the nearby *Ocean View Club* (☎ 242-331-2676).

Early Sunday evening, a preacher sets up his sound system under the shade of the Lazy Tree and raps his evangelical silliness over infectious contempo music.

Chris McLaughlin, director of the Underwater Photo Center at Guanahani Divers, offers a slide show on San Salvador at 8 pm every Saturday, plus shows on scuba diving on Wednesday and Friday evenings. Admission is free.

Things to Buy

Gwen, the 'Straw Lady,' sells shell crafts and plaited straw-work under the Lazy Tree. Iris Fernandez also sells straw goods, at her San Salvador Gift Shop.

Getting There & Away

Air The airport is 1 mile north of Cockburn Town. At press time it was being expanded to take jets from Europe and North America (the US$16 million project is bedeviled by political follies and may take some time).

Bahamasair flies between Miami and San Sal Thursday and Sunday (US$60 one way) and between Nassau and San Sal Friday and Sunday (US$72 one way). The Bahamasair agent has an office in the basement of the Riding Rock Inn Resort. If you want to buy a ticket or make any changes, you'll need to come here.

Club Med Columbus Isle operates charter flights. Scheduled flights depart Miami Friday, Saturday, and Sunday; fares vary according to season, but are included in the accommodations packages. One of Club Med's pilots, amiable and knowledgeable Khazik Kazni, flies local charters. He's based at the Riding Rock Inn Resort.

Riding Rock Inn Resort also offers private charters; at press time it was planning to buy its own 10-seater plane. Divers who are on prepaid diving packages are permitted to bring 70 lbs of luggage; everyone else gets 44 lbs.

Boat Riding Rock Inn Resort has a nine-slip marina with fuel, water, electricity, satellite TV connections, and groceries. Dockage costs US80¢ per foot daily and US$4.80 weekly. Water and electricity each begin at US$10 per day, depending on size of vessel.

The mail boat *Lady Francis* sails here from Nassau at 6 pm Tuesday (US$40 one way). It also calls at United Estates and Rum Cay.

Getting Around
You can rent cars for US$85 per day and scooters for US$50 at the airport. The Riding Rock Inn Resort rents bicycles for US$6.50/10 half-/full day.

NORTHWEST COAST
North of the airport, Queen's Hwy skirts the scrub-lined shore. Bonefish Bay has a fabulous beach that Club Med likes to claim as its own; you can gain access from Sue Point, 3 miles north of Cockburn Town, at the north end of the bay near the settlement of North Victoria Hill. The hamlet has the tiny New World Museum, displaying Lucayan Indian artifacts unearthed at the Palmetto Grove archaeological site north of town. You'll need to find the curator, Mervin Benson (☎ 242-331-2126), to be let in. Admission costs US$1.

See if you can hire a local and boat to take you bird watching on the lakes.

North of North Victoria Hill, the road swings around the north shore along sand-rimmed Graham's Harbour. The harbor is calm and good for swimming. A Columbus Day Homecoming is traditionally held here on the beach on Discovery Day (October 12). The island bursts into life with music, feasting, dinghy ('smack boat') races, and fun games.

Chrysostrom Schreiner, the Catholic missionary, is buried beneath a pile of rocks on a bluff at the west end of the harbor, where he was convinced Columbus

had first stepped ashore. Appropriately, the annual Columbus Day Regatta is held here. Graham's Harbour ends at North Point. The wreck of the *Columbia*, which ran aground in 1980, is just off the point.

Bahamian Field Station
This research station (☎ 242-331-2520, fax 242-331-2524), at the eastern end of Graham's Harbour, is on the former site of a US missile-tracking station. Visitors are welcome, although there's not much to see here.

The station, a branch of the New York state college system, is officially known as the Center for the Study of Archaeology, Biology, Geology & Marine Sciences. It primarily hosts scientific conferences and field courses for student groups. Scientists also run a coral-reef monitoring project. Its own two-week course in tropical marine biology, cosponsored by Oklahoma State University, is offered each June and is open to students worldwide for US$1320, including roundtrip airfare from Fort Lauderdale. The station also hosts an annual symposium on the natural history of The Bahamas. You can write the station c/o Twin Air, 1100 Lee Wagener Blvd, Suite 113, Fort Lauderdale, FL 33315.

Elderhostel (☎ 617-426-7788), 75 Federal St, Boston, MA 02110-1941, offers 11-day study trips at the staion for folks over 60.

Earthwatch (☎ 800-776-0188, fax 617-926-8532, info@earthwatch.org), 680 Mt Auburn St, Watertown, MA 02272, a non-profit organization, houses volunteers at the Bahamian Field Station on its programs to preserve San Sal's reefs. It needs volunteer divers to help set up and monitor underwater transections, identify and photograph coral species, and measure physical and chemical characteristics of the water. The 10-day program costs US$1195, including housing at the station. You supply your own diving gear. See the Internet Resources section in the back of the book for EarthCorps' website address.

Places to Stay & Eat

Cliff Fernandez (☎ 242-331-2676) rents three modern air-con cottages – *Ocean View Apartments* – in North Victoria Hill. A modern two-bedroom *oceanfront house* is also for rent (in the USA ☎ 719-574-5781).

Club Arawak, next to the New World Museum, has basic native fare and does duty as the local nightspot.

NORTHEAST COAST

The east shore is lined with lonesome beaches, including 5-mile-long East Beach, with its pinkish sands, and Snow Bay, at the far south, where you can be alone with the gentle lapping of the waves and the cry of seabirds. The road, however, runs inland from the shore for most of the way, passing a series of briny lakes scummed with orange algae blooms and smelling like backed-up toilets.

United Estates (locally called 'U-E'), the main settlement in the area, is a small village 8 miles' drive northeast of Cockburn Town. It's a motley affair strung out for a mile along Queen's Hwy and hemmed in between a limestone ridge and a brine pool that doubles as a resting place for dozens of rusting car hulks. The island's only high school is in the settlement of Reckley Hill, north of U-E. Note the blue house called 'Solomon's Hill,' decorated with dozens of plastic buoys. It's very photogenic, especially at Christmas, when the owner, Solomon Jones, adorns his home with lights.

Dixon Lighthouse

U-E is dominated by this magnificent lighthouse, nestled atop Dixon Hill (it's a stiff five-minute climb up a potholed road from Queen's Hwy). The gleaming-white structure rises 67 feet from its hilltop base, 163 feet above sea level. It was raised in 1856 and still puts out its beam twice every 25 seconds, fired by a superbly maintained Hood pelcum vapor burner, reflected and magnified to 400,000 candle-power by a huge Fresnel (or bull's-eye) lens. A poster dating from 1921 shows its workings.

The lighthouse is tended by Joyce Hanna, a delightful lady with pigtails who lives in the handsome cottage beneath the light. She is responsible for ensuring that the clocklike rotating mechanism that turns the light is wound by hand every 90 minutes throughout the night. You can climb the 80 steps to admire the internal workings and step out onto the balcony for a panoramic bird's-eye view of the entire island. It's open 9 am to noon and 2 to 5 pm daily.

The Bahamas' Port Dept is planning to replace the historic light with an automated light. You can help preserve the magnificent structure by contacting (and sending donations to) the Bahamas Lighthouse Preservation Society. Call David Gale (☎ 242-366-0282).

Chicago Herald Monument

This weather-worn monument stands at the south end of East Bay, 1 mile from Queen's Hwy and about 3 miles southeast of U-E. The crude stone marker, topped by a marble globe, sits on a slender isthmus named **Crab Cay**. A plaque reads: 'On this spot Christopher Columbus first set foot upon the soil of the New World. Erected by the *Chicago Herald*, June 1891.' There is no evidence whatsoever to support the lofty claim . . . and, in any event, the off-shore reefs make this an unlikely spot for anyone to come ashore! A dirt track leads to East Bay from the highway; you can slog south along the beach until you find the monument.

Places to Eat

If you're exploring the island, take water and snacks. The only two eateries in the area are *Three J's Take-Away* and *Ed's First & Last Bar*, both funky clapboard shacks. Both serve native dishes, such as cracked conch and peas 'n' rice, but neither is guaranteed to be open.

Getting There & Away

The *Lady Francis* mail boat calls at United Estates weekly from Nassau. See the Cockburn Town section for details.

SOUTHEAST COAST

Last century, this quarter of the island was the center of cotton and citrus plantations. Several small yet once-thriving settlements have all been abandoned in recent decades. Only their ghostly old stone houses remain, slowly turning to dust behind fieldstone boundary walls. It's a desolate stretch. The most notable site is the ruins of **Farquharson Plantation**, established in the 1820s by Charles Farquharson, a justice of the peace who recorded plantation life in his journals.

The road dips and rises inland, paralleling **Pigeon Creek**, an 8-mile-long ecological treasure (baby sharks, for example, swim here) that opens to the ocean at **Snow Bay**, to the south. The creek is good for bonefishing. There's an important but unmarked Lucayan Indian archaeological site along the shore at the north end of Pigeon Creek.

Breathtakingly beautiful Snow Bay has a snow-white beach and sheltered turquoise waters good for skinny-dipping. A dirt track leads to Snow Bay from Queen's Hwy at Blackwood Bay. The ruins of the Belmont Church are near the turnoff.

High Cay Land & Sea Park, offshore to the southeast, protects High Cay, Porus Cay, and Low Cay, important nesting sites for ospreys, boobies, and other seabirds. Endangered iguanas cling to Low Cay. The reef-girt cays, half a mile southeast of Snow Bay, have claimed several ships, notably the *Hinchinbrook*, which went down in 1913 and is today favored by scuba divers.

SOUTHWEST COAST

South of Cockburn Town, Fernandez Bay and Long Bay – boasting beautiful Sugar Loaf Beach – sweep south to Sandy Point, the hilly, pendulous southwest tip of the island, reached off Queen's Hwy by Sandcliff Rd. The peninsula's leeward shore is fringed by beautiful Grotto Beach. Several foreigners have built homes along the breezy coast. The residential community is known as Columbus Estates. There are several caves, notably Dripping Rock, which contains a well.

Watling's Castle

Columbus Estates occupies the site of a plantation said to have been established by George Watling but actually founded by a Loyalist settler, Cade Matthews, who named it for the pirate. It remained operational until 1925. The ruins sit atop a hill with good views of the sea. There's not much to see: just a lookout tower, ruined slave quarters, and other crumbling structures entwined with shrubbery. Long pants are a good idea to guard against thorny scrub.

Guanahani Landfall Park

Years ago some supposedly knowledgeable folks stuck a pin in a map to determine the *exact* spot of Columbus' first landfall and – *hey presto!* – here you are at Long Bay, 2 miles south of Cockburn Town. The historic event is commemorated by four uninspired monuments beside the shore. The oldest, a swirly plinth, was created in 1968 and also marks the Olympic Games in Mexico. The chunk of metal on top, which looks like it dropped from the *Challenger* disaster, is actually a bowl that held the Olympic flame on its journey from Greece to Mexico City.

Alongside it is a much-photographed, simple, 10-foot-tall cement cross. Dedicated on Christmas Day, 1956, it's prettified by a bougainvillea bush to its side. The government of Spain dedicated its own monument on the occasion of the visit of three Columbus caravel replicas on February 10, 1992. The cement block, with a ceramic plaque, is backed by an ugly metal sculpture.

"THIS PLAQUE WAS PRESENTED BY THE GOVERNMENT OF SPAIN ON THE OCCASION OF THE VISIT OF THE REPLICAS OF CHRISTOPHER COLUMBUS CARAVELS ON 10ᵀᴴ FEBRUARY, 1992 IN COMMEMORATION OF THE FIRST LANDFALL AT SAN SALVADOR IN 1492"

1492 - 1992

Lastly, there's a small chunk of concrete inset with a bronze plaque, dedicated in October 1991 when a replica of the *Santa María*, built by the Nao Santa María Foundation of Japan, made landfall here on its journey from Barcelona to Kobe. (An identical edifice – the Tappan Monument – was erected in 1951 half a mile farther north.)

A ceremony is held each Discovery Day, when the Olympic flame is rekindled.

Horseback Riding
You can ride horses at the New Columbus Horse-Riding Ranch (☎ 242-357-9527) at Sugar Loaf, about 4 miles south of Cockburn Town. The place is professionally run by Austrians Manfred and Margonda Roon. Ninety-minute beach and trail rides are offered at 9:30 am daily for US$40; a 2½-hour ride is offered at 5 pm for US$55. Individual lessons cost US$30 per hour. Group lessons, for US$25 hourly, are held at 5 pm weekdays and at

9, 10, and 11 am and 4, 5, and 6 pm on weekends. Lessons are also offered by appointment. Beginners are welcome. The ranch is open 7 am to sunset; its mailing address is Cockburn Town PO, San Salvador, Bahamas.

Places to Eat
There's a *grocery store* and the *Stansheka Bar* on Queen's Hwy in Sugar Loaf, half a mile south of Guanahani Landfall Park.

Rum Cay

Pop 60
This small island – incorrectly claimed by locals to be Santa María de la Concepción, Columbus' name for his second landfall – is 25 miles southwest of San Salvador but shares the same administration. Ten miles long and 5 miles wide, Rum Cay is entirely off the tourist beat. The coasts are lined by

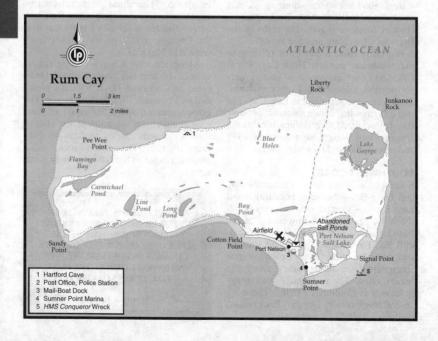

Rum Cay

0   1.5   3 km
0   1   2 miles

ATLANTIC OCEAN

Liberty Rock
Junkanoo Rock
Pee Wee Point
Flamingo Bay
Blue Holes
Lake George
Carmichael Pond
Line Pond
Long Pond
Bay Pond
Sandy Point
Cotton Field Point
Airfield
Port Nelson
Abandoned Salt Ponds
Port Nelson Salt Lake
Signal Point
Sumner Point

1 Hartford Cave
2 Post Office, Police Station
3 Mail-Boat Dock
4 Sumner Point Marina
5 *HMS Conqueror* Wreck

stunning beaches, and the entire isle wears a necklace of coral. There's a wreck, the HMS *Conqueror*, a 101-gun man o' war that sank in 30 feet of water off Signal Point.

The only settlement is **Port Nelson**, just west of Sumner Point on the south coast. This hamlet is still merging with the 20th century; electricity and telephone service had arrived by press time. It is backed by disused salt ponds that provided salt bound for the fishing fleets of Nova Scotia in the 19th century. Hurricanes in 1908 and 1926 destroyed the ponds and killed the industry; afterward many residents drifted away.

The rest of the isle is a virtual wilderness of rolling hills browsed by feral cattle and donkeys.

There's a post office and police station in Port Nelson.

Places to Stay & Eat
The *Rum Cay Club*, the island's only hotel, has closed and was for sale at press time, with no news on when it might reopen. The owner, David Melville (☎ /fax 242-357-7676), may be able to accommodate you. Constable Ted Bain and Hermie, the local midwife, rent *rooms*.

The choice eatery is the *Sumner Point Marina Restaurant*, highly recommended by yachters. Constable Bain's *Ocean View Restaurant* is also recommended for basic native fare, as is *Two Sisters Take-A-Way*, which sells fresh bread, conch, grouper, and chicken. Locals also hang out at *Toby's Bar*

and *Kay's Bar*, which host live music on weekends and get lively when boaters are in.

Getting There & Away
There's a private airstrip in Port Nelson. There are no scheduled flights.

The Sumner Point Marina (☎ 242-357-1000) has 18 slips, fuel, electricity, water, and ice. The *Lady Francis* mail boat calls weekly from Nassau. See the Cockburn Town section.

Conception Island

This uninhabited, reef-rimmed speck on the map, 15 miles northeast of Long Island and 25 miles southeast of Cat Island, is protected as the Conception Island Land & Sea Park under the jurisdiction of the Bahamas National Trust. The isle – a mere 3 miles by 2 miles – is an important nesting site for endangered green turtles as well as migratory seabirds, particularly boobies, which give their name to Booby Cay, east of the island.

A briny creek dominates the interior and opens to the sea. It's a haven for divers and yachters.

Amazing Grace, the supply ship for Windjammer Barefoot Cruises' sailing fleet, calls on Conception during its island-hopping voyages, offered twice monthly between Grand Bahama and Trinidad. See the Getting There & Away chapter for details.

CONCEPTION ISLAND

Long Island

Pop 3107

Long Island, 28 miles south of Cat Island, is relatively undeveloped, yet it's one of the prettiest Family Islands. The drive along its main road, the Queen's Hwy, offers stupendous sights, from deep caves and a fishing village where you can still see wooden sailing dinghies being made by hand, to plantation ruins and beautiful churches – the divinely inspired handiwork of Father Jerome (see the Father Jerome sidebar in the Cat Island chapter). The island is 60 miles north to south and less than 2 miles wide.

Scenic side roads lead to magnificent bays, blue holes, and miles and miles of beach. In places along the windward shore, Atlantic rollers crash against dramatic cliffs (other beaches are protected by offshore reefs). Cape Santa Maria, to the north, has especially superb beaches and reefs. The west coast consists of a string of shallow bays. (When you're given directions by locals, remember that they say 'up south' and 'down north,' the opposite of what you might expect.) In late spring hundreds of thousands of yellow butterflies appear, dancing merrily along in streams, like ribbons.

The island has Lucayan Indian caves to explore (they called their island 'Yuma'). The caves have yielded *duhos* (wooden seats) that archaeologists believe suggest chieftainship and ceremony, and *zemi* figurines bearing religious connotations. Columbus, whom evidence suggests made his third New World landfall here, believed that the Indians had 'no sect whatsoever' and that '[they] would very shortly become Christians, because they are of very good intelligence.' To the south, the island – Columbus' 'Fernandina' – ends at Cape Verde, where Columbus supposedly anchored on October 24, 1492.

The island's inhabitants are scattered among about 35 settlements. A large percentage are whites or 'brights' (people of

HIGHLIGHTS

- Cape Santa Maria's beach, blindingly white with bathtub-warm shallows extending forever
- Shark Reef, where you can watch sharks feast in front of your eyes
- Long Island Regatta, *the* time to party-hearty with locals
- Lochabar Beach Lodge, a cozy, unpretentious, down-home inn . . . and what a setting!
- Hamilton's Cave, boasting stalactites, stalagmites, and leaf-nosed fruit bats

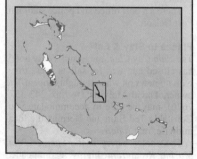

mixed black and white ancestry, with a distinct lobster-red hue to their complexions), including many descendants of the 18th-century Loyalists. The colonists established a plantation system that was as viable as any in the archipelago. Uniquely, sheep-rearing remained profitable well into this century. Farming endures today in large groves of bananas and rows of corn (especially around Deadman's Cay), in stock-rearing, and in production of vegetables and pineapples in limestone potholes.

Long Island is acclaimed as a diving paradise, most famously for its wall dives and the fast-paced action of Shark Reef. The island also has hot fishing year-round, thanks to the North Equatorial Current,

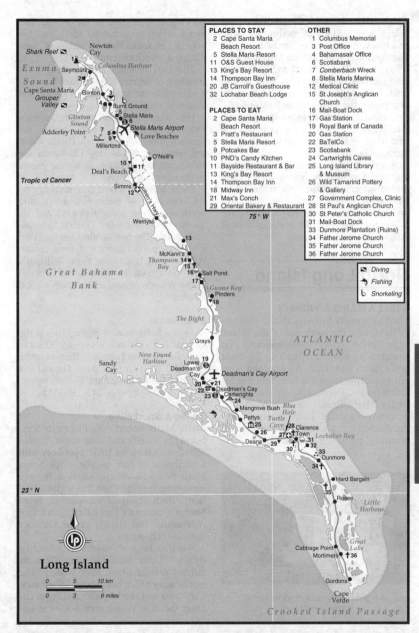

PLACES TO STAY
2 Cape Santa Maria
  Beach Resort
5 Stella Maris Resort
11 O&S Guest House
13 King's Bay Resort
14 Thompson Bay Inn
20 JB Carroll's Guesthouse
32 Lochabar Beach Lodge

PLACES TO EAT
2 Cape Santa Maria
  Beach Resort
3 Pratt's Restaurant
5 Stella Maris Resort
9 Potcakes Bar
10 PND's Candy Kitchen
11 Bayside Restaurant & Bar
13 King's Bay Resort
14 Thompson Bay Inn
18 Midway Inn
21 Max's Conch
29 Oriental Bakery & Restaurant

OTHER
1 Columbus Memorial
3 Post Office
4 Bahamasair Office
6 Scotiabank
7 Comberbach Wreck
8 Stella Maris Marina
12 Medical Clinic
15 St Joseph's Anglican
   Church
16 Mail-Boat Dock
17 Gas Station
19 Royal Bank of Canada
20 Gas Station
22 BaTelCo
23 Scotiabank
24 Cartwrights Caves
25 Long Island Library
   & Museum
26 Wild Tamarind Pottery
   & Gallery
27 Government Complex, Clinic
28 St Paul's Anglican Church
30 St Peter's Catholic Church
31 Mail-Boat Dock
33 Dunmore Plantation (Ruins)
34 Father Jerome Church
35 Father Jerome Church
36 Father Jerome Church

⚲ Diving
⌐ Fishing
♭ Snorkeling

Shark Reef ⚲
Newton
Cay
Seymours
Columbus Harbour
Exuma
Sound
Cape Santa Maria
Grouper
Valley ⚲
Glinton
Burnt Ground
Stella Maris
Stella Maris Airport
Glinton
Sound
Adderley Point
Love Beaches
Millertons
O'Neill's
Deal's Beach
Tropic of Cancer
Simms
Queen's Hwy
Wemyss
Great Bahama
Bank
McKann's
Thompson
Bay
Salt Pond
Guana Key
Pinders
The Bight
Grays
New Found
Harbour
Sandy
Cay
Lower
Deadman's
Cay
Deadman's Cay Airport
Deadman's Cay
Cartwrights
Mangrove Bush
Blue
Hole
Pettys
Turtle
Cove
Clarence
Town
Lochabar Bay
Deans
Dunmore
Hard Bargain
Roses
Little
Harbour
ATLANTIC
OCEAN
23° N
75° W
Long Island
0   5   10 km
0   3   6 miles
Cabbage Point
Great
Lake
Mortimers
Gordons
Cape
Verde
Crooked Island Passage

LONG ISLAND

which originates in the Canary Islands and brings huge schools of marlin, yellowfin and blackfin tuna, wahoo, and other game fish. Seasonal highs include March to May for rainbow runners, March to June for dolphin (dorado), April and May for yellowfin tuna, July to December for blackfin tuna, and September to November for wahoo.

Bottom fish are abundant year-round. And bonefishing is splendid; you can even cast while wading in 1 foot of water near the beaches.

A warning: There are no general currents that pull swimmers away from land, except during adverse weather, but wave action can be rough and certain beaches have undertows. Remember: Every *seventh* wave is much bigger than the previous waves! Ask locals about conditions.

North Long Island

STELLA MARIS & VICINITY

Most visitors fly to Stella Maris. This settlement, near the north end of the island, is an upscale residential community that stretches for about a mile along the coast amid palms and scrub. An irregular warren of narrow lanes has been laid out for future homes. Dominating the scene is the Stella Maris Resort, atop a bluff that descends to a rocky shoreline with beach-lined coves . . . a wonderful spot in early morning to watch stilt-legged waders

A typical Family Island 'slave home' from days of yore

picking at tidal life in the pools. The beach is not protected by reefs, and the waters can sometimes be turbulent, producing a severe undertow.

The best beaches are the four Love Beaches, at the end of a dirt road that runs a mile northeast from Ocean View Dr, the shoreline road.

For bonefishing enthusiasts, there's excellent sport in the shallow bay on the leeward shore off Adderley Point, where the remains of Adderley Plantation are smothered in vegetation, as are the graves in the slaves' cemetery.

Stella Maris is served commercially by the settlement of Burnt Ground (a mile north along the main highway) and its smaller twin community, Glinton, immediately north. The two hamlets are speckled with brine pools littered with town refuse. A side road leads east from William's Auto Garage (at the south end of Glinton) to the Atlantic shore, where there's good snorkeling.

Information

There's a Scotiabank in Stella Maris at the General & Food Store; it's open 9:30 am to 2 pm Tuesday and Thursday. The post office (☎ 242-338-2010) is in Burnt Ground just south of Pratt's Restaurant. For the police, call ☎ 242-337-0999 or 242-338-8555.

Diving & Snorkeling

Stella Maris Resort (see Places to Stay, below) is a dedicated dive resort. It also offers snorkeling for US$10 per hour with a minimum of four people. Cape Santa Maria Beach Resort also offers diving and snorkeling (see the Cape Santa Maria section). Both resorts participate in Jean-Michel Cousteau's Out Island Snorkeling Adventures (see details in the Outdoor Activities chapter).

Want to be with sharks in a feeding frenzy? Stella Maris Resort offers its famous dive at Shark Reef weekly. The exhilarating affair lasts about 15 minutes. Caribbean reef sharks gather and begin circling the dive vessel even before it has moored. (Nurse sharks and even hammer-heads sometimes visit, too.) Divers go down together – quickly! – accompanied by a divemaster. The sharks swim around and between the divers, expectantly antici-pating the moment, five minutes later, when a lead-weighted bucket of chum (fish remains) is thrown in. The frenzy is over almost before the bucket hits the bottom, 30 feet down. *Awesome!* Nondivers can watch events from above through a glass-bottomed bucket.

See the Dive & Snorkel Sites sidebar on the next page for details of Long Island's other underwater highlights.

Bonefishing & Sport Fishing

Guided bonefishing is offered by Stella Maris Resort for US$140/160 half-/full day for two people. Bottom fishing costs US$160 to US$300 full day; deep-sea fishing costs you US$550. Alternately, contact 'Dockie' (☎ 242-338-2018), one of the best local guides, in Burnt Ground.

Places to Stay

The *Stella Maris Resort* (☎ 242-338-2051, fax 242-338-2052; in the USA ☎ 954-359-8236, 800-426-0466, fax 954-359-8238), a mile north of the airport, enjoys a breezy perch atop the ridge and stunning views over the Atlantic. It is German-owned and run with Teutonic efficiency. The handsome stone-and-timber lodge has a fine dining room and large bar and lounge. There are 30 pink-and-white rooms and apartments on the ridge and two dozen cottages scattered in a half-mile arc on the coral shore. Rooms have ceiling fans, tile floors, rattan furni-ture, and glass sliding doors that open to patios or verandahs with marvelous views. Rates are US$195/245 low/peak season, including water sports and bicycle, plus 8% tax and US$6 per-person housekeeping gra-tuity nightly (you should challenge the housekeeping 'tax'). A two-bedroom villa costs US$295/350. A MAP (breakfast and dinner) plan costs US$64/45 adult/child. Four-day packages cost US$615/715 per person.

The resort features freshwater and salt-water pools, tennis courts, a card room, and a sunny atrium. It's a five-minute walk downhill to the beach, where the inn has a sun deck and swimming pool. It offers free trips to local beaches for guests. Its mailing address is Out Islands Promotion Board, 1100 Lee Wagener Blvd, No 319, Fort Lauderdale, FL 33315.

For details on other local accommoda-tions, see the Cape Santa Maria section.

Places to Eat

Nonguests can dine at *Stella Maris Resort*, which serves hearty breakfasts – the buffet costs US$12 – and native and continental cuisine. Dinners cost US$31; US$21 for entrée only.

To dine with locals, try *Pratt's Restaurant* (☎ 242-338-7022) in Burnt Ground near the post office. It serves Bahamian seafoods and native dishes. *Barbie's Ice Cream* (☎ 242-338-5009) is a modern, clean restaurant and ice cream parlor at the north end of Glinton.

Alternately, try *Potcakes Bar* (☎ 242-338-2018) next to the Stella Maris Marina. It has an upscale restaurant, and a bar by night.

Ed Knowles sells fresh bread and produce at *Rose Haven & Meat Market* (☎ 242-338-5017) in Glinton. You can get your fresh protein at *Long Island Meat & Fish* (☎ 242-338-2016) in Culmers, south of Stella Maris.

Adderley Supply, in Burnt Ground, sells pharmaceuticals and groceries, as does the *Burnt Ground Convenience Store*.

Also see the Cape Santa Maria section for additional places to eat.

Entertainment

Stella Maris Resort has a handsome bar where local residents gather. The resort uses a cave as a nightclub on Monday night, with a barbecue and dancing to a rake 'n' scrape band.

There are a few funky satellite lounges in Burnt Ground and in Glinton, good for supping with locals. You should check out both the *Playboy Club* and *Sabrina's Bar*.

LONG ISLAND

Dive & Snorkel Sites

Dive Sites

Most visitors to Long Island come for the acclaimed diving, based at Stella Maris. Prime sites include the following:

Cape Santa Maria Ship's Graveyard – Two wrecks, a small pleasure cruiser and the 103-foot *Comberbach*, lie 100 feet down.

Conception Island Wall – The wall begins just off a leeside beach at 45 feet and plunges down, down, down.

Grouper Valley – Every November thousands of groupers gather in this valley, which also draws other pelagic species.

Grouper Village – Don't arrive without food: The half-dozen or so resident groupers expect to be fed. 'Brutus,' a mammoth jewfish, also lives here.

Ocean Blue Hole – This cavern is a dramatic, ever-widening funnel.

Snorkel Sites

Coral Gardens – Hawksbill turtles favor these awesome caves, overhangs, and valleys.

Eagle Ray Reef – Yes, rays frequent this beautiful coral formation guarded by a friendly grouper.

Flamingo Tongue Reef – Countless species of corals and fish are on show.

Newton Cay – Scores of coral heads are found on this reef.

Poseidon Point – This is one of very few places to watch large tarpon amid the reefs.

Rainbow Reef – This reef is famous for elkhorn corals and sponges.

Rock Pools – Crabs inhabit these tidal pools and swim-in coral formations.

Turtle Cove – It's named for the turtle grass, not the animals. Still, there are lots of splendid shells.

Watermelon Beach – Plenty of colorful parrotfish and damsels are found amid acres of staghorn coral. ■

Things to Buy

Stella Maris has a well-stocked boutique, Tingum's. You can purchase handmade straw-work at Bert's Dry Goods in Burnt Ground and Adderley Straw Work in Glinton.

Getting There & Away

Air The Stella Maris Airport is about a mile south of the Stella Maris Resort. For Customs and Immigration, call ☎ 242-338-2012. See the Getting There & Away and Getting Around chapters for airline phone numbers in Nassau and abroad.

Bahamasair, which has an office in Burnt Ground (☎ 242-338-2015), flies from Miami on Thursday and Sunday and from Nassau four times per week (US$80 one way). Island Express flies from Fort Lauderdale.

Cat Island Air flies from Nassau at 9 am Wednesday and Friday (US$55 one way). Long Island Wings flies charters to Stella Maris.

Stella Maris Resort offers private charters for hotel guests (US$90 one way with hotel booking). If you are holding a Bahamasair ticket, you can use it to fly on the charter.

Boat The Stella Maris Marina – Long Island's only port of entry – is also the only full-service marina on the island. Boats up to 100 feet can be hauled.

Getting Around

Bus Matthias Pratt (☎ 242-338-7051/7022) operates a minibus charter service. He charges about US$150 for a ride for four people from Stella Maris to Mangrove Bush, in the southern part of the island.

Car & Scooter Stella Maris Resort rents cars for US$65 a day plus mileage (US25¢ a mile) using Wellington Taylor, who has a home-based car-rental agency in Burnt Ground. (My bill for use of a tiny Geo Metro for the day was US$110.) You'll do better to book directly and negotiate a price with Taylor or with Joe Williams (☎ 242-338-5002) in Glinton, who charges US$65 daily, including unlimited mileage, for Nissan Sentras or minivans. Weekly rentals cost US$55 per day.

Stella Maris Resort rents scooters for US$30/46 half-/full day. Inell Ditez, in Burnt Ground, rents scooters for US$40 daily.

Burnt Ground has a gas station, immediately north of the Bahamasair office.

Taxi Taxis meet all flights. A taxi to the Stella Maris Resort costs US$3 per person. A taxi to Cape Santa Maria Beach Resort costs about US$12 for two. Jerry and Jennifer Knowles (☎ 242-336-2106) will act as guides.

GLINTON TO NEWTON CAY

North of Glinton, the road continues 3 miles to Seymours – a hilltop settlement – then winds downhill and ends at the shores of Columbus Harbour, a shallow bay lined by mangroves. You can cross the narrow tidal creek on a footbridge to reach Newton Cay, a small island with a beach on the Atlantic shore. A trail leads to other beaches, and there are caves around the headland to the north.

The Model Boat Fest takes place at Bridge Beach, near Seymours, each August. For information, call Alvin Smith (☎ 242-338-5273).

The **Columbus Memorial**, a remote, 15-foot-tall stone obelisk, is surrounded by thick stands of thatch palm and sea grape at the northern tip of Long Island. It bears a plaque dedicated to 'the peaceful aboriginal people of Long Island and to the arrival of Christopher Columbus.' It is topped by a rusty globe that's skewered by a cross.

The windblown site is a contemplative spot to commune with nature. *Beware the steep cliffs!* The vistas out to sea are sublime, as are the views over a beautiful, flask-shaped, jade-colored, sand-rimmed bay. Snorkeling is good around the headlands, and you can body-float with the tide.

The track to the monument is signed at Seymours. The rocky path leads northwest 1 mile until you eventually reach the headland, ascended by a short yet steep trail that deposits you at the monument. I made it on a bicycle . . . but bring plenty of water!

The mail boat *Sherice M* calls at Seymours weekly from Nassau, also stopping at Salt Pond and Deadman's Cay (see the Salt Pond section for details). Matthias Pratt (☎ 242-338-7051/7022) charges about US$25 to drive four people from Stella Maris to the memorial.

CAPE SANTA MARIA

This pendulous 3-mile-long cape is connected to Long Island by a narrow isthmus with mangrove creeks. The cape's west shore is lined along its entire length with a gorgeous white-sand beach shelving into turquoise shallows. Snorkeling is especially good at the reef gardens at the south end. The Stella Maris Resort (see the Stella Maris & Vicinity section) has shade cabañas midway down the bay. It offers free shuttles each morning for its guests. Access is via a dirt road (signed) from Seymours.

Places to Stay & Eat

The plantation-style *Cape Santa Maria Beach Resort* (☎ 242-357-1006; in North America 250-598-3366, 800-663-7090, fax 250-598-1361) has a sublime setting at the north end of the bay. The resort's 20 deluxe air-con cottages, in 10 units, are widely spaced amid lawns a stone's throw from the beach. Each has beautiful tile floors, rattan furniture, ceiling fans, wooden ceilings, bright tropical prints, and simply yet colorfully tiled bathrooms. All rooms open to screened porches facing the beach. Wooden walkways lead to a handsome restaurant and bar. Facilities include catamarans, sailboats, and sailboards; you can play volleyball, dive, and snorkel. Fishing can be arranged. It participates in Jean-Michel Cousteau's Out Island Snorkeling Adventures (see the Outdoor Activities chapter). Rates are US$195 single or double mid-April to mid-December, US$245 the rest of the year. An extra bedroom costs US$100/125, respectively. A MAP plan costs US$65. All-inclusive packages are also offered.

Cape Santa Maria's restaurant is open for three meals daily, but 24-hour reservations are required for visitors at dinner. The resort has its own private airstrip and charters.

STELLA MARIS TO DEAL'S BEACH

Queen's Hwy runs south from Stella Maris along the leeward shore. The beach about 2 miles south of Stella Maris is backed by a 200-year-old cemetery where members of the Knowles family slumber beneath blankets of pine needles. You can snorkel around the island offshore. The cemetery is opposite Knowles Straw Works, just north of Millertons, where you can buy handbags and straw-work at the source from the Handicraft Manufacturing Outlet, which also makes Christmas gifts.

Another mile brings you to 2-mile-long Deal's Beach, where the Stella Maris Resort has a picnic cabaña and open grill, plus sailboats for hotel guests (free transfers are offered twice daily). The snorkeling, over a sea-fan garden, is splendid. You can follow a road east from here to O'Neill's, a tiny hamlet with two beaches that also offer good snorkeling.

Places to Stay & Eat

Sam Knowles has simple rooms at his *O&S Guest House* near Deal's Beach. His *Bayside Restaurant & Bar* serves native dishes.

PND's Candy Kitchen (☎ 242-338-8865), a twee little bar on Deal's Beach, is a cool place to sample Bahamian seafood washed down by a Kalik.

SIMMS

This quaint seaside hamlet is lent charm by its old cottages behind stone walls, dating back to the plantation era. It is dominated by well-kept **St Peter's Anglican Church** and a **Methodist church** across the road. The most endearing structure is a prim little **post office** and, nudging up behind it, an equally diminutive jail still bearing the sign 'HER MAJESTY'S PRISON.'

There's a medical clinic at the south end of Simms.

You can grab a bite to eat and drink at the *Blue Chip* and buy straw-work at Simm's Super Straw, next to the Methodist church.

THOMPSON BAY & McKANN'S

South of Simms, the road moves inland until it touches the shore again at Thompson Bay, about 15 miles south of Stella Maris. The bay is scenic, but far more spectacular is that at McKann's, about half a mile east; turn east at the sign for King's Bay Resort. Here a 200-yard-wide crescent beach is enclosed by low headlands, with a reef about 100 yards offshore. The tall dunes are backed by sea grape and palm and lagoons good for birding. Apparently there's a pirate's treasure cave here; ask Captain Bowe at the Thompson Bay Inn (see below).

Places to Stay & Eat

The roadside *Thompson Bay Inn* (☎ 242-337-1264) is favored by locals. It has eight basic rooms with no furnishings except a double bed and dressing table, with two shared bathrooms down the hall. Rates are US$45/55 single/double (US$5 more for air-con) in the summer, US$5 more in the winter. The hotel offers a fish-fry on Wednesday. It has a dark bar and restaurant, plus a large dance hall with a Ladies' Night on Thursday, happy hour at 7 pm on Saturday, and dancing on weekends. You can also 'enjoy a rollicking game of pool.' Its postal address is PO Box 30133, Thompson Bay, Long Island, Bahamas.

The grandly named *King's Bay Resort* (☎ 242-338-8945) enjoys a fabulous and breezy location atop the dunes on the Atlantic shore. There are eight meagerly furnished rooms; each costs about US$60. It has a large restaurant and bar serving three meals daily (Bahamian fare; typically US$5 to US$10), with a concrete patio overlooking the beach. The place is a bit rundown and gets little business . . . but what a setting for a reclusive no-frills escape! Free airport transfers and a free island tour are offered.

Dorothy Miller operates a *takeout* selling cracked conch and Bahamian specialties.

Getting Around

Captain Bowe at Thompson Bay Inn rents cars for US$65 daily (US$70/75 large sedan/minivan). He'll also take you bone-fishing and on guided cave tours.

SALT POND

Salt Pond, 20 miles south of Stella Maris, is the main commercial node of the island, despite its diminutive size. A small lobster fleet is based here, and a mail boat calls in weekly. When it arrives, islanders from miles around gather for the lively activity. There's a fish-processing plant, a major supply store (Harding's), and a gas station.

Just north of Salt Pond is St Joseph's Anglican Church, enjoying a sublime setting on a ridge above the beach and bone-flats. Break out your camera! You'll be astonished, too, by the sublime coastal vistas along the Atlantic shore. Immediately north of Harding's, a road leads east to the shore. It turns to sand after half a mile, but follow this through the thatch palm and sea grape and it will suddenly deposit you atop a headland, with blush-pink beaches and craggy, untouched shore-line spreading as far as the eye can see. Tall dunes back the shore. You can hike trails that lead south for several miles.

At Pinders, about 2 miles south of Salt Pond, another road (this one in terrible condition) leads to Guana Key, a beautiful, well-protected, shallow bay; Guana Key Island is a short swim offshore. The cay is unique for its semitame curly-tailed lizards, which you can hand-feed. In good weather you can snorkel over the wreck of an old freighter in 15 feet of water.

The highlight of the island's annual calendar is the Long Island Regatta, held at Salt Pond in mid-May. Up to 50 locally built sloops from throughout the islands compete during the festive four-day event, during which copious amounts of rum are consumed and rake 'n' scrape bands play. You can nip aboard the spectator boat for a close-up view of the action. For information, call Raphael Cartwright (☎ 242-393-3949), Larry Cartwright (☎ 242-337-0335), or Margo Harding (☎ 242-338-0333).

Places to Stay & Eat

Reportedly, there's a small roadside guest-house – *Windtryst* – with five air-con rooms, two with a kitchen.

The *Midway Inn*, 3 miles south of Salt Pond, has a fish-fry on Friday.

Getting There & Away

The *Sherice M* mail boat sails from Nassau to Salt Pond at 1 pm Tuesday (17 hours, US$45 one way), also stopping at Seymours and Deadman's Cay.

South Long Island

Deadman's Cay & Vicinity

Pop 1000

Deadman's Cay, 35 miles south of Stella Maris, is Long Island's main settlement and the site of its second airport. It stretches along Queen's Hwy for several miles. To the north is the subdivision of Lower Deadman's Cay, dominated by St Athanatius Church, which dates from 1929. The locals in this middle-class haven like to top their garden walls with cement griffins, lions, and swans. The sound west of Deadman's Cay is superb for bonefishing.

Information There's a Royal Bank of Canada (☎ 242-337-1044) in Lower Deadman's Cay; it's open 9 am to 1 pm Monday to Thursday and 9 am to 5 pm Friday. The Scotiabank branch in Deadman's Cay has similar hours.

There's a BaTelCo office in Deadman's Cay. You can whiten your undies at Cartwright's Laundromat. There's a clinic at the south end of Deadman's Cay.

Things to See History buffs might enjoy the overgrown ruins of **Grays Plantation**, 2 miles north of Lower Deadman's in Grays.

Cartwrights Caves, near the settlement of Cartwrights, immediately south of Deadman's Cay, were once used by Lucayan Indians. Harmless bats now live within the 150-foot-long caves. They're on private property, half a mile east of the main road. You'll see the sign. Leonard Cartwright (☎ 242-337-0235) offers guided tours of the caves for US$5.

Places to Stay & Eat The modest two-story *JB Carroll's Guesthouse*, next to JB Carroll's gas station (☎ 242-337-1048), has six rooms for rent; two have a kitchen.

For native dishes, try the *Dew Drop Inn Restaurant & Bar* (☎ 242-337-0044) at the north end of Deadman's Cay. At the south end, *Snack Corner* sells sandwiches, snacks, and desserts. Ask around for Max in Deadman's, who'll clean fresh-caught conch and prepare it for you for US$5.

Want to hang out with locals? Check out *Moonglow Bar* in Lower Deadman's or the *Twilight Club* (☎ 242-337-1076).

Things to Buy You can buy sponges from Roland Mattardy on Apple Pond Rd in Lower Deadman's, and straw-work and other locally made items from Richie Rich's Gift Shop, which is located between the settlements of Deadman's Cay and Lower Deadman's.

Getting There & Away The airport is between Lower Deadman's and Deadman's Cay, 1 mile east of the Queen's Hwy. It has a snack bar.

Bahamasair flies between Nassau and Deadman's four times weekly via Stella Maris.

The *Sherice M* mail boat sails from Nassau to Deadman's Cay each Tuesday (see the Salt Pond section for details).

Getting Around Gladstone Taylor (☎ 242-337-1055) rents cars at the airport. There's a gas station locaated near JB Carroll's Guesthouse.

Mangrove Bush
Reached from Queen's Hwy by a side road beginning at the Hillside Tavern, 1 mile south of Cartwrights, this fishing hamlet is a center for traditional boatbuilding. Today the wooden vessels are built exclusively for racing regattas, most notably by the descendants of Rupert Knowles, a foremost boatbuilder who died in 1986. His son, Mac, recently built a winner named *Rupert's Legend* in honor of his dad. Another local resident, Laurin Knowles (☎ 242-337-0025), builds boats commercially.

The *Hillside Tavern* (☎ 242-337-1628) is the local place to be. It's full of trophies won in local sailing regattas. There's also an oceanside tavern, *Kooter's Restaurant* (☎ 242-337-0340).

Pettys
This hamlet, 4 miles southeast of Deadman's Cay, has a few sites of interest. Hamilton's Cave is 1500 feet long, one of the largest caves in The Bahamas. It contains bats, stalactites, stalagmites, and a stone walkway with saltwater on one side and fresh water on the other. Leonard Cartwright (☎ 242-337-0235), in Deadman's Cay, offers tours.

You can visit the Natural Products Factory just south of Pettys; it makes 'Mellow Yellow' liqueurs of rum and lime.

The Long Island Library & Museum was scheduled to open by early 1998, with photographs and artifacts (glass bottles and the like) that chronicle the island's history and culture.

Wild Tamarind Pottery & Gallery This pottery studio is a *must see*. It displays the work of Denis Knight, a septuagenarian who came to The Bahamas from England

LONG ISLAND

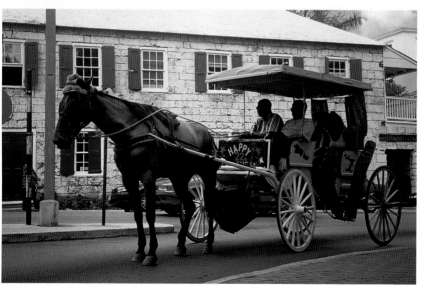

Top Left: Fort Fincastle and downtown Nassau from the water tower
Top Right: Bust of Sir Milo Butler, Rawson Square, Nassau
Bottom: Surrey trip through downtown Nassau

Top: Don Wood – 'carver, sailor, rum-barrel bailer' – finishing a cabinet in Marsh Harbour, Abacos
Bottom Left: Potter Denis Knight at work in the Wild Tamarind Pottery & Gallery on Long Island

Bottom Right: Vert Lowe and one of his shipshape treasures in New Plymouth, Abacos

in the 1960s and became head of the art department at the College of The Bahamas before retiring here. He conjures up exquisite ceramic miniatures of Bahamian cottages and outhouses (US$50 to US$120), as well as mugs, bowls, and vases fired in a propane kiln (or occasionally in an old wood-fired kiln). You can also buy painted sea-urchin shells, Junkanoo figurines, birdhouses shaped like bees' nests, *duhos* (replicas of concave Indian stools and corn-grinding tables), and tiny chickcharnies (US$7), the legendary mischiefmakers of Andros. His works are sold only on-site. Denis is also known throughout The Bahamas for his ceramic murals, which adorn several public buildings.

Denis' wife, Marina Darville, loves to show her marvelous collections of shells and old bottles. Marina was born on Long Island to a family that has lived here for 300 years.

The couple host local children for summer camps at their exquisite home, with inspirational views and a setting described as a 'sanctuary of plum, gumelemi, and wild tamarind.'

You'll see the sign for their place by Queen's Hwy south of town; it's 400 yards up a rocky dirt road.

Places to Stay & Eat *Hamilton's Inn* (☎ 242-337-1264) is a basic eatery that also rents no-frills rooms.

Turtle Cove
This 2-mile-wide bay near Deans, which is about 2 miles southeast of Pettys, is the future site of a hotel, golf course, and marina. It boasts a fabulous beach and turquoise shallows. Its real treasure, however, lies to the southeast beyond a headland, where the world's deepest blue hole (660 feet) leads to the world's eighth-largest underwater cavern. The setting is exquisite, surrounded on three sides by cliffs with a ledge favored by locals for shady snoozing and barbecues. The neck of the aquamarine hole opens to a beautiful cove rimmed by gorgeous white sands. *Magnificent!* Bring a picnic.

The turnoff from Queen's Hwy is marked by a walled double gateway topped by cannonballs. Turtle Cove can also be reached by a shoreline trail from Mangrove Bush, north of Pettys.

Clarence Town
This peaceful harbor town, Long Island's administrative headquarters, has a stupendous setting on a hillside that falls gently to the harbor, where jade-colored flats deepen to Atlantic blues. Two twin-spired mission-style churches rise above the town. St Paul's Anglican Church, on a hill north of town, is accented with red trim and is pretty enough, but it's outshined by its Catholic counterpart on a hill south of town (see below). Ironically, both were designed by Father Jerome, the enigmatic architect-hermit-cleric of Cat Island. The first was designed prior to, and the second after his conversion to Catholicism.

The post office and BaTelCo office are in the government complex (☎ 242-337-3030) on the north side of town. There's a clinic attended by an English doctor.

St Peter's Catholic Church Father Jerome conjured up a visionary confection in stone with this sparkling white church with blue trim, reminiscent of Greece. You can climb the ladders within one of the two medievalist spires for a marvelous bird's-eye view over Clarence Town. Portly folks should forgo the climb; they could get stuck! The church, beside Queen's Hwy, is open all hours.

Lochabar Bay This stunning half-mile-wide, flask-shaped cove, 2 miles southeast of town, is actually a vast blue hole. It is rimmed by a splendid pencil-thin beach, surrounded on three sides by dense thickets of thatch palm and scrub. Coral reefs lie just offshore, with staghorn at 30 feet.

Places to Stay & Eat The all-timber *Lochabar Beach Lodge* (☎ /fax 242-337-0331), a wonderfully lonesome cottage-inn nestling up to Lochabar Bay, is one of the sweetest finds in the Family Islands. This

St Peter's Catholic Church, Clarence Town

modern eatery down by Clarence Town harbor. For a more down-to-earth offering, try *Skieta's OK Bar*, where locals hang out under a shady palapa.

The *Oriental Bakery & Restaurant*, just west of town, specializes in pound cake, pizzas, and hot patties; it's open 6 to 10 am and 6 to 10 pm. It serves Asian cuisine on Wednesday and fresh bread every day.

Getting There & Away American Canadian Caribbean Line's *Niagara Prince* and *Mayan Prince* call at Clarence Town on twice-yearly 12-day cruises between Nassau and the Turks and Caicos. See the Getting There & Away chapter.

Henry Major, the dockmaster, can provide fuel and water for private boaters.

The *Abilin* mail boat sails from Nassau to Clarence Town at noon on Tuesday (17 hours, US$45 one way), also stopping at Great Inagua.

Dunmore to Cape Verde

The southern quarter of Long Island is scenically uninspired, although the 15-mile route leads past three exquisite Father Jerome churches, whitewashed and painted in trademark blue, in Dunmore, Hard Bargain, and Mortimers. The latter looks like it belongs in New Mexico.

It also passes overgrown plantation ruins, such as 'Dunmore,' named for a former governor of The Bahamas, who had an estate producing sisal, cotton, and pineapples. You can follow a dirt track half a mile to the ruined hilltop mansion; look for the gates beside the road just north of the church at Dunmore, about 3 miles southeast of Clarence Town.

Great salt ponds (accessible by side roads) lie hidden from view between the road and west shore. The Diamond Crystal Salt Co produced salt and shrimp here until the 1970s. A Taiwanese company reportedly plans to resurrect shrimping.

Another side road leads to Roses, a quaint hilltop village that overlooks Little Harbour, which Columbus described as 'a very wonderful port with . . . two entrances' created by an island in the middle.

small, utterly charming guesthouse is run by Dick and Dawn Meehan, Floridians for whom Lochabar is also home. They have two bedrooms with private bathroom downstairs (they live upstairs); one sleeps three, and the other sleeps four. One two-bedroom and two single-bedroom cottages were also planned. All are spacious and exquisitely decorated, with homemade furniture, fauxwash wooden walls, tile floors, fully stocked kitchen or kitchenette, and wide French doors that open to a patio facing the bay, which is rippled by near-constant breezes (you also have ceiling fans). The Meehans pamper you like long-lost family. They planned to offer sailboats and dinghies. Rooms cost US$85 single or double nightly, plus US$10 for each extra person; US$525 weekly, plus US$25 per extra person. *Highly recommended!* The mailing address is PO Box N-30330, Clarence Town, Long Island, Bahamas.

The best place to eat is the *Harbour Restaurant, Bar & Satellite Lounge*, a clean,

Income levels decrease progressively to the south, with modern bungalows giving way to mostly clapboard homes and tumbledown emancipation-era houses. The road ends at Gordons, a small, down-at-the-heels hamlet.

From Gordons, you can hike a mile to Cape Verde, which is the island's southernmost point.

Places to Stay & Eat At press time a new resort and 'bonefishing community' was slated to be built on the west coast at Mortimers.

There are several eateries to choose among, including *Carpenter's Arms* in Roses, *Red Door Restaurant* in Cabbage Point, and *Midway Restaurant & Bar* in Mortimers.

Crooked Island District

Crooked Island, Acklins Island, Long Cay, and outlying Samana and Plana cays make up the Crooked Island District. The three principal islands form a rough triangle enclosing the shallow Bight of Acklins – superb for tarpon and bonefish (it was favored by Franklin D Roosevelt) – to the north, east, and west, respectively. By all accounts, Columbus sailed down the leeward side of the islands in 1492, passing through the Crooked Island Passage, which later became a major highway for Spanish treasure fleets. Columbus called the islands the 'Fragrant Isles,' perhaps because of the aromatic scent of the cascarilla tree's bark (also called 'Eleuthera bark').

In the late 18th century the islands, like their northern neighbors, were settled by Loyalists from North America who tried to establish a cotton industry. About 50 plantations were founded, using more than 1000 slaves. By the 1830s depleted soils, weevils, and emancipation doomed the plantations forever. The white landowners left. The black laborers remained and turned to subsistence fishing and farming. Their descendants still fish, tend the land, and draw an income from stripping cascarilla bark and selling it to the manufacturers of Campari liquor (it is also used in medicines). Says one islander: 'Around 'ere everyone get up early to figure out a way to get by. You got to be creative, mon, to make a living 'ere.'

These southerly islands are relatively backward. Electricity still hasn't reached many areas, and tourism is almost nonexistent. But other adventurers come calling: Cubans and Haitians make the desperate run for a new life, and, not infrequently, drug-runners rush in aboard small planes (often approaching against the wind to conceal themselves) to offload bales of cocaine that some locals – despite their God-fearing ways – will disperse to Nassau and abroad. Many locals who, for example, won't eat

HIGHLIGHTS

- A trip to Bird Rock Lighthouse and the Bat Caves
- Shelling at Shell Beach and skinny-dipping at Bathing Beach
- Dining with locals at Ms Gibson's Lunch Room when the mail boat is in
- Diving the Million Dollar Mistake – maybe you'll rustle up some unclaimed money
- Bonefishing in the Bight of Acklins. It doesn't get better than this!

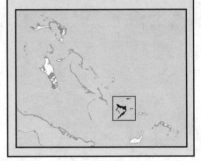

figs because Jesus cursed the fig tree are up to their necks in trafficking because Jesus never spoke out against drugs.

The islanders' idiosyncrasies are related in *Out Island Doctor*, the autobiography of Evans Cottman, a Yankee teacher who fell for the Crooked and Acklins spell in the 1940s and set up here, where he was adopted as a doctor. Many of the adult islanders were youngsters back then and scamper about in various chapters. Locals will tell you that the doctor stretched the truth: ''im spice it up so it sell well . . . he put a lot of tricks in that book.' Cottman, for example, tells deliciously of a judge on Acklins presiding over a divorce case. The judge tells the couple that they should be ashamed. He orders them to take hands. They hesitate. *BLAM!* Down comes the gavel. The lady giggles; the man bows his head. The judge orders them to walk out of the courtroom and continue down the road to their house, where he orders the man to make love to his wife like he used to before they were married; he tells the woman to return the man's love just as she did in the past. The two make haste down the road, picking up speed as they go.

A 50-mile barrier reef rings the entire island chain, offering drop-offs beginning at about 50 feet and plunging to 3600 feet in the Crooked Island Passage. I recommend bringing your own dive equipment.

In summer the mosquitoes are ferocious. Your arrival will be viewed by these ravenous hordes much as you might look upon the arrival of a succulent steak. Bring plenty of repellent.

Crooked Island

Pop 436
Crooked Island, about 250 miles southeast of Nassau, is the main island in the district, although only a few hundred souls inhabit

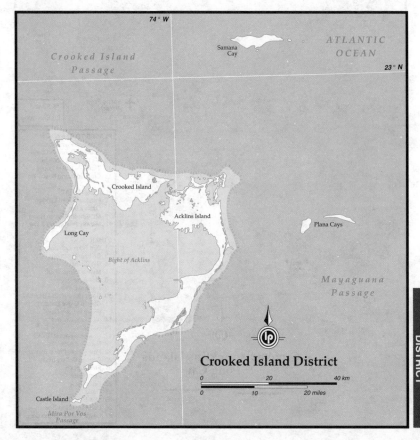

Crooked Island District

Bird Rock
Gun Bluff
Pittstown Point
Gordon's Bluff
Brine Pool
Landrail Point
Turtle Sound
Shell Beach
Cabbage Hill
Church Grove
Bathing Beach
French Wells
Rat & Goat Cays
Major's Cay Harbour
True Blue
Cove Point
Ferry Route
Chesters
Northeast Point
Colonel Hill
Major's Cay
Colonel Hill Airfield
Crooked Island
Lovely Bay
The Going Through
Acklins Island
Albert Town
Long Cay
Ferry Route
Windsor Point
Bight of Acklins
Fish Cay
Guana Cay
Snug Corner
Creek Point
Golden Grove
Spring Point Airfield
Spring Point
Pompey Bay
Jamaica Cay
Roker Cay
Rocky Point
Jim Point
Salinas Point
Salinas Point Settlement
South Bluff
Jamaica Bay
Castle Island
Mira Por Vos Passage

CROOKED ISLAND DISTRICT

Crooked & Acklins Islands & Long Cay

| 0 | 10 | 20 km |
| 0 | 5 | 10 miles |

↴ Fishing
b Snorkeling

PLACES TO STAY
2 Pittstown Point Landing
7 Scavella Bonefish Lodge
8 Ms Gibson's Cottage
13 Three Ps Guest House
16 Crooked Island Beach Inn

PLACES TO EAT
2 Pittstown Point Landing, Ozzie's Bar
8 Ms Gibson's Lunch Room
12 Midway Restaurant & Bar

OTHER
1 Bird Rock Lighthouse
3 Cottman's Cottage
4 Bat Caves
5 Marine Farms (Fort)
6 Mail-Boat Dock
9 Medical Clinic
10 Great Hope House (Ruins)
11 Church Grove Landing (Ferry to Long Cay)
14 All Saints Church
15 BaTelCo
17 St John's Baptist Church
18 Nurse's Office
19 Post Office, Police Station
20 Cannon Battery (Ruins)
21 Ferry Dock
22 Ferry Dock
23 Ferry Dock
24 Clinic
25 Mail-Boat Dock
26 Lucayan Indian Site
27 Castle Island Lighthouse

its 92 sq miles. Most of the population is concentrated in Landrail Point and Colonel Hill, the motley capital.

Locals on several other islands claim brazenly that Columbus landed on their pieces of turf. But Crooked Island, which recent evidence suggests was the explorer's second New World landfall (he named it Santa María de la Concepción after the Virgin Mary), modestly makes no claims. There are no plaques.

The island's irregular shoreline is indented with deep inlets and sounds and lined by beautiful beaches. The main road runs along the north shore. Inland, briny lagoons and swamps cover much of the island. The rest is scrub and dense pockets of woodland that have never been cleared. Bird watchers are in for a treat! Herons, ospreys, egrets, mockingbirds, finches, wild canaries, hummingbirds, and flamingos abound. And lepidopterists can spot approximately 28 endemic subspecies of butterflies. Spring is a good time to visit.

About 60% of the islanders are Seventh-day Adventists (the rest are Baptists and Presbyterians) . . . and a devout lot they are, too! From Friday sundown to Saturday sundown, the island virtually comes to a halt.

COLONEL HILL & VICINITY

The only major settlement flanks a hill midway along the north coast. The scrub-covered plain below slopes down to a bay rimmed by a beach. The village comprises a few dozen ramshackle clapboard huts, emancipation-era houses, and pastel-painted modern concrete homes. The only building of note is the St John's Baptist Church, atop the hill.

The road leads northwest 1.5 miles to the twin settlements of Cabbage Hill and Church Grove, and 2 miles farther, to Cripple Hill. The only buildings of interest in these villages are lime-green All Saints Church, surrounded by *Spathodea* (flame-of-the-forest) in Cabbage Hill, and the small Baptist church, fronted by a tiny bell tower, in Cripple Hill.

From All Saints Church, a hilly dirt road leads southwest to a small ferry dock –

Church Grove Landing – jutting into Turtle Sound, good for bonefishing.

Information

There are no banks in the Crooked Island District. The post office, beside the police station in the administration building in Colonel Hill, may provide basic banking transactions. The BaTelCo station (☎ 242-344-2590) is in Church Grove.

The medical clinic is in Landrail Point (see the Landrail Point & Vicinity section), but there's a nurse in Colonel Hill in the pink building opposite the school, at the base of the village.

The island is policed by a 'great whale of a man' named Constable Elijah (☎ 242-344-2197).

Places to Stay & Eat

Hardy budget travelers might check out Rev Ezekiel Thompson's spartan *Crooked Island Beach Inn* (☎ 242-344-2321), fronting a tiny beach half a mile east of Colonel Hill. It has six dark, meagerly furnished rooms, each with ceiling fan and shared bathrooms. Some have three beds. It's vastly overpriced at US$50/60 single/double (no credit cards). Meals, including breakfast, are offered by prearrangement.

The *Three Ps Guest House*, a cramped and dour place in Cabbage Hill, charges US$60 triple. There's a shared kitchen.

The *Midway Restaurant & Bar*, in Cabbage Hill, serves native lunches and dinners. You can buy groceries at the *Cabbage Hill Supermarket*, next to the *T&S Guest House* (☎ 242-336-2096), which was not open at press time.

Getting There & Away

The airfield is located 1.5 miles east of Colonel Hill.

Bahamasair offers flights between Nassau and Colonel Hill on Tuesday and Saturday (US$84 one way), also stopping at Acklins Island. Charter airlines also fly to Colonel Hill.

A small passenger ferry runs between Church Grove Landing and Albert Town (Long Cay) on Wednesday and Saturday.

CROOKED ISLAND DISTRICT

Getting Around

You can negotiate a car rental with locals, any of whom will also run you about for a small fee. Rev Ezekiel Thompson (see Places to Stay & Eat, above) rents cars for US$60 to US$80 per day, plus deposit. There are no taxis.

LANDRAIL POINT & VICINITY

Pop 50

This hamlet, 9 miles northwest of Colonel Hill, has a teeny harbor where the mail boat calls, announcing its arrival with two blasts of the horn. Then the entire town comes to a halt, and the enthusiastic islanders hop aboard before the vessel has had time to tether.

A sandy 4WD track leads north 1.5 miles to Pittstown Point, the northwestern tip of the island. Most local sites of interest are here.

Information

There's a medical clinic in Landrail Point. The local phone booth is at Ms Gibson's Lunch Room (☎ 242-344-2676). She'll time your call on a stopwatch!

Bird Rock Lighthouse

Crooked's most impressive site is a small, coral-encrusted, sand-edged cay a mile offshore from Pittstown Point. It is pinned by a stately 115-foot-tall lighthouse dating from 1876, erected to guide ships through the treacherous Crooked Island Passage. The rusting and partially decayed lighthouse – also known as the Crooked Island Passage Light – today struggles against the elements. The old Fresnel lens was long ago replaced by a modern battery-operated lantern. Alas, scores of disused car batteries lie scattered over the coral cay and inside the lighthouse, too, leaking their acid to God knows what harmful effect.

The cay is a prime nesting colony for snowy white terns and tropicbirds, which caterwaul a welcome to visitors. Fabulous shells are sprinkled about.

The cay is a five-minute boat ride from Pittstown Point.

Gun Bluff

The overgrown ruins of a British fort stand atop this shoreline bluff, just east of Pittstown Point. There's a quarry where the stone for Bird Rock Lighthouse was extracted. And Evans Cottman built his **octagonal home** beside the shore here.

You can hike or drive a 4WD vehicle to the bluff. Follow the track that leads from Landrail Point to Pittstown Point; at the Y-fork take the sandy trail to the right.

Bat Caves

These caves are 100 yards inland from the shore near Gordon's Bluff, 2 miles east of Pittstown Point. A small entrance opens to vast vaulted chambers linked by high tunnels. They're easily explored, and the walking is level. Some of the walls are festooned with mosses, and there are stalactites in the depths. Land crabs find the cool retreats accommodating, and bats squint down from their rooftop perches. The bats slumber by day inside the bell-shaped hollows that pit the ceiling. Take mosquito repellent; clouds of ravenous insects lick their proboscises at your approach, especially after heavy rains.

Brine Pool

This amoeba-shaped lagoon, stretching from Landrail Point north to Pittstown Point, is separated from the sea by a narrow tombolo (sandspit beach), along whose shore several expats have built modest homes. In years past the pool produced salt for export. Today stilt-legged waders pick in the shallows. Ducks paddle atop the glistening surface. Ospreys police the scene with sharp eyes. In summer flamingos sometimes flock from Long Cay, arriving about sunset and returning to Long Cay shortly after dawn.

Marine Farms, a salt farm on an island in the midst of the pond, has a long history. It began life as a cotton plantation and – amazingly – a Spanish or British fort (depending on whom you talk to) that is said to have managed a firefight with US warships in the War of 1812. Cannon can still be seen lying amid the ruins and salt pans.

Great Hope House
This mansion, about a mile south of Landrail Point, was once the centerpiece of a 19th-century plantation. The ruins are today embraced by towering jumby trees, blooming sage brushes, periwinkle vines, and scrub. It's a 30-minute hike along an overgrown track.

Shell Beach & Bathing Beach
These aptly named beauties stretch south from Landrail Point for 7 miles to **French Wells** at the southwestern tip of Crooked. The waters off Bathing Beach, as shallow and limpid as a spa pool, are known as the 'World's Largest Swimming Pool.' Snorkeling is divine, with fabulous coral heads just below the water. Alas, sharks are often present.

Activities
Robbie Gibson's Thunderbird Charters (c/o the marina ☎ 242-344-2676; c/o Gibson's wife at the BaTelCo office 242-344-2590) offers fishing for US$300/500 half-/full day for up to six people; he immodestly proclaims himself 'the best bonefishing guide in the world' after a few drinks. Elton 'Bonefish Shakey' McKinney also guides for US$140/240 half-/full day.

Gibson offers scuba diving for US$35 per dive and rents scuba gear (mask and snorkel, US$5; flippers, US$5; regulator, US$10).

Places to Stay
Daisy Scavella's *Scavella Bonefish Lodge* (☎ 242-344-2598) is a simple yet endearing little guesthouse facing the harbor in Landrail Point. The deep-turquoise building, which dates from 1884, has two sparsely furnished rooms downstairs, each with two beds and ceiling fans, for US$50/75 single/double. The upstairs room has six beds and dormer windows. There's a kitchen if you wish to cook meals

for yourself. The lodge also has several boats for bonefishing.

Ms Marina Gibson (☎ 242-344-2676) has a two-bedroom, one-bathroom *cottage* in Landrail Point, with wood paneling and hot and cold water. It costs US$75 per person, including three meals daily served at her restaurant across the road (see below).

Pittstown Point Landing (☎ 242-344-2507, VHF channel 16; in North America ☎ 704-878-8724, 800-752-2322, fax 704-881-0771) is a rare jewel in the rough, magnificently located at the northwestern tip of the island, with views toward Bird Rock Lighthouse. Cottages shaded by coconut palms and decorated in tropical pastels sit amid landscaped lawns edging up to a splendid beach. The 12 spacious, gleaming-white rooms are in four squat bungalows; they get hot, despite ceiling fans. Each room is sparsely furnished with two queen-size beds and large closets. Rooms cost US$85/95/105/115 single/double/triple/quad December 1 to mid-April. Ask about meal-plan rates.

There's a handsome little bar and restaurant, decorated with fishermen's nets. It has all-around windows through which breezes ease. Pittstown is totally laid-back, thanks to Cindy Lee Bates, the delightful, pixieish manager. The place has been splendidly restored since a devastating fire in 1995. Diving, snorkeling, sand volleyball, bicycles, and boat rental are offered. The kitchen was Crooked Island's first post office and, according to some accounts, a barracks during the 18th century for the nearby British fortress.

Places to Eat
Much of the local chit-chat occurs at *Ms Gibson's Lunch Room* (☎ 242-344-2676), or 'Mama's Kitchen,' an island institution that fills up when the mail boat calls. It's a teeny place with one long table for family-style dining. It's run by one of the nation's Distinguished Citizens (that's official), who – ably assisted by her daughter Willie – serves peas 'n' rice, fried fish, lobster, and

johnny cake. Dishes cost US$10 and up; a full meal costs US$20. There's no conch! The matriarch is a faithful Seventh-day Adventist and therefore considers the sea creature unclean. There's no alcohol, either . . . but you can bring your own. Call for reservations.

Pittstown Point Landing restaurant and on-site *Ozzie's Bar* are open daily and serve tasty native Bahamian fare. You'll need reservations for dinner. Locals call by for a takeout meal or to drink. You can also buy homemade bread for US$3.50 per loaf.

Getting There & Away

Pittstown Point Landing features its own 2000-foot airstrip, charging a US$5 landing fee, plus US$2 per day tie-down. It offers charter service to and from Nassau (US$670 for up to five passengers). On Thursday, when the plane makes its grocery run to Nassau, you can book individual seats for US$120 per person.

The *Lady Mathilda* mail boat sails from Nassau weekly (US$70 one way). Call the Potter's Cay dockmaster (☎ 242-393-1064) in Nassau for departure times. The boat also stops at Acklins Island and Maya-guana. It can sleep 50 passengers in saunalike bunkrooms with diminutive windows. The quasi-dining-room consists of two small tables with benches almost inside the engine room. Onboard conversation has been described as competing with 'a 100-ton truck dragging a heavy chain across a rocky road.'

Getting Around

Robbie Gibson (see the Activities section) will take you sightseeing by boat; he typically charges US$200/400 for a half-/ full-day trip.

There's a gas station in Landrail Point.

COLONEL HILL TO COVE POINT

East of Colonel Hill, the road follows the north shore 3 miles to **Major's Cay**, a weeny hamlet facing a magnificent flask-shaped boneflat with turquoise-jade waters rimmed by a narrow yet splendid beach.

Farther east, the road fades to dirt, growing steadily narrower until the scrub brushes up against the car. Just when you are convinced that you should turn around, the track deposits you at Cove Point, the tip of Crooked Island, 10 miles east of Major's Cay. There's nothing at this point but a tiny concrete wharf where the ferry for Acklins Island departs twice daily (see the Acklins Island section for details), as well as a two-seat outhouse.

There are no services east of the settlement of Colonel Hill.

Long Cay

Pop 30

This small island hangs like a wattle below Crooked Island, from which it is separated by a mile-wide channel. Columbus, it seems, landed here on October 19, 1492, in search of an 'island or city' named Saomete and ruled by a king rich in gold. The explorer named the island Isabela after the Spanish queen.

The island was later known as Fortune Island (it is still shown on charts as such, though few Bahamians know it by that name) and once boasted thriving sponging and salt industries. In the 19th century Long Cay was also used as the central Royal Mail station for mail traveling between England and the Caribbean.

Flamingos wade in the bight on the south side of the island. In summer they migrate – often daily – between Long Cay and Crooked Island. And an endemic sub-species of iguana inhabits two tiny cays that lie 7 and 10 miles southeast of Long Cay: Fish Cay and Guana Cay.

In the 19th century **Albert Town** (also called 'Windsor'), the island's only settlement, was the main base in the archipelago for transatlantic mail and freight ships hiring and dropping off stevedores, or 'coast crew.' The port town was lively with bars and, presumably, illicit brothels. In the

20th century the town's population fell from 3000 to just 30 people. Wild goats have taken over the intriguing ruins, though the largest Anglican church south of Nassau still stands.

Albert Town still has a clinic and post office, although they may be closed by the time you visit. Stephen Rose has a small grocery and acts as a bonefishing guide.

Million Dollar Mistake
This famous plane wreck lies in 12 feet of water about 50 yards offshore. The plane was on a drug run when it crashed at sea. Locals found a suitcase containing about US$1,000,000. It was handed to an official from Nassau who, it seems, pocketed the money and went on to live the life of Riley.

Places to Stay & Eat
There's talk that a Canadian company was planning to build a marina and resort with an airstrip. Meanwhile, Steven Rolles has a basic *guesthouse*.

Ruth May will prepare food with advance notice.

Getting There & Away
Robbie Gibson (c/o the marina ☎ 242-344-2676; c/o his wife at the BaTelCo office 242-344-2590) will take you to Long Cay by boat from Landrail Point (30 minutes, about US$100). He also includes Long Cay on a full-day sightseeing trip for US$400 that includes the Million Dollar Mistake, the flamingos, the settlement of Arthur Town, beachcombing on Shell Beach, and a picnic (you'll cook conch and fish that you've collected or speared yourself).

Acklins Island

Pop 428
Decidedly undeveloped and offbeat Acklins is separated from Crooked Island by a shallow passage called 'The Going Through.'

Acklins, recent evidence has suggested, is the second island by which Columbus passed in the New World. Columbus never actually set foot here, however, but continued to Crooked Island, his second true landfall.

The 45-mile-long island tapers southwest. It is low and sandy, except to the north and along the east coast, which is hilly and rugged areas. It is mostly covered by scrub.

Reefs lie offshore to the east, and there are fabulous and lonesome beaches along the shore. To the west, the bight extends for miles; bonefish gather in vast schools near shore, and catching 'em is a no-brainer. Bonefishing has come late to the island, which in 1997 saw the opening of two bonefishing lodges and the arrival of the first tourists.

Many of the local residents still rely on fishing and beating bark for Campari. Public electricity still had not arrived in 1997 (although plenty of homes have a small generator). And most people still use public wells for their water source; to bathe, most locals dip water from barrels. Alas, some wells are polluted by modern effluents that are poured onto the ground and leach into the soil.

The main settlement is **Spring Point**, midway down the west coast. A rugged dirt road leads north to the smaller settlements of Snug Corner, 12 miles from Spring Point, and Chesters, at the northern tip of Acklins. The road runs 20 miles south from Spring Point to Roker Cay.

A partially excavated Lucayan Indian site along the shore of Pompey Bay, immediately south of Spring Point, may have been the largest Lucayan settlement in The Bahamas. The only other site of interest here is the remote Castle Island Lighthouse, erected in 1867 at the southern tip of the island, near tiny, landlocked Salinas Point Settlement.

The annual Acklins Homecoming & Regatta is usually held during the first weekend in August.

Information
There's a public telephone in Chesters. There are medical clinics in Chesters and Spring Point, and there's a nurse in Mason's Bay.

Places to Stay & Eat
Two bonefishing lodges were to open by the end of 1997: *Gray Point Bonefish Lodge* in Pine Field and another in Snug Corner. A *scuba-diving resort* with eight rooms was slated to open by 1998 in Pine Field.

Locals gather at Curtis Hanna's *Airport Inn & Restaurant*, in Spring Point, with two rooms with ceiling fans and shared bathroom. Native dishes cost about US$6.

Getting There & Away
The airfield is immediately northeast of Spring Point. Bahamasair has flights from Nassau via Crooked Island on Tuesday and Saturday.

American Canadian Caribbean Line's *Mayan Prince* and *Niagara Prince* cruise ships stop here twice yearly during Nassau-to-Providenciales cruises; see the Getting There & Away chapter.

The government runs a free passenger ferry from Cove Point (Crooked Island) to Lovely Bay, 3 miles west of Chesters, at 8 am and 4 pm daily except Sunday, returning at 8:30 am and 4:30 pm.

The *Lady Mathilda* mail boat calls at Spring Point weekly from Nassau (see the Landrail Point & Vicinity section for details).

Getting Around
Leon Cooper (☎ 242-344-3534) acts as a local guide and may rent his car. Ethelyn Bain (☎ 242-344-3628) also has a car for rent.

Samana Cay

This uninhabited cay, 25 miles north of Acklins Island, still fits Columbus' description of the island that welcomed the explorer to the New World in 1492: 'quite large . . . flat . . . green . . . [with] many waters' and white cliffs facing south. The island's claim has been hotly disputed for two centuries (see the sidebar), but in 1986 a National Geographic Society field study concluded that Samana should wear the first-landfall crown. If the claim is true, the *Niña*, *Pinta*, and *Santa María* anchored on Samana's southwest side, at a spot where the reef opens. Columbus explored inside the reef in a rowboat and recorded the features of the island that he named San Salvador.

Archaeological digs led by the National Geographic Society have unearthed at least 10 Lucayan Indian sites (along with a Spanish earthenware vessel) and an ancient causeway of conch shells. With luck, *zemi* religious figures, shards of pottery, and other Indian mementos may yet be found.

Crooked and Acklins islanders visit seasonally to crab by torchlight and to collect conch meat and cascarilla bark. Otherwise no one has claimed the isle or settled it in the more than 500 years since Columbus landed.

The First Landfall

No one disputes that Columbus' first landfall was in The Bahamas (except residents of the Turks and Caicos). But the question of *which* island has aroused considerable controversy. Several islands claim the prize.

Columbus and the priest-historian Bartolomé de las Casas kept assiduous records, but, much to historians' regret, no evidence exists to prove where Columbus *first* stepped ashore. (The original record vanished after being dispatched to Queen Isabella.) Investigators have spent centuries sleuthing for clues to put the argument to rest.

Nine first landfalls have been proposed and defended. Today's Samana Cay was strongly favored at an early stage, but in 1942 Admiral Samuel Eliot Morison, a noted biographer of Columbus, declared that Watling Island (which was renamed San Salvador – the name that Columbus

Christopher Columbus

bestowed on his first landfall – in 1926) was the hallowed island. Watling Island was accepted for years as the first landfall, although, incredibly, no one had taken into account 'dead reckoning' – the cumulative effect of current and leeway (wind-caused slippage) on a vessel's course – in tracing the route of the round-bottomed fleet. Yet Columbus' course took him along the southern half of the North Atlantic gyre, a then-undiscovered slow clockwise swirl of winds and currents that sweeps in a southwestern direction from the Madeira Islands to The Bahamas.

In November 1986, following five years of extensive study by Joseph Judge and a team of scholarly interests under the aegis of the National Geographic Society, *National Geographic* magazine announced that it had solved the 'grandest of all geographic mysteries.' Judge ordered a new translation of the Columbus diaries, drew the first-ever track of the log, then input all the variables into a computer to adjust for leeway, current, and magnetic variation, and traveled to the islands to find actual evidence. See the Columbus' First Landfall map in the Facts about The Bahamas chapter for a comparison of Judge's and Morison's proposed tracks.

The Judge team was also the first to track Columbus' course using the Spanish league (2.82 nautical miles), *not* the English league (2.5 nautical miles) previously used. *Presto!* The *exact* landing spot turns out to be latitude 23°09'00"N and longitude 73°29'13"W . . . the island of Samana Cay. ∎

Plana Cays

This string of small cays, beginning 15 miles east of Acklins Island, is a protected reserve for the endangered hutia, The Bahamas' only endemic mammal. An estimated 5000 hutias survive here in splendid isolation. No dogs are allowed ashore.

Amazing Grace, the supply ship for Windjammer Barefoot Cruises' sailing fleet, calls on Plana Cays during its twice-monthly island-hopping voyages between Grand Bahama and Trinidad. American Canadian Caribbean Line's *Mayan Prince* and *Niagara Prince* cruise ships also stop here during their island-hopping trips. See the Getting There & Away chapter for details.

CROOKED ISLAND DISTRICT

Inaguas & Mayaguana

Great Inagua, suspended just above Cuba and Haiti, 325 miles from Nassau and virtually off the tourist map, is the southernmost Bahamian island and a tremendous offbeat escape. Little Inagua is a diminutive isle to its northeast. Mayaguana, the easternmost and one of the most lonesome of Bahamian islands, is 50 miles east of Acklins Island and 50 miles northwest of Providenciales (Turks and Caicos).

HIGHLIGHTS

- Taking a fascinating tour of Morton Salt Works
- Counting flamingos in Inagua National Park
- Volunteering at the marine turtle research station at Union Creek Reserve
- Bunking at Camp Arthur Vernay in the midst of Inagua National Park

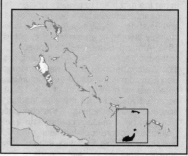

Great & Little Inagua

Great Inagua, 20 miles north to south at its widest and 35 miles east to west, is a parched limestone platform that narrows to the northeast. Uninhabited Little Inagua lies to the northeast.

Great Inagua's interior is covered in brush and cactus, with vast acres of exceedingly briny lakes. Though the trade winds blow here strongly and consistently, the island is scorchingly hot. About half of Great Inagua lies within Inagua National Park, protecting the hemisphere's largest flock of West Indian flamingos. The eastern two-thirds of the island are inaccessible except by arduous trek. There is only one settlement: Matthew Town, once a major seaport and trading center, which retains much of its rugged charm.

The human population is outnumbered five to one by wild horses and burros. By day they stay in the brush, wandering into the open at night to evade the mosquitoes, which don't breed in the brine lakes (in former years the mosquito plague was so bad that to escape it, the burros would wade up to their necks in the ocean). The burros are said to be descended from wild asses sent here laden with gold by Henri Christopher, the Haitian revolutionary, when France attempted to retake that island in 1802. Locals say the treasure is still

buried here. But in truth the burros were simply imported as beasts of burden.

Great Inagua's human settlement was financed and supported by salt. 'Crystal farming' was initiated in the late 18th century and the island became a major salt exporter. For the tale of salt and Great Inagua, read *Great Inagua* by Margery O Erickson (Capriole Press, New York).

By the turn of the 20th century the island's population exceeded 5000 people. Great Inagua also became a pony-breeding center; the Hamburg Steamship Line even brought monied Europeans to play polo! During the early 20th century, merchant vessels called in at Matthew Town to pick up coast crew, draining the population during a period when salt production was in decline.

In 1935 three Yankee brothers – the Ericksons – revived salt processing and

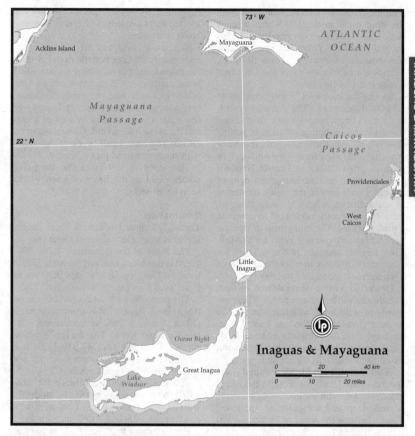

Inaguas & Mayaguana

began its mechanization. The industry was boosted during WWII by attempts to extract magnesium (a highly flammable metal) from brine. In 1954 the Ericksons' West Indian Chemical Company was bought by the Morton Salt Company, which still pretty much runs the island. Today Morton produces about 1 million tons of salt a year locally. Most is bulk-shipped for the industrial and chemical markets, for highway de-icing, and for northern European fisheries. The vast mountains of salt change hue throughout the day; they turn pastel-pink and even

purple at dawn and dusk. It makes you pine for a glass of water! Great Inagua, how-ever, has no potable water supply; water is currently shipped in aboard Morton's M/S *Cecile Erickson* salt freighter and distrib-uted by truck.

Lying only 50 miles north of Cuba and Haiti (Great Inagua is closer to both coun-tries than to its nearest Bahamian neigh-bor), the island sometimes sees refugees washing ashore. Great Inagua's southern-most position makes it a prime piece of real estate for drug-runners heading in from Colombia and other drug-producing nations. So many islanders profited from the drug trade in the 1980s that when a policeman became overzealous, locals burned down the police station and took him hostage. A riot squad was flown in. Things are calmer now that the US Coast Guard has a facility here.

So why the heck visit? Firstly, how about 50,000 flamingos? (The locals say 'fil-amingos.') Great Inagua's success in saving its resident flamingo population is putting the island on the map. In season – November through June – the birds can be seen in great flocks in Inagua National Park, strutting around like prima donnas, dabbling their toes in the water, clustering in great flocks, wheeling in to land, or, most magnificently, taking off en masse in a pink blizzard. The birds mate in December and January and nest February to April. They migrate annually to Cuba. There are other rare birds, too, to whet the appetite of even the most jaded bird watcher.

Hawksbill turtles come ashore to nest. Freshwater turtles inhabit ponds. There are plenty of wild boar, which the locals like to hunt (foreign visitors are barred from hunting). And the saltworks make an interesting study. There are few beaches. Sport fishing and scuba diving are embryonic.

When novelist Ian Fleming visited Great Inagua in the 1950s, he thought the island quite strange, with its lake 'only a couple of feet deep and the color of a corpse.' Thus it became the home of Dr No, the villain of the first James Bond film.

MATTHEW TOWN
Pop 1200
The island's only town is one of the largest, wealthiest, and most sophisticated settlements in the Family Islands, despite its unfavorable locale. It has been described as having 'the air of an Australian mining camp.' An Australian mining camp mellowed, perhaps, by money and age, and populated by more Godly residents – on any night, at least one of its fistful of churches is sure to be ringing out hymns – and an equal number of cockerels and hens. Just about every family in town is

supported by brine, specifically by the Morton Salt Company, which runs Matthew Town as its own.

The town, laid out in a large grid, endearingly features both modern US-style bungalows and old two-story whitewashed houses with green shuttered windows. One building stands out: the gleaming-white, two-story colonial structure on Gregory St (the main street), topped by a clock tower and housing the island Commissioner's Office. There's a small beach to the south, with shade trees and picnic benches.

The scoop in 1997 was that the noisy power plant in the heart of town would soon be moved.

Information
There's no tourist office. A local named David Hanna sells videos of Great Inagua.

The Bank of the Bahamas (☎ 242-339-1264) is one block north of the Main House hotel on Gregory St; it's open 9:30 am to 2 pm weekdays except Wednesday.

The post office (☎ 242-339-1248) is on the ground floor of the Commissioner's Office. Public telephone booths are scattered around town. The BaTelCo office (☎ 242-339-1000, fax 242-339-1323) is a half-mile north of the town's center; it's open 9 am to 5:30 pm weekdays.

The Erickson Public Library (☎ 242-339-1863), on Gregory St, is modestly stocked. It's open 10 am to 1 pm weekdays and 9 am to 1 pm and 3 to 7 pm Saturday.

Edna Barbes (☎ 242-339-1284) takes in laundry.

The medical clinic (☎ 242-339-1249) has a doctor and a nurse. It's housed in a building dating from 1904 on Victoria St between Cartwright and Meadows Sts.

The police station (☎ 242-339-1444) is on Gregory St, 200 yards north of the Main House.

Erickson Museum
This small museum, next to the library on Gregory St, is dedicated to the island's history and especially Morton's part in it. There's a simple re-creation of the saltworks, with salt samples, plus fascinating

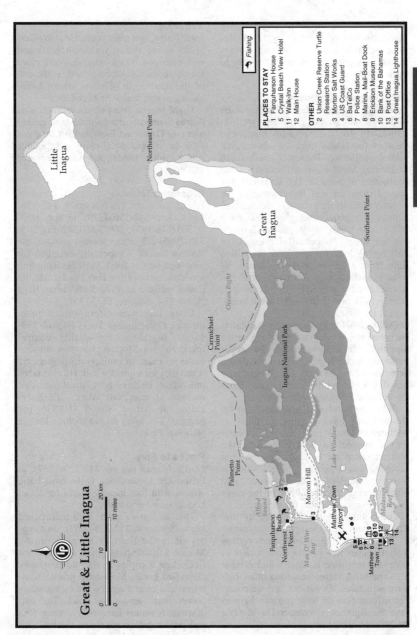

PLACES TO STAY
1 Farquharson House
5 Crystal Beach View Hotel
11 Walk-Inn
12 Main House

OTHER
2 Union Creek Reserve Turtle
  Research Station
3 Morton Salt Works
4 US Coast Guard
6 BaTelCo
7 Police Station
8 Marina, Mail-Boat Dock
9 Erickson Museum
10 Bank of the Bahamas
13 Post Office
14 Great Inagua Lighthouse

Fishing

profiles on salt production and native fauna, including the life cycle of flamingos. You can visit during library hours (see above); ask the librarian to open it for you.

Great Inagua Lighthouse

Be sure to climb the steep, winding stairs of this gleaming-white lighthouse (☎ 242-339-1370) for the splendid bird's-eye view of the island from the observation platform at the top. The tower, a mile south of central Matthew Town, occupies the southernmost point in The Bahamas. It's one of three ancient lighthouses in the country that feature a rotating mechanism, similar to a grandfather clock, that must be wound by hand every 90 minutes throughout the night. Its beautiful Fresnel (or bull's-eye) lens focuses and magnifies light from a kerosene vapor lantern; its light is visible up to 20 miles offshore. It's splendidly preserved by the keeper, who lives in one of two sextagonal buildings at the base.

Oddly, a Victorian-era wooden bathtub is anchored atop the lighthouse, along with a pipe to collect rainwater; does the keeper bathe up here? It gets darned windy up here, too – hang on tight! On an especially fine day, Cuba can be seen temptingly on the horizon, 50 miles to the south.

Below the lighthouse, note the cut in the shore where a noisy generator turns an Archimedes screw that 'pumps' seawater into a channel to be conveyed to the Morton salt pans. Pelicans may be seen scooping fish from the channel, which is often chockful of shad, barracuda, and other species. Locals gather in the early evening to cast their nets for supper.

The lighthouse is fighting for its life. The Bahamas' Port Dept plans to automate it. The Bahamas Lighthouse Preservation Society hopes to sway the government to save this maritime landmark and elevate it to the same status accorded other historic structures. Donations are welcome. For information on how you can help to save the lighthouse, contact David Gale (☎ 242-366-0282).

Activities

Isaac Cartwright rents boats. He also offers scuba diving (bring your own gear) and will take you bonefishing. A good place for snorkeling is Alfred Sound, at the end of the road north of town, where bonefishing is also said to be excellent.

Great Inagua Tours offers snorkeling at Alfred Sound as part of a three-hour guided tour (see Organized Tours, below). At press time the company had plans to introduce scuba diving, bonefishing, and deep-sea fishing.

Organized Tours

Island Vacations (in Nassau ☎ 242-356-1111, fax 242-356-4379; in the USA ☎ 305-748-1833, 800-900-4242, fax 305-748-1965) offers an escorted ecotour, the 'Inagua Safari' – especially designed for bird watchers – for US$1999, including roundtrip airfare from Fort Lauderdale. Its postal address is 4372 Reflections Blvd N, No 104, Sunrise, FL 33351.

Larry Ingraham offers guided tours through Great Inagua Tours (☎ 242-339-1862). Ingraham, the quality control inspector for Morton, has two 40-seat buses to cater to cruise-ship passengers when they infrequently call. He also takes individuals on three-hour island tours that include Morton Salt Works and snorkeling at Alfred Sound (US$35 per person). The tours do not include Inagua National Park.

Places to Stay

Ford's Inagua Inn (☎ 242-339-1277), at Prison and Victoria Sts, is the most basic option, with four meager rooms for about US$40 single or double.

The endearing and well-maintained *Main House* (☎ 242-339-1267), on Gregory St in the heart of town, is run by Morton Salt Company. There are six rooms (including a triple) in the old two-story clapboard home. Most have private bathrooms and central air-con fed by the noisy power plant across the road. The two downstairs rooms have only ceiling fans and private bathrooms down the hall. All rooms are spacious and adequately furnished, albeit with dated furniture. Bathrooms are clean and large with plenty of fluffy towels and – taking Bahamian religiosity to extremes – Gideon's Bibles in the loos! Meals were not being served at press time, but this may change. A small room costs US$45 single or double; a large room is US$60 single, double, or triple. No credit cards are accepted.

Main House also has a splendidly furnished two-story guesthouse nearby. Alas, it's for company executives and the like . . . definitely not for the traveling hoi polloi. An exception may be made for groups.

A more modern option is Kirk and Eleanor Walkine's *Walk-Inn* (☎ 242-339-1612), on Gregory St at the corner of Maud St. This sky-blue building has five well-maintained rooms, all with crisp, attractive decor, pin-neat bathrooms, and modern furniture, including TV. Light is limited by small windows. Rooms with two single/two double beds cost US$55/65; credit cards aren't accepted.

The *Pour-More Motel* (☎ 242-339-1361), on Kortwright St, planned to open by the end of 1997 with five air-con rooms, all with tile floors, private bathroom, and TV. They promise to be handsome but won't have much light. There's a restaurant, plus a bar with two pool tables. Rooms will cost US$60 to US$80, depending on size. The mailing address is PO Box 27, Matthew Town, Great Inagua, Bahamas.

The Colombian-owned *Crystal Beach View Hotel* (☎ 242-339-1550, fax 242-339-1670) is north of central Matthew Town, and it is the only beachside hotel. This modern structure has 14 pleasant albeit modestly furnished rooms for rent. There is also a TV lounge and restaurant on the premises.

Ezzard Cartwright (☎ 242-339-1362) also has self-catering beachside efficiencies for rent – *Sunset Apartments* – south of town.

Great Inagua Lighthouse

Places to Eat

Great Inagua is a bit of a culinary wasteland. Most fare is fried. Health food hasn't yet made it here, and since few locals make an income from the sea, don't expect a wide seafood menu. Vegetables are rare. Even peas 'n' rice is hard to come by. At least there's no shortage of salt.

Topp's Restaurant (☎ 242-339-1465/1293), on Astwood St between Albert and Russell Sts, is run by a happy-go-lucky fella named Cleveland Palacious. For breakfast, try pig's-feet souse or eggs and toast for US$5; for lunch or dinner, you can get okra soup and grouper or conch and fries for US$5.

Alternately, try *Traveller's Rest*, alias 'The Pit,' at Meadows and Victoria Sts. It serves basic, uninspired fare: conch fritters, grouper, and hamburgers, all with fries, for US$5. Similarly, there's *Cozy Corner*, on North St, which opens at 10 am. There's also *Last Stop Take-Away*, at Meadows and Russell Sts, where you can get good soup for US$5 (takeout only).

INAGUAS & MAYAGUANA

The *Morton Company Store*, on Gregory St, is well stocked (it absolutely will not accept US$100 bills). A *market* is held intermittently by the beach.

Entertainment
The place to hang out is *Traveller's Rest*, where the music is loud, the satellite TV is always on, and a pool table keeps locals amused. Decor is enhanced by subdued red lighting. It hops on weekends. *Topp's* is a less moody place with a jukebox and dartboard as well as satellite TV.

Alternatives include the *After Work Bar*, down by the shore on Gregory St at the foot of Astwood St. It has a pool table.

Things to Buy
You'll find a small array of local crafts at Sislyn Gift Corner at the corner of Victoria and Mortimer Sts, and at BBB's Souvenirs on Nesbit St, one block inland from Gregory St.

Getting There & Away
The airport is 2 miles north of town. It has a telephone but no other facilities.

Bahamasair has service between Nassau and Matthew Town Monday, Tuesday, Wednesday, and Friday (US$120 one way). The local office (☎ 242-339-1415) is on Gregory St at the foot of Astwood St.

Private pilots must clear immigration (☎ 242-339-1602) at the airport.

Private boaters can berth at the well-protected marina in town. You'll need to clear immigration; there's an office (☎ 242-339-1271) next to the Commissioner's Office on Gregory St.

The *Abilin* mail boat sails here from Nassau at noon Tuesday (17 hours, US$45 one way), stopping first at Clarence Town (Long Island).

Getting Around
There's no bus service on Great Inagua. Rocklyn 'Rockie' Barbes (☎ 242-339-1284) acts as an unofficial taxi driver in his beat-up old Yankee car that he drives at about 15 mph.

You can rent single-gear bicycles for US$10 daily from Bertram Ingraham at Ingraham's Variety Store (☎ 242-339-1232) on Kortwright St. At press time Bertram had plans to rent cars for US$60 a day. But with barely 30 miles of road on the island, what's the point?

NORTH OF MATTHEW TOWN
The paved road turns to dirt 2 miles north of Matthew Town. About 2 miles farther on, you pass between vast briny flats, the southernmost of the Morton Salt Works' mirrorlike salt pans, which are contained by dikes that connect them to equally briny natural lakes. Farther north, the dirt road passes sporadic beaches, the ruins of an old sisal plantation, and an abandoned Loyalist settlement.

About 4 miles north of Morton Salt Works, the road ends at Farquharson Beach, lining Albert Sound, a protected bay and a prime snorkeling and bonefishing spot where the abandoned US Aerostat station is located. Breakers crash over the coral reef about a mile from shore. A turnoff here leads east – inland – to the Union Creek Reserve (see the reserve's section in this chapter).

Morton Salt Works
This facility is the second-largest solar saline plant in North America. It comprises 34,000 acres of reservoirs and salt pans surrounding a cleaning, storage, and bulk-freight loading facility.

Seawater drains into canals that feed the lagoons (the canals teem with barracuda, lobster, and bonefish), which spread inland for miles, separated by low dikes that channel brine between the vast flats. As water circulates, algae (fostered by flamingo droppings) grow and darken the water, hastening evaporation by absorbing more sunlight. Meanwhile tiny brine shrimp feed on the algae, filtering and cleaning the water. More impurities are removed via controlled movement of water, which is eventually channeled into 60 huge rectangular pans. There the supersaturated brine is evaporated to a specific gravity at which sodium chloride precipitates out. The water is pumped back into the sea, leaving a vast carpet of snow-white salt crystals – called 'salina,' or solar salt – about 6 inches deep. This entire production process takes about seven months.

Each pan is 'harvested' once a year between March and June, and its salt is transported and washed. The soggy crystals are then stacked into huge mountains to dry in the sun (each stockpile might weigh up to 250,000 tons) before being loaded via conveyor belts into bulk-freighters tied up at the nearby wharf. Take a closer look and you'll note that each pile of salt contains crystals of a specific size and shape; the different grades of salt are each intended for a different purpose.

The Morton Salt Company doesn't offer a formal tour, but any of the senior executives that you're sure to bump into in town will be happy to show you around. Contact Carl Farquharson, the company president, or the general manager at ☎ 242-339-1847.

Places to Stay

Larry Ingraham (☎ 242-339-1204/1862) rents out the four-bedroom *Farquharson House* at Farquharson Beach – a splendidly lonesome setting if you want a self-catering option.

INAGUA NATIONAL PARK

This 287-sq-mile national park protects the world's largest breeding colony of roseate (or West Indian) flamingos. It owes its existence to Robert Porter Allen, research director of the National Audubon Society, who arrived on Great Inagua in 1952 and dedicated his life to saving what might have been the last breeding colony of endangered roseate flamingos (see Ecology & Environment in the Facts about The Bahamas chapter). The park was formally created in 1963 and is administered by the Bahamas National Trust. Most of the vegetation is thorny scrub, as drought-resistant as that of the US Southwest. Bonsai forest also graces much of the interior. However,

the brine concentration can overcome even the hardiest plants, and there are vast acres of deceased, leafless trees amid circular pools, looking like the Somme after an infernal bombardment.

The terrain may be hostile to humans, but it is perfect for birds and wildlife. The super-salty soup teems with brine shrimp and larval brine flies, foods favored by flamingos and a parade of other waders. Dominating the park is Lake Windsor, a precious mirror reflecting the antics of roseate spoonbills, endemic pink egrets, avocets, cormorants, tricolored Louisiana herons, and about 50,000 flamingos strutting around in hot pink.

The roseate is restricted to Great Inagua, the Turks and Caicos, Bonaire, portions of the Yucatán Peninsula, and Cuba. The gangly birds visit Lake Windsor each spring. They gather in groups numbering from a dozen to several hundred individuals. They feed by tilting their heads upside down and swishing their sievelike beaks through the shallows. During the breeding season, the birds go through an elaborate, noisy ceremony – a flamingo quadrille – prancing around shoulder to shoulder, long necks stiffly erect, while the

males flash their wings and the entire flock puts out a fearful hue and cry. Gradually pairs form and begin building nest mounds. The roseates divide their parental duties, some brooding the mud nests and others standing guard over a single egg. The youngsters can fly about 75 days after being born.

Flamingos have started to repopulate neighboring islands . . . a sure sign of success. The birds have been hunted ruthlessly for meat and milliners' stores during the past 200 years. Locals still have a taste for flamingo steak (it is said to taste like partridge) and occasionally shoot the birds for meat, despite a US$1000 fine and a penalty of three months' imprisonment. Hogs are the birds' other main enemies.

Sometimes you can see flamingos in the brine pools on the edge of the Morton Salt Works, outside the park boundary. But the large flocks are within the park, far from traffic and other disturbances. The best times to visit are early morning and late evening.

There are also burrowing owls, Bahamian pintails, endemic Bahamian woodstar hummingbirds, brown pelicans, striped-headed tanagers, American kestrels, and endangered Bahama parrots.

Each spring a bird count is undertaken. You're welcome to volunteer. Contact Henry Nixon, the warden (☎ 242-339-1616, fax 242-339-1850, VHF channel 16).

Places to Stay

There is a bunkhouse at *Camp Arthur Vernay* on Long Cay in Lake Windsor – a beautiful, silent place in the midst of a foreboding landscape. The bunkhouse sleeps nine people in a dormer room and has two shared showers with cold and lukewarm water. There's an outdoor kitchen with wood-fired stove. Sheets and mattresses are provided. It costs US$25 per person. Arrangements must be made through Henry Nixon (see above), who may or may not overnight with you. You should take your own food, but Nixon will cook for you on request; be prepared to tip extra.

Getting There & Away

The park entrance, 20 miles from Matthew Town, is reached via a dirt road that passes the southernmost of Morton's salt ponds and Maroon Hill (see below). The park gate is kept locked. You must be accompanied by Henry Nixon, the park warden, who charges US$50 for up to four people (US$10 each extra person) for a tour that includes the saltworks. Otherwise you can accompany Nixon on his rounds of the park 'for a donation.'

AROUND INAGUA NATIONAL PARK
Maroon Hill

This linear, cactus-covered limestone ridge stretches east to west at the south end of the Morton salt pans. Its ecosystem is different from that of the surrounding flats. There's a cave full of bats at its westernmost end, beside the road. The hill is a good vantage point for spying the location of flamingos, which can usually be seen in the brine ponds immediately to the west.

Union Creek Reserve

This separately administered area lies at Inagua National Park's northwest corner and encompasses 7 sq miles of tidal creeks and beach where sea turtles – notably green turtles – feed and come ashore to nest. The sanctuary is the only natural feeding grounds in the Caribbean region and mid-Americas where sea turtles are not hunted or exploited in any way.

Important research is undertaken at the **Archie Carr Research Center**, run by noted turtle expert Karen Bjorndal. Donations and volunteers are needed. Contact the Caribbean Conservation Corporation (☎ 800-678-7853), PO Box 2866, Gainesville, FL 32602.

Union Creek is accessed by a dirt road that leads 2 miles east from Albert Sound.

LITTLE INAGUA

This 30-sq-mile island, 5 miles northeast of Great Inagua, is uninhabited, despite its relatively rich soils, which support a dense stand of plump Cuban royal palm, the only such stand in The Bahamas. It, too, harbors a large population of wild burros and goats, as well as prolific birdlife. Marine turtles also nest here.

Amazing Grace, the supply ship for Windjammer Barefoot Cruises' sailing fleet, calls at Little Inagua during its island-hopping voyages, offered twice monthly between Grand Bahama and Trinidad. See the Getting There & Away chapter for details.

Mayaguana

Pop 308

Visiting Mayaguana, 65 miles north of Great Inagua, is about as offbeat an adventure as you can find in The Bahamas. The island is favored by occasional budget travelers, mostly European backpackers.

This remote, bow-tie-shaped island is 25 miles east to west and 6 miles at its widest, in the west. To the east, the deep Caicos (or Windward) Passage separates Mayaguana from the Turks and Caicos.

The ties between the two are strong, and many Turks and Caicos islanders settled on Mayaguana in the mid- and late 19th century.

NASA had a missile-tracking station – now defunct – here during the Apollo and Mercury programs (apparently it was initiated during the Cuban Missile Crisis). Since it closed, many islanders have drifted away. In 1993, however, the Bahamian government launched a 25,000-acre eco-tourism project (see Mayaguana Eco-Park, below) that, when completed, may boost Mayaguana's fortunes.

Abraham Bay, on the south coast, is the largest of three small settlements on the island. Islanders have erected the motley Mayaguana Aerospace Park & Museum around NASA's theodolite pedestal, which once helped keep US astronauts on track.

Roads lead to the other settlements: Pirate's Well, 10 miles northwest, and Betsy Bay, 12 miles northwest.

BaTelCo has a station. Everyone else communicates by radio on VHF channel 16. Electricity and full telephone service were scheduled to arrive in 1997.

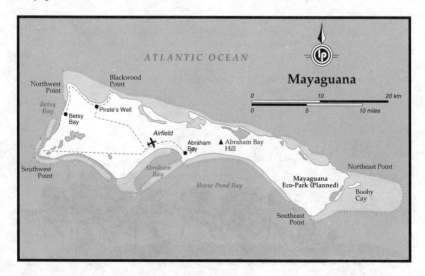

Mayaguana Eco-Park

Still in the planning stages at press time, this vast park, at the virtually pristine east end of the island, will have a botanical garden, an experimental farm, nature trails for hikers and cyclists, and sea kayaks for canoeing through the mangrove creeks.

There are beaches, rocky shores, and reefs good for snorkeling, plus **Booby Cay**, an important nesting site for seabirds, offshore.

It will be several years before the planned tourist facilities are in place.

Places to Stay & Eat

Reggie's has six rooms and a restaurant. Doris and Cap Brown run the *Sheraton Guest House*, also with a restaurant. *Paradise Village* and *Camelot House* also have rooms and a restaurant.

Leon Edwards has a small seaside *guesthouse* at Pirate's Well, where a 15-room motel was to be built.

Latitude 22, next to Reggie's, serves Bahamian breakfasts, lunches, and dinners.

Getting There & Away

The airfield is located 2 miles west of Abraham Bay.

Bahamasair offers flights from Nassau to Mayaguana three times weekly en route to, or via, Great Inagua.

American Canadian Caribbean Line's *Niagara Prince* and *Mayan Prince* spend three days at Abraham Bay during their 12-day cruises through the Family Islands between Nassau and Providenciales (Turks and Caicos) in December and April. See the Getting There & Away chapter.

'Papa' Charlie and Bosie Brooks both offer water-taxi service.

The mail boat *Lady Mathilda* sails from Nassau weekly, calling at Abraham Bay after stopping at Crooked and Acklins islands (US$70 one way). For departure times, call the Dockmaster's Office (☎ 242-393-1064) on Potter's Cay in Nassau.

Turks and Caicos

Though constitutionally separate from The Bahamas, the Turks and Caicos are geographically part of the Bahama Banks. This oddity is a British crown colony with its own government, yet the US dollar is the coin of the realm. The islands are not quite The Bahamas and not quite the Caribbean. They have their own identity, different from that of The Bahamas.

The chain consists of eight islands and 41 small cays, of which only nine are inhabited. Though it's just a 75-minute flight from Miami (closer than Puerto Rico or the US Virgin Islands), this obscure outpost has begun to appear on tourist maps only in the past few years. The Turks and Caicos are like a hidden pearl, and an offbeat one at that. For many years the islands' tourist slogan was 'Where on earth are the Turks and Caicos?' The islands began to boom only when Club Med opened a property on Providenciales in 1984.

Ashore, they are not the prettiest of the region's islands, being rocky, semibarren, and covered with cacti and thorny acacia trees. But there *are* notes of astounding beauty, such as Chalk Sound (Providenciales). The islands are also a bird-watcher's and whale-watcher's paradise. There are 200 miles of powdered-sugar beaches. (It's still an item of local lore – endorsed by Turks and Caicos tourism officials – that in 1962 John Glenn sighted the beaches from space and maneuvered his Mercury capsule to splash down in paradise.) The beaches shelve gently into emerald-green, sand-bottomed shallows that grade into Prussian blues where the ocean floor falls

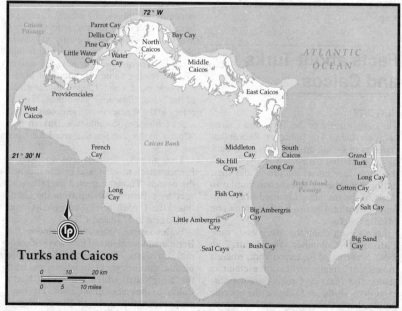

Turks and Caicos

off into the depths. The waters offer fishing to rival The Bahamas. Wahoo, dolphin fish, sailfish, and kingfish are among the many game species that cruise the troughs within a half-mile of shore. The bonefishing is both superb and untapped. And a 230-mile-long coral reef with plummeting walls explains why the Turks and Caicos are listed as one of the world's top 10 dive sites. If you're not an investment banker, reinsurance executive, or drug smuggler, chances are you've traveled to the Turks and Caicos in order to dive the wall.

'Development' has come late to the islands. As late as 1965, in Cockburn Town (Grand Turk), the funky capital, the telephone operator was the jailer . . . and the telephone exchange was a hand-cranked phone in a wooden shack! Karaoke has arrived. But no major cruise ship has yet called. And though resort development is proceeding apace on Providenciales (locally known as 'Provo'), the other islands retain a sleepy, bucolic mood. And even Provo hasn't become spoiled. You don't come to the Turks and Caicos to live it up.

Facts about Turks and Caicos

HISTORY

The early history of the Turks and Caicos parallels that of The Bahamas. Recent discoveries of Indian artifacts on Grand Turk have shown that the islands evolved much the same indigenous culture as did their northern neighbors. A ballcourt similar to those of the far more advanced Maya culture in Central America has been found on Middle Caicos.

Locals even claim that the islands were Christopher Columbus' first landfall in 1492. Some argue for Grand Turk, where a monument attempts to cast the claim in stone. The *Turks & Caicos Pocket Guide* even goes so far as to define the specific point where Columbus came ashore on

October 16: at Malcolm Roads, just south of Provo's Northwest Point. Experts, however, have debunked the theory.

Colonial Era

The island group was a pawn in the power struggles between the French, Spaniards, and British. For several centuries, ownership bounced like a ping-pong ball, landing finally with Great Britain. But lying to windward of the main sailing routes, possessing no gold or decent anchorages, and lacking sufficient rain for growing sugar, the islands were viewed as unimportant specks. They remained virtually uninhabited until 1678, when a group of Bermudians settled and started extracting salt and timber. Salt traders cleared the land and created the salinas (salt-drying pans) that still exist on several islands. Most of this salt went aboard swift sloops to supply the cod-fishing industries of New England and Canada's Maritime Provinces.

In 1710 the Spaniards captured the islands, then sailed away. The Bermudians returned and prospered. Similar to their northerly neighbors, the islands became a base for notorious pirates, who were not averse to sacking the wealthy salt merchants' homes. Some people claim that piracy accounts for the islands' name: 'Turks' for the name of a group of Mediterranean pirates and 'Caicos' for the name of the boats. *'Baloney!'* say others. 'Turks' refers to the species of native cactus whose scarlet blossom resembles a Turkish fez; 'Cayos' is for the Spanish word for 'tiny isles.'

The pirates' depredations invoked a French attack in 1753, and France claimed the islands. Though repelled the following year by a British warship from the Carolinas, the French briefly occupied Grand Turk again in 1778 and 1783.

Following the American Revolution, the Bermudians were joined by a wave of colonial Loyalists. They established cotton plantations throughout the islands and built the King's Rd, which ran across North Caicos to the end of East Caicos. The Loyalists brought their slaves. But the plantation era was short-lived. By 1820 the cotton crop had failed. The majority of planters moved on. Many left their slaves behind, and eventually they, too, became salt rakers. About the middle of the 19th century, a whaling industry flourished, with its base in the Ambergris Cays, southwest of South Caicos.

The islands became a formal part of the Bahamas in 1799, but in 1848, following a petition by Turks and Caicos residents, they became self-governing, under the supervision of the governor of Jamaica. In 1872 the islands were annexed by Jamaica.

Modern Era

The islands remained tied to Jamaica until well into the 20th century. The US military built airstrips during WWII, bringing brief prosperity to the islands. Otherwise the Turks and Caicos' history during the past five decades has been unremarkable. The islands slumbered in obscurity until 1962, when John Glenn splashed down just off Grand Turk, putting the islands in the international spotlight. That same year, the islands again became linked to the Bahamas.

About the same time, the islands were 'discovered' by seven millionaires (including Teddy Roosevelt III and a couple DuPonts) who leased land from the British government, built a small airstrip for their private planes, and constructed a deep-water anchorage for their yachts and those of friends escaping the rigors of East Coast winters. When those friends arrived in larger numbers than their hosts could accommodate, the intimate Third Turtle Inn was built to relieve the pressure. By the 1970s Provo was the near-private domain of a group of wealthy escape artists from long-john climates.

In 1973 the Turks and Caicos became a separate crown colony of Great Britain. Meanwhile, Count Ferdinand Czernin, the son of the last prime minister of the Austro-Hungarian Empire, ferreted out a miniscule dot on the map – Pine Cay, which is northeast of Provo – on which he planned a Walden-Pond-like resort. After

his death, the resort became the exclusive Meridian Club, a prize-winning resort still frequented by the sophisticated elite.

In 1984 Club Med opened its doors on Provo, and the Turks and Caicos started to boom. In the blink of an eye, the islands, which had had no electricity, acquired satellite TV. Today bulldozers and half-poured foundations line the roads of Provo, which is the center of the tourism boom.

See the Government & Politics section for other recent events of interest.

GEOGRAPHY

The Turks and Caicos are separated from the Bahamian islands of Great Inagua and Mayaguana by the 30-mile-wide, deep-ocean Caicos Passage. The group of islands lies 575 miles southeast of Miami. Haiti and the Dominican Republic are some 90 miles due south. The islands total 193 sq miles.

To the west is the Caicos group, an arc comprising – west to east – West Caicos, Providenciales, North Caicos, Middle Caicos, East Caicos, and South Caicos. These islands are separated from one another by narrow waterways. To the east, separated from the Caicos group by the 7000-foot-deep, 22-mile-wide Turks Island Passage (also called the Columbus Passage), is the Turks group: Grand Turk and tiny Salt Cay.

Much of the Turks and Caicos islands, most notably the southern halves of North, Middle, and East Caicos, is composed of creeks, sand flats, lagoons, and marshy wetlands. Most of the sandy beaches are found on the north and west shores, facing the open ocean.

GEOLOGY

Like the rest of the Bahamian archipelago, the two island groups each sit atop a flat underwater mountain surrounded by its own barrier reef. Separating the islands are shallow, sand-covered banks that cover an area 10 times larger than the islands' land area. As in The Bahamas, there are sinkholes, notably Ocean Hole, a

1200-foot-wide, 200-foot-deep blue hole off the south shore of Middle Caicos.

See the Geology section in the Facts about The Bahamas chapter for details on geological formation in the region.

CLIMATE

The Turks and Caicos' climate is similar to that of the southern Bahamas, though slightly warmer and drier. Temperatures average 77°F in winter and rise to an average of 90°F in summer. The hottest months are August to November, when trade winds can die and temperatures can soar to 100°F or more. Average humidity is 35% (significantly less than on most Bahamian islands). Average annual rainfall is 21 inches. Most of the rain falls in summer.

Official announcements of hurricanes are broadcast on Turks & Caicos Radio (on Grand Turk 99.4 FM; on Provo 105.9 FM). Hurricane-shelter locations are listed on page 26 of the telephone directory. There is a Hurricane Command Centre (☎ 649-94-61425) on Grand Turk and another on Provo, at the Myrtle Rigby Health Complex.

ECOLOGY & ENVIRONMENT

The Turks and Caicos bear similarities to the southernmost Bahamian islands, notably Great Inagua and Crooked and Acklins islands. They are predominantly semiarid, notably Salt Cay and much of South Caicos and Grand Turk, which were denuded of vegetation to dissuade rainfall during the heyday of the salt industry. The larger, middle islands of North, Middle, and East Caicos are lusher. Many species are also found in The Bahamas.

More than 30 protected areas have been set aside to conserve delicate ecosystems and wildlife habitat (see the National Parks section). Spearfishing, diving for lobster and conch, and jet-skiing are outlawed within the preserves.

FLORA

Everything makes do on about 21 inches of rain a year (less in the Turks group and

The unique Turk's head cactus

slightly more on North, Middle, and East Caicos). That ain't a lot of rain in these hot climes. The vegetation is tenacious and well adapted to drought. Cacti thrive. Native vegetation varies from island to island, according to variations in rainfall; North Caicos is the lushest island. Salt Cay and West Caicos are virtual deserts.

Typical species include the sweet acacia pork, prickly pear, doughboy cactus, and cinicord, with its fuzzy, lollipoplike yellow flowers. Unique to the islands is the Turk's head cactus, which you will see on the national flag. It's easily recognizable: a short, stubby cactus topped by a red flower shaped like a fez. Aloe and sisal are also common.

You'll recognize wild cotton plants by the lint given off in spring, and the gumbo limbo tree by its coppery bark. Buttonwood, candlewood, and poisonwood are abundant. Dwarf silver palm is common along the shore. Wild mahogany, bay cedar, and lignum vitae can still be found. The coconut palm is not native. It was only recently introduced by resort developers.

There are many flowering trees and bushes, including the false frangipani and the bonsai-like red mangrove, whose white and yellow blossoms emit a deep fragrance in summer. Wild orchids bloom in winter. The bougainvillea, the magnificent royal poinciana, and casuarina are among the more common exotic species introduced to the islands, as is the Geiger tree, with its bright orange blossoms, and the golden shower tree, a native of India named for its cascade of brilliant yellow blossoms in late spring.

Other trees bear fruits, such as the pigeon plum (good for making jams), passion flower, canip (known in the Florida Keys as 'Spanish lime'), and wild dilly, whose gummy fruit is favored by iguanas (humans prefer its domesticated cousin, which produces chicle, once the main ingredient in chewing gum).

Seagrasses and seaweeds flourish in the vast banks south of the Caicos islands. The dense meadows extend for miles. The most common species is turtle grass, so-called because it is eaten by green turtles. The grassy meadows support huge populations of mollusks, sea urchins, sea cucumbers, and other animals, notably conch, a favorite food of stingrays, octopi, and loggerhead turtles.

FAUNA
Donkeys, wild horses, and cattle far outnumber humans, though they stay in the wilds. Their forebears once carried 25-lb burlap bags of salt from the ponds to the warehouses and docks. Having earned their rest, they were set free.

Marine Life
A flourishing population of bottle-nosed dolphins lives in these waters. The Turks and Caicos' unofficial and much-cherished mascot is JoJo, a 7-foot male bottle-nosed dolphin, who has been playing with tourists off Provo's Grace Bay beach and Pine Cay since leaving his pod in 1983 (only a handful of wild dolphins worldwide are recorded as having left their pods to cohabit with humans). See the sidebar.

As many as 7000 North Atlantic humpback whales use the Turks Island Passage and the Mouchoir Banks, south of Grand Turk, as their winter breeding grounds between January and March (these are the only known breeding grounds for North Atlantic humpbacks). And manta rays are commonly seen during the spring plankton blooms off Grand Turk and West Caicos.

Reptiles
Iguanas once inhabited much of the Turks and Caicos. The colonies on larger islands were wiped out by development, which destroyed their natural habitats, and by newly introduced predators – domestic cats

---

JoJo, the Friendly 'Flipper'
For over a decade, a 7-foot male bottle-nosed dolphin called 'JoJo' has cruised the waters off Provo and North Caicos. When he first appeared, he was shy and limited his human contact to following or playing in the bow waves of boats. He soon turned gregarious and has become an active participant whenever people are in the water. In 1995 JoJo crossed the Turks Island Passage and appeared off Grand Turk, where he spent a month.

JoJo is now so popular that he has been named a national treasure by the Ministry of Natural Resources. JoJo even has his own warden, who studies his behavior and looks out for him as part of the 'JoJo Dolphins Project' (☎ 649-94-15610), Box 153, Providenciales, Turks and Caicos, BWI.

It is important to remember that JoJo is wild and therefore unpredictable. See the cautions in the Outdoor Activities chapter. ■

and dogs. Today their habitat is limited, and they're endangered.

In 1996 the Turks & Caicos National Trust (see National Parks, below) launched a 'Little Water Cay Initiative' to raise US$50,000 annually for preservation of the rock iguana *(Cyclura carnata)*, the endangered endemic species found only on Little Water Cay, northeast of Provo. The 1500 or so iguanas have become a major tourist lure for the island, attracting an estimated 17,000 people in 1996. The 150-acre cay is part of Princess Alexandra National Park, which also comprises Mangrove Cay and Donna Cay. Fort George Cay (near Little Water) and the Ambergris Cays (south of South Caicos) also are protected iguana reserves.

The waters are favored by four species of turtle. Hawksbills are an endangered species, although locally they are a dime a dozen and nest on many of the cays; alas, the Turks and Caicos do *not* recognize the hawksbill's endangered status. Green turtles visit the inshore waters and tidal creeks of North and Middle Caicos to graze on seagrass beds. Loggerheads are also common, and even leatherbacks are occasionally seen.

Birds

The vast wetlands in the southern portions of the Caicos islands are ideal feeding grounds for shorebirds and for waders, and the numerous uninhabited cays throughout the chain make perfect nesting sites for seabirds. More than 175 species of birds have been sighted, of which 78 are migratory land birds. Ospreys are numerous and easily spotted; so, too, are sparrow hawks and barn owls. Flamingos – once numerous throughout the chain – are now limited to West, North, and South Caicos, where you may also see Cuban herons.

Frigate birds are more commonly seen here than in The Bahamas. The most important nesting site is at Vine Point (Middle Caicos), but they also nest on Penniston Cay (near Grand Turk) and other islands. Pelicans are ubiquitous, more so than in

The Bahamas. Many cays are important nesting sites for sooty and roseate terns, Audubon's shearwaters, and brown noddy terns.

NATIONAL PARKS

The 33 areas set aside as national parks, nature reserves, sanctuaries, and sites of historical interest protect native flora and fauna. Much of the thanks goes to Chuck Hesse, creator of the Society to Protect Our Reefs and Islands from Degradation and Exploitation (☎ 649-94-65849). Hesse has spent two decades crusading for the creation of national parks. His efforts were rewarded in 1988, when the first 19 national parks and sanctuaries were approved. (Hesse also runs the Caicos Conch Farm on Provo; see the Caicos Islands chapter.)

The Turks & Caicos National Trust has two offices. The first is at Harbour House on Grand Turk; the second (☎ 649-94-61723) is in Butterfield Square on Provo. In 1997 the trust embarked on construction of three underwater snorkeling trails: one on the Bight reef off Provo and two on reefs off Grand Turk.

The Turks & Caicos Dept of Environment & Coastal Resources (☎ 649-94-62855) has jurisdiction over some reserves, including the protected Mouchoir Banks.

Parks and reserves include the following (west to east):

West Caicos
   West Caicos Marine National Park – Superb diving can be had amid the coral reefs.
Providenciales
   Northwest Point Marine National Park – Majestic stands of elkhorn coral and superb wall diving. Inland saline ponds attract roseate spoonbills and other waterfowl.
   Chalk Sound National Park – A cay-studded lagoon of stunning turquoise.
   Princess Alexandra National Park – Protects the shore and offshore environment along Grace Bay and cays northeast of Provo.
   Leeward Land & Sea Park – Protects the north coast from Dodson Hill to Little Water Cay, and extends from the high tide line to the offshore deep. Ashore, there are iguanas, ospreys, and flamingos.

North, Middle, & East Caicos

Ramsar Site – Protects a vast expanse of marsh and intertidal wetlands, a breeding site and nursery for waterfowl, lobster, conch, and fish.

North Caicos

Three Mary Cays National Park – Another important seabird nesting site.

East Bay Islands National Park – Protects numerous small cays off North Caicos, favored sites for seabirds.

Middle Caicos

Conch Bar Caves National Park – An extensive cave system, some with lagoons and most with colonies of resident bats and Indian petroglyphs.

Middle Caicos Reserve & Trail System – Pristine beaches, freshwater lakes, and pine forests are accessed by 10 miles of trails.

Vine Point & Ocean Hole Nature Reserve – Protects vast intertidal swamplands along the south shore, a frigate-bird breeding colony, and a huge blue hole.

South Caicos

Admiral Cockburn Land & Sea Park – Protects the scrub-covered shore and offshore coral reefs of western South Caicos.

Belle Sound & Admiral Cockburn Cays Nature Reserve – Encompasses the mangroves and bonefish flats west of South Caicos.

Grand Turk

Columbus Landfall National Park – Protects the foreshore and coral reefs of Cockburn Town, which some argue was the site of Columbus' first landing in the New World; the ocean deep begins within 400 yards of shore.

South Creek National Park – Protects mangroves and wetlands along the island's south shore, home to migrating shorebirds and waders.

Grand Turk Cays Land & Sea Park – Comprises a series of tiny cays – Gibb's, Penniston, Long, and Martin Alonza Pinzon – off the southeast shore, important nesting sites for seabirds, with abundant iguanas and Turk's head cactus.

GOVERNMENT & POLITICS

The Turks and Caicos are a British crown colony, a dependency of the UK. The existing constitution dates from 1988. A governor from the UK is appointed as the Queen's representative, with responsibility for internal security, external affairs, and certain judicial matters. The governor also presides over the Executive Council of Ministers.

Local self-government is administered by the 13-member Legislative Council, an elected body headed by the chief minister and empowered to enact local statutes. The legal system is based upon common English law, supplemented by UK statutes designed to apply to the islands and local ordinances of the Legislative Council that are approved by the UK government. The judicial system is administered by a resident magistrate and a nonresident judge who visits at quarterly intervals.

Relations between the islanders and the governor have been strained for some years. Governor Martin Bourke was appointed in 1993 with a US$35 million budget to combat corruption. In January 1996 Bourke suggested that government and police corruption had turned the islands into a haven for drug trafficking. When his comments appeared in the *Offshore Finance Annual*, opponents accused him of harming investment. The growing opposition threatened to spill over into civil unrest. In April 1996 the British government sent the warship HMS *Brave* to cruise the coast, and a squad of specially trained policemen arrived. In the end the much-ballyhooed popular uprising turned out to be just another lazy day in the sun. The issue revived calls for independence,

---

The Turks and Caicos Crest

In 1860 artists were asked to submit a design to be used as the territory's colonial crest. The selected design showed a schooner in the background and two men in the foreground, raking heaps of salt – a typical island scene of the 19th century. The London flagmaker assumed that the salt heaps were igloos and added entrances to the white mounds.

In 1967 the flag was changed to include a new crest, depicting the country's indigenous spiny lobster, the queen conch, and the Turk's head cactus. ■

but so far these have been just agitated conversation over rum cocktails. There has even been talk of joining Canada as its 11th province.

In October 1996 Bourke was recalled to England after his stormy term. He was replaced by John Kelly. A Jamaican national, Kipling Douglas, was appointed chief justice (another Jamaican, Caesar Campbell, was appointed as director of tourism). At press time the chief minister was Derek Taylor.

The government offices are in Cockburn Town, the capital, on Grand Turk.

ECONOMY
Historically the Turks and Caicos relied upon salt export and, to a lesser degree, upon whatever booty came their way from pirates. Salt remained the backbone of the British crown colony until the 1950s, when the industry collapsed.

Today the finance, tourism, and fishing industries generate most private-sector income. Despite their history as pirates' lairs, the islands are a safe place to put your money. The Turks and Caicos are a tax-free offshore finance center, offering services such as company formation, offshore insurance, banking, trusts, and limited partnerships. Still, the industry is a mere minnow compared to that of The Bahamas, and you will no doubt be astonished to discover that Grand Turk, the financial center, is just a dusty backwater in the sun.

The Turks and Caicos experienced an 11% increase in visitors in 1996, when 87,794 visitors called. According to the Caribbean Tourism Organization, of all the region's islands, only Cuba reported a larger increase in tourist arrivals for that year. The government has grand plans for tourism, including a much-touted cruise-ship terminal on East Caicos, to be linked to Provo by a major causeway.

Still, income from tourism and offshore investment is not yet sufficient for the Turks and Caicos to survive without aid from Britain. Practically all consumer goods and foodstuffs are imported.

Agriculture is limited to small family gardens and teeny farms. The islands' most important exports are conch and lobster (about 750,000 lbs annually). Commemorative coins and souvenir-issue stamps bring in considerable revenue.

Illegal drug trafficking, a major problem, is also a source of significant revenue for many islanders.

POPULATION & PEOPLE
The population totals a mere 14,000. About half live on Provo, the main island, and Grand Turk. The growth rate is 3.7% per annum. Most residents are black descendants of African slaves that were brought over by Loyalist settlers in the late 18th century.

Turks and Caicos islanders (called 'TIs' or 'belongers') are descended from the early Bermudian settlers, Loyalist settlers, slave settlers, and salt rakers. The 21-page telephone directory reflects this heritage, with long listings under the names Astwood, Butterfield, Forbes, Lightbourne, Stubbs, and Williams.

Many whites are 'retirement-aged swashbucklers and goldbugs' and shady expat characters who, if you ask their profession, will tell you, 'Uh, I have some – er – investments.' Many expatriates, particularly Brits, are employed in the hospitality and finance industries.

ARTS
Though slow to develop, the arts scene in the Turks and Caicos has begun to blossom. Traditional music, folklore, and sisal weaving evolved during colonial days and have been maintained to this day, as is true in The Bahamas. However, fine art is a modern notion. The first gallery – the Bamboo Gallery on Provo – didn't open until 1990.

The local art scene is dominated by the Haitian community. However, now other artists are also well represented. Much of the work is inspired by the islands' scenery and marine life, with vibrant colors redolent of the Caribbean. The Bamboo Gallery promotes work by local artists, including

EDA ROGERS

Top Left: Spotted dolphins
Bottom Left: Mangrove swamp, Lucayan National Park, Grand Bahama

Top Right: Blue as far as the eye can see in the Abacos
Bottom Right: More than a million cruise-ship passengers visit The Bahamas each year.

Top: Christmas decorations? Nope . . . a modern take on obeah at Solomon Jones' house, San Salvador
Bottom Left: Checking out the local crafts in Dunmore Town, Eleuthera

Bottom Right: Drinkin', fishin', writin', and fightin': Papa Hemingway's favorite Biminis haunt

that of Dwight Outten, from Middle Caicos, whom some people consider to be the leading artist in the islands. Another family member, Phillip Outten, a Rastafarian, produces naive acrylic works (some in gay primary colors, others more somber) inspired, he says, by his meditations and 'concept of daily reality.'

The North Caicos Art Society in Whitby (North Caicos) sponsors local art, emphasizing silkscreen painting. Perhaps the leading artist in this genre is Anna Bourne, one of many expatriate artists, who lives on Providenciales and paints on silk with French dyes.

SOCIETY & CONDUCT

Turks and Caicos islanders are an intriguing contrast to Bahamians. Some are gracious, warm-spirited, and friendly, and there are many who are entrepreneurial and eager to provide good service. But some are less courteous, and they may be more cantankerous and confrontational than their northern neighbors. Could this characteristic, which is so distinct from the islanders immediately to the north, be inherited from the strong linkages that have traditionally existed with Jamaica, to which the Turks and Caicos were politically bound from 1872 to 1962? (See Lonely Planet's *Jamaica travel survival kit.*)

The islanders, however, are as devoutly religious as their northern neighbors. This doesn't stop some from philandering or having a tipple, for example, on Sunday, when the pubs (strictly speaking) aren't serving: 'We might be drinking, but we are conscious of our religion.'

Also see the Society & Conduct section in the Facts about The Bahamas chapter for more information.

LANGUAGE

The official language of the Turks and Caicos is English. The local islanders' distinct dialect bears much resemblance to that of Bahamians (see the Facts about The Bahamas chapter).

Haitian residents speak their own French-based creole patois.

Facts for the Visitor

See The Bahamas' Facts for the Visitor chapter for tips on planning your trip, such as when to go and what to bring.

SUGGESTED ITINERARIES

The overwhelming majority of visitors restrict their stay to Provo and, to a lesser degree, Grand Turk. A few offbeat travelers make it to the remoter cays. If you really want to experience the heart and soul of the islands, take time to explore South Caicos or Salt Cay, and venture out to at least one uninhabited cay.

Here's a recommended offbeat approach to taking in the best of the islands, assuming a 10-day itinerary. Any combination will do.

Day One – Arrive on Provo. Sunbathe, drink cocktails, make love.

Day Two – Hire a 4WD jeep. Explore the island, visiting the Caicos Conch Farm, Chalk Sound, and Northwest Point Marine National Park. Take snorkel gear and a picnic lunch to be enjoyed at the Tiki Huts.

Day Three – Enjoy water sports at Grace Bay. This afternoon, perhaps you'll play a round of golf or go horseback riding. Or you can sunbathe, drink cocktails, and make love.

Day Four – Take a flight excursion to North and Middle Caicos (be sure to take time to visit the flamingos) or a dive excursion to West Caicos.

Day Five – Fly to South Caicos for bonefishing at Belle Sound or diving the wall.

Day Six – Fly to Grand Turk. Explore Cockburn Town. Hire a boat for sport fishing, or dive the wall.

Day Seven – Charter a boat for an excursion to Salt Cay for a prearranged lunch at Mount Pleasant Guest House. Take a tour with Bryan Sheedy or dive the wall. If you're visiting in winter, go whale watching . . . or even *swimming* with whales!

Day Eight – Sunbathe, drink cocktails, and make love.

Day Nine – Treat yourself to a one-day excursion to Cuba!

Day 10 – 'Home, James!'

THE BEST

Salt Cay – This tiny cay, the southernmost major isle, retains an otherworldly charm loaned by the architectural remains of the salt industry and historic Balfour Town. Making it all come alive is Bryan Sheedy, who offers tours for guests at his Mount Pleasant Guest House, one of the finest in the islands. Alternately, Windmills Plantation offers laid-back, deluxe charm for the wealthy. There's whale watching in winter.

Cockburn Town (Grand Turk) – The colony's capital is a charming enclave of old Bermudian architecture, including old inns. The beaches are nice. And there's great sport fishing and windsurfing. But it ain't for everyone. You'll either love it or hate it (see The Worst, below).

Whale Watching – Humpback whales mate and give birth in the warm waters north and east of Salt Cay . . . close enough for you to swim out from the scintillating beaches to be in their midst. *Wow!*

Swimming with JoJo – The islands' resident mascot is sure to put a smile on your face if he shows up unannounced while you're snorkeling off Provo.

Diving the Wall – What a rush to don scuba gear and drop down the sheer-faced walls – festooned with gorgonians and other corals – of the submarine plateaus upon which the islands sit. You dangle unsupported with miles of blue nothing below, like Wile E Coyote after he has accidentally run off the edge of a cliff. Fortunately, the plummet never comes! See the Outdoor Activities chapter for details.

Chalk Sound (Provo) – It's hard to believe the beauty of this narrow, 3-mile-long inlet, whose waters are colored an impossibly uniform turquoise and studded with a zillion mushroomlike islets.

Grace Bay – Who couldn't love Provo's miles-long stretch of white sand?

Flamingo Pond – This brine lake, the highlight of North Caicos, is named for the flock of flamingos that is resident year-round.

Cuba Excursions – For a description, see the *¡Cuba Sí!* sidebar in the New Providence chapter in the Bahamas section.

THE WORST

Grand Turk – Despite my comments above, there's a second side to Grand Turk. Too many of the locals are sullen, the island's sights can be seen in a day, hovels abound, and it gets infernally hot and barren in summertime. You can almost read the thought – 'Oh, my God . . . what have I gotten myself into?' – on the dismayed faces of expatriates who believed the glossy brochures and have just arrived here for a two-year posting.

TOURIST OFFICES

The headquarters of the Turks & Caicos Islands Tourist Board (☎ 649-94-62321, fax 649-94-62733) is on Pond St in Cockburn Town; its mailing address is PO Box 128, Cockburn Town, Grand Turk, Turks and Caicos, BWI. The board is under the jurisdiction of the Ministry of Tourism (☎ 649-94-62801, fax 649-94-61120).

The board also has two information bureaus on Provo: at Providenciales Airport (☎ 649-94-15496) and at Turtle Cove Marina Plaza (☎ 649-94-64970).

The board maintains offices abroad at the following locales:

UK
> Turks & Caicos Information Office, International House, 47 Chase Side, Enfield, Middlesex EN2 6NB (☎ 0181-364-5188, fax 0181-367-9949)

USA
> Turks & Caicos Islands Tourist Board, 11645 Biscayne Blvd, Suite 302, Miami, FL 33181 (☎ 800-241-0824)
> Trombone Associates, 420 Madison Ave, New York, NY 10017 (☎ 212-223-2323, fax 212-223-0260)

VISAS & DOCUMENTS

Citizens of the United States will need proof of citizenship (a valid passport, voter's registration card, or birth certificate will suffice) and photo identification to enter the Turks and Caicos. Everyone else, including UK citizens, needs to have a valid passport. No visas are required for citizens of the USA, Canada, the UK and Commonwealth countries, Ireland, and most Western European countries. Citizens of most other countries require visas, which can be obtained from British embassies, High Commissions, or consulates abroad (see the Embassies & Consulates section, below).

For information on work, residence, or stays longer than three months, you should contact the Turks & Caicos Immigration Dept (☎ 649-94-64233/63355, fax 649-94-62924), South Base, Grand Turk, Turks and Caicos.

Proof of onward transportation is required upon entry.

Citizens of the USA, Canada, the UK, and Commonwealth countries require valid driver's licenses for stays of up to three months. Everyone else requires an International Driving License (see the Facts for the Visitor chapter in the Bahamas section for information on how to obtain one).

EMBASSIES & CONSULATES
Turks and Caicos
Representation Abroad

As a British crown colony, the Turks and Caicos are represented through British embassies and consulates abroad.

In the USA contact the British Embassy (☎ 202-462-1340), 3100 Massachusetts Ave NW, Washington, DC 20008-3600, or the Consular Section (☎ 202-588-7800, fax 202-797-2929), Observatory Circle, Washington, DC 20008-3600. Or you can contact any of the following consulates:

California
    Consulate-General, 11766 Wilshire Blvd, Suite 400, Los Angeles, CA 90025 (☎ 310-477-3322, fax 310-575-1450)
    Consulate-General, 1 Sansome St, Suite 850, San Francisco, CA 94104 (☎ 415-981-3030, fax 415-434-2018)
Georgia
    Consulate-General, Marquis One Tower, 245 Peachtree Center Ave, Suite 2700, Atlanta, GA 30303 (☎ 404-524-5856, fax 404-524-3153)
Illinois
    Consulate-General, Wrigley Bldg, 400 N Michigan Ave, Suite 1300, Chicago, IL 60611 (☎ 312-346-1810, fax 312-464-0661)
Massachusetts
    Consulate-General, Federal Reserve Plaza, 600 Atlantic Ave, Boston, MA 02210 (☎ 617-248-9555, fax 617-248-9578)
New York
    Consulate-General, 845 Third Ave,

New York, NY 10022 (☎ 212-745-0200, fax 212-754-3062)
Texas
    Consulate-General, First Interstate Bldg, 1000 Louisiana, Suite 1900, Houston, TX 77002-5506 (☎ 713-659-6270, fax 713-659-7094)

Embassies & Consulates in Turks and Caicos

There are no foreign embassies or consulates in the Turks and Caicos.

The US Embassy & Consulate (☎ 242-322-1181, 242-328-2206, fax 242-328-7838), on Queen St in Nassau in The Bahamas, also serves the Turks and Caicos.

CUSTOMS

Visitors may each bring in duty free one carton of cigarettes or 50 cigars, one bottle of liquor or wine, and 50 grams of perfume. The importation of all firearms is forbidden, except upon written authorization from the Commissioner of Police. Spear guns, drugs, and pornography are also illegal.

For further information, contact Turks and Caicos Customs (☎ 649-94-62801).

MONEY

The Turks and Caicos are unique: a British-dependent territory with the US dollar as its official currency. The treasury also issues a Turks and Caicos crown and quarter. There are no restrictions on the amount of money that visitors can bring in.

The country is pricey. Values are difficult to find.

Most credit cards are readily accepted on Provo and Grand Turk, as are traveler's checks. Elsewhere you may need to operate on a cash-only basis.

Foreign currency can be changed at local banks, which can also issue credit-card advances. Barclays has branches on Provo, Grand Turk, and South Caicos. Scotiabank has branches on Provo and Grand Turk.

There are no direct taxes on income or capital for individuals or companies. Indirect taxation is limited to telephone charges (10%), customs duties (33%), car and motorcycle rental, plus the 7% hotel tax and US$20 air departure tax.

POST & COMMUNICATIONS
Sending & Receiving Mail

The post office headquarters (☎ 649-94-62801) is on Grand Turk. There's at least one post office on each island. Most are open 8 am to 12:30 pm and 2 to 4:30 pm Monday to Thursday and 8 am to 12:30 pm Friday. All the caveats mentioned regarding sending and receiving mail in The Bahamas apply here as well (see the Facts for the Visitor chapter in the Bahamas section).

DHL Worldwide Express (☎ 649-94-64352) has an office on Provo; Federal Express (on Provo ☎ 649-94-64682; on Grand Turk 649-94-62515) is also represented in the Turks and Caicos.

Telephone & Fax

Cable & Wireless operates a digital network using state-of-the-art equipment. Its offices are on Grand Turk and Provo. Direct dial is standard.

Public phone booths are located throughout the islands. Many booths require phonecards, issued in denominations of US$5, US$10, and US$20 (plus a standard 10% government tax).

You can also bill calls to your American Express, Discover, Visa, or MasterCard by dialing ☎ 111 on any touchtone phone and giving the operator your card details (there's a three-minute minimum).

Phone calls to the USA and Caribbean cost US$2.50 per minute; to the UK and Canada, US$3.30; to The Bahamas, US$1.95; to Europe, US$4; and to the rest of the world, US$5. Rates drop on weekdays between 7 pm and 6 am, and all day on weekends.

When calling from abroad, dial the country code (☎ 649), then 94, and then the five-digit local number. When dialing within the Turks and Caicos, dial the five-digit local number only.

For the local operator, call ☎ 110; for the international operator, call 115.

Cellular Phones You can rent a cellular phone at Cable & Wireless offices for US$10 a day. If you bring your own phonecard, you'll be charged US$5 for a connection. National calls cost US$1 per minute. Calls to the USA and Caribbean will cost you US$3.75 per minute; to Canada and the UK, US$4.60; and to Western Europe, US$5.40.

Fax Most major hotels have a fax machine. Faxes can also be sent via Cable & Wireless offices, as can telexes. Telexes are billed at the same rate as telephone calls. Telegrams cost US55¢ a word. A 10% government tax is charged.

BOOKS

The *Turks & Caicos Pocket Guide*, edited by Julia Blake (Domy Graphix, Providenciales), is a handy compendium-style guide to the islands. It is not a sightseeing guide.

Diving and Snorkeling Guide to the Turks & Caicos Islands by Susanne and Stuart Cummings (Pisces Books) includes detailed, illustrated descriptions of 30 dive sites, with ratings.

Water and Light by Stephen Harrigan is a splendid memoir by a Texan who 'followed his bliss' and spent several months diving off Grand Turk. For a rollicking tale, read *Don't Stop the Carnival* by Herman Wouk, about an expat American who sets out to run a hotel on the fictional island of Amerigo.

Doing Business in the Turks & Caicos Islands is a 32-page booklet published by Times Publications, PO Box 234, Providenciales, Turks and Caicos, BWI. The company also publishes *Turks & Caicos Islands Real Estate Guide*. Each costs US$6, including shipping.

Several stores and hotel shops stock books. The largest selection is at Unicorn Bookstore in the Market Place on Provo (see the Caicos Islands chapter).

NEWSPAPERS & MAGAZINES

There are two newspapers: the biweekly *Free Press* and the weekly *Turks & Caicos*

News. Times of the Islands is a slick, full-color, quarterly magazine serving both the tourist and the investor. Subscriptions cost US$28, plus US$4 for orders *outside* the USA; write PO Box 234, Providenciales, Turks and Caicos, BWI.

Provo and Grand Turk are each served by a free monthly visitors' guide: *Where, When, How . . .*

RADIO & TV

The official government radio station is Radio Turks & Caicos (106 FM) on Grand Turk. There are several private stations. For contemporary light rock, try 92.5 FM. You'll find country and western on 90.5 FM, easy listening on 89.3 FM, and classical music on 89.9 FM. WPRT at 88.7 is a religious and public announcement channel, as is WIV at 96.7 FM.

Multichannel satellite television is received from the USA and Canada. The islands have one private television station.

TIME

The Turks and Caicos are on Eastern Standard Time, which is five hours behind Greenwich Mean Time.

ELECTRICITY

The Turks and Caicos use 110 volts, 60 cycles, suitable to all US appliances.

HEALTH

There are no endemic tropical diseases in the Turks and Caicos. No vaccinations are required. See the Facts for the Visitor chapter in the Bahamas section for general travel-health advice.

The only full-service hospital is the Grand Turk Hospital (☎ 649-94-62333), which has an emergency room. On Provo there are two private medical centers. There's the MBS Medical Clinic (☎ 649-94-64242) on Leeward Hwy and the New Era Medical Centre in Blue Hills. Also, there is the government-run Myrtle Rigby Health Clinic (☎ 649-94-13000).

There are also government clinics on each of the islands:

Grand Turk	☎ 649-94-62328
Middle Caicos	☎ 649-94-66145
North Caicos	☎ 649-94-67194
Provo	☎ 649-94-13000
South Caicos	☎ 649-94-63216

A government doctor pays a weekly visit to Salt Cay.

In medical emergencies beyond the capacity of the local hospital, patients are flown by air-ambulance to full-service hospitals in Nassau or Miami.

The MBS Medical Clinic on Provo has a recompression chamber.

EMERGENCY

For the police, fire, or ambulance, call ☎ 999 or 911.

Other important numbers include the following:

Island	Police	Fire
Grand Turk	☎ 649-94-62299	649-94-62233
Middle Caicos	☎ 649-94-66111	
North Caicos	☎ 649-94-67116	
Provo	☎ 649-94-64259	649-94-64444
South Caicos	☎ 649-94-63299	

DANGERS & ANNOYANCES

The biggest annoyance is the surly attitude of many locals, notably on Grand Turk, where one renowned resident likes to push tourists around, and on South Caicos. But crime is rare and muggings virtually unknown. The odd incident of drunkenness is about as bad as things get, and even the most mundane crimes make the headlines. Nonetheless, you should be cautious of petty theft.

The most sinister – dare I say asinine – threat may be the donkeys. Occasionally an unruly villain such as Buster, a frisky black jackass on Grand Turk, will think it quite fun to strike terror into unsuspecting pedestrians and cyclists. One day a tourist was nipped on the butt and the Royal Turks and Caicos Police were summoned to apprehend the beast. Four motorcycle policemen armed with lassos sped the wrong way down Front St in hot pursuit, but Buster got away.

Watch those teeth – Buster,
Grand Turk's spirited jackass

BUSINESS HOURS & PUBLIC HOLIDAYS

Government offices are usually open 8 am to 12:30 pm and 2 to 4 pm Monday to Friday. Private offices and businesses are usually open 8:30 am to 5 pm. Banks are open 8:30 am to 2:30 pm Monday to Thursday and 8:30 am to 12:30 pm and 2:30 to 4:30 pm Friday.

Holidays that fall on either Saturday or Sunday are usually observed on the following Monday.

January 1	New Year's Day
March 10	Commonwealth Day
Friday before Easter	Good Friday
Monday after Easter	Easter Monday
May 26	National Heroes' Day
June 14 (or nearest weekday)	Her Majesty The Queen's Official Birthday
August 1	Emancipation Day
September 26	National Youth Day
October 13	Columbus Day
October 24	International Human Rights Day
December 25	Christmas Day
December 26	Boxing Day

There are also numerous local special events; see the island chapters for details.

ACCOMMODATIONS

Lodgings in the Turks and Caicos, as in The Bahamas, range from quaint inns up to fancy all-inclusive resorts. The variety is greatest on Provo, where you can choose among modern 'boutique' hotels, intimate guesthouses, condominiums, and Club Med and other all-inclusive resorts.

Information on lodgings is available through the Turks & Caicos Hotel Reservation Centre (☎ 305-667-0966, fax 305-667-2494), 4197 Braganza St, Coconut Grove, FL 33133. Also see Accommodations in the Facts for the Visitor chapter in the Bahamas section; most of those comments apply in the Turks and Caicos as well.

Room rates range from about US$60 to over US$300 nightly. A 7% hotel-room tax applies. Most hotels impose a surcharge (usually about 20%) during the Christmas season. Many hotels also add a 10% to 20% service charge, also assessed on anything charged to your room. A 50% deposit is a standard requirement.

Elliot Holdings (☎ 649-94-65355, fax 649-94-65176) rents luxury villas, houses, and apartments in the Turks and Caicos. Its local mailing address is PO Box 235, Providenciales, Turks and Caicos, BWI; in the USA write 2985 Biscayne Blvd, Suite 410, Miami, FL 33137.

FOOD

Be advised: You are not coming to the Turks and Caicos for the cuisine. Sure, international dishes run the gamut from Mexican and Italian to burgers and fries. But with few exceptions, local fare is unnoteworthy. Conch, lobster, softshell crab, and fresh fish (often blackened with Cajun seasoning) are the island favorites, along with spicy Jamaican jerk chicken and fresh fruits, such as sapodillas and sugar apples. See the Bahamas section for more details on local cuisine.

ENTERTAINMENT

Entertainment is relatively subdued, except on Provo, where a large number of lively bars and other offerings cater to the tourist trade. Several bars – especially on Grand Turk – are filled with chummy English expats and their colorful 'mates.' On Provo bars range from quiet cocktail lounges to Texan-style sports bars with live bands. All the islands have funky bars where bands play traditional rake 'n' scrape music and the locals (mostly men) engage in dominoes or watch TV. The bars catering predominantly to Haitians can get rough as the night wears on.

The only cinema complex is on Provo, although South Caicos has a small cinema on Stubbs Rd. Several resort hotels on Provo feature dance clubs. Live bands also do the hotel rounds.

Those who like to gamble can try their hand with Lady Luck at the Port Royale Casino on Provo. Here you can play a variety of games, including roulette, blackjack, and Caribbean stud poker.

THINGS TO BUY
The handcrafted plait-and-sew style of straw weaving survives. Handmade rag rugs and baskets are a great buy. The art scene is lively on Provo; you can pick up some splendid Haitian art.

Getting There & Away

AIR
There are international airports on Grand Turk and Provo. Other islands have local airstrips. Most international flights arrive at Provo. See the island chapters for fares and schedules.

A departure tax of US$20 is payable on all international flights. No tax is levied on children under 12.

American Airlines (☎ 649-94-15700; in the USA 800-433-7300), at press time, flew daily to Provo from Miami. Interisland Airways (☎ 649-94-61548) has service between Fort Lauderdale and Provo.

Lynx Air International (in the USA ☎ 954-772-9808, 888-596-9247) flies to Grand Turk from Fort Lauderdale. Turks & Caicos Airways (☎ 649-94-64255) flies to Provo from Miami.

Sandals' Beaches Turks & Caicos resort offers charter flights to Provo from New York.

From most European countries, you'll need to fly to Miami or New York and connect to flights to the Turks and Caicos. A charter company serves Provo from Italy.

Air Jamaica (☎ 800-523-5585) flies to Provo from Montego Bay, Jamaica, the new Caribbean hub. Bahamasair (in the USA ☎ 800-222-4262, fax 305-937-6461) serves Provo from Nassau. Turks & Caicos Airways flies to Provo from Nassau and from a number of Caribbean countries.

From the Turks and Caicos, you can charter a plane with Sky King (☎ 649-94-15464, fax 649-94-15127) and hop over to Cuba by five-seater charter planes for US$350 roundtrip. The trips are open – *legally* – to US citizens as long as they don't spend money in Cuba. It also has charters to Haiti and Dominican Republic.

If you're piloting a private plane, you can buy aerial charts in the Turks and Caicos at the Unicorn Bookstore on Provo.

SEA
Cruise Ship
The major cruise lines bypass the Turks and Caicos, although this may soon change – at press time the government planned to begin construction of a cruise-ship terminal on East Caicos in 1998.

At press time, two cruise companies offered regular cruises to the islands: American Canadian Caribbean Line and Windjammer Barefoot Cruises. See the Getting There & Away chapter in the Bahamas section for details.

Private Yacht
Yachters are welcome and served by marinas in the Turks and Caicos. Yachters are permitted seven days in the islands, after which they can obtain a cruising permit good for three months.

Strict regulations are enforced. Many of the approaches and landfalls, for example, lie within protected areas where anchoring is strictly controlled (moorings within such areas are for dive boats only, although visiting yachts can moor while diving). No firearms may be brought into the Turks and Caicos (you must surrender them for the duration of your stay). And no conch or lobster may be taken. The latest regulations can be obtained from the Dept of Environment & Coastal Resources (☎ 649-94-62855).

The main marinas on Provo are the Leeward Marina, the South Side Basin Marina, the Caicos Marina, and Turtle Cove Marina. South Caicos has the Sea View Marina in Cockburn Harbour. See details on each marina in the island chapters.

An excellent guide to sailing the Turks and Caicos is the *Yachtsman's Guide to The Bahamas and Turks & Caicos,* edited by Meredith Helleberg Fields (Tropic Isle Publishers). See the Getting There & Away chapter in the Bahamas section for details and ordering information.

Tides swirl across the shallow sea bottom and around the sand banks, making the shallows treacherous for boaters. You should obtain US Defense Mapping Agency charts 25720, 26260/1/2, and 26268, or British Admiralty charts 409, 1266, and 1441. You can order them from Bluewater Books & Charts (☎ 954-763-6533, 800-942-2583), 1481 SE 17th St, Fort Lauderdale, FL 33316. Nautical charts are sold in the Turks and Caicos at the Unicorn Bookstore on Provo.

For communications, boaters should use VHF channel 16 (and VHF 09 or 13 as a last resort).

ORGANIZED TOURS

A few companies offer air-hotel packages to the Turks and Caicos. Check with the companies listed under Organized Tours in the Getting There & Away chapter in the Bahamas section.

Scuba operators also offer packages from the USA, including Caradonna Caribbean Tours (☎ 800-328-2288, fax 407-682-6000), PO Box 3299, Longwood, FL 32779, and Caribbean Adventures

(☎ 800-934-3483, fax 954-434-4282), 10400 Griffin Rd, Suite 303, Fort Lauderdale, FL 33328. Otherwise organized tours to the Turks and Caicos are few and far between.

From the Turks and Caicos, daylong excursions to the Dominican Republic are offered by travel agencies; see the Caicos Islands chapter for details.

Getting Around

AIR

All the islands except for West and East Caicos are served by air from Grand Turk and Provo. Most flights island-hop; planes land merely to drop off and pick up passengers, and they're usually back in the air before you can blink. Flights are often fully booked, and you may be placed on a waiting list. Planes often leave early.

Three local companies have flights between the islands on a quasischeduled basis. The largest and most professional operator is Sky King (on Provo ☎ 649-94-15464; on Grand Turk 649-94-61520; on South Caicos 649-94-63376), with about 10 flights daily between Provo and Grand Turk.

Turks & Caicos Airways (on Provo ☎ 649-94-64255; on South Caicos 649-94-63279) offers regular scheduled interisland service between all the inhabited islands.

Interisland Airways (on Provo ☎ 649-94-15481; on Grand Turk 649-94-61667) also offers regular interisland flights. I've experienced professional piloting with Interisland, but one of their pilots was a bit cavalier for my liking! All three companies also offer charter flights.

The smaller cays can only be accessed by charter plane. Fares are usually based on five passengers. The three airlines listed above offer charter flights between all islands and nearby destinations. Provo Air Charter (☎ 649-94-64296), on Provo, also offers interisland flights.

BUS
Public bus service is limited to a single line on Provo. There are no buses on the other islands.

CAR
Driving is on the *left*. Speed limits in the Turks and Caicos are 20 mph in settlements and 40 mph on main highways.

Because local transportation is limited, renting a car or motorcycle makes sense on Provo if you plan to explore the island. Otherwise, stick to taxis or bicycles for 'scooting' around locally.

Only one leading US car-rental company – Budget – has an office on Provo. Several local companies also rent cars on Provo and Grand Turk. Elsewhere car-rental options are virtually nil. See island chapters for details.

A government tax of US$10 is levied on car rentals (US$5 on scooter rentals). Mandatory insurance costs US$14.

BICYCLE
As in The Bahamas, bicycles can be rented at many hotels and concessions, but they're unwieldy beach cruisers. They're fine for tootling around but not for serious touring.

TAXI
Taxis are available on all the inhabited islands. Most taxis will be minivans. They are a good bet for touring the islands, since most taxi drivers double as tour guides.

Make sure you negotiate an agreeable price with the driver before setting out in the taxi. The fares are generally quoted according to the number of passengers; each additional passenger will reduce the per-capita fare.

Taxi drivers on Provo are members of the Providenciales Taxi Association (☎ 649-94-65481). This association can order a taxi for you by radio dispatch.

ORGANIZED TOURS
Both Sky King and Turks & Caicos Airways (see the Air section, above) offer island-hopping excursions.

J&B Tours at the Leeward Marina on Provo offers various excursions using its fleet of 11 boats. Boat excursions include half-day and full-day fishing, snorkeling, sightseeing, and beach-cruising.

See island chapters for more details. For information on special-interest and outdoor activities, see the Outdoor Activities chapter.

Caicos Islands

The Caicos chain is an arc that comprises, west to east, the islands of West Caicos, Providenciales (the main tourist gateway and hot spot), North Caicos, Middle Caicos, East Caicos, and South Caicos, as well as numerous small isles and cays.

Providenciales

Pop 7000

As recently as 1964, the island of Providenciales (colloquially called 'Provo') did not have a single wheeled vehicle. In 1990 the 230-room Turquoise Reef Resort & Casino opened on Grace Bay, giving the island both its first large hotel and a long-awaited casino. Provo is now the most developed island for tourism, boasting many resort hotels, an 18-hole golf course, and miles of roads. This development darling of the chain is suddenly popular with retirees from around the world; the past decade has seen blossoming residential development, especially luxurious villas along Sapodilla Bay. Given its recent evolution, the island has an atmosphere that's more reminiscent of the Florida Keys than of Nassau, and it has little of the character of other Caribbean islands. Provo has a trump card, however: its diving. Miles and miles of coral reefs are temptingly close to shore.

The island is shaped like a wedge, narrowing to the northeast. The north shore is a gentle, concave curve lined with beaches. The south shore is indented by sounds and lakes.

The main town, sprawling, soulless namesake Providenciales, sits in the middle of the island. It's a modern town with an irregular layout. Most of the island's services are here, including snazzy shopping malls strung along Leeward Hwy. There are pockets of makeshift shacks – the

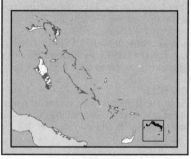

HIGHLIGHTS

- Parasailing over Grace Bay
- Diving the wall at West Caicos or South Caicos
- Northwest Point Marine National Park and the beach at Malcolm Roads
- Stunning Chalk Sound National Park . . . bring your camera!
- Hiking and bird watching on Middle Caicos and North Caicos
- Bonefishing in Belle Sound, South Caicos

homes of Haitians – interspersed among the more upscale homes. Turtle Cove, about a mile northeast of downtown, is a node for tourist services, and it has Provo's premier marina.

The resort scene is 5-mile-long Grace Bay, with its blindingly white sand and unbelievably turquoise waters. The bay begins east of Turtle Cove and is lined with an unbroken, snow-white beach backed by well-spaced hotels. Smith's Reef lies off-shore, providing good snorkeling. Grace Bay curves toward the northeastern tip of the island, ending at Leeward Marina. The marina is home to Josiah Marvel, who, along with Jamaican-born Bertie Sadler, has spent years studying the question of exactly where Christopher Columbus made his first New World landfall (they are heavily partisan toward the Turks and Caicos). Secluded Leeward Beach is good for beachcombing. The entire north shore and offshore waters are protected within Princess Alexandra National Park.

Juba Point Salina, a large lake surrounded by mangrove flats, spreads along the south shore inland of the coast. East of the lake, the Long Bay Hills, an upcoming residential area, rise over the shore. Long Bay Beach, 3 miles long, is accessible by trails from Long Bay Beach Dr.

Away from the beaches, Provo's charm lies in its rugged hills and ridges, carpeted with prickly pear cacti and scrub unfolding down to the sea. The western half of Provo is mostly barren wilderness, dramatic and well worth exploring, with two national parks.

Provo is surrounded by uninhabited cays that you can easily reach by chartered boat or excursion.

Orientation
The main highway, Leeward Hwy, runs east from downtown along the island's spine, ending near Bird Rock. A coastal highway, Grace Bay Rd, parallels Grace Bay.

A separate coast road runs northwest from downtown to Blue Hills and Wheeland settlements, beyond which it continues as a dirt track to Northwest Point. A fourth road runs south from downtown to Sapodilla Bay.

Information
Tourist Offices The tourist office (☎ 649-94-64970) is at Turtle Cove Marina Plaza; it's open 9 am to 5 pm weekdays. There's also a tourist information booth in the arrivals hall at Provo's airport.

Money Barclays Bank (☎ 649-94-64245) is in Butterfield Square, the main downtown plaza, on Leeward Hwy. Scotiabank (☎ 649-94-64750, fax 649-94-64755), also in Butterfield Square, has a 24-hour ATM. You can receive money by wire transfer through Western Union (☎ 649-94-13702) on Leeward Hwy.

Post & Communications The post office (☎ 649-94-64676) is next to the police station on Old Airport Rd; it's open 8 am to noon and 2 to 4 pm Monday to Thursday and 8 am to 12:30 pm and 2 to 5:30 pm Friday. Federal Express (☎ 649-94-64682) has an office in the Center Complex on Leeward Hwy. DHL Worldwide Express (☎ 649-94-64352) has an office in Butterfield Square.

There are public phone booths at several roadside locations. Dial ☎ 111 to place credit-card calls. A telephone exchange is on Leeward Hwy near Turtle Cove.

Travel Agencies Try Provo Travel in Central Square Plaza on Leeward Hwy. There are several other agencies downtown.

Bookstore For a large selection of books, newspapers, and magazines, try the Unicorn Bookstore (☎ 649-94-15458, fax 649-94-15510, unicorn@caribsurf.com), at the Market Place on Leeward Hwy. Most resort boutiques sell a small supply of books and magazines.

Laundry Try Pioneer Cleaners in Butterfield Square.

Medical Services The MBS Medical Clinic (☎ 649-94-64242), on Leeward Hwy, has several private doctors. Try Dr Steven Bourne (☎ 649-94-10000), Dr Euan Menzies (☎ 649-94-64242), or Dr Sam Slattery (☎ 649-94-10525). The clinic has a recompression chamber.

The New Era Medical Centre is in Blue Hills.

The Myrtle Rigby Health Clinic (☎ 649-94-13000, pager 6-9000 #1094, VHF channel 82), downtown on Leeward Hwy, is government-run.

The Provo Discount Pharmacy, in Central Square Plaza on Leeward Hwy, is open 8 am to 10 pm daily.

Diane Hawkins of Aromatome, at the Turquoise Reef Resort & Casino (see the Places to Stay section), offers massage and aromatherapy by appointment. She also offers yoga classes.

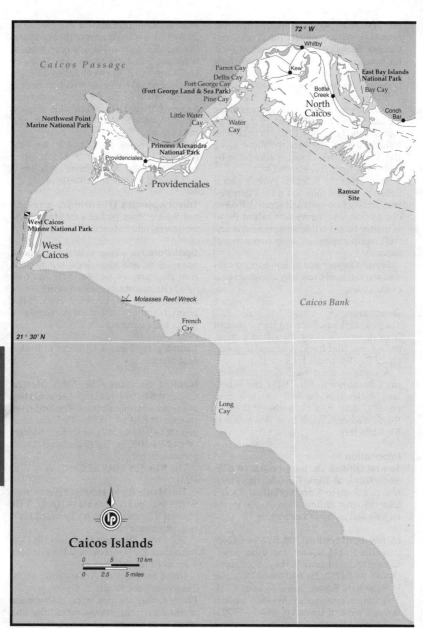

CAICOS ISLANDS

72° W

Caicos Passage

Whitby

Kew

Parrot Cay
Dellis Cay
Fort George Cay
(Fort George Land & Sea Park)
Pine Cay

East Bay Islands
National Park

Bay Cay

Bottle
Creek

Conch
Bar

Little Water
Cay

Water
Cay

North
Caicos

Northwest Point
Marine National Park

Providenciales

Princess Alexandra
National Park

Providenciales

Ramsar
Site

West Caicos
Marine National Park

West
Caicos

Molasses Reef Wreck

Caicos Bank

French
Cay

21° 30' N

Long
Cay

Caicos Islands

0   5   10 km

0   2.5   5 miles

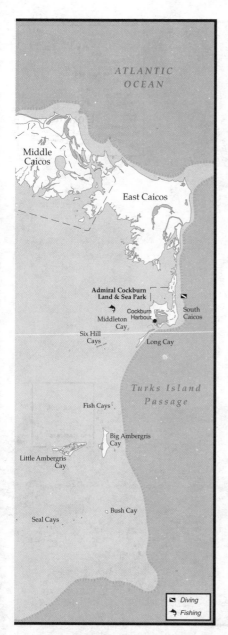

ATLANTIC
OCEAN

Middle
Caicos

East Caicos

**Admiral Cockburn
Land & Sea Park**

Cockburn   South
Middleton   Harbour   Caicos
Cay

Six Hill
Cays

Long Cay

*Turks Island
Passage*

Fish Cays

Big Ambergris
Cay

Little Ambergris
Cay

Bush Cay

Seal Cays

↘ Diving
↖ Fishing

CAICOS ISLANDS

Emergency Dial ☎ 999 for emergencies, 649-94-64259 for the police, and 649-94-64444 for the fire department.

Cheshire Hall
Pickings for sightseers are rather slim downtown, but history buffs might check out the ruins of this 1790s plantation house, constructed by British Loyalists. It's on Leeward Hwy.

West Providenciales & Northwest Point Marine National Park
A rugged dirt road (for 4WD vehicles only) leads from Wheeland, a settlement northwest of downtown, to **Malcolm Roads**, a superb 2-mile-long beach good for snorkeling and popular with locals on weekends. Following this arduous, windy, hilly, rocky track, you're soon amid cacti, with views over the inland saline lakes.

The **Tiki Huts**, at the south end of the beach, is a tumbledown Polynesian village sitting over a coral shore. It was erected by a French TV company, which used it for an adventure game show until a contestant was killed while diving for conch. There are no facilities.

Another dirt road leads from Crystal Bay Resorts, northwest of Wheeland, to **Northwest Point**. From here you can walk east to a lighthouse. It's a desperate drive, with deep sand and potholes, and you shouldn't attempt it unless you have a large 4WD. Many people who attempt the track in small jeeps get stuck!

Protecting reefs off Provo's west shore, Northwest Point Marine National Park also encompasses several saline lakes that attract breeding and migrant waterfowl. The largest is **Pigeon Pond**, inland. Other ponds – notably Northwest Point Pond and Frenchman's Creek – encompass tidal flats and mangrove swamps along the west coast, attracting fish and fowl in large numbers. You'll have to hike to get here.

Chalk Sound National Park
The waters of this incredible 3-mile-long bay, about 2 miles southwest of downtown, define 'turquoise.' The color is uniform: a

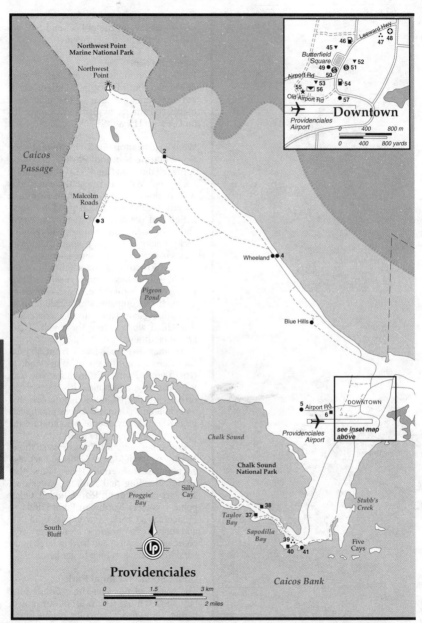

Northwest Point
Marine National Park

Northwest
Point

Caicos
Passage

Malcolm
Roads

Pigeon
Pond

Wheeland

Blue Hills

Leeward Hwy

Butterfield
Square

Airport Rd

Old Airport Rd

Downtown

Providenciales
Airport

0   400   800 m
0   400   800 yards

Airport Rd

DOWNTOWN

Providenciales
Airport

see inset map
above

Chalk Sound

Chalk Sound
National Park

Stubb's
Creek

Proggin'
Bay

Silly
Cay

Taylor
Bay

Sapodilla
Bay

Five
Cays

South
Bluff

Providenciales

Caicos Bank

0   1.5   3 km
0   1   2 miles

CAICOS ISLANDS

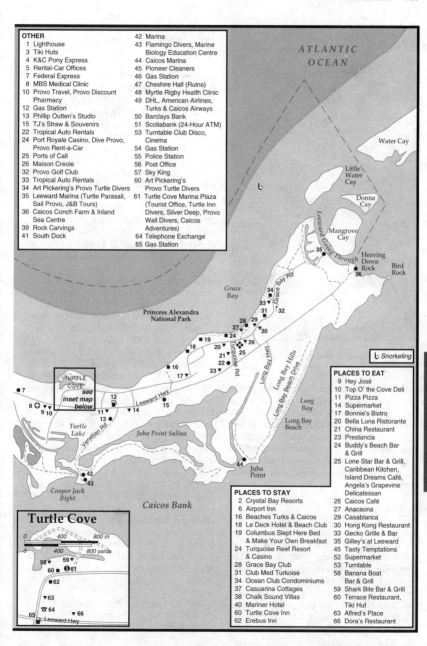

OTHER
1 Lighthouse
3 Tiki Huts
4 K&C Pony Express
5 Rental-Car Offices
7 Federal Express
8 MBS Medical Clinic
10 Provo Travel, Provo Discount Pharmacy
12 Gas Station
13 Phillip Outten's Studio
15 TJ's Straw & Souvenirs
22 Tropical Auto Rentals
24 Port Royale Casino, Dive Provo, Provo Rent-a-Car
25 Ports of Call
26 Maison Creole
32 Provo Golf Club
33 Tropical Auto Rentals
34 Art Pickering's Provo Turtle Divers
35 Leeward Marina (Turtle Parasail, Sail Provo, J&B Tours)
36 Caicos Conch Farm & Inland Sea Centre
39 Rock Carvings
41 South Dock

42 Marina
43 Flamingo Divers, Marine Biology Education Centre
44 Caicos Marina
45 Pioneer Cleaners
46 Gas Station
47 Cheshire Hall (Ruins)
48 Myrtle Rigby Health Clinic
49 DHL, American Airlines, Turks & Caicos Airways
50 Barclays Bank
51 Scotiabank (24-Hour ATM)
53 Turntable Club Disco, Cinema
54 Gas Station
55 Police Station
56 Post Office
57 Sky King
60 Art Pickering's Provo Turtle Divers
61 Turtle Cove Marina Plaza (Tourist Office, Turtle Inn Divers, Silver Deep, Provo Wall Divers, Caicos Adventures)
64 Telephone Exchange
65 Gas Station

ATLANTIC OCEAN

Water Cay

Little Water Cay

Donna Cay

Mangrove Cay

Heaving Down Rock

Bird Rock

Leeward Going Through

Grace Bay

Princess Alexandra National Park

Grace Bay Rd

Long Bay Hills Rd

Long Bay Beach Drive

Long Bay

Long Bay Beach

Turquoise Rd

TURTLE COVE see inset map below

Leeward Hwy

Turtle Lake

Juba Point Salina

Venetian Rd

Cooper Jack Bight

Caicos Bank

Juba Point

Snorkeling

CAICOS ISLANDS

PLACES TO EAT
9 Hey José
10 Top O' the Cove Deli
11 Pizza Pizza
14 Supermarket
17 Bonnie's Bistro
20 Bella Luna Ristorante
21 China Restaurant
23 Prestancia
24 Buddy's Beach Bar & Grill
25 Lone Star Bar & Grill, Caribbean Kitchen, Island Dreams Café, Angela's Grapevine Delicatessan
26 Caicos Café
27 Anacaona
29 Casablanca
30 Hong Kong Restaurant
33 Gecko Grille & Bar
35 Gilley's at Leeward
45 Tasty Temptations
52 Supermarket
53 Turntable
58 Banana Boat Bar & Grill
59 Shark Bite Bar & Grill
60 Terrace Restaurant, Tiki Hut
63 Alfred's Place
66 Dora's Restaurant

PLACES TO STAY
2 Crystal Bay Resorts
6 Airport Inn
16 Beaches Turks & Caicos
18 Le Deck Hotel & Beach Club
19 Columbus Slept Here Bed & Make Your Own Breakfast
24 Turquoise Reef Resort & Casino
28 Grace Bay Club
31 Club Med Turkoise
34 Ocean Club Condominiums
37 Casuarina Cottages
38 Chalk Sound Villas
40 Mariner Hotel
60 Turtle Cove Inn
62 Erebus Inn

Turtle Cove

0   400   800 m
0   400   800 yards

58
59
60 61
62
63
64
65   66
Leeward Hwy

The Tiki Huts at Malcolm Roads

vast, unrippled, electric-blue carpet eerily and magnificently studded with countless tiny islets, like mushrooms.

A slender peninsula separates the sound from the sea. The peninsula is scalloped with beach-lined bays, notably **Sapodilla Bay**. A horribly potholed road runs along the peninsula, which is lined with vacation homes.

Rock Carvings
At the far eastern end of the Sapodilla Bay peninsula, a rocky hilltop boasts carvings on slabs of rock, like God's Ten Commandments. In fact they date back only to 1844. The slabs are intricately carved with Roman lettering that records the names of sailors apparently shipwrecked here and the dates of their sojourns. The carvings are reached via a rocky trail that begins 200 yards east of the Mariner Hotel; the

trail leads uphill 200 yards to the summit, which offers wonderful views over the island and Chalk Sound.

Caicos Conch Farm & Inland Sea Centre
This smelly place (☎ 649-94-65330, fax 649-94-65849), near the northeastern tip of Provo, claims to be 'the world's only conch farm.' It strives to protect the Caribbean queen conch *(Strombus gigas)* from extinction and also raises the mollusks commercially for export and local use. The farm was the brainchild of Chuck Hesse, an environmentalist who after years of research can now produce a consumable mollusk in 28 months, from egg to adult conch. Chuck reckons he has 2 million conchs in the ponds and an additional 1 million offshore in 80 acres of 'pasture' fenced to keep predators at bay. (He reckons that in the wild only one in 500,000 conch eggs matures to adulthood, due to predation; at the farm more than 80% of larvae survive.) Annual production is over 750,000 conchs a year, with 10,000 harvested weekly. They're worth US$1 apiece!

You can learn how conchs are grown from eggs to adults on a tour. You'll see the hatchery and metamorphosis facility, onshore nursery ponds, 'sub-sea maturation pasture,' and conch-processing facility. The facility is rather boring unless you have a guide to bring it to life. Call ahead. It's open 9 am to 5 pm daily; the tour costs US$6. The mailing address is PO Box 286, Providenciales, Turks and Caicos, BWI.

J&B Tours (☎ 649-94-65047, fax 649-94-65288, jbtours@caribsurf.com) offers an excursion to the farm.

Diving & Snorkeling
There's no shortage of dive operators on Provo, and they offer everything from resort courses to PADI instruction. Most offer free hotel pick-up. See the Dive Sites sidebar for highlights of Provo's underwater world.

Art Pickering's Provo Turtle Divers (☎ 649-94-64232; in the USA 954-467-3460, 800-833-1341, fax 954-467-7544), with facilities at both the Ocean Club and the Turtle Cove Inn (see the Places to Stay section), offers a full range of dives and courses. It offers a free introductory class and has two 30-foot and one 41-foot dive boats. This dive operator also has week-long packages (US$650 per person double) and rents dive equipment; its mailing address is PO Box 219, Providenciales, Turks and Caicos, BWI.

Caicos Adventures (☎ 649-94-13346, divucrzy@caribsurf.com; in the USA ☎ 800-513-5822), at the Turtle Cove Marina Plaza, specializes in custom trips to uncharted dive sites and uses a 36-foot dive boat. It also has a full range of dives and courses, plus a 'Dive West Caicos' trip for US$70, including hotel transfers, two dives, and lunch at a beach.

Club Med Turkoise (see Places to Stay), on Grace Bay, specializes in diving, but its superb facilities are for guests only. It charges US$35 per day, including two dives plus a night dive. An 'Open Water Certification' course costs US$225. Other Club Med facilities have been criticized for taking out too many divers together. The club's 'Dedicated Dive Program,' however, is not a cattle drive: Only 50 certified divers a week are permitted.

Dive Provo (☎ 649-94-65029; in the USA 800-234-7768), at the Turquoise Reef Resort & Casino, is a PADI Dive Center. It offers weeklong packages starting at US$810 per person double. It has three 40- to 42-foot dive boats and offers photo and video services.

There's also Turtle Inn Divers (☎ 649-94-15389; in the USA 800-359-3483), at Turtle Cove Marina Plaza, which runs certification courses and uses a 45-foot motor catamaran and 28-foot dive boat. It also offers snorkeling, charging US$25 to US$30 a trip. Turtle Inn Divers' postal address is PO Box 152, Providenciales, Turks and Caicos, BWI.

Other operators include Provo Wall Divers (☎ 649-94-15595) and Silver Deep (☎ 649-94-65612, fax 649-94-64527), both at Turtle Cove Marina Plaza. There's also Flamingo Divers at the Marine Biology

---

Dive Sites

Amphitheater – This bowl-shaped undercut at 85 feet curves into the Caicos Passage. Whales, sharks, and manta rays often pass by.

Chimney – Garden eels populate this 10-foot-wide cut in the plate coral.

Coral Stairway – A series of coral steps leads to a sand cellar that is Grand Central Station for schooling eagle rays.

Shark Hotel – Check in at this 'hotel' to commune with reef and blacktip sharks. The wall has a sponge-encrusted coral chimney that descends 130 feet.

French Cay, south of Providenciales, also features superb diving:

Dax Canyon – The wall starts at 45 feet and drops to a shelf at 150 feet. Large eagle rays are frequent visitors.

Rock 'n' Roll – A huge coral mound marks this wall dive, renowned for eagle rays, sharks, moray eels, and a rainbow of sponges. ■

Education Centre (☎ /fax 649-94-64193) on Cooper Jack Bight.

There are several live-aboard dive boats based in Provo. *Sea Dancer* (☎ /fax 649-94-65276; in the USA ☎ 305-669-9391, fax 305-669-9475) and *Turks & Caicos Aggressor* (in the USA ☎ 504-385-2628, 800-348-2628, fax 504-384-0817) both offer weeklong dive charters.

The MBS Medical Clinic has a recompression chamber; see the Information section.

Golf

The Provo Golf Club (☎ 649-94-65991, fax 649-94-65992, provgolf@caribsurf.com) is an 18-hole course across from Club Med Turkoise on Grace Bay. The beautiful, Karl Litton-designed championship course has been rated one of the 10 best golf courses in the Caribbean. The course features rocky outcroppings, four sets of tees, unrelenting water hazards, and plenty of palms and bougainvilleas lining the tight, lush

CAICOS ISLANDS

fairways. The course's vital statistics: par 72, 6529 yards.

The course charges US$95/55 for 18/nine holes. Club rental costs US$15/10. Cart rental costs US$15/9. There's also a driving range; a bucket of 50 balls costs US$5. Lessons are offered to nonmembers for US$40. The Fairways Bar & Grill, in the clubhouse, serves breakfast and lunch. The Turks & Caicos Islands Amateur Open is held here each October. The club's postal address is PO Box 124, Providenciales, Turks and Caicos, BWI.

Sport Fishing & Bonefishing
Captain Bob Collins (☎ 649-94-64065, fax 649-94-64141) offers his 43-foot Hatteras, *Sakitumi*, for half- and full-day deep-sea fishing charters. Captain Barr Gardiner (☎ 649-94-64874, fax 649-94-64960) offers two daily bonefishing charters; write PO Box 241, Providenciales, Turks and Caicos, BWI. J&B Tours (☎ 649-94-65047, fax 649-94-65288, jbtours@caribsurf.com), at Leeward Marina, also has bonefishing excursions.

Two events comprise the Turks & Caicos Billfish Challenge: the Invitational Billfish Tournament and the Turks & Caicos International Billfish Tournament. Both are held in July.

Boat Excursions
Sail Provo (☎ 649-94-64783), at Leeward Marina, offers half-day (Sunday, Tuesday, Thursday; US$39) and full-day (Monday, Wednesday, Friday; US$69) excursions to Little Water Cay aboard the 52-foot catamaran *Arielle* or the *Two Fingers*, a 36-foot catamaran. It also offers sunset cruises on Wednesday and Thursday for US$29.

Michael Robertson (☎ 649-94-65122, VHF channel 74) offers charters aboard his 41-foot trimaran, *Minx*. He also offers a full-day cruise with catered lunch, plus a sunset champagne cruise with gourmet dinner for just you and your loved one!

J&B Tours (see contact information above), at Leeward Marina, has a variety of powerboat cruises to outlying cays, including a beach cruise, the 'Provo Native

Tour,' and the 'Iguana Island Shuttle.' It also offers a nocturnal trip to see the phosphorescent mating display of glowworms off Pine Cay (see the X-Rated Antics sidebar in this chapter).

Other Activities
Most resorts have tennis courts. Club Med Turkoise is particularly noted for its tennis facilities.

K&C Pony Express (☎ 649-94-10073), in Wheeland, 3 miles northwest of downtown, offers horseback riding along the beach at 9 and 11 am and 3 and 5 pm daily (US$35, including transfers).

Turtle Parasail (☎ 649-94-15389), at Leeward Marina, offers parasailing.

Organized Tours
Executive Tours (☎ 649-94-64524) offers half-day island tours for US$10 to US$12. The Island Network Fitness Centre (☎ 649-94-65822), in the Ports of Call shopping complex at Grace Bay, offers a 'fitness trek.' Provo Air Charter (☎ 649-94-65040) offers an 'Aerial Photography Safari' for US$50.

Ocean Outback (☎ 649-94-15810) will take you and 'just one other person' (presumably your loved one) to Silly Cay, at the mouth of Chalk Sound. A full-day trip (Tuesday or Thursday only) costs US$65. The company guarantees that you'll have this beautiful cay to yourselves. You can even overnight, with a tent, dinner, and breakfast provided, for US$75. Ocean Outback also offers a daylong 'Ultimate Getaway' excursion for US$75, including transfers, breakfast, snorkeling, barbecue lunch, and all drinks.

Special Events
The archipelago's biggest bash is held on Provo each July. The Provo Summer Festival features regattas, parades, partying, and a 'Miss Turks and Caicos Beauty Pageant,' all spread over a week.

Places to Stay
Downtown & Turtle Cove The *Airport Inn* (☎ 649-94-13514, fax 649-94-13281),

in the Airport Plaza at the airport, is perfect if you're in transit between islands. It has 12 rooms with ceiling fans, calming modern decor, cable TV, and phone. A restaurant is in the works. Rates are US$65/75 without/with air-con. It offers special rates for airline crew, plus 15% off car-rental rates for guests.

The *Turtle Cove Inn* (☎ 649-94-64203, fax 649-94-64141; in the USA ☎ 800-887-0477), near the marina, is an intimate property centered on an amoeba-shaped pool and stone-paved sun deck surrounded by lush tropical gardens. It bills itself as a dive and tennis center and has its own dock. There are 30 air-con rooms, all with tile floor, patio, a lively tropical motif, cable TV, phone, and ceiling fan. Rates (summer/winter) are US$85/95 at poolside, US$90/105 marina, US$100/115 ocean-view, and US$115/130 suite. A nine-night minimum stay is required at Christmas, when prices rise 20%. There are two restaurants – the Tiki Hut is a lively little spot – a dive shop, and scooter rentals on-site. The postal address is PO Box 131, Providenciales, Turks and Caicos, BWI.

For the best views, check into *Erebus Inn* (☎ 649-94-64240, fax 649-94-64704; in the USA ☎ 800-323-5655), amid landscaped grounds on the hill overlooking Turtle Cove. It has 21 spacious air-con rooms with a tropical motif, tile floors, cable TV, rattan furniture, ceiling fans, and a choice of king-size beds or two doubles. Sliding glass doors open to patios with fine views along the coast. Better yet are the four handsome chalets and the two-bedroom villa perched on the hillside. They have marvelous ambiance, with large French doors opening to wooden decks. The inn's facilities include a panoramic restaurant and sun deck, two pools, clay tennis courts, miniature golf, and a shuttle service by boat to the nearby beach. Rates are US$105 to US$150 April through December and US$140 to US$165 the rest of the year. The villa costs US$315 and US$420, respectively. The inn's mailing address is PO Box 238, Providenciales, Turks and Caicos, BWI.

Grace Bay & East Providenciales The guesthouse *Columbus Slept Here Bed & Make Your Own Breakfast* (☎ /fax 649-94-65878), on Grace Bay, is equipped with one bedroom with en-suite bathroom and kitchen privileges. There are also two small 'efficiency' units, each with private bathroom. One has twin beds; the other has a double bed. Rates are US$75/500 daily/monthly and include continental breakfast, 'guard cats and swimming dogs,' 'waking to boisterous mockingbirds and whistling ospreys,' 'gazing at sextillion stars,' and 'basking on a nearly deserted beach of quintillion grains of white sand.' The place is run by a convivial Canadian, Louise Fletcher. The guesthouse's mailing address is PO Box 273, Providenciales, Turks and Caicos, BWI.

Le Deck Hotel & Beach Club (☎ 649-94-65547, 800-528-1905, fax 649-94-65770, ledeck@caribsurf.com), just southwest of Columbus Slept Here, is a small, informal inn with 26 luxury air-con rooms set around a flower garden. Each has an iron-framed bed, telephone, cable TV, and ceiling fan. Bathrooms are small. Junior suites, upstairs, have vaulted ceilings. The hotel has a dive center offering certification courses. There's a freshwater pool, plus a restaurant and bar overlooking the beach. Standard rooms cost US$110/160 single/double in summer; junior suites cost US$170/185 in winter. One-bedroom condos cost US$210/260 in winter and US$295 in peak season. Dive and golf packages are offered. The postal address is PO Box 144, Providenciales, Turks and Caicos, BWI.

The graceful *Turquoise Reef Resort & Casino* (☎ 649-94-65555, fax 649-94-65629; in the USA ☎ 305-670-4911, 800-992-2015, fax 305-670-4948) has 228 air-con rooms centered on a huge sun deck and pool. Each has a tropical motif, contemporary rattan furniture, terra-cotta tile floors, fans, and patios or balconies. All have ocean views. The place is peaceful and attracts a mixed clientele of oldsters and young couples as well as families. It boasts the 'Kids on Vacation Club' (8 am to 9 pm Monday to Friday) where kids from two to 12 years old are catered to with activities such as puppet-making and pool games. There's supervised babysitting at night. Garden-view rooms cost US$130 to US$200 and deluxe beachfront rooms cost US$185 to US$270, depending on season. The local postal address is Grace Bay Rd, PO Box 205, Providenciales, Turks and Caicos, BWI; in the USA, c/o Icon Hotel Marketing, 9200 S Dadeland Blvd, Suite 518, Miami, FL 33156.

Club Med Turkoise (☎ 649-94-65500, 800-258-2633, fax 649-94-65497) is spread over 70 acres toward the eastern end of Grace Bay. The club is built around a central complex with open-air bar, theater, casino and nightclub, and asymmetric pool with volleyball and water-polo area. It's more downscale and less luxurious than many other Club Meds. Still, it has more facilities than you can shake a stick at, including eight tennis courts, a dive center, and an 'Intensive Circus Workshop.' Specialty weeks are offered, such as 'Comedy Club Month' in March and a Pro-Beach Volleyball week in January. The club has a panoply of excursions.

The club has a strongly Gallic flavor. Overseeing your happiness are the predominantly French 'GOs' (*gentil organizateurs*; guests are GMs, or *gentil membres*). The 298 air-con double rooms are in two-story beachfront units. Each has a king-size or two single beds. Per-person nightly rates range from US$140 to US$235, depending on season. Single supplements (for a private room) cost 20% to 100% extra. Special package rates are offered, including airfare from various US gateways.

Nearby, the *Ocean Club Condominiums* (☎ 649-94-65880, fax 649-94-65845; in the USA ☎ 800-457-8787) is a deluxe all-suite oceanfront resort centered on two attractive amoeba-shaped pools set amid beautifully manicured grounds. There are shaded hammocks slung between the palms, a swim-up bar, fitness room, and night-lit tennis court. There's also the Gecko Grille & Bar (in the Ocean Club Plaza), an on-site dive operation, fashion boutique, duty-free store, and Tropical Auto Rentals office (also in the plaza).

It has a range of 83 suites, from a studio suite (US$155/170 in summer/winter) to three-bedroom deluxe suites for up to six people (US$460/695). All have a telephone, cable TV, en-suite kitchen, and washer and dryer. Children under 12 stay free with parents when sharing a suite. Seniors over 55 get a 10% discount in low season. May through June and September through November, all guests receive a 'Caicos Treasure Chest' card that entitles them to discounts on interisland flights and at local businesses. The mailing address is PO Box 240, Providenciales, Turks and Caicos, BWI.

Beaches Turks & Caicos, formerly Royal Bay Resort & Villas, is now part of Sandals Resort, the chain that has been voted 'Top Caribbean Hotel Group' *every* year in the World Travel Awards. To contact Sandals, call the following numbers:

Turks and Caicos	☎ 649-94-68000
	fax 649-94-68001
Canada	☎ 416-223-0028,
	800-545-8283
	fax 416-223-3306
UK	☎ 0171-581-9895
	fax 0171-823-8758
USA	☎ 305-284-1300,
	800-726-3257
	fax 305-667-8996

Beaches Turks & Caicos has 177 large, elegantly furnished, air-con, ocean-view rooms in seven categories, including two standards of suites (the suites all have two bathrooms – one with a Roman tub and shower). All have two double beds or king-size bed and a private verandah. There are also 36 one- and two-bedroom villas, each with fully equipped kitchen. A cable TV, clock radio, and telephone are standard. It offers three restaurants, bars and lounges (including a lively piano bar), and a full range of water sports and recreational activities. Rates for a seven-night package begin at US$1472/1592 double low/peak season (US$100 per night single supplement). Everything inside the resort, including diving and alcohol, is included for a single package price.

Unlike Sandals' other resorts – it has always been a *couples-only* resort chain – Beaches accepts singles, couples, and families with children. But it feels like a deluxe adult resort to which kids have been admitted. It broke my heart to see infants crawling on the full-size snooker table and youngsters dragging pool cues through the restaurants and shooting ivory balls onto the terra-cotta floors.

Sandals offers charter flights; see the Getting There & Away section for details. The postal address is Light Bight Rd, Providenciales, Turks and Caicos, BWI.

The most luxurious offering is the *Grace Bay Club* (☎ 649-94-65757, 800-94-65757, fax 649-94-65758), a lush 5-acre world centered on an Andalusian-style mansion and a plaza with a tinkling fountain. The entire complex – brimful of tasteful artwork and antiques – is like stepping inside the Louvre or British Museum. The rooms are done up in cool igloo-white, with exquisite furnishings and artwork, monogrammed bathrobes, fine toiletries, and cable TV/VCR.

Other temptations include the clover-shaped swimming pool, exquisite patios, a Jacuzzi, two tennis courts, water sports (including Sunfish and Hobie Cats), a waterfall with real frogs, and an outside thatched restaurant serving acclaimed cuisine. The club also features the spiffy Anacaona Restaurant for intimate candle-lit dinners. Service is impeccable. There are eight types of rooms, from junior suites (US$355 to US$455, depending on the season) to a two-bedroom penthouse (US$895 to US$1255). The postal address is PO Box 128, Providenciales, Turks and Caicos, BWI.

There's no shortage of private cottages for rent. Consider *Treasure Beach Villas* (☎ 649-94-64325, fax 649-94-64108), with 18 units in two concrete-block 'villas.' Each features tile floors, tasteful furnishings, fully equipped kitchen, cable TV, and tropical landscaping. Rates range from US$112 to US$175, including a free rental car, which you pick up at the airport.

Try *The Cottage* (☎ 649-94-65376, fax 649-94-65792), a one-bedroom bungalow near Turquoise Reef Resort & Casino. It has a king-size bed, full kitchen, and cozy down-home furnishings. The bungalow rents for US$125/800 daily/weekly April to September and US$150/1000 daily/weekly October to March (additional people are charged US$25 each). Write c/o Kit and Colin Sanders, PO Box 92, Providenciales, Turks and Caicos, BWI.

Platinum Resort Villas (☎ 649-94-65539, fax 649-94-65421) has four fully furnished units (with one, two, three, or four bedrooms) in the prestigious Leeward neighborhood, a five-minute walk from the beach. Rates are US$143 to US$357 daily, US$1000 to US$2500 weekly. Another one-bedroom *guesthouse* (in the USA ☎ 609-983-1811, fax 609-983-3661), with cable TV and deck, rents for US$850 to US$1200 weekly; write c/o Coral House, 19 Saw Mill Rd, Medford, NH 08055. A larger property is *Villa Camilla* (in the USA ☎ 617-232-1370), a luxurious oceanfront three-bedroom home with a separate one-bedroom guesthouse.

Comfort Suites was due to open a 100-unit hotel in early 1998 next to Turquoise Reef Resort & Casino.

West Providenciales A new upscale condominium resort complex – *Crystal Bay Resorts* (☎ 649-94-64929, fax 649-94-64825) – was due to open in late 1997 on 98 acres near the far northwestern end of the island. The project will be completed by 2000, when it will have 160 privately owned deluxe units, most available for rent. These include junior suites and one-, two-, and three-bedroom apartments along the shore amid the low scrub. The bay is smothered with seagrasses and is not a prime spot. The resort will have two freshwater pools, a Jacuzzi, and a restaurant and bar. Its postal address is PO Box 101, Providenciales, Turks and Caicos, BWI.

Chalk Sound Villas (in the USA ☎ 404-351-2200, fax 404-351-2615), located in

CAICOS ISLANDS

southwest Provo, offers nine handsome, tastefully decorated units in a residential compound between Sapodilla and Taylor bays. Weekly rates start at US$1800. One is a true stunner: Rockspray, a charming and romantic stone villa with cathedral beamed ceilings that looks like it came from the Middle Ages. It sits on a tiny peninsula overlooking Chalk Sound and has open decks with hammocks for admiring the spectacular views. Its interior has fine furnishings, a TV, and a stereo. The mailing address is PO Box 550509, Atlanta, GA 30355.

Casuarina Cottages (☎ 649-94-64474), on the Sapodilla peninsula, has three small yet handsome cottages that rent for US$800 to US$1000 weekly.

At press time, the 25-room *Mariner Hotel* (☎ /fax 649-94-64488), at the east end of Sapodilla Bay, was closed, but ground had been broken on an upscale resort and marina – *Silly Creek Estate & Marina* – at the south end of the peninsula.

Places to Eat

Downtown & Turtle Cove A good place for breakfast is the congenial *Tiki Hut* cabaña bar and grill at the Turtle Cove Inn. It has a wide menu, from Belgian waffles to 'El Tiki Burritos.' The lunch menu is heavy on burgers and salads, for US$6 to US$8. Pastas and pizzas are the dinner specialties and average US$15. The inn's *Terrace Restaurant* specializes in creative conch dishes and seafoods; it's closed Sundays.

My favorite spot is the *Turntable* (☎ 649-94-13673), downtown near Butterfield Square, a quaint Haitian-run restaurant popular with locals. It serves barbecue, seafood, and chicken from US$9, plus Jamaican patties, fish and chips, and sandwiches, for US$2 to US$8. *Fast Eddie's* (☎ 649-94-13176), on Airport Rd, serves island dishes, as does unpretentious *Dora's Restaurant* (☎ 649-94-64558) on Leeward Hwy near Turtle Cove; the ambiance is somewhat forlorn until the evening crowd arrives. Dora's offers a seafood buffet at 6:30 pm Monday to Thursday for US$22,

including taxi transfers (for a minimum of four people).

The atmospheric and gaily painted *Banana Boat Bar & Grill* (☎ 649-94-15706), near Turtle Cove Marina, specializes in seafood and steaks. It also has burgers for US$6. It has an oyster bar, plus a happy hour 4 to 7 pm. Tuesday night is seafood night.

For cafe cuisine, try the *Top O' the Cove Deli* (☎ 649-94-64694), on Leeward Hwy. If you have a pizza craving, head to *Pizza Pizza* to the east, in Provo Plaza on Leeward Hwy.

You can even find Mexican food at *Hey José* (☎ 649-94-64812) in Central Square Plaza on Leeward Hwy; it's well run by Californians. Meals cost US$6 to US$15.

Alfred's Place (☎ 649-94-64679), on the hill overlooking Turtle Cove Marina, is a favorite of yachters, who flock for chef Alfred Holzfiend's gourmet cuisine, blending French with Asiatic and Caribbean flavors; meals cost US$6 to US$30. Also try *Shark Bite Bar & Grill* (☎ 649-94-15090), just east of Turtle Cove Marina.

Tasty Temptations (☎ 649-94-64049), in Butterfield Square, serves coffee, cappuccinos, and pastries, plus sandwiches and cold cuts for lunch.

Grace Bay & East Providenciales *Jimmy's on the Beach* (☎ 649-94-15575) has an all-you-can-eat breakfast, lunch, and dinner from US$10. It has nightly specials. For US$20 you can even indulge in all-you-can-drink!

Gilley's at Leeward (☎ 649-94-65094) has a waterfront setting but uninspired decor. It serves up breakfast and lunch (mostly salads and sandwiches) for about US$5. Budget US$20 for a seafood dinner.

The lively, German-run *Caribbean Kitchen* (☎ 649-94-65884), upstairs in Ports of Call, specializes in local cuisine: everything from lobster salad and boiled fish and grits to steamed conch and oxtail. Prices start at US$5. Fish and chips are served on Wednesday night English-style in newspaper for US$9. It's open 6 am to midnight daily (Wednesday to Saturday only in summer). Next door the same owners operate *Marco Polo* (☎ 649-94-65129), featuring cuisine reflecting the Italian explorer's travels . . . from borscht for US$4 to curried salads for US$7.

The *Lone Star Bar & Grill* (☎ 649-94-65832), in the Ports of Call shopping complex, is a sports bar with three large-screen TVs. It serves Tex-Mex food and has special theme nights. Monday and Thursday are all-you-can-eat 'Fajita Rita' nights, and a prime rib special is offered on Friday.

My favorite eatery is the *Caicos Café* (☎ 649-94-65278), opposite the Grace Bay Club. This charmer has tremendous ambiance, assisted by lively artwork, tasteful music, and the chic (predominantly French) clientele. You dine on a deck shaded by a dazzling, flamboyant tree. It serves entrées from steak au poivre to seafoods, averaging US$20. The lunch menu features lobster-salad sandwiches, grilled fish, and hamburgers. Plan on spending about US$10 for lunch.

For uncommon, sophisticated creations, head to *Gecko Grille & Bar* (☎ 649-94-65885) in the Ocean Club Plaza. It's renowned for such dishes as Chilean salmon, 'Voodoo Jalapeño Shooters,' and grouper macadamia with pureed avocado and pineapple-tomato salsa. It also serves traditional West Indian fare such as spicy conch chowder and flame-roasted pork chops. Entrées begin at US$15. Soups, salads, and appetizers average US$7. You can choose air-con indoor dining in upscale, contemporary surrounds or romantic alfresco dining in a courtyard shaded by trees sparkling with myriad lights. The bar claims the largest choice of rums on the island. It's open 6 to 9:30 pm nightly except Wednesday. In summer it's open Wednesday to Sunday only.

Buddy's Beach Bar & Grill (☎ 649-94-65555), at the Turquoise Reef Resort & Casino, serves seafood and steaks; it has an outdoor oyster bar.

You can go Asian at *China Restaurant* (☎ 649-94-65377) on Turquoise Road. It serves Szechwan cuisine amid suitably Oriental decor. The house specialty is pork in hot sauce. The simple, unpretentious *Hong Kong Restaurant*, on Grace Bay Rd, is also good, with over 100 dishes on its menu.

For Italian, head to the *Portofino Restaurant* at the Turquoise Reef Resort & Casino; entrées cost about US$20. It has nightly specials, including pizzas on Monday. My favorite is the elegantly casual *Bella Luna Ristorante* (☎ 649-94-65214), a futuristic purple building with massive plate-glass windows all around, on Grace Bay Rd. Entrées average US$15. The *Pasta House Restaurant* aims 'to provide good, healthy meals at family-affordable prices.' Go on Monday or Thursday nights, when it offers all-you-can-eat.

Mediterranean cuisine has also found its way to Provo at *Prestancia* (☎ 649-94-65900) on Leeward Hwy. You can dine in the lounge or on the terrace overlooking Grace Bay. Ottoman delights include kebabs, pita bread, and pizza. Reservations are recommended. *Coco Bistro* (☎ 649-94-65369), on Grace Bay Rd, also serves Mediterranean dishes. The decor is delightful, with walls festooned with art; jazz typically adds to the romantic ambiance.

Casablanca (☎ 649-94-65449), also on Grace Bay Rd, boasts less sophisticated international fare, mostly seafoods and grilled meats from US$16 to US$25, but also has a wide selection of desserts for US$5. It opens at 6:30 pm. *Bonnie's Bistro* (☎ 649-94-65777) is another good option for seafood.

The smartest – and most expensive – place is the ultraelegant *Anacaona* (☎ 649-94-65050) by the Grace Bay Club. It serves nouvelle cuisine with a Caribbean flair. Very romantic . . . but I've heard conflicting reviews, from 'sublime' to 'poor.'

Beaches Turks & Caicos has a Tuesday-night poolside buffet.

For cafes, try *Island Dreams Café* in Ports of Call, which serves ice cream, cappuccinos, and espressos. *Angela's Grapevine Delicatessen*, also in Ports of

Call, sells pastries, meats, cheeses, etc, as well as cappuccinos and dinners-to-go.

Entertainment
Dance Clubs & Casinos Most of the upscale resorts in Grace Bay have dance clubs, including *Beaches* and *Turquoise Reef*. *Club Med Turkoise* permits outside visitors with a pass for US$22, including US$20 worth of bar tokens. It gives you full access to the dance club, bars, and nightly show. Club Med is about as wild as things get on Provo.

You can gamble at the *Port Royale Casino* (☎ 649-94-65555) at Turquoise Reef. It has roulette, blackjack, Caribbean stud poker, and slot machines.

Pubs/Bars For local color, head to the *Turntable Club Disco* on Airport Rd. It has a dartboard, pool table, and one-armed bandits. The disco on Thursday night is popular with Haitians and can sometimes get rowdy. Bingo is offered at 8 pm Saturday and on Sunday afternoons. It also has a cinema.

The *Banana Boat Bar & Grill* has live music on Tuesday. A rake 'n' scrape band sometimes plays at *Alfred's Place* (see Places to Eat, above).

In Turtle Cove, the *Shark Bite* has live entertainment most nights; it's *the* in spot on Saturday night. The unpretentious and distinctly Texan *Lone Star Bar & Grill* is probably the number-one sports bar; sports fanatics can watch three games at once on the separate satellite TVs. Happy hour is 5 to 6:30 pm Monday to Friday.

The *Caribbean Kitchen* has a live band on Saturday, as does the *Anacaona*.

Things to Buy
You can pick up a free map with discount coupons for the Ports of Call shopping complex at Grace Bay, where a large selections of beachy items, casual clothing, and batiks is offered at Tattooed Parrot (☎ 649-94-65829), Marilyn's Crafts, and the Night & Day Boutique. To put some spice into your island love life, nip into Teddy Bare and surprise your lover with lingerie or other intimate gifts.

The Caribbean Art Gallery, also in Ports of Call, sells mostly naive Haitian art, including painted wooden animals. More traditional works are represented at Lionheart Gallery, 100 yards east of Ports of Call. While here, check out the Maison Creole, boasting fabulous contemporary art, model ships, and an eclectic miscellany of home decorative pieces. It's open 10 am to 5 pm Tuesday to Saturday and 7 to 9 pm Thursday to Friday.

If you're driving east along Leeward Hwy, look for the sign saying 'Local Artist's Studio' opposite the Shell gas station. The sign points the way to the studio of Phillip Outten, a Rastafarian whom some people consider the leading artist in the Turks and Caicos. Take the first right onto Venetian Rd; his home – gaily painted in Rasta colors – is the first house on the right. (See the Turks and Caicos introductory chapter for more information on Outten.)

You can buy Cuban cigars and jewelry at Koko Tok, next to Maison Creole. The best places for duty-free jewelry are The Goldsmith's in Central Square Plaza on Leeward Hwy and the jewelry store in the Turquoise Reef Resort & Casino.

To support the local economy, pop into Nell's Gift Shop, Winnie's Gifts, or TJ's Straw & Souvenirs, all on Leeward Hwy.

Getting There & Away
Air The small and provincial Providenciales Airport is 1 mile west of town on Airport Rd. See the Turks and Caicos introductory chapter for airline telephone numbers.

American Airlines flies two daily nonstops from Miami for as little as US$160 roundtrip in low season (fares may double in peak season). American has an office in Butterfield Square. Turks & Caicos Airways has daily service from Miami.

Interisland Airways flies from Fort Lauderdale; you can also make connections through Nassau and Freeport in The Bahamas.

Sandals' Beaches Turks & Caicos offers nonstop charter flights, called 'Beaches Express,' departing John F Kennedy International Airport in New York every Sunday morning. Fares include complimentary meals.

A weekly charter flight arrives at Provo from Italy, serving Club Vacanze, an Italian-run resort on North Caicos.

Air Jamaica flies twice weekly (from US$210 roundtrip for a seven-day excursion) from Montego Bay, the airline's new Caribbean hub.

Bahamasair flies from Nassau on Friday and Sunday (US$157 one way). Turks & Caicos Airways also operates between Provo and Nassau, plus the Dominican Republic, Haiti, Jamaica, and Puerto Rico.

Provo Travel (☎ 649-94-64035, fax 649-94-64081), in Central Square Plaza, has tours to the Dominican Republic.

Boat Provo is the final stopping point on American Canadian Caribbean Line's *Niagara Prince*'s 12-day cruise through the Bahamian islands in December. A similar cruise begins in Provo in April. Windjammer Barefoot Cruises' *Amazing Grace* calls in Provo twice monthly during 13-day cruises between Grand Bahama and Trinidad (see the Getting There & Away chapter in the Bahamas section).

Turtle Cove Marina (☎ 649-94-64303) has 32 slips, plus fuel, water, electricity, showers, laundry, and grocery. Caicos Marina (☎ 649-94-65600), at Long Bay, has 12 slips and similar facilities. Leeward Marina (tel 649-94-65553), at the eastern end of the island, has similar services but no berths. There's also the South Side Basin Marina (☎ 649-94-64200).

Getting Around
To/From the Airport There are no buses from the airport. A taxi to Grace Bay costs US$10 to US$15 one way for two people; each extra person costs US$5.

Bus There's a public bus that runs along Leeward Hwy; it also runs southwest as far as South Dock and Sapodilla Bay. The fare for a one-way ride is US$2.

Car, Motorcycle & Scooter If you plan to tour, you'll want a 4WD vehicle, as many of Provo's best beaches are reached by unpaved tracks. Driving on the beaches is prohibited; if you get stuck, you'll be charged US$500 for recovery! Mandatory insurance costs US$14. Most rental companies offer free drop-off and pick-up.

Provo Rent-a-Car (☎ 649-94-64404, fax 649-94-64993) is at the airport. It also has an office (☎ 649-94-65610) at Turquoise Reef Resort & Casino. It rents cars and jeeps from US$48 (US$10 less in summer).

Tropical Auto Rentals (☎ 649-94-65300, fax 649-94-65456) charges US$49 to US$80 for nine types of vehicles, including minivans. It has an office in the Ocean Club Plaza on Grace Bay and another at Tropicana Plaza; they're open 8 am to 5 pm daily. Turks & Caicos National Car Rental (☎ 649-94-64701), with an office at the airport, charges US$37 to US$59. Island Rent-a-Car (☎ 649-94-64475) also has an office at the airport.

Suzuki Jeep Rental (☎ 649-94-64158), on Leeward Hwy, rents jeeps from US$52/312 daily/weekly.

One US-based company, Budget, has a Provo office (☎ 649-94-64079, fax 649-94-64108; in the USA ☎ 800-527-0770).

Provo Fun Cycles (☎ 649-94-65863) rents Honda scooters for US$25/39 single/double seat. It also has 250cc enduro motorcycles, plus jeeps for US$59.

Scooter Bob's (☎ 649-94-64684), in Turtle Cove Marina Plaza, rents Yamaha scooters.

Taxi There are several taxi companies. Most use minivans. You can call VHF channel 06 for the dispatcher or contact companies at the numbers below:

Island's Choice Taxi	☎ 649-94-10409
Nell's Taxi Service	☎ 649-94-13228
Paradise Taxi	☎ 649-94-13555
Providenciales Taxi Association	☎ 649-94-65481

CAICOS ISLANDS

Bicycle Provo Fun Cycles and Scooter Bob's (see the Car, Motorcycle & Scooter, section, above) both rent single-gear beach cruisers for US$13 daily. Tropical Auto Rentals has 10-speed mountain bikes for US$3.50/12 hourly/daily.

Boat Boat trips can be arranged from Leeward Marina. You can charter *Beluga*, a 37-foot catamaran (☎ /fax 649-94-64396). Ocean Outback (☎ 649-94-15810) rents out 14-, 18-, and 24-foot boats for US$20 to US$50 per hour, US$120 to US$280 daily, including snorkel gear, beach umbrella, and water skis.

West Caicos

This small island, about 6 miles southwest of Provo, is renowned for its diving. The 10-mile-long, 2-mile-wide island is fringed by the **Molasses Reef**, which harbors the remains of the oldest known shipwreck in the Western Hemisphere, dating from 1509. The reefs off the west shore are protected within **West Caicos Marine National Park**.

Other prime dive sites include Elephant Ear Canyon, named for the biggest sponges found in the Turks and Caicos, at 95 feet. One 10-foot-wide monster masks a cave. There's also the Magic Mushroom: A sand chute leads to a precipice where sponges and black coral anchor the coral buttresses. Lobsters pack the cracks.

Inland, **Lake Catherine** is a nature reserve that attracts flamingos, ospreys, ducks, and waders.

Cays East of Providenciales

Little Water Cay

This cay, which is northeast of Provo and separated from it by the 400-yard-wide Leeward Going Through channel, is a popular destination for day-trippers. (See the Providenciales map.)

Visitors can bathe, snorkel, line-fish, or walk the nature trails, which have boardwalks and interpretive signs. The 170-yard-long **North Shore Trail** leads from the beach to a shallow mangrove estuary where you can learn about this vital ecosystem. A lookout deck offers views over a pond and large osprey nest. Iguanas frequently forage along the 225-yard-long **South Shore Trail**, which passes through a lush coastal coppice and also has a lookout deck.

The Turks & Caicos National Trust and the Turks & Caicos Dept of Environment & Coastal Resources have developed a management plan in an effort to minimize the impact of visitors. For example, it's illegal and harmful to feed the approximately 2000 or so endangered rock iguanas, though so many people do it that they'll come waddling down to the boat to greet you. *Don't feed or touch the iguanas!* And stay to the trails to avoid trampling the iguanas' burrows and the ecologically sensitive plants.

Visitors on private boats are not charged; people arriving by commercial boat pay a US$3 fee. See Boat Excursions in the Providenciales section for details on tours to Little Water.

Mangrove Cay

This isle was joined to Little Water Cay before a hurricane in 1960 gouged out the channel that now separates the two. The cay (also known as Big Water Cay) boasts an unbroken span of sand where the 1987 *Sports Illustrated* swimsuit edition was shot. Staring at the dazzling sands, blinded by the glare of the sun, you may succumb to the mirage that supermodels in bikinis are reclining in supine splendor at the margin of sand and sea.

Pine Cay

This cay, 2 miles northeast of Provo, is a Central Park-size, 800-acre private cay that welcomes visitors by prior arrangement. (See the chapter map.) It has a small cadre of seasonal residents that includes Bill Cosby, Denzel Washington, and Jimmy Buffett, who has a passion for bonefishing here.

The cay was the site of the first tourist development in the islands – the snooty Meridian Club – planned in the 1950s by Count Ferdinand Czernin but not brought to fruition until the '70s by his widow, Helen Czernin, and the Polish-born architect George Nipanich (both of whom still live on the island). Today there's a second hotel and about 30 affiliated houses, but no cars, roads, TVs, or telephones (there *is* a fax, however). Marvelously, after a few days you'll forget what a telephone sounds like. Indeed, so far out is the cay that it doesn't take note of daylight saving time, thereby constituting its own little time zone.

The vegetation is lusher than Provo's. About two-thirds of the island – which is named for the native Cuban pine that thrives at the edge of the freshwater ponds – are set aside as a nature preserve, accessed by 9 miles of nature trails. There are semi-tame iguanas and 120 species of birds, including white-tailed tropic birds.

A fabulous beach runs almost the full length of the west shore. At its northern end, Sand Dollar Point, you can wade out 400 yards in knee-deep water, searching for the eponymous shells. A 70-foot wreck lies partially submerged a stone's throw from shore, with cannon on the seabed. And snorkeling is superb at the Aquarium, a cove on the east shore of Pine Cay, with two coral arms embracing a sandy floor covered with anemones pulsing like little translucent green hearts.

Places to Stay The cay's *ultra*exclusive *Meridian Club* (in the USA ☎ 212-696-4566, 800-331-9154, fax 212-689-1598), which has acquired a cult status among the super-rich, is both barefoot casual – even the manager hangs out in rumpled shorts – and pricey, appealing to travelers with a taste for luxurious and unpretentious isolation. There are 12 one-bedroom cabañas tucked in amid the dunes, each with a

lounge and a private screened porch fronting directly onto the beach. Rooms are grandly austere (imagine coat hooks made of driftwood and wall decorations fashioned from sand dollars), with neither telephones nor TVs. For total seclusion, you can opt for the one-room Sand Dollar Cottage nestled under casuarinas on the beach. There's also a pool and tennis court.

Rates are US$475 to US$650 double, depending on season. Single occupancy costs US$75 extra, as does the Sand Dollar Cottage. Rates include roundtrip transfers from Provo for some (but not all) flights, plus the use of sailboats, sailboards, and

---

X-Rated Antics

No, I'm not talking sex on the beach. I'm referring to glowworm sex, which takes place in the channel between Pine Cay and Fort George Cay, not far from the Aquarium.

Here millions of the teeny glowworm (*Odontosyllis enopla*) copulate by the clock, 55 minutes after sundown, five days after each month's full moon. Lesser displays are seen on the fourth and sixth nights. Voyeurs may journey here by boat to witness this fabulous 15-minute-long performance. First the females, then the randy males, light up in an outburst of phosphorescent fireworks as the males chase the glowing white egg sacs enclosed within the ejected hindquarters of the females. Talk about a sexual flush! Alas, the males' brief but ecstatic neon-green display is their last gasp: The females devour the males after mating. ■

Ready for love

bicycles, and boating excursions on the spiffy launch, with crew decked out in yachting whites. Special package rates are offered. The club won't take credit cards or kids under 12. Meals are said to be a let-down. Write the club c/o RMI Marketing, The Carriage House, 201 E 29th St, New York, NY 10016.

Getting There & Away Pine Cay has a packed-sand airstrip.

The Meridian Club will take guests to a variety of deserted cays.

Fort George Cay

This tiny cay, a stone's throw north of Pine Cay, is a national historic site, with the remains of an 18th-century British fort built to protect the Caicos islands from attack. Divers and snorkelers can inspect barnacle-encrusted cannon lying on the bottom of the ocean. The site is protected within **Fort George Land & Sea Park**.

Dellis Cay

Next north in the necklace, Dellis is one of the best isles for shelling, thanks to a combination of tide patterns and current. *No shells may be taken away!* Leave them for others to admire.

Parrot Cay

This uninhabited cay, just west of North Caicos, is said to have been the lair of the pirate Calico Jack in the 1720s. The only guarded treasure today is a deluxe resort (nonoperational at press time) once owned by a shah. The resort gained new ownership in 1996 and is scheduled to be expanded and reopened in December 1998 under the management of the Four Seasons hotel chain.

North Caicos

Pop 1275

Little-visited North Caicos is of prime interest to ecotourists. It gets more rainfall than other islands and hence has lusher

(though unspectacular) vegetation. It has traditionally been the bread basket of the island chain. Farms evolved in colonial times and fine sloops were built to transport the crops to the other islands. Mangoes, oranges, and other fruits and vegetables still thrive beside sugar apples and sea grapes.

There are four tiny settlements, notably Kew, near the island's center, and Bottle Creek, on a breezy coastal bluff 2 miles south of the airport. A major planned community, King's Landing, is slated for a huge chunk of land north of Bottle Creek.

North Caicos hosts the Festarama Festival each July.

Information

There's a post office in Kew, and Bottle Creek has a small public library. The police station is in Bottle Creek; to reach the police, call ☎ 649-94-67116.

Things to See & Do

The Kew area has several historic ruins, including the **Wades Green Plantation**, granted to a British Loyalist by King George III. The owners struggled to grow sisal and sea-island cotton until drought, hurricanes, and pernicious bugs drove them out. The plantation lasted for only 25 years; the owners abandoned their slaves and left. Nearby is **Kew Farm**, where a Canadian nicknamed 'Farmer John' raises okra and cantaloupe fertilized with seaweed raked from the shore and irrigated by wind-pumped water.

The **West Indian Mariculture Crab Farm** (☎ 649-94-67213), on the northeast shore, is a commercial venture where you can observe crabs in various stages of development. Visitors are welcome. It supposedly has a daily boat tour.

Beaches include Pumpkin Bluff, Horsestable, and, most importantly, Whitby Beach. On any one, yours will be the only Robinson Crusoe footprints, and I guarantee you will find pluperfect shells.

Cottage Pond, a 150-feet-deep blue hole on the northwest coast, attracts waterfowl such as West Indian whistling

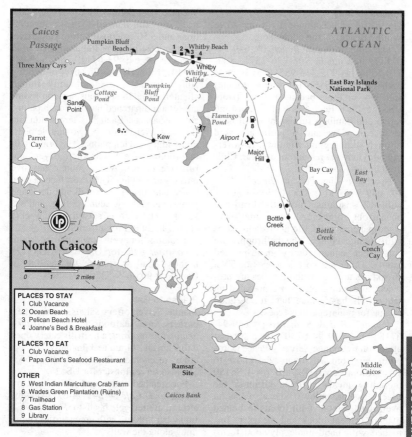

North Caicos

| 0 | 2 | | 4 km |
| 0 | 1 | | 2 miles |

PLACES TO STAY
1 Club Vacanze
2 Ocean Beach
3 Pelican Beach Hotel
4 Joanne's Bed & Breakfast

PLACES TO EAT
1 Club Vacanze
4 Papa Grunt's Seafood Restaurant

OTHER
5 West Indian Mariculture Crab Farm
6 Wades Green Plantation (Ruins)
7 Trailhead
8 Gas Station
9 Library

ducks, grebes, and waders. And Belle-field Landing Pond, Pumpkin Bluff Pond, and Dick Hill Creek also attract flamingos. A series of small cays off the northeast shore are protected within **East Bay Islands National Park**, and a trio of cays to the northwest form **Three Mary Cays National Park**. Vast bonefish flats extend east of the island.

The entire south shore is encompassed by the **Ramsar Site** sanctuary, comprised of a vast series of marsh and intertidal wetlands. It extends to East Caicos and

protects an important breeding site and nursery for waterfowl, lobster, conch, and fish. The creeks are full of schooling bonefish and tarpon.

A large brine lake, **Flamingo Pond**, floods the center of the island. Here the gangly birds strut around in hot pink. You can see them from a distance: Three cabañas have been erected on the main road, and they offer views over the pond, 400 yards away. You'll need binoculars. To get closer, follow the dirt track that leads east from Kew to the edge of the pond.

Places to Stay

The fistful of accommodations are all at Whitby Beach, on the north shore.

The homey *Ocean Beach* (☎ 649-94-67113; in Canada 905-336-2876, 800-710-5204, fax 905-336-9851) has 10 units with rooms (US$98/110 single/double) and two- or three-bedroom suites (from US$155/165). Each has ceiling fans and rattan and bamboo furnishings. All have an ocean view and a patio accessed through sliding glass windows. It's overpriced. There's a restaurant and bar. Children under 12 stay free.

Nearby is the *Pelican Beach Hotel* (☎ 649-94-67112, fax 649-94-67139), with 12 spacious, modestly furnished oceanfront rooms and two suites with wood-paneled walls, tile floors, and patios with lounge chairs. The bathrooms are small but enhanced by hand-painted motifs. There are no telephones or TVs. Breakfasts and sandwich lunches are provided, and native meals are prepared on request. It has a nice bar. It's a good escape for nongregarious types.

Joanne's Bed & Breakfast (☎ 649-94-67184, fax 649-94-67301) is a modest affair run by Joanne Selver, a Peace Corps volunteer from Michigan who chose to stay. Rooms cost US$110 (or US$150 including meals at Papa Grunt's; see Places to Eat, below). She also has an overpriced 'motel' with rooms fashioned of bare cement block and meagerly furnished with hand-made plywood furniture, though there are some romantic touches. Two rooms – one without windows – share an outside bathroom and cost US$60. Six rooms have private bathroom and cost US$70. She was adding two euphemistically termed 'executive suites' (US$100) with ocean views. The B&B also has a two-bedroom 'villa' for US$200, including housekeeping service, and a two-bedroom apartment complete with kitchen for US$120/600 daily/weekly. The beach is a 15-minute walk away. Joanne also offers a courtesy van service and runs a small gift shop at Club Vacanze (see below). She does *not* take walk-ins: You'll need to make reservations and a 50% deposit before you arrive.

The nicest place is Italian-owned *Club Vacanze* (☎ 649-94-67119, fax 649-94-67114), formerly the Prospect of Whitby Hotel. It has a predominantly Italian clientele. The 28 spacious, air-con rooms are set amid parched lawns, thatch palms, and casuarinas. Each has terra-cotta tile floors, wicker furniture, two double beds, minifridge, and telephone. The brightly lit bathrooms have bidets, hair dryer, and full-size mirror. A TV lounge has live music some nights. The resort faces a deep beach and also has a small sun deck and pool, plus archery, scuba diving, and sea kayaks. The club is served by a weekly charter flight to Provo from Italy.

Looking for your own two-bedroom *oceanfront villa* for US$100 to US$125 nightly? Call ☎ /fax 649-94-67308; in Canada ☎ 905-649-5220.

Places to Eat

Joanne Selver offers salads, sandwiches, burgers, and seafoods at *Papa Grunt's Seafood Restaurant*, a no-frills eatery open 7 to 9 am and 11 am to 3 pm daily. Dinners are by reservation. Pizza slices cost US$3. She also serves lobster for US$23.

For steamed conch and native fare, try the *Super D Cafe* (☎ 549-94-67124) at the airport. Better yet, head to *The Shoal*, a funky bar in Kew, with green turtles swimming along the walls.

The restaurants in the *Pelican Beach Hotel* and *Ocean Beach* serve lunch and dinner by reservation only. *Club Vacanze* serves quality meals catering to Italian tastes; expect to pay US$30 for dinner.

You can buy produce and groceries at *KH's Food Store* in Whitby and at *Al's Grocery* in Bottle Creek.

Getting There & Away

North Caicos' airport is just north of Major Hill.

Sky King (with offices on North Caicos) flies several times per day from

Provo (US$25 one way). Turks & Caicos Airways (also with an office on the island) and Interisland Airways have several flights daily from Provo.

Getting Around

A taxi from the airport to Club Vacanze costs US$10 one way. Mac of M&M Tours (☎ 649-94-67338) offers island tours for US$25 per hour. You won't need more than three hours to see the entire island.

At Club Vacanze and Whitby Plaza, Joanne Selver rents beach-cruiser bicycles for a steep US$18 a day! She won't rent by the hour.

Middle Caicos

Pop 270

The largest of the Caicos islands (with an area of 48 sq miles) is also one of the least developed, with barely a handful of vehicles and no convenience stores or nightclubs. But the fishermen and farmers in the tiny hamlets of Conch Bar, Bambarra, and Lorimers give visitors a warm welcome.

Bambarra is named for people from the Bombarras tribe of the Niger River, who were shipwrecked here in 1842 when a slavetrader, the *Gambier*, ran aground.

The island hosts the Middle Caicos Expo each August.

Things to See & Do

The southern half of the island is composed of vast intertidal swamplands. Offshore, **Vine Point & Ocean Hole Nature Reserve** protects a frigate-bird breeding colony, plus a 210-foot-deep, 400-yard-wide marine blue hole favored as a hangout by turtles and sharks.

The paved road from the airfield to Lorimers is good for bicycling, with plenty of beachside stops along the way.

Middle Caicos Reserve & Trail System

The island boasts miles of beaches, large freshwater lakes and lavish pine forests accessed by 10 miles of trails along the north coast, created in conjunction with the Turks & Caicos National Trust. One trail leads from Mudjen Harbour Beach to join the historic **Crossing Over Trail** that leads from Middle to North Caicos. En route, it

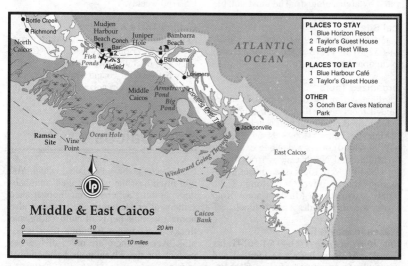

passes the ruins of several Loyalist cotton plantations, as well as brine pools favored by cranes and flamingos.

The north coast is dramatically scenic, with long sandy beaches and scalloped bays held in the cusps of rugged limestone cliffs. The spectacular coastal scenery at Mudjen Harbour Beach features a huge amphitheater carved from the raw limestone bluffs. Here the long unfurling of turquoise waves is broken by tiny **Dragon Cay**, connected to the shore by a sand spit and surrounded by placid sea pools for warm-water bathing.

Plans call for the trail to be extended eastward along almost the entire north coast.

Conch Bar Caves National Park This park protects 15 miles of underground caverns – one of the largest cave systems in the Caribbean region. Some have lagoons and stalactites and stalagmites, often dramatically pliated in curtains. Most have colonies of bats. They were used as sacred sanctuaries by the Lucayan Indians, who left petroglyphs on the walls. There are at least 38 pre-Columbian Lucayan sites on the island, many of which have been excavated by archaeologists. The most notable is the **Armstrong Pond Village Historical Site**.

J&B Tours (☎ 649-94-65047, fax 649-94-65288) in Provo offers daylong cave excursions here.

Organized Tours
Cardinal Arthur (☎ 649-94-66107) offers guided tours, as well as bonefishing, reef fishing, snorkeling, and bird watching.

Majestic Tours (☎ 649-94-64999, fax 649-94-64040) offers a daylong excursion to Middle and North Caicos from Provo for US$149. J&B Tours (see contact information above) offers a daylong 'Cave Safari' excursion to Middle Caicos from Provo; the trip includes a picnic lunch.

Places to Stay & Eat
Blue Horizon Resort (☎ 649-94-66141, fax 649-94-66139) is both a residential and vacation community in Mudjen Harbour,

overlooking Dragon Cay. It opened in November 1996 and includes studio-type rental cottages with screened porches and full modern kitchens. Rates are US$150 per night or US$750 to US$950 weekly. Its *Blue Harbour Café* offers lunch and dinner by reservation only.

Taylor's Guest House (☎ 649-94-66118; in the USA 305-667-0966), in Conch Bar about 300 yards from the beach, has four rooms for US$45 to US$50. It has a small restaurant. Likewise, *Arthur's Guest House* (☎ 649-94-66122) has two simple rooms. Mrs Arthur will cook for an extra fee.

There are *villas* to rent, too (in the USA ☎ 215-322-0505, fax 215-322-0593), including a luxury three-bedroom home with cathedral ceiling and 2 acres of private beachfront; weekly rates begin at US$925. *Eagles Rest Villas* (in the USA ☎ 800-484-1882, fax 813-793-7157) is a duo of oceanfront two-bedroom units near Bambarra, each sleeping up to six and costing US$750 to US$1000 weekly. Also consider staying at a two-bedroom *waterfront villa* (in the USA ☎ 604-736-6717, fax 604-736-3241, sundial@mindlink.bc.ca) with covered verandah. It rents for US$575 to US$750 weekly.

Getting There & Away
Sky King flies several times daily from Provo (US$35 one way). Turks & Caicos Airways operates two roundtrip flights daily between Provo and Middle Caicos.

Also see the Organized Tours section, above.

East Caicos

East Caicos is the least-visited island. You will often hear the island called 'uninhabited,' although there is an impoverished settlement of Haitians. The island is also home to small herds of wild cattle and flocks of flamingos flaunting their neon-pink liveries. There are miles of beaches perfect for the adventurous beachcomber in you.

The island could soon boom, thanks to a proposal to build a cruise-ship terminal here. The proposed US$450 million project includes plans for a bridge link with South Caicos, part of the planned pan-Caicos highway with bridges linking the entire Caicos chain.

There is no air service; East Caicos can only be reached by boat.

South Caicos

Pop 1400

South Caicos, 22 miles west of Grand Turk, is the easternmost and smallest Caicos island. It's ladle-shaped, with its 'handle' to the northeast. First impressions are of an arid wasteland and forlorn, sand-blasted streets roamed by wild horses and donkeys. But read on.

The big attraction is diving: A reef and wall run the length of the east coast. South Caicos' only settlement, **Cockburn Harbour**, is also a perfect spot to launch across the 40-mile-wide Caicos Bank in search of bonefish. Flamingos inhabit the vast salinas (salt ponds) on the northeast edge of Cockburn Harbour; the birds – about 60 total – are resident year-round. And the Annual Commonwealth Regatta is held on South Caicos each May.

South Caicos was historically the most productive isle during the 19th-century heyday of salt raking. The population now lives exclusively off conch and lobster fishing, but the lobstering industry is in crisis. Lobster sells for US$2.75 a pound (compared to about US35¢ a pound for conch), and a handful of the most successful fishermen can make as much as US$1000 a day during the four-month season. But they are the exception. It is highly competitive, and the last few seasons have not been good. Locals have even begun using bleaches to drive scarce lobster out of their hiding places, destroying the coral reefs and lobster stock together. Many islanders have drifted to Provo in the past decade.

South Caicos is soon to be put on the map by a massive 1000-room resort development, High Point, atop the Sail Rock Hills.

The town of Cockburn Harbour is a rough-edged place with a somewhat sullen population and a rakishly appealing down-in-the-dumps shantytown feel. Corrugated-tin-and-driftwood shacks are interspersed amid modern bungalows and handsome, albeit weathered, colonial-era wooden structures left from salt-trade days.

Drug traffic is a problem (signs posted in town remind locals that trade or possession of drugs is good for 14 years in the pokey). In the 1980s the trade was fostered by the annual Plane Exchange, when aircraft came in from South and North America, ostensibly for an aircraft swap-meet . . . a customs nightmare! The pilots gathered at the former Admiral Arms Hotel (now the Center for Marine Resource Studies), where aircraft serial numbers are etched on the roof beams.

Barclays Bank has a branch in town, open 9 am to 1 pm on Thursday. For the police, call ☎ 649-94-63299.

Center for Marine Resource Studies

This research facility, in the center of Cockburn Harbour, undertakes ecological studies with the aim of helping Turks and Caicos islanders to develop sustainable fishing practices. It is run by the School for Field Studies (☎ 508-927-7777, fax 508-927-5127, sfshome@igc.apc.org), at 16 Broadway, Beverly, MA 01915-4499, a nonprofit organization that gives young students practical education in environmental studies. Visitors are welcome; the director, Tomas Vergel Jamir, will be happy to give you a tour. Donations (including computers and books) are welcomed.

In addition to sponsoring independent research, the school offers two courses: A semester-long course in marine resource management is given twice yearly and a monthlong marine parks management course is offered June through July and July through August. Participants who wish to use scuba equipment (a major part

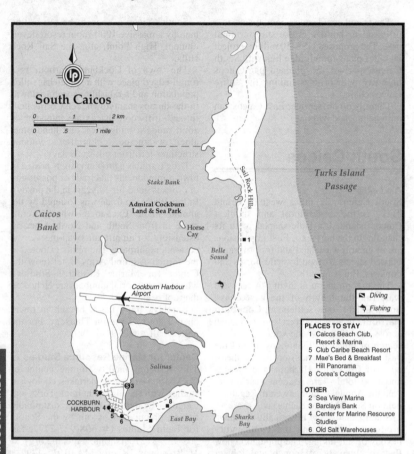

South Caicos

0   1   2 km
0   .5   1 mile

Stake Bank

**Admiral Cockburn
Land & Sea Park**

*Caicos
Bank*

*Horse
Cay*

*Belle
Sound*

Sail Rock Hills

*Turks Island
Passage*

*Cockburn Harbour
Airport*

Salinas

⑤③

COCKBURN
HARBOUR   ④②
⑤
⑥

⑦   ⑧

East Bay   *Sharks
Bay*

☒ Diving
↝ Fishing

PLACES TO STAY
1 Caicos Beach Club,
   Resort & Marina
5 Club Caribe Beach Resort
7 Mae's Bed & Breakfast
   Hill Panorama
8 Corea's Cottages

OTHER
2 Sea View Marina
3 Barclays Bank
4 Center for Marine Resource
   Studies
6 Old Salt Warehouses

CAICOS ISLANDS

of the research undertakings) must be certified prior to arrival.

Town Landmarks
Mand of the island's historic buildings are at the southeast end of town, centered on the old **Wesleyan church** with its tall spire.

On its lonesome atop Tucker's Hill at the south end of town is the **old commissioner's house**. The house is now home to Mae's Bed & Breakfast Hill Panorama (see Places to Stay, below).

Admiral Cockburn Land & Sea Park
Much of the island is within this park, north and west of Cockburn Harbour. It encompasses the **Sail Rock Hills**, a ridge extending along the panhandle and rising to 178 feet. The hills offer spectacular views east over the Turks Island Passage and west over **Belle Sound**, a vast turquoise bay opening to the flats of the Caicos Bank. The reserve extends west for several miles to protect the mangroves and bonefish flats, and extends windward to protect the offshore coral reefs.

Activities

South Caicos is known for its wall diving, although you're sure to see plenty of pelagics: eagle rays, Atlantic rays, blacktip sharks, and – the highlight – humpback whales in January and February.

Club Caribe Beach Resort (see Places to Stay, below) is a full-service dedicated dive resort offering advanced diving, with three dives daily. It does *not* offer resort or certification courses.

At press time both Club Caribe and the new Caicos Beach Club, Resort & Marina (see Places to Stay) planned to offer bonefishing in Belle Sound and beyond. Until they do, Julius 'Goo the Guide' Jennings (☎ 649-94-63444) at Club Caribe will take you out.

Organized Tours

J&B Tours (☎ 649-94-65047) in Provo offers a full-day powerboat excursion here from Provo. The trip includes diving for conch and lobster in season and a visit to a frigate-bird colony; it costs US$168, including a barbecue lunch.

Places to Stay

A basic option is *Corea's Cottages*, east of town. It offers simple bunk-type beds for about US$50 nightly.

Mae's Bed & Breakfast Hill Panorama (☎ 649-94-63207) is an off-beat gem in the old commissioner's house atop Tucker's Hill. The place is run by a delightful old dear named Mae, who has a renewable lease on the government-owned property that she shares with three dogs and three cats. An old horse-drawn buggy stands outside. The exterior is badly in need of renovation, but the interior is thoroughly charming, with a parlor and music room and three clean, well-lit bedrooms (two with shared bathroom) offering views over town. They're simply furnished, with romantic lace bedspreads and pillowcases, and cost US$65 each, including breakfast. Mae makes lunch and dinner on request and will even give up her splendid large bedroom. The breezy patios in front and back are perfect for relaxing and savoring the sunrise and sunset.

Club Caribe Beach Resort (☎ 649-94-63444, fax 649-94-63466, helene@club carib.com; in the USA ☎ 305-258-1177, 800-581-2582, fax 305-257-2072), a dedicated dive resort that's also perfect for non-divers, sits over the ocean at the edge of town. It has 16 modestly furnished air-con rooms, each with ceiling fan, couch, and small bathroom. Rates are US$100/175 town-view/ocean-view, including meals. There are two large elevated sun decks and a pool. Bicycles and kayaks are available. The place is well run by a Californian couple.

Club Caribe also has two octagonal two-story 'villas,' each with four units, about a mile north on a lonesome beach. They have fans but no air-con or kitchens.

At press time a new, large-scale resort – *Caicos Beach Club, Resort & Marina* (☎ 649-94-66606) – was being built atop the Sail Rock Hills on 200 acres, with views over the Atlantic Ocean and Belle Sound. The first phase – 200 rooms and a conference center – was due to open by the spring of 1998. The resort, known locally as High Point, will have a hilltop horizon pool and its own 100,000-gallon-a-day desalination plant. Plans include a large marina for charter fishing.

Places to Eat

Club Caribe serves set meals; they're tasty and filling. Reservations are required for nonguests. The basic *Eastern Inn Restaurant* (☎ 649-94-63301) serves seafoods and chicken.

The *Hillside View Restaurant* is the place to eat conch with the locals. Locals also like *Dora's Restaurant* (☎ 649-94-63247) at the Cockburn Harbour airport. Dora's serves a great lobster sandwich.

Entertainment

The tiny *Trench Town Club*, 100 yards from the Club Caribe, has a pool table and music (usually cranked up to full bore). There's a *cinema* on Stubbs Rd.

Getting There & Away

The airport is about a mile north of town.

Lynx Air International flies to South Caicos from Fort Lauderdale three times weekly. Interisland Airways flies between South Caicos and all the other inhabited islands. Sky King flies several times daily between Provo and South Caicos (US$40 one way). It also flies between Grand Turk and South Caicos (US$20 one way). Turks & Caicos Airways has daily flights from Provo and Grand Turk.

Sea View Marina (☎ 649-94-63219) in Cockburn Harbour has a fuel dock, water, and the Sea View grocery.

Also see the Organized Tours section, above, for details on trips to the island.

Getting Around

There are usually no taxis at the airport when you arrive; you will have to call for a taxi on arrival. The unofficial resident historian, 'Cornelius,' can also show you around the island.

Turks Islands

The Turks group comprises Grand Turk and its smaller southern neighbor, Salt Cay, in addition to several other tiny cays. The islands lie east of the Caicos, separated from them by the 22-mile-wide Turks Island Passage.

Grand Turk

Grand Turk is a treeless, brush-covered, bean-shaped dot of an island, just 6.5 miles long and 1.5 miles across at its widest. Cockburn Town, the main settlement, has been the administrative and political capital of the archipelago for more than 400 years. Today it also claims to be the business and financial center, yet it remains as

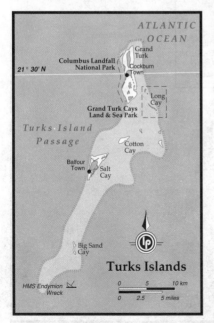

Turks Islands

sleepy as a capital can be. Don't be surprised to see semiwild donkeys roaming the main street.

The island's middle is dominated by several salinas, or salt ponds, from which an odor will sometimes arise (salt – 'white gold' – was Grand Turk's most important export until the industry collapsed in 1962). Pocketed limestone cliffs rise along the north and east shores. There are nice beaches along all shores; inland, caves once used by Lucayans await your discovery. A series of tiny isles – Gibb's, Penniston, Long, and Martin Alonza Pinzon cays – begins about 1 mile off the southeast shore, forming Grand Turk Cays Land & Sea Park.

A few hundred yards off Grand Turk's leeward shore, the ocean abruptly changes hue. The line is precise: You can easily note where the luminous turquoise sea

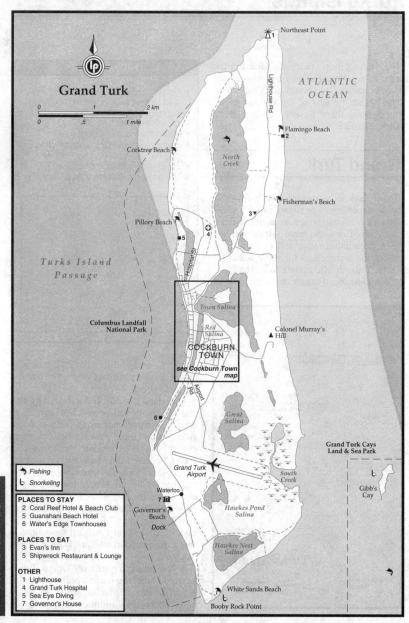

Grand Turk

0   1   2 km
0   .5   1 mile

Northeast Point

ATLANTIC
OCEAN

Lighthouse Rd

Flamingo Beach

North
Creek

Corktree Beach

Fisherman's Beach

Pillory Beach

Turks Island
Passage

Hospital St

Columbus Landfall
National Park

Town Salina

Red Salina

COCKBURN
TOWN
see Cockburn Town
map

Colonel Murray's
Hill

Airport Rd

Great
Salina

Grand Turk Cays
Land & Sea Park

Grand Turk Airport

South
Creek

Gibb's
Cay

Waterloo

Governor's
Beach
Dock

Hawkes Pond
Salina

Hawkes Nest
Salina

White Sands Beach

Booby Rock Point

↰ Fishing
b Snorkeling

PLACES TO STAY
2 Coral Reef Hotel & Beach Club
5 Guanahani Beach Hotel
6 Water's Edge Townhouses

PLACES TO EAT
3 Evan's Inn
5 Shipwreck Restaurant & Lounge

OTHER
1 Lighthouse
4 Grand Turk Hospital
5 Sea Eye Diving
7 Governor's House

TURKS ISLANDS

becomes an abyssal shade of Prussian blue and the shallow seabed opens into a chasm more than 8000 feet deep. There's excellent diving and fishing. Tuna, wahoo, and dolphin fishing are all fabulous, and bonefish can be caught in North Creek and off Long Cay. North Creek also offers great windsurfing.

The island's dowdy image may soon be improved somewhat by the planned addition of a deluxe resort, the Governor's Beach Hotel.

COCKBURN TOWN
Pop 3500

Cockburn Town has a compact, picturesque heart that belies all notions of a nation's 'capital.' Everything happens on the two main streets, lined with old street lamps and pastel-painted colonial buildings, some of them salt warehouses built of limestone. Others are fine wooden structures that are usually painted white, with steep roofs, shuttered windows, and shaded doorways. These were erected by the wealthy Bermudian expatriates who once dominated the salt trade. Many of the houses are hemmed in by stone walls to keep out wild cattle and donkeys.

Sand smothers the streets, blowing into the yards and gathering against walls. Shanties – huts fashioned of cardboard, bits of wood, and tin – have been erected on spare plots in the heart of the dusty downtown. It's like a vision of the poverty-stricken Sahel! Expats arriving here in hopes of bettering their financial careers must feel like they're the victims of a cruel joke.

Immediately inland, a latticework of old salt ponds runs the length of downtown. The ponds (they're long disused) are quite smelly. On the west side of town is a white beach that curves off toward the blue horizon. There are salt piers which jut toward the reef, one quarter-mile from shore. Most people live in the outlying 'suburbs,' notably to the east, where the land rises to Colonel Murray's Hill, a trysting spot for lovers (please don't peer through the steamed-up windows).

Pillory Beach runs along the Cockburn Town shorefront and to the north of town.

Adding color to the scene are characters such as John Houseman, a well-known island expert and self-styled eccentric raconteur. An English journalist turned Turks and Caicos 'belonger,' this strange old fox is a walking encyclopedia on the islands.

Another local to seek out is Bertie Sadler, an avid historian who has a store in the Pond St market, where a flag bearing the original crest of the islands (see the Turks and Caicos Crest sidebar in the introductory chapter) still hangs.

Orientation

The heart of town is sandwiched between the ocean and the salt pond named Red Salina. Front St runs along the waterfront. Front St narrows and becomes Duke St three blocks south of the government plaza. Pond St runs parallel 50 yards to the east, along Red Salina. Osborne Rd, Mission Folly, and Moxie Folly run east from Pond St to the residential area known as Back Salina.

To the north Pond St divides: Hospital St runs north to the hospital; Lighthouse Rd runs northeast to the lighthouse at Northeast Point. Pond St divides to the south, too: One road follows the waterfront to Governor's Beach and the dock; the other – Airport Rd – runs southeast to the airport.

Most hotels have basic maps. *Where, When, How Grand Turk & Salt Cay* has accurate maps of both islands, as does the *Turks & Caicos Pocket Guide* (see Books in the Turks and Caicos introductory chapter).

Information

The Turks & Caicos Islands Tourist Board (☎ 649-94-62321, fax 649-94-62733) is on Pond St near Victoria St; its mailing address is PO Box 128, Cockburn Town, Grand Turk, Turks and Caicos, BWI.

Scotiabank (☎ 649-94-62506, fax 649-94-62667), on Front St at Osborne Rd, is open 8:30 am to 2:30 pm Monday to Thursday and 8:30 am to 4:30 pm Friday.

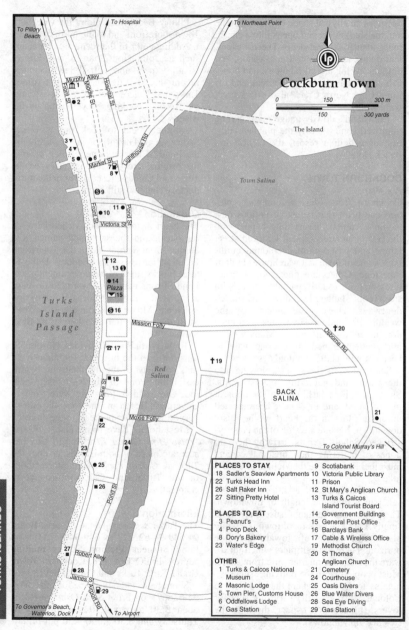

Cockburn Town

0   150   300 m
0   150   300 yards

The Island

Town Salina

Turks Island Passage

Red Salina

BACK SALINA

To Pillory Beach

To Hospital

To Northeast Point

Murphy Alley

Maple St

Hospital St

Front St

Market St

Lighthouse Rd

Pond St

Victoria St

Plaza

Mission Folly

Duke St

Moxie Folly

Osborne Rd

To Colonel Murray's Hill

Pond St

Robert Alley

James St

Airport Rd

*To Governor's Beach,
Waterloo, Dock*

To Airport

PLACES TO STAY
18 Sadler's Seaview Apartments
22 Turks Head Inn
26 Salt Raker Inn
27 Sitting Pretty Hotel

PLACES TO EAT
3   Peanut's
4   Poop Deck
8   Dory's Bakery
23 Water's Edge

OTHER
1   Turks & Caicos National
    Museum
2   Masonic Lodge
5   Town Pier, Customs House
6   Oddfellows Lodge
7   Gas Station
9   Scotiabank
10 Victoria Public Library
11 Prison
12 St Mary's Anglican Church
13 Turks & Caicos
    Island Tourist Board
14 Government Buildings
15 General Post Office
16 Barclays Bank
17 Cable & Wireless Office
19 Methodist Church
20 St Thomas
    Anglican Church
21 Cemetery
24 Courthouse
25 Oasis Divers
26 Blue Water Divers
28 Sea Eye Diving
29 Gas Station

TURKS ISLANDS

There's a Barclays Bank (☎ 649-94-62831) a few blocks south.

The post office (☎ 649-94-62801) is on Front St next to Barclays Bank. Federal Express (☎ 649-94-62515) has an office, as does UPS (☎ 649-94-62030). There's a Cable & Wireless telephone office on Front St, open 8 am to 4 pm Monday to Thursday and 8 am to 3:30 pm Friday.

T&C Travel (☎ 649-94-62592), on Pond St, provides full travel services.

The modestly stocked Victoria Public Library is on Front St; it is open 8 am to 5 pm Monday to Thursday, 8 am to 4 pm Friday, and 9 am to 1 pm Saturday. It has a selection of recent international newspapers and magazines.

The small, well-equipped Grand Turk Hospital (☎ 649-94-62333) is a mile north of town. It has an emergency room. There's also a clinic (☎ 649-94-62328). An expat named David Bown (c/o the Sitting Pretty Hotel, ☎ 649-94-62232) offers bodywork massage for US$30 per hour.

Some of the locals are a bit surly, including one well-known character who goes around with a guitar slung around his neck. He's likely to bum from you and has been known to threaten visitors. Give him a wide berth.

For the police, call ☎ 649-94-62299. For the fire department, call ☎ 649-94-62233.

Front St

Most sites of interest are on the waterfront. The town's historic government buildings – notably the handsome blue-faced **General Post Office** – surround a small plaza where the Columbus Monument – a small plinth with a plaque, dedicated in 1990 – claims cheekily and definitively that the explorer landed here on October 12, 1492. Nearby, four large cannon point to sea. The fringing coral reef is protected within **Columbus Landfall National Park**. Nip into the post office to admire the Philatelic Bureau, displaying scores of the beautiful stamps for which the Turks and Caicos are justly famous.

Important historic buildings farther north include little St Mary's Anglican Church, the pink-faced Victoria Public Library, the Oddfellows Lodge, and the weathered Masonic Lodge.

Turks & Caicos National Museum This little gem, at Front St and Murphy Alley, is in the restored Guinep House (named for the imposing guinep tree in its forecourt), a historic building constructed of salvaged ship's timbers. It displays eclectic miscellany such as shell tools, beads, stamps, locks, and greenstone celts (tools) dug up from the past. Other sections are devoted to the salt industry and life on the coral reef. Its central exhibit is the remains from the Molasses Reef, the oldest authenticated shipwreck in the Americas. Ships of Discovery, a Texas-based nonprofit archaeological research group, has devoted over a decade to the wreck, whose hull is on display alongside the world's largest collection of wrought-iron breech-loading cannon.

Museum founder and manager Brian Riggs and his assistant, Deniece Smith, make you feel at home. Riggs leads a tour at 2 pm weekdays (you can find him next door in his old Bermuda-style cottage when he's not riding his rusting motorcycle). Hours are 9 am to 4 pm weekdays (9 am to 6 pm Wednesday) and 9 am to 1 pm Saturday; US$5/2 nonresidents/residents. Students can get in for US50¢.

Duke St

Duke St, south of the downtown heart, is lined by stone walls behind which several mansions of the wealthy have been turned into rakish little inns, notably the **Turks Head Inn** and **Salt Raker Inn**.

Diving & Snorkeling

See the Dive Sites sidebar for a description of Grand Turk's best underwater spots.

Blue Water Divers (☎ 649-94-62432), at the Salt Raker Inn on Duke St, offers a full range of dives, including blue holes and tunnels on the lee side of the wall. It has weeklong packages for US$650, including 12 dives. It uses two 26-foot boats and also offers full PADI instruction.

Dive Sites

Black Forest – Five types of black coral cling to an undercut festooned with sponges.

McDonald's – Everything from groupers to angelfish hang out near this coral arch.

Tunnels – Sand chutes slope down to the entrance of twin tunnels that drop to 100 feet and emerge in a sponge theme park. ∎

Oasis Divers (☎ 649-94-61128; in the USA 800-892-3995, 770-645-8163, fax 770-640-7461), also on Duke St, specializes in three- to seven-day dive packages. Prices start at US$295. Its mailing address is PO Box 137, Grand Turk, Turks and Caicos, BWI.

Sea Eye Diving (☎ /fax 649-94-61407, ci@caribsurf.com; in the USA ☎ 305-670-6149, 800-725-2822), at the Guanahani Beach Hotel at Pillory Beach and in town on Duke St, offers dives off 24-foot Carolina Skiffs with Bimini tops. It's geared toward photographers and has a full-service photo center with rental gear. It offers a full range of dives (prices start at US$30 for a one-tank dive) and courses, including specialty courses costing US$100. Snorkel trips to Gibb's Cay, east of Grand Turk, cost US$35 and include lunch. The postal address is PO Box 67, Grand Turk, Turks and Caicos, BWI.

Bring a mask, fins, and snorkel. Rentals are scarce.

Sport Fishing
Ossie Virgil (☎ 649-94-62018, cellular 649-94-10199) will take you deep-sea fishing aboard 21-foot and 34-foot boats; write him c/o Sand Dollar Tours, PO Box 78, Grand Turk, Turks and Caicos, BWI. You can charter a boat for fishing from Dutchie's (☎ 649-94-62244) on Airport Rd.

The annual Grand Turk Game Fishing Tournament is held at the end of July or in early August. The annual Turks & Caicos International Billfish Tournament was initiated in 1996 and is held each August. Contact Ossie Virgil for details.

Special Events
The island hosts a two-day 'Summerjam' every June, featuring live bands, beauty contests, and general festivities. Other special events include the following:

April
Spring Garden Festival

June
Queen's Official Birthday Celebrations – Features the police marching band playing with jingoistic fervor; it's really an excuse to imbibe.

July
Rake 'n' Scrape Festival

August
Cactus Fest
Carnival – A weeklong festival with reggae music, salacious dancing, and general festivities.

December
Christmas Tree Lighting Ceremony – The lights go on in mid-December at this event.

Places to Stay
Grand Turk relies upon water shipped in from The Bahamas and frequently experiences drought and acute water shortages.

Sadler's Seaview Apartments, on Duke St, has three one- and two-bedroom bungalow units, each with kitchen, living room, cable TV, ceiling fans, and outdoor patio, for US$45 to US$80. Housekeeping service is provided, and there's a laundry. Write c/o Marjorie Sadler, PO Box 31, Grand Turk, Turks and Caicos, BWI.

The *Beachcomber House* (☎ 649-94-62470) offers one room for rent, for US$60/80 single/double.

The governor's mansion, later the US ambassador's home, metamorphosed some years back into the dowdy *Turks Head Inn* (☎ 649-94-62466, fax 649-94-62825, tophotel@grand-turk.com), an 1840s charmer on Duke St with spacious rooms with lofty ceilings and creaky wooden floors. New management had taken it over when I reviewed it, and a much-needed renovation was underway with the intent of creating a Deep South plantation feel. Rooms were to be substantially upgraded and TV, phones, and minibars added to attract a more upscale clientele. Eventually the inn will have 12 rooms. Three rooms on the ground floor will have their own garden. The new managers – Alan Tatham and Edward Clotworthy – hoped to train locals in higher levels of service. Rates will be US$65/80 single/double. You can write the inn at PO Box 58, Grand Turk, Turks and Caicos, BWI.

Grand Turk Hotels (☎ 649-94-62666, fax 649-94-62888, gthotels@caribsurf.com; in the USA ☎ 800-577-3872) has four local properties under its umbrella: the Guanahani Beach Hotel, Sitting Pretty Hotel, Water's Edge Townhouses, and the Coral Reef Hotel & Beach Club (see the Coral Reef listing in the North of Cockburn Town section). The postal address is PO Box 156, Grand Turk, Turks and Caicos, BWI.

The modern *Guanahani Beach Hotel* (☎ 649-94-62135, fax 649-94-61460), at the north end of Front St, faces powder-white Pillory Beach. It has 16 spacious aircon rooms, each with two double beds, telephone and cable TV, ceiling fans, and ocean-view balcony. The Sea Eye dive center is here, and there's a handsome pool, sun deck, and stone-and-timber beach bar. Rates are US$80/95 single/double mid-April to mid-December and US$115/130 the rest of the year. Special three- to seven-night dive packages are offered.

The *Sitting Pretty Hotel* (☎ 649-94-62231, 800-418-4704, fax 649-94-62668) on Duke St, formerly the Kittina Hotel, has 43 nicely decorated rooms, some in an older, bougainvillea-framed building. The oceanfront units each have a tile floor, wooden ceiling, rattan furniture, ceiling fan, and glass sliding doors opening to a patio or balcony facing the beach. Some have a tiny kitchenette. The hotel is a gathering spot for residents and itinerants. Should you desire, you can even sleep in the same bed slept in by Mariel Hemingway or Princess Alexandra. Rooms cost

US$90/105 single/double mid-April to mid-December and US$135/150 the rest of the year. Suites cost US$125/195 and US$170/285, respectively. The mailing address is PO Box 42, Grand Turk, Turks and Caicos, BWI.

Water's Edge Townhouses (☎ 649-94-62055, fax 649-94-62911), a half-mile south of town, is a self-catering option. It comprises three two-bedroom units with dining room and full kitchen. Each costs US$2500 weekly for up to four people.

The *Salt Raker Inn* (☎ 242-94-62260, fax 242-94-62432), on Duke St, is a 150-year-old Bermudian shipwright's home turned into an intimate, 12-room oceanfront inn. Modern conveniences meld with Caribbean charm. Some rooms have telephone and cable TV. Upstairs suites have an ocean-view balcony with hammocks. The Secret Garden Restaurant is set in a quaint flower garden. The inn has package rates beginning at US$196 double for garden-view rooms. Its mailing address is PO Box 1, Grand Turk, Turks and Caicos, BWI. The inn also has a website. See Internet Resources in the back of the book.

Places to Eat

For conch and native fare, try *Regal Beagle*, *The Diplomat*, or *Touch of Class* (☎ 649-94-62071) on Airport Rd. Or try *Peanut's*, on Front St near Market St, named for the culinary queen of Cockburn Town. Peanut's claims to sell the best conch fritters (or 'rhythm pills,' named for their aphrodisiac properties), served with Jamaican beer. Peanut herself says, 'Dragon Stout and rhythm pills puts it back.' The restaurant serves hearty lobster, too. The *Poop Deck*, just to its south, is said to have the best fried chicken in the islands.

The *Water's Edge* (☎ 649-94-61680), on Duke St, is an atmospheric restaurant and bar with a wooden deck overhanging the beach. It's a good place for snacks such as buffalo wings, nachos, and conch salad, starting at US$5, and entrées such as grilled meats and grouper, starting at US$11. Try the key lime pie or carrot cake for US$4. It also has pizzas from US$7, a 'brown bag special' lunch, and nightly specials: all-you-can-eat spaghetti and lasagne (Monday), Tex-Mex (Tuesday), pizza (Wednesday), and a fish fry (Thursday).

Sandpiper Room, at the Sitting Pretty Hotel, serves continental dinners and native seafood dishes. The hotel also has a breezy courtyard cafe and a bougainvillea-shaded patio bar where you can sip a Roosterbasher, the hotel's wicked house drink. A poolside barbecue is held on Friday night.

The *Turks Head Inn* serves island and continental cuisine, including conch creole, fish and chips (US$8), lamb shanks, and tuna and crab salad. It offers a Sunday brunch. I expect the menu will become more sophisticated. You can opt for the breezy outdoor terrace or the English pub, with its brass plaques, sea charts, and china. A two-tier air-con restaurant was being added at press time.

The Salt Raker Inn's *Secret Garden Restaurant* has creative entrées such as grouper in beer batter for US$16 and jumbo shrimp in garlic for US$23. It serves a fish and lobster barbecue on Wednesday and Saturday and hosts a dinner-and-dancing special on Friday for US$20. Breakfast is served from 7:15 am. Dinner reservations are required.

The elegant *Shipwreck Restaurant & Lounge*, at the Guanahani Beach Hotel, is known for its lobster dinners in season (August to March).

You can buy freshly baked items at *Dory's Bakery* on Pond St next to the gas station.

Entertainment

Nookie Hill (named for the highest point of the island or for the activity?) has disco from 10 pm to 5 am on weekends.

Mitch Rollings, the dive guide, plays guitar at local bars (he has an album, appropriately on the Manta Ray label). About the only live music in town is at the *Salt Raker Inn*. Inevitably the guys behind the guitars are Mitch and other local divemasters.

The *Turks Head Inn* sometimes has live music. It's planning a new garden bar that will feature live music more often. The 'boys' club,' a clique of prominent males that many consider a kind of informal government, meets every Friday night on the patio to debate the week's events and plot the island's future. All comers are welcome to join the games of intellect.

A more earthy place to drink with locals is the *Poop Deck* on Front St.

Things to Buy

You'll be hard put to find souvenir items. There are boutiques at the Guanahani Beach Hotel. There's also a store selling fine batiks, T-shirts, and resortwear at Sea Eye Diving at the south end of Duke St. You can buy naive Haitian art at the Sitting Pretty Hotel. The Turks Head Inn was planning to add a boutique.

A-1 Business, on Front St, sells cameras, but they're *not* duty free.

Getting There & Away

Air Grand Turk Airport is 1 mile south of Cockburn Town. See airline numbers in the Turks and Caicos introductory chapter.

Lynx Air International flies to Grand Turk from Fort Lauderdale three times weekly. If you're traveling to Grand Turk from abroad with other carriers, you'll need to transfer in Provo.

Sky King flies several times daily between Provo and Grand Turk (US$50 one way). Some flights stop en route at South Caicos.

Majestic Tours (☎ 649-94-64999, fax 649-94-64040) offers a daylong excursion to Grand Turk from Provo (US$149) and another to Grand Turk and Salt Cay (US$209).

Boat Windjammer Barefoot Cruises' *Amazing Grace* includes Grand Turk on its cruises. See the Getting There & Away chapter in the Bahamas section for details.

Getting Around

To/From the Airport A taxi may be at the airport to meet incoming flights. If not, you can call for one from the airport. A taxi to or from downtown costs US$4 one way. There are no buses.

Car & Scooter You're hardly likely to need a car, but you *can* hire one from Dutchie's Car Rental (☎ 649-94-62244, fax 649-94-62799) or Tropical Auto Rentals (☎ 649-94-61000), both near the airport on Airport Rd. If you do drive, pay attention to the one-way system.

Island Fun Cycles (☎ 649-94-61680), near Water's Edge on Duke St, rents scooters for US$25 (single) and US$40 (double) per day.

Taxi Several locals operate taxis. Try Jack Williams (☎ 649-94-62239). If you hire a taxi for an island tour, be sure to negotiate the fare beforehand.

Bicycle You can rent a bicycle at the Sitting Pretty Hotel for US$10 a day. Island Fun Cycles has bicycles for the same price.

NORTH OF COCKBURN TOWN
North of town, the island divides like a tuning fork, with the prongs divided by North Creek, a 2-mile-long lagoon opening to the sea via a pencil-thin mouth. Northeast Point, to windward, is pinned by a small cast-iron lighthouse. Fisherman's Beach and Flamingo Beach run south from Northeast Point; seaweed and choppy waters detract from swimming. The leeward shore is lined by Corktree Beach.

Places to Stay & Eat
The *Coral Reef Hotel & Beach Club* (☎ 649-94-62055, fax 649-94-62911), on Flamingo Beach 2 miles northeast of Cockburn Town, is the only resort on the windward side of the island. It has 19 oceanfront self-catering units set amid palms and hibiscus. The bungalow-style air-con units each have a private bathroom, kitchen, cable TV, radio, refrigerator and telephone, plus a wide wooden deck. The resort has a freshwater pool and Jacuzzi, fitness room, and tennis court. Studios cost US$80 mid-April to

mid-December and US$105 the rest of the year; suites cost US$105/135, respectively. You can write the Coral Reef Hotel at PO Box 156, Grand Turk, Turks and Caicos, BWI.

Island House (☎ 649-94-61519, fax 649-94-62646) is a Mediterranean-style villa-hotel on the ridge overlooking Flamingo Beach. It has spacious air-con suites with kitchen and balcony. There's a swimming pool.

Evan's Inn is a popular eatery on Lighthouse Rd, northeast of Cockburn Town.

SOUTH OF COCKBURN TOWN
The town of Waterloo, 1.5 miles south of Cockburn Town, boasts beautiful Governor's Beach, the most popular picnic and party spot for locals. Its other highlights are St Thomas Anglican Church and Governor's House, built in 1815, the year of the famous battle for which the village is named. The island's dock is here. The US missile-tracking station where John Glenn was debriefed is here; so, too, is a disused US Navy facility.

Dirt roads lead south to White Sands Beach (good for snorkeling) and east to three prime bird-watching spots: Hawkes Pond Salina, Hawkes Nest Salina, and South Creek National Park, which protects the mangroves and wetlands along the island's southeast shore.

Places to Stay
The modern *Arawak Inn* (☎ 649-94-62277, fax 649-94-62279) has 15 self-catering air-con suites. Each has a kitchen and sofa bed and can sleep up to four people. There's a freshwater pool. Horseback riding is offered. The inn has a daily shuttle service to town. Weeklong package rates range from US$490 to US$563 double per person. The postal address is PO Box 140, Grand Turk, Turks and Caicos, BWI.

A 50-room luxury resort, the *Governor's Beach Hotel*, was slated to open by late 1998 in Waterloo. The plantation-style resort will have a casino and on-site dive operation.

TURKS ISLANDS

GRAND TURK CAYS LAND & SEA PARK

Gibb's, Penniston, Martin Alonza Pinzon and Long cays make up this small park southeast of Grand Turk (see the chapter map). It protects important nesting sites for seabirds. There are also large numbers of Turk's head cacti. Penniston Cay is an important nesting site for frigate birds, and boobies and noddy and sooty terns abound on Gibb's Cay. The terns come to Gibb's Cay each May and June to breed (the females lay a single egg in a thick carpet of cactus spines). Human visitation is discouraged during these months. Long Cay is a separate sanctuary. A population of iguanas lives on this tiny isle.

Salt Cay

Pop 125

Sun-drenched Salt Cay, 8 miles southwest of Grand Turk, is shaped like a triangle. It's a mere speck of land, but it's steeped in character and to my mind is the most interesting Turks and Caicos island. The modern history of the archipelago began here in the 17th century, when Bermudian salt traders settled and a salt industry emerged. They constructed ponds linked to the sea by canals and sluice gates and built windmills to control water flow. Salt Cay was once the world's largest producer of salt – in the industry's heyday over 100 vessels a year departed the isle for the USA, bulging with 'white gold.'

The island provides a picturesque vision of 19th-century life. It could be a living museum of industrial archeology, with its decrepit windmills, salt sheds, and salinas, now smelly and scummed by wind-whipped froth.

The main settlement, historic **Balfour Town**, boasts several old two-story homes with wide verandahs and jalousied windows, like buildings from a Tennessee Williams play. Many have been bought of late by expats, who are gradually bringing them back to life.

The island still awaits its first asphalt. But what's the point? The island has barely half a dozen cars! Donkeys and wild cattle far outnumber human inhabitants, as do iguanas, including 'Iggy,' a semitame giant who resides at the north end of the island. The beaches and swimming are superb.

Big Sand Cay, 8 miles south of Salt Cay (see the chapter map), was once a habitat for now-endangered West Indian monk seals and manatees. Both have long since disappeared here, due to hunting and habitat destruction. The cay has a small population of iguanas, and it is a haven for diminishing numbers of green and hawksbill turtles, which come ashore to lay their eggs in the sand.

Salt Cay has a small clinic with two nurses; a doctor visits once every other week. The Fun in the Sun Festival is held on Salt Cay each June.

Things to See

The most noteworthy attraction ashore is the splendidly preserved **White House** in north Balfour Town, a salt merchant's stately manor with a stepped (Bermudian) stone roof and chimney. It is still owned by the Harriott family, which built the house in 1835 from stone brought here as ballast. Next door is the old wooden **Treasury Building**, where salt workers once collected their pay. Nearby are **St John's Anglican Church** and, housing the old jail, the **District Commissioner's Office**.

Balfour Town's White House

About 100 yards south of the White House is a derelict building beside the shore. It once ground salt to a powdery fineness to supply Cape Cod's fisheries. There's an underwater tombstone offshore that dates from 1812.

Activities

Choice dive sites include Wanda Lust, known for its plankton-rich waters that attract whales and eagle rays; Kelly's Folly, a rolling coral garden with hawksbill turtles, morays, and parrotfish; and HMS *Endymion*, a recently discovered, never-salvaged, 18th-century British warship bristling with cannon and massive anchors in a coral canyon just 25 feet down. The sea mound here has swimthroughs. The wreck is south of Big Sand Cay. There's also the Northwest Wall, plunging from 50 feet to 120 feet and covered with corals, and Point Pleasant, a shallow cove crowded with coral heads topped with elkhorn.

Salt Cay Divers, at the Mount Pleasant Guest House (see Places to Stay, below), uses two boats, including a 38-foot WWII-era landing craft. It specializes in diving

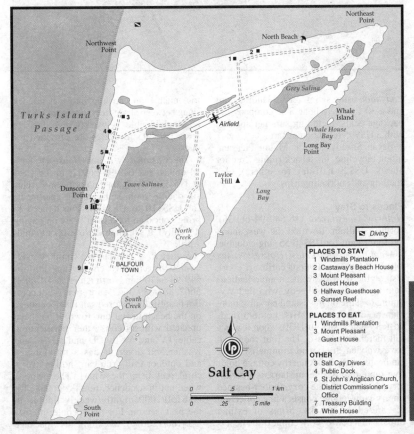

Salt Cay

0   .5   1 km
0   .25   .5 mile

PLACES TO STAY
1 Windmills Plantation
2 Castaway's Beach House
3 Mount Pleasant
   Guest House
5 Halfway Guesthouse
9 Sunset Reef

PLACES TO EAT
1 Windmills Plantation
3 Mount Pleasant
   Guest House

OTHER
3 Salt Cay Divers
4 Public Dock
6 St John's Anglican Church,
   District Commissioner's
   Office
7 Treasury Building
8 White House

Diving

TURKS ISLANDS

Humpback Whales

Salt Cay is perhaps the best spot in the Caribbean region to see humpback whales during the winter months. Scores of leviathans arrive to breed in the warm waters of the Silver and Mouchoir Banks, east and south of Salt Cay. They gather each January, February, and March to mate and give birth in these waters, so close to shore that you can literally swim out to touch them!

Whaling was an important industry on the cay in the late 19th century, when whales were dragged ashore and butchered at Whale House Bay. ■

Endymion using swim-aboard landing craft and a 30-foot dive boat. The company has package deals, including summer specials with a US$95 rebate on airfare.

Bryan Sheedy, also at Mount Pleasant, offers bicycling, horseback riding (free for guests, US$20 half-day for others), plus shelling and snorkeling trips.

Places to Stay

Halfway Guesthouse (☎ 649-94-66936), north of Balfour Town on the west shore, has four rooms for US$40/55 single/double.

Mount Pleasant Guest House (☎ /fax 649-94-66927, scdivers@caribsurf.com), also on the west shore, is an unpretentious gem run by Bryan Sheedy, who fled Wyoming to settle on this island paradise more than a decade ago. His home-turned-hostelry dates back to 1830, when it was a salt merchant's house. The four rooms all have wooden floors and minimalist decor but heaps of charm. A nearby cottage holds four more rooms; one, upstairs, is a dormitory sleeping six. The cozy, timber-beamed library-cum-lounge boasts a fine collection of rare-edition books, prints of extinct birds, and a pewter collection. If the heat is

too much, you can hop into a hammock slung between shade trees. Rates are US$65/85 single/double. A weekly dive package costs US$895. Bicycles are provided for guests.

The *Castaway's Beach House* (☎ 649-94-66921, fax 649-94-66922; in the USA ☎ 315-536-7061), on the north shore, rents six one-bedroom self-catering apartments for US$110 to US$160. You'll need to bring your own food (don't rely on buying it locally). It's open mid-November to mid-April.

Sunset Reef (c/o Nathan Smith ☎ 649-94-66928; on Provo c/o JoAnne Phillips 649-94-64109; in North America 410-889-3662, 888-889-3662, sunsetreef@aol.com) is a beautifully restored salt raker's cottage on the beach in Balfour Town. It has been updated with air-con, water purification, cable TV and VCR, CD and stereo, and washer and dryer. It has a full kitchen and outdoor grill. You can snorkel over a coral reef from the wharf. The owners, when not in residence, rent the cottage for US$150/1000 nightly/weekly double in the peak season. For four people, it costs US$180/1200. A weeklong dive package costs US$895. Rates include a bicycle, but you can rent an electric golf cart for US$35 daily. The US mailing address is 3501 Clipper Rd, Baltimore, MD 21211.

The *Windmills Plantation* (☎ 649-94-66962, 800-822-7715, fax 649-94-66930) is a small, superdeluxe resort in a stunning beachside location about 1.5 miles northeast of Balfour Town. It was designed by owner-architect Guy Lovelace and his interior designer wife, Patricia, who employed a delightfully bizarre West Indian motif and a palette of Caribbean pastels to evoke the plantation era (you may recognize it as the locale of a Victoria's Secret fashion shoot). It has eight luxuriously and romantically appointed suites with terra-cotta floors, hand-carved four-poster beds (king-size), old lanterns, and private outdoor patio with shower and Jacuzzi. Columned walkways, lined by alcoves with hammocks, radiate out from the Romanesque pool. It has its own restaurant and bar, and diving and water sports are offered. Daily rates range from US$495 to US$685. Weekly packages (including airfare from Provo) are US$3595 to US$4495. It's open mid-October to May only.

Places to Eat

The choice option is *Mount Pleasant Guest House*, serving native seafood and other gourmet fare. Bryan claims the restaurant is the 'best in the country.' Reservations are recommended, as they are at *Windmills Plantation*, whose owners pride themselves on their Caribbean cuisine.

For local color, head to *Leggatts' Brown House* in town.

Getting There & Away

The airfield is northeast of Balfour Town. The terminal is a building the size of a Nissen hut.

Interisland Airways and Sky King both have flights from Provo. A private charter flight from Grand Turk will cost about US$75.

The trip to the cay is much more fun by boat. Sand Dollar Tours (☎ 649-94-62018) offers trips from Grand Turk. Eldon Talbot or Perry Seymour, both with the Ministry of Fisheries, might take you in their launch (on my journey they took time out for a spot of sport fishing en route). Expect a fast, bumpy ride.

Getting Around

One of the island's only two taxis will inevitably show up after the driver sees the plane land at the Salt Cay airfield.

Bryan Sheedy – a treasure-trove of knowledge – takes guests on island tours in his electric golf cart.

TURKS ISLANDS

Internet Resources

There are numerous sites on The Bahamas, offering information on everything from lodging and eats to real-estate tips and cheap plane fares. There is also a handful of sites focusing on the Turks and Caicos.

Websites listed below are only a sampling of what's available online.

Remember that websites may be updated frequently, occasionally, or not at all. Follow up your online research with phone calls.

GENERAL WEBSITES

The Invented City
www.invented-city.com

A website for those interested in home exchanges; includes destinations all over the world, plus details on availability and rates.

The Official Club Med Website
www.clubmed.com/

Home page providing a complete listing of Club Meds around the world.

US Customs Service Website
www.customs.ustreas.gov/

Website offering useful travel information, from things you should know before you go to US Customs office locations to regulations to international programs and activities.

US State Department Travel Warnings & Consular Information Sheets
travel.state.gov/travel_warnings.html

Lists current travel warnings issued by the State Dept, plus pertinent information on every US embassy and consulate in the world.

Where to Stay in the Caribbean
www.where2stay.com/islands/

Website focusing on accommodations in The Bahamas, the Turks and Caicos, and Caribbean countries, from budget to top end; also has restaurant information and general facts about individual islands.

WEBSITES ON THE BAHAMAS

Bahamas – A Guide to Moving There
www.escapeartist.com/bahamas/bahamas.htm

Provides numerous links to all sorts of other sites – home pages of airlines, towns and cities, local publications, schools, and business organizations – that provide a dizzying amount of information on the country; also provides real-estate company links.

Bahamas On-Line
TheBahamas.com/

Website offering general information on where to stay, what to eat, and things to do throughout the islands.

Bill & Nowdla Keefe's Bimini Undersea
www.biminiundersea.com/

Provides information on the Biminis-based dive operator and its offerings.

Blue Lagoon Island
dolphinswims.com/

Provides information on dolphin encounters at Blue Lagoon Island, just off New Providence.

Earthwatch Institute
gaia.earthwatch.org/

Earthwatch's website, with information on EarthCorps volunteer opportunities, international expeditions, scientific field research, and news and events.

The Islands of The Bahamas
www.interknowledge.com/bahamas/

Website of the Bahamas Ministry of Tourism/ Bahamas Tourist Office, with useful information on each island, accommodations, and travel tips.

Small Hope Bay Lodge
web.SmallHope.com/SHB/

Home page of the Andros resort, with details on its outdoor activities offerings (including fishing and diving), rates, and calendar of events.

WEBSITES ON TURKS AND CAICOS
Accenting the Turks and Caicos Islands
www.interknowledge.com/turks-caicos/

Provides general information on the islands, thumbnail sketches of individual islands, rough maps, details on outdoor activities, and tourist board addresses and phone numbers.

The Best of Grand Turk, Turks and Caicos Islands, British West Indies
www.grand-turk.com/

Offers information on deep-sea fishing, dive packages, and other island activities offered by the Turks Head Inn, plus links to useful websites that provide island history, travel information, and details on car and bike rentals.

Blue Water Divers and the Salt Raker Inn
www.microplan.com/bluerake.htm

Home page of the intimate oceanfront inn on Grand Turk, with details on its dive offerings.

Caicos Adventures
www.fortmyers.com/turks/caicosad.html

Home page of Caicos Adventures, a Provo-based dive operator; offers good information on dive and snorkel excursions in the Turks and Caicos, including rates, accommodations, and special package deals.

Dick Zebo's Turks and Caicos Reservations Center
www.fortmyers.com/turks/t-chome2.html

Website offering information on getting there and away; accommodations; dive, snorkel, and golf packages; car and scooter rentals; and honeymoon packages; plus an opportunity to listen to 'the sounds of the islands.'

Interisland Airways
www.empg.com/interisland/

Schedules and fares for Provo-based airline specializing in charter flights within the Turks and Caicos and to/from Miami, plus information on tour packages.

Islands
www.atsea.com/islands/islands.htm

Lists numerous hotels, restaurants and car-rental companies in the Turks and Caicos.

Lynx Air International
www.lynxair.com/

Home page for carrier offering service from Fort Lauderdale to the islands; provides current flight schedules.

Index

SIDEBARS

LONELY PLANET TRAVEL ATLASES

Lonely Planet has long been famous for the number and quality of its guidebook maps. Now we've gone one step further and produced a handy companion series: Lonely Planet travel atlases–maps of a country produced in book form.

Unlike other maps, which look good but lead travelers astray, our travel atlases have been researched on the road by Lonely Planet's experienced team of writers. All details are carefully checked to ensure the atlas corresponds with the equivalent Lonely Planet guidebook.

The handy atlas format means no holes, wrinkles, torn sections or constant folding and unfolding. These atlases can survive long periods on the road, unlike cumbersome fold-out maps. The comprehensive index ensures easy reference.

- full-color throughout
- maps researched and checked by Lonely Planet authors
- place names correspond with Lonely Planet guidebooks –no confusing spelling differences
- legend and traveling information in English, French, German, Japanese and Spanish
- size: 230 x 160 mm

Available now:
Chile & Easter Island • Egypt • India & Bangladesh • Israel & the Palestinian Territories • Jordan, Syria & Lebanon • Kenya • Laos • Portugal • South Africa, Lesotho & Swaziland • Thailand • Turkey • Vietnam • Zimbabwe, Botswana & Namibia

---

LONELY PLANET TV SERIES & VIDEOS

Lonely Planet travel guides have been brought to life on television screens around the world. Like our guides, the programs are based on the joy of independent travel, and look honestly at some of the most exciting, picturesque and frustrating places in the world. Each show is presented by one of three travelers from Australia, England or the USA and combines an innovative mixture of video, Super-8 film, atmospheric soundscapes and original music.

Videos of each episode–containing additional footage not shown on television–are available from good book and video shops, but the availability of individual videos varies with regional screening schedules.

Video destinations include: Alaska • American Rockies • Australia (Southeast) • Baja California • Brazil • Central Asia • Chile & Easter Island • Corsica, Sicily & Sardinia • East Africa, Tanzania & Zanzibar • Ecuador & the Galápagos Islands • France • Greenland & Iceland • Indonesia • Israel & the Sinai Desert • Jamaica • Japan • La Ruta Maya • Morocco • New York City • North India (Varanasi to the Himalayas) • Pacific Islands • South India • Southwest China • Turkey • Vietnam • West Africa • Zimbabwe, Botswana & Namibia

The Lonely Planet TV series is produced by:
Pilot Productions
The Old Studio
18 Middle Row
London W10 5AT UK

For video availability and ordering information contact your nearest Lonely Planet office.

Music from the TV series is available on CD & cassette.

PLANET TALK

Lonely Planet's FREE quarterly newsletter

We love hearing from you and think you'd like to hear from us.
When... is the right time to see reindeer in Finland?
Where... can you hear the best palm-wine music in Ghana?
How... do you get from Asunción to Areguá by steam train?
What... is the best way to see India?

For the answer to these and many other questions read PLANET TALK.

Every issue is packed with up-to-date travel news and advice including:

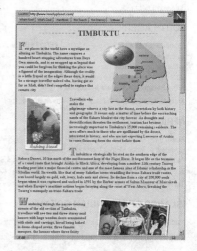

- a letter from Lonely Planet founders Tony and Maureen Wheeler
- travel diary from a Lonely Planet author–find out what it's really like out on the road
- feature article on an important and topical travel issue
- a selection of recent letters from our readers
- the latest travel news from all over the world
- details on Lonely Planet's new and forthcoming releases

To join our mailing list contact any Lonely Planet office .

Also available: Lonely Planet T-shirts. 100% heavyweight cotton (S, M, L, XL)

LONELY PLANET ONLINE

Get the latest travel information before you leave or while you're on the road

Whether you've just begun planning your next trip, or you're chasing down specific info on currency regulations or visa requirements, check out Lonely Planet Online for up-to-the-minute travel information.

As well as travel profiles of your favorite destinations (including maps and photos), you'll find current reports from our researchers and other travelers, updates on health and visas, travel advisories, and discussion of the ecological and political issues you need to be aware of as you travel.

There's also an online travelers' forum where you can share your experience of life on the road, meet travel companions and ask other travelers for their recommendations and advice. We also have plenty of links to other online sites useful to independent travelers.

And of course we have a complete and up-to-date list of all Lonely Planet travel products including guides, phrasebooks, atlases, Journeys and videos and a simple online ordering facility if you can't find the book you want elsewhere.

www.lonelyplanet.com or AOL keyword: lp

LONELY PLANET PRODUCTS

Lonely Planet is known worldwide for publishing practical, reliable and no-nonsense travel information in our guides and on our web site. The Lonely Planet list covers just about every accessible part of the world. Currently there are eight series: *travel guides, shoestring guides, walking guides, city guides, phrasebooks, audio packs, travel atlases* and *Journeys*–a unique collection of travel writing.

EUROPE

Amsterdam • Austria • Baltic States & Kaliningrad • Baltic States phrasebook • Britain • Central Europe on a shoestring • Central Europe phrasebook • Czech & Slovak Republics • Denmark • Dublin • Eastern Europe on a shoestring • Eastern Europe phrasebook • Finland • France • French phrasebook • Germany • German phrasebook • Greece • Greek phrasebook • Hungary • Iceland, Greenland & the Faroe Islands • Ireland • Italy • Italian phrasebook • Lisbon • London • Mediterranean Europe on a shoestring • Mediterranean Europe phrasebook • Paris • Poland • Portugal • Portugal travel atlas • Prague • Romania & Moldova • Russia, Ukraine & Belarus • Russian phrasebook • Scandinavian & Baltic Europe on a shoestring • Scandinavian Europe phrasebook • Slovenia • Spain • Spanish phrasebook • St Petersburg • Switzerland • Trekking in Greece • Trekking in Spain • Ukrainian phrasebook • Vienna • Walking in Britain • Walking in Italy • Walking in Switzerland • Western Europe on a shoestring • Western Europe phrasebook

NORTH AMERICA

Alaska • Backpacking in Alaska • Bahamas • Baja California • Bermuda • California & Nevada • Canada • Chicago • Deep South • Florida • Hawaii • Honolulu • Los Angeles • Mexico • Mexico City • Miami • New England • New Orleans • New York City • New York, New Jersey & Pennsylvania • Pacific Northwest USA • Rocky Mountain States USA • San Francisco • Seattle • Southwest USA • USA phrasebook • Washington, DC & The Capital Region

CENTRAL AMERICA & THE CARIBBEAN

Bahamas, Turks & Caicos • Central America on a shoestring • Costa Rica • Cuba • Eastern Caribbean • Guatemala, Belize & Yucatán: La Ruta Maya • Jamaica

SOUTH AMERICA

Argentina, Uruguay & Paraguay • Bolivia • Brazil • Brazilian phrasebook • Buenos Aires • Chile & Easter Island • Chile travel atlas • Colombia • Ecuador & the Galápagos Islands • Latin American Spanish phrasebook • Peru • Quechua phrasebook • Rio de Janeiro • South America on a shoestring • Trekking in the Patagonian Andes • Venezuela

Travel Literature: Full Circle: A South American Journey

AFRICA

Arabic (Moroccan) phrasebook • Africa on a shoestring • Africa The South • Cape Town • Cairo • Central Africa • East Africa • Egypt & the Sudan • Egypt travel atlas • Ethiopian (Amharic) phrasebook • Kenya • Kenya travel atlas • Malawi, Mozambique & Zambia • Morocco • North Africa • South Africa, Lesotho & Swaziland • South Africa travel atlas • Swahili phrasebook • Trekking in East Africa • West Africa • Zimbabwe, Botswana & Namibia • Zimbabwe, Botswana & Namibia travel atlas

Travel Literature: The Rainbird: A Central African Journey • Songs to an African Sunset: A Zimbabwean Story

ISLANDS OF THE INDIAN OCEAN

Madagascar & Comoros • Maldives & Islands of the East Indian Ocean • Mauritius, Réunion & Seychelles

Also Available: Travel with Children • Traveller's Tales

MAIL ORDER

Lonely Planet products are distributed worldwide. They are also available by mail order from Lonely Planet, so if you have difficulty finding a title please write to us. North American and South American residents should write to Embarcadero West, 155 Filbert St, Suite 251, Oakland CA 94607, USA; European and African residents should write to 10A Spring Place, London NW5 3BH, UK; and residents of other countries to PO Box 617, Hawthorn, Victoria 3122, Australia.

NORTH-EAST ASIA

Beijing • Cantonese phrasebook • China • Hong Kong • Hong Kong, Macau & Canton • Japan • Japanese phrasebook • Japanese audio pack • Korea • Korean phrasebook • Mandarin phrasebook • Mongolia • Mongolian phrasebook • North-East Asia on a shoestring • Seoul • Taiwan • Tibet • Tibet phrasebook • Tokyo

Travel Literature: Lost Japan

MIDDLE EAST & CENTRAL ASIA

Arab Gulf States • Arabic (Egyptian) phrasebook • Cairo • Central Asia • Central Asia phrasebook • Iran • Israel & the Palestinian Territories • Israel & the Palestinian Territories travel atlas • Istanbul • Jerusalem • Jordan & Syria • Jordan, Syria & Lebanon travel atlas • Lebanon • Middle East • Turkey • Turkey travel atlas • Turkish phrasebook • Trekking in Turkey • Yemen

Travel Literature: The Gates of Damascus • Kingdom of the Film Stars: Journey into Jordon

INDIAN SUBCONTINENT

Bengali phrasebook • Bangladesh • Delhi • Goa • Hindi/Urdu phrasebook • India • India & Bangladesh travel atlas • Indian Himalaya • Karakoram Highway • Nepal • Nepali phrasebook • Pakistan • Rajasthan • Sri Lanka • Sri Lanka phrasebook • Trekking in the Indian Himalaya • Trekking in the Karakoram & Hindukush • Trekking in the Nepal Himalaya

Travel Literature: In Rajasthan • Shopping for Buddhas

SOUTH-EAST ASIA

Bali & Lombok • Bangkok • Burmese phrasebook • Cambodia • Ho Chi Minh • Indonesia • Indonesian phrasebook • Indonesian audio pack • Jakarta • Java • Laos • Lao phrasebook • Laos travel atlas • Malay phrasebook • Malaysia, Singapore & Brunei • Myanmar (Burma) • Philippines • Pilipino phrasebook • Singapore • South-East Asia on a shoestring • Thailand • Thailand's Islands and Beaches • Thai phrasebook • Thailand travel atlas • Thai audio pack • Thai Hill Tribes phrasebook • Vietnam • Vietnamese phrasebook • Vietnam travel atlas

ANTARCTICA

Antarctica

AUSTRALIA & THE PACIFIC

Australia • Australian phrasebook • Bushwalking in Australia • Bushwalking in Papua New Guinea • Fiji • Fijian phrasebook • Islands of Australia's Great Barrier Reef • Melbourne • Micronesia • New Caledonia • New South Wales & the ACT • New Zealand • Northern Territory • Outback Australia • Papua New Guinea • Papua New Guinea phrasebook • Queensland • Rarotonga & the Cook Islands • Samoa • Solomon Islands • South Australia • Sydney • Tahiti & French Polynesia • Tasmania • Tonga • Tramping in New Zealand • Vanuatu • Victoria • Western Australia

Travel Literature: Islands in the Clouds • Sean & David's Long Drive

THE LONELY PLANET STORY

Lonely Planet published its first book in 1973 in response to the numerous 'How did you do it?' questions Maureen and Tony Wheeler were asked after driving, bussing, hitching, sailing and railing their way from England to Australia.

Written at a kitchen table and hand collated, trimmed and stapled, *Across Asia on the Cheap* became an instant local best seller, inspiring thoughts of another book.

Eighteen months in South-East Asia resulted in their second guide, *South-East Asia on a shoestring*, which they put together in a backstreet Chinese hotel in Singapore in 1975. The 'yellow bible', as it quickly became known to back-packers around the world, soon became the guide to the region. It has sold well over half a million copies and is now in its 9th edition, still retaining its familiar yellow cover.

Today there are 240 titles, including travel guides, walking guides, language kits & phrasebooks, travel atlases and travel literature. The company is the largest independent travel publisher in the world. Although Lonely Planet initially specialized in guides to Asia, today there are few corners of the globe that have not been covered.

The emphasis continues to be on travel for independent travelers. Tony and Maureen still travel for several months of each year and play an active part in the writing, updating and quality control of Lonely Planet's guides.

They have been joined by over 70 authors and 170 staff at our offices in Melbourne (Australia), Oakland (USA), London (UK) and Paris (France). Travelers themselves also make a valuable contribution to the guides through the feedback we receive in thousands of letters each year and on our website.

The people at Lonely Planet strongly believe that travelers can make a positive contribution to the countries they visit, both through their appreciation of the countries' culture, wildlife and natural features, and through the money they spend. In addition, the company makes a direct contribution to the countries and regions it covers. Since 1986 a per-centage of the income from each book has been donated to ventures such as famine relief in Africa; aid projects in India; agricultural projects in Central America; Greenpeace's efforts to halt French nuclear testing in the Pacific; and Amnesty International.

'I hope we send people out with the right attitude about travel. You realize when you travel that there are so many different perspectives about the world, so we hope these books will make people more interested in what they see. Guidebooks can't really guide people. All you can do is point them in the right direction.'

– Tony Wheeler

LONELY PLANET PUBLICATIONS

Australia
PO Box 617, Hawthorn 3122, Victoria
☎ (03) 9819 1877 fax (03) 9819 6459
e-mail talk2us@lonelyplanet.com.au

USA
155 Filbert St, Suite 251
Oakland, California 94607
☎ (510) 893 8555, TOLL FREE (800) 275 8555
fax (510) 893 8563
e-mail info@lonelyplanet.com

UK
10A Spring Place, London NW5 3BH, UK
☎ (0171) 428 4800 fax (0171) 428 4828
e-mail go@lonelyplanet.co.uk

France
71 bis rue du Cardinal Lemoine, 75005 Paris
☎ 01 44 320620 fax 01 46 347255
e-mail bip@lonelyplanet.co.fr

World Wide Web: www.lonelyplanet.com or *AOL keyword: lp*